NEW
PERSPECTIVES
SERIES

Computer Concepts

SECOND EDITION

COMPREHENSIVE

June Jamrich Parsons

University of the Virgin Islands

Dan Oja

GuildWare, Inc.

A Susan Solomon Book

CTI

A DIVISION OF COURSE TECHNOLOGY
ONE MAIN STREET, CAMBRIDGE, MA 02142

an International Thomson Publishing company IP

Albany • Bonn • Boston • Cambridge • Cincinnati • London • Madrid • Melbourne
Mexico City New York • Paris • San Francisco • Singapore • Tokyo • Toronto • Washington

New Perspectives on Computer Concepts Second Edition—Comprehensive is published by CTI.

Managing Editor	Mac Mendelsohn
Series Consulting Editor	Susan Solomon
Product Manager	Susan Solomon
Production Editor	Debbie Masi
Art Direction and Design	Ella Hanna
Prepress Production and PhotoResearch	Hanna Design+Company
Interior Illustrators	Network Graphics and Tarragon Interactive, Inc.

© 1996 by CTI.
A Division of Course Technology - ITP.

For more information contact:

Course Technology
One Main Street
Cambridge, MA 02142

International Thomson Publishing Europe
Berkshire House 168-173
High Holborn
London WCIV 7AA, England

Thomas Nelson Australia
102 Dodds Street
South Melbourne, 3205
Victoria, Australia

Nelson Canada
1120 Birchmount Road
Scarborough, Ontario
Canada M1K 5G4

International Thomson Editores
Campos Eliseos 385, Piso 7
Col. Polanco
11560 Mexico D.F. Mexico

International Thomson Publishing GmbH
Kônigswinterer Strasse 418
53227 Bonn, Germany

International Thomson Publishing Asia
211 Henderson Road
#05-10 Henderson Building
Singapore 0315

International Thomson Publishing Japan
Hirakawacho Kyowa Building, 3F
2-2-1 Hirakawacho
Chiyoda-ku, Tokyo 102 Japan

Trademarks
Course Technology and the open book logo are registered trademarks of Course Technology.
I(T)P The ITP logo is a trademark under license.
Microsoft and Windows 95 are registered trademarks of Microsoft Corporation.

Some of the product names and company names used in this book have been used for identification purposes only and may be trademarks or registered trademarks of their respective manufacturers and sellers.

Disclaimer
CTI reserves the right to revise this publication and make changes from time to time in its content without notice.

ISBN 0-7600-3440-0

Printed in the United States of America

10 9 8 7 6 5 4 3

From the

New Perspectives Series Team

We believe that technology is transforming the way people teach and learn, and we are excited about providing instructors and students with materials that use technology to teach about technology.

Our development process is unparalleled in the higher education publishing industry. Every product we create goes through an exacting process of design, development, review, and testing.

Reviewers give us direction and insight that shape our manuscripts and bring them up to the latest standards. Every manuscript is quality tested. Students whose backgrounds match the intended audience work through every keystroke, carefully checking for clarity and pointing out errors in logic and sequence. Together with our own technical reviewers, these testers help us ensure that everything that carries our name is error-free and easy to use.

We show both *how* and *why* technology is critical to solving problems in college and in whatever field you choose to teach or pursue. Our time-tested, step-by-step instructions provide unparalleled clarity. Examples and applications are chosen and crafted to motivate students.

As the New Perspectives Series team at Course Technology, our goal is to produce the most timely, accurate, creative, and technologically sound product in the entire college publishing industry. We strive for consistent high quality. This takes a lot of communication, coordination, and hard work. But we love what we do. We are determined to be the best. Write us and let us know what you think. You can also e-mail us at newperspectives@course.com.

The New Perspectives Series Team

Joseph Adamski	Kathy Finnegan	Harry Phillips
Judy Adamski	Robin Geller	Sandra Poindexter
Roy Ageloff	Roger Hayen	Mark Reimold
David Auer	Charles Hommel	Ann Shaffer
Rachel Bunin	Chris Kelly	Susan Solomon
Joan Carey	Terry Ann Kremer	Christine Spillett
Patrick Carey	Melissa Lima	Susanne Walker
Barbara Clemens	Nancy Ludlow	John Zeanchock
Kim Crowley	Mac Mendelsohn	Beverly Zimmerman
Kristin Duerr	Dan Oja	Scott Zimmerman
Jessica Evans	June Parsons	

Preface to the Instructor

An Integrated System of Instruction: Five Components

You hold in your hands a textbook that is one component of an integrated system of instruction. And what do we mean by an integrated system of instruction? We mean text, graphics, video, sound, animation, and simulations that are linked and that provide a flexible, unified, and interactive system to help you teach and to help your students learn. Specifically, the *New Perspectives Integrated System of Instruction* consists of five components: a Course Technology textbook (on computer concepts and/or microcomputer applications), Course Labs, Course Online, Course Presenter, and Course Test Manager. These components have been developed to work together to provide a complete, integrative teaching and learning experience.

The Textbook: The New Paradigm for Concepts Courses

This textbook–*New Perspectives on Computer Concepts*—is unique in many ways. It taps into the learning styles of today's students, and it empowers students to be self-sufficient computer users. It emphasizes the practical aspects of today's computing environment, such as the basics of installing software, expanding a computer system, defragmenting a disk, or decompressing a file. It contains Super Figures—illustrations that students can read and that employ the well-known fact that people always look at the pictures first. And it includes a rich collection of end of chapter materials—Review, Projects, Resources, and Lab Assignments—that are thought-provoking and encourage critical thinking. Taken together these features propelled the first edition of *New Perspectives on Computer Concepts* to become the best-selling new first edition concepts book in over a decade.

The second edition of *New Perspectives on Computer Concepts* has retained all of the show-stopping features that made the first edition so popular. And now it includes more ways to choose your coverage, a reorganization of topics, new coverage, entirely new art and photographs, student notes, Internet Projects, and much, much more. Here are *only a sampling* of the changes we've made to this feature-rich second edition:

- You can now choose the amount of coverage you want. Three editions are available—the Brief Edition (Chapters 1 through 5), the Introductory Edition (Chapters 1 through 8), or the Comprehensive Edition (Chapters 1 through 14). Also we are pleased to be the first computer concepts textbook to offer chapters (6 through 14) *available as separate modules* so you can order only the coverage you want. See below for more details about our Custom Editions and Course Kits.

- We've reorganized. The more technical topics have been delayed to Chapters 9 through 14. One example is how we moved coverage of topics formerly in Chapter 3 to Chapter 9.

- We've added new coverage. Obviously, we've updated our coverage to the latest technology; but we also now have two new chapters—one devoted entirely to buying a computer (Chapter 5) and one devoted entirely to the Internet and the information superhighway (Chapter 7). New *User Focus* sections—covering topics such as installing software, getting connected to the Internet, and setting up a modem—now conclude each chapter. We've beefed up our coverage of hardware, especially mainframes and peripheral devices.

■ We have all new art and photographs. Many of these new figures were developed using state-of-the-art object-oriented technology. See for example, Figures 1-20, 2-14, 5-7 and 10-20.

■ We've divided the chapters into numbered sections that always begin at the top of a page. This affords several tangible benefits, among them: Learning is broken up into more assimilatable chunks. You can more accurately allocate time in your syllabus. The numbers make it easier to navigate and communicate about the chapter. Look on pages 1-4 and 3-4 for examples.

■ We've added focus questions. Every major heading in each section is followed by new focus questions designed to engage students, to pique their interest, and to establish the relevance of the material that follows. Look for examples on pages 2-8, 5-22 and 9-24.

■ We've put student notes in the margins. Throughout the text these notes direct students' attention to concepts and activities that maximize learning. You can find examples on pages 2-48, 6-8 and 9-23.

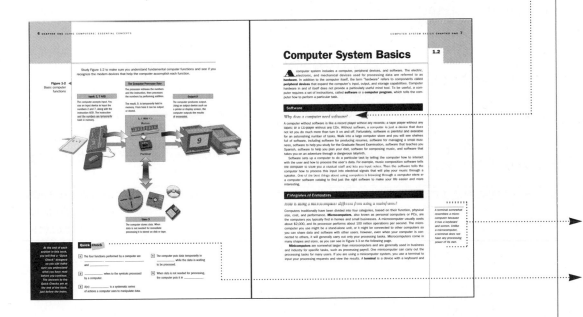

A terminal somewhat resembles a micro- computer because it has a keyboard and screen. Unlike a microcomputer, a terminal does not have any processing power of its own.

■ At the end of each section we've added meaningful, conceptual questions—called Quick Checks—that test students' understanding of what they read in the section. Answers to Quick Check questions are at the back of the book preceding the Glossary/Index. You can find examples of Quick Checks on pages 5-16, 8-15 and 14-27.

■ We now have Internet Projects. Icons in the Projects section designate those projects that have been carefully designed to require use of the Internet, or to permit use of the Internet and/or traditional library resources to complete the Project. Some representative examples are Project 4 in Chapter 1, Project 12 in Chapter 5, Project 6 in Chapter 9, and Project 3 in Chapter 10.

Remember, this list includes only a few of the many changes and enhancements to this new second edition.

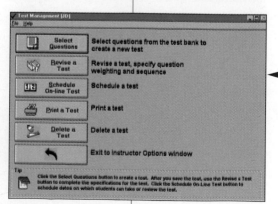

Course Labs: Now, Concepts Come to Life

Computer skills and concepts come to life with these New Perspectives Course Labs—25 highly interactive tutorials that combine illustrations, animation, digital images, and simulations. The Labs guide students step-by-step, present them with Quick Check questions, allow them to explore on their own, test them on their comprehension, and provide printed feedback. All of the Labs are either new or completely revised. *The Labs show students what textbooks can only talk about.* See pages xx and xxii for a complete list and brief description of the Labs.

Course Online: A Site Dedicated to Keeping You and Your Students Up-To-Date

Once again Course Technology ushers technology into the classroom by providing a dedicated site on the World Wide Web for users of *New Perspectives on Computer Concepts*. Instructors may visit the *password-protected* Faculty Online Companion for additional assignments with solutions, "Hot Tips" from other users, most commonly asked questions with answers, articles, content updates, and more. Students may visit the Student Online Companion where they'll find resources such as content updates to the text, links to interesting sites, additional graphics and exercises, and Internet Projects. Please see your Instructor's Manual or call your Course Technology customer service representative for more information.

Course Presenter: Ready-Made or Customized Dynamic Presentations

Course Presenter is a CD ROM-based presentation tool that provides you a wealth of resources for use in the classroom, replacing traditional overhead transparencies with computer generated screenshows. Presenter includes a structured presentation for each chapter of the textbook and also provides the flexibility to create your own custom presentations, complete with matching students notes and lecture notes pages.

Course Test Manager: Testing and Practice Online or On Paper

Course Test Manager is cutting edge Windows-based testing software that helps instructors design and administer pre-tests, practice tests, and actual examinations. The full-featured program allows students to randomly generate practice tests that provide immediate online feedback and detailed study guides for questions incorrectly answered. Online pre-tests help you assess student skills and plan instruction. You can use Course Test Manager to generate traditional paper tests. Also students can take tests at the computer that can be automatically graded and generate statistical information on student individual and group performance.

Integrating the Five Components: The Formula for Successful Teaching and Learning

The text, graphics, video, sound, animation, and simulations contained in the Textbook, Labs, and Presenter, Test Manager and Web Pages are linked to provide a flexible, unified, and interactive system of instruction. How are they linked? The diagram here helps answer that question.

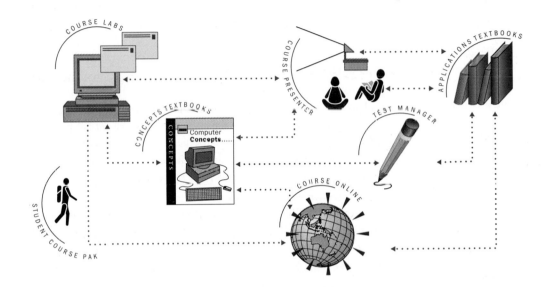

Start with the link between the Computer Concepts textbook and the Course Labs. The Labs teach skills and concepts that are introduced in the textbook. Each Lab is identified by an icon, and the icons appear throughout the text adjacent to the text material they reinforce. Quick Checks appears in both the textbook and the Labs. The textbook contains Lab Assignments that students complete using the Course Labs. These are only a few examples of how these two components are linked.

All of the components are linked in similar ways. Here are some examples. While using Course Presenter, you can click a button and launch a Lab. Presenter also contains Quick Checks that you can display for student interaction. Students see the same figures in Presenter that they see in the textbook and in Course Test Manager. The Practice Tests in the Test Manager generate a study guide of pages in the textbook to help students study the topics of those questions they incorrectly answered. Some of the Projects in the textbook require students to visit the *New Perspectives on Computer Concepts* Web page. And so on...

You can choose to integrate these components as much or as little as you like. Used in total this integration provides a powerful teaching and learning system.

Instructor's Manual: Your Help System

For each chapter the authors provide a chapter outline; suggestions for instruction on the chapter content, for integrating the Labs, and for using the Resources; answers to the Review, Projects, and Labs Assignments; Quick Quizes: and numerous teaching tips.

Student Course Pak: For Students With Computers and Distance Learners

We are pleased to present another Course Technology first—the Student Course Pak. It is available to students who have their own computers or who have access to computers with CD-ROM drives. It is also ideal for instructors and students in distance learning programs.

The Student Course Pak includes:
— the textbook *New Perspectives on Computer Concepts Second Edition* (Brief, Introductory, or Comprehensive Editions)
— a CD which contains:
  - the 25 Course Labs
  - the Practice Test component of Course Test Manager

The New Perspectives Series: A Wide Selection of Application Software Texts

New Perspectives on Computer Concepts is part of the New Perspectives Series, which includes microcomputer applications textbooks. These applications textbooks are also part of the integrated system of instruction. For example, they include Quick Checks and Lab Assignments; they link to Course Presenter and Course Test Manager; and they have home pages.

The applications textbooks are available in different lengths, platforms, and releases. They are also available with the concepts textbooks in bound editions, in Course Kits, and in our new Custom Editions. Contact your CTI sales representative or customer service representative for the most up-to-date details. The following list shows the programs available in the New Perspectives Series.

dBASE	Microsoft PowerPoint	Perfect Office
Internet and World Wide Web	Microsoft Windows 3.1	Paradox
Lotus 1-2-3	Microsoft Windows 95	Presentations
Microsoft Access	Microsoft Word	Quattro Pro
Microsoft Excel	Microsoft Works	Microsoft Visual Basic
Microsoft Office Professional	Netscape Navigator	WordPerfect

Course Kits and Custom Editions: Exactly What You Want, the Way You Want It

If you want to customize your textbook to fit your course *exactly*, Course Technology offers you two ways to combine the materials you want and save students money. With Course Kits you can choose two or more New Perspectives or other Course Technology textbooks to use in one course; they will be packaged together in a box and sold to your students for a deeply discounted price. Or, if you want your New Perspectives course materials bound together in one volume, you can choose from our Custom Editions—select the materials and the binding (spiral or three-ring binder) and order at a discounted price. Contact your CTI sales representative or customer service representative for more details.

Acknowledgments

This integrated system of instruction works because of a powerful system of talented people. Many thanks to Mark Ciampa, Gail Miles, Cathy Moore, Dave White and Roy Ageloff whose comments were invaluable. Sandi Poindexter and John Zeanchock deserve special recognition for their review of the instructional design. The extraordinary talents of Debbie Masi, Ella Hanna, and Kim Munsell are woven throughout this system of instruction. Coco and Claire hounded the team until everything was perfect. And still, no thanks to Marilyn.

Brief Contents

Table of Contents

CHAPTER THIRTEEN

Managing the Data in Files and Databases

Course Labs

Course Labs offer the absolute best when it comes to interactive learning reinforcement. The newly designed Labs now offer:

- Steps, which guide students step-by-step as they learn/review basic concepts
- Quick Checks, which appear as students work through the Steps and which draw attention to key points
- Quick Check Summary Reports, which can be printed as homework and as validation that students have completed the Steps
- Explore, in which students can experiment, practice skills, and complete the Lab Assignments at the end of each chapter.

CHAPTER ONE

Using a Mouse

This Lab guides students through basic mouse functions and operations. Interactive exercises using dialog boxes allow students to practice mouse skills by creating posters.

Using a Keyboard

Students learn the parts of the keyboard and basic keyboard operations. They practice basic keyboarding with interactive typing exercises, including a self-paced typing tutor that helps improve speed and accuracy.

User Interfaces

Students are presented with user interfaces on a general/conceptual level, and then have the opportunity to interact with menu driven, prompted dialog, command line, graphical, and combination interfaces.

DOS Command-Line Interface

This Lab presents students with concepts and basic skills associated with the DOS command line, and provides hands-on practice entering commands at a live DOS prompt.

Peripheral Devices

Descriptions, drawings, and animations explain the functions of many popular peripheral devices.

CHAPTER TWO

Word Processing

This Lab guides students through essential word processing skills, such as typing and editing text, formatting, saving, and opening a document. They interact with a word processing program, specially designed for this Lab, that offers a hands-on introduction to word processors.

Spreadsheets

Students are introduced to essential spreadsheet skills. A spreadsheet program, specially designed for this Lab, allows students to practice and explore these skills on their own.

Databases

After learning essential database concepts, students learn to use query by example to search a visual database for specific records.

Computer History Hypermedia

This dynamic Lab contains descriptions, drawings and photos related to the history and development of computing devices. Students learn to use hypertext links to research historical events and trends.

CHAPTER THREE

Using Files
Students see what happens on the screen, in RAM, and on disk when they save, open, revise, and delete files.

Defragmentation and Disk Operations
In this Lab, students interact with simulated disks, files, and FATs to discover how the computer physically stores files. This Lab demonstrates how files become fragmented and how defragmentation utilities work.

Windows Directorie, Folders, and Files
Students work with a directory tree to learn basic concepts of directory hierarchies and file types.

DOS Directories and File Management
Students learn the basics of DOS file managment, including subdirectories, copying, and moving files.

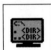

CHAPTER FOUR

Troubleshooting
Students use a simulated computer to step through the boot process. They learn to identify and troubleshoot the most common boot-related problems.

Binary Numbers
This Lab introduces students to binary numbers, demonstrates how data is stored electronically using 1s and 0s, and provides practice converting between binary and decimal.

CPU Simulator
Students use a microprocessor simulation to see what happens in the ALU, control unit, and register during execution of simple assembly language programs. They can run prepared programs or write their own to see how a microprocessor actually works.

CHAPTER FIVE

Buying a Computer
In this Lab an online glossary helps students interpret the technical specifications and advertisements to compare features and make purchase decisions.

CHAPTER SIX

E-mail
Students use a simple e-mail simulation to learn essential e-mail skills including creating, sending, forwarding, replying, printing and saving mail.

CHAPTER SEVEN

The Internet: World Wide Web
Students interact with a simulated Web browser to explore home pages, URLs, linking, and hypertext. You can assign this Lab even if an Internet connection is not available.

CHAPTER EIGHT

Data Backup
Using a simulated business environment, this Lab teaches basic backup procedures. Students experience data loss, attempt to restore lost data, and learn first-hand the value of regular backup procedures.

CHAPTER NINE

Data Representation

This Lab consists of multiple sections that build upon students' understanding of binary numbers. It demonstrates how 0s and 1s are used to represent all types of data, including text, numbers, graphics and animations. This Lab also explains the concept of data compression.

CHAPTER TEN

Building a Network

This Lab begins with a basic network consisting of a file server and two workstations. Students, playing the part of the Network Manager, are guided through a hands-on process of adding devices and modifying the network.

CHAPTER TWELVE

System Testing

Students play the role of a beta tester who must systematically test an information system to determine if it processed data correctly.

CHAPTER THIRTEEN

SQL Queries

Students learn how to use relational and logical operators and how to locate specific records or groups of records in a database.

CHAPTER FOURTEEN

Visual Programming

Students use a simple visual programming environment to write elementary programs. This Lab introduces programming fundamentals and event-driven visual programming in a Visual Basic style environment.

Credits

Cover Photographed by Durvin & Co., designed by Hanna Design+Company. **Chapter One** Opener: Photofest. Figure 1-1: UPI/Bettmann. Figure 1-3 a-c: Courtesy of International Business Machines Corporation. Figure 1-3d: ©Frank Pryor/Courtesy of Apple Computer, Inc. Figure 1-4 and 1-5: Courtesy of International Business Machines Corporation. Figure 1-6: ©Charles Thatcher/Tony Stone Images. **Chapter Two** Opener: AP/Wide World Photos. Figure 2-2 and 2-5: Courtesy of Microsoft Corporation. Photographed by Durvin & Co. Figure 2-11a: Courtesy of International Business Machines Corporation. Figure 2-11b: Courtesy of Apple Computer, Inc. Figure 2-17: Courtesy of Berkeley Systems, Inc. Figure 2-22: Courtesy of Creative Labs, Inc. ©1995. Figure 2-24: Compliments of Microsoft Corporation. Photographed by Durvin & Co. **Chapter Three** Opener: ©Dilip Meta/Contact Press Images, Inc. **Chapter Four** Opener: James Kaczman. **Chapter Five** Opener: Bonnie Kamin Photography. Figure 5-1: Courtesy Midwest Micro, Fletcher Ohio. Figure 5-7a-b: Courtesy EPSON Americas, Inc. Figure 5-7c: Courtesy Hewlett-Packard Company. Figure 5-8: PC-3050 Courtesy of Sharp Electronics Corporation. Figure 5-9: Mobile Communications Division of U.S. Robotics. Figure 5-10, 5-11 and 5-12a: Courtesy of International Business Machines Corporation. Figure 5-12b: PC-3050 Courtesy of Sharp Electornics Corporation. Figure 5-12c: Toshiba America Information Systems, Inc. Figure 5-13a: James P. Dawson/NYT Pictures. Figure 5-13b-c: Images reprinted with permission from Microsoft Corporation. Figure 5-15: Micron Electronics, Inc. Figure 5-19: Reprinted by permission of Wall Street Journal. ©1995 Dow Jones & Company, Inc. All Rights Reserved Worldwide. **Chapter Six** Opener: Spencer Jones 1995/FPG International. Figure 6-14a: Courtesy of International Business Machines Corporation. Figure 6-14b (Lotus Notes): Courtesy of Lotus Development Corporation. Figure 6-14c (ProshareVideo 200): Courtesy of Intel Corporation. Figure 6-14d (Collabra Share): Courtesy of Netscape Communications Corporations. Figure 6-14e: ©Steven Peters/Tony Stone Images. **Chapter Seven** Opener: Created by Dan Oja, Guildware, Inc. Figure 7-6 and 7-7: Prodigy Services Company. Figure 7-20: Drawing by P. Steiner, ©1993 The New Yorker Magazine, Inc. Figure 7-21: ©1990 Peter Menzel Photography. **Chapter Eight** Opener: Ducal Palace, Mantua/Mauro Magliani/SuperStock, Inc. Figure 8-11: Source: *Understanding Computers: Computer Security.* Alexandria, VA: Time-Life Books, 1986. Figure 8-14: I. Essa, T. Darrell, A. Pentland, ©MIT, Medial Library 1994. **Chapter Nine** Opener: The Granger Collection, New York. **Chapter Ten** Opener: Photographed by Carol Palmer Photography. Figure 10-2a: Third Coast StockPhotography. Figure 10-2b: Stock Market Photo. **Chapter Eleven** Opener: Photographed by Durvin & Co. Figure 11-2: Source: Reprinted with permission of the Free Press, a Division of Macmillan, Inc. from *Competitive Advantage: Creating and Sustaining Superior Performance*, p.5 ©1985 by Michael E. Porter. Figure 11-6a-g: International Business Machines Corporation. **Chapter Twelve** Opener: Minden Pictures. Figure 12-3a,b,c: International Business Machines Corporation. **Chapter Thirteen** Opener: Photofest. **Chapter Fourteen** Opener: ©Ken Reid 1991/FPG International.

CHAPTER ONE

Using Computers:

Essential Concepts

In the classic science-fiction film *2001: A Space Odyssey*, astronaut Dave Bowman and four crew members depart on a mission to Jupiter. The mission objective: to discover the source of a mysterious object from space. Midway through the mission, the onboard computer, named HAL, begins to exhibit strange behavior. Dave leaves the spacecraft to make some external repairs. When he is ready to reboard, he speaks to the computer, "Open the pod bay door, HAL." HAL's reply is chilling, "I'm sorry, Dave, I'm afraid I can't do that."

This dialog between a human and a computer raises some intriguing questions. How realistic is it? Can humans and computers communicate this fluently? What went wrong with the communication? Why won't the computer let Dave back into the spaceship?

To use a computer effectively, you must communicate tasks to the computer and accurately interpret the information the computer provides to you. The means by which humans and computers communicate is referred to as the *user interface*, and this is the central theme of Chapter 1.

In this chapter you will learn which computer components are necessary for communication between humans and computers. You will also learn about the user interfaces typically found on today's computer systems and how to respond to what you see on the computer screen. The chapter concludes with a discussion about manuals, reference guides, and tutorials that will help you learn how to interact with a specific computer system or software package.

CHAPTER**PREVIEW**

This chapter is a practical introduction to computers that you can immediately apply in the Lab component of this course: starting a computer, logging into a network, starting programs, and using a variety of user interfaces. When you have completed this chapter you should be able to:

- Define the term "computer"

- Describe the relationship between computer hardware and software

- Identify the parts of a typical microcomputer system

- List the peripheral devices that are typically found on microcomputer systems

- Define the term "user interface"

- Describe how you use interface elements such as prompts, commands, menus, and graphical objects

- Describe the resources you can use to learn how to use computers and software

LABS

Peripheral Devices

User Interfaces

DOS Command-Line User Interface

Using a Mouse

Using a Keyboard

Computers: Mind Tools

Computers have been called "mind tools" because they enhance our ability to perform tasks that require mental activity. Computers are adept at performing activities such as making calculations quickly, sorting large lists, and searching through vast information libraries. Humans can do all these activities, but a computer can often accomplish them much faster and more accurately. Our ability to use a computer complements our mental capabilities and makes us more productive. The key to making effective use of the computer as a tool is to know what a computer does, how it works, and how you can use it. That is the focus of this book.

Von Neumann's Definition

What is a computer?

If you look in a dictionary printed before 1940, you might be surprised to find a computer defined as a *person* who performs calculations! Machines also performed calculations back then, but they were referred to as calculators, not computers. The modern definition and use of the term "computer" emerged in the 1940s when the first electronic computing devices were developed as a response to World War II military needs.

In 1945, a team of engineers began working on a secret military project to construct the Electronic Discrete Variable Automatic Computer, referred to by the acronym EDVAC. At the time, only one other functioning computer had been built in the United States. Plans for the EDVAC were described in a report by the eminent mathematician John von Neumann, pictured in Figure 1-1.

Figure 1-1
John von Neumann

When this photo was published in 1947, the caption read, "Dr. John von Neumann stands in front of a new Electronic 'Brain,' the fastest computing machine for its degree of precision yet made. The machine which can do 2,000 multiplications in one second and add or subtract 100,000 times in the same period was displayed today for the first time at the Institute for Advanced Study. Its fabulous memory can store 1,024 numbers of 12 decimal places each. Dr. von Neumann was one of the designers of the wonder machine."

Von Neumann's report has been described as "the most influential paper in the history of computer science." It was one of the earliest documents to specifically define the components of a computer and describe their functions. In the report, von Neumann used the term "automatic computing system." Today, popular usage has abandoned this cumbersome terminology in favor of the shorter terms "computer" or "computer system." Based on the concepts presented in von Neumann's paper, we can define a **computer** as a device that accepts input, processes data, stores data, and produces output. Let's look more closely at the elements of this definition.

A Computer Accepts Input

What kinds of input can a computer use?

Computer **input** is whatever is put into a computer system. "Input" is also used as a verb that means to feed information into a computer. Input can be supplied by a person, by the environment, or by another computer. Some examples of the kinds of input a computer can process are the words and symbols in a document, numbers for a calculation, instructions for completing a process, pictures, audio signals from a microphone, and temperatures from a thermostat.

An **input device** gathers and translates input into a form that the computer can process. As a computer user you will probably use the keyboard as your main input device.

A Computer Processes Data

In what ways can a computer process data?

Data refers to the symbols that describe people, events, things, and ideas. Computers manipulate data in many ways, and we call this manipulation "processing." In the context of computers, then, we can define a **process** as a systematic series of actions a computer uses to manipulate data. Some of the ways a computer can process data include performing calculations, sorting lists of words or numbers, modifying documents and pictures according to user instructions, and drawing graphs. A computer processes data in a device called the **central processing unit** or **CPU**.

You will get a more technical perspective on data in Chapter 3 and learn more about the way the central processing unit works in Chapter 4.

A Computer Stores Data

Why does a computer store data?

A computer must store data so it is available for processing. The places a computer puts data are referred to as **storage**. Most computers have more than one location for storing data. The place where the computer stores data depends on how the data is being used. The computer puts data in one place while it is waiting to be processed and another place when it is not needed for immediate processing. **Memory** is an area that holds data that is waiting to be processed. **Storage** is the area where data can be left on a permanent basis while it is not needed for processing.

A Computer Produces Output

What kinds of output does a computer produce?

Computer **output** is the results produced by a computer. "Output" is also used as a verb that means the process of producing output. Some examples of computer output include reports, documents, music, graphs, and pictures. An **output device** displays, prints, or transfers the results of processing from the computer memory.

The distinction between memory and storage is particularly useful for understanding how computers work. Make sure you understand that "memory" is a holding area used while the data is waiting to be processed. "Storage" is a more permanent location for data when it is not needed for processing.

Study Figure 1-2 to make sure you understand fundamental computer functions and see if you recognize the modern devices that help the computer accomplish each function.

Figure 1-2
Basic computer functions

Input: 2, 7 ADD

The computer accepts input. You use an input device to input the numbers 2 and 7, along with the instruction ADD. The instruction and the numbers are temporarily held in memory.

The Computer Processes Data

The processor retrieves the numbers and the instruction, then processes the numbers by performing addition.

The result, 9, is temporarily held in memory. From here it can be output or stored.

Output 9

The computer produces output. Using an output device such as a printer or display screen, the computer outputs the results of processing.

2, 7 ADD = 9

Memory

CPU

Processor

9

Store 9

The computer stores data. When data is not needed for immediate processing it is stored on disk or tape.

Quick Check

1 The four functions performed by a computer are
_____, _____, _____,
and _____.

2 _____ refers to the symbols processed by a computer.

3 A(n) _____ is a systematic series of actions a computer uses to manipulate data.

4 The computer puts data temporarily in
_____ while the data is waiting to be processed.

5 When data is not needed for processing, the computer puts it in _____.

Computer System Basics

A computer system includes a computer, peripheral devices, and software. The electric, electronic, and mechanical devices used for processing data are referred to as **hardware**. In addition to the computer itself, the term "hardware" refers to components called **peripheral devices** that expand the computer's input, output, and storage capabilities. Computer hardware in and of itself does not provide a particularly useful mind tool. To be useful, a computer requires a set of instructions, called **software** or a **computer program**, which tells the computer how to perform a particular task.

Software

Why does a computer need software?

A computer without software is like a record player without any records; a tape player without any tapes; or a CD-player without any CDs. Without software, a computer is just a device that does not let you do much more than turn it on and off. Fortunately, software is plentiful and available for an astonishing number of tasks. Walk into a large computer store and you will see shelves full of software, including software for producing resumes, software for managing a small business, software to help you study for the Graduate Record Examination, software that teaches you Spanish, software to help you plan your diet, software for composing music, and software that takes you on an adventure through a dangerous labyrinth.

Software sets up a computer to do a particular task by telling the computer how to interact with the user and how to process the user's data. For example, music composition software tells the computer to show you a musical staff and lets you input notes. Then the software tells the computer how to process this input into electrical signals that will play your music through a speaker. One of the best things about using computers is browsing through a computer store or a computer software catalog to find just the right software to make your life easier and more interesting.

Categories of Computers

How is using a microcomputer different from using a mainframe?

Computers traditionally have been divided into four categories, based on their function, physical size, cost, and performance. **Microcomputers**, also known as personal computers or PCs, are the computers you typically find in homes and small businesses. A microcomputer usually costs about $2,000, and its processor performs about 100 million operations per second. The microcomputer you use might be a stand-alone unit, or it might be connected to other computers so you can share data and software with other users. However, even when your computer is connected to others, it will generally carry out only your processing tasks. Microcomputers come in many shapes and sizes, as you can see in Figure 1-3 on the following page.

Minicomputers are somewhat larger than microcomputers and are generally used in business and industry for specific tasks, such as processing payroll. One minicomputer can carry out the processing tasks for many users. If you are using a minicomputer system, you use a terminal to input your processing requests and view the results. A **terminal** is a device with a keyboard and

A terminal somewhat resembles a microcomputer because it has a keyboard and screen. Unlike a microcomputer, a terminal does not have any processing power of its own.

Figure 1-3
Microcomputers

A standard **desktop microcomputer** fits on a desk and runs on power from an electrical outlet. The display screen is usually placed on top of the horizontal "desktop" case.

Desktop Microcomputer

Microcomputer with Tower Case

A microcomputer with a **tower case** contains the same basic components as a standard desktop microcomputer, but the vertically-oriented case is large and allows more room for expansion. The tower unit can be placed on the floor to save desk space.

Notebook Computer

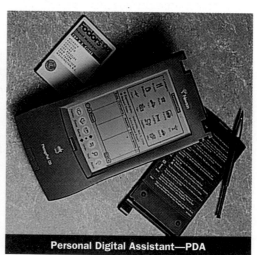

Personal Digital Assistant—PDA

A **notebook computer** is small and light, giving it the advantage of portability that a standard desktop computer does not have. A notebook computer can run on power from an electrical outlet or batteries.

To achieve even more portability, a **personal digital assistant** (PDA) eliminates the size and weight of a keyboard. PDAs accept input written with a special stylus.

▶ **Figure 1-4**
A typical
minicomputer

A minicomputer handles processing tasks for multiple users. This minicomputer can handle up to 20 users, but only three terminals are currently connected.

Terminals act as each user's main input and output device. The terminal has a keyboard for input and a display screen for output, but it does not process the user's data. Instead, processing requests must be transmitted from the terminal to the minicomputer.

The minicomputer stores data for all the users in one centralized location.

screen used for input and output, but not for processing. Your terminal transmits your processing request to the minicomputer. The minicomputer sends back results to your terminal when the processing is complete. The minicomputer system with three terminals in Figure 1-4 is fairly typical and carries a price tag of $68,000.

Mainframes are large, fast, and fairly expensive computers, generally used by business or government to provide centralized storage, processing, and management for large amounts of data. As with a minicomputer, one mainframe computer carries out processing tasks for multiple users who input processing requests using a terminal. However, a mainframe generally services more users than a minicomputer. To process large amounts of data, mainframes often include more than one processing unit. One of these processing units directs overall operations. A second processing unit handles communication with all the users requesting data. A third processing unit finds the data requested by users.

When you use a mainframe, your processing requests are transmitted from your terminal to the computer. At the same time, other users may also transmit requests. The computer processes each request in turn and transmits back the results. Mainframes service user requests quickly. Even though there might be 200 people submitting processing requests, the speed of the computer's response makes it seem as if you are the only user.

Mainframes remain the computer of choice in situations where reliability, data security, and centralized control are necessary. The price of a mainframe computer system is typically several hundred thousand dollars. A mainframe computer is housed in a closet-size cabinet, and its peripheral devices are contained in separate cabinets, as shown in Figure 1-5 on the following page.

Supercomputers are the largest, fastest, and most expensive type of computer. Unlike minicomputers and mainframes, supercomputers are not designed to optimize processing for multiple users. Instead, supercomputers use their significant processing power to solve a few very difficult problems such as predicting the weather and modeling nuclear reactions. The speed of a supercomputer can reach one trillion instructions per second. The cost of a supercomputer, like the one in Figure 1-6 on the following page, tops out at about $35 million.

If you were a scientific researcher using a supercomputer, you would probably need to make an appointment and provide an estimate of the time needed to complete your processing task.

Both mainframes and supercomputers are large, expensive, and powerful. However, a mainframe usually supports many users doing relatively simple processing tasks, whereas a supercomputer supports only a few users who have complex processing tasks.

Figure 1-5
IBM mainframe
computer

The mainframe processor and storage
units are housed in the large cabinets.
The four terminals in the foreground
are used for computer maintenance.
Additional terminals are located in other
areas of the building.

Figure 1-6
A Cray
supercomputer

The processing unit of this Cray computer
is just over six feet tall. The terminals are
located in other areas of the building.

When your appointment arrives, you input your problem from a terminal. While the supercomputer works on your problem, other users have to wait.

Today the lines that divide the different computer categories are fuzzy and tend to shift as more powerful computers become available. For example, the definition of minicomputers in technical dictionaries published in the early 1980s specified performance features that more accurately describe today's microcomputers. Because the characteristics of each computer category shift and change as technology advances, it is difficult to categorize a particular computer unless you have up-to-date technical expertise. So, if you want to know whether a particular computer is a micro, a mini, a mainframe, or a supercomputer, look at the sales literature to find out how the manufacturer classifies it.

This book focuses on microcomputers because that is the category of computers you are likely to use. Although the focus is on microcomputers, most of the concepts you will learn apply to the other categories of computers as well.

Computer System Components

When I use a computer system, what hardware components will it include?

Microcomputer, minicomputer, mainframe, and super-computer systems include devices to input, output, process, and store data. Study Figure 1-7 to learn about the hardware components you are likely to use on a typical microcomputer system.

The primary output device on a microcomputer is the **monitor**; a display device that converts electrical signals from the computer into points of colored light on the screen to form an image.

The **system unit** is the case or box that contains the main circuit board of the computer system. In a typical microcomputer, the system unit contains the power supply, storage devices, and the main circuit board with the computer's main processor and memory.

A **CD-ROM** is a high-capacity storage medium with a capacity of up to 680 million characters. Most CD-ROMs contain information when you purchase them and do not allow you to add or change the information they contain.

A **floppy disk drive** is a storage device that writes data on floppy disks. A typical microcomputer system has a 3¹/₂-inch floppy disk drive that stores up to 1.44 million characters of data on a single floppy disk. Some microcomputer systems also have a 5¹/₄-inch drive to accommodate programs supplied on 5¹/₄ inch disks. A light indicates when the floppy disk drive is in use—a warning not to remove your disk until the light goes out.

A **CD-ROM drive** is a storage device that uses laser technology to read data from a CD-ROM.

A **mouse** is a pointing device that you use to manipulate objects on the screen. Mice are rapidly becoming a standard input device on most microcomputer systems.

Storage media are physical materials that provide long-term storage for computer data. **Floppy disks** are popular microcomputer storage media that come in 3¹/₂-inch or 5¹/₄-inch sizes to match the two sizes of microcomputer disk drives. Floppy disks also come in high-density or low-density versions, again to match the capacity of the disk drive.

A **hard disk drive** can store billions of characters on a non-removable disk platter. A hard disk drive is mounted inside the system unit; an external light indicates when the hard disk drive is in use.

Most computers are equipped with a **keyboard** as the primary input device. A computer keyboard includes the letter and number keys, as well as several additional keys that control computer-specific tasks.

Microcomputer Compatibility

Can all computers use the same software?

Hundreds of companies manufacture microcomputers, but there are only a small number of microcomputer designs or **platforms**. Today there are two major microcomputer platforms: IBM-compatibles and Macintosh-compatibles. **IBM-compatible computers**, also referred to as **PC-compatibles**, are based on the architecture of the first IBM microcomputer. IBM-compatible computers are manufactured by Compaq, Dell, Gateway, and hundreds of other companies. The second major microcomputer platform is based on the Macintosh computer, manufactured by Apple Computer, Inc.

Computers that operate in essentially the same way are said to be **compatible**. Two computers are compatible if they can communicate with each other, share the same software, share data, and use the same peripheral devices.

Not all microcomputers are compatible with each other. The IBM platform and the Macintosh platform are not regarded as compatible because they cannot use the same hardware devices or

Because about two-thirds of the microcomputers in use today are IBM-compatible, the examples in this book focus on the IBM platform.

Figure 1-8 ◀
Peripheral devices

A **bar code reader** gathers input data by reading bar codes, such as the universal product codes on supermarket products. Bar code readers are also used at library circulation desks to track books.

An **LCD projection display panel** is placed on an overhead projector to produce a large display of the information shown on the computer screen.

A **hand scanner** converts a 4–6″ section of text or graphics into electronic format. To use the scanner, you pull it over the text you want to convert.

A **modem** transfers data from one computer to another over telephone lines. External modems have their own case. Internal modems are installed inside the computer system unit.

A **scanner** converts text or images on paper documents into an electronic format that the computer can display, print, and store.

use the same programs without hardware or software to translate between them. Apple is trying to overcome compatibility problems with a new platform called the **PowerPC** that uses a built-in translation process to run both IBM and Macintosh software.

Peripheral Devices

Is it possible to expand or modify a basic computer system?

The term "peripheral device" designates equipment that is used with a computer, but is not a necessary or integral part of it. For example, a printer is a popular peripheral device used with micro, mini, and mainframe computers, but the computer can function without one. Keyboards, monitors, mice, and disk drives are peripheral devices, even though they are included with most basic computer systems. Figure 1-8 shows some of the more popular peripheral devices used with microcomputers.

Peripheral devices allow you to expand and modify your basic computer system. For example, you might purchase a computer that includes a mouse, but you might prefer to use a trackball,

Lab

Peripheral Devices

A **monitor** is an output device the computer uses to display the results of processing.
A **touch sensitive screen** displays options you can select by touching them on the screen.

A **sound card** can be installed inside the system unit to give a computer the capability to accept audio input from a **microphone**, play sound files stored on disks or CD-ROMs, and produce audio output through **speakers** or earphones.

A **trackball** is a pointing device that you might use as an alternative to a mouse. You roll the ball to position the pointer on the screen. Unlike a mouse, a trackball doesn't move on the desk and therefore requires less space.

A **keyboard** is the main input device for most computer systems.

A **mouse** is a pointing device you use to manipulate on-screen objects.

Figure 1-8
Peripheral devices
continued

A **laser printer** uses the same technology as a photocopier to print professional-quality text and graphics. Heat fuses a fine dark powder, called toner, onto paper to create text and images.

A **disk drive** stores data.

A **dot matrix printer** creates characters and graphics by printing a fine pattern of dots using a 9-pin or 24-pin print mechanism. A 9-pin printer creates a coarser image than a 24-pin printer.

A **plotter** uses pens to draw an image on paper. Plotters are often used by architects and engineers to produce multicolor line drawings.

A **computer projector** generates a large image of what's on the computer screen suitable for conference and lecture presentations.

or you might want to expand your computer's capabilities by adding a scanner so you can input photographs.

Most microcomputer peripheral devices are designed for installation by users without technical expertise. When you buy a peripheral device it usually comes with installation instructions and specially designed software. You should carefully follow the instructions to install the device. Also make sure the computer is turned off before you attempt to connect a peripheral device so you don't damage your computer system. The instructions will also give you directions on how to install any software that might be necessary to use the peripheral device.

What's the difference between the terms computer *and* computer system*? A computer does not include peripheral devices, but a computer system does.*

Computer Networks

Our school has a computer network. Is using a network going to be difficult?

A **computer network** is a collection of computers and other devices connected to share data, hardware, and software. A network can connect microcomputers, minicomputers, and mainframes. A network has advantages for an organization and its users. For example, if users share a printer on a network, the organization saves money because it does not have to purchase a printer for every user. Network users can send messages to others on the network and retrieve data from a centralized storage device. Using a computer on a network is not much different from using a stand-alone computer, except that you usually have access to more data and software. On a network you might also have to be more aware of security.

Networks must be secured against unauthorized access to protect the data they store. Most organizations restrict access to the software and data on a network by requiring users to log in. To **log in** you enter a unique user ID and password. A **user ID** is a combination of letters and numbers that serve as your "call sign" or "identification." You can let people know your user ID so they can send you messages over the network, but you don't want to reveal your password. A **password** is a special set of symbols known only to you and the person who supervises the network. You should not reveal your password because it would violate your responsibility to help maintain network security. Also, you should understand that if someone logs into a network using your user ID and sends offensive messages or erases important files, it will look as if you did it. In addition to logging into a network, you might have to log in to use some software; the login procedure is similar. Figure 1-9 shows you what to do when a computer asks you to log in.

If your school has a computer network, Project 3 at the end of this chapter will help you learn how to use it.

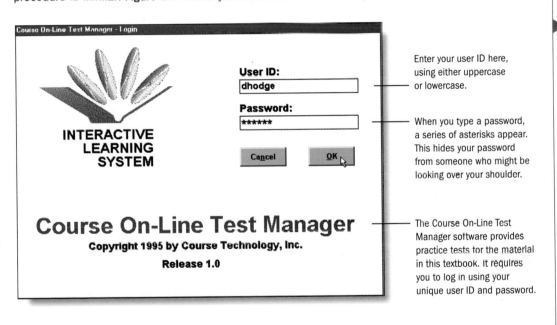

Figure 1-9
Entering a user ID and password

Enter your user ID here, using either uppercase or lowercase.

When you type a password, a series of asterisks appear. This hides your password from someone who might be looking over your shoulder.

The Course On-Line Test Manager software provides practice tests for the material in this textbook. It requires you to log in using your unique user ID and password.

Quick Check

1. Most microcomputers are equipped with a(n) _____ as the primary input device and a(n) _____ as the primary output device.

2. A(n) _____ is generally devoted to carrying out the processing tasks of only one user, even when it is connected to other computers.

3. A(n) _____ is a device that resembles a microcomputer but does not have any processing capability.

4. What two types of computers are designed to perform processing tasks for many users?

5. If an organization wants to provide processing for more than 200 users and reliability, security, and centralized control are necessary, a(n) _____ computer would best meet its needs.

6. An IBM computer is _____ with a Compaq computer because it operates in essentially the same way.

7. A computer _____ allows you to send messages to other computer users and access data from a centralized storage device.

1.3

The User Interface

To effectively use the computer as a mind tool, you must communicate with it; you must tell the computer what tasks to perform, and you must accurately interpret the information the computer provides to you. The means by which humans and computers communicate is referred to as the **user interface**. Through the user interface, the computer accepts your input and presents you with output. This output provides you with the results of processing, confirms the completion of the processing, or indicates that data was stored.

The user interface is a combination of software and hardware. The software that controls the user interface defines its characteristics. For example, software controls whether you accomplish tasks by manipulating graphical objects or typing commands. The hardware controls the way you physically manipulate the computer to establish communication, for example, whether you use a keyboard or your voice to input commands. After you have a general understanding of user interfaces, you will be able to figure out quickly how to make the computer do what you want it to do.

Lab

User Interfaces

Interacting with the Computer

What kinds of user interfaces are typically found on computers?

Donald Norman, a well-known cognitive scientist, wrote a delightful book called *The Psychology of Everyday Things* in which he says, "Well-designed objects are easy to interpret and understand. They contain visible clues to their operation. Poorly designed objects can be difficult and frustrating to use. They provide no clues—or sometimes false clues. They trap the user and thwart the normal process of interpretation and understanding." A classic example of a poorly designed computer "object" is the screen message, "Press any key to continue." Apparently, some users have become frustrated when they can't find a key on the keyboard labeled "Any Key"!

User interfaces have changed and evolved in response to the needs of a rapidly growing community of computer users. Yet interface design and development are still in an early stage. Using computers can be enjoyable. However, as with many objects in everyday life, some computer user interfaces are not well conceived, and using them is frustrating.

A user interface is constructed using hardware and software interface elements, such as a mouse, menus, and graphics. In this section of the chapter you are going to look at several basic interface elements, so you will recognize them and understand how to use them. With this background, you can make some intelligent guesses about how to proceed when you use an unfamiliar computer or a new software package.

In Project 5 at the end of this chapter, you have a chance to make your own evaluation of a user interface.

As you read the descriptions of the interface elements, consider not only how to use them, but also the positive and negative aspects of each design. Which interface elements are easy to interpret and understand? Which provide clues about what to do and how to do it? If you have used computers, you should remember using some or all of these user interface elements, and you might recall your own reaction to them.

Prompts

Why is it sometimes hard for me to figure out what the computer wants me to do?

A **prompt** is a message displayed by the computer that asks for input from the user. In response to a computer prompt, you enter the requested information or follow the instruction. Some prompts, such as "Enter your name:," are helpful and easy to understand, even for beginners. Other prompts, like A:\>, are less helpful.

A sequence of prompts is sometimes used to develop a user interface called a **prompted dialog**. In a prompted dialog, a sort of conversation takes place between the computer and user. Here is an example of a prompted dialog that tells you how much money will accumulate in your savings account. The computer's prompts are in uppercase. The user's responses are in bold.

HOW MUCH MONEY IS CURRENTLY IN YOUR ACCOUNT?
1000
HOW MUCH MONEY WILL YOU DEPOSIT EACH MONTH?
100
WHAT IS THE YEARLY INTEREST RATE PERCENT?
6
WHAT IS THE LENGTH OF THE SAVINGS PERIOD IN MONTHS?
36
O.K. AFTER 36 MONTHS YOU WILL HAVE $5149.96 IN YOUR SAVINGS ACCOUNT.

A prompted dialog is rarely found in commercial software packages. There are two reasons why. First, the process of interacting with such a dialog is very linear. You must start at the beginning of the dialog and respond sequentially to each prompt. It is difficult to back up if you make an error.

The second reason that a prompted dialog is difficult to use is due to the ambiguity of human language. If a prompt is not clear and you respond to it with something unexpected, the dialog will not function correctly. In Figure 1-10 you can see an example of this difficulty in the dialog with a computer-based library card catalog system.

Do Project 6 to apply what you know about user interfaces to an evaluation of your school's library card catalog.

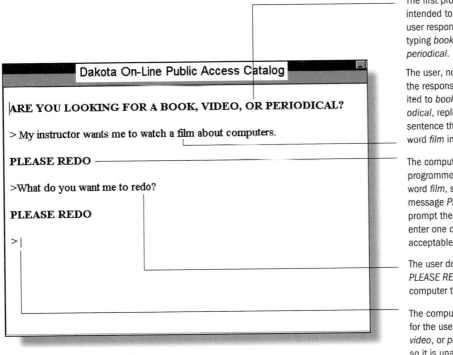

The first prompt is intended to have the user respond by typing *book*, *video*, or *periodical*.

The user, not realizing that the response should be limited to *book*, *video*, or *periodical*, replies with a sentence that include the word *film* instead of *video*.

The computer was not programmed to accept the word *film*, so it displays the message *PLEASE REDO* to prompt the user to enter one of the three acceptable responses.

The user doesn't understand *PLEASE REDO* and asks the computer to explain.

The computer is still waiting for the user to type *book*, *video*, or *periodical*, and so it is unable to continue the dialog.

Figure 1-10
An unsuccessful dialog

The difficulty with the dialog in Figure 1-10 is not necessarily the fault of the user. The prompts should have provided more specific instructions, and the computer program should have accepted a wider vocabulary. Unfortunately, if this were the interface on your on-line library card catalog, you would need to learn how to work within its limitations.

Today's commercial software tends to use "wizards" instead of prompted dialogs. A **wizard** is a sequence of screens that direct you through multi-step software tasks such as creating a graph, a list of business contacts, or a fax cover sheet. Wizards, like the one in Figure 1-11, use graphics to help explain the prompts and allow users to back up and change their responses.

Figure 1-11
Using a wizard to make a list of business clients

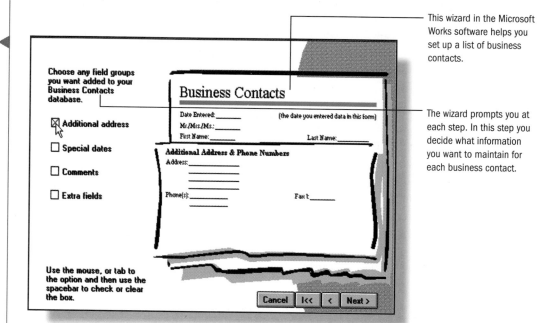

This wizard in the Microsoft Works software helps you set up a list of business contacts.

The wizard prompts you at each step. In this step you decide what information you want to maintain for each business contact.

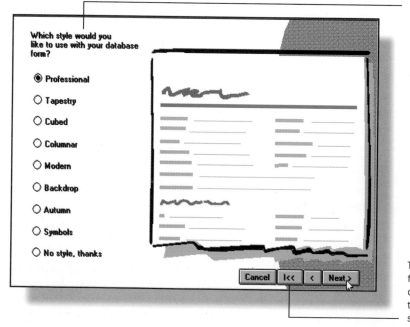

In the next step, the wizard helps you decide how you want the list to look— you can select from several professionally designed styles.

The wizard lets you move forward or backup and change your responses until the business contacts list is set up to your satisfaction.

Commands

Is it true that I have to memorize lots of commands to use a computer?

A **command** is an instruction you input to tell the computer to carry out a task. When you use many older microcomputer interfaces and many mainframe interfaces, you must type commands, then press the Enter key to indicate that the computer should now carry out the command. Each word in a command results in a specific action by the computer. Command words are often English words, such as *print*, *begin*, *save*, and *erase*, but command words can also be more cryptic and might even use special symbols. Some examples of cryptic command words include *ls*, which means list; *cls*, which means clear the screen; and *!*, which means quit. Figure 1-12 shows how you might use a command to find out what is on your disk.

The phrases "enter a command" and "enter data" probably originated because pressing the Enter key signals the end of the input data.

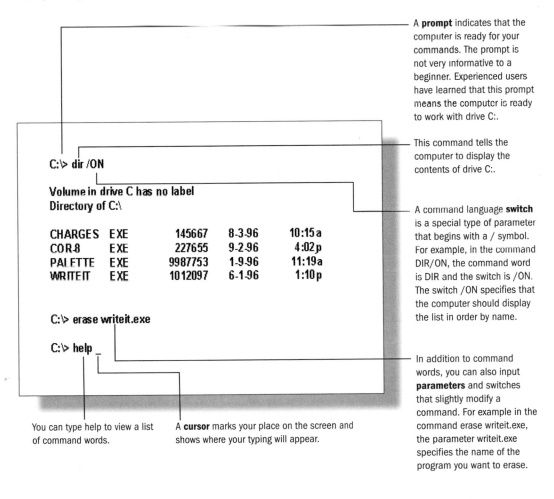

A **prompt** indicates that the computer is ready for your commands. The prompt is not very informative to a beginner. Experienced users have learned that this prompt means the computer is ready to work with drive C:.

This command tells the computer to display the contents of drive C:.

A command language **switch** is a special type of parameter that begins with a / symbol. For example, in the command DIR/ON, the command word is DIR and the switch is /ON. The switch /ON specifies that the computer should display the list in order by name.

In addition to command words, you can also input **parameters** and switches that slightly modify a command. For example in the command erase writeit.exe, the parameter writeit.exe specifies the name of the program you want to erase.

You can type help to view a list of command words.

A **cursor** marks your place on the screen and shows where your typing will appear.

► **Figure 1-12**
Using commands

```
C:\> dir /ON

Volume in drive C has no label
Directory of C:\

CHARGES   EXE      145667    8-3-96    10:15a
COR-8     EXE      227655    9-2-96     4:02p
PALETTE   EXE     9987753    1-9-96    11:19a
WRITEIT   EXE     1012097    6-1-96     1:10p


C:\> erase writeit.exe

C:\> help _
```

The commands you input must conform to a specific syntax. **Syntax** specifies the sequence and punctuation for command words, parameters, and switches. If you misspell a command word, leave out required punctuation, or type the command words out of order, you will get an **error message** or **syntax error**. When you get an error message or syntax error, you must figure out what is wrong with the command and retype it correctly.

An interface that requires the user to type in commands is referred to as a **command-line user interface**. Some people like to use command-line interfaces. They believe that once you have become fluent with the command words and syntax, the commands are easy to construct, quick

Lab

DOS Command- Line User Interface

to type, and have the versatility to accomplish a wide variety of tasks. Learning to use a command line user interface is not easy. You must memorize the command words and know what they mean. To make the situation even more difficult, there is no single set of commands that you can use for every computer and every software package. Instead, there are many different sets of commands.

If you forget the correct command word or punctuation, or if you find yourself using an unfamiliar command-line user interface, you should type HELP and press the Enter key. With some command-line user interfaces, the HELP command provides you with a list of commands. If on-line help is not available, you need to use a reference manual to find out how to proceed.

Menus

Are menus easier to use than commands?

Menus were developed as a response to the difficulties many people experienced trying to remember the command words and syntax for command-line user interfaces. A **menu** displays a list of commands or options. Each line of the menu is referred to as a **menu option** or a **menu item**. Figure 1-13 shows you how to use a menu.

Figure 1-13
Using a menu

To use this **pull-down** menu, you first select which menu you want to use from a **menu bar**. The menu bar for this software package includes File, Edit, View, Insert, Format, and Help menus.

When you click the menu title, the menu appears and shows you a list of menu options.

You can select the option you want using the mouse or keyboard.

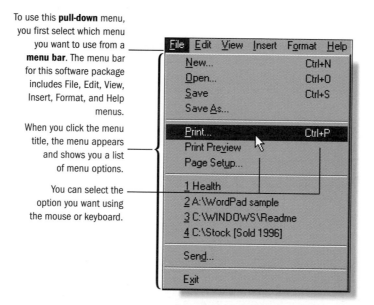

Menus are popular because when you use them, you do not have to remember command words. You just choose the command you want from a list. Also, because all the commands on the list are valid commands, it is not possible to make syntax errors.

You might wonder how a menu can present all the commands you might want to input. Obviously, there are many possibilities for combining command words, so there could be hundreds of menu options. Two methods are generally used to present a reasonably sized list of menu options. One method uses a menu hierarchy. The other method uses a dialog box.

A **hierarchy** is an organization of things ranked one above the other. For example, an organizational chart shows the hierarchy of the people in a business. As the name implies, a **menu hierarchy** arranges menus in a hierarchical structure. After you make a selection from one menu, a submenu appears, and you can make additional choices by selecting an option from the submenu. Some software has a fairly complex menu hierarchy, making it difficult to remember how to find a particular menu option. Visualizing the menus as a hierarchy, as shown in Figure 1-14, makes a complex menu structure easier to use.

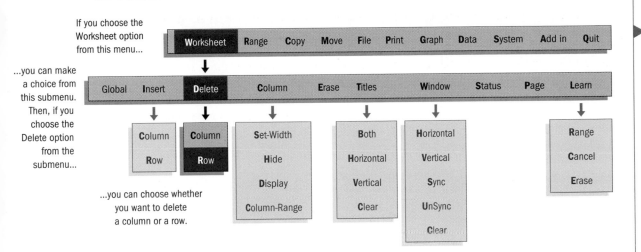

If you choose the Worksheet option from this menu...

...you can make a choice from this submenu. Then, if you choose the Delete option from the submenu...

...you can choose whether you want to delete a column or a row.

Figure 1-14
A menu hierarchy

Although a dialog box appears in conjunction with a menu, it is really a different type of user interface element. It combines the characteristics of both menus and prompts.

Instead of leading to a submenu, some menu options lead to a dialog box. A **dialog box** displays the options associated with a command. You fill in the dialog box to indicate specifically how you want the command carried out, as shown in Figure 1-15.

When you select Print, the Print dialog box appears. The dialog box prompts you to enter specifications about how the computer should carry out the Print task.

Click this button to display a list of printers you can use.

Change the number of copies by clicking these buttons.

Figure 1-15
Using a dialog box

The Print option displays three dots to indicate that this menu leads to a dialog box.

Indicate how much of your document you want to print by clicking *one of these buttons.*

When you are satisfied with the print specifications, click the OK button.

Graphical Objects

Why are GUIs so popular?

A **graphical object** is a small picture on the screen that you can manipulate using a mouse or other input device. Each graphical object represents a computer task, command, or a real-world object. You show the computer what you want it to do by manipulating an object instead of entering commands or selecting menu options. Graphical objects include icons, buttons, tools, and windows, as explained in Figure 1-16.

Mainframe computers have been slow to incorporate GUIs. You will find out why when you read about monitors at the end of Section 1.3.

Figure 1-16
Graphical objects

A **window** usually contains a specific piece of work. For example, a window might contain a document you are typing or a picture you are drawing. You can think of windows as work areas, analogous to different documents and books that you might have on your desk. Just as you switch between the documents and books you have on your desk, you can switch between windows on the computer screen to work on different tasks.

People generally communicate with each other using what we might call a "speech" or "verbal" user interface. The use of voice input and output to communicate with computers, however, has taken a back seat to the development of graphical user interfaces. You'll discover some of the problems with verbal interfaces if you do Project 9 at the end of this chapter.

A **button** helps you make a selection. When you select a button, its appearance changes to indicate that it has been activated. The button labeled "Document-WordPad" is selected and it appears to be pushed in. The button labeled "untitled-Paint" is not selected so it does not appear to be pushed in.

An **icon** is a small picture that represents an object. When you select an icon, you indicate to the computer that you want to manipulate the object. A selected icon is highlighted. The My Computer icon on the right is selected, so it is highlighted with dark blue.

Some buttons are labeled with pictures. These buttons are often referred to as **tools**.

An example of manipulating on-screen objects is the way you delete a document using Windows 95. The documents you create are represented by icons that look like sheets of paper. A Recycle Bin represents the place where you put documents you no longer want. Suppose you used your computer to write a report named "Sport Statistics," but you no longer need the report stored on your computer system. You use the mouse to drag the Sport Statistics icon to the Recycle Bin and erase the report from your computer system, as shown in Figure 1-17.

The Sport Statistics document is no longer needed.

Using the mouse, you can drag the Sport Statistics document icon to the Recycle Bin.

Once in the Recycle Bin, the document will no longer appear in the My Document window. Periodically, you can empty the Recycle Bin to permanently get rid of the documents it contains.

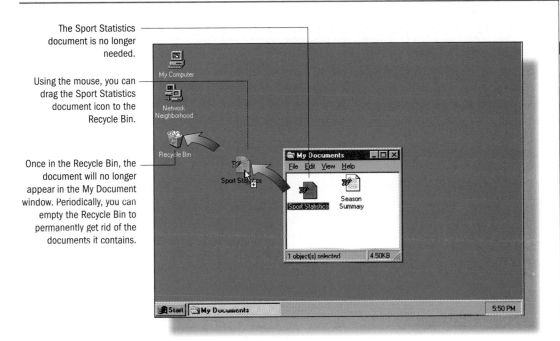

Figure 1-17
Directly manipulating on-screen objects

Graphical objects are a key element of **graphical user interfaces** or **GUIs** (pronounced "gooies") found on most of today's microcomputers. GUIs are based on the philosophy that people can use computers intuitively—that is, with minimal training—if they can manipulate on-screen objects that represent tasks or commands.

Graphical user interfaces often contain menus and prompts in addition to graphical objects because graphical user interface designers found it difficult to design icons and tools for every possible task. Figure 1-18 shows how a graphical user interface incorporates menus and prompts in addition to graphical objects.

For more information on the design principles for graphical user interfaces, refer to the Schneiderman article listed in the Resources section at the end of this chapter.

The **menu bar**, usually at the top of the screen, displays menu titles. Selecting a menu title displays its pull-down menu.

Tool bars display buttons or tools that provide shortcuts to the commands on the menus.

This **wizard** appears when you click the ChartWizard button. The ChartWizard prompts you through the steps to create a chart or graph.

The **ChartWizard** button starts a wizard.

The **window** in the background contains the data for the chart.

The **status bar** gives you brief help about what you're doing.

The **task bar** contains buttons that show you which software programs you are using.

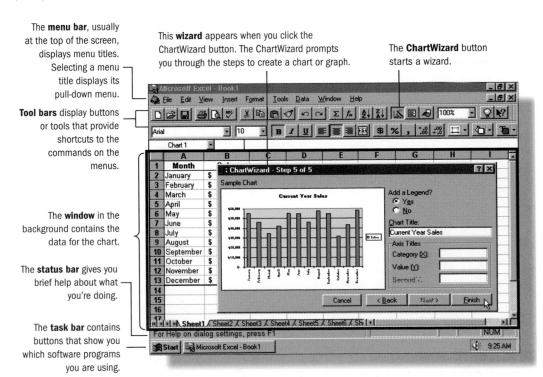

Figure 1-18
Graphical user interface elements for Windows 95 software

Most graphical user interfaces are based on a metaphor in which computer components are represented by real-world objects. For example, a user interface with a **desktop metaphor** might represent documents as file folders and storage as a filing cabinet. Metaphors are intended to make the tasks you perform with computers more concrete, easier to explore, and more intuitive.

Pointing Devices

Some mice have three buttons, while others have only one or two—why?

Lab

Using a Mouse

A **pointing device** such as a mouse, trackball, or lightpen helps you manipulate objects and select menu options. The most popular pointing device is the mouse. The mouse was developed by Douglas Engelbart in the early 1970s to provide an input method more efficient than the keyboard. Englebart's work coincided with efforts to construct graphical user interfaces. The popularity of the mouse and graphical user interfaces grew slowly, until Apple Computer, Inc. produced the Macintosh computer in 1983. Now virtually every computer is equipped with a mouse.

When you move the mouse on your desk, a **pointer**—usually shaped like an arrow—moves on the screen in a way that corresponds to how you move the mouse. You select an object on the screen by pressing the left mouse button a single time. This is referred to as **clicking**. Some operations require you to click the mouse twice in rapid succession. This is referred to as **double-clicking**. You can also use the mouse to **drag** objects from one screen location to another by clicking the object, holding down the mouse button, and moving the mouse to the new location for the object. When the object is in its new location, you release the mouse button. Figure 1-19 shows you how to hold a mouse and use it to manipulate graphical objects.

The mouse moves the pointer only when the mouse is in contact with a hard surface like a desk. If you pick up the mouse and move it, the pointer will not move. This is handy to know. Suppose you are dragging an object, but your mouse runs into an obstacle on your desk. You can just pick up the mouse, move it to a clear space, and continue dragging.

The mouse you use with a Macintosh computer only has one button. IBM-compatible computers use either a two- or three-button mouse. A two-button mouse allows you to **right click** an object and provides another way of manipulating it. For example, if clicking the left button selects an object, clicking the right button might bring up a menu of actions you can do with the object. On a three-button mouse you rarely use the third button.

Figure 1-19 ◀

Using a mouse

A pointer on the screen, usually shaped like an arrow, moves as you move the mouse.

To select an object, use the mouse to position the pointer on the object, then click the left mouse button.

If you move the mouse to the right on your desk, the pointer moves to the right on your screen. When you pull the mouse toward you, the pointer moves toward the bottom of the screen.

To hold the mouse, rest the palm of your right hand on the mouse so your index finger is positioned over the left mouse button. Lightly grasp the mouse using your thumb and ring finger.

MOUSEPAD

Some three-button mice, however, allow you to click the middle button once instead of double-clicking the left mouse button. This feature is useful for people who have trouble double-clicking. It also helps prevent some muscular stress injuries that result from excessive clicking.

Keyboard

Do I need to be a good typist to use a computer?

Virtually every computer user interface requires you to use a keyboard. You don't have to be a great typist, but to use a computer effectively you should be familiar with the computer keyboard because it contains special keys to manipulate the user interface. Study Figure 1-20 on the following page before you read the rest of this section.

You use the typing keys to input commands, respond to prompts, and type the text of documents. A cursor or an insertion point indicates where the characters you type will appear. The **cursor** appears on the screen as a flashing underline. The **insertion point** appears on the screen as a flashing vertical bar. You can change the location of the cursor or insertion point using the arrow keys or the mouse.

The **numeric keypad** provides you with a calculator-style input device for numbers and arithmetic symbols. You can type numbers using either the set of number keys at the top of the typing keypad or the keys on the numeric keypad. However, notice that some keys on the numeric keypad contain two symbols. When the Num Lock key is activated, the numeric keypad produces numbers. When the Num Lock key is not activated, the keys on the numeric keypad move the cursor in the direction indicated by the arrows on the keys.

The Num Lock key is an example of something called a toggle key. A **toggle key** switches back and forth between two modes. The Caps Lock key is also a toggle. When you press the Caps Lock key you switch or "toggle" into uppercase mode. When you press the Caps Lock key again you toggle back into lowercase mode.

Now here's an interesting problem that faced the designers for word processors that use command-line interfaces. Suppose someone is typing in the text of a document and wants to issue a command to save the document on a disk. If the user types SAVE, it will just appear as another word in the document. How does the computer know that SAVE is supposed to be a command and not just part of a sentence such as "Save your money." Interface designers solved this problem by introducing function keys, control keys, and Alt keys.

Function keys, like those numbered F1 through F12, are located at the top of your keyboard. They do not exist on the keyboard of a standard typewriter but were added to computer keyboards to initiate commands. For example, with many software packages F1 is the key you press to get help. The problem with function keys is that they are not standardized. In one program, you press F7 to save a document, but in another program, you press F5.

There are 12 function keys, but you usually need more than 12 commands to control software. Therefore, you can use the Ctrl, Alt, and Shift keys in conjunction with the function keys to expand the repertory of available commands. For example, if you hold down the Ctrl key while you press F1, instead of issuing the command to get help, you might issue the command to change margins. If you see <Alt F1>, Alt+F1, [Alt F1], Alt-F1, or Alt F1 on the screen or in an instruction manual, it means to hold down the Alt key and press F1. You might see similar notation for using the Ctrl or Shift keys.

If you are left handed, you can hold the mouse in your left hand and click the right mouse button after selecting the left-handed mouse option in your software.

Lab

Using a Keyboard

The Alt and Ctrl keys also work in conjunction with the letter keys. For example, Ctrl+C has been used since the early days of computing to tell the computer to stop what it is doing. Even in a graphical user interface, you can use Ctrl and Alt key "shortcuts" instead of using menus. For example, when you use the Windows 95 software, Ctrl+X is a shortcut for clicking the Edit menu and then clicking the Cut option. Or, if you see an underlined menu title such as Edit, you can open the menu using Alt+E instead of clicking Edit.

Ctrl+C rarely works in today's graphical user interfaces, but the Esc key often cancels your last command.

Figure 1-20 ◄
The computer keyboard

COLOR KEY

☐ Typing Keypad

☐ Function Key Array

☐ Editing Keypad

☐ Numeric Keypad

The **Esc** or "escape" key cancels an operation.

The **function keys** execute commands, such as centering a line of text or bold-facing text. The command associated with each function key depends on the software you are using.

Each time you press the **Backspace** key, one character to the left of the cursor is deleted. If you hold down the backspace key, multiple characters to the left are deleted one by one until you release it.

The **Caps Lock** key capitalizes all the letters you type when it is engaged, but does not produce the top symbol on keys that contain two symbols. This key is a **toggle key**, which means that each time you press it, you switch between uppercase and lowercase modes. There is usually an indicator light on the keyboard to show which mode you are in.

You hold down the **Shift** key while you press another key. The Shift key capitalizes letters and produces the top symbol on keys that contain two symbols.

You hold down the **Ctrl** key while you press another key. The result of Ctrl key combinations depends on the software you are using.

You hold down the **Alt** key while you press another key. The result of Alt key combinations depends on the software you are using.

Monitor

How are the monitor and user interface related?

A monitor is a required output device for just about every computer user interface. Whereas you manipulate the keyboard and mouse to communicate with the computer, the monitor is what the computer manipulates to communicate with you by displaying results, prompts, menus, and

The **Print Screen** key prints the contents of the screen when you use some software. With other software, the Print Screen key stores a copy of your screen in memory that you can manipulate or print with draw or paint software.

The function of the **Scroll Lock** key depends on the software you are using. This key is rarely used with today's software.

The **Pause** key stops the current task your computer is performing. You might need to hold down both the Ctrl key and the Pause key to stop the task.

Indicator lights show you the status of each toggle key: Num Lock, Caps Lock, and Scroll Lock. The Power light indicates whether the computer is on or off.

Home takes you to the beginning of a line or the beginning of a document, depending on the software you are using.

The **Num Lock** key is a toggle key that switches between number keys and cursor keys on the numeric keypad.

Page Up displays the previous screen of information. **Page Down** displays the next screen of information.

The **cursor keys** move your position on the screen up, down, right, or left.

End takes you to the end of the line or the end of a document, depending on the software you are using.

graphical objects. Monitor display technology determines whether the interface designer can include color and graphical objects.

The first microcomputer monitors and the displays on many terminals still in use today were character-based. A **character-based display** divides the screen into a grid of rectangles, which can each display a single character. The set of characters that the screen can display is not modifiable; therefore, it is not possible to display different sizes or styles of characters. The only graphics possible on character-based displays are those composed of underlines, exclamation points, and other symbols that already exist in the character set. One of the reasons that mainframes rarely support graphical user interfaces is because of the legacy of character-based terminals connected to mainframe systems.

Character-based displays use only one color to display text on a black background. Green is probably the most frequently used color, followed by amber and white. Even though there appears to be "color" on the screen of a character-based display, it is technically classified as a monochrome display.

A **graphics display** or **bit-map display** divides the screen into a matrix of small dots called **pixels**. Any characters or graphics the computer displays on the screen must be constructed of dot patterns within the screen matrix. The more dots your screen displays in the matrix, the higher the **resolution**. A high-resolution monitor can produce complex graphical images and text that is easier to read than a low-resolution monitor. Most of the monitors on microcomputers have bit-map display capabilities. This provides the flexibility to display characters in different sizes and styles as well as the graphical objects needed for GUIs.

Monochrome or gray-scale monitors display text and graphics in shades of gray. Color monitors allow the interface designer to use the impact of color to create pleasing screen designs and use color as a cue to direct the user's attention to important screen elements.

A User Interface Comparison: Starting Programs

Now that you have learned about user-interface elements, let's see how they work for a typical computer activity. One of the most frequent computer activities is starting a program. Figure 1-21 illustrates the different ways you could start a program— using commands, using graphical objects, and using a menu.

`C:>works`

To start Microsoft Works using the DOS command-line user interface, you need to know the name the computer has given the program. In this case, the computer calls Microsoft Works "Works." At the C:> prompt, type **works** then press the Enter key.

To start Microsoft Works using the Windows 3.1 user interface, you must move the pointer to the Microsoft Works graphical object and double-click the left mouse button.

2. Next, you move the pointer to the Programs menu item to display a list of program folders.

3. Select the Microsoft Works for Windows folder from the menu.

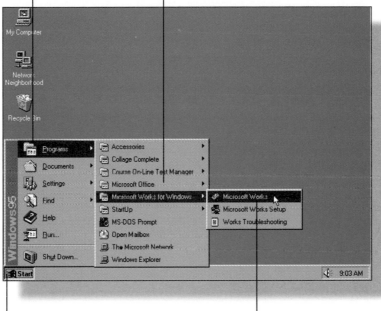

1. To start Microsoft Works using the Windows 95 interface, you click the Start button to view a menu of categories.

4. Use the mouse to click Microsoft Works.

Figure 1-21
Starting programs with different types of user interfaces

Quick Check

1. A(n) _____, such as "Enter your name:," is one way a computer can tell the user what to do.

2. Instead of prompted dialogs, today's software tends to use _____ to direct a user through multi-step software tasks, such as creating a graph or creating a fax cover sheet.

3. When you use a command-line interface, you press _____ when you are done typing a command.

4. If you type a command, but leave out a required space, you have made a _____ error.

5. When you make a menu selection, a(n) _____ or a(n) _____ might appear to let you enter more details on how you want the computer to do a task.

6. Most _____ are based on a metaphor, such as a desktop metaphor in which documents are represented by folder icons.

7. The flashing underline that marks your place on the screen is called the _____; the flashing vertical bar is called the _____.

8. You can use the _____ key and the _____ key in conjunction with letter keys instead of using the mouse to control menus.

9. _____ are work areas on the screen analogous to different documents and books you might have open on your desk. (Hint: Don't forget to read the figure captions!)

10. A(n) _____ display cannot be used in conjunction with a GUI.

1.4

User **Focus:**

Help, Tutorials, and Manuals

Many resources are available to help you learn how to use computers; look for those that suit your budget, time, and learning style.

No class can ever teach you all you need to know about using computers or every-thing about one software package. You should not feel frustrated if you don't "know" how something on your computer works. One of the most important skills you can develop as a computer user is the ability to figure out how to do new computing tasks. But don't expect to figure things out in a flash of inspiration! You usually have to get some additional information.

You can find information about installing computer hardware and using computer software in books, on your computer screen, on videotapes, and on audio cassettes. We can refer to these books, tapes, and so forth as "resources." To use these resources effectively, you need to know they exist, you need to know where to find them, and you need to develop some strategies for applying the information they contain. Let's take a look at some of the resources you can use to do this.

On-line Help

If I'm using a program and I "get stuck," what help can I get from the computer?

The term "on-line" refers to resources that are immediately available on your computer screen. Reference information is frequently available as on-line Help, accessible from a Help menu or by typing HELP at a command-line prompt. Figure 1-22 shows how you access on-line Help for the Microsoft Windows 95 software.

In Windows 95 software. Help is available on the menu bar or from the Start button. Help appears in a help window.

Help has three sections: Contents, Index, and Find. To select the section you want, click one of the tabs.

Figure 1-22 ◄
Using on-line Help for the Windows 95 software

If you are using the Contents section of help, look through the list of "books." Each book covers a help subject.

Once you open a Help book, you will see a list of specific Help topics. Click the topic you want, then click the Display button.

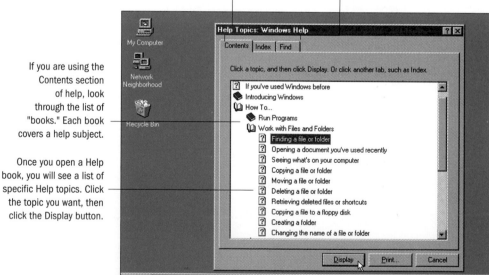

Tutorials

How can I get the most out of a tutorial?

A **tutorial** is a guided, step-by-step learning experience. Usually this learning experience teaches you the generic skills you need to use specific hardware or software. For example, suppose you purchase CorelDRAW software, and the first thing you want to draw is your company logo. When you use a tutorial that teaches you how to use CorelDRAW, you learn how to do such things as draw straight lines and wavy lines, use color in the drawing, and change the sizes of the pictures you draw. The tutorial does not teach you exactly how to draw your company logo. To get the most out of a tutorial, therefore, you need to think about how you can *generalize* the skills you are learning so you can apply them to other tasks.

When you use a tutorial, don't try to cover too much ground at once. Two 60-minute sessions each day are probably sufficient. As you work on a tutorial, take notes on those techniques you expect to apply to your own projects. When you have completed enough of the tutorial to do your own project, put the tutorial aside. You can complete the rest of the tutorial later if you need to learn more. Tutorials come in a variety of forms, as shown in Figure 1-23.

Computer-based tutorials display a simulation of the hardware or software and display tutorial instructions in boxes or windows on the screen. Computer-based tutorials have an advantage over their printed counterparts because they can demonstrate procedures using computer animation.

Figure 1-23
Tutorials and reference resources

Video tutorials on videotape visually illustrate how the software or hardware works. Some video tutorials are designed so that you watch them, take notes, then try the steps on the computer later. Other video tutorials are designed to be used while you are sitting at the computer. As with audio tutorials, you can stop and rewind video tutorials if you miss something.

Printed tutorials are very popular. To use a printed tutorial, you read how to do a step, then you try to do it on the computer.

Audio tutorials on cassette verbally walk you through the steps of the tutorial. An advantage to this type of tutorial is that you do not have to read instructions. However, you must stop the tutorial and rewind, if you do not hear or understand the instructions. You might like audio tutorials if you easily retain information presented in lectures.

Reference Manuals

When should I use a reference manual instead of a tutorial?

Reference manuals are usually printed books or on-line resources that describe each feature of a hardware device or software package. They might also include examples of how to use these features. A reference manual is organized by features, rather than in the lesson formats.

Think of reference manuals as encyclopedias, containing descriptions of all features of the software and how to use them. You can do Project 7 to become more familiar with reference manuals.

Do not assume that you should read a reference manual from cover to cover. Instead, leaf through it to get a quick overview of all the features. A reference manual can be quite long, sometimes thousands of pages.

You should use a reference manual to find out if a feature exists or to find out how to use a feature. When you use a reference manual, you should first check the table of contents or index to locate the information you need, then turn to the appropriate section and read it carefully.

Reference manuals are usually included with the hardware or software that you buy. Most often, reference manuals are printed documents, but a recent trend is to provide computer-based reference manuals that you can read on the computer screen. Computer-based reference manuals are extensive and are often distributed on CD-ROMs.

You can usually find independent publishers who produce reference manuals for popular hardware and, particularly, for popular software. You might want to purchase one of these reference manuals if it is easier to understand or better organized than the manual included with the hardware or software you purchased.

Other Sources of Information

Who needs a manual?

Although it is sometimes possible to dispense with manuals to learn software, you should not throw aside your hardware installation manual. You could damage equipment if you do not install it correctly, so read and follow the manual carefully whenever you are installing hardware.

If you like reading and easily remember the things you read in books, you will probably like using printed reference manuals and tutorials. If you are a visual learner, you will probably like video tutorials. If you are an adventurous learner, you might enjoy exploring software applications without referring to printed materials or video tutorials. Graphical and menu-driven user interfaces make this sort of exploration possible, as do interfaces that include on-line Help.

Another approach to learning how to use computers is to take a course. Because you're reading this book, you are probably enrolled in an introductory computer course. Courses are available from schools, manufacturers, and private training firms and might last from several hours to several months. Courses about software packages tend to be laboratory-based with an instructor leading you through steps. Some courses might be lecture only, however; you might want to ask about the course format before you register.

If you run into a problem and are pressed for time, the best course of action might be to ask an expert. You might have a friend who knows a lot about computers, or on the job you might know a computer "guru." These are both good sources of information, as long as you don't overuse them.

You might also seek help from the support line of a software or hardware company. A **support line** is a service offered over the phone by a hardware manufacturer or software publisher to customers who have questions about how to use a software or hardware product. Sometimes these support line calls are toll-free; sometimes they are not. In addition to paying for the phone call, you might also pay a fee for the time it takes the support person to answer your question.

End Note
Learning to use computers is a challenging activity, heightened by the fact that computer hardware and software change rapidly. Just when you master one software package, a better one appears. You then face the challenge of learning something new. Happily, you will discover that many concepts you learned previously carry over to new hardware and software technologies. To maintain a good attitude about computers, it is important to view the learning process itself as an interesting challenge. Approach this challenge as if you were a detective—gather information, make hypotheses, explore and test your hypotheses, and when you've solved one case, look forward to the challenge of the next.

Review

1. Using your own words, write out the answers to the questions in italics below each heading in the chapter.

2. List each of the boldface terms used in the chapter, then use your own words to write a short definition of each term. If you would like clarification of one or more terms, refer to a computer dictionary or a computer science encyclopedia such as those listed in the Resources section of this chapter. You can also refer to the Glossary/Index at the back of this book.

3. At the top of a sheet of paper write "Definition of the term *computer*," then make a list of important words, names, and phrases that are related to your list.

4. Use lines to divide a sheet of paper into four equal sections. In the top left corner write "microcomputer." Write "minicomputer" in the top right corner, "mainframe" in the bottom left corner, and "supercomputer" in the bottom right corner. Place words, phrases, and definitions in each section that describe and differentiate each type of computer.

5. Draw a sketch of a microcomputer system, without referring to the book. Then label as many components as you can. When you have finished, look at Figure 1-7 to see if you omitted anything.

6. List as many peripheral devices as you can, without referring to the book. Indicate whether each peripheral is an input device, an output device, or both. When you have finished, refer to Figure 1-8 and review any devices you omitted.

7. Make a list of the user interface elements covered in this chapter. Write at least three terms or phrases associated with each. For example, User interface element: Prompt. Associated terms and phrases: (a) prompted dialog, (b) wizards, (c) can be ambiguous or confusing.

8. Make a list of information resources that might help you install hardware and learn to use software. Write a one-sentence description of each resource.

Projects

1. Your Computer Draw a sketch of a computer system in your computer lab, home, or office and do the following:

   a. Title the sketch appropriately, for example, "My Computer at Home."

   b. List its brand name and model number, for example, "Dell 486/50."

   c. Label the following parts, if applicable:

monitor	screen
keyboard	3½-inch disk drive
5¼-inch disk drive	hard drive light
CD-ROM drive	power switch
power light	system unit
mouse	printer

2. Microcomputers: Input and Output Devices Look in a computer magazine and photocopy one ad for each of the following types of microcomputers: desktop, tower, notebook, and PDA. On the computer in each ad, label each component and indicate if it is an input, output, processing, or storage device.

3. Getting Started on Your Network Do this project only if your school has a computer network for student use. If the network requires a user ID and password, get them. Learn how to log in. Your school might have a short tutorial that teaches you how to use the network, or your instructor might provide a demonstration. Write a one- to two-page step-by-step tutorial on how to log into the network. Your tutorial should include the following:

   a. A title

   b. An introductory paragraph explaining where the network is located, who can access it, and how students can get a user ID and password

   c. Numbered steps to log into the network (if your lab policy requires that you turn on the computer each time you log in, you should include instructions for doing this in your tutorial)

   d. Numbered steps for logging out of the network

 4. Research Tool: The Internet Do this project only if your school provides you with access to the Internet. The Internet is a worldwide computer network that provides access to a wealth of information including a World Wide Web site designed to accompany this textbook. Using the Internet can come in handy right from the start of this course. Several of the end-of-chapter projects refer you to information resources on the Internet. If you would like to use the Internet for these projects, this is a good time to get started.

There are several software tools to help you use the Internet, such as Mosaic, Netscape, and Lynx. It is not possible to cover all these software tools here. Therefore, this is an exploratory project that you can accomplish with the help of your instructor or with a tutorial prepared by your school. Find out how to use the Internet at your school and then answer the following questions:

a. What is the name of the software tool you use to access the Internet?

b. How do you access the "home page" for your school?

c. Use your Internet software to access the World Wide Web site *http://www.vmedia.com/ cti/concepts2*. How can the information at this site help you with the end-of-chapter Projects in this textbook?

d. List at least five other locations or "sites" that are available from your home page. How do you get to these other sites?

e. How can you keep track of where you have been on the Internet? (In other words, is there a way to backtrack to sites?)

f. When you are finished browsing on the Internet, how do you quit?

5. Evaluate a User Interface Select a computer interface with which you are familiar. For example, you might select your bank's ATM machine or your favorite arcade game. Using the terminology you learned in this chapter, write a complete description of the user interface and its features. Your description might answer questions such as: Does the interface use menus? If so, what type? What hardware elements are required for the user interface? Is the interface intuitive? Does the interface use a metaphor? If so, what? Don't limit yourself to answering just these questions.

6. Your Library Card Catalog Find out if your library has a computerized card catalog. If it does, use it to answer the following questions:

a. What is the name of the software your library uses for its computerized card catalog?

b. What type of user interface does it have?

c. Explain the steps you would take to find the call number for the book *War and Peace*.

d. Is the computerized card catalog efficient to use, or do you need to enter a lot of extra information to find a book?

e. What kind of on-line help is available?

f. Is the computerized card catalog easy to learn to use?

g. How much had you used the computerized card catalog before this assignment?

7. Reference Manuals Locate a software reference manual in your computer lab, home, or library; then answer the following questions:

a. What is the title of the reference manual?

b. How many pages does it have?

c. What are the titles of each section of the manual? For example, there might be a "Getting Started" section or an "Installation" section, and so on.

d. Does the reference manual include an index? If so, does it look complete? You should be suspicious of a large reference manual with a short index—it might be difficult to find the information you need.

e. Does the reference manual contain a list of features? If so, is this list arranged alphabetically? If not, how is it arranged?

f. Read a few pages of the reference manual. Write one or two sentences describing what you read. Does the reference manual seem to be well written and easy to follow? Why or why not?

8. Identify Your Learning Style In this chapter, you learned that you can take many approaches to learning how to use hardware and software. For this project, think about your own learning style and how it might affect the resources you select for learning about computers and software. Write a one-page paper and include the following:

a. Describe the way you like to learn things in general—do you like to read about them, take a class, listen to a cassette, watch a video, think about them, do library research, or take a different approach?

b. If you had to learn how to use a new software application, which approach would you like best: working through a tutorial, using a reference manual, exploring on your own, taking a class, or asking an expert? Why?

c. How does this relate to the way you like to learn other things?

9. Why Not Just Talk to It? Computer scientists have discovered that it is quite difficult to develop a "conversational" user interface that you could use to simply "talk" to a computer. One of the stumbling blocks is the ambiguity of human speech. For example, if someone tells you "My friend was looking at a bicycle in the store window, and she wanted it," you assume that "it" refers to the bicycle, not the *store window*. But English grammar does not make the meaning of "it" explicit, so a com-

Resources

puter would have a hard time understanding what you mean. Hurbert Dreyfus discusses this problem in the video *The Machine That Changed the World* and in the book entitled *What Computers Can't Do*. To pursue this topic, do one or more of the following activities:

a. With a small group of other students, try to think of other examples of ambiguity in human conversation that a computer would probably have difficulty understanding. You can share your list with the rest of the class or turn it in to your instructor.

b. Watch Episode IV of the video *The Machine That Changed the World*, if it is available, and use your library to research this topic so you more fully understand the problem. Write a term paper summarizing your research.

10. Super Fast, Major Price Tag
In 1995, the NEC Corp. announced technology for the fastest super computer in the world, capable of one trillion calculations per second. However, the *Communications of the ACM* reported that the supercomputer would "sell for more than $100 million, virtually guaranteeing it will never be built." Is this price exorbitant compared to other supercomputers? How much does the average supercomputer cost? Who owns them? What tasks do supercomputers perform that make them cost effective? Write a two-page paper addressing these questions about supercomputers. You can use books and periodicals in your library or, if you have access to the Internet, a list of supercomputing resources is at *http://www.yahoo.com/Computers/ Supercomputing_and_Parallel_Computing*.

■ **Clarke, A.C.** *2001: A Space Odyssey*. New York: New American Library, 1968. *2001* is a science-fiction classic that takes a bold perspective on how computers might develop in the future. Perhaps Clarke's writing is so powerful because of his strong background in science and research. Clarke is well known for his contribution to the invention of the communications satellite.

■ *Computer Dictionary*, 2nd ed. Redmond, WA: Microsoft Press, 1994. It is useful to have a dictionary of computer terms when you read articles in computer magazines. Microsoft Press publishes this up-to-date dictionary that will help you make sense of computer jargon.

■ **Dreyfus, H.** *What Computers Can't Do: the limits of artificial intelligence*. Rev. ed. New York: Harper & Row, 1979. *What Computers Can't Do* is a classic contribution to the ongoing discussion about computer intelligence. Dreyfus updated his arguments against computer intelligence in the 1992 book, *What Computers Still Can't Do: a critique of artificial reason*, published by MIT Press.

■ **Graham, N.** *The Mind Tool: Computers and Their Impact on Society*, 5th ed. St. Paul, MN: West Publishing, 1989. This well-respected text provides broad coverage of the history of computing, how computers work, and the impact computers have on society.

■ **Norman, D.** *The Psychology of Everyday Things*. New York: Basic Books, 1988. Donald Norman says, "This is the book I have always wanted to write, but I didn't know it." The book is an entertaining account of the predicaments caused by poor engineering of everyday objects, such as stoves and revolving doors, as well as more technological devices, such as computer interfaces and nuclear power plants.

■ **Ralston, A., and E. D. Reilly**. *Encyclopedia of Computer Science and Engineering*, 3rd ed. New York: Van Nostrand Reinhold, 1993. A definitive reference work on computer concepts, this single-volume encyclopedia is arranged alphabetically by topic and is extensively indexed. You can find information on the first computers, biographies of people who made key contributions to the computer industry, and explanations of many simple and complex computer concepts. Check your library to find this book or a similar computer reference resource.

- **Reinhardt, A.** "Your Next Mainframe." *Byte Magazine*, May 1995, pp. 48-58. Reinhardt points out that "the blurring of computer architectures is erasing the relevance of terms like *mainframe, minicomputer*, and *microcomputer*," and supports this thesis by comparing microcomputer and mainframe specifications. He suggests some alternative ways of categorizing computers, for example, by the software they run or by the functions they perform within a system. Particularly interesting are his charts "What PCs have that mainframes don't" and "Where mainframes still excel."

- **Schneiderman, B.** "Direct Manipulation: A Step Beyond Programming Languages." *Computer*, August 1983, IEEE publication. Ben Schneiderman, one of the gurus of computer interface design, summarized four principles of direct manipulation interfaces, now popularized as GUIs: (1) continuous representation of available objects, (2) physical actions replace typed commands, (3) manipulation of an object results in immediate feedback, and (4) users can explore the environment and learn to use features gradually.

- *The Machine That Changed the World.* (video) Boston: WGBH Television in cooperation with the British Broadcasting Corp., 1991. An excellent collection of five videos about computers. Episode IV, "The Thinking Machine," focuses on research in the field of artificial intelligence. It presents both sides of the controversy over whether computers can ever be intelligent.

- **von Neumann, J.** "First Draft of a Report on the EDVAC" [unpublished report written in 1945] in Stern, N. B. *From ENIAC to UNIVAC: An Appraisal of the Eckert-Mauchly Computers.* Bedford, MA: Digital Press, 1981. John von Neumann's report on the EDVAC computer is printed in full as an appendix to Nancy Stern's well-researched book about the earliest efforts to build a working electronic computer. The book contains some fascinating photos of one-of-a-kind computing equipment, as well as detailed circuit diagrams showing how these machines worked.

Lab Assignments

The New Perspectives Labs are designed to help you master some of the key computer concepts and skills presented in each chapter of the text. If you are using your schoolís lab computers, your instructor or technical support person should have installed the Labs software for you. If you want to use the Labs on your home computer, ask your instructor for the appropriate software.

Each Lab has two parts: Steps and Explore. Use Steps first to learn and review concepts. Read the information on each page and do the numbered steps. As you work through the Lab, you will be asked to answer Quick Check questions about what you have learned. At the end of the Lab, you will see a Summary Report of your answers to the Quick Checks. If your instructor wants you to turn in this Summary Report, click the Print button on the Summary Report screen.

When you have completed Steps, you can click the Explore button to complete the Lab Assignments. You can also use Explore to practice the skills you learned and to explore concepts on your own.

The instructions for starting the Labs depend on whether your computer has Windows 3.1 or Windows 95. Use the appropriate set of steps for your computer system. Your instructor or technical support person might help you get started.

To begin the Lab from Windows 3.1 Program Manager:

1. Double-click the Course Labs group icon to open the Course Labs window.

2. Double-click the New Perspectives Course Labs Concepts icon to open a window containing icons for all the Labs.

3. Click the icon for the Lab you want to use.

4. Follow the instructions on the screen to enter your name and class section.

5. Read the instructions for using the Lab by clicking the Instructions button.

6. When you are ready to begin the Lab, click the Steps button.

To begin the Lab from Windows 95:

1. Click the Start button.

2. Point to Programs.

3. Point to Course Labs.

4. Click New Perspectives Concepts to open a window containing icons for all the Labs.

5. Click the name of the Lab you want to use.

6. Read the instructions for using the Lab by clicking the Instruction button.

7. When you are ready to begin the Lab, click the Steps button.

Peripheral Devices

 A wide variety of peripheral devices provide expandability for computer systems and provide users with the equipment necessary to accomplish tasks efficiently. In the Peripheral Devices Lab you will use an on-line product catalog of peripheral devices.

1. Complete the Steps to find out how to use the on-line product catalog. Click the Steps button and begin the Steps. As you work through the Steps, answer all of the Quick Check questions that appear. When you complete the Steps, you will see a Summary Report that summarizes your performance on the Quick Checks. Follow the directions on the screen to print the Summary Report.

2. After you know how to use the product catalog to look up products, features, and prices, use Explore to:

a. List the characteristics that differentiate printers.

b. List the factors that differentiate monitors.

c. Describe the factors that determine the appropriate type of scanner for a task.

d. List the peripheral devices in the catalog that are specially designed for notebook computers.

3. Suppose that the company that produces the peripheral devices catalog selected your name from its list of customers for a free scanner. You can select any one of the scanners in the catalog. Assume that you own a notebook computer to which you could attach any one of the scanners. Click the Explore button and use the catalog to help you write a one-page paper explaining which scanner you would select, why you would select it, and how you would use it.

4. Suppose you are in charge of information systems in a metropolitan hospital. Twenty nursing stations need printers. The printers will be used for a variety of reports. High print quality is not essential; but, of course, the reports must be readable. Some reports require more than one copy. Because they will be situated near patients, the printers must be quiet. Use the catalog in the Explore portion of the Lab to write a one-page paper in which you recommend a printer from the catalog for the nursing stations. Support your recommendation by explaining the advantages of the printer you selected and the disadvantages of the other printers available.

5. Suppose you own a basic computer system, such as the one in Figure 1-7 of this text book. You have an idea that you can earn the money for your college tuition by using your computer to help other students produce spiffy reports with color graphs and scanned images. Your parents have agreed to "loan" you $1,000 to get started. Click the Explore button and look through the on-line peripheral devices catalog. List any of the devices that might help you with this business venture. Write a one-page paper explaining how you would spend your $1,000 to get the equipment you need to start the business.

User Interfaces

 You have learned that the hardware and software for a user interface determine how you interact and communicate with the computer. In the User Interfaces Lab, you will try five different user interfaces to accomplish the same task—creating a graph.

1. Begin with the Steps to find out how each interface works. Click the Steps button and begin the Steps. As you work through the Steps, answer all of the Quick Check questions that appear. When you complete the Steps, you will see a Summary Report that summarizes your performance on the Quick Checks. Follow the directions on the screen to print the Summary Report.

2. In Explore, use each interface to make a 3-D pie graph using data set 1. Title your graphs "Bike U.S. Sales." Use the percent style to show the percent of each slice of the pie. Print each of the five graphs (one for each interface).

3. In Explore, select one of the user interfaces. Write a step-by-step set of instructions for how to produce a line graph using data set 3. This line graph should show lines and symbols, and have the title "Home Budget."

4. Using the user interface terminology you learned in this Lab and in Chapter 1 of the text book, write a description of each of the interfaces you used in the Lab. Then, suppose you worked for a software publisher and you were going to create a software package for producing line, bar, column, and pie graphs. Which user interface would you use for the software? Why?

DOS Command-Line User Interface

 The DOS command-line user interface provides a typical example of the advantages and disadvantages of command-line user interfaces. DOS was included with the original IBM PC computers to provide users with a way to accomplish system tasks such as listing, moving, and deleting files on disk. Although todayís typical computer user prefers to use a graphical user interface such as Windows, DOS commands still function on most IBM-compatible computers.

1. Begin with Steps to learn how to use the DOS command-line interface. Click the Steps button and begin the Steps. As you work through the Steps, answer all of the Quick Check questions that appear. When you complete the Steps, you will see a Summary Report that summarizes your performance on the Quick Checks. Follow the directions on the screen to print the Summary Report.

2. In Explore, write out your answers to a through d.

a. Explain the different results you get when you use the commands DIR, DIR /p, and DIR /w.

b. What happens if you make a typing error and enter the command DUR instead of DIR? What procedure must you follow to correct your error?

c. Enter the command, DIR /? and explain what happens. Enter the command VER /? and explain what happens. What generalization can you make about the /? command parameter?

d. Enter the command VER /p. Why do you think /p does not work with the VER command word, but it works with DIR?

3. Write a one-page paper summarizing what you know about command line user interfaces and answering the following questions:

a. Which DOS commands do you now know how to use?

b. How do you know which commands to use to accomplish a task?

c. How do you know what parameters work with each command?

d. What kinds of mistakes can you make that will produce an error message?

e. Can you enter valid commands that don't produce the results you want?

Using a Mouse

 A mouse is a standard input device on most of today's computers. You need to know how to use a mouse to manipulate graphical user interfaces and to use the rest of the Labs.

1. The Steps for the Using a Mouse Lab show you how to click, double-click, and drag objects using the mouse. Click the Steps button and begin the Steps. As you work through the Steps, answer all of the Quick Check questions that appear. When you complete the Steps, you will see a Summary Report that summarizes your performance on the Quick Checks. Follow the directions on the screen to print the Summary Report.

2. In Explore, demonstrate your ability to use a mouse and to control a Windows program by creating a poster. To create a poster, select a graphic, type the caption for the poster, then select a font, font styles, and a border. Print your completed poster.

Using a Keyboard

 To become an effective computer user, you must be familiar with your primary input device—the keyboard.

1. The Steps for the Using a Keyboard Lab provide you with a structured introduction to the keyboard layout and the function of special computer keys. Click the Steps button and begin the Steps. As you work through the Steps, answer all of the Quick Check questions that appear. When you complete the Steps, you will see a Summary Report that summarizes your performance on the Quick Checks. Follow the directions on the screen to print the Summary Report.

2. In Explore, start the typing tutor. You can develop your typing skills using the typing tutor in Explore. Take the typing test and print out your results.

3. In Explore, try to improve your typing speed by 10 words per minute. For example, if you currently type 20 words per minute, your goal would be 30 words per minute. Practice each typing lesson until you see a message that indicates you can proceed to the next lesson. Create a Practice Record as shown on page 1-39 to keep track of how much you practice. When you have reached your goal, print out the results of a typing test to verify your results.

Practice Record

Name: _____

Section: _____

Start Date: _____ Start Typing Speed: _____ wpm

End Date: _____ End Typing Speed: _____ wpm

Lesson #: _____ Date Practiced/Time Practiced _____

 Quick Check

Answers

1.1

1. accepts input, processes data, stores data, produces output

2. data

3. process

4. memory

5. storage

1.2

1. keyboard, monitor

2. microcomputer

3. terminal

4. minicomputers, mainframes

5. mainframe

6. compatible

7. network

1.3

1. prompt

2. wizards

3. Enter

4. syntax

5. submenu, dialog box

6. graphical user interfaces

7. cursor, insertion point

8. Ctrl, Alt

9. Windows

10. character-based

Glossary/Index

Special Characters

/ (slash), 1-19

 A

Alt key A key that you hold down with another key. The result of the Alt key combinations depend on the software used, 1-25, 1-26

Apple Computer, Inc., 1-12, 1-13. *See also* Macintosh computers

architecture. *See* memory

audio tutorials A cassette that verbally walks you through the steps of a tutorial, 1-31

B

Backspace key A key that when pressed deletes one character to the left of the cursor, 1-26

bar code reader A device that gathers input data by reading bar codes, 1-12, 1-12–1-13

bit-map displays, 1-28

button An object that helps you make a selection, 1-22
    commands, 1-22
    mouse, 1 24–25

C

Caps Lock key A key that when engaged, capitalizes all the letters you type, but does not produce the top symbol on keys that display two symbols, 1-25, 1 26

CD-ROM A high capacity storage medium with a capacity of up to 680 million characters. Most CD-ROMs do not allow you to add or change the information on them, 1-11

CD-ROM drive A storage device that uses laser technology to read data from a CD-ROM, 1-11

central processing unit (CPU) The circuitry in a computer that performs arithmetic and logic operations and executes instructions. Also called the CPU or processor, 1-5 *See also* microprocessor.

ChartWizard button A button that when pressed starts a wizard, 1-23

character-based display A screen display in which the screen is divided into a grid of rectangles, which each display a single character; the characters cannot be modified, 1-28

clicking Pressing the left mouse button once to select an object on the screen, 1-24

command A combination of words, parameters, and punctuation that tells the computer what you want it to do, 1-19, 1-20

Print Screen key When pressed, this key prints the contents of the screen or stores a copy of your screen in memory depending on the software being used, 1-27, 1-27–1-28

printed tutorial A tutorial that you read on paper and then try to do on a computer, 1-31

printers, 1-14

process A systematic series of actions a computer uses to manipulate data, 1-5

processing, 1-6

programs. *See* software

prompt A message displayed by the computer to request information or help you proceed, 1-16, 1-16–1-18, 1-19

prompted dialog A type of user interface in which the computer presents prompts one at a time and waits for a response after each one. Also called prompted conversation, 1-16, 1-16–1-17

The Psychology of Everyday Things (Norman), 1-16

pull-down menus, 1-20

R

Recycle Bin, 1-22–23

reference manual A printed book or on-line resource that contains the information about installing and using software or hardware, 1-32

resolution The number of pixels that can be displayed horizontally or vertically on the screen, 1-28

right clicking A technique used with a two-button mouse to manipulate objects, 1-24

S

scanner A device that converts text or images on paper into an electronic format that a computer can display, print, and store, 1-12, 1-12–1-13

screens, 1-27–28. *See also* monitors
    touch sensitive, 1-13

Scroll Lock key A key that is rarely used today, but whose function depends on the software being used, 1-27, 1-27–1-28

Shift key A key that you hold down while you press another key. The Shift key capitalizes letters and produces the top symbol on keys that contain two symbols, 1-25, 1-26

slash (/), command language switches, 1-19

software, 1-7
    operating systems. *See* Windows 3.1; Windows 95
    starting programs, 1-28–29

sound card A device that can be installed inside a system unit to give a computer the capability to accept audio input, play sound files, and produce audio output, 1-13

speakers Devices that are used with a sound card to produce audio output, 1-13

starting
    Microsoft Works, 1-28–29
    programs, 1-28–29

status bar A bar that gives you brief help about what you're doing on screen, 1-23

storage Electronic circuitry that holds data on a permanent basis while it is not needed for processing, 1-5, 1-6
    disks. *See* floppy disks; hard disks
    drives. *See* floppy disk drives; hard disks
    memory versus, 1-5
    primary. *See* memory

storage devices. *See* floppy disks; hard disks

storage media Physical materials that provide long-term storage for computer data, 1-11

supercomputer The largest, fastest, and most expensive type of computer, used to handle specialized information analysis, 1-9

support line A telephone number maintained by a software or hardware company that users can call to get assistance, 1-32

switch A special type of command language parameter that begins with a / symbol, 1-19

syntax The rules of a command language that specify the order of the command words and parameters and the punctuation that is required for valid commands, 1-19

syntax error An error caused by misspelling a command word, leaving out required punctuation, or typing the command words out of order, 1-19

system unit A case or box that contains the power supply, storage devices, and the main circuit board of the computer system, 1-11

T

task bar A bar on screen that contains buttons that show you which software programs you are using, 1-23

terminal An input and output device for a host computer, 1-7, 1-9

toggle key A key on the computer keyboard that is used to switch back and forth between two modes, 1-25, 1-26

Computer Files and Data Storage

Software
and **Multimedia**
Applications

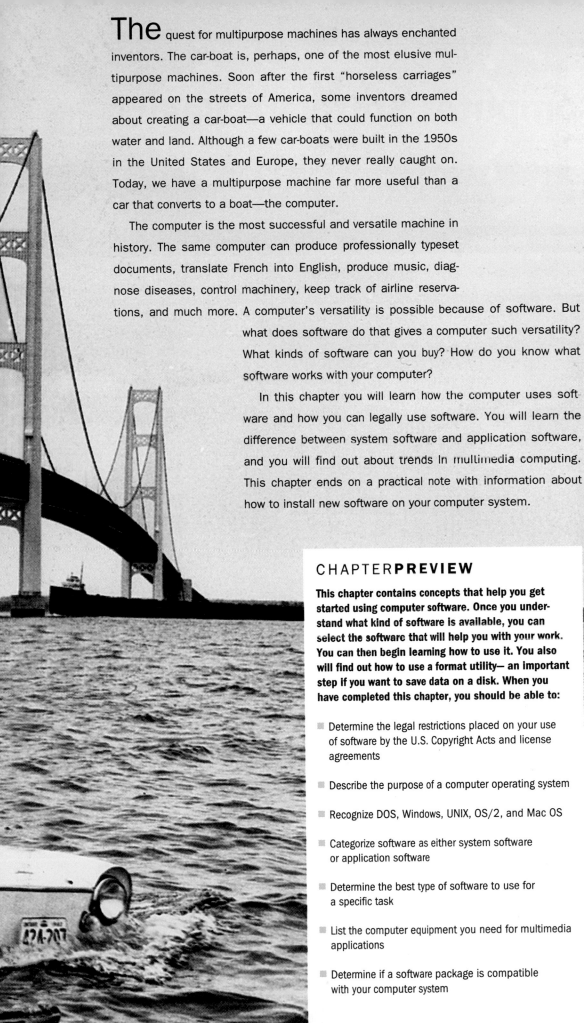

The quest for multipurpose machines has always enchanted inventors. The car-boat is, perhaps, one of the most elusive multipurpose machines. Soon after the first "horseless carriages" appeared on the streets of America, some inventors dreamed about creating a car-boat—a vehicle that could function on both water and land. Although a few car-boats were built in the 1950s in the United States and Europe, they never really caught on. Today, we have a multipurpose machine far more useful than a car that converts to a boat—the computer.

The computer is the most successful and versatile machine in history. The same computer can produce professionally typeset documents, translate French into English, produce music, diagnose diseases, control machinery, keep track of airline reservations, and much more. A computer's versatility is possible because of software. But what does software do that gives a computer such versatility? What kinds of software can you buy? How do you know what software works with your computer?

In this chapter you will learn how the computer uses software and how you can legally use software. You will learn the difference between system software and application software, and you will find out about trends In multimedia computing. This chapter ends on a practical note with information about how to install new software on your computer system.

CHAPTER**PREVIEW**

This chapter contains concepts that help you get started using computer software. Once you understand what kind of software is available, you can select the software that will help you with your work. You can then begin learning how to use it. You also will find out how to use a format utility— an important step if you want to save data on a disk. When you have completed this chapter, you should be able to:

■ Determine the legal restrictions placed on your use of software by the U.S. Copyright Acts and license agreements

■ Describe the purpose of a computer operating system

■ Recognize DOS, Windows, UNIX, OS/2, and Mac OS

■ Categorize software as either system software or application software

■ Determine the best type of software to use for a specific task

■ List the computer equipment you need for multimedia applications

■ Determine if a software package is compatible with your computer system

LABS

Word Processing

Spreadsheets

Databases

Computer History Hypermedia

Computer Software Basics

Computer software determines what a computer can do. In a sense, software transforms a computer from one kind of machine to another—from a drafting station to a typesetting machine, from a flight simulator to a calculator, from a filing system to a music studio.

Computer Programs

Do I need to write programs for my computer?

A **computer program** is a set of detailed, step-by-step instructions that tells a computer how to solve a problem or carry out a task. Some computer programs handle simple tasks, such as converting feet and inches to centimeters. Longer and more complex computer programs handle very complicated tasks, such as reconstructing photographs sent back from a spacecraft flyby of Jupiter.

The steps in a computer program are written in a language that the computer can interpret and process. As you read through the simple computer program in Figure 2-1, notice the number of steps required to perform a relatively simple calculation.

Computer magazines are a great source of information about the rich variety of computer software available. Project 4 at the end of this chapter helps you learn how to use this information resource.

Figure 2-1 ◀
A computer program that converts feet and inches to centimeters

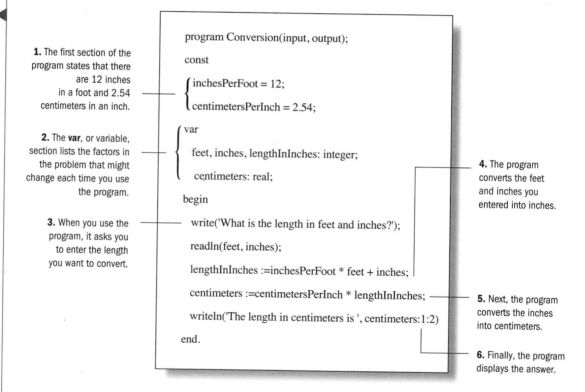

1. The first section of the program states that there are 12 inches in a foot and 2.54 centimeters in an inch.

2. The **var**, or variable, section lists the factors in the problem that might change each time you use the program.

3. When you use the program, it asks you to enter the length you want to convert.

4. The program converts the feet and inches you entered into inches.

5. Next, the program converts the inches into centimeters.

6. Finally, the program displays the answer.

```
program Conversion(input, output);

const
    inchesPerFoot = 12;
    centimetersPerInch = 2.54;

var
    feet, inches, lengthInInches: integer;
    centimeters: real;

begin
    write('What is the length in feet and inches?');
    readln(feet, inches);
    lengthInInches :=inchesPerFoot * feet + inches;
    centimeters :=centimetersPerInch * lengthInInches;
    writeln('The length in centimeters is ', centimeters:1:2)
end.
```

Although most computer users do not write computer programs, computer programming is a challenging career. Project 9 at the end of this chapter helps you discover more about computer programming careers.

At one time organizations and individuals had to write most of the computer programs they wanted to use. A team of programmers might have spent several years writing a program for a task such as billing clients for insurance premiums. A program like that could easily contain more than 100,000 steps.

Today many organizations purchase commercially written programs to avoid the time and expense of writing their own programs. Individuals rarely write computer programs for their personal computers, preferring to select from thousands of commercially written programs. Most computer users are not computer programmers.

Computer Software

Are computer programs, data, and software the same thing?

Software is a basic part of a computer system, but "software" is a term that has more than one definition. In the early days of the computer industry, it became popular to use the term "software" for all the non-hardware components of a computer. In this context, software referred to computer programs and to the data used by the programs.

The U.S. Copyright Act of 1980 defines software as "a set of statements or instructions to be used directly or indirectly in a computer in order to bring about a certain result." This definition implies that computer software is essentially the same as a computer program. It also implies that a collection of data, such as a list of dictionary words, is not software.

In practice, the term "software" is usually used to describe a commercial product, which might include more than a single program and might also include data, as shown in Figure 2-2.

As you read articles about computers, scan computer ads, and listen to people talk about computers, you will begin to understand the different shades of meaning associated with computer terms such as "software." A good computer dictionary helps, too.

The disks contain one or more **programs**, and possibly some data. For example, the Microsoft Windows 95 software includes programs that help you draw graphics, write documents, and keep track of what's on your disks. The software also includes some data, such as information on time zones that you can use to set your computer's clock.

▶ **Figure 2-2**
Software products

A **software package** contains disks and a reference manual.

In this textbook, we define **software** as instructions and associated data, stored in electronic format, that direct the computer to accomplish a task. Under this definition, computer software may include more than one computer program, if those programs work together to carry out a task; software also can include data, but data alone is not software. For example, word processing software might include the data for a dictionary, but the data *you create* using a word processor is not called software. Suppose you write a report using a software package, then store the report on a disk. Your report consists of data rather than instructions for the computer to carry out. Because your report does not contain instructions, it is not software.

"Software" is a plural noun, so there is no such thing as "softwares" or "one software." How, then, do we talk about software in the singular? We often use the term "software package" when we want to talk about a particular example of software.

The distinction between software, programs, and data is important. Try Quick Check Questions 1 through 3 to see if you can use these terms correctly.

Copyrighted Software

Is it illegal to copy software?

Just because you can copy software doesn't make it legal to do so. Like books and movies, most computer software is protected by a copyright. A **copyright** is a form of legal protection that grants certain exclusive rights to the author of a program or the owner of the copyright. The owner of the copyright has the exclusive right to copy the software, to distribute or sell the software, and to modify the software. If you are not the owner of the copyright, it is illegal for you to copy, distribute, or sell the software unless you obtain permission from the copyright owner.

When you purchase copyrighted software, you do not become the owner of the copyright. Instead, you own only a copy of the software. Your purchase allows you to use the software on your computer, but you cannot make additional copies to give away or sell. People who illegally copy, distribute, or modify software are sometimes called **software pirates**, and the illegal copies they create are referred to as **pirated software**.

The restrictions stated by the Copyright Act apply only to the programs and data included as part of the original software. The data you enter—the documents, files, and graphics you create—can be copied without restriction.

Copyrighted materials such as software display a copyright notice that contains the word "Copyright" (or the © symbol), the year of publication, and the name of the copyright holder. For example, the copyright notice on the software that accompanies this book is "Copyright 1996

Figure 2-3
Sections 106 and 117 of the 1980 Copyright Act

Only the copyright owner can reproduce, sell, or distribute the copyrighted software. Note that this section was written before computer software copyright became an issue, thus the reference to phonorecords, but not to software.

Section 106. Exclusive Rights in Copyrighted Works
Subject to sections 107 through 118, the owner of copyright under this title has the exclusive rights to do and to authorize any of the following:

(1) to reproduce the copyrighted work in copies or phonorecords;
(2) to prepare derivative works based upon the copyrighted work;
(3) to distribute copies or phonorecords of the copyrighted work to the public by sale or other transfer of ownership, or by rental, lease, or lending...

Section 117 - Right to Copy or Adapt Computer Programs in Limited Circumstances
Notwithstanding the provisions of section 106, it is not an infringement for the owner of a copy of a computer program to make or authorize the making of another copy or adaptation of the computer program provided:

1. that such a new copy or adaptation is created as an essential step in the utilization of the computer program in conjunction with a machine that is used in no other manner; or

2. that such new copy or adaptation is for archival purposes only and that all archival copies are destroyed in the event that continued possession of the computer program should cease to be rightful. Any exact copies prepared in accordance with the provisions of this section may be leased, sold or otherwise transferred, along with the copy from which such copies were prepared, only as part of the lease, sale, or other transfer of all rights in the program. Adaptations so prepared may be transferred only with the authorization of the copyright owner.

It is legal to copy the software from the distribution disks to the hard disk of your computer system so you can access the software from the hard disk.

It is legal to make an extra copy of the software in case the copy you are using becomes damaged.

If you give away or sell the software, you cannot legally keep a copy.

You cannot legally sell or give away modified copies of the software without permission.

Course Technology, Inc." When you start a computer program, the copyright notice usually appears on the first screen; it is also usually printed in the reference manual. The Copyright Acts of 1976 and 1980 address software copyright issues and allow you to copy or modify software only under certain circumstances. If you read the sections of the Copyright Act shown in Figure 2-3, you will discover under what circumstances you can and cannot legally copy copyrighted software.

Licensed Software

Do I need to read the small print before I buy software?

In addition to copyright protection, computer software is often protected by the terms of a software license. A **software license** is a legal contract that defines the ways in which you may use a computer program. For microcomputer software, you will find the license on the outside of the package, on a separate card inside the package, or in the reference manual. Mainframe software licenses are usually a separate legal document, negotiated between the software publisher and a corporate buyer.

Software licenses are often lengthy and written in "legalese," but they are generally divided into manageable sections that you can understand by reading them carefully. To become familiar with a typical license agreement, you can read through the "No-Nonsense License Statement" used for software published by Borland International, shown in Figure 2-4.

► **Figure 2-4**
A software license

The book analogy explained here is a useful way to think about software use.

This section explains how you are allowed to use the software.

These sections make provisions for multiple users.

Here, Borland essentially says that you use this software at your own risk.

This software is protected by both United States copyright law and international copyright treaty provisions. Therefore, you must treat this software just like a book, except that you may copy it onto a computer to be used and you may make archival copies of the software for the sole purpose of backing-up our software and protecting your investment from loss.

By saying "just like a book," Borland means, for example, that this software may be used by any number of people, and may be freely moved from one computer location to another, so long as there is no possibility of it being used at one location while it's being used at another or on a computer network by more than one user at one location. Just like a book can't be read by two different people in two different places at the same time, neither can the software be used by two different people in two different places at the same time. (Unless, of course, Borland's copyright has been violated or the use is on a computer network by up to the number of users authorized by additional Borland licenses as explained below.)

LAN PACK MULTIPLE-USE NETWORK LICENSE

If this is a LAN Pack package, it allows you to increase the number of authorized users of your copy of the software on a single computer network by up to the number of users specified in the LAN Pack package (per LAN Pack — see LAN Pack serial number).

USE ON A NETWORK

A "computer network" is any electronically linked configuration in which two or more users have common access to software or data. If more than one user wishes to use the software on a computer network at the same time, then you may add authorized users either by (a) paying for a separate software package for each additional user you wish to add or (b) if a LAN Pack is available for this product, paying for the multiple-use license available in the LAN Pack. You may use any combination of regular software packages or LAN Packs to increase the number of authorized users on a computer network. (In no event may the total number of concurrent users on a network exceed one for each

software package plus the number of authorized users installed from the LAN Pack(s) that you have purchased. Otherwise, you are not using the software "just like a book.") The multiple-use network license for the LAN Pack may only be used to increase the number of concurrent permitted users of the software logged onto the network, and not to download copies of the software for local workstation use without being logged onto the network. You must purchase an individual copy of the software for each workstation at which you wish to use the software without being logged onto the network.

FURTHER EXPLANATION OF COPYRIGHT LAW PROVISIONS AND THE SCOPE OF THIS LICENSE STATEMENT

You may not download or transmit the software electronically (either by direct connection or telecommunication transmission) from one computer to another, except as may be specifically allowed in using the software on a computer network. You may transfer all of your rights to use the software to another person, provided that you transfer to that person

(or destroy) all of the software, diskettes and documentation provided in this package, together with all copies, tangible or intangible, including copies in RAM or installed on a disk, as well as all back-up copies. Remember, once you transfer the software, it may only be used at the single location to which it is transferred and, of course, only in accordance with the copyright laws and international treaty provisions. Except as stated in this paragraph, you may not otherwise trans-

fer, rent, lease, sub-license, time-share, or lend the software, diskettes, or documentation. Your use of the software is limited to acts that are essential steps in the use of the software on your computer or computer network as described in the documentation. You may not otherwise modify, alter, adapt, merge, decompile or reverse-engineer the software, and you may not remove or obscure Borland copyright or trademark notices.

L I M I T E D   W A R R A N T Y

Borland International, Inc. ("Borland") warrants the physical diskette(s) and physical documentation enclosed herein (but not any diskettes or documentation distributed by the Paradox Runtime Licensee) to be free of defects in materials and workmanship for a period of sixty days from the purchase date. If Borland receives notification within the warranty period of defects in materials or workmanship, and such notification is determined by Borland to be correct, Borland will replace the defective diskettes(s) or documentation. DO NOT RETURN ANY PRODUCT UNTIL YOU HAVE CALLED THE BORLAND CUSTOMER SERVICE DEPARTMENT AND OBTAINED A RETURN AUTHORIZATION NUMBER.

The entire and exclusive liability and remedy for breach of the Limited Warranty shall be limited to replacement of defective diskette(s) or documentation and shall not include or extend to any claim for or right to recover any other damages, including but not limited to, loss of profit, data, or use of the software, or special, incidental, or consequential damages or other similar claims, even if Borland has been specifically advised of the possibility of such damages. In no event will Borland's liability for any damages to you or any other

person ever exceed the lower of suggested list price or actual price paid for the license to use the software, regardless of any form of the claim.

BORLAND INTERNATIONAL, INC. SPECIFICALLY DISCLAIMS ALL OTHER WARRANTIES, EXPRESS OR IMPLIED, INCLUDING BUT NOT LIMITED TO, ANY IMPLIED WARRANTY OF MERCHANTABILITY OR FITNESS FOR A PARTICULAR PURPOSE. Specifically, Borland makes no representation or warranty that the software is fit for any particular purpose and any implied warranty of merchantability is limited to the sixty-day duration of the Limited Warranty covering the physical diskette(s) and physical documentation only (and not the software) and is otherwise expressly and specifically disclaimed.

This limited warranty gives you specific legal rights; you may have others which may vary from state to state. Some states do not allow the exclusion of incidental or consequential damages, or the limitation on how long an implied warranty lasts, so some of the above may not apply to you.

BUSINESS PRODUCTS (With Network Provisions): NO-NONSENSE LICENSE STATEMENT

BUSINESS PRODUCTS (With Network Provisions): NO-NONSENSE LICENSE STATEMENT

This section restates the basic copyright restrictions about transferring software.

Although you pay for a software license, your legal right to use the software continues only as long as you abide by the terms of the software license. Therefore, reading the terms of the software license agreement included with any software package you use is important. The software license agreement explains whether you may make copies, modify the software, or transfer it to another person. A software license often extends the rights given to you by the U.S. Copyright Act. For example, although the Copyright Act makes it illegal to copy software for use on more than one computer, the license for Claris Works software allows you to buy one copy of the software and install it on your home computer and your office computer as long as you are the primary user of both computers.

It is important to distinguish the concept of licensing from that of purchasing a copy of software. When you pay for licensed software, you do not buy and then own a copy of the software. Instead, you buy permission to use the software. You can think of it as renting software, rather than buying it.

Shrink Wrap Licenses

Do I have to sign a software license for it to be valid?

Signing and submitting a license agreement every time you purchase software would be inconvenient, so the computer industry makes extensive use of **shrink wrap licenses**. When you purchase computer software, the disks or CD-ROM in the package are usually sealed in an envelope or plastic shrink wrapping. A notification, such as the one in Figure 2-5, states that opening the wrapping signifies your agreement to the terms of the software license.

Figure 2-5
A typical shrink wrap license

When you open the package, you agree to the terms of the software license agreement. If you do not agree with the terms, you should return the software unopened.

ATTENTION! Use of the software program on the enclosed disks is subject to the terms of the Microsoft License Agreement printed on the license card, in the multilingual License booklet, or in the user's documentation. You should not open this packet until you have read the Microsoft License Agreement. By opening this packet, you signify that you have read the Microsoft License Agreement and accept its terms.

With a shrink wrap license, the software publisher avoids the lengthy process of negotiating the terms of the license and obtaining your signature. It is essentially a "take it or leave it" approach to licensing. Although the courts have yet to provide a definitive ruling on its validity, shrink wrap licensing is one of the most frequently used methods for providing legal protection for computer software.

Licenses for More Than One User

If my company has a computer network, does it still have to pay for a license for each user?

Most software publishers offer a variety of license options; some are designed for a single user, others for more than one user. A **single-user license** limits the use of the software to one user at a time. Most commercial software is distributed under a single user license.

A **multiple-user license** allows more than one person to use a particular software package. This type of license is useful in cases where users each have their own personalized version of the software. An electronic mail program would typically have a multiple-user license because users each have their own mailbox. Multiple-user licenses are generally priced per user, but the price for each user is typically less than the price of a single-user license.

A **concurrent-use license** allows a certain number of copies of the software to be used at the same time. For example, if an organization with a computer network has a concurrent-use license for five copies of a word processor, at any one time as many as five employees may use the software. Concurrent-use licenses are usually priced in increments. For example, a company might be able to purchase a concurrent-use license for up to 50 users for $2,500, or up to 250 users for $10,000.

A **site license** generally allows the software to be used on any and all computers at a specific location, such as within a corporate office building or on a university campus. A site license is priced at a flat rate, for example, $5,000 per site.

Public Domain Software

Isn't some software free?

Sometimes an author abandons all rights to a particular software title and places it in the public domain, making the program available without restriction. Such software, referred to as **public domain software**, is owned by the public rather than by the author.

Public domain software may be freely copied, distributed, and even resold. The primary restriction on public domain software is that you are not allowed to apply for a copyright on it. Public domain software is fairly rare. It is frequently confused with shareware because it is legal to copy and distribute both public domain software and shareware.

What's the difference between a multiple-user license and a concurrent-use license? With a multiple-user license, each individual who uses the software must be assigned a license. If five employees use mail software under a multiple-user license, a five-user license is required even if they are not all using the software at the same time. With a concurrent-use license for five users, any five employees can use the software at the same time even if there are hundreds of employees in the firm.

Shareware

My friend gave me a copy of something called "shareware." Was that illegal?

Shareware is copyrighted software marketed under a "try before you buy" policy. Shareware usually includes a license that allows you to use the software for a trial period. If you want to continue to use it, you must send in a registration fee. Take a look at the shareware license in Figure 2-6 and notice the rights it includes.

Figure 2-6
A typical shareware license

To avoid problems, be sure you're clear on your rights to copy, use, and distribute software. Many programs provide this information when you click Help and then select the Help About menu option.

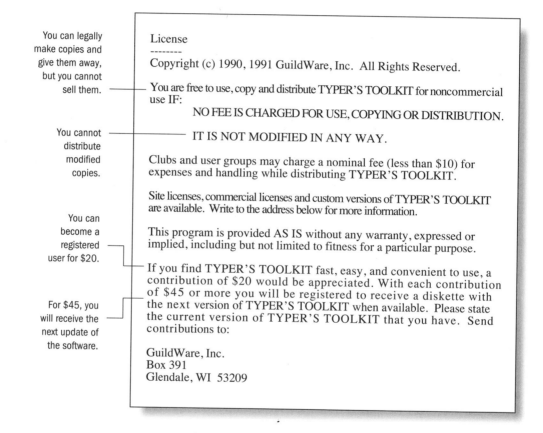

You can legally make copies and give them away, but you cannot sell them.

You cannot distribute modified copies.

You can become a registered user for $20.

For $45, you will receive the next update of the software.

License

Copyright (c) 1990, 1991 GuildWare, Inc. All Rights Reserved.

You are free to use, copy and distribute TYPER'S TOOLKIT for noncommercial use IF:
        NO FEE IS CHARGED FOR USE, COPYING OR DISTRIBUTION.

        IT IS NOT MODIFIED IN ANY WAY.

Clubs and user groups may charge a nominal fee (less than $10) for expenses and handling while distributing TYPER'S TOOLKIT.

Site licenses, commercial licenses and custom versions of TYPER'S TOOLKIT are available. Write to the address below for more information.

This program is provided AS IS without any warranty, expressed or implied, including but not limited to fitness for a particular purpose.

If you find TYPER'S TOOLKIT fast, easy, and convenient to use, a contribution of $20 would be appreciated. With each contribution of $45 or more you will be registered to receive a diskette with the next version of TYPER'S TOOLKIT when available. Please state the current version of TYPER'S TOOLKIT that you have. Send contributions to:

GuildWare, Inc.
Box 391
Glendale, WI 53209

When you send in the fee to become a registered shareware user, you are granted a license to use the software beyond the trial period. You might also receive a free copy of the latest version of the software or printed documentation for the program.

When you read the shareware license in Figure 2-6, you might have noticed that you are allowed to make copies of the software and distribute them to others. This is a typical shareware policy and a fairly effective marketing strategy that provides low-cost advertising. Unfortunately, registration fee payment relies on the honor system, so many shareware authors collect only a fraction of the payment they deserve for their programming efforts.

Software Categories

What's the difference between system software and application software?

Because there are so many software titles, categorizing software as either system software or application software is useful. **System software** helps the computer carry out its basic operating tasks. **Application software** helps the human user carry out a task.

System software and application software are further divided into subcategories. As you continue to read this chapter, use Figure 2-7 to help you understand the differences between system and application software and to help you distinguish among the various subcategories of system and application software.

Remember the key difference between system software and application software: system software helps the computer, application software helps you.

▶ **Figure 2-7**
Software categories

Quick Check

1. If you use a computer to write a report, the report is considered software. True or false?

2. When you type a report or enter the information for a mailing list, you are creating _____.

3. The instructions that tell a computer how to convert inches to centimeters are a computer _____.

4. To use a computer to write and edit documents, you need word processing _____.

5. The "try before you buy" policy refers to _____ licenses.

6. A(n) _____ for microcomputer or mainframe software is a contract by which the software publisher grants the buyer permission to use the software.

7. _____ software helps the *computer* carry out its basic operating tasks.

2.2 System Software

System software is the category of software containing programs that perform tasks essential to the efficient functioning of computer hardware. System software includes the programs that direct the fundamental operations of a computer, such as displaying information on the screen, storing data on disks, sending data to the printer, interpreting commands typed by users, and communicating with peripheral devices.

Let's look at some of the specific functions of the four subcategories of system software: operating systems, utilities, device drivers, and computer programming languages.

Operating Systems

Why does a computer need an operating system?

An **operating system** is the software that controls the computer's use of its hardware resources such as memory and disk storage space. An operating system works like an air traffic controller to coordinate the activities within the computer. Just as an airport cannot function without air traffic controllers, a computer cannot function without an operating system. When you purchase a microcomputer, the operating system is usually pre-installed on the hard disk and ready to use. You "see" the operating system each time you turn on your computer, and the operating system helps you start the application software you want to use.

If you envision computer hardware as the core of your computer system, then the operating system provides the next layer of functionality by assisting the computer with its basic hardware operations. The operating system also interacts with the next layer—application software—to carry out application tasks such as printing and saving data. Figure 2-8 helps you envision the relationship between your computer hardware, the operating system, and application software.

You might be familiar with the names of the most popular microcomputer operating systems: DOS, Microsoft Windows, OS/2, and Mac OS. You are less likely to be familiar with the names of minicomputer and mainframe operating systems such as UNIX, VMS, and MVS. Operating systems for micro, mini, and mainframe computers perform many similar tasks. An operating system helps you start an application, then works "behind the scenes" while application software is running to perform tasks essential to the computer system's efficient functioning. It controls input and output, allocates system resources, manages the storage space for programs and data, maintains security, and detects equipment failure. Study Figure 2-9 to discover more about what an operating system does.

Figure 2-8
The relationship among hardware, operating system, and application software

Application Software

Operating System

Computer Hardware

The **computer hardware** is the core of the system, but the hardware cannot function without an operating system.

The **operating system** acts as a liason between the computer hardware and application software.

Application software requires the operating system to carry out hardware related tasks such as printing reports and storing data on disks.

Figure 2-9
Operating system functions

Control Basic Input and Output

An operating system controls the flow of data into and out of the computer, as well as the flow of data to and from peripheral devices. It routes input to areas of the computer where it can be processed and routes output to the screen, a printer, or any other output device you request.

Allocate System Resources

A **system resource** is any part of a computer system, such as a disk drive, memory, printer, or processor time, that can be used by a computer program. The operating system allocates system resources so programs run properly.

For example, each program instruction takes up space inside the computer and each instruction requires a certain amount of time to complete. The operating system ensures that adequate space is available for each program that is running and makes sure the processor quickly performs each program instruction.

The operating system also manages the additional resources required for using multiple programs or for providing services to more than one user at the same time. For example, if you want to run two or more programs at the same time, a process called **multitasking**, the operating system ensures that each program has adequate space and that the computer devotes an appropriate amount of time to the tasks prescribed by each program.

To accommodate more than one user at a time, an operating system must have multiuser capabilities. You typically find **multiuser** operating systems on mainframe and minicomputer systems, where users each have their own terminal but share the processing capability of a single main computer. Multiuser operating systems typically provide speedy service so users each think they are the only ones using the computer.

Manage Storage Space

The operating system keeps track of the data stored on disks and CD-ROMs. Think of your disks as filing cabinets, your data as papers stored in file folders, and the operating system as a filing clerk. The filing clerk takes care of filing a folder when you finish using it. When you need something from your filing cabinet, you ask the filing clerk to get it. The filing clerk knows where to find your folder. On your computer system, the operating system stores your data at some location on a disk. Although you might not know exactly where your data is stored on the disk, when you need the data again, you only need to ask the operating system to retrieve it.

Detect Equipment Failure

The operating system monitors the status of critical computer components to detect failures that affect processing. When you turn on your computer, the operating system checks each of the electronic components and takes a quick inventory of the storage devices. For example, if an electrical component inside your computer fails, the operating system displays a message identifying the problem and does not let you continue with the computing session until the problem is fixed.

Maintain Security

The operating system also helps maintain security for the data on the computer system. For example, the operating system might not allow you to access the computer system unless you have a user ID and password.

Let's look at a specific example of how the operating system works as a liaison between the computer hardware and application software. The operating system provides a foundation so that application software operates correctly and uses peripheral devices properly. For example, suppose you use application software to write a letter and then you want to print it. The operating system helps the application software communicate with your computer's printer, as shown in Figure 2-10.

Figure 2-10
The operating system: a liaison between the computer hardware and application software

1. The user tells the word processing application to print the document.

2. The word processing application signals the operating system that a document must be sent to the printer.

3. The operating system sends the document to the printer.

Microcomputer Operating Systems

As a computer user, why is it important for me to know which operating system is on my computer?

Today's popular operating systems for IBM-compatible microcomputers include DOS, Windows, and OS/2. The Macintosh operating system is called Mac OS. UNIX is available for both IBM-compatible and Macintosh computers. Versions of UNIX and Windows are also available for some minicomputers and mainframes.

You interact directly with your computer's operating system to start programs and manage the data on your disks. You need to know which operating system your computer uses so you can enter the appropriate instructions to accomplish these tasks. How can you tell which operating system your computer uses? Many microcomputer users can recognize an operating system by looking at the first screen that appears when they turn the computer on or by recognizing the operating system prompt. If you study Figure 2-11, you can identify the DOS, Mac OS, Windows 3.1, Windows 95, UNIX, and OS/2 operating systems when you encounter them in the future.

Microsoft Windows 3.1 is sometimes referred to as an "operating environment," rather than an operating system; newer versions of Windows such as Windows NT and Windows 95 are generally classified as operating systems.

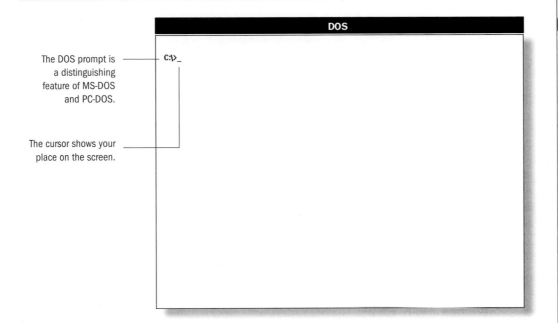

The DOS prompt is a distinguishing feature of MS-DOS and PC-DOS.

The cursor shows your place on the screen.

Figure 2-11
Microcomputer operating systems

DOS, which stands for Disk Operating System, is marketed under the trade names PC-DOS and MS-DOS. Both PC-DOS and MS-DOS were developed primarily by Microsoft Corporation and are essentially the same operating system. DOS was introduced in 1981 with IBM's first personal computer. Since the first version of DOS appeared, this operating system has gone through six major versions.

Early versions of DOS provided only a command-line user interface, but more recent versions include a menu-driven user interface called the DOS Shell. The DOS Shell provides menu access to the most frequently used operating system features, so you do not have to memorize the DOS commands.

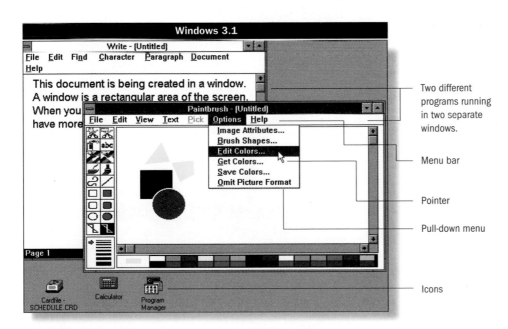

Two different programs running in two separate windows.

Menu bar

Pointer

Pull-down menu

Icons

Microsoft took a more graphical approach to operating systems when it designed Windows.

Microsoft Windows 3.1 provides icons that you can directly manipulate on the screen using a pointing device, and pull-down menus you can use to easily issue a command. The applications you use with Windows 3.1 all have a consistent look, so it is easy to learn how to use new software. Windows 3.1 also lets you run more than one program at a time in separate windows on the screen, and lets you easily transfer data between them. While using Windows 3.1, you can still run DOS software.

Figure 2-11
Microcomputer
operating systems
continued

My Computer icon

Disk drive icon

Windows

The Start button is
a unique feature
of Windows 95.

Title bar

Menu Bar

Document
icon

Task bar

Microsoft introduced a new version of Windows in 1995 that offers better operating efficiency than Windows 3.1. The user interface design for Windows 95 is based on extensive usability testing by both novice and expert computer users.

Windows 95 has a graphical user interface that uses icons to represent objects such as computers, disk drives, and documents.

In addition to programs designed specially for Windows 95, the operating system also runs software designed for Windows 3.1 and DOS. Windows 95 support multitasking, networking, and electronic mail.

Icons

Windows

Menu bar

OS/2 was designed jointly by Microsoft and IBM. Their goal was to create an operating system that would take advantage of newer, more powerful computers, plus offer a graphical user interface while retaining the ability to run DOS

programs. As with other graphical user interfaces, OS/2 allows you to manipulate objects on the screen to perform tasks and select commands from menus. As with Microsoft Windows, OS/2 lets you work with more than one

application at a time and easily transfer data between them. If your computer uses OS/2, you can run most DOS and Windows software, as well as software designed specifically for OS/2.

Apple Icon — Menu bar
Icons
Windows
UNIX prompt

Figure 2-11
Microcomputer
operating systems
continued

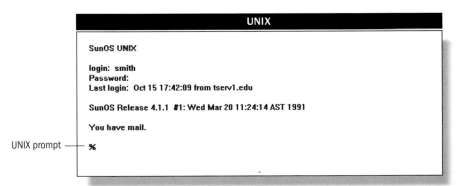

In 1984, Apple Computer, Inc. took a revolutionary step when it introduced the Apple Lisa computer with a new operating system based on a graphical user interface featuring pull-down menus, icons, and a mouse. The Lisa computer was not a commercial success, but Apple's next product, the Macintosh computer, was very successful and defined a new direction in operating system user interfaces that became an industry standard.

The **Macintosh Operating System** is usually referred to by its version number. For example, version eight of the operating system is called System 8. The Macintosh operating system has multitasking capability and offers network support.

UNIX is an operating system that was developed at AT&T's Bell Laboratories in 1969. UNIX was originally designed for minicomputers, but is now also available for microcomputers and mainframes. Many versions of UNIX exist, such as AIX from IBM, XENIX from Microsoft, and ULTRIX from Digital Equipment Corporation, but these other versions are essentially the same operating system adapted for different computers. UNIX features a command-line user interface, but you can purchase add-on software that provides a graphical user interface with direct object manipulation and pull-down menus. UNIX is a multi-user operating system, which means that many users can run programs on a single computer at the same time. UNIX also supports multitasking.

Utilities

Does the operating system include all the system software I need?

Utilities are a subcategory of system software designed to augment the operating system by providing a way for a computer user to control the allocation and use of hardware resources. Some utilities are included with the operating system; they perform tasks such as preparing disks to

Figure 2-12
Using the Windows 95 format utility

1. Insert the disk you want to format and click the **My Computer** icon to select it, then press **Enter**.

2. Click the **3½ Floppy (A:)** icon in the My Computer window.

3. Click **File** on the menu bar, then click **Format** to open the Format window.

4. Make sure the Capacity box matches the size of the disk you want to format, then click Start.

5. When the format is complete, the computer displays this window. Click the **Close** button.

hold data, providing information about the files on a disk, and copying data from one disk to another. Additional utilities can be purchased separately from software publishers and vendors. For example, Norton Utilities, published by Symantec, is a very popular collection of utility software. It retrieves data from damaged disks, makes your data more secure by encrypting it, and helps you troubleshoot problems with your computer's disk drives.

One of the important tasks performed by an operating system utility is formatting a disk. Each disk must be formatted before you can store data on it. Think of formatting as creating the electronic equivalent of storage shelves. Before you can put things on the shelves, you must assemble the shelves. In a similar way, before you can store data on a disk, you must make sure the disk is formatted.

You can buy preformatted disks, but you still might need a disk format utility if you use a disk that has not been preformatted or a disk that was formatted previously for a different type of computer. To run a format utility, you either type the name of the utility or select the format option from a menu. Figure 2-12 shows how to use the format utility for Windows 95.

Device Drivers

How do I use a device driver?

In Chapter 1, you learned that when you purchase a new peripheral device, such as a CD-ROM drive or a mouse, you often need to install software that tells your computer how to use the device. The system software that helps the computer control a peripheral device is called a **device driver**.

When you purchase a new peripheral device, its installation instructions usually tell you how to install both the device and the necessary device drivers. The way you "use" a device driver is to install it according to the instructions. Once the device driver is installed correctly, the computer uses it to communicate with the device.

If you have followed the instructions for installing a new device and its device driver, but the device does not work, check with the manufacturer. You might need an updated version of the device driver.

Computer Programming Languages

Is a computer programming language part of the system software included with a basic computer system?

As you know, a computer program is a series of instructions that the computer follows to perform a task. However, the list of instructions written by a human programmer is quite different from the instructions that the computer actually follows. The programmer's instructions must be translated into electrical signals that the computer can manipulate and process.

A **computer programming language** allows a programmer to write programs using English-like instructions, such as those you saw in Figure 2-1. The programming language then translates the instructions created by a programmer into a format the computer can interpret and directly process.

As mentioned earlier in this chapter, most computer users do not need to write programs. Therefore, most computers do not include a computer programming language. If you want to write programs, you must purchase programming language software. Today some of the most popular programming languages are BASIC, Visual Basic, C, C++, COBOL, Ada, and FORTRAN.

Quick Check

1. If you want to run more than one program at a time, you must use an operating system with _____ capability.

2. _____ is a multiuser operating system.

3. The DOS, Windows, Mac OS, and OS/2 operating systems are typically used on _____ computer systems.

4. _____ software helps the computer accomplish such tasks as preparing a disk for data, providing information about the files on a disk, copying data from one disk to another, and retrieving data from damaged disks.

5. You install a(n) _____ to tell the computer how to use a new peripheral device.

6. A(n) _____ translates a programmer's instructions into instructions the computer can interpret and directly process.

2.3 | # Application Software

Now let's return to the idea presented at the beginning of this chapter—that the computer is a multipurpose machine. Although system software handles internal computer functions and helps the computer use peripheral devices, it doesn't transform the computer into the different kinds of machines you need to write reports, "crunch" numbers, learn how to type, or draw pictures. It is application software that enables the computer to become a multipurpose machine and to perform many different tasks.

Software categorized as **application software** helps you accomplish a specific task using the computer. Application software helps you produce documents, perform calculations, manage financial resources, create graphics, compose music, play games, maintain files of information, and so on. Application software packages are sometimes referred to simply as **applications**.

The vast amount of application software makes classifying it convenient. Keep in mind, though, that the categories are neither formal nor standard. You might see word processing software categorized as business software in one software catalog, but as productivity software in another.

One way to classify application software is to use four categories: productivity, business, education and reference, and entertainment. Figure 2-13 shows you an expanded view of the application software branch of the software hierarchy chart you saw in Figure 2-7.

Figure 2-13 ◀
Application software

Productivity Software

What productivity software is right for me?

As you might expect from its name, **productivity software** helps you work more effectively. The most popular types of productivity software are word processing, spreadsheet, and database management. We'll look at these first, then take a look at some additional types of productivity software. As you read the descriptions, consider which types would be most useful for you.

Word processing software helps you produce documents such as reports, letters, papers, and manuscripts. Word processing is the most popular type of application software. Individuals use word processing software for correspondence, students use it to write reports and papers, writers use it for novels, reporters use it to compose news stories, and scientists use it to write research reports.

Word processing software gives you the ability to create, spell check, edit, and format your document on the screen before you commit it to paper. Therefore, when you begin typing the text of a document, you can let your ideas flow without worrying about making typing errors. After you have entered your first draft, word processing software gives you the flexibility to improve the quality of your document by changing the wording or rearranging topics. When you are satisfied with the content of your document, you can use formatting and page layout features of your word processing software to create a professional-looking printout.

Word processing software also gives you the ability to easily reuse documents. For example, if you have a resume that you send out periodically, it is easy to retrieve it, make necessary updates, and print it. In a law office, many standard documents such as wills, rental agreements, and premarital agreements are created using word processing software. These documents can be modified and reused for many clients.

Most word processing software has **mail merge**—the capability to merge a list of names and addresses with a form letter, then print a personalized version of the letter. Corporations use mail merge on a large scale to produce mass mailings about their services, new products, and latest sweepstakes. On a smaller scale, individuals can use mail merge to send out job applications, holiday letters, announcements, and invitations. Figure 2-14 on pages 60 and 61 explains how word processing software helps you write, edit, format, and print documents.

Spreadsheet software helps you work with numbers. The software displays a grid of rows and columns on the screen. You enter numbers and mathematical formulas in the grid and the computer automatically calculates the result. To visualize how this works, think about a simple hand held calculator. Suppose you need to add five numbers: 10234, 77654, 23411, 765487, and 341112. You enter the first number, press the + key, enter the second number, and so on. But when the calculation is complete, how do you know if you entered all the numbers correctly? You can't go back and check. Now, suppose the numbers you entered were somehow displayed in a column on a computer screen and the computer automatically added up the column and displayed the result. By looking at the numbers, you could be sure they were entered correctly. You could even change a number if you had made a mistake when you entered it.

Let's look at another example. Suppose you are buying a car and you have narrowed the choice to two cars. One car is less expensive, but the interest rate is higher. The other car is more expensive, but the interest rate is lower. Which car is the better deal? With a hand-held calculator, you have to do the entire calculation twice—once for each car. But, if you could type the formula for the calculation so it would appear on a computer screen, you could first plug in the numbers for one car. After you see the result, you could plug in the numbers for the second car.

When you use your spreadsheet software you can set up your own formulas for calculation or you can use built-in formulas, called functions, similar to the square root and log functions built into a hand-held calculator. You can use a spreadsheet function just by plugging in numbers—you don't have to know the details of the formula.

Figure 2-14
Word processing
software

Looking for better word to use

Thesaurus menu option

Spelling menu option

Spelling dialog box

This word is not in the dictionary

List of synonyms for "saga"

Thesaurus dialog box

Suggested correct spellings

Click Ignore to leave the word as it is.

Click change to replace continus with continues.

2 As you write, you can use the on-line **Thesaurus** to find a word with just the right meaning to convey your ideas. To use the Thesaurus, click the word you want to change and then select the Thesaurus options from the menu. You can then select the word you want from a list of synonyms.

3 An on-line **spell checker** helps you proofread your document. When you select the spell check option from the menu, the software compares each word in your document to the words in the software's dictionary. Words that can't be found in the dictionary are highlighted so you can change them to the correct spelling. Some words, such as proper names, are not in the dictionary. When the spell checker highlights one of these words in your document, you can skip the word.

1 **Word processing** software helps you produce documents such as reports, letters, papers, and manuscripts. To use a word processor, you type in the text of the document. The cursor or **insertion point** shows where the next charactyer you type will appear. As you type, you can edit your work by using the Backspace, Insert, and Delete keys. You can also highlight a block of text and delete, move, or copy it.

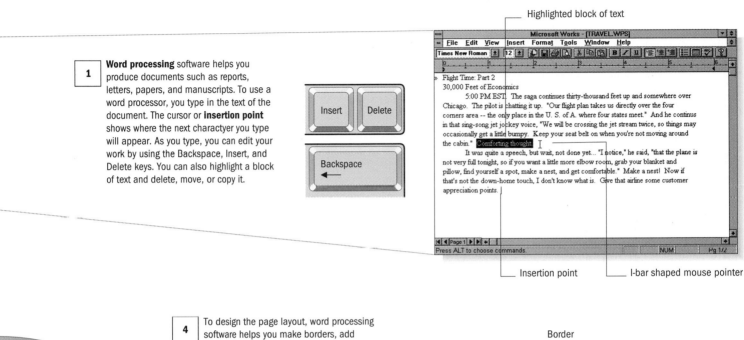

Highlighted block of text

Insertion point

I-bar shaped mouse pointer

4 To design the page layout, word processing software helps you make borders, add headers and footers, autromatically number each page, add graphics, create columns, add footnotes, and justify the margins.

5 Word processing software has many formatting features to help you design the appaerance of your printed document. You can use formatting features to adjust the line spacing, boldface text, italicize text, center text, change the font, and change the font size.

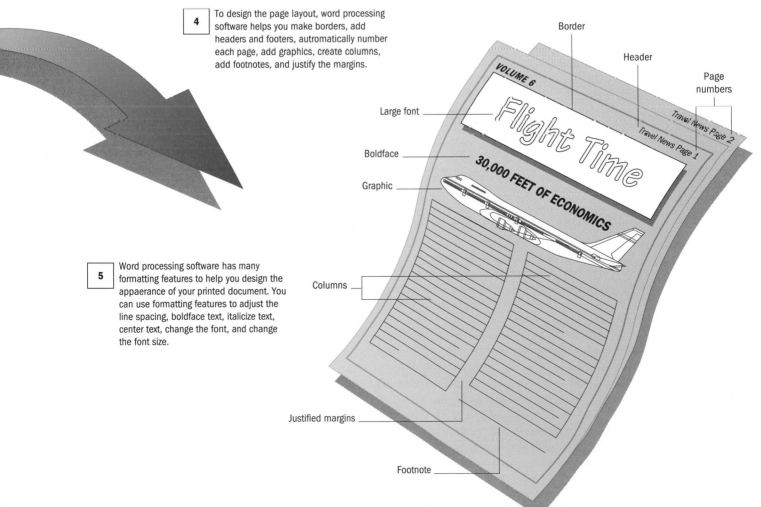

Border

Header

Page numbers

Large font

Boldface

Graphic

Columns

Justified margins

Footnote

Figure 2-15 on pages 64 and 65 explains more about spreadsheet software.

Spreadsheet software is frequently used by financial analysts to examine investment opportunities, by managers to create budgets, by entrepreneurs to create business plans, and even by educators to keep track of student grades. Individuals use spreadsheet software to track household budgets, calculate retirement investments, calculate loan payments, and compare investment opportunities.

Lab

Databases

Database management software helps you store, find, update, organize, and report information. Usually, this information is stored as **records** similar to the file cards or Rolodex cards you might use to store names and addresses. When information is in a computerized database, it is easy to search through it—even in a database containing thousands of records. To find information in a database, you enter a **query** that tells the computer exactly what you want to find. For example, when you use a library card catalog database, you can enter a query to find all the books written by Mark Twain.

You can also easily update the information in a record. For example, a computerized library card catalog keeps track of which books are checked out, by placing "out" in the Status field. When the book Tom Sawyer is checked out, its status field is updated to "out."

One of the most useful features of database management software is its ability to organize information by sorting it alphabetically or numerically. For example, if you have a database of all the names and birth dates of your friends, you can enter a query to find all your friends who have birthdays this month.

You can easily update the information in a record. For example, Latisha Smith gets married and changes her last name to Billings. When you give your database management software a command such as "update Latisha for Lastname—Billings" the software searches for Latisha's record, then changes her last name to Billings.

One of the most useful features of database management software is its ability to organize information by sorting it alphabetically or numerically. For example, suppose your insurance company requires an inventory of your household possessions, their date of purchase, and their value. You find it easy to make a list of the items one room at a time. However, your insurance company requires an *alphabetized* list of items in the entire house. After you enter the items room by room, you can have the database management software quickly alphabetize your list for the insurance company. You could even create a list of your possessions organized by their value or date of purchase.

Database management software also has sophisticated reporting features that help you produce professional-looking printouts. Usually reports are organized in a column or table format. You can print a report containing all the records in the database or just selected records. Most database management software will automatically calculate totals for your reports, such as the entire value of your household inventory.

Database management software helps hospitals and doctors keep track of patient records. The IRS uses database management software to keep track of tax payments. The phone company keeps track of names, addresses, and phone numbers using database software. Record clubs and book clubs keep track of members and sales using database software. Figure 2-16 on pages 66 and 67 explains more about using database management software to store, find, update, organize, and report information.

Although word processing, spreadsheet, and database management software are the most popular productivity software, you might find that other types of productivity software are also useful—electronic mail, desktop publishing, graphics, and scheduling.

Electronic mail software provides you with a computerized mailbox that collects documents or "mail" you receive electronically from other computer users. You can send electronic mail messages, read your electronic mail on your computer screen, save or throw away your electronic mail after you read it, and compose electronic replies to the mail you receive.

Graphics software helps you draw pictures, 3-D images, and animations. If you have limited artistic ability, you can use graphics software to retrieve predrawn images called **clip art**, which you can use as-is or modify. **Presentation graphics software** helps you present business information using screen-based slide shows of bulleted lists, graphs, and charts.

Desktop publishing software provides you with computerized tools for page layout and design that combine text and graphics. Although many desktop publishing features are available in today's sophisticated word processing software, desktop publishing software provides additional features to help you produce professional, quality output for newspapers, newsletters, and brochures.

Scheduling software helps you keep track of appointments, due dates, and special dates such as birthdays and holidays. You can use scheduling software to print a daily, weekly, or monthly calendar.

A software publisher sometimes combines several productivity software applications into a single package called **integrated software**. Typically, integrated software includes word processing, spreadsheet, database, and presentation graphics applications. Electronic mail is also included in some integrated software. The applications in an integrated software package are sometimes referred to as **modules**. Integrated software is often called a **suite**, **office**, or **works**. Some popular integrated software packages include Microsoft Works, Claris Works, Lotus Smart-Suite, Novell Perfect Office, and Microsoft Office.

Integrated software makes it easy to cut and paste data between applications. For example, you can easily incorporate budget figures from a spreadsheet module into a document you are writing using a word processing module. Another handy feature of integrated software is that the modules have a consistent user interface, so it is more like using one large application than using several smaller ones.

Business Software

What's the difference between horizontal-market and vertical-market software?

A second major category of application software, called **business software**, helps organizations efficiently accomplish routine tasks. Software in the business category is different from productivity software because its emphasis is on organization-wide tasks such as accounting, personnel management, and inventory control. Often, business software is divided into two categories: horizontal-market software and vertical-market software.

A horizontal market is a group of different types of businesses that, despite their differences, have some of the same software needs. **Horizontal-market software** refers to generic software packages that can be used by many different kinds of businesses. Accounting and payroll applications are good examples of horizontal-market software. Every business needs to maintain a set of books to track income and expenses and generate financial reports. Accounting software is designed to computerize the bookkeeping and financial reporting tasks typically required in most businesses. Almost every business has employees and needs to maintain payroll records. Payroll software keeps track of employee hours and produces the reports required by the government for income tax reporting.

A vertical market is a group of similar businesses—travel agencies, for example—that need specialized software. **Vertical-market software** is designed for specialized tasks in a specific market or business. Tasks in the construction industry include estimating the cost of labor and materials for a new building and providing the customer with a bid or estimate of the price for the finished building. Vertical-market software, such as estimating software designed specifically for construction businesses, can automate the task of gathering labor and materials costs and perform the calculations needed to arrive at an estimate. Other examples of vertical market software include the software that handles billing and insurance for medical practices and software that tracks the amount of time attorneys spend on each case.

Some productivity software, such as word processing applications, can also be categorized as horizontal-market software because they can be used in virtually any business.

Figure 2-15
Spreadsheet
software

Column B — Cell B3

Row 3

1 **Spreadsheet software** displays a grid of rows and columns on the screen. Each box formed by this grid is called a **cell**. Each cell has an **address** that indicates its row and column position. For example, cell address B3 means a cell in column B, row 3.

Function Categories

Financial

Date & Time

Math & Trig

Statistical

Lookup & Reference

Database

Text

Logical

3 To make your work easier, spreadsheet software includes many built-in formulas, called **functions**. Functions help you do financial, scientific, and statistical calculations. For example, the **pmt** function calculates loan payments. The **log** function calculates logarithms. The **stdev** function calculates standard deviations.

4 By plugging different numbers into the formulas on your worksheet, you can examine the outcome of different **"what if" scenarios**, such as "What if 1997 sales of the Huntsman stoves are $300,000?" or "What if they are $100,000 or $400,000?" A spreadsheet automatically calculates the results for each scenario, so you don't have to do the calculations over and over again by hand.

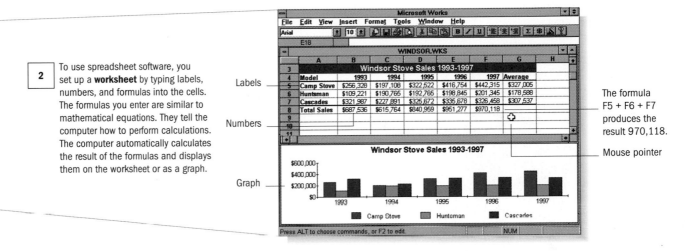

2 To use spreadsheet software, you set up a **worksheet** by typing labels, numbers, and formulas into the cells. The formulas you enter are similar to mathematical equations. They tell the computer how to perform calculations. The computer automatically calculates the result of the formulas and displays them on the worksheet or as a graph.

Labels

Numbers

Graph

The formula F5 + F6 + F7 produces the result 970,118.

Mouse pointer

5 Most spreadsheet software lets you create graphs and charts from the numbers in your worksheet. Graphing options are generally quite sophisticated. For example, the Microsoft Excel spreadsheet software has 15 types of graphs. You need to be careful to select the type of graph that accurately depicts your data.

6 Spreadsheet software creates professionally formatted reports of your worksheets. Formatting options help you automatically number pages, add headers, and position graphics. Because many spreadsheets are wider than thay are long, a landscape print option lets you print a "sideways" worksheet.

Header

Worksheet

Graph

Automatic page numbering

Figure 2-16
Database
management
software

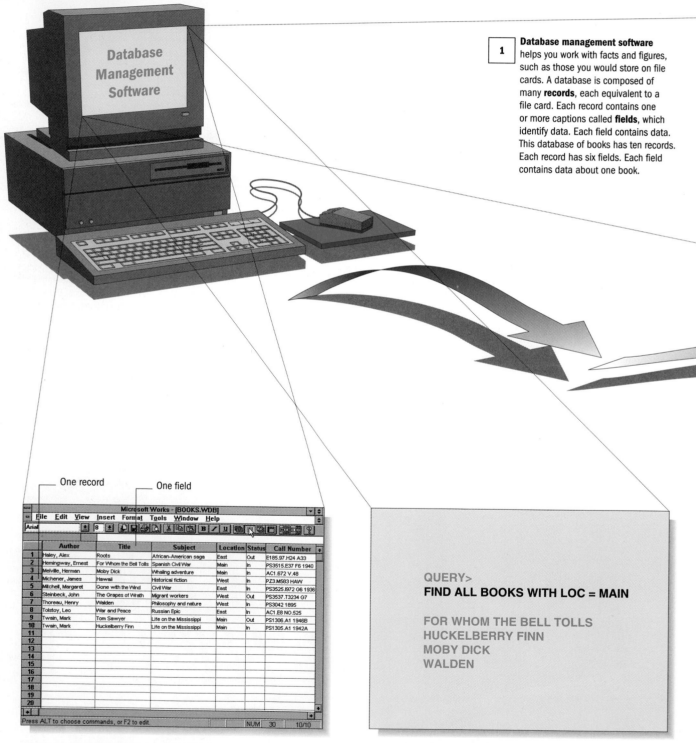

1 **Database management software** helps you work with facts and figures, such as those you would store on file cards. A database is composed of many **records**, each equivalent to a file card. Each record contains one or more captions called **fields**, which identify data. Each field contains data. This database of books has ten records. Each record has six fields. Each field contains data about one book.

— One record   — One field

Microsoft Works - [BOOKS.WDB]

File   Edit   View   Insert   Format   Tools   Window   Help

Arial

	Author	Title	Subject	Location	Status	Call Number
1	Haley, Alex	Roots	African-American saga	East	Out	E185.97 .H24 A33
2	Hemingway, Ernest	For Whom the Bell Tolls	Spanish Civil War	Main	In	PS3515.E37 F6 1940
3	Melville, Herman	Moby Dick	Whaling adventure	Main	In	AC1.672 V.48
4	Michener, James	Hawaii	Historical fiction	West	In	PZ3.M583 HAW
5	Mitchell, Margaret	Gone with the Wind	Civil War	East	In	PS3525.I972 G6 1936
6	Steinbeck, John	The Grapes of Wrath	Migrant workers	West	Out	PS3537.T3234 G7
7	Thoreau, Henry	Walden	Philosophy and nature	West	In	PS3042 1895
8	Tolstoy, Leo	War and Peace	Russian Epic	East	In	AC1.E8 NO.525
9	Twain, Mark	Tom Sawyer	Life on the Mississippi	Main	Out	PS1306.A1 1946B
10	Twain, Mark	Huckelberry Finn	Life on the Mississippi	Main	In	PS1305.A1 1942A
11						
12						
13						
14						
15						
16						
17						
18						
19						
20						

Press ALT to choose commands, or F2 to edit.   NUM   30   10/10

QUERY>
FIND ALL BOOKS WITH LOC = MAIN

FOR WHOM THE BELL TOLLS
HUCKELBERRY FINN
MOBY DICK
WALDEN

3 Another way to visualize a database is as a list or table. Each row of the table is a record. Each column of the table is a field.

4 You can make a **query** to find one or more records. For example, a query to "find all the books where Location = Main" produces four titles.

One record

Roots

Title: Roots
Author: Haley, Alex
Subject: Afro-American saga
Location: East
Status: Out
Catalog #: E185.97.H24 A33

Fields

Data

Files or database

TITLE
A-Z

2 You can organize the records by sorting or indexing. Here the records are arranged in alphabetical order by title.

Sorted by title

Microsoft Works - [BOOKS.WDB]

File Edit View Insert Format Tools Window Help

Arial   10

	Author	Title	Subject	Location	Status	Call Number
1	Hemingway, Ernest	For Whom the Bell Tolls	Spanish Civil War	Main	In	PS3515.E37 F6 1940
2	Mitchell, Margaret	Gone with the Wind	Civil War	East	In	PS3525.I972 G6 1936
3	Michener, James	Hawaii	Historical fiction	West	In	PZ3.M503 HAW
4	Twain, Mark	Huckelberry Finn	Life on the Mississippi	Main	In	PS1305.A1 1942A
5	Melville, Herman	Moby Dick	Whaling adventure	Main	In	AC1.672 V.48
6	Haley, Alex	Roots	African-American saga	East	Out	E185.97.H24 A33
7	Steinbeck, John	The Grapes of Wrath	Migrant workers	West	Out	PS3537.I3234 G7
8	Twain, Mark	Tom Sawyer	Life on the Mississippi	Main	Out	PS1306.A1 1946B
9	Thoreau, Henry	Walden	Philosophy and nature	West	In	PS3042 1895
10	Tolstoy, Leo	War and Peace	Russian Epic	East	In	AC1.E8 NO.525
11						
12						
13						
14						
15						
16						
17						
18						
19						
20						

Press ALT to choose commands, or F2 to edit.   NUM   14   10/10

Page numbering

Page 1

Print date: 2/4/96

Date

Title

All Books (Grouped by Status)

Title

For Whom the Bell Tolls
Gone with the Wind
Hawaii
Huckelberry Finn
Moby Dick
Walden
War and Peace

Roots
The Grapes of Wrath
Tom Sawyer

Author

Hemingway, Ernest
Mitchell, Margaret
Michener, James
Twain, Mark
Melville, Herman
Thoreau, Henry
Tolstoy, Leo

Haley, Alex
Steinbeck, John
Twain, Mark

Call Number

PS3515.E37 F6 1940
PS3525.I972 G6 1936
PZ3.M583 HAW
PS1305.A1 1942A
AC1.672 V.48
PS3042 1895
AC1.E8 N0. 525

Subtotal

E185.97.H24 A33
PS3537.T3234 G7
PS1306.A1 1946B

Subtotal

Total

Status

In
In
In
In
In
In
In

7

Out
Out
Out

3

10

Column titles

Grouped by status

Subtotal for each group

Total for all groups

5 Database management software provides sophisticated options for creating sorted or grouped reports. A **control-break report** groups the data by category. In this case, the data is sorted by status so that all the books that have been checked out are listed together.

Figure 2-17
Software toys

Screen saver software such as *After Dark* puts a moving image on the screen when you are not using your computer. On older monitors, screen savers prevented an image from "burning" into the screen if it was left on too long. Newer monitors are not so susceptible to burned images, but many users still have fun watching screen saver images such as these flying toasters.

If you are using the New Perspectives Labs that accompany this text book, you will have a first-hand experience with computer-aided instruction.

Entertainment Software

Are computers changing the way we spend our spare time?

Entertainment software included games and software designed for entertainment. Using entertainment software, you can fly a simulated jet, play 18 holes of golf, solve a Sherlock Holmes mystery, battle monsters, or explore new worlds. Although games are plentiful, not all entertainment software is in game format. With "software toys" there is no competition, no score, no winner, no loser. Software toys have a certain appeal to computer users who are looking for low-stress diversions. One software toy is a computerized fish tank application that lets you catch, breed, and watch a collection of brilliantly realistic tropical fish inside the glass "tank" of your computer monitor. Another is "Paper Planes," software that shows you how to construct several types of paper airplanes. Figure 2-17 shows some examples of software toys.

In 1993, entertainment software generated more than $500 million in sales. Considering that about 37% of U.S. households have one or more personal computers, you might expect to see significant changes in the pattern of leisure-time activity. The average person, however, spends about 2 hours a week using entertainment software, but spends about 17 hours watching television. Clearly, the computer industry has some work to do to make inroads on television's appeal.

Education and Reference Software

Can I use educational and reference software to improve my grades?

Education and reference software is designed to help you learn more about a particular topic. One subcategory of education software is called **CAI** or **tutorial software**. CAI stands for "computer-aided instruction." CAI software can help you learn how to type, fix your car, use your word processor, speak French, or prepare for the GMAT exam.

Educational simulations let you work with a computerized model of something in the real world, manipulate it, and see what happens. Some students use computerized simulations in introductory chemistry classes so they can experiment with chemical reactions without using real, and sometimes dangerous, chemicals.

Reference software, such as an electronic encyclopedia, helps you look up facts on any topic. Other reference software includes collections of classic literary works, electronic dictionaries, the phone directories for every city in the United States, a trip planner with maps of the entire United States, and medical reference guides.

Quick Check

1. The three most popular types of productivity software are _____, _____, and _____.

2. When several productivity software modules are sold as a package, it is referred to _____.

3. Personnel management software designed to be used in businesses as varied as hospitals, schools, and restaurants would be considered _____ market software.

4. Simulators and tutorials would be classified as _____ software.

5. Although word processing software helps you produce documents, _____ software is often used to produce professional-looking brochures and newsletters.

Multimedia

In the 1960s, a group of mop-haired musicians called the Beatles burst onto the music scene. Millions of screaming fans sent "I Want to Hold Your Hand" rocketing to the top of the charts. The Beatles formed their own record company called Apple Corps, Ltd.

In 1976, two young Californians, Steve Jobs and Steve Wozniak, started a computer company in a garage. Before the decade was out, their company had one of the most successful public stock offerings in history. Both Wozniak and Jobs became instant millionaires. Unfortunately, they named their company Apple Computer, Inc. According to the lawyers who represented Apple Corps, Ltd., that was a problem. The computer makers were charged with copyright infringement for using the Apple name.

In 1981, after lengthy negotiations, Apple Corps agreed to let Wozniak and Jobs use the Apple name. In return, Wozniak and Jobs agreed not to manufacture musical products. At the time, this arrangement seemed perfectly reasonable because computer technology and record companies had very little in common.

Today, however, the distinction between computer technology and record companies is not so clear. Consumer electronic inventions—radio, telephone, photography, sound recording, television, video recording, and computers—are merging and creating a new technology called multimedia.

Multimedia's Roots

Is multimedia the same as CD-ROM?

The term "multimedia" isn't really anything new—it refers to the integrated use of multiple media, such as slides, videotapes, audiotapes, records, CD-ROMs, and photos. School children sometimes still watch multimedia presentations that synchronize a tape-recorded sound track with a series of slides. As you can imagine, coordinating such a multimedia presentation is not easy. The teacher typically has difficulty getting the slides to synchronize with the sound track. If one slide is out of order or upside down, the teacher has to stop the tape, fix the slide, then restart the tape. The technology is cumbersome, and it is virtually impossible to go back to review segments of the presentation that students did not understand.

Today, the computer is replacing or controlling many of the technologies and media previously used for multimedia presentations. Advances in computer technology have made it possible to combine text, photo images, speech, music, animated sequences, and video into a single interactive computer presentation. A new definition of multimedia has emerged from this blend of technology. Today, **multimedia** is defined as an integrated collection of computer-based media including text, graphics, sound, animation, photo images, and video.

Envision a multimedia encyclopedia, for example. Like a traditional encyclopedia, it contains articles and pictures on a wide range of topics. But a multimedia encyclopedia has more. Suppose you're writing a research paper that explains the reasons for the European conflict in the country formerly known as Yugoslavia. You can pull up an article about Yugoslavia on your screen, listen to the Yugoslav national anthem, and view a map of eastern Europe. As you read the article, you can instantly access a cross-reference to an article about the Bosnia-Herzegovina conflict. A narrated video segment gives you some background on the causes of the conflict. A multimedia encyclopedia provides you with a rich selection of text, graphics, sound, animation, and video, as shown in Figure 2-18 on the next page.

Most multimedia applications are shipped on a CD-ROM because the graphics, sound, and video require large amounts of storage space. However, not everything shipped on CD-ROM is multimedia. Many software publishers distribute large data files and non-multimedia software on CD-ROM because one CD-ROM is more convenient and more cost-effective than 20 or 30 floppy disks. For example, one software company sells a CD-ROM that contains more than 200 classic works of literature—but only the text of the classics, not any graphics or sound. In this case, the CD-ROM contains data, not a multimedia application.

Figure 2-18 ◄
Compton's
multimedia
encyclopedia

To initially find information, you can use the Menu,
Contents list, Idea Search, Info Plot, or Topic Tree.

You control the
video clip of
the Bosnia-
Herzegovina
conflict using
on-screen
controls
modeled
after a VCR.

Topics related
to the main
article are listed
here. You jump
to a related
topic by clicking
here.

This status bar
tells you how to
use the
controls.

Click here
to see a map
of Yugoslavia.

Click here
to listen to
the Yugoslav
national
anthem.

Articles
explain
topics.

Multimedia Applications

Are multimedia applications better than plain old software?

Multimedia technology adds pizzazz to all types of computer applications: productivity, business, entertainment, and education and reference. You can use a multimedia scheduler to remind you of appointments and due dates. Instead of flashing a message on your screen, the multimedia scheduler reminds you of appointments by displaying a video image of a "personal assistant." "Excuse me," your personal assistant might say, "but I believe you have an appointment in five minutes."

You can use a multimedia presentation application to create a motivational business presentation that includes a short video message from the company president, pictures of a new product line, graphs of projected sales, sound effects of cheering crowds, and text that lists the features and benefits of the new products.

You can use multimedia entertainment applications to have an animated adventure in the far reaches of space. You control the animated instrument panel of your spacecraft from your computer keyboard, discuss tactics with video images of your crew members, and hear the sounds of your engines, instrument warnings, and weapons.

You can use multimedia computer-aided instruction to learn a foreign language. You can watch and listen to a short foreign-language video segment and view a synchronized translation. Then you can practice your pronunciation by speaking into a microphone so the computer can compare your pronunciation with a native speaker's.

Many "plain old" software applications can be improved by adding multimedia features. Multimedia technology also opens possibilities for new and creative applications. However, all multimedia products do not necessarily make effective use of multimedia technology. Multimedia product designers have not always considered which technologies would actually enhance their product.

Some multimedia products can be faulted for an incomplete use of multimedia technology. For example, one multimedia product was criticized for including "photos with brief titles but no

There are many more multimedia applications than we can describe in this chapter. Project 7 at the end of this chapter helps you find out what's available, what's popular, and what's useful in multimedia.

explanatory text…sketchy text, discontinuity, and almost total lack of sound." On the other hand, overuse of multimedia elements can sometimes detract from the contents. A reviewer pans one multimedia encyclopedia as "big on photos and animations, small on info." So, multimedia has the *potential* to improve an application, if the multimedia product is well designed.

Hypertext and Hypermedia

How do hypertext and hypermedia help me use multimedia applications?

Hypertext, a key element of many multimedia products, has been used effectively in non-multimedia products as well. Because you are likely to use hypertext with many computer applications, it is useful to learn what it's all about. The term **hypertext** was coined by Ted Nelson in 1965 to describe the idea of documents that could be linked to each other. Linked documents make it possible for a reader to jump from a passage in one document to a related passage in another document. Figure 2-19 will help you visualize a hypertext.

Lab

Computer History Hypermedia

► **Figure 2-19**
A hypertext of linked documents

A reference in the document about "Planes" links to an "Air Force Report."

The references in the "Air Force Report" link two other documents: one about helicopters and one about B-52 bombers.

A link from the Helicopters document to a dictionary shows the definition of the word "allocate."

al•lo•cate /'al-e-kat/*vt* **1.** to apportion for a specific purpose or to particular persons or things: DISTRIBUTE **2.** ASSIGN, DESIGNATE **syn** see ALLOT

Nelson wanted to create a giant hypertext that encompassed virtually every document on library shelves. His goal was not achievable with the technology of the sixties, and little was heard about hypertext for about 20 years. Then in 1987 Apple shipped a software product called Hypercard. It provided users a way to create the electronic equivalent of a stack of note cards. Each card could contain text, graphical images, or sounds; the cards could be linked to each other. Users jumped from one card to another by clicking buttons or specially marked *hot spots* in the text or graphics. The Hypercard-style implementation of hypertext developed over the next 10 years and became an important element of on-line Help, computer-based learning systems, and multimedia applications.

To try hypermedia, and follow links between text, graphics, and sounds, use the Computer History Hypermedia Lab.

The links in today's applications often involve graphics, sound, and video, as well as text. This type of multimedia hypertext is referred to as **hypermedia**. Hypertext and hypermedia are important computer-based tools because they help you easily follow a path that makes sense to you through a large selection of text, graphical, audio, and video information. Figure 2-20 shows you how to use hypermedia links to view film clips, compare critical reviews, and listen to sections of dialog with Microsoft's Cinemania application.

Figure 2-20 ◀
Using hypermedia

While looking at a biography of Humphrey Bogart, you can jump to information about the movie *Casablanca*. The blue lettering used for "Casablanca" indicates it is a link. The hand pointer indicates that you can click the link to jump to the *Casablanca* topic.

To read Leonard Maltin's review of the movie, click the Maltin button. Hypermedia buttons such as this help you jump to major sections of the hypermedia.

To hear a sound clip from the movie, click the speaker icon. Hypermedia links to sounds are usually indicated by a speaker icon.

To read sections of the script, click the document icon.

From the credits, you can select any topic indicated by blue lettering. For example, select the director's name to see his biography.

Multimedia Equipment

How do I know if my computer can use multimedia applications?

Today's multimedia applications require a computer system that can display graphic images, run video clips, and play sounds. Because most multimedia applications are shipped on a CD-ROM disk, your computer needs to have a CD-ROM drive. Your computer system must be able to quickly manipulate and transfer large amounts of data so you need a fast computer with a lot of memory. To display realistic graphical and video images, your computer system must have a high-resolution monitor capable of displaying a wide range of colors. To play realistic sounds, your computer needs a sound card and speakers. Figure 2-21 shows a computer well equipped for multimedia.

Just about every computer has a built-in internal speaker, but its sound capabilities are very primitive. Even though your computer can "beep" through the internal speaker, you need an additional sound card for multimedia applications.

A fast processor and lots of memory can speedup searches and video displays.

A high-resolution color monitor displays graphics, animations, and videos.

Earphones can be used as an alternative to speakers.

Speakers are attached to a sound card for audio playback.

A CD-ROM drive plays the multimedia software.

CD-ROMs contain multimedia software.

▶ **Figure 2-21**
A multimedia PC

Most computer companies produce one or more computer models equipped for multimedia applications. If you are in the market for a new computer, it makes sense to get one equipped for multimedia because of the many excellent multimedia applications available today. If you already have a computer, but it is not equipped for multimedia, you can add multimedia capabilities by purchasing a multimedia kit that contains a CD-ROM drive and sound card. A multimedia kit, like the one shown in Figure 2-22, is designed for non-technical users and usually can be installed in a few hours. Instead of using a multimedia kit, you can purchase a CD-ROM drive and sound card individually, but installing these individual components usually requires more technical expertise.

Figure 2-22
A multimedia kit

Speakers

Sound card

Disk containing device drivers

CD-ROM drive

In Chapter 5 you will learn technical terminology that will let you compare the capability of computer systems, including those equipped for multimedia.

The Multimedia PC Marketing Council publishes what is known as the MPC standard, which specifies the computer equipment you need to successfully use multimedia applications on your computer system. You will sometimes see the MPC logo on the box of multimedia applications, along with a description of the computer hardware required. The MPC logo is shown in Figure 2-23.

Figure 2-23
MPC Logo

Multimedia applications are available for both the Macintosh and IBM-compatible platforms. When you purchase a multimedia CD-ROM, read the package to make sure it will work with your computer. You might be surprised that Apple Computers, Inc. is active in the multimedia market after promising Apple Records that it would not manufacture musical products. In fact, Apple is an industry leader in multimedia technology. Considering past disagreements, it is somewhat ironic that the multimedia version of the Beatles' 1964 movie *A Hard Day's Night* is available exclusively for Macintosh computers.

Quick Check

1 Multimedia applications combine media such as _____, _____, _____, _____, _____, and _____.

2 Multimedia is the same as CD-ROM. True or false?

3 _____ and _____ are important computer-based tools because they help you easily navigate through a large selection of text, graphical, audio, and video information by following a path you choose.

4 The _____ standard specifies the minimum hardware requirements you need to successfully use multimedia applications on your computer system.

5 Most multimedia applications require equipment such as _____, _____, _____, _____, and _____.

6 You can add multimedia capability to your computer by purchasing a(n) _____ designed to be installed in a few hours by a non-technical user.

User **Focus:**

Installing Software

Many microcomputers are sold with pre-installed system and application software, but eventually most computer users want to install additional software.

Software Compatibility

How do I know what software will work on my computer?

Before you install software or a multimedia application, you must make sure it is compatible with your computer system. To be compatible, the software must be written for the type of computer you use and for the operating system installed on your computer. You must also make sure your computer meets or exceeds the system requirements specified by the software. **System requirements** specify the minimum hardware and operating system requirements needed for a software product to work correctly. The system requirements are usually listed on the outside of a software package, as shown in Figure 2-24. They might also be explained in more detail in the software reference manual.

You need multimedia hardware that complies with the basic MPC standard.

To run Encarta, your computer must have Microsoft Windows version 3.1 or later.

► **Figure 2-24**
System requirements

Your computer must have DOS version 3.1 or later.

Determining Compatibility

Does the version of my computer's operating system affect compatibility?

Suppose you want to purchase software for your IBM-compatible computer. First, you need to make sure the software is written for IBM-compatible computers, rather than for the Apple Macintosh. Sometimes the same software title is available for more than one type of computer. For example, Microsoft Word is available for both IBM-compatible and Apple Macintosh computers, but these are two distinct versions of the software. You cannot use the Macintosh version of Microsoft Word on your IBM-compatible.

Once you know the software is compatible with your computer, you must make sure the software will work with your operating system. If your IBM-compatible computer uses the DOS operating system, you must select DOS software. If your computer uses the Microsoft Windows operating system, you can select DOS or Windows software because Windows can run software designed for both of these operating systems. If your computer uses OS/2, you can select OS/2, DOS, or Windows software because OS/2 can run software designed for all three operating systems.

Operating systems go through numerous revisions. A higher version number indicates a more recent revision; for example, DOS 6.0 is a more recent version than DOS 5.0. Windows 95 is a more recent version than Windows 3.1. Operating systems are usually **downwardly compatible**, which means that you can use application software designed for earlier versions of the operating system, but not those designed for later versions. For example, if Windows 95 is installed on your computer, you can generally use software designed for earlier versions of Windows, such as Windows 3.1. However, your software might not work correctly if it requires Windows 95 but you have Windows 3.1 on your computer. If you want to use software that requires a newer version of your operating system, you must first purchase and install an operating system upgrade. Figure 2-25 on the next page summarizes the concept of downward compatibility.

Figure 2-25
Downward
compatibility

Windows 95 maintains downward compatibility by running software designed for earlier versions of Windows.

This software application requires Windows 3.1. It should work with Windows 3.1 and with Windows 95.

This software application requires Windows 95, so it is not likely to work with earlier versions of the operating system.

Software Setup

When I purchase software, what do I do with the disks?

Computer software is usually shipped on floppy disks, called **distribution disks**, or on CD-ROMs. In the years when personal computers first appeared on the market, you could often use the software directly from the distribution disk. Now that is rarely possible because the programs are so large they take up many disks. Today, instead of using software directly from the distribution disk, you usually install it on your hard disk. During the installation process, programs and data for the software are copied to the hard disk of your computer system.

When you install software using a command-line operating system, such as DOS, you should carefully follow the installation instructions provided in the reference manual. There is no consistent installation procedure for DOS software, so each software application might require different steps. On the other hand, for Microsoft Windows applications, the installation process is more consistent and usually much easier. Figure 2-26 shows you how to install Windows applications.

Installing software from a CD-ROM frequently differs from the installation process for software shipped on floppy disks. Software shipped on a CD-ROM is usually too large to fit on a hard disk. As you learned in Chapter 1, a CD-ROM stores up to 680 million characters of data, but a typical hard disk stores approximately 500 million characters of data. Because of the large size of CD-ROM software, you generally access the CD-ROM programs and data directly from the CD-ROM instead of from a hard disk. In this case, a very limited amount of information must be copied to your hard disk during the installation process. As with any software, you should read the installation instructions to find out how to install software distributed on a CD-ROM.

▶ **Figure 2-26**
The installation
process

1. Insert the setup disk and start the setup program.

2. Select full or customized installation. The number of programs and data files that the setup program copies to your hard disk depends on which features of the software you want available. For a full installation, the setup program copies all the files and data from the distribution disks to the hard disk of your computer system. A full installation provides you with access to all the features of the software.

During a customized installation, the setup program displays a list of software features for your selection. After you select the features you want, the setup program copies only the selected program and data files to your hard disk. A customized installation can save space on your hard disk.

☒ **Full Installation**
☐ **Customized Installation**

3. Insert each disk in the specified drive when the setup program tells you to do so. Each disk is numbered, and messages on the screen will tell you which disk to insert.

4. When the setup program is finished, start the program you have just installed to be sure it works.

5. Fill out the registration card and send it in. When you send in the card, you become a registered user. The perks of being a registered user vary with each software publisher, but they might include receiving free technical support, product information, or discounts on new versions of the software.

End Note Software is the key to the computer's versatility. System software and application software work together to help you accomplish an incredible variety of tasks. You might think it is "corny" to follow copyright laws and license restrictions, but ethical software use benefits everyone. Software publishers use revenues from software sales to improve current software, provide technical support, and develop new applications. By resisting the temptation to use illegal copies of software, you can help provide software publishers with the resources they need to develop more of the software that makes the computer such a versatile machine.

Review

1. Write a sentence or two explaining the most important concept you learned from this chapter.

2. Below each heading in this chapter, there is a question. Look back through this chapter and answer each of these questions using your own words.

3. Select 10 terms in this chapter that you believe are most important, then use your own words to write a definition of each term.

4. Under U.S. copyright law, what are the two major rights granted to the copyright holder? What are the three rights granted to the user of copyrighted materials?

5. Complete the following "legal" matrix to clarify the difference between copyrighted software, licensed software, shareware, and public domain software.

Suppose you are not the author of a software package. Is it...	Copyrighted Software	Licensed Software	Shareware	Public Domain Software
Legal to make a backup copy?				
Legal to sell a copy?				
Legal to give a copy to a friend?				
Protected by U.S. Copyright Law?				

6. For each of the following descriptions, indicate whether the software is copyrighted, licensed, shareware, or public domain. For some descriptions, there is more than one answer.

   a. The software does not have a copyright notice

   b. You must send in money to become a registered user

   c. The software is shrink wrapped and there is a message about your rights and responsibilities

   d. When you start the software you see a message "©1994 Course Technology, Inc."

   e. When you start the program you see a message, "Copyright 1986, 1987 SupRSoft, Inc. All Rights Reserved. You are free to use, copy, and distribute this software for non-commercial use if no fee is charged for use, copying, or distribution, and if the software is not modified in any way."

7. Create a sentence outline of Section 2.2 System Software. Your outline should have at least three levels. You can use I., A., and 1. for the outline levels. Be sure that the sentence you write for each outline level focuses on a single, important point.

8. Fill in the following table by using a check mark to indicate which operating systems are available for each type of computer.

Operating System	IBM Compatible	Macintosh	Minicomputer	Mainframe
DOS				
WINDOWS				
OS/2				
MVS				
VMS				
UNIX				

9. At the top of a sheet of paper, write "Productivity Software." Next, list all the terms you associate with productivity software. You can include terms that are not in the chapter; for example, if you use a productivity software package that is not mentioned in the chapter, you might still list it.

10. Review Section 2.3 on software applications. Then make a list of what you think are the three most important features of word processing, spreadsheet, and database software.

11. For each of the following applications, indicate what software tool would be best to use—word processing, spreadsheet, database, graphics, electronic mail, desktop publishing, or scheduling.

   a. Working with numbers and examining "what-if" scenarios

   b. Producing documents

c. Working with facts and figures, such as customer names and addresses

d. Drawing pictures, 3-D images, and animations

e. Sending electronic messages between two computers

f. Producing professional-looking brochures and newsletters

g. Creating pie charts, line graphs, and bar graphs

h. Determining times for meetings, tracking special events, and maintaining a to-do list

12. Make a two-column list to summarize multimedia. The left column of the list should include multimedia features such as sound, animation, and so on. The right column should indicate the computer equipment that is needed to implement the features you listed in the left column.

13. Suppose you're thinking of purchasing spreadsheet software, and you read a very favorable review of Microsoft Excel for Windows. The article indicates that the software requires "an IBM-PC/AT, PS/2, or compatible; graphics compatible with Microsoft Windows version 3.0 or later; MS-DOS version 3.1 or later; optional printer; a mouse or compatible pointing device is recommended." You have a Compaq computer with Windows 95, a Hewlett-Packard printer, and a Microsoft mouse. Explain whether you can expect the Microsoft Excel spreadsheet software to work on your computer after you install it.

Projects

1. Format a Disk In this chapter you learned how utility software helps you direct the operating system to accomplish tasks such as formatting a disk. This is a good time to try it out. If your lab computers have the Windows 95 operating system, you can do this project on your own by referring to Figure 2-12. Otherwise, your instructor will need to help you.

2. The Operating System in Your School's Lab In this chapter you learned how to identify microcomputer operating systems by looking at the main screen and prompt. In this project you will explore more about the operating system in your school computer lab. If you have more than one lab or your computer uses more than one operating system, your instructor should tell you which one to use for the project.

Find out which operating system is used in your school computer lab. Be sure you find out the type and version. You can go into the lab and obtain this information from one of the computers. If you see a command-line user interface, try typing "ver" and then pressing the Enter key. If you see a graphical user interface, try clicking the Apple menu, or click the Help menu, then select Help About. Once you know the operating system used in your school lab, use the operating system reference manual and library resources to answer the following questions:

a. Which operating system and version are used in your school lab?

b. What company publishes the operating system software?

c. When was the first version of this operating system introduced?

d. Does this operating system have a command-line user interface or a graphical user interface?

e. Does this operating system support multitasking?

f. Do you need a password to use the computers in your school lab? Even if you do not need to use a password, does the operating system provide some way to secure access to the computers?

g. What is the anticipated arrival date for the next version of this operating system?

h. How much does the publisher of this operating system usually charge for upgrades if you are a registered user?

3. The Legal Beagle: Analyzing a License Agreement When you use a software package, it is important to understand the legal restrictions on its use. In this project you have an opportunity to practice reading a real software license agreement and making decisions based on how you interpret what it says. You can do this project on your own or discuss it in a small group, as specified by your instructor. To extend this project, you can locate another license agreement, answer the same questions, then write a short paper about which license is better for the software user.

Read the IBM Program License Agreement in Figure 2-27 on the next page, then answer the questions in a through h that follow:

a. Is this a "shrink wrap" license? Why or why not?

b. After you pay your computer dealer for the program this license covers, who owns the program?

c. Can you legally have one copy of the program on your computer at work and another copy of the program on your computer at home if you use the software only in one place at a time?

d. Can you legally sell the software? Why or why not?

e. Under what conditions can you legally transfer possession of the program to someone else?

f. If you were the owner of a software store, could you legally rent the program to customers if you were sure they did not keep a copy after the rental period was over?

g. Can you legally install this software on one computer, but give more than one user access to it?

h. If you use this program for an important business decision and you later find out that a mistake in the program caused you to lose $500,000, what legal recourse is provided by the license agreement?

4. Software Applications: What's Available? There are so many software packages that it is difficult to get an idea of what's available unless you take a look through current computer magazines and software catalogs. This project has two parts.

Figure 2-27 ◀

You can do either one or both as your instructor assigns. Part A helps you discover the variety of available software applications. Part B helps you research an application or operating system in more depth. You will be able to find the information for this project in the computer magazines listed in the Resources section at the end of the chapter. If you have access to the Internet, check out Computer Express at *http://www.cexpress.com.*

Part A. Find an ad for a computer vendor that sells a large variety of software. Jot down the name of the vendor and where you found the ad. List the categories the vendor uses to classify software and the number of software packages in each category.

Part B. Select one type of software from the following categories: operating systems, disk utilities, word processing, graphics, presentation graphics, electronic mail, desktop publishing, spreadsheets, database, accounting, or scheduling. Read a comparison review of software packages in the category you select. Next try to locate and photocopy ads for each of the products in the review. Look through the software vendor ads to find the best price for each product. Finally, write a one- or two-page summary explaining your purchase recommendation.

5. What Software Tool Would You Recommend? Folk wisdom tells us to use the appropriate tool for a job. This is true for software tools, too. In this project you decide what software tool is most appropriate for a task. You can do this project on your own or discuss it in a small group.

For each of the scenarios that follow, decide if word processing, spreadsheet, database, desktop publishing, graphics, scheduling, electronic mail, or accounting software is the best tool.

International Business Machines Corporation   *Armonk, New York 10504*

IBM Program License Agreement

BEFORE OPENING THIS PACKAGE, YOU SHOULD CAREFULLY READ THE FOLLOWING TERMS AND CONDITIONS. OPENING THIS PACKAGE INDICATES YOUR ACCEPTANCE OF THESE TERMS AND CONDITIONS. IF YOU DO NOT AGREE WITH THEM, YOU SHOULD PROMPTLY RETURN THE PACKAGE UNOPENED AND YOUR MONEY WILL BE REFUNDED.

This is a license agreement and not an agreement for sale. IBM owns, or has licensed from the owner, copyrights in the Program. You obtain no rights other than the license granted you by this Agreement. Title to the enclosed copy of the Program, and any copy made from it, is retained by IBM. IBM licenses your use of the Program in the United States and Puerto Rico. You assume all responsibility for the selection of the Program to achieve your intended results and for the installation of, use of, and results obtained from, the Program.

The Section in the enclosed documentation entitled "License Information" contains additional information concerning the Program and any related Program Services.

LICENSE
You may:
1) use the Program on only one machine at any one time, unless permission to use it on more than one machine at any one time is granted in the License Information (Authorized Use);
2) make a copy of the Program for backup or modification purposes only in support of your Authorized Use. However, Programs marked "Copy Protected" limit copying;
3) modify the Program and/or merge it into another program only in support of your Authorized Use; and
4) transfer possession of copies of the Program to another party by transferring this copy of the IBM Program License Agreement, the License Information, and all other documentation along with at least one complete, unaltered copy of the Program. You must, at the same time, either transfer to such other party or destroy all your other copies of the Program, including modified copies or portions of the Program merged into other programs. Such transfer of possession terminates your license from IBM. Such other party shall be licensed, under the terms of this Agreement, upon acceptance of the Agreement by its initial use of the Program.

You shall reproduce and include the copyright notice(s) on all such copies of the Program, in whole or in part.
You shall not:
1) use, copy, modify, merge, or transfer copies of the program except as provided in this Agreement;
2) reverse assemble or reverse compile the Program; and/or
3) sublicense, rent, lease, or assign the Program or any copy thereof.

LIMITED WARRANTY
Warranty details and limitations are described in the Statement of Limited Warranty which is available upon request from IBM, its Authorized Dealer or its approved supplier and is also contained in the License Information. IBM provides a three-month limited warranty on the media for all Programs. For selected Programs, as indicated on the outside of the package, a limited warranty on the Program is available. The applicable Warranty Period is measured from the date of delivery to the original user as evidenced by a receipt.

Certain Programs, as indicated on the outside of the package, are not warranted and are provided "AS IS."
Z125-3301-02 4/87

SUCH WARRANTIES ARE IN LIEU OF ALL OTHER WARRANTIES, EXPRESS OR IMPLIED, INCLUDING, BUT NOT LIMITED TO, THE IMPLIED WARRANTIES OF MERCHANTABILITY AND FITNESS FOR A PARTICULAR PURPOSE.
Some states do not allow the exclusion of implied warranties, so the above exclusion may not apply to you.

LIMITATION OF REMEDIES
IBM's entire liability and your exclusive remedy shall be as follows:
1) IBM will provide the warranty described in IBM's Statement of Limited Warranty. If IBM does not replace defective media or, if applicable, make the Program operate as warranted or replace the Program with a functionally equivalent program, all as warranted, you may terminate your license and your money will be refunded upon the return of all your copies of the Program.
2) For any claim arising out of IBM's limited warranty, or for any other claim whatsoever related to the subject matter of this Agreement, IBM's liability for actual damages, regardless of the form of action, shall be limited to the greater of $5,000 or the money paid to IBM, its Authorized Dealer or its approved supplier for the license for the Program that caused the damages that is the subject matter of, or is directly related to, the cause of action. This limitation will not apply to claims for personal injury or damages to real or tangible personal property caused by IBM's negligence.
3) In no event will IBM be liable for any lost profits, lost savings, or any incidental damages or other consequential damages, even if IBM, its Authorized Dealer or its approved supplier has been advised of the possibility of such damages, or for any claim by you based on a third party claim.

Some states do not allow the limitation or exclusion of incidental or consequential damages so the above limitation or exclusion may not apply to you.

GENERAL
You may terminate your license at any time by destroying all your copies of the Program or as otherwise described in this Agreement.
IBM may terminate your license if you fail to comply with the terms and conditions of this Agreement. Upon such termination, you agree to destroy all your copies of the Program.

Any attempt to sublicense, rent, lease or assign, or, except as expressly provided herein, to transfer any copy of the Program is void.

You agree that your are responsible for payment of any taxes, including personal property taxes, resulting from this Agreement.

No action, regardless of form, arising out of this Agreement may be brought by either party more than two years after the cause of action has arisen except for the breach of the provisions in the Section entitled "License" in which event four years shall apply.

This agreement will be construed under the Uniform Commercial Code of the State of New York.

a. You want to keep track of your monthly expenses and try to figure out ways to save some money.

b. As the leader of an international team of researchers studying migration patterns of Canadian geese, you want all the team members to communicate their findings to each other quickly.

c. You are the office manager for a department of a large Fortune 500 company. One of your responsibilities is to arrange meetings and schedule facilities for the employees in your department.

d. As a partner in a law firm, you need to draft and modify legal briefs.

e. You are in charge of a fund-raising campaign and you need to track the names, addresses, phone numbers, and donations made by contributors.

f. You are going to design and produce the printed program for a community theater play listing the actors, director, lighting specialists, and so on.

g. A sales manager for a cosmetics company wants to motivate the sales force by graphically showing the increases in consumer spending in each of the past five years.

h. The marketing specialist for a new software company wants to send out announcements to 150 computer magazines.

i. The owners of five golf courses in Jackson County want to design a promotional brochure that can be distributed to tourists in restaurants and hotels.

j. The owner of a small business wants to keep track of ongoing income and expenses and print out monthly profit and loss statements.

k. The superintendent of a local school system wants to prepare a press release explaining why student test scores were 5% below the national average.

l. A contractor wants to calculate his cost for materials needed to build a new community center.

m. A college student wants to send out customized letters addressed to 20 prospective employers.

n. The parents of three children want to decide whether they should invest money for their children's education in the stock market or whether they should buy into their state's prepaid tuition plan.

o. The director of fund-raising for a large nonprofit organization wants to keep a list of prospective donors.

INTERNET OPTIONAL

6. Where's the Shareware? You learned in this chapter that shareware can be less expensive than commercial software; it also lets you try the software before you buy it. But is shareware as available as commercial software? In this project you will find out.

Use computer magazines and/or Internet sites to find a shareware program and a commercial program for each of the categories in the table below. For each shareware package, indicate the program name, the name of the retailer or vendor, and the selling price. In the reference column, indicate the name, date, and page of the magazine, or the Internet site, where you found the information. Shareware vendors frequently advertise in the back pages of computer magazines. If you have access to the Internet, you might try the Virtual Software Library at *http://www.acs.oakland.edu/oak.html.*

Software Type	Title	Price	Vendor	Reference
Shareware productivity				
Commercial productivity				
Shareware system utility				
Commercial system utility				
Shareware education				
Commercial education				
Shareware games				
Commercial games				

7. Multimedia "Top 10" In the last two years the multimedia market has exploded. For this project, create your own list of "top 10" multimedia titles. Look in recent editions of computer magazines and select the 10 multimedia applications that are most interesting or useful to you. For each multimedia application you select, list its title, publisher, and a short description of what it does. Also list the name of the computer magazine you used and the page on which you found the information about each multimedia application.

8. The Great Scheduler Problem Using a computer to maintain your schedule—what could be better? The computer warns you if you try to make two appointments at the same time, gives you advance notice of your appointments, and keeps track of your "To Do" list by bringing forward the tasks you didn't complete yesterday. Well, one slight problem—where is your computer when you see a friend in the "caf" and you set up a date, or when your colleague stops you in the hall to let you know about the sales meeting next Tuesday? Better switch to one of those pocket schedulers, right? No, too limiting—not enough memory and a small screen. Why not carry around a small device that communicates to your computer using an infrared beam? Is this the solution? What other solutions have been tried? Can you think of a better one?

This project is suitable for a term paper. You will need to research the software packages that give you scheduling capabilities, along with some of the hardware innovations that give you the option of running scheduling software on something other than a desktop computer. When you write your paper, be sure to include references to the resources you use.

9. Programming as a Career You learned in this chapter that most people do not need to write programs to use their computers. You also learned that computer programming is a challenging career field. In this project you will find out more about computer programming careers.

Computer programming jobs are often listed in the back pages of computer magazines, in professional journals, and on career bulletin boards on the Internet. Some of the best sources of information are the following:

InfoWorld magazine

The professional journal *Communications of the ACM*

The newspaper *San Jose Mercury News*, and its Internet site *http://www.sjmercury.com*

The Internet Monster Board *http://www.monster.com*

The Internet Career Mosaic *http://www.careermosaic.com*

To complete this project first locate three advertisements for computer programming jobs. Photocopy or print out a copy of the ads. Create a table like the one that follows, and fill it in for each of the three job openings you found.

Programming Jobs	Job 1	Job 2	Job 3
Educational requirements			
Work experience required			
Programming languages required			
Mainframe, mini, or microcomputer			
Company name			
Starting salary			

Resources

- *A Hard Day's Night*, The Voyager Co., 1351 Pacific Coast Highway, Santa Monica, CA 90401, 310-451-1383, $39.95. This CD-ROM contains the entire 90-minute Beatles film, *A Hard Day's Night*, along with an annotated script.

- **Nelson, T.** *Literary Machines.* Southbend, MI: The Distributors, 1981. Nelson describes project Xanadu as "the most audacious and specific plan for knowledge, freedom, and a better world yet to come out of computerdom: the original (and perhaps the ultimate) hypertext system." The details are here in Nelson's book, *Literary Machines.* You might also look for these other books by Nelson: *Computer Lib* (1987 edition published by Microsoft Press) and *The Home Computer Revolution* (published by the author in 1977).

- **Software Publishers Association** The Software Publishers Association provides public information on the legal use of software. SPA estimates that one-third of the software currently in use is pirated; its goal is to make software piracy a major issue in the computer industry. It publicizes its campaign slogan "Don't copy that floppy" in magazines, pamphlets, and videotapes. You can contact the organization at 1-800-388-7478 to obtain information or to report copyright violations.

- **White, R.** *How Software Works.* Emeryville, CA: Ziff-Davis Press, 1993. Browse through this book if you would like to look "under the hood" to see how a computer runs software, but you don't want to get lost in technical detail. Some of the topics related to the chapter you just finished include how Windows runs more than one program at a time, how programming languages translate ideas into software, and how spreadsheet formulas work.

■ **Wodaski, R.** *Multimedia Madness*. Carmel, IN: Sams Publishing, 1992. This 616-page book provides a good background in multimedia applications and hardware. The book includes a disk and CD-ROM containing hundreds of multimedia samples.

Computer Magazines

It's a good idea to become familiar with computer magazines, journals, and newsletters because they carry the most current information about the fast-moving computer industry. Although computer books are excellent for explaining concepts and history, computer magazines contain more up-to-date information on the latest hardware and software.

■ **Byte**
One of the oldest and most respected computer publications, *Byte*'s main focus is on computer hardware, although it also contains software reviews and a variety of regular columns. Jerry Pournelle, a science fiction writer and venerable computer columnist, provides product reviews and opinions in a column called "Chaos Manor."

■ **Computer Select**
If your library has CD-ROM databases, it might also have the *Computer Select* CD. Published quarterly, *Computer Select* contains abstracts and articles from many computer magazines. It is easy to search the entire CD for all articles on a specific topic.

■ **Computer Shopper**
If nothing else, this magazine must be the largest monthly computer publication! Each edition is about 800 pages. The articles are somewhat overshadowed by the numerous and lengthy (some up to 10 pages) computer ads. If you are going to buy a computer via mail order, this is the definitive resource.

■ **InfoWorld**
This weekly publication in tabloid format reports the latest industry news and is required reading for all computer "gurus."

■ **Macworld**
Macintosh users like the hardware and software reviews they find in this monthly magazine, which is dedicated to the Apple Macintosh computer.

■ **PC Computing**
The focus of this magazine is on IBM-compatible computers and software. Featured columnist John Dvorak usually presents an interesting perspective on new developments in the computer industry.

■ **PC World**
Similar in focus to *PC Computing*, *PC World* is distinguished by its "Consumer Watch" column, which acts as an industry watchdog and consumer advocate. "Consumer Watch" answers reports on product bugs, clarifies deceptive advertising, and prints consumer complaints.

■ **Windows**
This publication is especially for Microsoft Windows users. Each issue contains hardware and software reviews, as well as hints and tips on customizing the Microsoft Windows operating environment.

Lab Assignments

Word Processing

 Word processing software is the most popular computerized productivity tool. In this Lab you will learn how word processing software works. When you have completed this Lab, you should be able to apply the general concepts you learned to any word processing package you use at home, at work, or in your school lab.

1. Click the Steps button to learn how word processing software works. As you proceed through the Steps, answer all of the Quick Check questions that appear. After you complete the Steps, you will see a Quick Check Summary Report. Follow the instructions on the screen to print this report.

2. Click the Explore button to begin. Click File, then click Open to display the Open dialog box. Click the file **Timber.Doc**, then press the Enter key to open the letter to Northern Timber Company. Make the following modifications to the letter, then print it out. You do not need to save the letter.

   a. In the first and last lines of the letter, change "Jason Kidder" to your name.

   b. Change the date to today's date.

   c. The second paragraph begins "Your proposal did not include..." Move this paragraph so it is the last paragraph in the text of the letter.

   d. Change the cost of a permanent bridge to $20,000.

   e. Spell check the letter.

3. In Explore, open the file **Stars.Doc**. Make the following modifications to the document, then print it out. You do not need to save the document.

   a. Center and boldface the title.

   b. Change the title font to size 16 Arial.

   c. Boldface the DATE, SHOWER, and LOCATION.

   d. Move the January 2-3 line to the top of the list.

   e. Number the items in the list 1., 2., 3., etc.

   f. Add or delete tabs to re-align the columns.

   g. Double-space the entire document.

4. In Explore, compose a one-page double-spaced letter to your parents or to a friend. Make sure you date the letter and check your spelling. Print the letter and sign it. You do not need to save your letter.

Spreadsheets

 Spreadsheet software is used extensively in business, education, science, and humanities to simplify tasks that involve calculations. In this Lab you will learn how spreadsheet software works. You will use spreadsheet software to examine and modify worksheets, as well as to create your own worksheets.

1. Click the Steps button to learn how spreadsheet software works. As you proceed through the Steps, answer all of the Quick Check questions that appear. After you complete the Steps, you will see a Quick Check Summary Report. Follow the instructions on the screen to print this report.

2. Click the Explore button to begin this assignment. Click OK to display a new worksheet. Click File, then click Open to display the Open dialog box. Click the file **Income.Xls**, then press the Enter key to open the **Income and Expense Summary** worksheet. Notice that the worksheet contains labels and values for income from consulting and training. It also contains labels and values for expenses such as rent and salaries. The worksheet does not, however, contain formulas to calculate Total Income, Total Expenses, or Profit. Do the following:

   a. Calculate the Total Income by entering the formula =sum(C4:C5) in cell C6.

   b. Calculate the Total Expenses by entering the formula =sum(C9:C12) in C13.

   c. Calculate Profit by entering the formula =C6-C13 in cell C15.

   d. Manually check the results to make sure you entered the formulas correctly.

   e. Print your completed worksheet showing your results.

3. You can use a spreadsheet to keep track of your grade in a class. Click the Explore button to display a blank worksheet. Click File, then click Open to display the Open dialog box. Click the file **Grades.Xls** to open the Grades worksheet. This worksheet contains all the labels and formulas necessary to calculate your grade based on four test scores.

Suppose you receive a score of 88 out of 100 on the first test. On the second test, you score 42 out of 48. On the third test, you score 92 out of 100. You have not taken the fourth test yet. Enter the appropriate data in the **Grades.Xls** worksheet to determine your grade after taking three tests. Print out your worksheet.

4. Worksheets are handy for answering "what if" questions. Suppose you decide to open a lemonade stand. You're interested in how much profit you can make each day. What if you sell 20 cups of lemonade? What if you sell 100? What if the cost of lemons increases?

In Explore, open the file **Lemons.Xls** and use the worksheet to answer questions a through d, then print the worksheet for question e:

   a. What is your profit if you sell 20 cups a day?

   b. What is your profit if you sell 100 cups a day?

   c. What is your profit if the price of lemons increases to $.07 and you sell 100 cups?

   d. What is your profit if you raise the price of a cup of lemonade to $.30? (Lemons still cost $.07 and assume you sell 100 cups.)

   e. Suppose your competitor boasts that she sold 50 cups of lemonade in one day and made exactly $12.00. On your worksheet adjust the cost of cups, water, lemons, and sugar, and the price per cup to show a profit of exactly $12.00 for 50 cups sold. Print this worksheet.

5. It is important to make sure the formulas in your worksheet are accurate. An easy way to test this is to enter 1's for all the values on your worksheet, then check the calculations manually. In Explore, open the worksheet **Receipt.Xls**, which calculates sales receipts. Enter 1 as the value for Item 1, Item 2, Item 3, and Sales Tax %. Now, manually calculate what you would pay for three items that cost $1.00 each in a state where sales tax is 1% (.01). Do your manual calculations match those of the worksheet? If not, correct the formulas in the worksheet and print out a *formula report* of your revised worksheet.

6. In Explore, create your own worksheet showing your household budget for one month. You may use real or made up numbers. Make sure you put a title on the worksheet. Use formulas to calculate your total income and your total expenses for the month. Add another formula to calculate how much money you were able to save. Print a formula report of your worksheet. Also, print your worksheet showing realistic values for one month.

Databases

The Database Lab demonstrates the essential concepts of file and database management systems. You will use the Lab to search, sort, and report the data contained in a file of classic books.

1. Click the Steps button to review basic database terminology and to learn how to manipulate the classic books database. As you proceed through the Steps, answer the Quick Check questions that appear. After you complete the Steps, you will see a Quick Check Summary Report. Follow the instructions on the screen to print this report.

2. Click the Explore button. Make sure you can apply basic database terminology to describe the classic books database by answering the following questions:

   a. How many records does the file contain?

   b. How many fields does each record contain?

   c. What are the contents of the Catalog # field for the book written by Margaret Mitchell?

   d. What are the contents of the Title field for the record with Thoreau in the Author field?

   e. Which field has been used to sort the records?

3. In Explore, manipulate the database as necessary to answer the following questions:

   a. When the books are sorted by title, what is the first record in the file?

   b. Use the Search button to search for all books in the West location. How many do you find?

   c. Use the Search button to search for all books in the Main location that are checked in. What do you find?

4. In Explore, use the Report button to print out a report that groups the books by Status and sorted by title. On your report, circle the four field names. Put a box around the summary statistics showing which books are currently check in and which books are currently checked out.

Computer History Hypermedia

The Computer History Hypermedia Lab is an example of a multimedia hypertext, or hypermedia that contains text, pictures, and recordings that trace the origins of computers. This Lab provides you with two benefits: first, you learn how to use hypermedia links, and second, you learn about some of the events that took place as the computer age dawned.

1. Click the Steps button to learn how to use the Computer History Hypermedia Lab. As you proceed through the Steps, answer all the Quick Check questions that appear. After you complete the Steps, you will see a Quick Check Summary Report. Follow the instructions on the screen to print this report.

2. Click the Explore button. Find the name and date for each of the following:

   a. First automatic adding machine.

   b. First electronic computer.

   c. First fully electronic stored-program computer.

   d. First widely used high-level programming language.

   e. First microprocessor.

   f. First microcomputer.

   g. First word processing program.

   h. First spreadsheet program.

3. Select one of the following computer pioneers and write a one-page paper about that person's contribution to the computer industry: Grace Hopper, Charles Babbage, Augusta Ada, Jack Kilby, Thomas Watson, or J. Presper Eckert.

4. Use this Lab to research the history of the computer. Based on your research, write a paper explaining how you would respond to the question, "Who invented the computer?"

Quick Check

Answers

2.1

1. false
2. data
3. program
4. software
5. shareware
6. license
7. system

2.2

1. multitasking
2. UNIX
3. micro
4. Utility
5. device driver
6. programming language

2.3

1. word processing, spreadsheet, database management
2. integrated software
3. horizontal market software
4. education software
5. desktop publishing

2.4

1. text, graphics, sound, animation, photo images, video
2. false
3. hypertext, hypermedia
4. MPC
5. speakers, sound card, CD-ROM drive, high-resolution color monitor, fast processor (high memory capacity is also acceptable)
6. multimedia kit

Glossary/Index

Computer Files and Data Storage

Computer Files and **Data** Storage

How much data can you pack into a small area? In 1968, Frederick Watts hand-printed 9,452 characters on a piece of paper the size of a postage stamp. In 1983, Tsutomu Ishii of Tokyo, Japan wrote the Japanese characters for *Tokyo, Japan* on a human hair. A few years later, Surendra Apharya of Jaipur, India managed to squeeze 241 characters on a single grain of rice.

That seems like a lot of data packed into a small area, but a computer can store hundreds of times as much data in the same area. For example, an entire encyclopedia, complete with illustrations, can fit on a single CD-ROM disk.

Of course, a computer does not achieve such storage capability by making letters smaller! How, then, can computers store so much data in such a small area? How can you search through all that data to find what you want? Can you change data once it is stored? What happens if you run out of space on a disk?

In this chapter you will learn the answers to these and many more questions. First, you'll learn the definitions of the terms *file*, *data*, and *information*. You will learn that there are different types of files, and you will find out how to use each type. This chapter explains how computers store and retrieve data.

You will find out that the operating system provides you with a metaphor to help visualize and manipulate files. But you will see that this metaphor is quite different from the way the computer itself actually stores and keeps track of files.

This chapter also provides information about the speed, cost, and storage capacity of popular microcomputer storage media. With this information, you can make decisions about the storage devices that are right for your computing needs.

CHAPTER**PREVIEW**

The information in this chapter provides you with a practical foundation for using a computer to manage your own data. You will find out which disk drive to use when you store data and how to create a valid filename that the computer will accept. You will learn how to use DOS, Windows 3.1, or Windows 95 to organize the files on your disk so they are easy to locate. You will also learn what happens in the computer when you save, retrieve, or modify a file, so you will know what to do when the computer asks if you want to "Replace file?" After you have completed this chapter you should be able to:

■ Correctly use the terms *data* and *information*

■ Determine if a file is an executable file, data file, or source file

■ Create valid filenames under DOS, Windows 3.1, and Windows 95

■ Explain how file extensions and wildcards simplify file access

■ Describe the difference between logical and physical file storage

■ Discuss how the directory and the FAT help you access files

■ Select a storage device based on characteristics such as its capacity and access speed

■ Understand the process of saving, retrieving, revising, deleting, and copying files

LABS

DOS Directories and File Management

Windows Directories, Folders, and Files

Defragmentation and Disk Operations

Using Files

Data, Information, and Files

Computer professionals have special definitions for the terms *data*, *information*, and *file*. Although we might refer to these as technical definitions, they are not difficult to understand. Knowing these technical definitions will help you communicate with computer professionals and understand phrases such as "data in, information out."

Data and Information: Technically Speaking

Aren't data and information the same thing?

In everyday conversation, people use the terms *data* and *information* interchangeably. However, some computer professionals make a distinction between the two terms. **Data** is the words, numbers, and graphics that describe people, events, things, and ideas. Data becomes information when you use it as the basis for initiating some action or for making a decision. **Information**, then, is defined as the words, numbers, and graphics used as the basis for human actions and decisions.

To understand the distinction between data and information, consider the following: AA 4199 ORD 9:59 CID 11:09. These letters, numbers, and symbols, which describe an event—a flight schedule—are typical of the data stored in a computer system. Along with other flight schedules, this data can be sorted or transmitted to other computers.

Now, let's say that you decide to take a trip from Chicago (ORD) to Cedar Rapids, Iowa (CID). You ask your travel agent to make your reservation. Your agent requests information on flights from Chicago to Cedar Rapids and sees the following on the computer screen:

Carrier	Flight Number	From	Departs	To	Arrives
AA	4199	ORD	9:59	CID	11:09

Here, the letters, numbers, and symbols displayed on the screen are considered *information* because your travel agent is using them to make your reservation.

The distinction between data and information might seem somewhat elusive, because "AA 4199 ORD 9:59 CID 11:09" can be both data and information. Remember that the distinction is based on usage. Usually, if letters, numbers, and symbols are stored in a computer, they are referred to as data. If letters, numbers, and symbols are being used by a person to complete an action or make a decision, they are referred to as information.

Incidentally, in Latin, the word *data* is the plural for *datum*. According to this usage, it would be correct to say "The January and February rainfall *data* are stored on the disk," and "The March *datum* is not yet available." Most English dictionaries accept the use of *data* as either singular or plural. In this text *data* is used with the singular verb, as in "The *data is* stored on the disk."

Computer Files

What kinds of files will I have on my computer?

A **file** is a named collection of program instructions or data that exists on a storage medium such as a hard disk, a floppy disk, or a CD-ROM. Suppose you use a computer to write a memo to your employer. The words contained in the memo are stored on a disk in a file. The file has a name to distinguish it from other files on your disk.

Although there are several kinds of files, a typical computer user deals mainly with two kinds of files: executable files and data files. Executable files contain the commands that the computer follows to perform tasks. Data files contain data. Understanding the difference between these two kinds of files is important because you use them in different ways. Let's take a closer look at the differences between executable files and data files.

Executable Files

How do I use executable files?

An **executable file** contains the instructions that tell a computer how to perform a specific task. For example, the word processing program that tells your computer how to display and print text is stored on disk as an executable file. Other executable files on your computer system include the operating system, utilities, and application software programs.

To use an executable file, you *run* it. In Chapter 1 you learned how to run programs. In DOS you type the name of the program, in Windows 3.1 you double-click a program icon, and in Windows 95 you select the program from a menu. The programs you run are one type of executable file.

Your computer also has executable files that you cannot run. These files are executed at the request of a computer program, not the user. For example, a word processing program may request that the computer use an executable file called **Grammar.Dll** to check the grammar in a document.

Most operating systems help you identify the executable files you can run. DOS uses part of the filename to indicate an executable file. You will learn more about this later in the section "Filenaming Conventions." Windows 3.1 and Windows 95 use icons to indicate which files you can run. Figure 3-1 shows how Windows 95 uses icons to indicate which files you can run.

There are two types of executable files: some that you can run and some that you cannot run.

Figure 3-1
Program icons

You can run files represented by a "generic" icon of a blank window.

You can also run files represented by unique icons such as these.

You cannot run folders

You cannot run the data files represented by icons that look like note pads or pages.

The instructions in an executable file are directly executed by the computer. The instructions are stored in a format that the computer can interpret, but this format is not designed to be readable to humans. If you try to look at the contents of an executable file using word processing software, the file will appear to contain meaningless symbols such as ☺□¬%□□.

You can try to look at the contents of an executable file and compare it to the contents of a data file. Project 6 helps you do this.

Data Files

How do I use data files?

Think of data files as passive: The data does not instruct or direct the computer to do anything. Think of executable files as active: The instructions stored in the file cause the computer to do something.

A **data file** contains words, numbers, and pictures that you can view, edit, save, send, and print. Typically, you create data files when you use application software. For example, you create a data file when you store a document you have written using word processing software or a picture you have drawn using graphics software. You also create a data file when you store the numbers for a spreadsheet, a statistical analysis, or a graph. When you store a list using database software, a sound clip, or a video, you also create a data file. Once you create a data file and store it on a disk, you can later view it, modify it, copy it to another disk, print it, erase it, or save it again.

You probably won't create all the data files you use. You might receive data files as part of a software package you purchase. For example, word processing software often includes a dictionary data file that contains a list of words the software uses to check spelling.

You can also purchase specific data files that contain information you need. Suppose you own a business and want to mail product information to prospective customers. You could purchase a data file that contains the names and addresses of people in your geographical area who fit the age and income profile of consumers who are likely to buy your product.

Whether you create or purchase a data file, you typically use it in conjunction with application software. The application software helps you manipulate the data in the file. You usually view, revise, and print a data file using the same software you used to create it. For example, if you create a data file using word processing software such as Microsoft Word, you would usually use Microsoft Word to edit the file.

If you purchase a data file, how do you know what application software to use it with? Usually, a software product that contains data files will also contain the program you need to manipulate the data. If the program that manipulates the data is not included, the user manual indicates which program you can use. For example, if you purchase a collection of data files that contain graphical images, the user manual might indicate that you need a program such as Microsoft Paintbrush to view and modify the images.

Source Files

*Is **Autoexec.Bat** an executable file or a data file?*

*The **Autoexec.Bat** file is important, so don't delete it! Project 6 helps you learn more about the **Autoexec.Bat** file on the computers you use.*

If you look at the files on most DOS or Windows computers, you will see a file named **Autoexec.Bat**. This is an example of a batch file. A **batch file** is a series of operating system commands that you use to automate tasks you want the operating system to perform.

When you first turn on an IBM-compatible computer, it looks for a batch file called **Autoexec.Bat**. If it finds this file, the computer automatically executes any instructions the file contains. Usually the **Autoexec.Bat** file contains instructions that customize your computer configuration. For example, **Autoexec.Bat** might tell your computer that you have a CD-ROM drive or that the computer should establish connection with a network.

Because batch files contain instructions, you might assume that they are executable files. However, unlike most executable files, a batch file does not contain instructions in a format that the computer can directly carry out. Instead, a batch file contains instructions that computer users can read and modify. The commands in a batch file must go through a translation process before they can be executed.

Batch files belong to a third category of files called source files. A **source file** contains instructions that must be translated before a computer can execute them. The computer does the translation, so it seems as if the source file is being executed just like an executable file. But this is not the case; behind the scenes, a translation program converts the source file into commands the computer can execute. When you use a computer language such as BASIC to write a computer program, you create a source file that must be translated into executable instructions.

The Documentcentric Approach to Files

How important is it for me to distinguish between executable files, data files, and source files?

Understanding the difference between executable, data, and source files helps you understand how a computer works. Once you understand the characteristics of these file types, you understand that the computer performs the instructions in executable files to help you create data files. It follows, then, that the way you use a computer is to run an application program and use it to create data files. For example, you run the WordPerfect word processing program, then you use it to create a report.

The problem with this model is that to revise a document, you must remember what software you used to create it. Suppose you create a list of people who contributed to your organization's 1995 fund-raising campaign. The next year, you want to use this list again. You remember you called the file Contributors 95, but what program did you use to create it? Did you use Microsoft's Excel spreadsheet or Access database? Or did you use a word processing program such as Microsoft Word?

An alternative approach to using files is referred to by the term *documentcentricity*. The term is derived from two words: document and centric. **Documentcentricity** means that the *document* is *central* to the way you use a computer. Under the documentcentric model, once you indicate the document you want to revise, the computer automatically starts the appropriate application program. For example, if you are using Windows 95, when you click the Contributors 95 document, the computer starts the Microsoft Word application, then retrieves the data file Contributors 95, as shown in Figure 3-2.

Under the documentcentric approach, you select the data file you want to revise and the computer automatically runs the appropriate application program. Under the traditional model, you run an application program first, then select the file you want to revise.

Clicking the document starts the appropriate program.

Windows 95 supports a documentcentric approach, as well as the traditional approach to using files. With the documentcentric approach, you select the *data* file you want to revise. The operating system automatically starts the appropriate application software and opens the data file you selected.

Figure 3-2
Using the documentcentric approach

The operating system on your computer determines whether you can use the documentcentric approach. The trend with the latest versions of Windows and the Mac OS is to provide the tools you need to use the documentcentric approach. However, many people will continue with the traditional approach for using programs and files even with these new operating systems.

Filenaming Conventions

May I use any name I want when I create my own files?

When you study
Figure 3-4, pay
particular attention to
the naming
conventions for the
operating system you
use. You should learn
those filenaming
conventions so you
can create filenames
the computer will
accept.

A **filename** is a unique set of letters and numbers that identifies a file and usually describes the file contents. For example, **Excel** is the name of one of the main files for the Microsoft Excel spreadsheet software.

The filename might be followed by a **filename extension** that further describes the file contents. Filename extensions are also referred to as *file extensions* or *extensions*. The filename **Excel.Exe**, with the **.Exe** extension, indicates it is an executable file. The extension is separated from the filename with a period, called a *dot*. So, if you were to tell someone the name of this file, you would say "Excel dot E-x-e."

As a computer user, you are not usually responsible for naming executable files. These files are included with the application software you purchase, and the files are named by the programmers who write them. It is useful to know, however, that the executable files you can run generally have either a **.Com** (for *command*) extension or **.Exe** (for *executable)* extension. Executable files that you cannot run have extensions such as **.Sys**, **.Dll**, **.Drv**, and **.Vbx**. When you look through a list of files on a disk, you can quickly identify executable files by their file extensions. See Figure 3-3.

Figure 3-3
Executable file
extensions

File Type	File Extension
Files you can run	.EXE, .COM
Flles you cannot run	.SYS, .DLL, .DRV, .VBX

On the other hand, you get to name the data files you create. When you create a data file or rename an existing file, you must assign it a valid filename. A **valid filename** is created by following specific rules. The rules for creating a valid filename are referred to as **filenaming conventions**. Each operating system has a unique set of filenaming conventions; the filenaming conventions of several operating systems are listed in Figure 3-4. Can you determine why **Aux**, **My File.Doc**, and **Bud93/94.Txt** are not valid filenames under some operating systems?

Figure 3-4
Filenaming
conventions

	DOS and Windows 3.1	Windows 95	MacOS	UNIX
Maximum length of filename	8 character filename plus 3 character extension	255 character filename including the 3 character extension	32 characters No extensions used	14 characters (depends on the version of UNIX), including an extension of any length
Character to separate filename from extension	. (period)	. (period)	No extensions	. (period)
Spaces allowed	No	Yes	Yes	No
Numbers allowed	Yes	Yes	Yes	Yes
Characters not allowed	/[]:="\:,|*?	\?:"<>|	None	!@#$%^&*()[]{}'"\/|;<>
Reserved words	AUX, COM1, COM2, COM3, COM4, CON, LPT1, LPT2, LPT3, PRN, or NUL	AUX, COM1, COM2, COM3, COM4, CON, LPT1, LPT2, LPT3, PRN, or NUL	None	Depends on version of UNIX
Case sensitive	No	No	Yes	Yes—use lower case

Using DOS or Windows 3.1 filenaming conventions, **Aux** is not a valid filename because it is a reserved word. **My File.Doc** is not valid because it contains a space between My and File. The filename **Bud93/94.Txt** is not valid because it contains a slash. Filenames such as **Session**, **Report.Doc**, **Budget1.Wks**, and **Form.1** are valid under all the operating systems listed in Figure 3-4.

It is sometimes difficult to select a DOS or Windows 3.1 filename that is unique and descriptive within the eight-character limit. You should try, however, to choose filenames that help you remember what is in the file. When DOS was originally introduced, many computer users added a three-letter extension to each filename to further describe the file contents. For example, **.Mem** was a popular extension to use for data files that contained memos.

Some file extensions do not tell you what application was used to create the file; instead they tell you a general file category. For example, a **.Txt** extension tells you that the file is in the general category of text data files. A **.Bmp** extension tells you that that file contains a graphic.

Figure 3-5 lists some of the extensions that indicate the general category or type of data file.

File Type	File Extension
Text	.Txt
Sound	.Wav, .Mid, .Voc
Graphics	.Bmp, .Pcx, .Tif, .Wmf, .Pic
Animation	.Flc, .Fli, .Avi

Figure 3-5
Extensions that indicate a general category or type of data file

Increasingly, however, software automatically assigns a file extension. For example, when you create a file with the word processing software Microsoft Word for Windows, the software assigns a **.Doc** extension to your filename. By automatically assigning an extension, the application helps you identify the files you created using that application. Suppose that you had many files on a disk—some created using Word and others created using a spreadsheet program and a graphics program. Now you want to view or edit one of the files you created using Microsoft Word. The Word software searches through all the files on your disk and shows you a list of only those filenames that have a **.Doc** extension. Because you see only the files you created using Word, you do not have to wade through a long list of files that include your spreadsheets and graphics. Figure 3-6 on the following page lists some of the file extensions automatically assigned to data files by application software.

When you create files using Windows applications, don't add a filename extension. The application software will automatically add the appropriate extension for you.

Figure 3-6
Extensions used
by application
software

Application Category	Application Software	File Extension
Database	Lotus Approach	.Apr
	Microsoft Cardfile	.Crd
	Microsoft Access	.Mdb
	Microsoft Works	.Wdb
	Paradox	.Db
	dBase V	.Dbf
Spreadsheet	Lotus 1-2-3	.Wk4
	Microsoft Excel	.Xls
	Microsoft Works	.Wks
	Quattro Pro	.Wb1
Word Processing	WordPerfect	.Wrd
	Microsoft Word and Wordpad	.Doc
	Microsoft Write	.Wri
	Microsoft Works	.Wps
	Lotus Ami Pro	.Sam

Wildcards

*Wildcards provide a
handy shortcut for
managing many files
at once. Exercise 7
in the Chapter Review
will help you practice
using wildcards.*

What's *.* ?

Files have unique names, but sometimes you want to refer to more than one file. For example, suppose you want to list all the files on your disk with an .Exe extension. You can specify *.Exe (pronounced "star dot e-x-e"). The asterisk is a **wildcard character** used to represent a group of characters. *.Exe means all the files with an .Exe extension. Suppose your disk contains the files: **Excel.Exe**, **Spell.Exe**, **Excel.Cfg**, and **Budget.Dat.** You could use *.Exe to represent **Excel.Exe** or **Spell.Exe** and **Excel.*** to represent **Excel.Exe** and **Excel.Cfg**.

. (pronounced "star dot star") means all files. When you use DOS, the command DEL *.* will delete all the files in a directory. Be careful if you use this command!

Most operating systems use wildcards to make it easier to manipulate a collection of files. For example, using wildcards, you can delete all the files on a disk in one operation, instead of deleting each file individually. You will use wildcards even with a graphical user interface such as Windows 3.1, as shown in Figure 3-7.

When you want to retrieve a file in Microsoft Word, the Open dialog box appears.

The *.doc in the File Name box means that the files list displays any file with a .doc extension.

Only those files with the .doc extension appear.

Figure 3-7
Wildcards help you locate files in Microsoft Word for Windows

Logical File Storage

How do I keep track of all the files on my disks?

Your computer system might contain hundreds, even thousands, of files stored on disks and storage devices. To keep track of all these files, the computer has a filing system that is maintained by the operating system. Once you know how the operating system manages your computer's filing system, you can use it effectively to store and retrieve files.

Most computers have more than one storage device that the operating system uses to store files. Each storage device is identified by a letter and a colon. Floppy disk drives are usually identified as A: and B:. The hard disk drive is usually identified as C:. Additional storage devices can be assigned letters from D: through Z:. Figure 3-8 on the following page shows some microcomputer configurations and the letters typically assigned to their storage devices. Does one of these match the configuration for the computer you use?

This **desktop model computer** has a 3½-inch floppy disk drive as drive A:. Inside the case is the hard disk drive, drive C:.

3½-inch drive A:

Hard drive C: is inside the case.

Hard drive C: is inside the case.

3½-inch drive A:

CD-ROM drive D:

This **tower model** has a 3½-inch floppy disk drive as drive A: and a hard disk drive as drive C:. There is no drive B:, but the CD-ROM drive is drive D:.

Figure 3-8
Storage device letter assignments

Hard disk drive C: is inside the case.

This **desktop model** has an impressive array of storage devices. The 3½-inch floppy drive is drive A:, and the 5¼-inch floppy drive is drive B:. The hard disk drive is C:, and the CD-ROM drive is D;. The tape storage device does not have a drive letter because it is not a storage device you can use to store individual files from within your applications.

3½-inch drive A:

5¼-inch drive B:

CD-ROM drive E:

Tape drive is not assigned a letter.

This **notebook computer** has one 3½-inch floppy disk drive as drive A:. The hard disk drive, C:, is inside the case. There is no drive B:. Because of space restrictions it is difficult to fit many storage devices in a notebook computer.

Hard drive C: is inside the case.

3½-inch drive A:

The operating system maintains a list of files called a **directory** for each disk or CD-ROM. The directory contains information about the files such as the filename, the file extension, the date and time the file was created, and the size of every file on a storage device. You can use the operating system to view the directory of a disk. Study Figure 3-9 on the next two pages to learn how a directory looks in DOS, Windows 3.1, and Windows 95.

Figure 3-9
Directories

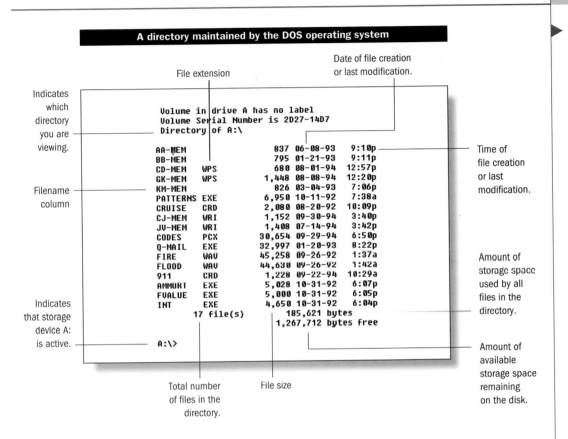

A directory maintained by the DOS operating system

Indicates which directory you are viewing.

File extension

Date of file creation or last modification.

```
        Volume in drive A has no label
        Volume Serial Number is 2D27-14D7
        Directory of A:\

        AA-MEM              837  06-08-93   9:10p
        BB-MEM              795  01-21-93   9:11p
        CD-MEM    WPS       680  08-01-94  12:57p
        GK-MEM    WPS     1,448  08-08-94  12:20p
        KM-MEM              826  03-04-93   7:06p
        PATTERNS  EXE     6,950  10-11-92   7:38a
        CRUISE    CRD     2,080  08-20-92  10:09p
        CJ-MEM    WRI     1,152  09-30-94   3:40p
        JV-MEM    WRI     1,408  07-14-94   3:42p
        CODES     PCX    30,654  09-29-94   6:50p
        Q-MAIL    EXE    32,997  01-20-93   8:22p
        FIRE      WAV    45,258  09-26-92   1:37a
        FLOOD     WAV    44,630  09-26-92   1:42a
        911       CRD     1,228  09-22-94  10:29a
        AMMORT    EXE     5,028  10-31-92   6:07p
        FVALUE    EXE     5,000  10-31-92   6:05p
        INT       EXE     4,650  10-31-92   6:04p
                17 file(s)       185,621 bytes
                               1,267,712 bytes free

        A:\>
```

Filename column

Indicates that storage device A: is active.

Time of file creation or last modification.

Amount of storage space used by all files in the directory.

Amount of available storage space remaining on the disk.

Total number of files in the directory.

File size

A directory maintained by Windows 3.1

Date of file creation or last modification.

Time of file creation or last modification.

Icon indicates which directory you are viewing.

```
                    File Manager - [A:\*.*]
  File  Disk  Tree  View  Options  Window  Help

  a    c    f    i    z                            A:

  a:\         911.crd       1228   9/22/94  10:29:28am   a
              aa-mem         837    6/8/93   9:10:58pm   a
              ammort.exe    5028  10/31/92   6:07:36pm   a
              bb-mem         795   1/21/93   9:11:36pm   a
              cd-mem.wps     680    8/1/94  12:57:56pm   a
              cj-mem.wri    1152   9/30/94   3:40:48pm   a
              codes.pcx    30654   9/29/94   6:50:58pm   a
              cruise.crd    2080   8/20/92  10:09:32pm   a
              fire.wav     45258   9/26/92   1:37:08am   a
              flood.wav    44630   9/26/92   1:42:16am   a
              fvalue.exe    5000  10/31/92   6:05:00pm   a
              gk-mem.wps    1448    8/8/94  12:20:50pm   a
              int.exe       4650  10/31/92   6:04:48pm   a
              jv-mem.wri    1408   7/14/94   3:42:06pm   a
              km-mem         826    3/4/93   7:06:18pm   a
              patterns.exe  6950  10/11/92   7:38:30am   a
              q-mail.exe   32997   1/20/93   8:22:12pm   a




  A: 1,238KB free, 1,423KB total        Total 17 file(s) (185,621 bytes)
```

Icons indicate file type.

File size

Filename and extension

Amount of available storage space remaining on the disk.

Total number of files in the directory.

Amount of storage space used by all files in the directory.

When you type directory names, don't confuse the backslash \ with the regular slash /.

Figure 3-9
Directories
(continued)

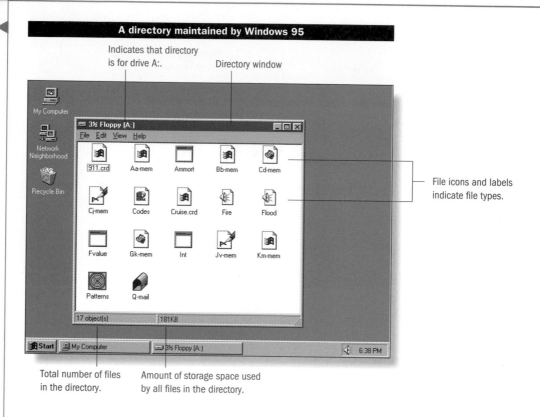

A directory maintained by Windows 95

Indicates that directory is for drive A:.

Directory window

File icons and labels indicate file types.

Total number of files in the directory.

Amount of storage space used by all files in the directory.

Lab

Windows Directories, Folders, and Files

The main directory of a disk, sometimes referred to as the **root directory**, provides a useful list of files. It could be difficult, however, to find a particular file if your directory contains several hundred files. To help you organize a large number of files, most operating systems allow you to divide your directory into smaller lists called **subdirectories**. For example, you can create one subdirectory to hold all your files that contain documents and another subdirectory to hold all your files that contain graphical images.

A subdirectory name is separated from a drive letter and a filename by a special symbol. In DOS and Microsoft Windows, this symbol is the backslash \. For example, the root directory of drive C: might have a subdirectory called **Graphics**, written as **C:\Graphics**.

A **file specification** is the drive letter, subdirectory, and filename that identifies a file. Suppose you create a subdirectory on drive A: named Word for your word processing documents. Now suppose you want to create a list of things to do called **To-do.Doc** and put it on drive A: in the Word subdirectory. The file specification is:

Drive letter → **A:\Word\To-do.Doc** ← Extension

Subdirectory   Filename

Subdirectories can be further divided into what you might think of as *sub-subdirectories*. As you create more and more subdirectories on a disk, it becomes important to pay attention to the structure of the directories. Metaphors, such as those shown in Figure 3-10 can help you visualize this structure.

Metaphors of directory structures are sometimes called *logical models* because they represent the way you logically conceive of them. **Logical storage** is a conceptual model of the way data is stored on your disk. This logical view of storage is a convenient mental model that helps you understand the computer's filing system; however, it is not how the data is actually stored. **Physical storage** refers to how data is actually stored on the physical disk. To find out more about how computers physically store data, it is useful to understand a bit about storage media and storage devices. That is the topic of Section 3.2.

► **Figure 3-10**
Metaphors of
directory structures

You can mentally visualize the directory of a disk as a tree on its side. The trunk and branches are directories and the leaves are files.

Windows 3.1 displays the directory as a hierarchical structure of file folders.

The root directory is the base or trunk of the tree.

A subdirectory, such as Word, is a branch of the tree. It is called A:\Word.

Reports is a subdirectory of Word, written as A:\Word\Reports.

Files, such as To-Do and Budget, are the leaves of the tree. To-Do and Budget are in the Reports subdirectory. The file specification for To-Do is A:\Word\Reports\To-Do.

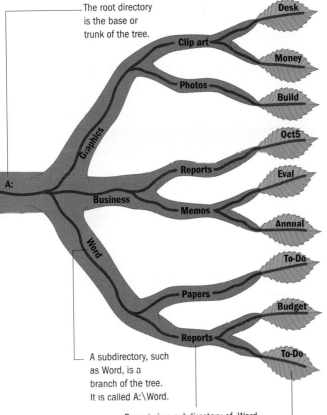

The root directory a:\ is represented by a file folder.

The files in A:\ Word \ Reports are listed here.

Word is a subdirectory of a:\.

Letters, memos, and reports are subdirectories of Word.

The red line shows the path for files in A:\Word\Reports.

When you use Windows 95 you can visualize the directory of a disk as boxes within boxes. Here, nested windows show the files and directories on A:\.

The root directory is the title for a window that holds the file folders representing files and subdirectories in A:.

By clicking the Word file folder, you open the window for the

By clicking the Reports folder, you open the window for the Reports directory.

The files in A:\Word\Reports are shown here.

Quick Check

1 To differentiate between data and information, use the rule: _____ is used by computers; _____ is used by humans.

2 Name each part of the file specification A:\Research\Primates\Jan5.Dat.

  ↑   ↑   ↑   ↑ ↑

__ _____ _____ ___ __

3 Executable files that you can run have _____ or _____ extensions.

4 When you use software designed for Windows 3.1 to create a data file, why don't you add a file extension?

5 Nested file folders and directory trees are ways of representing _____ storage.

6 The main directory for a disk is called the _____ directory.

7 **Autoexec.Bat** is an example of a(n) _____ file that needs to be translated by the computer before its instructions are executed.

3.2

Storage Technologies

The terms reading and writing make sense if you imagine you are the computer. As the computer you write a note and save it for later. You retrieve the note and read it when you need the information it contains.

When it comes to computer storage, users have two questions: How much data can I store? How fast can I access it? The answers to these questions depend on the storage medium and the storage device. A **storage medium** (storage *media* is the plural) is the disk, tape, paper, or other substance that contains data. A **storage device** is the mechanical apparatus that records and retrieves the data from the storage medium. When we want to refer to a storage device and the media it uses, we can use the term **storage technology**.

The process of storing data is often referred to as **writing data** or **saving a file** because the storage device *writes* the data on the storage medium to *save* it for later use. The process of retrieving data is often referred to as **reading data**, **loading data**, or **opening a file**. The terms *reading data* and *writing data* are often associated with mainframe applications. The terms *save* and *open* are standard Windows terminology.

Storage Specifications

How do I compare storage technologies?

Knowing the characteristics of a storage device or storage medium helps you determine which one is best for a particular task. Storage technology comparisons are often based on storage capacity and speed.

A byte is a unit of information equivalent to a single character—a letter, punctuation mark, space, or numeral.

Data is stored as bytes—each **byte** usually represents one character. The phrase "profit margin" requires 13 bytes of storage space because the phrase contains 12 characters and the space between the two words requires an additional byte of storage space. **Storage capacity** is the maximum amount of data that can be stored on a storage medium and is usually measured in kilobytes, megabytes, or gigabytes. A **kilobyte** (KB) is 1,024 bytes, but this is often rounded to one thousand bytes. A **megabyte** (MB) is approximately one million bytes. A **gigabyte** is approximately one billion bytes. When you read that the storage capacity of a computer is 850 MB, it means the hard disk on that computer can store up to 850 million bytes of information. This is equivalent to approximately 225,000 single-spaced pages of text.

In addition to storage capacity, users are concerned with access time. **Access time** is the average time it takes a computer to locate data on the storage medium and read it. Access time for a microcomputer storage device, such as a disk drive, is measured in milliseconds. One **millisecond** (ms) is a thousandth of a second. When you read, for example, that disk access time is 11 ms, it means that on average, it takes the computer eleven thousandths of a second to locate and read data from the disk.

It is fairly easy to compare two storage technologies based on storage capacity and access time; these specifications are usually included in advertisements and product descriptions. However, additional characteristics of storage technologies must be considered. The durability and access methods of a storage technology are also important characteristics to compare.

Magnetic or Optical Storage?

Will the metal detector in an airport erase the data on my disks?

Magnetic and optical storage technologies are used for the majority of today's micro, mini, and mainframe computers. Each of these technologies has advantages and disadvantages.

Magnetic surface

Read-write head

Mylar disk

Before the data is stored, the particles in the magnetic surface of the disk are scattered in random patterns.

The read-write head magnetizes the particles. The positive poles of the magnetized particles point toward the negative pole of the read-write head.

The read-write head can reverse polarity to align the next row of particles in the opposite direction. The patterns of magnetized particles represent data.

With **magnetic storage** the computer stores data on disks and tape by magnetizing selected particles of an oxide-based surface coating. The particles retain their magnetic orientation until that orientation is changed, thereby making disks and tape fairly permanent but modifiable storage media. Figure 3-11 shows how a computer stores data on magnetic media.

You can intentionally change or erase files stored on magnetic media. If you run out of storage space on a disk, you can erase files you no longer need to make more space available.

Data stored on magnetic media such as floppy disks can also be unintentionally altered by the environment and by device or media failure.

In the environment, magnetic fields, dust, mold, smoke particles, and heat are the primary culprits causing data loss. Placing a magnet on your disk is a sure way of losing data. The metal detectors in an airport use a magnetic field, but the field is not strong enough to disrupt the data on your floppy or hard disks. The x-ray machine on the conveyer belt is even less disruptive—x-rays do not affect the magnetic particles. You are more likely to damage your disks by leaving them on the dashboard of your car in the sun or carrying them around in your backpack where they will pick up dust and dirt. At many mainframe installations, magnetic media are stored in climate-controlled vaults to protect against environmental hazards such as dust, extreme temperatures, smoke, and mold.

Media failure is a problem with the storage media that results in data loss. Magnetic media gradually lose their magnetic charge, resulting in lost data. Some experts estimate that the reliable life span of data stored on magnetic media is about three years, and they recommend that you refresh your data every two years by recopying it.

A device failure can damage a disk and result in data loss. A **device failure** is a problem with a mechanical device such as a disk drive. Storage devices fail as a result of power or circuitry problems.

With **optical storage**, data is burned into the storage medium using beams of laser light. The burns form patterns of small pits in the disk surface to represent data. The pits on optical media are permanent, so the data cannot be changed. Optical media are very durable—the useful life of

Figure 3-11
Storing data on magnetic media

The data stored on optical media cannot be changed, but the data stored on magnetic media can.

a CD-ROM is estimated to exceed 500 years. Optical media do not, however, give you the flexibility of magnetic media for changing the data once it is stored. CD-ROMs are the most popular type of optical storage. Figure 3-12 shows how a laser burns pits onto an optical disk.

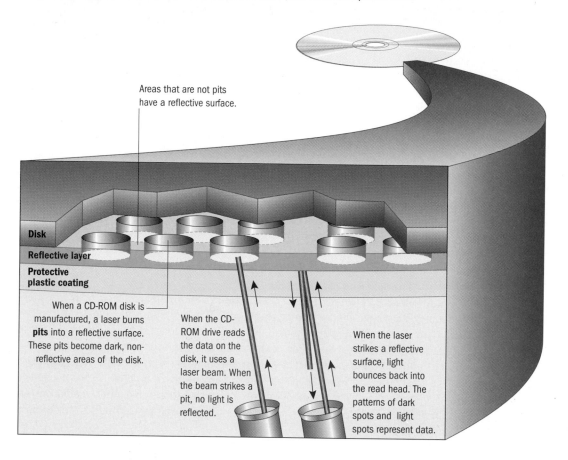

Figure 3-12
Storing data on an optical disk

Areas that are not pits have a reflective surface.

Disk

Reflective layer

Protective plastic coating

When a CD-ROM disk is manufactured, a laser burns **pits** into a reflective surface. These pits become dark, non-reflective areas of the disk.

When the CD-ROM drive reads the data on the disk, it uses a laser beam. When the beam strikes a pit, no light is reflected.

When the laser strikes a reflective surface, light bounces back into the read head. The patterns of dark spots and light spots represent data.

Floppy Disks

Why is it called a floppy disk?

A **floppy disk** is a flexible mylar plastic disk covered with a thin layer of magnetic oxide. Floppy disks get their name from this thin mylar disk. If you cut open the disk casing (something you should never do unless you want to ruin the disk), you would see that the mylar disk inside is thin and, well, floppy. Floppy disks are also called **floppies** or **diskettes**.

Floppy disks come in several sizes: 3½ inch, 5¼ inch, and 8 inch. The disk size most commonly used on today's microcomputers is 3½ inch. A 3½-inch circular disk made of flexible mylar is housed inside a protective case of rigid plastic. When the disk is inserted in the disk drive, the spring-loaded access cover slides to the side to expose the disk surface for reading and writing data. Figure 3-13 shows the construction of a 3½-inch disk.

A common misconception is that a 3½-inch disk is a "hard disk" because it has a hard plastic case. A 3½-inch disk is a floppy disk, not a hard disk.

The **disk label** often wraps around to the underside of the disk. When you affix the label, make sure it does not stick to the access cover.

Only high-density disks have this **high-density indicator hole.**

The rigid plastic **disk jacket** protects the inner disk.

The spring-loaded **access cover** slides to the left when the disk is inserted in the drive.

When the disk is in the drive, this head aperture is aligned with the opening in the access cover to expose the disk surface to the read-write head.

The disk drive engages the **drive hub** to rotate the disk.

Oxide-coated **mylar disk**

When the **write-protect window** is open, the disk is write protected and the computer cannot write data on the disk. You usually keep the window closed so you can store files on your disk.

The **disk liner** removes dirt and dust from the disk surface.

Figure 3-13
3½-inch floppy disk

In the past, floppy disks stored data only on one side; but today most store data on both sides. As you might guess, a **double-sided disk**, sometimes abbreviated as DS, stores twice as much data as a single-sided disk.

The amount of data a computer can store on each side of a disk depends on the way the disk is formatted. In Chapter 2 you learned that a disk must be formatted before you can store data on it. The formatting process creates a series of concentric **tracks** on the disk, and each track is divided into smaller segments called **sectors**, as shown in Figure 3-14.

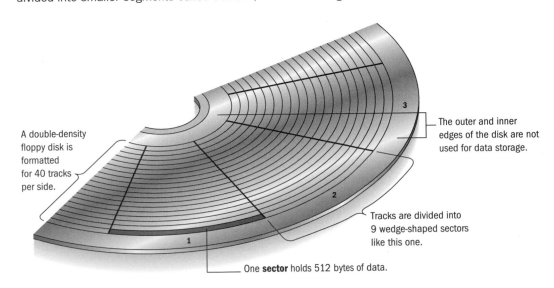

A double-density floppy disk is formatted for 40 tracks per side.

The outer and inner edges of the disk are not used for data storage.

Tracks are divided into 9 wedge-shaped sectors like this one.

One **sector** holds 512 bytes of data.

Figure 3-14
A formatted disk

A double-sided disk that is formatted with 40 tracks per side and 9 sectors per track has 720 sectors. On IBM-compatible computers, each sector of a track holds 512 bytes of data. A file that is 512 bytes or less fits in a single sector. Larger files are stored in more than one sector.

In addition to being doubled-sided, floppy disks are available in both double-density and high-density versions. **Disk density** refers to the size of the magnetic particles on the disk surface. The disk density limits the amount of data you can reliably store on the disk. **Double-density disks**, abbreviated as DD, are also referred to as *low-density* disks. A double-density 3½-inch disk is usually formatted with 80 tracks per side and 9 sectors per track; it stores 720 kilobytes. A **high-density disk**, abbreviated as HD, stores more data than a double-density disk. A high-density 3½-inch disk is usually formatted for 80 tracks and 18 sectors per side, for a storage capacity of 1.44 megabytes. Figure 3-15 summarizes floppy disk capacities by size and density.

Figure 3-15
Floppy disk capacities

Disk Size	3½ Inch		5¼ Inch	
Density	High	Low	High	Low
Capacity	1.44 MB	720 KB	1.2 MB	360 KB .
Sectors per side	18	9	18	9
Tracks per side	80	40	80	40

The higher the disk density, the smaller the magnetic particles it stores, and the more data it can store. Think of it this way: Just as you can put more lemons than grapefruit in a basket, you can store more data on a disk coated with smaller magnetic particles than with larger magnetic particles.

When you purchase and use floppy disks, you must make sure the disk size and storage density match the capacity of your disk drive. You can tell the size of the disk drive by looking at the size of the opening where you insert the disk. You might need to refer to the reference manual for your computer to find out whether the drive can use high-density disks. For example, if you have a high-density 3½-inch disk drive, you should purchase and use high-density 3½-inch disks.

Floppy Disk Drives

Does a floppy disk drive give me fast access to my data?

The storage device that records and retrieves data on a floppy disk is a **floppy disk drive**. Refer to Figure 3-16 to find out how the rotation of the disk, combined with the lateral movement of the read-write head, allows the drive mechanism to access any sector of the disk.

The read-write head can read or write data from any sector of the disk, in any order. This ability to move to any sector is referred to as **random access** or **direct access**. Random access is a handy feature of disk-based storage that provides quick access to files anywhere on a disk. Even with random access, however, a floppy disk drive is not a particularly speedy device. It takes about 0.5 seconds for the drive to spin the disk up to speed and then move the read-write head to a particular sector.

The **drive spindle** engages the hub on the disk to rotate the disk inside of its protective jacket.

A 3 1/2-inch drive does not write data on a disk if a photo diode detects light through the write-protect window. If this window is open and light shines through it, the disk has been **write protected** and you cannot modify the data it contains.

The **read-write head** moves close to the disk surface in order to react to the magnetic fields generated by the magnetic particles. By distinguishing positive and negative magnetic fields, the drive head reads the byte pattern that represents each character. To write data on the disk, a low voltage current in the read-write head magnetizes the particles that form each byte.

The read-write head moves in or out to a specific track.

Figure 3-16
How a 3½-inch floppy disk drive works

Uses for Floppy Disk Storage

For what kinds of projects are floppy disks the best kind of storage technology?

Today, floppy disk storage is used for three purposes: distribution, sharing data, and backup.

The most prevalent use of floppy disks is for software distribution. When you purchase software, the package usually includes floppy disks containing programs and data files. However, floppy disks are used less frequently for distribution than they were in the past. Large applications and multimedia are frequently shipped on CD-ROM instead.

The second use for floppy disks is to share data with other computer users. For example, if you want to give a copy of a report to several colleagues, you can copy the report to several floppy disks. Today, instead of floppy disks, many computer users use computer networks or electronic mail to share data.

Another use for floppy disks is to make duplicate copies of your data files in case something happens to the originals, a process known as **backup**. The role of floppy disk storage for backup is being taken over, to some extent, by tape storage.

In the university setting, floppy disks are also used to hold student data. If you have your own computer, you would store most of your data on the hard disk. In a student lab, because you don't have your own computer and you never know which computer you will be assigned, you need to carry your data with you on a floppy disk.

In the past, floppy disks were the primary storage medium for microcomputer systems, but today hard disk storage has taken over that role.

Whether you use floppy disks or other storage media, making a backup of your data is important. Make sure you make regular backups of your data.

Hard Disk Storage

How can a hard disk be the same size as a floppy, but store so much more data?

Hard disk storage provides faster access to files than a floppy disk and is the preferred type of storage for most computer systems. A **hard disk platter** is a flat, rigid disk made of aluminum or glass and coated with a magnetic oxide. A **hard disk** is one or more platters and their associated read-write heads. You will frequently see the terms *hard disk* and *hard disk drive* used interchangeably. You might also hear the term *fixed disk* used to refer to hard disks.

Microcomputer hard disk platters are typically 3½ inches in diameter—the same size as the circular mylar disk in a floppy. However, the storage capacity of a hard disk far exceeds that of a floppy disk. Also, the access time of a hard disk is significantly faster than a floppy disk's. Hard disk storage capacities of 850 MB and access speeds of 11 ms (.0011 seconds) are not uncommon. Figure 3-17 explains how is it possible to pack so much data on a hard disk and access it so quickly.

Figure 3-17 ◄
How a hard disk
drive works

Each data storage surface has its own **read-write head**. Read-write heads move in and out from the center of the disk to locate a specific track. The head hovers only five microinches above the disk surface so the magnetic field is much more compact than on a floppy disk. As a result, more data is packed into a smaller area on a hard disk platter.

The platter surfaces are formatted into cylinders and sectors. A **cylinder** is a vertical stack of tracks. A hard disk could have between 312 and 2,048 cylinders. To find a file, the computer must know the cylinder, sector, and platter in which the file is stored.

The **drive spindle** supports one or more **hard disk platters**. Both sides of the platter are used for data storage. More platters mean more data storage capacity. Hard disk platters rotate as a unit on the drive spindle to position a specific sector under the read-write heads. The platters spin continuously making thousands of revolutions per minute.

Like a floppy disk drive, a hard drive is a random (or direct) access storage device. To locate data, the disks spin to the specified sector and the heads move to the specified cylinder.

Like floppy disks, hard disks provide random access to files by positioning the read-write head over the sector that contains the requested data. Unlike floppy disks, which begin to rotate only when you request data, hard disks are continually in motion, so there is no delay as the disk spins up to speed. As a result, hard disk access is faster than floppy disk access. You can ask your computer operating system to tell you the capacity of your hard disk and how much of the capacity is currently used for data. To do this in DOS, you can type CHKDSK at the C:\> prompt. In Windows 3.1, you can look at the status bar at the bottom of the File Manager window to find your hard disk's capacity. In Windows 95 you can select your hard disk drive icon under My Computer to view a graph of disk capacity and utilization. Figure 3-18 on this page and the next shows you how to find out your disk capacity and utilization under DOS, Windows 3.1, and Windows 95.

It is important to keep track of how much space is available on your disk, so you don't inadvertently fill it up. In Project 2 you can find out how much space is available on your computer's hard disk.

▶ **Figure 3-18**
Hard disk capacity and utilization

When you are using DOS, you can type **chkdsk** at the C:\> prompt to view information on disk capacity and utilization

```
C:\>chkdsk

    851,296,256 bytes total disk space
     20,332,544 bytes in 4 hidden files
      3,637,248 bytes in 220 directories
    459,112,448 bytes in 7,697 user files
    368,197,632 bytes available on disk

         16,384 bytes in each allocation unit
         51,959 total allocation units on disk
         22,473 available allocation units on disk

        655,360 total bytes memory
        475,904 bytes free
```

Total disk capacity

Space available on the disk

This section provides information about *memory*, not disk storage

1. When you are using Windows 3.1, you must double-click the File Manager icon to open the File Manager window.

2. The File Manager window contains information about your computer's storage devices.

3. Click the icon for one of the storage devices shown in this row.

4. Capacity and utilization statistics are shown here.

Space available on disk

Total disk capacity

Figure 3-18
Hard disk capacity
and utilization
(continued)

1. When you are using Windows 95, you must double-click the **My Computer** icon to open the My Computer window.

2. In the My Computer window, click the storage device icon for which you want information.

3. Click **File**, then click **Properties** to display the properties of the storage device.

4. The properties are summarized in the Properties window.

Space available on disk

Total disk capacity

Graph shows the percentage of disk capacity used.

The read-write heads in a hard disk hover a microscopic distance above the disk surface. If a read-write head runs into a dust particle or some other contaminant on the disk, it might cause what is called a **head crash**. A head crash damages some of the data on the disk. To help eliminate contaminants from contacting the platters and causing head crashes, a hard disk is sealed in its case. A head crash can also be triggered by jarring the hard disk while it is in use. Although hard disks have become considerably more rugged in recent years, you should still handle and transport them with care.

Figure 3-19
How a removable
hard disk works

Drive activity light

The drive latch secures or releases the cartridge.

The removable hard disk cartridge slides into place.

Hard disk platter

Some hard disks are removable. **Removable hard disks** or hard disk cartridges, such as the one pictured in Figure 3-19, contain platters and read-write heads that can be inserted and removed from the drive much like a floppy disk. Removable hard disks increase the potential storage capacity of your computer system, although the data is available on only one disk at a time. Removable hard disks also provide security for your data by allowing you to remove the hard disk cartridge and store it separately from the computer.

Mainframe users refer to disk storage as DASD (pronounced "daz-dee"). **DASD** stands for direct access storage device. As a direct, or random, access device, DASD can directly access data, much like a microcomputer hard disk drive. The DASD at most mainframe installations is either disk packs—high-capacity fixed disks—or a redundant array of inexpensive disks (RAID).

Many mainframe installations still use removable disk packs, although they are a fairly old technology. A **disk pack** contains from 6 to 20 hard disks. Each disk is a little larger than 10 inches. The entire pack can be removed and replaced with another pack. Disk packs are gradually being replaced by high-capacity fixed disk drives. **High-capacity fixed disk drive** technology is similar to a microcomputer hard disk with its platters and read-write heads, but the storage capacity of a high-capacity fixed disk drive is measured in gigabytes (billions of bytes), rather than megabytes (millions of bytes). Each high-capacity fixed disk drive is housed in a cabinet. A mainframe computer system might include as many as 100 fixed disk drive cabinets.

RAID, another type of hard disk storage, is found in an increasing number of mainframe and microcomputer installations. RAID stands for redundant array of inexpensive disks. A **RAID** storage device contains many disk platters, provides redundancy, and achieves faster data access than conventional hard disks. The **redundancy** feature of RAID technology protects data from media failures by recording data on more than one disk platter.

To further increase the speed of data access, your computer might use a disk cache. A **disk cache** (pronounced "cash"), illustrated in Figure 3-20, is a special area of computer memory into which the computer transfers the data you are likely to need from disk storage.

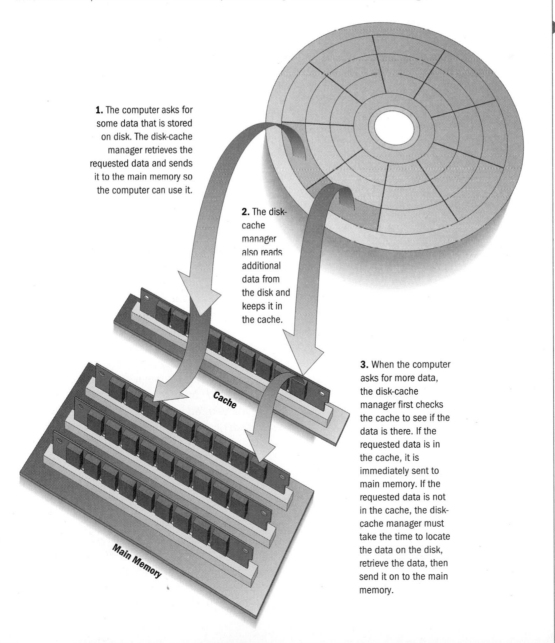

1. The computer asks for some data that is stored on disk. The disk-cache manager retrieves the requested data and sends it to the main memory so the computer can use it.

2. The disk-cache manager also reads additional data from the disk and keeps it in the cache.

3. When the computer asks for more data, the disk-cache manager first checks the cache to see if the data is there. If the requested data is in the cache, it is immediately sent to main memory. If the requested data is not in the cache, the disk-cache manager must take the time to locate the data on the disk, retrieve the data, then send it on to the main memory.

Cache

Main Memory

▶ **Figure 3-20**
How disk caching works

To understand cache, think of the disk as a supermarket. When you go to the supermarket, you have a shopping list. You need a package of chicken for dinner tonight, but you buy two packages of chicken and put one in the freezer. The freezer is like the cache—it stores something until you need it, and you don't have to go all the way to the store again to get it.

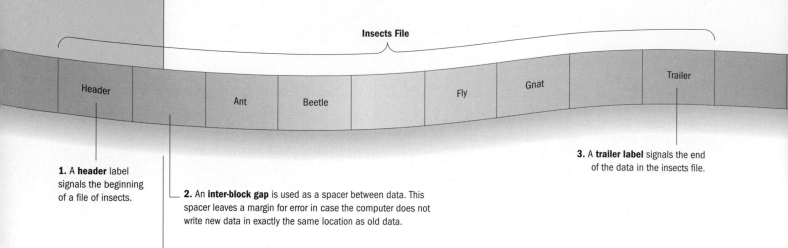

1. A **header** label signals the beginning of a file of insects.

2. An **inter-block gap** is used as a spacer between data. This spacer leaves a margin for error in case the computer does not write new data in exactly the same location as old data.

3. A **trailer label** signals the end of the data in the insects file.

Figure 3-21
Sequential file access on magnetic tape

How does a disk cache help speed things up? Suppose your computer retrieves the data from a particular sector of your disk. There is a high probability that the next data you need will be from an adjacent sector—the remainder of a program file, for example, or the next section of a data file. The computer reads the data from nearby sectors and stores it in the cache. If the data you need next is already in the cache, the computer doesn't need to wait while the mechanical parts of the drive locate and read the data from the disk.

Tape Storage

Do they still use those big tape drives on computers that you see in old movies?

In the 1960s, magnetic tape was the most popular form of mainframe computer storage. When IBM introduced its first microcomputer in 1981, the legacy of tape storage continued in the form of a cassette tape drive, similar to those used for audio recording and playback.

Using tape as a primary storage device instead of a hard disk would be slow and inconvenient because tape requires sequential, rather than random, access. With **sequential access**, data is stored and read as a sequence of bytes along the length of the tape. To find a file stored on a microcomputer tape storage device, you advance the tape to the approximate location of the file, then wait for the computer to slowly read each byte until it finds the beginning of the file. Study the sequential access diagram in Figure 3-21 to learn how computers store data on tape.

Microcomputer users quickly abandoned tape storage for the convenience and speed of random access disk drives. Recently, however, tape storage for microcomputers has experienced a revival—not as a principal storage device, but for making backup copies of the data stored on hard disks. As you have learned in this chapter, the data on magnetic storage can be easily destroyed, erased, or otherwise lost. Protecting the data on the hard disk is of particular concern to users because it contains so much data—data that would be difficult and time-consuming to reconstruct. Therefore, it is a good idea to have a copy of the data tucked safely away as a backup.

A **tape backup** is a copy of the data on a hard disk, stored on magnetic tape, and used to restore lost data. A tape backup is relatively inexpensive and can rescue you from the overwhelming task of trying to reconstruct lost data. If you lose the data on your hard disk, you can copy the data from the tape backup back to the hard disk. Typically, you do not use the data directly from the tape backup because the sequential access is too slow to be practical.

Make sure you understand the difference between sequential access and random access. It is the key to the popularity of disk storage technology and the limitation of tape storage technology.

Although tape storage devices are useful for data backup, many computer users still back up their data to floppy disks.

Animals File

Header   Cat   Dog

4. Another header label signals the beginning of a file of animals. On a sequential medium like this tape, to reach the animal file, the computer must forward through the entire insect file.

The most popular type of tape drive for microcomputers uses tape cartridges, but there are different tape specifications and cartridge sizes. The specifications for tape storage include tape length and width. When you purchase tapes, check the tape drive manual to make sure the tapes you purchase are the correct type for your tape drive. Figure 3-22 illustrates the basic concepts of tape storage.

▶ **Figure 3-22**
Cartridge tape storage

Tape drive

Tape cartridge

The drive wheel pulls the tape from the supply reel over the read-write head.

Supply reel

Tape

Head aperture

The take-up reel holds the recorded tape segments.

Tape cartridges are available in different sizes and contain tapes of different lengths and thicknesses. Check the manual for your tape drive to make sure you purchase the correct type of cartridge.

An elastic band that stretches around the tape reels and the drive reel maintains a constant tension on the tape so the data is recorded accurately.

CD-ROM Storage

If CD-ROMs are read only, doesn't that limit their use?

CD-ROMs are based on the same technology as the audio CDs you buy at your favorite music store. Their technology is derived from the compact disc digital-audio recording system. CD-ROM (pronounced "cee dee rom") stands for Compact Disc Read Only Memory. A computer CD-ROM disk, like its audio counterpart, contains data that has been stamped on the disk surface as a series of pits. To read the data on a CD-ROM, an optical read head distinguishes the patterns of pits that represent bytes. Figure 3-23 shows how you load a CD into the CD-ROM drive.

A CD-ROM drive supplements, rather than replaces, a hard disk drive because a CD-ROM is a read-only device.

Figure 3-23
CD-ROM storage

The printed side of the disk does not contain data. It should be face up when you insert the disk because the lasers read the bottom of the disk.

Compton's Interactive Encyclopedia

Data is stored on the bottom of a CD-ROM disk in one continuous track that spirals out from the center of the disk. The track is divided into equal-length sectors.

Earphone jack

Drive activity light

Disk carrier

Volume control

Push-button slides disk carrier in or out.

CD-ROMs provide tremendous storage capacity. A single CD-ROM disk holds up to 680 megabytes, equivalent to more than 300,000 pages of text, and is quite durable. The surface of the disk is coated with a clear plastic, making the data permanent and unalterable.

CD-ROM disks are limited by the fact that they are *read only*. **Read only** means that the computer can retrieve data from a CD-ROM but cannot save any new data on it. In this respect, CD-ROM technology differs from hard disk storage, on which you can write, erase, and read data. A read-only CD-ROM drive does not generally serve as the sole storage device for a microcomputer.

A CD-ROM disk is relatively inexpensive to manufacture, making it an ideal way for software publishers to distribute large programs and data files. CD-ROM is the media of choice for delivery of multimedia applications because it provides the large storage capacity necessary for sound, video, and graphics files.

A recent technological development is the creation of CDs on which you can write data. **CD-R** (compact disc-recordable) technology allows the computer to record data on a CD-R disk using a special CD-R recording device. Disks that have been produced with the CD-R device can be used on a regular CD-ROM drive, like the one you might have on your computer. As with regular CD-ROMs the data on the disk cannot be erased or modified. An earlier device called a WORM drive also stored data on CDs using optical technology. The CDs, however, could not be used in regular CD-ROM drives, so their use did not become widespread.

CD-R is a useful technology for archiving data. **Archiving** refers to the process of moving data off a primary storage device when that data is not frequently accessed. For example, a business might archive its accounting data for previous years or a hospital might archive billing records once the accounts are paid. What's the difference between an archive and a backup? Archived data does not generally change, but the data you back up might change frequently.

Physical File Storage

Do I need to know exactly where each file is stored on a disk?

Although a disk is formatted into tracks and sectors that provide physical storage locations for data, files are actually stored in clusters. A **cluster** is a group of sectors; it is the smallest storage unit the computer can access. The number of sectors that form a cluster depends on the type of computer. IBM-compatible microcomputers form a cluster from two sectors. Each cluster is numbered and the operating system maintains a list of which sectors correspond to each cluster.

When the computer stores a file on a random-access storage medium, the operating system records the cluster number that contains the beginning of the file in a file allocation table (FAT). The **FAT** is an operating system file that maintains a list of files and their physical location on the disk. The FAT is such a crucial file that if it is damaged by a head crash or other disaster, you generally lose access to all the data stored on your disk. This is yet another reason to have a backup of the data on your hard drive.

When you want to store a file, the operating system looks at the FAT to see which clusters are empty. The operating system then puts the data for the file in empty clusters. The cluster numbers are recorded in the FAT. The name of the new file and the number of the first cluster that contains the file data are recorded in the directory.

A file that does not fit into a single cluster will spill over into the next adjacent or *contiguous* cluster unless that cluster already contains data. If the next cluster is full, the operating system stores the file in a nonadjacent cluster and sets up instructions called *pointers*. These "point" to each piece of the file, as shown in Figure 3-24 on the following page.

When you want to retrieve a file, the operating system looks through the directory for the filename and the number of the first cluster that contains the file data. The FAT tells the computer which clusters contain the remaining data for the file. The operating system moves the read-write head to the cluster that contains the beginning of the file and reads it. If the file is stored in more than one cluster, the read-write head must move to the next cluster to read more of the file. It takes longer to access a file stored in nonadjacent clusters than one stored in adjacent clusters because the disk or head must move farther to find the next section of the file.

To differentiate between physical and logical file storage, remember that physical file storage refers to the way data is electronically stored on the storage medium. Logical file storage refers to the metaphor you use to visualize the organization of your files.

Lab

Defragmentation and Disk Operations

Figure 3-24 ◄
How the FAT works

1. The directory is a file maintained by the operating system that contains a list of files on the disk and the number of the cluster that contains the start of the file. The directory and FAT work together to keep track of the files on a disk.

2. The directory contains the filenames and the cluster number that contains the beginning of the file. Here the directory shows that a file called **Jordan.Wks** begins in cluster 7.

Directory	
Filename	**Starting Cluster**
Bio.Txt	**3**
Jordan.Wks	**7**
Pick.Wps	**9**

3. The file allocation table (FAT) is a file maintained by the operating system to keep track of the physical location of files on a disk.

4. Each cluster is listed in the FAT, along with a number that indicates the status of the cluster. If status is "1," the cluster is reserved for technical files. If status is "0," the cluster is empty, so new data can be stored there. If the status is "999," the cluster contains the end of a file. Other status numbers indicate the sector that holds more data for a file.

5. Looking at the FAT entry for cluster 7, you see that the **Jordan.Wks** file continues in cluster 8.

6. The FAT entry for cluster 8, shows that the **Jordan.Wks** file continues in the cluster 10. The file is stored in **non-contiguous** clusters 7, 8, and 10.

7. The FAT entry for cluster 10 shows that this is the end of the **Jordan.Wks** file.

Fat		
Cluster	**Status**	*Comment*
1	**1**	*Reserved for operating system*
2	**1**	*Reserved for operating system*
3	**4**	*First cluster of Bio.Txt. Points to cluster 8 which holds more data for Bio.Txt.*
4	**999**	*Last cluster of Bio.Txt*
5	**0**	*Empty*
6	**0**	*Empty*
7	**8**	*First cluster for Jordan.Wks. Points to cluster 8 which holds more data for the Jordan.Wks file.*
8	**10**	*Points to cluster 10 which holds more data for the Jordan.Wks file.*
9	**999**	*First and last cluster containing Pick.Wps*
10	**999**	*Last cluster of Jordan.Wks*

As you use random-access storage, files tend to become **fragmented**, that is, each file is stored in many nonadjacent clusters. Drive performance generally declines as the drive works harder to locate the clusters that contain the parts of a file. To regain peak performance, you can use a **defragmentation utility** to rearrange the files on a disk so that they are stored in adjacent clusters. Study Figure 3-25, which explains more about fragmentation and defragmentation.

Figure 3-25 ◄
Defragmenting a disk

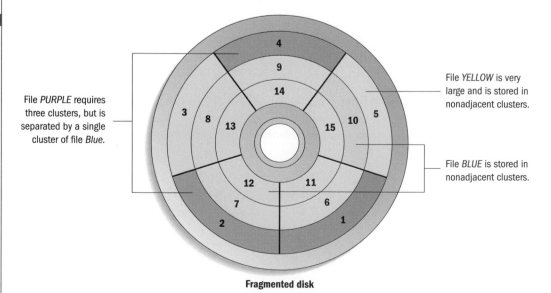

File *PURPLE* requires three clusters, but is separated by a single cluster of file *Blue*.

File *YELLOW* is very large and is stored in nonadjacent clusters.

File *BLUE* is stored in nonadjacent clusters.

Fragmented disk

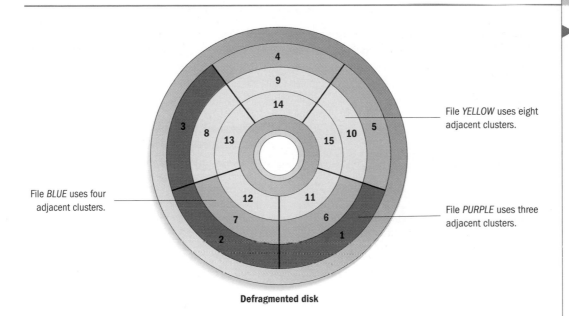

Figure 3-25
Defragmenting
a disk
(continued)

File *YELLOW* uses eight adjacent clusters.

File *BLUE* uses four adjacent clusters.

File *PURPLE* uses three adjacent clusters.

Defragmented disk

When you erase a file, the operating system changes the status of the appropriate clusters in the FAT. For example, if a file is stored in clusters 1, 2, 5, and 7 and you erase it, the operating system changes the status for those four clusters to "empty." The data is not physically removed or erased from those clusters. Instead, the old data remains in the clusters until a new file is stored there. This rather interesting situation means that if you inadvertently erase a file, you might be able to get it back using the operating system's undelete utility. Of course, you can only undelete a file if you haven't recorded something new over it, so undelete works only if you discover and correct mistakes immediately. Not all operating systems provide an undelete utility. To find out if one is available, you can consult the reference manual for your operating system.

Quick Check

1. Storage capacity is measured in _____, and access time is measured in _____ .

2. A magnet can disrupt data on _____ storage, but _____ storage technology is more durable.

3. The formatting process creates a series of concentric _____ and triangle-shaped _____ on the disk.

4. The computer can move directly to any file on a(n) _____ access device, but must start at the beginning and read through all the data on a(n) _____ access device.

5. When software is sold, it is typically distributed on either _____ or _____ media.

6. The primary storage device on a microcomputer is _____ .

7. The _____ keeps track of the physical location of files on a disk.

8. True or False: Data files that are entered by the user, changed often, or shared with other users are generally stored on optical media.

User **Focus:**
Using Files

3.3

Figure 3-26
File operations
for a typical
word processing
session

Now that you have learned about logical and physical file storage, let's apply what you've learned to how you typically use files when you work with application software. Using word processing software to produce a document illustrates the way you use files on a computer, so let's look at the file operations for a typical word processing session. Examine Figure 3-26 to get an overview of the file activities of a typical word processing session.

| 1 | Running an Application |

Suppose you want to create a document about the summer vacation packages your company offers. You decide to create the document using the word processing software, Microsoft Word. Your first step is to start the Microsoft Word program. When you run Microsoft Word, the program file is copied from the hard drive to the memory of the computer.

| 2 | Creating a File |

You begin to type the text of the document. As you type, your data is stored in the memory of the computer. Your data will not be stored on disk until you initiate the Save command.

Word.Exe is loaded into memory from hard disk

Your data is stored in memory while you type

| 3 | Saving a Data File |

When you create a file and save it on disk for the first time, the application or the operating system prompts you to name the file so you can later retrieve it by name. You know from earlier in this chapter that the name you give to a file must follow the naming convention for the operating system. You name the file **A:Vacation.Doc.** By typing A: you direct the computer to save the file on the floppy disk in drive A: The computer looks for empty clusters on the disk where it can store the file. The computer then adds the filename to the directory, along with the number of the cluster that contains the beginning of the file. Once you have saved your file, you can exit the Word program or work on another document.

When you save your revisions they overwrite the old contents of **Vacation.Doc** on the disk.

The changes you make to **Vacation.Doc** the document are stored in memory

Word.Exe is loaded into memory

A:Vacation.Doc is copied from disk into memory

A:Vacation.Doc is copied from memory to the floppy disk

4   Revising a Data File

When you see the **Vacation.Doc** file on the screen, you can make modifications to it. Each character that you type and each change that you make is stored temporarily in the main memory of the computer, but not on the disk. The main memory retains data only as long as the computer power is on. So to store your data on a more permanent basis, you must tell the computer to copy the data from the memory of the computer to the disk.

The **Vacation.Doc** file is already on the disk, however, so when you are done with the modifications you have two options. Option one is to store the revised version in place of the old version. Option two is to create a new file for your revision and give it a different name, such as **Holiday**.

If you decide to go with option one—store the revised version in place of the old version—the operating system copies your revised data from the computer memory to the same clusters that contained the old file. You do not have to take a separate step to delete the old file—the operating system automatically records the new file over it.

If you decide to go with option two—create a new file for the revision—the application prompts you for a filename. Your revisions will be stored under the new filename. The original file, **Vacation.Doc**, will still remain on the disk in its unrevised form. ,

5   Retrieving a Data File

Now suppose that a few days later, you decide that you want to revise **Vacation.Doc**. You need to start Microsoft Word. Once the Word program is running, you can retrieve the **Vacation.Doc** file from the disk on which it is stored.

When you wat to use a data file that already exists on disk storage, you must tell the application to open the file. In Microsoft Word you either type the name of the file, **A:Vacation.Doc**, or select the filename from a list of files stored on the disk. The application communicates the filename to the operating system. The operating system looks at the directory and FAT to find which clusters contain the file, then moves the read-write head to the appropriate disk location to read the file. The electronics on the disk drive transfer the file data into the main memory of the computer where your application software can manipulate it. Once the operating system has retrieved the file, the word processing software displays it on the screen.

Lab

**DOS Directories
and File Management**

Copying Files

Can I copy a file from the hard disk to my floppy disk and vice versa?

You can copy a file from one storage medium to another. When you copy a file, the original file remains intact. You'll find that copying files is a task you will do frequently. Making copies of important files as backup, copying files from your hard disk to a floppy disk to share with a friend, or transferring files you receive on a floppy disk to your hard disk are only a few of the tasks that require you to know how to copy files.

Suppose you want to copy the **Vacation.Doc** file from a floppy disk to your hard disk. The operating system is responsible for maintaining the list of files on your disk, so you usually use the operating system to copy files. With a graphical operating system such as Microsoft Windows, you can drag the icon that represents **Vacation.Doc** from its place in the directory of drive A: to the icon that represents drive C:, as shown in Figure 3-27.

Figure 3-27 ◀
Using
Windows 3.1
to copy a file

Drive c: icon

To copy the file
vacation.doc to drive
c:, drag the file icon to
the drive c: icon.

File icon

With the DOS operating system, you use the Copy command to copy a file. Let's assume that the disk containing **Vacation.Doc** is in drive A: and your hard disk drive is drive C:. The DOS command to copy **Vacation.Doc** from drive A: to a subdirectory called Plans on drive C: is:

COPY A:Vacation.Doc C:\Plans\Vacation.Doc

Deleting Files

What if I delete a file that I still need?

Eliminating files that you no longer need opens space for new files. If you want to eliminate a file that you have saved on disk, you **delete** or **erase** the file. As you know, when you delete a file, the operating system does not physically erase the cluster that contains the data belonging to that file. Instead, it changes the entries in the FAT to indicate that the clusters are available for storing other files. As additional files are stored on the disk, the sectors that formerly contained the deleted file are gradually overwritten.

To delete the file **Vacation.Doc** from the disk in drive A: using DOS, you type: DEL A:Vacation.Doc. To delete a file using Windows 3.1, you highlight the file in the File Manager window, then press the Delete key. Using Windows 95 you delete a file by pressing the Delete key to delete the icon that represents the file.

If you accidentally erase a file, you should stop using the computer immediately. Do not store anything else on the drive that contains the erased file until you have successfully used an undelete utility program to restore the file.

End Note Having access to many files stored on hard disks or CD-ROMs is a valuable advantage of today's computer technology. To use files effectively, you should know how to interact with the computer's filing system: how to name, save, retrieve, copy, and erase files. You should now understand how storage devices, the operating system, and application software interact to help you maintain a filing system for your data.

Review

1. Answer the questions in italics below each heading in this chapter, using your own words.

2. List the three most *practical* things you learned from this chapter. Why do you think they are the most practical?

3. List each of the boldface terms used in this chapter, then use your own words to write a short definition of each term. If you would like clarification of one or more terms, refer to a computer dictionary or a computer science encyclopedia such as those listed in the Resources section of Chapter 1. You can also refer to the Glossary/Index on page 3-42.

4. Copy the following chart on paper. Place an X in the Data Files column if the feature applies to data files. Place an X in the Executable Files column if the feature applies to executable files. If a feature applies to both, put an X in both columns.

Feature	Data Files	Executable Files
Created by you, the user		
Created by programmers		
Use an application to view it		
Supplied with software		
Has an .EXE or .COM extension		
Referred to as a program or application		

5. Indicate which filenames in the following list are invalid under the operating system used in your school's computer lab. Which filenaming convention does each nonvalid filename violate?

Wp.Exe	Ppr	Win.Exe
Autoexec.Bat	Results*.Wks	Monthly.Wk1
Report#1.Txt	Smith&Smith.Doc	Sep/94.Wri
Aaia map.Doc	Ocean.Tif	Mn43-44.Dbf

6. Examine the directory listing in Figure 3-28 and answer the following questions:

Figure 3-28

a. What is the size of the file **Stoves.Crd**?

b. On what date was **911.Crd** last modified?

c. How many program files are on the disk?

d. Approximately how many megabytes of storage are available on the disk?

e. What application was used to create **Cj-mem.Wri**?

f. How many of these files are data files?

g. What is the largest file on the disk?

h. Does **Codes.Pcx** contain text or graphics?

i. What type of data does the file **Fire.Wav** contain?

j. How many of the files appear to be memos?

k. How would you use a wildcard to get a directory of all the files with .Wri extensions?

l. How many files match the specification S*.*?

m. How many files match the specification *.*?

7. Suppose you have a disk with the following files:

Minutes.Doc	Report.Doc	Budget.Xls
Jacsmemo.Doc	Report1.Doc	Shipjan.Xls
Shipfeb.Xls	Shipmar.Xlx	Shipapr.Xls
Minutes.Txt	Roger.Txt	Roadmap.Bmp

If you could specify all the files with a .Doc extension by *.Doc. How would you specify the following files?

a. All the files with .Xls extensions

b. All the files that contain minutes

c. All the files that begin with "Ship"

d. All the files on the disk

e. All the files that begin with the letter "R"

8. Suppose you need to retrieve a file from Sarah's computer. She tells you that the file is stored as

C:\Data\Monthend.Doc.

   a. What is the filename?

   b. What is the file extension?

   c. On which drive is the file stored?

   d. In which directory is the file stored?

   e. What type of file is it likely to be?

   f. Will you need a specific software program to retrieve and view the file?

9. On each of the following three lines, indicate the relative position of floppy disk, hard disk ,tape, and CD-ROM storage by placing these storage types along the line. The first one is completed for you.

   a. Access time (slowest to fastest):

      Tape   CD-ROM   Floppy disk   Hard disk

      slow ——————————————————→ fast

   b. Capacity (smallest to largest):

      small ——————————————————→ large

   c. Reliability (least reliable to most reliable):

      easy to lose data ——————→ data is very secure

10. How would you explain the difference between physical storage and logical storage to someone who is not "computer literate?" Can you think of noncomputer analogies in which the way we think about something (logical view) is different from the way it really is (physical view)?

11. Suppose you need to defragment the files manually on the disk shown in Figure 3-29. Using the disk on the right, show how the files are arranged after you complete the defragmentation. Use colored pencils or different patterns to show each file clearly.

Figure 3-29 ◄

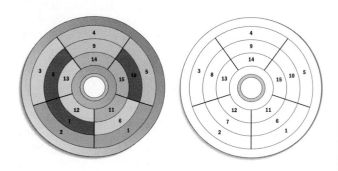

Projects

1. File Extensions Many software applications use a specific file extension for data files created with that application. Determine the extensions used by five applications on your own computer or a lab computer. Run each software application and attempt to retrieve a file. If the software application uses a specific file extension, you will usually see the extension indicated in a box on the screen. For example, you might see *.Doc if you are using Microsoft Word for Windows.

For each of the five programs you select:

   a. Specify the program name.

   b. Sketch a picture of the program icon (if you are using Windows) or indicate the executable filename (if you are using DOS).

   c. Indicate the filename extension the program uses. If the program does not use a specific filename extension, indicate that this is the case.

2. Storage Devices You Use You should be aware of the storage devices on your computer so that you use the best device for each task. You will need to take a hands-on look at your computer at home or a computer in your school lab to answer the following questions:

   a. Where is this computer located?

   b. What is the hard disk capacity? (Hint: Refer to Figure 3-18.)

   c. What is the hard disk drive letter?

   d. What is the floppy disk size?

   e. What is the floppy disk capacity?

   f. What is the floppy disk drive letter?

   g. Is there a tape storage device?

   h. Is there a CD-ROM drive?

   i. Which storage device do you usually use for the data files you create?

   j. Which storage device holds most of the applications software that you use?

   k. Which storage device would you use for backups?

3. Calculating Storage Requirements How much storage space would be needed to store this textbook? To calculate approximately how many bytes of storage space this text (not including pictures) requires:

   a. Count the number of lines on a typical page.

   b. Count the number of characters (including blanks) in the longest line of text on the page.

   c. Multiply the number of lines by the number of characters in the longest line to calculate the number of characters (bytes) per page.

   d. Multiply this figure by the number of pages in the book.

e. What do you estimate is the computer storage space required for this text?

4. Calculating Hard Disk Capacity Most manufacturers list the storage capacity of their hard disk drives on the drive itself or in the user manual. The manufacturer calculates storage capacity in bytes using the formula:

capacity = cylinders × surfaces × sectors × 512

The 512 in the formula is the number of bytes stored in each sector of each cylinder. Suppose you have a hard disk with 615 cylinders, 4 surfaces (two platters), and 17 sectors. What is the capacity in bytes of this disk?

5. Shopping for Storage Use a recent computer magazine or an Internet site such as Computer Express at *http://www.cexpress.com* to fill in the following "shopping list:"

Item	Brand	Merchant	Price
Package of 10 3½-inch floppy disks			
High-density 3½-inch floppy disk drive			
850 MB 10 ms hard disk drive			
Tape drive			
Quad-speed CD-ROM			

6. What's in That File? Earlier, you learned to distinguish between executable, data, and source files. In this project, you will look at the contents of each file type. When you view an executable file, you should see meaningless symbols. When you view a data file, you should be able to read the data applications. When you view a source file, you should be able to read the commands it contains. The Type command lets you view the contents of a file without changing it. You can use the Type command to look at the **Autoexec.Bat** source file, the **Command.Com** executable file, and the **Country.Txt** data file.

If you are using DOS, make sure you are at the C:\> prompt. If you are using Windows 3.1, double-click the MS-DOS prompt icon in the Main window. If you are using Windows 95, click the Start button, select Programs, then select MS-DOS prompt. Do each of the following steps, and write down the first line you see on the screen:

a. Type the following command (including "type"), then press the Enter key:
type c:\autoexec.bat | more

b. Type the following command, then press the Enter key: **type c:\command.com**

c. Type the following command, then press the Enter key: **type c:\dos\country.txt | more**

7. Troubleshooting a Storage Problem Read the following scenario and determine what went wrong, then write a paragraph describing what you would do to correct the problem. Your instructor will indicate if you should do this project individually or discuss it in a small group.

Toni's 80 MB hard disk contained about 75 MB of files on February 18. On that day, she made a tape backup of the entire disk. On February 19, Toni moved to a company office one block away. The company maintenance staff moved the computer, along with Toni's paper files, in the late afternoon. The people on the maintenance crew left the computer on the desk in the new office.

On February 20, Toni set up the computer and turned it on. Everything seemed fine. She used the computer to write a few memos using WordPerfect for Windows. On February 21, Toni tried to open a data file containing the names and addresses of her clients. The computer displayed a message—something about an error on drive C:. Toni turned off her computer and then turned it back on, hoping the error would go away, but the computer wouldn't let her access any data on the hard disk.

8. CD-Mania What's the difference between the CDs that contain your favorite music album and the CD-ROMs you use in a computer? You might be surprised to learn that some computer CD-ROM drives can play your music CDs. In fact, there are several CD formats, including CD-DA, CD-I, CD-ROM, PhotoCD, and CD-R. For this project, use your library and Internet resources to write a paper describing these CD formats. The length of your paper will depend on the scope of the project: a three-page paper is suitable for a short project, a term paper might require 10-15 pages. Be sure you include a bibliography.

Your paper can deal with CDs from the technical perspective or from the applied perspective. If you take the technical perspective, you should look for answers to questions such as, but not limited to:

a. What are the capacity and storage format for each type of CD?

b. Why did these specifications originate?

c. What are the advantages and disadvantages of each?

If you take the applied perspective, you should try to find the answers to questions such as, but not limited to:

a. What are the primary uses for each type of CD?

b. What are the advantages and disadvantages of each?

c. How do the costs of each format compare?

9. Data Storage in Organizations Organizations take different approaches to data storage, depending on the volume of their data, the value of their data, and the need for data security. The purpose of this Project is to interview the person responsible for maintaining the data for an organization and discover the answers to the following questions:

a. What is the position title of the person responsible for this organization's data storage?

b. What preparation did this individual have to qualify for this position?

c. What are this individual's job responsibilities?

d. How does this individual keep up with trends that affect data storage?

e. What type of data does the organization store?

f. What percent of this data is stored on a computer system?

g. What types of storage devices are used in this organization?

h. What is the capacity of each storage device?

i. What happens when the storage devices are full?

j. What problems are associated with maintaining the data for this organization?

This project works well if the class is divided into teams and each team interviews a person from a different organization. Each team can then present a 15-minute report to the rest of the class, along with a two- to three-page written report of its findings.

10. The Future of Computer Storage Ten years ago, the idea of 500 MB of storage on a personal computer seemed incredible. But technology turned that dream into reality. What storage technologies might we use in the future? Will optical storage cubes the size of a nine-volt battery hold gigabytes of data? Will *smart* credit cards hold all our financial data? Will magneto-optical devices combine the flexibility of magnetic media with the permanence of optical media? Will data be stored as holograms?

Use recent computer magazines and journals to research trends and projections for computer storage technology.

You might want to do a survey and write a paragraph or two on each new technology, or you might want to take an in-depth look at a technology that you find interesting.

The paper you write as the result of your research can be as short as 3 pages or as long as 25 pages, depending on the scope of the project specified by your instructor.

Resources

■ **IBM's Internet Web site** This Web site contains information on micro, mini, and mainframe computer storage. Look at the section on product information and select Storage from the list of product categories. Access this site at *http://www.ibm.com*.

■ **The Internet Yahoo Directory** This directory is a list of Internet sites with information on CD-ROM and hard disk drives. Access this site at *http://yahoo.com/ Computers/Hardware/Peripherals*.

■ **Rosch, W.** *The Winn L. Rosch Hardware Bible*. 3rd ed. Indianapolis: Sams Publishing, 1994. This book is one of the definitive references on microcomputer hardware. The emphasis is on technical details, but most of the explanations are clearly written for users who don't necessarily have a degree in electrical engineering or computer science. Chapters 21 through 25 cover microcomputer storage technology, including specifications for CD formats. This is a good source of information for Project 8.

■ *Understanding Computers: Memory and Storage*. Alexandria, VA: Time-Life Books, 1987. Time-Life Books has produced a lavishly illustrated series of books on computers that provide substantial detail in an easy-to-understand format. One of the books, Memory and Storage, contains an excellent section on storage devices—how they were developed and how they work.

Lab Assignments

DOS Directories and File Management

DOS is an operating system used on millions of computers. Even if your computer has a graphical user interface, such as Microsoft Windows, understanding DOS commands helps you grasp the basic concepts of computer file management. In this Lab, you learn how to use basic DOS commands.

1. Click the Steps button to learn basic DOS commands. As you proceed through the Steps, answer all of the Quick Check questions that appear. After you complete the Steps, you will see a Quick Check Summary Report. Follow the instructions on the screen to print this report.

2. Go through the Steps for this Lab once again. This time, create a mini DOS manual by listing each DOS command and its function. For each command, you should also provide a sample of a valid command, for example:

DIR   Provides a listing of all the files on a disk

Example: DIR A:

3. Click the Explore button and make a new disk. (You can copy over the disk you used for Steps.) Do each of the following tasks and record the command you used:

a. Display the directory for drive A:.

b. Display only those files on drive A: that begin with the letter "T."

c. Erase all the files that have names beginning with "New."

d. Create a directory called PAPERS.

e. Move all the files with .DOC extensions into the PAPERS directory.

f. Rename OPUS27.MID to SONG.MID.

g. Delete all the files with names that start with "Budget."

4. In Explore, make a new disk. (You can copy over the disk you used for earlier Lab activities.) Do each of the following tasks, then give your disk to your instructor. Don't forget to put your name on the disk label.

a. Make two subdirectories on your disk: PICS and BUDGETS.

b. Move all the files with .BMP extensions into the PICS directory.

c. Move all the files with .WKS extensions into the BUDGETS directory.

d. Delete all the files except README.TXT from the root directory. (Do not delete the files from PICS or BUDGETS.)

e. Rename the file README.TXT to READ.ME.

5. Use the TYPE command to view the contents of the START.BAT file. Describe the file contents. Use the TYPE command to view the contents of OPUS27.MID. Describe what you see? Explain the different results you obtained when you used the TYPE command with START.BAT and OPUS27.MID.

Windows Directories, Folders, and Files

 Graphical user interfaces such as MacOS, Windows 3.1, and Windows 95 use a filing system metaphor for file management. In this Lab, you will learn the basic concepts of these file system metaphors. With this background, you will find it easy to understand how to manage files with graphical user interfaces.

1. Click the Steps button to learn how to manipulate directories, folders and files. As you proceed through the Steps, answer all of the Quick Check questions that appear. After you complete the Steps, you will see a Quick Check Summary Report. Follow the instructions on the screen to print this report.

2. Click the Explore button. Make sure drive a: is the default drive. Double-click the a:\ folder to display the folder contents, then answer the following questions:

a. How many files are in the root directory of drive a:?

b. Are the files on drive a: data files or program files? How can you tell?

c. Does the root directory of drive a: contain any subdirectories? How can you tell?

3. Make sure you are in Explore. Change to drive c: as the default drive. Double-click the c:\ folder to display its contents, then answer the following questions:

a. How many data files are in the root directory of drive c:?

b. How many program files are in the root directory of drive c:?

c. Does the root directory of drive c: contain any subdirectories? How can you tell?

d. How many files are in the dos folder?

e. Complete the diagram in Figure 3-30 to show the arrangement of folders on drive c:. Do not include files.

▶ **Figure 3-30**

4. Open and close folders, and change drives as necessary to locate the following files. After you find the file, write out its file specification:

a. config.sys, b. win.ini, c. toolkit.wks, d. meeting.doc

e. newlogo3.bmp, f. todo.doc

Defragmentation and Disk Operations

 In this Lab you will format a simulated disk, save files, delete files, undelete files to see how the computer updates the FAT. You will also find out how the files on your disk become fragmented and what a defragmentation utility does to reorganize the clusters on your disk.

1. Click the Steps button to learn how the computer updates the FAT when you format a disk and save, delete, and undelete files. As you proceed through the Steps, answer all of the Quick Check questions that appear. After you complete the Steps, you will see a Quick Check Summary Report. Follow the instructions on the screen to print this report.

2. Click the Explore button. Click the Format button to format the simulated disk. Try to save files 1, 2, 3, 4, and 6. Do they all fit on the disk?

3. In Explore, format the simulated disk. Try to save all the files on the disk. What happens?

4. In Explore, format the simulated disk. Save FILE-3, FILE-4, and FILE-6. Next, delete FILE-6. Now, save FILE-5. Try to undelete FILE-6. What happens and why?

5. In Explore, format the simulated disk. Save and erase files until the files become fragmented. Draw a picture of the disk to show the fragmented files. Indicate which files are in each cluster by using color, crosshatching, or labels. List which files in your drawing are fragmented. Finally, defragment the disk and draw a new picture showing the unfragmented files.

Using Files

 In this Lab you manipulate a simulated computer to view what happens in memory and on disk when you create, save, open, revise, and delete files. Understanding what goes on "inside the box" will help you quickly grasp how to perform basic file operations with most application software.

1. Click the Steps button to learn how to use the simulated computer to view the contents of memory and disk

when you perform basic file operations. As you proceed through the Steps, answer all of the Quick Check questions that appear. After you complete the Steps, you will see a Quick Check Summary Report. Follow the instructions on the screen to print this report.

2. Click the Explore button and use the simulated computer to perform the following tasks.

a. Create a document containing your name and the city in which you were born. Save this document as NAME.

b. Create another document containing two of your favorite foods. Save this document as FOODS.

c. Create another file containing your two favorite classes. Call this file CLASSES.

d. Open the FOOD file and add another one of your favorite foods. Save this file without changing its name.

e. Open the NAME file. Change this document so it contains your name and the name of your school. Save this as a new document called SCHOOL.

f. Write down how many files are on the simulated disk and the exact contents of each file.

3. In Explore, use the simulated computer to perform the following tasks.

a. Create a file called MUSIC that contains the name of your favorite CD.

b. Create another document that contains eight numbers and call this file LOTTERY.

c. You didn't win the lottery this week. Revise the contents of the LOTTERY file, but save the revision as LOTTERY2.

d. Revise the MUSIC file so it also contains the name of your favorite musician or composer, and save this file as MUSIC2.

e. Delete the MUSIC file.

f. Write down how many files are on the simulated disk and the exact contents of each file.

Quick Check

Answers

3.1

1. data, information

2. drive letter, subdirectory, subdirectory, filename, filename extension

3. exe, com

4. Most Windows software automatically adds a specific extension to each file created with it.

5. logical

6. root

7. source

3.2

1. kilobytes (megabytes or gigabytes also acceptable), milliseconds

2. magnetic, optical

3. tracks, sectors

4. random, sequential

5. floppy disk, CD-ROM

6. hard disk drive

7. FAT (File Allocation Table)

8. false

Glossary/Index

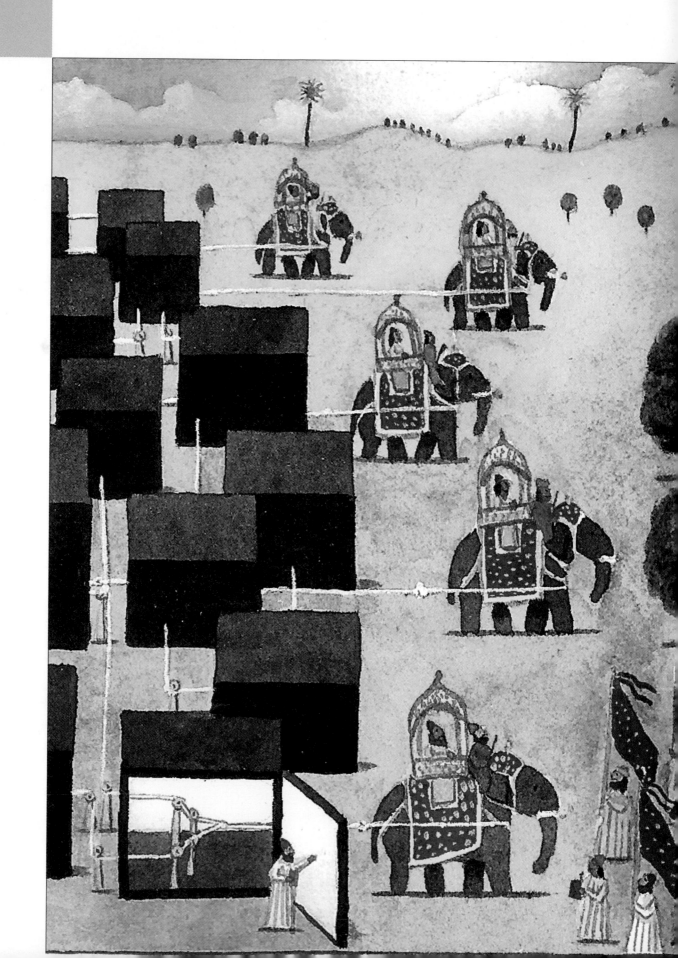

Computer Architecture

Readers of the April 1985 issue of *Scientific American* were somewhat surprised by an article about a group of archaeologists who had discovered an ancient computer constructed from ropes and pulleys. The article explained that "archaeologists have discovered the rotting remnants of an ingenious arrangement of ropes and pulleys thought to be the first working digital computer ever constructed." The article continued to describe in detail how the people of an ancient culture, known as the Apraphulians, built complex devices of ropes and pulleys, housed these devices in huge black wooden boxes, and used them to perform complex mathematical computations. Some of the devices were so colossal that elephants were harnessed to pull the enormous ropes through the pulley system.

A computer constructed of ropes and pulleys? As you might have guessed, this was an April Fools' article. And yet, such a device, if it were constructed, could accurately be called a digital computer. That you could build a computer out of ropes and pulleys reinforces the notion that a computer is, in many respects, a very simple device.

In this chapter, we'll take a more detailed look inside the case of a modern computer system. The basic concepts you learn in this chapter apply to micro, mini, and mainframe computers.

Once you understand how a computer works, you will have more success troubleshooting problems you encounter in the lab, at work, or at home. You'll learn how, when, and why you should expand your computer system. You'll be better equipped to understand much of the jargon you read in computer ads and hear in conversations with computer professionals.

CHAPTER**PREVIEW**

In previous chapters you focused on how computers and software help you accomplish tasks. Now it is time to look under the hood and tackle some technical concepts about how computers store and process data. Can you apply these technical concepts? Of course! You'll find that the concepts you learn in this chapter will help you when you set up a new computer. You can also use the information to identify the source of hardware problems when your computer does not seem to work. When you have completed this chapter you should be able to:

- Identify the components that are on the main circuit board of a microcomputer

- Explain how RAM, virtual memory, CMOS, and ROM differ

- Explain how the CPU performs the instructions contained in a computer program

- List the factors that affect CPU performance

- Describe how the data bus and expansion bus work

- List the components necessary to connect a peripheral device to a computer and describe each component's role

- Trace the boot process of your computer system

LABS

Binary Numbers

CPU Simulator

Troubleshooting

Digital Electronics

Computer architecture refers to the design and construction of a computer system. The architecture of any computer can be broadly classified by considering two characteristics: what the computer uses for power and how the computer physically represents, processes, stores, and moves data. Most modern computers are electronic devices, that is, they are powered by electricity. Also, a modern computer uses electrical signals and circuits to represent, process, and move data.

Inside the System Unit

Figure 4-1
Inside the system unit

Today, most integrated circuits are manufactured on a chip of silicon crystal. Silicon Valley in California is so named because many of the computer companies located there either produce or use silicon chips in their products.

What does the inside of a computer look like?

If you have never looked inside a computer, you might stop reading for a moment and try to visualize the inside of a computer's system unit. Did you picture a maze of wires and other electronic gizmos? Many people do. But you might be surprised to find that the inside of a computer looks pretty simple. We took the cover off the microcomputer in Figure 4-1 to show you what's inside.

Most of the components inside a computer are integrated circuits, commonly called *chips* or *microchips*. An **integrated circuit** is a thin slice of crystal packed with microscopic circuit elements such as wires, transistors, capacitors, and resistors. A single integrated circuit less than a quarter-inch square could contain more than 100,000 microscopic circuit elements. The completed circuit is packaged in a ceramic carrier that provides connection pins, as shown in Figure 4-2.

Inside the system unit, integrated circuits are housed on a circuit board called the **main board** or **motherboard**. The main board is connected to peripheral devices that collect input and produce output. Use Figure 4-3 as a "map" to the electronic components you will learn about in this chapter.

Power supply
Wires and ribbon cables
Hard disk drive
Floppy disk drive
Main board
Expansion slots
Expansion cards
Microprocessor chip
Memory

Fine wires connect the chip to metal leads called *pins*.

A plastic or ceramic case protects the chip.

Metal pins plug into a socket on a circuit board.

The silicon chip is less than .25″ square. The chip contains thousands of microscopic electronic components such as transistors, resistors, and capacitors.

▶ **Figure 4-2**
An integrated circuit

If you are interested in how the computer industry might have developed without the invention of the integrated circuit, complete Project 3 at the end of this chapter.

▶ **Figure 4-3**
Microcomputer main board

ROM chips contain the programs that start the computer, run system diagnostics, and control low-level input and output activities.

RAM temporarily holds data that is waiting to be processed.

A **bus** transports data between components on the main board.

A battery powered **real-time clock** chip keeps the current date and time.

The **microprocessor** contains the circuitry that performs arithmetic and logical operations.

An **expansion card** plugs into a slot to provide the circuitry to control printing, video display, disk storage, or telecommunications.

An **expansion slot** provides a way to add devices to a computer system.

A **port** provides a plug for a cable that leads to a device, such as a printer, monitor, disk drive, or modem.

Digital Data Representation

But if a computer is just a bunch of electrical circuits, how can it manipulate numbers and letters?

Data representation refers to the form in which information is conceived, manipulated, and recorded. When you want to add a column of numbers or sort a list of names, you represent the numbers and names by writing symbols such as 2, G, a, and 8. A computer is an electronic device, so it doesn't write down the data it works with. A computer somehow needs to use electrical signals to represent data. How does a computer do this?

The way a computer represents data depends on whether the computer is a digital or an analog device. A **digital device** works with discrete, that is, distinct or separate numbers or digits, such as 0 and 1. An **analog device** operates on continuously varying data. For example, a digital watch displays the time 12:20 for an entire minute before switching to 12:21—the 0 changes to a 1 without intermediate steps. An analog watch, on the other hand, positions its hands to show you that it is 12:01, but then moves the minute hand very slowly through the space between the minute marks. Think about what's different about the analog and digital versions of the devices shown in Figure 4-4.

Figure 4-4
Examples of analog and digital devices

In an analog computer, the number 5 might be represented by .05 volts, the number 6 might be represented by .06 volts, and so on. An analog computer could add 5 + 5 by combining .05 volts and .05 volts. The resulting .10 volts would represent 10, the sum of 5 + 5.

In a digital computer, each number or letter is represented by a series of electrical signals. Think about the way Morse code uses dashes and dots to represent letters. In a similar way, digital computers represent numbers, letters, and symbols with a code that uses a series of 0s (zeros) and 1s.

A digital computer represents the number 5 with the code 00000101. The letter A could be represented with the code 01000001. Why 0s and 1s? A digital computer is an electronic device, and you know that electricity can be on or off. If you equate the on state with 1 and the off state with 0, you can grasp the basic principle of how a digital computer works. Data that is represented by a series of 1s and 0s can easily be moved or stored electronically as a series of "ons" and "offs."

Each 1 or 0 that represents data is referred to as a **bit**. Most computer coding schemes use eight bits to represent each number, letter, or symbol. A series of eight bits is called a **byte**. Study Figure 4-5 to make sure you understand how the term *byte* is related to the terms *bits* and *characters*.

A digital computer uses the electronic equivalent of 1s and 0s to represent data.

Figure 4-5
Bits, bytes, and characters

The smallest unit of information on a computer is a **bit**. A bit can be a 0 or a 1. The electronic circuits in a computer carry one bit as a pulse of electiricity through a circuit.

A collection of eight bits is called a **byte**. This byte is composed of eight bits: 01111001

0 1 1 1 1 0 0 1

y

A byte represents one **character**—a letter, numeral, or punctuation symbol. This byte, 01111001, represents a lowercase Y.

Data Representation Codes

Do all digital computers use the same code to represent data?

Digital computers use many different coding schemes to represent data. The coding scheme the computer uses depends on whether the data is numeric data or character data.

Numeric data consists of numbers that represent quantities and that might be used in arithmetic operations. For example, your annual income is numeric data. You use it in arithmetic operations every April when you calculate your income taxes.

Character data is composed of letters, symbols, and numerals that will not be used in arithmetic operations. Examples of character data include your name, hair color, and Social Security number. Are you surprised that your Social Security *number* is considered character data? Because you are not going to use your Social Security number in arithmetic operations it is considered character data.

Digital computers represent numeric data using the **binary number system**, or base two. In the binary number system, there are only two digits: 0 and 1. The numeral 2 cannot be used in the binary number system, so instead of writing "2," you would write "10." The first eight

Lab

Binary Numbers

Your phone number is considered character data because you don't manipulate it arithmetically.

numbers in the binary number system are 1, 10, 11, 100, 101, 110, 111, 1000. If you need to review binary numbers, study Figure 4-6.

Figure 4-6
Binary numbers

Decimal		Binary			
Place	Place	Place	Place	Place	Place
10	**1**	**8**	**4**	**2**	**1**
	0				0
	1				1
	2			1	0
	3			1	1
	4		1	0	0
	5		1	0	1
	6		1	1	0
	7		1	1	1
	8	1	0	0	0
	9	1	0	0	1
1	0	1	0	1	0

1. In the decimal number system, there are ten digits: 0, 1, 2, 3, 4, 5, 6, 7, 8, 9. When we put one of these digits in the column for the 1's place, it represents a different number than when we put it in the column for the 10's place. For example, the digit 1 in the 1's column is worth 1, ...but the digit 1 in the 10's column is worth 10. As you know, after you use the digit 9, you must "carry" a one to the next column and use a zero as a placeholder to represent the number 10.

2. The columns or "places" for the binary number system are 1s, 2s, 4s, 8s, and so on. To find out the value of the next place, you double the value of the previous place. The next place to the left would be 16s.

3. In the binary number system there are only two digits: 0 and 1. When you are counting in binary, you run out of digits when you get to the number 2. To represent "2" in binary, you must move the digit 1 left into the next column and use a zero for a place holder. In binary, the number 10 (pronounced "one zero") means "2".

4. Suppose you want to convert the binary number 11001 into its decimal equivalent.

? 11001 ?

5. You can set up a conversion table like this one, using the the place values for the binary number system. Because the binary number 11001 has five places, our conversion table also needs five places: 16, 8, 4, 2, and 1.

16	8	4	2	1
1	1	0	0	1

16 + 8   + 1 = 25

6. Next, add the place values for any column that contains the digit 1. The sum is the decimal equivalent of the binary number. Here you see that binary 11001 is equivalent to the decimal number 25.

Digital computers use the binary number system to represent numeric data, but use either the ASCII or EBCDIC code to represent character data.

Digital computers typically represent character data using either the ASCII or EBCDIC codes. ASCII is the data representation code used on most microcomputers, on many minicomputers, and on some mainframe computers. **ASCII** stands for American Standard Code for Information Interchange and is pronounced "ASK ee." The ASCII code for an uppercase "A" is 01000001. Look at Figure 4-7 and notice that the ASCII code is used to represent symbols and numerals as well as uppercase and lowercase letters.

SYMBOL	ASCII	EBCDIC	SYMBOL	ASCII	EBCDIC	SYMBOL	ASCII	EBCDIC
(space)	0100000	01000000	?	0111111	01101111	^	1011110	
!	0100001	01011010	@	1000000	01111100	_	1011111	
"	0100010	01111111	A	1000001	11000001	a	1100001	10000001
#	0100011	01111011	B	1000010	11000010	b	1100010	10000010
$	0100100	01011011	C	1000011	11000011	c	1100011	10000011
%	0100101	01101100	D	1000100	11000100	d	1100000	10000100
&	0100110	01010000	E	1000101	11000101	e	1100101	10000101
'	0100111	01111101	F	1000110	11000110	f	1100110	10000110
(	0101000	01001101	G	1000111	11000111	g	1100111	10000111
)	0101001	01011101	H	1001000	11001000	h	1101100	10001000
*	0101010	01011100	I	1001001	11001001	i	1101001	10001001
+	0101011	01001110	J	1001010	11010001	j	1101010	10010001
,	0101100	01101011	K	1001011	11010010	k	1101011	10010010
-	0101101	01100000	L	1001100	11010011	l	1101000	10010011
.	0101110	01001011	M	1001101	11010100	m	1101101	10010100
/	0101111	01100001	N	1001110	11010101	n	1101110	10010101
0	0110000	11110000	O	1001111	11010110	o	1111111	10010110
1	0110001	11110001	P	1010000	11010111	p	1110100	10010111
2	0110010	11110010	Q	1010001	11011000	q	1110010	10011000
3	0110011	11110011	R	1010010	11011001	r	1110010	10011001
4	0110100	11110100	S	1010011	11100010	s	1110011	10100010
5	0110101	11110101	T	1010100	11100011	t	1110100	10100011
6	0110110	11110110	U	1010101	11100100	u	1110101	10100100
7	0110111	11110111	V	1010110	11100101	v	1110110	10100101
8	0111000	11111000	W	1010111	11100110	w	1110111	10100110
9	0111001	11111001	X	1011000	11100111	x	1111000	10100111
:	0111010	01111010	Y	1011001	11101000	y	1111001	10101000
;	0111011	01011110	Z	1011010	11101001	z	1111010	10101001
<	0111100	01001100	[	1011011	01001010	{	1111011	
=	0111101	01111110	\	1011100		}	1111101	
>	0111110	01101110	]	1011101	01011010			

Figure 4-7
ASCII and EBCDIC codes

IBM-brand mainframe computers often use the EBCDIC code. **EBCDIC** stands for extended binary coded decimal interchange code (pronounced "EB seh dick"). Figure 4-7 shows the EBCDIC codes in addition to the ASCII codes. See if you can spot some of the differences between the ASCII and EBCDIC coding schemes.

Data Transport

What happens to the data in a computer?

You now know that data exists in the computer as a series of electronic signals. These signals often must travel from one chip to another, so that the computer can process or store them.

Typically, data travels from one location to another within the computer on an electronic pathway or circuit called a **data bus**. The data bus is a series of electronic circuits that connect the various electrical elements on the main board. The bus contains data lines and address lines. **Data lines** carry the signals that represent data. **Address lines** carry the location of the data to help the computer find the data that it needs to process.

The term *bus* fairly accurately describes its function. Picture a school bus that goes to a neighborhood and picks up a load of children, drops them off at school, then goes to the next neighborhood on its route to pick up a second busload. After school, the bus transports loads of children home. A computer bus works in a similar way.

A computer data bus "picks up" a load of bits from one of the components on the main board, then transfers these bits to another main board component. After dropping off this load of bits, the bus collects another load, as shown in Figure 4-8.

Figure 4-8
How a data
bus works

Quick Check

1 A(n) _____ is a collection of microscopic circuit elements such as wires, transistors, capacitors, and resistors packed onto a very small square of silicon.

2 The smallest unit of information in a computer is a(n) _____ .

3 A series of eight bits is referred to as a(n) _____ .

4 A computer uses the _____ or _____ codes to represent character data.

5 The _____ number system represents numeric data as a series of 0s and 1s.

6 A(n) _____ is an electronic pathway that links the chips on the main board of a computer.

Memory

S o far in this chapter you have learned that digital computers represent data using electronic signals. You know that the data bus transports these electronic signals from one place to another inside the computer. Now you will find out where the computer puts data when it is not being transported from one place to another.

Memory is electronic circuitry that holds data and program instructions. Memory is sometimes called *primary storage*, but this term is easily confused with disk storage. It is preferable to use the term *memory* to refer to the circuitry that has a direct link to the processor and to use the term *storage* to refer to media, such as disks, that are not directly linked to the processor.

There are four major types of memory: random access memory, virtual memory, CMOS memory, and read-only memory. Each type of memory is characterized by the kind of data it contains and the technology it uses to hold the data.

Usually, RAM addresses are numbered using the binary number system. In this chapter, however, we use addresses such as M1, M2, and M3 to help you more easily grasp the basic concepts of RAM technology.

Random Access Memory

How does RAM work?

Random access memory, or **RAM**, is an area in the computer system unit that temporarily holds data before and after it is processed. For example, when you enter a document, the characters you type usually are not processed right away. They are held in RAM until you tell your software to carry out a process such as printing.

In RAM, microscopic electronic parts called **capacitors** hold the electronic signals for the ASCII, EBCDIC, or binary code that represents data. A charged capacitor represents an "on" bit. A discharged capacitor represents an "off" bit.

You can visualize the capacitors arranged in banks of eight. Each bank of capacitors holds eight bits, or one byte of data. A **RAM address** on each bank helps the computer locate the data contained in the bank, as shown in Figure 4-9.

In some respects, RAM is like a chalkboard. You can use a chalkboard to write mathematical formulas, erase them, and then write an outline for a report. In a similar way, RAM can hold numbers and formulas when you use a spreadsheet, then hold the text of your English essay when you use a word processor. The contents of RAM can change just by changing the charge of the capacitors. Because its contents can be changed, RAM is a reusable resource.

Unlike hard disk or floppy disk storage, most RAM is *volatile*. In other words, if the computer is turned off or the power goes out, all data stored in RAM instantly and permanently disappears. When someone unhappily says, "I have lost all my data!" it often means that the person was entering data for a document or worksheet, and the power went out before the data was saved on disk.

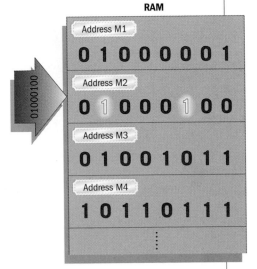

Figure 4-9
How RAM works

In the context of RAM, volatile means that data is lost if the power goes out.

RAM Functions

Why is RAM so important?

The contents of RAM are necessary for the computer to process any data. The central processing unit receives instructions from RAM, uses the data in RAM for processing, and keeps the results of processing temporarily in RAM until they are needed again or are stored on disk.

RAM stores user data, operating system instructions, and program instructions. As you have already learned, RAM holds data. When you type a document, each character you type is held in RAM until you save the document on a disk.

Every time you turn on your computer, it copies a set of operating system instructions from disk into RAM. These instructions, which help control basic computer functions, remain in RAM until you turn the computer off.

The computer keeps programs, data, and parts of the operating system in RAM.

RAM also holds program instructions. When you use a word processing program, the computer copies the instructions that turn your computer into a word processor from the disk into RAM.

RAM Capacity

How much RAM does my computer need?

The storage capacity of RAM is measured in megabytes. Today's microcomputers typically have between 4 and 32 megabytes of RAM, which means they can hold between 4 and 32 million bytes of data.

The amount of RAM your computer needs depends on the software you use. The amount of RAM required to run a software package is usually specified on the outside of the software box. What if the software you want to use requires more RAM than your computer has? You can purchase additional RAM to expand the memory capacity of your computer up to the limit set by the computer manufacturer.

When you purchase additional RAM, you must make sure it is the correct type, configuration, and speed for your computer system. The technical reference manual for your computer should contain the information you need to purchase the right type of RAM. Figure 4-10 explains the types of RAM that are available for microcomputers.

Figure 4-10 ◀
Microcomputer RAM types

A typical **DIP** (dual in-line pin) memory module stores 256 kilobits of data. Note, that's kilobits, not kilobytes. Although RAM is measured in megabytes, the capacity of the memory modules that make up RAM is measured in bits. DIPs are not used for main memory in most of today's computer systems, but they were popular in the first generation of microcomputers.

A DIP plugs into a special socket on the main board, or it might be soldered directly to the main board circuitry.

A **SIMM** (single in-line memory module) is a small circuit board that contains three to nine DIP packages. It is the memory module of choice on today's microcomputers.

The edge of the SIMM circuit board plugs into a special SIMM slot in the main board.

Virtual Memory

What if I run out of RAM?

Suppose you use a word processing program that requires 4 MB of RAM and a spreadsheet program that requires 2 MB of RAM. You might suspect that you would run out of RAM if you tried to run both programs at the same time. However, you need only 4 MB to run both programs. How can this be so?

With today's operating systems, you won't run out of RAM because the computer uses space on your computer's hard disk as an extension of RAM. A computer's ability to use disk storage to simulate RAM is called **virtual memory**. Figure 4-11 explains how virtual memory works.

The term virtual is associated with many computer technologies. In the context of computing, virtual usually means simulated.

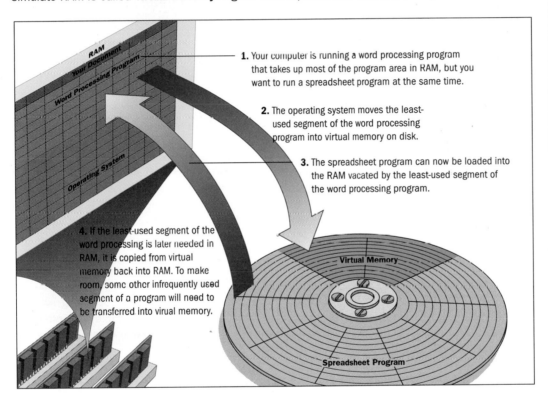

Figure 4-11
How virtual memory works

1. Your computer is running a word processing program that takes up most of the program area in RAM, but you want to run a spreadsheet program at the same time.

2. The operating system moves the least-used segment of the word processing program into virtual memory on disk.

3. The spreadsheet program can now be loaded into the RAM vacated by the least-used segment of the word processing program.

4. If the least-used segment of the word processing is later needed in RAM, it is copied from virtual memory back into RAM. To make room, some other infrequently used segment of a program will need to be transferred into virual memory.

Virtual Memory

Spreadsheet Program

Normally disks do not lose data when the power goes off. Data in virtual memory is not erased from the disk if the power fails, but the computer can no longer access it, even after the power is restored.

Virtual memory allows computers without enough real memory to run large programs, manipulate large data files, and run more than one program at a time. One disadvantage of virtual memory is reduced performance. It takes longer to retrieve data from virtual memory than from RAM because the disk is a mechanical device. Another disadvantage is that any data in virtual memory becomes inaccessible if the power goes off.

Read-only Memory

If a computer has RAM, why does it need ROM?

Read-only memory, or **ROM**, is a set of chips containing instructions that help a computer prepare for processing tasks. The instructions in ROM are permanent, and the only way to change them is to remove the ROM chips from the main board and replace them with another set. You might wonder why the computer includes chips with programs permanently stored in them. Why not use the more adaptable RAM?

You'll find out more about the role ROM plays in the boot process later in Section 4.5.

The answer to this question is that when you turn on your computer, the central processing unit receives electrical power and is ready to begin executing instructions. But because the computer was just turned on, RAM is empty—it doesn't contain any instructions for the central processing unit to execute. This is when ROM plays its part. ROM contains a small set of instructions that tell the computer how to access the disk drives and look for the operating system. When you turn on your computer, the central processing unit performs a series of steps by following the instructions stored in ROM. This series of steps is called the *boot process*.

CMOS Memory

If the boot instructions are permanent, does that mean I can't change any hardware on my computer system?

CMOS memory is more permanent than RAM, but less permanent than ROM.

The computer is not ready to process data until it has copied certain operating system files from the hard disk into RAM. But, the computer can only find data on the hard disk if it has some information about how the hard disk is formatted. The computer must know the number of tracks and sectors and the size of each sector, or it cannot know where to look for the operating system files.

If information about the hard disk was permanently stored in ROM, you would never be able to replace your hard disk drive with a larger one. The computer could not access the new hard disk using information about the old disk. Therefore, a computer must have some semipermanent way of keeping boot data, such as the number of hard disk drive tracks and sectors. For this, a computer needs a type of memory more permanent than RAM, but less permanent than ROM.

To remember the difference between memory types, remember:
- *RAM is temporary.*
- *Virtual memory is disk-based.*
- *ROM is permanent.*
- *CMOS is battery powered.*

CMOS memory (complementary metal oxide semiconductor, pronounced "SEE moss") holds data, but requires very little power to retain its contents. Because of its low power requirements, a CMOS chip can be powered by battery. CMOS uses battery power to retain vital data about your computer system configuration, even when your computer is turned off.

When your system configuration changes, the data in the CMOS memory must be updated. To change the CMOS data, you usually run a CMOS configuration, or setup, program. The reference manual for your computer indicates how to start the setup program. Some operating systems have special utilities that help you update the CMOS settings. For example, the **plug-and-play** feature of the Windows 95 operating system helps you update CMOS if you install a new hard drive.

Quick Check

1. _____ is electronic circuitry that holds data and programs.

2. Having a steady power source is important for a computer because RAM is _____.

3. RAM is measured in _____.

4. In RAM, microscopic electronic parts called _____ hold the electrical signals that represent data.

5. Most of today's microcomputers use _____ instead of DIP memory modules.

6. If your computer does not have enough RAM to run several programs at once, your computer operating system might simulate RAM with disk-based _____ memory.

7. The series of instructions that a computer performs when it is first turned on are permanently stored in _____.

8. System configuration information, such as the number of the hard disk tracks and sectors, is stored in battery-backed _____ memory.

Central Processing Unit

o far in this chapter you have learned that digital computers represent data using a series of electrical signals. You know that data can be transported over the data bus or held in memory. But a computer does more than transport and store data. A computer is supposed to process data—perform arithmetic, sort lists, format documents, and so on. The computer processes data in the central processing unit (CPU). In this section of the chapter you will learn how the central processing unit works.

The **central processing unit** is the circuitry in a computer that executes instructions to process data. The central processing unit retrieves instructions and data from RAM, processes those instructions, then places the results back into RAM so they can be displayed or stored. Figure 4-12 will help you visualize the flow of data and instructions through the processor.

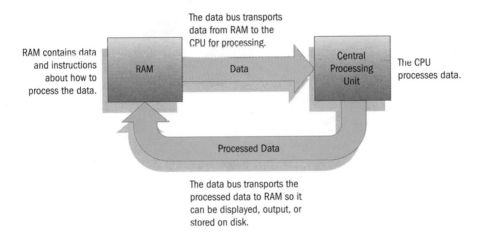

RAM contains data and instructions about how to process the data.

RAM

The data bus transports data from RAM to the CPU for processing.

Data

Central Processing Unit

The CPU processes data.

Processed Data

The data bus transports the processed data to RAM so it can be displayed, output, or stored on disk.

Figure 4-12
The data bus transports data and instructions between RAM and the CPU

Central Processing Unit Architecture

What does the CPU look like?

The central processing unit consists of one or more integrated circuits. The central processing unit of a mainframe computer usually contains several integrated circuits. In a microcomputer the central processing unit is a single integrated circuit called a **microprocessor**. Figure 4-13 shows a microprocessor similar to the one that is probably in the computer you use.

A microprocessor is not the same as a microcomputer. A microprocessor is the CPU chip found on the main board of a microcomputer.

The central processing unit of a microcomputer is a microprocessor. The microprocessor plugs into the main board and connects to the data bus.

Figure 4-13
A microprocessor

The central processing unit has two main parts: the arithmetic logic unit and the control unit. Each of these units perform specific tasks to process data.

The **arithmetic logic unit (ALU)** performs arithmetic operations such as addition and subtraction. It also performs logical operations such as comparing two numbers to see if they are the same. The ALU uses **registers** to hold the data that is being processed. In the ALU the result of an arithmetic or logical operation is held temporarily in the **accumulator**, as shown in Figure 4-14.

Figure 4-14
How the ALU works

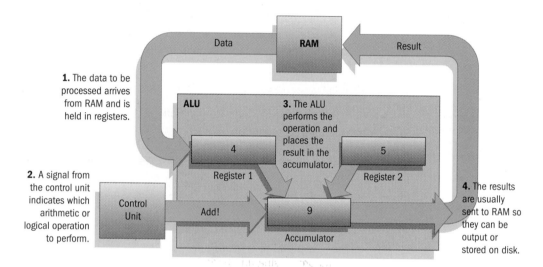

1. The data to be processed arrives from RAM and is held in registers.

ALU

3. The ALU performs the operation and places the result in the accumulator.

4

Register 1

5

Register 2

2. A signal from the control unit indicates which arithmetic or logical operation to perform.

Control Unit

Add!

9

Accumulator

4. The results are usually sent to RAM so they can be output or stored on disk.

Data   RAM   Result

How does the ALU get its data, and how does it know which arithmetic or logical operation it must perform? The **control unit** directs and coordinates processing. It retrieves each instruction in sequence from RAM and places it in a special **instruction register**. The control unit then interprets the instruction to find out what needs to be done. According to its interpretation, the control unit sends signals to the data bus to fetch data from RAM, and to the arithmetic logic unit to perform a process, as shown in Figure 4-15.

Figure 4-15
How the control unit works

Control Unit

1. The control unit retrieves an instruction from RAM and puts it in the **instruction register**.

Instruction pointer

M1

Instruction register

Add two numbers

2. The RAM address of the instruction is kept in the **instruction pointer**. When the instruction has been executed, the address in the instruction pointer changes to indicate the RAM address of the next instruction to be executed.

RAM

Address M1
Add two numbers

Address M2
Put result in M3

Address M3

3. The control unit interprets the instruction in its instruction register.

This instruction requires addition

ALU

Add!

4. Depending on the instruction, the control unit will get data from RAM, tell the ALU to perform an operation, or change the memory address in the instruction pointer.

Instructions

What specifies the steps that the CPU must perform to accomplish a task?

A computer accomplishes a complex task by performing a series of very simple steps, referred to as instructions. An **instruction** tells the computer to perform a specific arithmetic, logical, or control operation.

An instruction has two parts: the op code and the operands. An **op code**, which is short for operation code, is a command word for an operation such as add, compare, or jump. The **operands** for an instruction specify the data or the address of the data for the operation. Let's look at an example of an instruction:

op code ⟶ **JMP M1** ⟵ **operand**

In the instruction JMP M1, the op code is JMP and the operand is M1. The op code JMP means *jump* or go to a different instruction. The operand M1 is the RAM address of the instruction to which the computer is supposed to go. The instruction JMP M1 has only one operand, but some other instructions have more than one operand. For example, the instruction to add the contents of register 1 and register 2 has two operands:

op code ⟶ **ADD REG1 REG2** ⟵ **second operand**

↑

first operand

The list of instructions that a central processing unit performs is known as its **instruction set**. Every task a computer performs must be described in terms of the limited list of instructions in the instruction set. As you look at the list of instructions in Figure 4-16, consider that the computer must use a set of instructions such as this for all the tasks it helps you perform—from word processing to database management.

> An instruction tells the computer how to perform a single operation. Many instructions are required to accomplish a task such as adding a column of numbers.

▶ **Figure 4-16**
A simple microcomputer instruction set

Op Code	Operation	Example
INP	Input the given value into the specified memory address	INP 7 M1
CLA	Clear the accumulator to 0	CLA
MAM	Move the value from the accumulator to the specified memory location	MAM M1
MMR	Move the value from the specified memory location to the specified register	MMR M1 REG1
MRA	Move the value from the specified register to the accumulator	MRA REG1
MAR	Move the value from the accumulator to the specified register	MAR REG1
ADD	Add the values in two registers, place result in accumulator	ADD REG1 REG2
SUB	Subtract the value in the second register from the value in the first register, place the result in the accumulator	SUB REG1 REG2
MUL	Multiply the values in two registers, place the result in the accumulator	MUL REG1 REG2
DIV	Divide the value in the first register by the value in the second register, place the result in the accumulator	DIV REG1 REG2
INC	Increment the value in the register by 1	INC REG1
DEC	Decrement the value in the register by 1	DEC REG1
CMP	Compare the values in two registers; values are equal, place 1 in the accumulator, otherwise place 0 in the accumulator	CMP REG1 REG2
JMP	Jump to the instruction at the specified memory address	JMP P2
JPZ	Jump to the instruction at the specified address if the accumulator holds a 0	JPZ P3
JPN	Jump to the instruction at the specified address if the accumulator does not hold a 0	JPN P2
HLT	Halt program execution	HLT

Figure 4-17
Instruction cycle

Figure 4-18
Processing an
instruction

Instruction Cycle

How does a computer process instructions?

The term **instruction cycle** refers to the process in which a computer executes a single instruction. The instruction cycle is repeated each time the computer executes an instruction. The steps in this cycle are summarized in Figure 4-17.

You have all the pieces you need to understand the details of the instruction cycle. You know how the ALU performs arithmetic and logical operations and how the control unit retrieves data from RAM and tells the ALU which operation to perform. Figure 4-18 shows how the ALU, control unit, and RAM work together to process instructions.

1. The instruction pointer indicates the memory location that holds the first instruction (M1).

2. The computer fetches the instruction and puts it into the instruction register.

3. The computer executes the instructions in the instruction register; it moves the contents of M6 into register 1 of the ALU.

4. The instruction pointer changes to point to the memory location that holds the next instruction.

5. The computer fetches the instruction and puts it into the instruction register.

6. The computer executes the instructions; it moves the contents of M7 into register 2 of the ALU.

7. The instruction pointer changes to point to the next instruction.

Control Unit

Instruction pointer

M3

8. The computer fetches the instruction and puts it in the instruction register.

M1 MMR M6 R1
M2 MMR M7 R2
M3 ADD

Control Unit

Instruction pointer

M3

Instruction register

ADD

9. The computer executes the instruction. The result is put in the accumulator.

Control Unit

ALU

Accumulator

300

R1

100

Instruction register

ADD

R2

200

Study Figure 4-18 carefully so you understand the instruction execution cycle. You can test your understanding by answering Questions 8 and 9 in the Chapter Review.

CPU Performance

How does the architecture of a computer contribute to its performance?

All CPUs are not created equal; some process data faster than others. CPU speed is influenced by several factors including clock rate, word size, cache, and instruction set size. Specifications for these factors allow you to compare different CPUs.

Before you learn more about the factors that affect CPU performance, you should understand that a computer system with a high-performance CPU might not necessarily provide great overall performance. You know the old saying that a chain is only as strong as it weakest link. A computer system might also have weak links. Even with a high-performance processor, a computer system with a slow hard disk, no disk cache, and a small amount of RAM is likely to be slow at tasks such as starting programs, loading data files, printing, and scrolling through long documents.

Lab

CPU Simulator

Most microcomputers keep track of the date and time using a CMOS chip that runs on battery power.

Clock Rate

Do all computer clocks have to operate at the same rate to keep the right time and date?

A computer contains a **system clock** that emits pulses to establish the timing for all system operations. The system clock is not the same as a "real-time clock" that keeps track of the time of day. The system clock operates at a speed quite different from that of a clock that keeps track of minutes and seconds.

The system clock sets the speed for data transport and instruction execution. To understand how this works, visualize a team of oarsmen on a Viking ship. The ship's coxswain beats on a drum to coordinate the rowers. A computer's system clock and a ship's coxswain accomplish essentially the same task—they set the pace of activity. Boom! A stream of bits takes off from RAM and heads to the CPU. Boom! The control unit reads an instruction. Boom! The ALU adds two numbers together.

The clock rate of a computer is measured in MHz, millions of instructions per second.

The clock rate set by the system clock determines the speed at which the computer can execute an instruction and, therefore, limits the number of instructions the computer can complete within a specific amount of time. The time to complete an instruction cycle is measured in megahertz (MHz), or millions of cycles per second.

Although some instructions require multiple cycles to complete, you can think of processor speed as the number of instructions the processor can execute in one second. For example, the 4.77 MHz microprocessor in the very first model of the IBM PC executed 4.77 million instructions per second. Today, microprocessor speeds exceed 100 million instructions per second. If all other specifications are identical, higher megahertz ratings mean faster processing.

Word Size

Which is faster, an 8-bit processor or a 64-bit processor?

Word size refers to the number of bits the central processing unit can manipulate at one time. Word size is based on the size of the registers in the CPU and the number of data lines in the bus. For example, a CPU with an 8-bit word size is referred to as an 8-bit processor; it has 8 bit registers and manipulates 8 bits at a time.

Word size is measured in bits, not bytes.

Computers with a large word size can process more data in each instruction cycle than computers with a small word size. Processing more data in each cycle contributes to increased performance. For example, the first microcomputers used 8-bit microprocessors, but today's faster computers use 32-bit or 64-bit microprocessors.

Cache

Disk cache speeds up access to data on disk; is there a similar process that speeds access to data from RAM?

Disk cache, explained in Chapter 3, and RAM cache are not the same. Disk cache works between the disk and memory. RAM cache works with data between RAM and the central processing unit.

Another factor that affects CPU performance is cache. **Cache,** sometimes called **RAM cache** or **cache memory,** is special high-speed memory that gives the CPU more rapid access to data. A high-speed CPU can execute an instruction so quickly that it often waits for data to be delivered from RAM; this slows processing. The cache ensures that data is immediately available whenever the central processing unit requests it.

As you begin a task, the computer anticipates what data the central processing unit is likely to need and loads or *caches* this data into the cache area. Then, when an instruction calls for data, the central processing unit first checks to see if the required data is in the cache. If the required data is there, the central processing unit takes the data from the cache instead of fetching it from RAM, which takes longer. All other factors being equal, more cache means faster processing.

Instruction Set Complexity

What's the difference between CISC and RISC?

As programmers developed various instruction sets for computers, they tended to add more and more complex instructions that took up many bytes in memory and required several clock cycles for execution. A computer based on a central processing unit with a complex instruction set came to be known as a **complex instruction set computer**, or **CISC**.

In 1975 John Cocke, an IBM research scientist, discovered that most of the work done by a microprocessor requires only a small subset of the available instruction set. Further research showed that only 20% of the instructions of a CISC machine do about 80% of the work. Cocke's research resulted in the development of microprocessors with streamlined instruction sets, called RISC machines.

The microprocessor of a **reduced instruction set computer**, or **RISC**, has a limited set of Instructions that it can perform very quickly. In theory, therefore, a RISC machine should be faster than a CISC machine for most processing tasks. Some computer scientists believe, however, that a balance or hybrid of CISC and RISC technologies produce the most efficient and flexible computers.

Pipelining and Parallel Processing

Can a CPU increase its performance by executing more than one instruction at a time?

Computers with a single processor execute instructions "serially," that is, one instruction at a time. Usually, the processor must complete all four steps in the instruction cycle before it begins to execute the next instruction. However, with a technology called **pipelining**, the processor begins executing an instruction before it completes the previous instruction. Pipelining speeds up processing in computers with a single processor; it is also implemented on computers with multiple processors.

A computer that has more than one processor can execute multiple instructions at the same time. This method of executing instructions is called **parallel processing**. Parallel processing increases the amount of processing a computer can accomplish in a specific amount of time.

You learned about John von Neumann in Chapter 1. The type of computers he defined in his 1945 paper are referred to as von Neumann machines.

To take advantage of parallel processing, however, requires special software. Computers that are capable of parallel processing are called parallel computers or non-von Neumann machines. Figure 4-19 explains the concept of parallel processing.

Figure 4-19
How parallel processing works

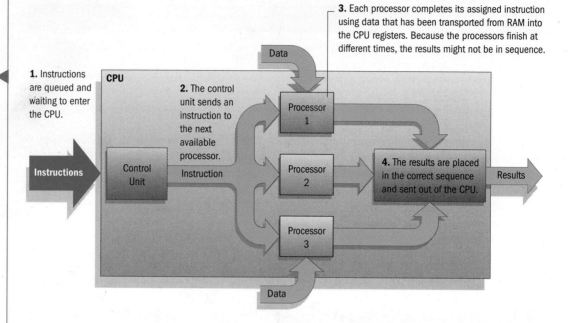

1. Instructions are queued and waiting to enter the CPU.

2. The control unit sends an instruction to the next available processor.

3. Each processor completes its assigned instruction using data that has been transported from RAM into the CPU registers. Because the processors finish at different times, the results might not be in sequence.

4. The results are placed in the correct sequence and sent out of the CPU.

CPU

Instructions

Control Unit

Instruction

Data

Processor 1

Processor 2

Processor 3

Data

Results

To get a clearer picture of serial, pipelining, and parallel processing techniques, consider an analogy—baking pizzas. Serial processing is like a pizzeria with only one oven that can bake only one pizza at a time. Just as this oven bakes only one pizza at a time, a serial processor processes only one instruction at a time.

Pipelining is similar to a pizza conveyor belt. A pizza starts moving along the conveyor belt, but before it reaches the end of the belt, another pizza starts moving along the belt. Likewise, a pipelining computer starts processing an instruction; but before it completes the instruction, it begins processing another instruction.

Finally, parallel processing is similar to a pizzeria with many ovens. Just as these ovens can bake more than one pizza at a time, a parallel processor can execute more than one instruction at a time.

Quick Check

1 A microcomputer uses a(n) _____ chip as its CPU.

2 The _____ in the CPU performs arithmetic and logical operations such as adding or comparing two numbers.

3 The _____ in the CPU directs and coordinates the operation of the entire computer system.

4 A computer instruction has two parts: the _____ and the _____.

5 What are the four steps in the instruction cycle?

6 What factors affect the speed of a CPU?

I/O

When you purchase a computer, you can be fairly certain that before its useful life is over, you will want to add equipment to expand its capabilities. If you understand computer I/O, you will see how it is possible to expand a computer system.

I/O, pronounced "eye-oh," is computer jargon for input/output. I/O refers to collecting data for the microprocessor to manipulate and transporting results to display, print, and storage devices. I/O between the central processing unit and peripheral devices often involves a long path that moves data over the expansion bus, slots, cards, ports, and cables. Figure 4-20 is an overview of the I/O architecture described in the rest of this section.

▶ **Figure 4-20**
I/O architecture

Data originates in RAM.

The expansion bus transports data.

An expansion slot provides a socket for expansion cards.

An expansion card is plugged into the expansion slot.

The expansion card contains a port.

A data cable from a peripheral device plugs into the port.

Expansion Bus

The expansion bus is an extension of the data bus.

What's the difference between the expansion bus and the data bus?

You already learned that a data bus transports data between RAM and the CPU. The data bus also extends to other parts of the computer. The segment of the data bus that transports data between RAM and peripheral devices is called the **expansion bus**.

Expansion Slots

How do I use expansion slots?

On the main board, the expansion bus terminates at an expansion slot. An **expansion slot** is a socket into which you can plug a small circuit board called an expansion card. The expansion slots on mainframes, minicomputers, and microcomputers provide a way to connect a large variety of peripheral devices.

Most microcomputers have four to eight expansion slots, but some of these slots usually contain expansion cards when you purchase the computer. The number of empty slots in your computer dictates its expandability.

Suppose that a few months after you purchase your computer, you decide you want to add sound capability. To find out if you have adequate expansion capability, turn your computer off, unplug it, then open the system unit case. Some computers contain more than one type of expansion slot, so the slots in your computer might appear to be different sizes. If you have an empty expansion slot, you can insert an expansion card, as shown in Figure 4-21.

Figure 4-21 ◀
Inserting an expansion card into a slot

An expansion card has a *card edge* connector with metal contacts that connect to the circuitry on the card.

A computer often contains several sizes of expansion slots.

When the card is inserted into the slot, the metal card edge connector contacts the connector in the slot to make a circuit for data transport.

An expansion slot contains metallic contacts that connect to the expansion bus.

Expansion bus

Expansion Cards

What kinds of expansion cards are available?

An **expansion card**, also referred to as an **expansion board** or a **controller card**, is a circuit board that plugs into an expansion slot. An expansion card provides the I/O circuitry for peripheral devices and sometimes contains an expansion device. For example, if you want to add sound capability, you would purchase and install an expansion card called a sound card. The sound card contains the circuitry to convert digital signals from your computer to sounds that play through speakers. Once you have inserted the sound card into an expansion slot, you can connect speakers or headphones. Microcomputer users can select from a wide variety of expansion cards, such as those shown in Figure 4-22.

A **graphics card** connects your monitor and computer.

Figure 4-22
Expansion cards

A **network card** connects your computer to the other computers on a local area network.

A **modem card** connects your computer to the telephone system so you can transport data from one computer to another.

A port is not the same as a slot. A port is located on the outside of the system unit, whereas a slot is located inside the unit.

Expansion Ports

How do I connect a peripheral device to an expansion card?

To connect a peripheral device to an expansion card, you plug a cable from the peripheral device into the expansion port on the expansion card. An **expansion port** is a location that passes data in and out of a computer or peripheral device. An expansion port is often housed on an expansion card in a way that it is accessible through a hole in the back of the computer system unit. A port might also be connected directly to the main board, instead of to an expansion card.

To many computer users, the back of a computer is a confusing array of unlabeled ports, connectors, and cables. Study Figure 4-23 to become familiar with the shapes of the most frequently used expansion ports.

Figure 4-23 ◀
Microcomputer
expansion ports

A **parallel port** provides a connection for transmitting data eight bits at a time over a cable with eight separate data lines. Because all eight bits travel at the same time, parallel transmission is relatively fast. Parallel transmission is typically used to send data to a printer.

In a microcomputer the parallel port is either built into the main board or mounted on an expansion card. The cable that connects two parallel ports contains 25 wires. Eight of these wires carry data and the remaining wires carry control signals that help maintain orderly transmission and reception.

Because the wires that carry data run parallel to each other for the full length of the cable, the signals in the cables tend to interfere with each other over long distances. Parallel cables can provide reliable connections for relatively short distances—from 10 to 50 feet, depending on how well the cable is shielded from electrical interference.

A **SCSI port** provides a connection for one or more peripheral devices. SCSI (pronounced "scuzzy") stands for small computer system interface. Unlike a parallel port, to which you can connect only one device, you can connect many devices to a single SCSI port by connecting one device to another in a chain. SCSI ports are particularly popular on Macintosh computers for attaching hard disk drives, CD-ROMs, and scanners.

A **serial port**, sometimes referred to as an **RS-232C port**, provides a connection for transmitting data one bit at a time. A serial port connects your computer to a device such as a modem, which requires two-way data transmission, or to a device such as a mouse, which requires one-way data transmission. A serial cable contains one data line and an assortment of control lines.

Because a serial cable requires fewer data lines, it is less susceptible to interference than a parallel cable. This makes serial connections more suitable than parallel connections for devices that are located greater distances from the computer.

A **MIDI port** is a special type of serial interface for connecting a computer to music synthesizers and musical instruments. MIDI (pronounced "middy") stands for musical instrument digital interface. Most of the keyboards used by rock musicians have a MIDI port so they can be connected to a computer to record, manipulate, and play back music.

Quick Check

1. A(n) _____ is an electronic path that transports data between RAM and expansion slots.

2. A(n) _____ is a small circuit board that plugs into an expansion slot.

3. An expansion _____ is located inside the system, whereas an expansion _____ is located on the exterior of the system unit.

4. Four types of expansion ports are _____, _____, _____ and _____.

User Focus:

The Boot Process

4.5

Now that you have an understanding about how I/O, RAM, ROM, and the CPU operate, you're ready to learn how they all work together to prepare a computer for accepting commands each time you turn it on.

The sequence of events that occurs between the time you turn on a computer and the time it is ready for you to issue commands is referred to as the **boot process**. Micro, mini, and mainframe computers all require a boot process. In this section of the chapter you'll learn about the microcomputer boot process because that is the type of computer you are most likely to use.

You'll find out what happens during each step of the boot process for a typical IBM-compatible computer and what you should do when the boot process doesn't proceed smoothly. Of course, even when you know how to troubleshoot computer problems, you should always follow the guidelines provided by your school or employer when you encounter equipment problems.

An Overview

If the computer memory is blank when I turn it on, how does it know how to start up?

As you learned earlier, one of the most important components of a computer—RAM—is volatile, so it cannot hold any data when the power is off. It also cannot hold the operating system instructions when the power is off. Therefore, the computer cannot use RAM to "remember" many basic functions, such as how to deal with input and communicate output to the external world. A computer needs some way to get operating system files into RAM. That's one of the main objectives of the boot process. In general, the boot process follows these six steps:

1. **Power Up**—When you turn on the power switch, the power light is illuminated, and power is distributed to the internal fan and main board.

2. **Start Boot Program**—The microprocessor begins to execute the instructions stored in ROM.

3. **Power-On Self-Test**—The computer performs diagnostic tests of crucial system components.

4. **Load Operating System**—The operating system is copied from a disk to RAM.

5. **Check Configuration and Customization**—The microprocessor reads configuration data and executes any customized start-up routines specified by the user.

6. **Ready for Commands and Data**—The computer is ready for you to enter commands and data.

Figure 4-24
Power up

Fan

Power Up

What's the first thing that happens when I turn the power on?

The first stage in the boot process is the power-up stage. The fan in the power supply begins to spin, and the power light on the case of the computer comes on, as shown in Figure 4-24.

If you turn on the computer and the power light does not come on, the system is not getting power. You can do several things to fix this problem. First, you can check the power cord at the back of the computer to make sure it is firmly plugged into the wall and into the system unit. If the plugs are in place, test the wall outlet by plugging in another electrical device, such as a lamp. If the wall outlet is supplying power, the power cord is plugged in, and the power light still does not come on, then the computer's power supply might have failed. If you encounter this problem, you need to contact a technical support person for assistance.

Start Boot Program

What happens if the ROM is malfunctioning?

When you turn on the computer, the microprocessor begins to execute the boot program stored in ROM, as shown in Figure 4-25.

Figure 4-25
ROM boot program activated

When ROM receives power, the programs it contains are activated.

Power flows through the power supply to the main board components.

If the ROM chips, RAM modules, or microprocessor are malfunctioning, the microprocessor is unable to run the boot program and the computer stops or "hangs." You know you have a problem at this stage of the boot process if the power light is on and you can hear the fan, but there is no message on the screen and nothing else happens. This problem requires the assistance of a technical support person.

Power-On Self-Test

Can the computer check to determine if all its components are functioning correctly?

The next step in the boot process is the **power-on self-test (POST)**, which diagnoses problems in the computer, as shown in Figure 4-26.

The POST first checks the graphics card that connects your monitor to the computer. If the graphics card is working, a message such as "Video BIOS ver 2.1 1995" appears on the screen. Many computers beep several times if the graphics card fails the test. The number of beeps depends on the ROM used in your computer. If your computer beeps and does not display the graphics card message, the graphics card is probably malfunctioning. You should contact a technical support person to have the graphics card checked.

If the graphics card passes the diagnostic test, the computer next tests RAM by placing data in each memory location, then retrieving that data to see if it is correct. The computer displays the amount of memory tested. If any errors are encountered during the RAM test, the POST stops and displays a message that indicates a RAM problem.

The POST then checks the keyboard. On most computers you can see the keyboard indicator lights flash when the keyboard test is in progress. If the keyboard is not correctly attached or if a key is stuck, the computer beeps and displays a keyboard error message. If a keyboard error occurs, you should turn the computer off and make sure that nothing is holding down a key on the keyboard. Next, unplug the keyboard and carefully plug it back into the computer. Finally, turn on the computer again to repeat the boot process. If the problem recurs, you might need to have your keyboard repaired or replaced.

The final step in the POST is the drive test. If you watch the hard disk drive and floppy disk drives during this test, you will see the drive activity lights flash on for a moment, and you will hear the drives spin. The drive test should only take a second or two to complete. If the computer

Figure 4-26 ◀
Power-on self-test

1. The POST checks if the graphics card is working.

Power supply

2. All RAM addresses are tested to make sure they can hold data.

4. The POST tests the hard disk and floppy disk drives.

3. The keyboard check makes sure a keyboard is attached to the computer.

pauses on this test, there might be a problem with one of the drives, and you should consult a technical support person.

Load Operating System

How does the computer find the operating system to load it into RAM?

After successfully completing the POST, the computer continues to follow the instructions in ROM to load the operating system, as shown in Figure 4-27.

Figure 4-27
Loading the operating system

1. If the computer finds a disk in drive A:, it uses A: as the default drive.

2. If the computer cannot find a disk in drive A:, it uses drive C: as the default drive. With drive C: as the default, the computer looks for the operating system files on drive C:.

3. The computer loads the operating system from the default drive into RAM.

The computer first checks drive A: to see if it contains a disk. If there is a disk in this drive, drive A: becomes the **default drive**. The computer uses the default drive for the rest of the computing session unless you specify a different one.

If there is no disk in drive A: but the computer has a drive C:, the computer uses drive C: as the default drive. If your computer has a hard disk, you generally want drive C: to be the default drive, so it is best not to put disks in any of the floppy disk drives until the boot process is complete. Otherwise, the computer recognizes the floppy disk drive as the default.

Next, the computer tries to locate and load operating system files from the default drive. First, the computer looks for two operating system files: **Io.Sys** and **Msdos.Sys**. If these files do not exist on the disk, the boot process stops and displays a message such as "Non-system disk or disk error" or "Cannot load a file." If you see one of these messages, there is probably a disk in drive A: that should not be there—remember that you want your computer to use drive C: as the default. Remove the disk from drive A: so your computer looks at the hard drive for the operating system files.

The microprocessor next attempts to load another operating system file, **Command.Com**. Two problems could occur at this stage of the boot process, and both problems have the same error message—"Bad or missing command interpreter." First problem: the file **Command.Com** might be missing because someone inadvertently erased it. Second problem: your disk might contain the wrong version of **Command.Com** because someone inadvertently copied a different version onto the computer.

If you encounter either problem, you should turn off the computer and make sure drive A: is empty, then turn the computer on again. If the "Bad or missing command interpreter" message appears when you turn the computer on again, you should turn the computer off, then find a bootable floppy disk. A **bootable floppy disk**, such as the one that came with the computer, contains operating system files. Put this floppy disk in drive A: and turn on the computer again. Even if you are successful using a floppy disk to boot your system, you need to correct the **Command.Com** problem on your hard disk. A technical support person or experienced user can help you do this.

Check Configuration and Customization

Does the computer get all its configuration data from CMOS?

Early in the boot process, the computer checks CMOS to determine the amount of installed RAM and the types of available disk drives. Often, however, more configuration data is needed for the computer to properly access all available devices. In the next stage of the boot process, the computer searches the root directory of the boot disk for configuration files, as shown in Figure 4-28.

Figure 4-28
Load configuration
data

The computer searches the
hard disk for files such as
Config.Sys and **Autoexec.Bat.**

Config.sys Autoexec.bat

Configuration files are copied
into RAM, then executed.

The computer also searches the default drive for customized startup instructions. On some computers these instructions are stored in a file called **Autoexec.Bat** or a Windows startup group, which you can modify to customize your computing environment. For example, you might customize the startup instructions so your To-do list document appears every time you start your computer.

Ready for Commands and Data

How do I know when the computer has finished booting?

The boot process is complete when the computer is ready to accept your commands. Usually the computer displays the operating system main screen or prompt at the end of the boot process. If you are using Windows, you will see the Windows desktop. If you are using DOS, you will see the operating system prompt shown in Figure 4-29.

When the computer displays the operating system prompt, you can enter commands and launch programs.

▶ **Figure 4-29**
The boot process is complete

End Note Today's computers are digital electronic devices that accomplish complex tasks by performing a fairly limited set of instructions at breakneck speed. Understanding how a computer manipulates data coded as 1s and 0s should help dispel some of the mystery about what goes on "under the hood" of a microcomputer. Also, you can apply this understanding to troubleshooting your way past computer equipment problems.

Troubleshooting is not difficult if you follow a logical procedure and think creatively. When you have a problem with a computer, first try to make a specific statement that describes the problem. Saying "It's broken!" is not very useful. A more specific description might be something like, "I turned my computer on, but the monitor is blank."

Try to make some hypotheses, or guesses, about the cause of the problem. Be creative—try to think of at least three potential causes. For the monitor problem you might hypothesize that the monitor isn't getting power, that it is not getting a video signal, or that it has somehow "burned out."

Ask yourself which of these potential causes would have the simplest solution. Start with the simple solution first—the monitor might not be getting power because it's not turned on or because the power cable isn't plugged in. These are the things you check first. Of course, you should follow the repair policies of your school or place of employment by not trying to fix equipment that must be repaired by a qualified service agent. And remember the golden rule of troubleshooting: Try at least three things before you call for help.

Review

1. Below each heading in this chapter, there is a question. Look back through this chapter and answer each of these questions using your own words.

2. Make a list of the boldface terms in this chapter, and use your own words to define each term.

3. Place an X in the following table to indicate which characteristics apply to each type of memory.

	RAM	Virtual Memory	ROM	CMOS
Holds user data such as documents		ʔ		
Holds program instructions such as word processor				
Holds boot program				
Holds configuration data for hard disk type				
Temporary	X			
Permanent				
Battery powered				ʔ
Disk-based				

4. Label the microcomputer components shown in a through g.

a.

b.

c.

d.

e.

f.

g.

5. Use Figure 4-7 to write out the ASCII code for the following phrase: **Power Up!**

6. Create a conceptual diagram like the one in Figure 4-9 to show how the phrase **Power Up!** is stored in RAM.

7. Imagine you are a teacher. Write a one- or two-page script explaining the instruction cycle to your class, and design at least three visual aids you would use as illustrations.

8. In Figure 4-30, after the processor executes the three instructions in RAM, what are the final values in Register 1, Register 2, and the accumulator? (Hint: Refer to Figure 4-16.)

▶ **Figure 4-30**

Program			
P1	MMR	M1	REG1
P2	MMR	M2	REG2
P3	ADD	REG1	REG2
P4	MAM	M3	
P5	HLT		
Data			
M1	5		
M2	3		
M3	0		

CONTROL UNIT	
INSTRUCTION POINTER	P1
INSTRUCTION REGISTER	

ALU	
ACCUMULATOR	
REG1	
REG2	

9. What are the values in Register 1, Register 2, and the accumulator when the computer has completed the instructions in the RAM of Figure 4-31?

Figure 4-31

Program			
P1	MMR	M1	REG1
P2	MMR	M2	REG2
P3	INC	REG1	
P4	DEC	REG2	
P5	MUL	REG1	REG2
P6	MAM	M3	
P7	HLT		
Data			
M1	7		
M2	4		
M3	0		

CONTROL UNIT	
INSTRUCTION POINTER	P1
INSTRUCTION REGISTER	

ALU	
ACCUMULATOR	
REG1	
REG2	

10. Suppose you are using the Microsoft Word for DOS word processor, and you are creating a document called **Report1.Doc**. Describe the contents of RAM.

11. Compare the specifications for Computer 1 and Computer 2 below. Is 100 MHz better than 75 MHz? Is a 32-bit word size better than a 64-bit word size? Circle the best performance rating in each category.

Performance Factor	Computer 1	Computer 2
Clock Rate	100 MHz	75 MHz
Word Size	32 bits	64 bits
Cache	256 K	32 K
Instruction Set	CISC	RISC
Pipelining	Yes	No
Parallel Processing	No	Yes

12. Use your own words to write a one-paragraph description of pipelining.

13. Label each of the I/O components illustrated in Figure 4-32.

▶ **Figure 4-32**

14. Think about the concepts in the first four sections of this chapter: Digital Electronics, Memory, Central Processing Unit, and I/O. Using these concepts, put together your own description of how a computer processes data. You can use a narrative description and/or sketches.

Projects

1. The Araphulians' Computer Read the article about the Araphulian computer in the April 19, 1988 issue of *Scientific American*, entitled "An Ancient Rope-and-Pulley Computer is Unearthed in the Jungle of Araphulia," then answer the following questions:

    a. The Araphulians did not use electricity. How then did they represent 0s and 1s?

    b. What did the Araphulian's *inverter box* accomplish?

    c. The archaeologists excavating the Araphulian site found a large overgrown field where several thousand rotting flip-flop boxes were buried. What part of the computer was at this site?

    d. Redraw the flip-flop diagram from the article and label it to show how it worked.

2. Looking From the Inside Out After disconnecting the power cable, carefully open the case of a computer system unit. Draw a sketch and label each of the components you see inside. Try to locate and label all the components shown in Figure 4-1.

3. The History of the IC Computers would not be available to individuals today if not for the invention of the integrated circuit. Just four months apart in 1959, Jack Kilby and Robert Noyce independently created working models of the circuit that was to transform the computer industry. Jack Kilby worked at Texas Instruments, and you can find reproductions of his original research notes on the Web site *http://www.ti.com/corp/docs/history/firstic.htm*. Robert Noyce developed the integrated circuit while CEO of Fairchild Semiconductor, but he left Fairchild to form Intel.

Use your library and Internet resources to research the impact of the integrated circuit on the computer industry, then do one of the following:

a. Write a two- to three-page paper summarizing how the integrated circuit was used in the first five years after it was invented.

b. Write two one-page biographical sketches; one of Jack Kilby and one of Robert Noyce.

c. Create a diagram of the "family tree" of computer technologies that resulted from the development of the integrated circuit.

d. Based on the facts you have gathered about the development of the computer industry, write a two- to three-page paper describing the computer industry today if the integrated circuit had not been invented.

4. Scanning a Computer Ad for Key Terms Photocopy a full-page computer ad from a current issue of a computer magazine, such as *Computer Shopper*. On the copy of the ad use a colored pen and circle any of the key terms that were presented in this chapter. Make sure you watch for abbreviations; they are frequently used in computer ads. On a separate sheet of paper, or using a word processor, make a list of each term you circled and write a definition of each.

5. Researching and Writing about RAM Suppose you are a computer industry analyst preparing an article on computer memory for a popular computer magazine. Gather as much information as you can about RAM, including current pricing, the amount of RAM that comes installed in a typical computer, tips for adding RAM to computers, and so forth. If you have Internet access, you might find useful information at sites such as *http://www.micron.com*. Use a word processor to write a one- to two-page article that would help your magazine's readers understand all about RAM.

6. Researching and Writing about RISC Write a one- to two-page paper about RISC technology. You might want to explore the history of the concept beginning with John Cocke's research. You can also look at the use of RISC processors for the type of powerful workstations typically used for engineering and CAD applications. You might also research Apple's new PowerPC computer that uses the PowerPC RISC chip. If you have Internet access check IBM's site: *http://www.ibm.com*.

7. Expansion Ports Look in computer magazines to find advertisements for three peripheral devices that connect to a computer using different ports or buses. For example, you might find a modem that connects to the serial port. Photocopy each of these three ads. For each device circle on the photocopy the device's brand name, model name and/or number, and the port or bus it uses. Also make sure you provide your instructor with the name and publication date of the magazine and the page number on which you found the information.

8. Interview with a Computer User Complete the following steps to interview one of your friends who has a computer, and write a report that describes how your friend could expand his or her computer system.

a. Find out as many technical details as you can about your friend's computer, including the type of computer, the type and speed of the microprocessor, the amount of memory, the configuration of disk drives, the capacity of the disk drives, the resolution of the monitor, and so on.

b. Find out how your friend might want to expand his or her computer system either now or sometime in the future. For example, your friend might want to add a printer, a sound card, CD-ROM drive, memory, or a monitor.

c. Look through computer magazines to find a solution for at least one of your friend's expansion plans. What you would recommend as a solution? If money was no object would your recommendation change? Why or why not? And what would your new recommendation be?

d. Write a two-page report describing your friend's computer and his or her expansion needs. Then describe the solution(s) you found.

9. Observing the Boot Process Using Section 4.5 as your guide, make a detailed list of each step in the boot process. Take your list into the computer lab and boot one of the computers. As the computer boots, read your list to make sure it is correct. For which steps in the boot process can you see or hear something actually happening?

Resources

10. Can a Computer Make Errors?

In 1994 Intel released the Pentium microprocessor. Within a matter of weeks, rumors began to circulate that the Pentium chip had a bug that caused errors in some calculations. As the rumors spread, corporate computer users became nervous about the numbers that appeared on spreadsheets calculated on computers with the Pentium processor. How can a computer make such mistakes? Are computers with Pentium processors destined for the dumpster? Is there any way users can save the money they have invested in their Pentium computers?

Suppose you own a computer store that sold many computers with the flawed Pentium microprocessor. Your customers are calling you to get the straight facts. Use your library and Internet resources to gather as much reliable information as you can about the Pentium flaw. Use this information to write a one-page information sheet for your customers. You might find the following resources useful:

- Intel's Internet site: *http://www.intel.com*

- "The Truth Behind the Pentium Bug" *Byte*, March 1995.

11. Troubleshooting Scenarios—What Would You Do?

Your instructor might want you to do this project individually or in a small group. For each of the following scenarios, indicate what might be wrong.

a. You turn on the computer's power switch and nothing happens—no lights, no beep, nothing. What's the most likely problem?

b. You turn on your computer and the computer completes the POST test. You see the light on drive A: and you hear the drive power up, but you get a message on the screen that says "Cannot load file." Explain what caused this message to appear and explain exactly what you should do to complete the boot process.

c. You are using a word processor to write an essay for your English composition course. You have completed eight pages, and you have periodically saved the document. Suddenly, you notice that when you press a key nothing happens. You try the mouse, but it no longer moves the pointer on the screen. What should you do next?

d. You turn on your computer, see the power light, and hear the fan. Then, the computer begins to beep repeatedly. What would you suspect is the problem?

- **Advanced Micro Devices, Inc. Web site**, *http://www.amd.com* AMD is one of the industry leaders in microprocessor research and production. At its Web site you'll find information on current and future microprocessor technology.

- **Dewdney, A. K.** "Computer Recreations: An ancient rope-and-pulley computer is unearthed in the jungle of Apraphul." *Scientific American*, April 1985, pp. 118–121. What begins as an April Fools' joke turns out to be an excellent explanation of the basic circuitry in a digital computer.

- **Foster, C.** *Computer Architecture*. New York: Van Nostrand Reinhold, 1970. If you want to learn more about computer architecture, this is one of the classics. Be warned, it's not easy reading.

- **Intel web site**, *http://www.intel.com* Intel is the world leader in microprocessor development and production. At its Web site you'll find information about the newest microprocessors. Intel has devoted substantial research efforts into parallel processing, and you can find information on this topic at the Intel site.

- **Kidder, T.** *The Soul of a New Machine*. Boston: Little, Brown, 1981. Kidder writes insightfully about the heady days when the computer industry was venturing into brave new worlds. This book describes a team of researchers who are consumed by a project to build the best computer.

- **Micron, Inc. Web site**, *http://www.micron.com* Micron, Inc. manufactures memory, main boards, and computer systems. Its Internet site contains useful information on memory technology.

- **Motorola Web site**, *http://www.motorola.com* Apple Computer introduced RISC architecture in its PowerPC products in 1994. The PowerPC microprocessor is manufactured by Motorola. At the Motorola Web site, you can find more information on RISC architecture.

- **Rosch, W. L.** *The Winn L. Rosch Hardware Bible*, 3rd ed. New York: Prentice Hall, 1994. Voted as one of the 20 all-time best microcomputer books by *Computer Magazine*, this 1,097-page book is packed with facts about personal computers.

- **Shurkin, J.** *Engines of the Mind: A History of the Computer*. New York: W. W. Norton & Company, 1984. This book is a lively account of the pioneers of the computer industry. It focuses on people and personalities, rather than on machines, and gives the reader a human perspective on the nature of creativity and invention.

■ **Texas Instruments Web site,** *http://www.ti.com* Jack Kilby, an employee of Texas Instruments, was one of the pioneers in the invention of the integrated circuit. Texas Instruments' Web site contains some historical information on integrated circuits as well as information about current developments in memory and processor technology.

■ **White, R.** *How Computers Work.* Emeryville, CA: Ziff-Davis Press, 1993. This book might be called the illustrated guide to how computers work because it contains so many great diagrams. If you are interested in what happens inside the system unit, this is the place to begin.

■ **Wyant, G. and Hammerstrom, T.** *How Microprocessors Work.* Emeryville, CA: Ziff-Davis Press, 1994. If you want to understand microprocessors in more detail, you can pick up this book at most bookstores. Full-page diagrams help to explain technical concepts clearly.

Lab Assignments

Binary Numbers

 Computers process and store numbers using the binary number system. Understanding binary numbers helps you recognize how digital computers work by simply turning electricity on and off. In this Lab, you learn about the binary number system and you learn how to convert numbers from binary to decimal and from decimal to binary.

1. Click the Steps button to learn about the binary number system. As you proceed through the Steps, answer all of the Quick Check questions that appear. After you complete the Steps, you will see a Quick Check Summary Report. Follow the instructions on the screen to print this report.

2. Click the Explore button, then click the Conversions button. Practice converting binary numbers into decimal numbers. For example, what is the decimal equivalent of 00010011? Calculate the decimal value on paper. To check your answer, enter the decimal number in the decimal box, and then click the binary boxes to show the 1s and 0s for the number you are converting. Click the Check It button to see if your conversion is correct.

Convert the following binary numbers into decimals:

   a. 00000101

   b. 00010111

   c. 01010101

   d. 10010010

   e. 11111110

3. In Explore, click the Conversions button. Practice converting decimal numbers into binary numbers. For example, what is the binary equivalent of 82? Do the conversion on paper. To check your answer, enter the decimal number in the decimal box, and then click the binary boxes to show the 1s and 0s of its binary equivalent. Click the Check It button to see if your conversion is correct.

Convert the following decimal numbers to binary numbers:

   a. 77

   b. 25

   c. 92

   d. 117

   e. 214

4. In Explore, click the Binary Number Quiz button. The quiz provides you ten numbers to convert. Make each conversion and type your answer in the box. Click the Check Answer button to see if you are correct. When you have completed all ten quiz questions, follow the instructions on the screen to print your quiz results.

CPU Simulator

 In a computer central processing unit (CPU), the arithmetic logic unit (ALU) performs instructions orchestrated by the control unit. Processing proceeds at a lightning pace, but each instruction accomplishes only a small step in the entire process. In this Lab you work with an animated CPU simulation to learn how computers execute assembly language programs. In the Explore section of the Lab, you have an opportunity to interpret programs, find program errors, and write your own short assembly language programs.

1. Click the Steps button to learn how to work the simulated CPU. As you proceed through the Steps, answer all of the Quick Check questions that appear. After you complete the Steps, you will see a Quick Check Summary Report. Follow the instructions on the screen to print this report.

2. Click the Explore button. Use the File menu to open a program called **add.cpu**. Use the Fetch Instruction and Execute Instruction buttons to step through the program. Then answer the following questions:

   a. How many instructions does this program contain?

   b. Where is the instruction pointer after the program is loaded but before it executes?

   c. What does the INP 3 M1 instruction accomplish?

   d. What does the MMR M1 REG1 instruction accomplish?

   e. Which memory location holds the instruction that adds the two numbers in REG1 and REG2?

   f. What is in the accumulator when the program execution is complete?

   g. Which memory address holds the sum of the two numbers when program execution is completed?

3. In Explore, use the File menu to open a program called **count5.cpu**. Use the Fetch Instruction and Execute Instruction buttons to step through the program. Then answer the following questions:

   a. What are the two input values for this program?

   b. What happens to the value in REG1 as the program executes?

   c. What happens when the program executes the JPZ P5 instruction?

   d. What are the final values in the accumulator and registers when program execution is complete?

4. In Explore, click File, then click New to make sure the CPU is empty. Write a program that follows these steps to add 8 and 6:

   a. Input 8 into memory address M3.

   b. Input 6 into memory address M5.

   c. Move the number in M3 to Register 1.

   d. Move the number in M5 to Register 2.

   e. Add the numbers in the registers.

   f. Move the value in the accumulator to memory address M1.

   g. Tell the program to halt.

Test your program to make sure it produces the answer 14 in address M1. When you are sure your program works, use the File menu to print your program.

5. In Explore, use the File menu to open a program called **Bad1.cpu**. This program is supposed to multiply two numbers together and put the result in memory location M3. However, the program contains an error.

   a. Which memory location holds the incorrect instruction?

   b. What instruction will make this program produce the correct result?

6. In Explore, use the CPU simulator to write a program to calculate the volume, in cubic feet, of the inside of a refrigerator. The answer should appear in the accumulator at the end of the program. The inside dimensions of the refrigerator are 5 feet, by 3 feet, by 2 feet. Make sure you test your program, then print it.

Troubleshooting

 Computers sometimes malfunction, so it is useful to have some skill at diagnosing, if not fixing, some of the hardware problems you might encounter. In the Troubleshooting Lab, you use a simulated computer that has trouble booting. You learn to make and test hypotheses that help you diagnose the cause of boot problems.

1. Click the Steps button to learn how to make and test hypotheses about hardware malfunctions during the boot process. As you proceed through the Steps, answer all of the Quick Check questions that appear. After you complete the Steps, you will see a Quick Check Summary Report. Follow the instructions on the screen to print this report.

2. Click the Explore button. Use the File menu to load **System11.trb**. Click the Boot Computer button and watch what happens on the simulated computer (in this case, actually, what does not happen!). Make your hypothesis about why this computer does not boot. Use the Check menu to check the state of various cables and switches. When you think you know the cause of the problem, select it from the Diagnosis list. If you correctly diagnosed the problem, write it down. If your diagnosis was not correct, form another hypothesis and check it, until you have correctly diagnosed the problem.

Answers

3. Sometimes problems that appear very similar, result from different causes. In Explore, use the File menu to load **System03.trb**, then diagnose the problem. Do the same for **System06.trb**. Describe the problems with these two systems. Then describe the similarities and differences in their symptoms.

4. In Explore, use the File menu to load System02 and System08. Both systems produce keyboard errors, but these errors have different causes. Describe what caused the problem in System02, and what caused the problem in System08. Once you have diagnosed these problems, what can you do about them?

5. In Explore, use the File menu to load Systems 04, 05, 07, 09, and 14. These systems produce similar symptoms on boot up. However, these systems have different problems. Diagnose the problem with each of these systems and indicate the key factor (the symptom or what you checked) that led to your diagnosis.

4.1

1. integrated circuit

2. bit

3. byte

4. ASCII, EBCDIC

5. binary

6. bus (or data bus)

4.2

1. Random access memory (RAM)

2. volatile

3. megabytes

4. capacitors

5. SIMM

6. virtual

7. ROM

8. CMOS

4.3

1. microprocessor

2. ALU

3. Control unit

4. opcode, operand

5. fetch, interpret, execute, increment instruction pointer

6. clock rate, word size, cache, instruction set

4.4

1. expansion bus

2. expansion card

3. slot, port

4. parallel, SCSI, serial, MIDI

Glossary/Index

The Computer Marketplace

The Computer

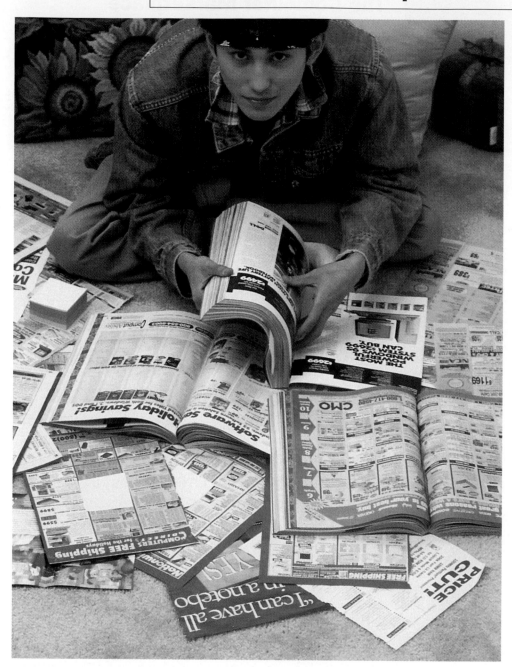

CHAPTER**PREVIEW**

When you have completed this chapter, you should be able to:

- Read a computer ad and understand how the technical specifications affect price and performance

- Explain why there are so many models of computers at so many different prices

- Research reliable information about computer products

- Determine which products are of good quality and value

- Take a systematic approach to shopping for a computer

- Explain how buying hardware is different from buying software

Marketplace

It is one of those dreary afternoons when the rain fogs up the windows. Your friend Matt is sprawled on the floor, tearing Post-it™ notes into tiny pieces of confetti.

"Hey, what's up?" you ask.

"I'm depressed or frustrated or something," he complains. "I finally have enough money to buy a computer, but now I also have one big headache!"

"What do you mean?"

"See all these magazines! See all these ads! How's a person supposed to know what to buy? The more I look, the more confused I get!" He opens the latest issue of *Computer Shopper*—all 800 pages of it—and you see that he has marked at least 30 ads with Post-it notes!

"Look," he says, "here's a computer with a Pentium processor...$1,995. Here's another one from a different company...$2,295."

"There's got to be some difference between them." You try to help.

Matt frowns. "Yeah. That's the trouble. This one for $1,995 has 8 megs of RAM, but the $2,295 computer has 16 megs."

"Well, that accounts for the price difference, right?" It seems simple to you.

But it is not so simple to Matt. "Hah!" he exclaims. "The cheaper computer has a 15-inch monitor, but the more expensive computer only has a 14-inch monitor." His eyes glaze over, and his voice becomes high-pitched. "And look. Here I can get one with 16 megs and all kinds of software for $2,395."

"Well, that sounds good." You try to encourage him.

"Yeah, but have you ever heard of this company?" he asks, pointing to the ad. "What if they go out of business right after I buy a computer from them? What am I going to do?"...

Sometime in the not-too-distant future you are likely to participate in a computer purchase decision—if not for your own computer, then one for your friend, your parents' small business, your employer, or your children. Buying the right computer and keeping within your budget are challenges.

The purpose of this chapter is to help you learn about computers and software from the consumer's perspective and to help you discover what you need to know to be a smart computer shopper. In Chapter 4 you learned how computers work. You know the purpose of computer components such as the processor, RAM, bus, expansion cards, and disk drives. In Chapter 5 you will learn about different options and models of these components and how they affect the pricing and performance of today's microcomputers.

Buying a Computer

5.1

Consumer's Guide to Desktop Computer Systems

Figure 5-1
MicroPlus
computer ad

S uppose you decide to buy a computer. You'll probably look at computer ads to get an idea of features and prices. Most computer ads list technical **specifications** describing the computer's components, capabilities, and special features. Do you need to understand the technical specifications to make an intelligent purchase decision? The answer is definitely "yes!" Suppose, for example, that you consider buying the MicroPlus computer advertised in Figure 5-1. It costs $2,295. Would it be a good "deal"?

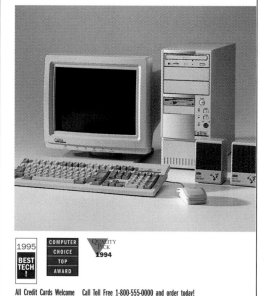

MicroPlus Home PC's

MicroPlus award-winning computers offer strong performance at a reasonable price. Simply the fastest Windows machines you can buy. MicroPlus computers feature superior engineering, starting with a genuine Intel processor and a motherboard designed specifically to take advantage of the latest technological advancements. Of course, you are covered by our one-year on-site parts and labor warranty.*

*ON-SITE SERVICE AVAILABLE FOR HARDWARE ONLY AND MAY NOT BE AVAILABLE IN CERTAIN REMOTE AREAS. SHIPPING AND HANDLING EXTRA. ALL RETURNS WILL BE EXCHANGED FOR LIKE PRODUCT ONLY. ALL RETURNS MUST BE IN ORIGINAL BOX WITH ALL MATERIALS. CALL FOR AN RMA NUMBER. DEFECTIVE PRODUCTS WILL BE REPAIRED AT MICROPLUS DISCRETION. THE COST FOR RETURNED MERCHANDISE IS NOT INCLUDED WITH ANY MONEY-BACK GUARANTEE. PRICES AND AVAILABILITY SUBJECT TO CHANGE WITHOUT NOTICE.

1995 BEST TECH! | COMPUTER CHOICE TOP AWARD | QUALITY PICK 1994

All Credit Cards Welcome   Call Toll Free 1-800-555-0000 and order today!

- Intel Pentium-133 with 256 K cache
- 8 MB RAM expandable to 128 MB
- 528 MB 11 MS Local bus enhanced EIDE hard drive with 120 K cache
- 4X CD-ROM Drive
- 3 1/2-inch 1.44 MB floppy drive
- 16-bit Sound Blaster®-compatable sound card and Koss® speakers
- 64-bit PCI local bus SVGA color graphics card with 1 MB DRAM
- 15-inch 1024 x 768 non-interlaced SVGA color monitor, .28 dot pitch
- Six -bay tower case
- Mouse
- MS-DOS 6.2, Windows 95
- Three PCI & four ISA slots
- Two high-speed serial ports and one parallel port
- 14.4 bps fax/modem with software

Sections 5.1 and 5.2 will help you understand the most frequently used terminology that you might encounter in computer ads. You can learn additional terms and practice comparison shopping in the Buying a Computer Lab.

You can't tell if the Micro Plus computer is a good deal unless you can compare its specifications to those of computers from other vendors. Let's take a closer look at what the specifications mean in terms of price and performance.

Comparing Microprocessors

Which microprocessor is best for my computing needs?

The microprocessor is the core component in a computer and is featured prominently in product descriptions. Computer ads typically indicate the type of microprocessor and its speed. Most of today's microcomputers are designed around a microprocessor from one of three product families: x86, 68000-series, or PowerPC.

In 1981 the original IBM PC used the Intel 8088 microprocessor, a slightly modified version of the 8086 model. The descendants of the 8086 microprocessors are often referred to as the **x86** family of microprocessors. Today's IBM-compatible computers still contain processors in the x86 **family**. Most of these processors are manufactured by Intel, but a few companies, such as Cyrix and AMD, have produced what are called "work-alike" processors. Computers with work-alike processors are generally less expensive than an equivalent model with an Intel processor. How can you tell what brand of processor a computer contains? Look for the "Intel Inside" logo in computer ads.

The **68000-series** microprocessors are manufactured by Motorola and used by Apple in its Macintosh Classic, SE, Quadra, and Performa computers. The instruction set for the 68000-series is different from that for the x86 family, which is why software written for x86 IBM-compatible computers does not work on 68000-based computers.

The **PowerPC** microprocessor implements RISC architecture to provide relatively fast performance at a low cost. The PowerPC chip is used by both Apple and IBM in their PowerPC computers. Although the PowerPC chip cannot directly execute the x86 or 68000 instruction set, PowerPC computers with an emulator can run software designed for IBM-compatible or Macintosh 68000-series computers. An **emulator** is software or hardware that enables one device to behave as if it were another.

The MicroPlus computer in the ad is a 133 MHz Pentium. The genealogy tree in Figure 5-2 will help you compare the specifications of this microprocessor to 68000-series and PowerPC microprocessors.

Figure 5-2
Microprocessor families

The microprocessor, to a great extent, determines the software titles you will be able to use. If you want to run Windows software, select a computer with an x86 microprocessor. If you want to use software designed for Macintosh computers, select a computer with a 68000-series or PowerPC microprocessor.

The Cost and Benefits of RAM Cache

Does a RAM cache affect the price of a computer?

A RAM cache is very important for optimum performance of computers with high-speed processors because the CPU can process data faster than it can retrieve it from the regular RAM area. A computer with an 80486 microprocessor should have at least 128 K of RAM cache; Pentium systems should have at least 256 K. Cache memory chips add to the cost of a computer system—a 256 K cache adds about $100.

Recall from Chapter 4 that microprocessor speed is measured in megahertz (MHz), and higher MHz ratings mean a faster processor. A Pentium 133 MHz processor, therefore, is faster than a Pentium 75 MHz processor.

In Chapter 4 you learned that a RAM cache speeds up processing by placing data in a special high-speed memory area.

RAM: Requirements and Cost

How much RAM is enough?

Recall from Chapter 4 that most of today's computers use SIMM modules for RAM. To expand the RAM capacity of these computers, you would purchase additional SIMMs and install them in empty SIMM sockets.

The amount of RAM a computer needs depends on the operating system and applications software you plan to use. It is theoretically possible to run Windows 3.1 in as little as 2 MB of RAM. Most Windows 3.1 applications, however, require at least 4 MB and perform even better with 8 MB or more. Windows 95 requires at least 4 MB of RAM, but performs better with 8 to 16 MB.

RAM costs about $50 per megabyte, so a 16 MB computer costs significantly more than an 8 MB system. Although some computer systems have 4 MB of RAM, 8 MB is the recommended minimum for the computing needs of today's typical computer user.

It is possible to add RAM after you purchase a computer system. For example, the MicroPlus computer includes 8 MB of RAM, but additional memory modules can be added up to a maximum of 128 MB. Before you purchase additional RAM, you must check the computer manual to find out the type of memory modules your computer uses and what memory configurations are possible.

Floppy Disk Drives: How Many?

Do I need more than one floppy disk drive?

Recall that a high-density disk drive stores up to 1.44 MB on a high-density floppy disk.

Most microcomputers today are configured with a single 3½-inch high-density floppy disk drive. Older computers often were configured with a 5¼-inch disk drive in addition to a 3½-inch drive. These two disk drive sizes were useful during the transition from the earlier 5¼-inch disks to the newer 3½-inch disks. Today, most software is shipped on 3½-inch disks or on CD-ROMs, so a 5¼-inch drive is unnecessary.

A popular misconception is that a computer needs two disk drives to copy the contents of one disk to another, but this is not the case. Both Windows and DOS allow you to make a copy of an entire disk by reading data from the original disk into memory, then inserting the destination disk and copying the data from memory to the destination disk. One 3½-inch floppy disk drive should be sufficient for your computing needs.

CD-ROM Drive: Worth the Cost?

Do I need a CD-ROM drive?

A CD-ROM drive is a worthwhile investment that lets you use multimedia, game, educational, and reference applications that are available only on CD-ROM disks.

Most microcomputers are configured with a double-speed (2x), quad-speed (4x), or six-speed (6x) CD-ROM drive. A faster CD-ROM drive will deliver data at a faster rate and provide better performance, especially with multimedia applications. You should purchase the fastest CD-ROM drive that you can afford.

If you plan to use multimedia software, you should be aware of current MPC standards. **MPC standards** specify the recommended computer configuration for running current multimedia software. These standards change about every two years. The chart in Figure 5-3 shows you the current MPC standard, MPC3, as well as earlier versions.

	MPC1	MPC2	MPC3
Date introduced	March 1991	May 1993	June 1995
Processor	16 MHz 386X	25 MHz 486SX	75 MHz Pentium
RAM	2 MB	4 MB	8 MB
Hard drive capacity	30 MB	160 MB	540 MB
CD-ROM drive speed	single-speed	double-speed	quad-speed
Sound board	8-bit	16-bit	16-bit
System software	Windows 3.0	Windows 3.0	Windows 3.1 or 3.11

▶ **Figure 5-3**
MPC standards

Try not to confuse memory and storage. Memory is on the main board; storage is handled by the disk drive.

Hard Drive Specifications

Why do computer ads include specifications on the hard drive bus and controller?

The factors that influence hard drive performance and price include storage capacity, controller type, cache capacity, and bus speed. Figure 5-4 provides an overview of these factors.

The hard disk circuit board, called a **controller**, contains the electronics that control the mechanical drive mechanism and data transfer. Controllers such as EIDE and SCSI are faster than IDE, MFM, or RLL.

A cable connects the controller to an expansion card. The expansion card is connected to a special high-speed local bus or the slower-speed expansion bus. Fast **bus speed** means faster data access

The controller often contains the chips for a disk cache. A large **cache capacity** contributes to fast data access times.

The hard disk and read/write heads are sealed inside the drive case. The size of the magnetic particles on the disk surface and their density determines the drive's **storage capacity**.

▶ **Figure 5-4**
Hard drive storage overview

As explained in Chapter 3, the access time of a hard disk drive is measured in milliseconds. A drive with a 13 ms access time is slightly slower than a drive with a 10 ms access time.

The more storage space you have, the better, so when comparing computer systems, the hard drive capacity is a significant factor. Most computers today are shipped with at least 500 MB hard disk drives.

Computer ads usually specify hard disk access time as an indication of drive performance. Access times of 9 to 13 ms are typical for today's microcomputer hard drives.

The two most popular types of hard drives are EIDE and SCSI. A drive mechanism includes a circuit board called a **controller** that positions the disk and read-write heads to locate data. Disk drives are categorized according to the type of controller they have. An **EIDE** (Enhanced Integrated Device Electronics) drive features high storage capacity and fast data transfer. **SCSI** drives provide a slight performance advantage over EIDE drives and are recommended for high-performance microcomputer systems and minicomputers.

In addition to drive capacity, access time, and type, most ads provide information about disk cache capacity and bus type. Disk cache, such as the 120 K cache in the MicroPlus computer, is an advantage because it will speed up system performance. A local bus, such as the one featured in the MicroPlus ad, increases data transport speed by providing a separate high-speed bus to carry data between storage devices and RAM.

Microcomputer Bus and Slot Types

Why do I need to pay attention to the bus type?

Computer ads generally specify the type of expansion bus the computer uses to transport data. The capacity of the expansion bus is determined by its speed and the number of bits that can be transported during each clock cycle. Bus speed is measured in megahertz, as is the microprocessor. A 33 MHz bus is faster than a 4.77 MHz bus, for example.

In some computers, the expansion bus is supplemented by special-purpose high-speed buses. The **VESA Local Bus** and the **PCI Local Bus** provide high-speed 32-bit or 64-bit paths that transfer data to display and storage devices. The local bus specified in the MicroPlus ad increases data transfer rates between the hard disk drive and RAM. The PCI Local Bus in the MicroPlus ad speeds up data transfer from RAM to the display.

A local bus is built into the main board and adds to the cost of a computer system. You cannot add a local bus to a computer unless you replace the main board. If your computer applications require extensive data access or graphics displays, you should make sure the system you purchase includes the appropriate local buses. The initial cost of including a local bus is far less than the cost of replacing your computer's main board if you later discover you need additional data transfer speed. Figure 5-5 summarizes the important features about microcomputer data buses.

Chapter 3 explained that a disk cache speeds up access to data by temporarily placing data where it can be accessed more quickly than from the drive. The cache area can be on the circuit board in the disk drive, on the controller card, or in RAM.

In a computer system with a high-speed local bus, the amount of data carried on the regular expansion bus is reduced, but it continues to carry data for slower devices such as the printer and mouse.

Figure 5-5 ◄
Microcomputer data bus summary

Bus Name	Number of Bits	Speed
XT Bus	8 bits	4.77 MHz
ISA Bus	16 bits	8 MHz
EISA Bus	32 bits	6–8.33 MHz
Micro Channel Bus	16 or 32 bits	10 MHz
VESA Local Bus	32 bits	33–66 MHz
PCI Local Bus	32 or 64 bits	33–66 MHz

Many computers provide one to three local bus slots for video adapter cards and hard disk controller cards. The MicroPlus computer has three high-speed PCI slots and four slower ISA slots. This sounds like a reasonable amount of room for expansion, but be careful. Some of these slots might be used by the devices shipped with the computer. When you are considering a particular computer, it is a good idea to ask how many of the expansion slots are *free*, that is, available for devices that you might want to install later.

Selecting a System Unit Case

What are bays, and why are they important?

The system unit case holds the main board and provides openings, called **bays**, for mounting disk, CD-ROM, and tape drives. Some bays are external, and some are internal.

An **external bay** provides an opening for installing a device that you need to access from the outside of the case. For example, you would install a floppy disk drive in an external bay because you need to insert and remove the floppy disks. An **internal bay** provides a mounting bracket for devices that do not need to be accessible from outside the system unit case. Hard disk drives typically use internal bays because you don't need to access them while using the computer.

A system unit with many bays provides greater expansion capability. Notice in Figure 5-1 that the MicroPlus computer tower case has six bays. From the picture in the ad, it appears that there are four external bays, so two of the bays must be internal. The hard disk drive occupies one internal bay, while the floppy disk drive and CD-ROM each occupy one external bay. That leaves one internal bay and two external bays for expansion—probably adequate for most home and business uses.

Video Adapters and Monitors

What is the relationship between the video adapter and the monitor?

You learned in Chapter 1 that many of today's graphical user interfaces require high-resolution graphics. As a consumer, your goal is to buy the best display that fits your budget. The quality of a computer display depends on two interrelated factors: the specifications of the monitor and the features of the video display adapter.

Monitor specifications include screen size, maximum resolution, and dot pitch. **Screen size** is the measurement in inches from one corner of the screen diagonally across to the opposite corner. Most computer systems are packaged with a 14-inch or 15-inch screen. You might want to consider paying an additional $300 to $500 for a 17-inch monitor if you have a vision problem or if you like to work with more than one program at the same time. With a 17-inch monitor you can use 1024×768 resolution to fit more windows on the screen, and the text will still be reasonably large.

Dot pitch is a measure of image clarity; a smaller dot pitch means a crisper image. Technically, dot pitch is the distance in millimeters between like-colored pixels. A .28 dot pitch is typical for today's monitors.

The specifications for a monitor include its **maximum resolution**, typically 1024×768. It is important to realize that the maximum resolution you can use is determined by both the video adapter and the monitor. If your video adapter supports 1280×1024 resolution, but your monitor supports only 1024×768, the maximum resolution you can use will be 1024×768.

Many older high-resolution monitors displayed an undesirable strobe-light effect called **flicker** at resolutions higher than 640×480. Most monitors sold today are non-interlaced. A **non-interlaced** (often abbreviated in ads as NI) monitor provides an image with less flicker at higher resolutions than an interlaced monitor. Figure 5-6 explains the difference between interlaced and non-interlaced monitor technology.

Figure 5-6
Producing an image

Red, green, and blue electron guns each shoot out a stream of electrons, which converge to form pixels on the screen. The color of the pixel is determined by the intensity of the beam from each of the guns.

The electron gun begins in the upper-left corner and moves rapidly across each line of the screen to create the image you see.

Interlaced technology means that the electron gun sweeps across all the even numbered lines on one pass, then scans all the odd numbered lines on the next pass. This sometimes creates a flicker at high resolutions, when there are many more pixels to scan.

When the electron gun reaches the bottom-right corner of the screen, it returns back to the top and begins again.

A video adapter is required for your computer to display any kind of text, graphics, or animations. It is not only for watching video segments on your computer screen.

Imagine the impact millions of computers have on electricity usage. Computer companies have responded to the concerns of environmentalists by designing **energy star compliant** monitors and computer systems. These systems use less energy by switching to a low-power stand-by mode after a specified period of inactivity. You can help save energy and reduce pollution by looking for the EPA pollution prevention logo on energy-saving products. Some people believe that radiation from monitors might have long-term health effects. Low-radiation monitors are advertised as meeting MPR-II and TCO standards for reduced radiation emission.

A **video display adapter**, also called a **video card** or graphics card, is an expansion card that provides a data pathway from the main board to the monitor. Most video display adapters use special graphics chips to boost performance. These **accelerated video adapters** can greatly increase the speed at which images are displayed. An accelerated video adapter connected to a fast VESA or PCI local bus can move data between the microprocessor and the video adapter as fast as the microprocessor can process it. Your computer will perform better, especially for graphical user interfaces, if it has an accelerated video adapter connected to a VESA or PCI bus.

Display resolution depends on the video display adapter that connects the monitor to the computer. Today, most computers have a **super VGA** (SVGA) video adapter that supports resolutions of 640×480, 800×600, and 1024×768. Older computers with VGA, not super VGA, video adapters do not support 800×600 or 1024×768 resolutions.

The amount of memory on the video adapter limits the number of colors that can be displayed at each resolution. Video adapter memory capacity is an important consideration if you are using multimedia software with photographic-quality images. To display photographic-quality images at 640×480 resolution, a video adapter should have at least 1 MB of memory. If you plan to display such images at 800×600 or 1024×768 resolutions, the video adapter should have 2 to 4 MB of memory.

Why Buy a Sound Card?

Should I spend extra money for a sound card?

If you want to run games or multimedia software, you should purchase a computer system that includes a sound card. A basic sound card adds less than $100 to the price of a computer system. A 16-bit sound card costs slightly more, but it provides higher quality sound output than an 8-bit sound card.

Most games and many multimedia applications require a Sound Blaster-compatible sound card. The original Sound Blaster card was manufactured by Creative Labs. Many software manufacturers designed their software to use these cards. Now, so called "Sound Blaster-compatible" cards from other manufacturers also work with this software and are popular with consumers.

Selecting a Modem

Does a fax/modem turn my computer into a fax machine?

Many computer systems include a modem that transmits to and receives data from other computers over telephone lines. The speed of transmission is usually expressed as baud rate or as bits per second. The **baud rate** is the number of signal changes that occurs in one second during data transmission. **Bits per second**, abbreviated bps, is the number of data bits transmitted by the modem in one second. When comparing computer system specifications, you just need to remember that faster modem speeds mean faster data transmission. A 14,400 or 28,800 bps modem is typical for today's computer systems.

A **fax/modem** is a modem that includes fax capability. This means that it can send a document that is in the memory of your computer to any standard fax machine—where the document is printed on paper. Modems with fax capability can also receive fax transmissions from standard fax machines or other fax/modems. You can view the received fax on your monitor or print it on your computer printer.

A modem requires communication software that helps you enter the settings required to establish communications with a variety of different computers. When you buy a computer system that includes a modem, the computer vendor has probably installed the communications software needed to operate the modem. But it's a good idea to check to be sure that the software is included in the system price.

A fax/modem does not provide a way for you to feed a piece of paper through your computer, so the documents you fax must be in electronic form, not on paper.

The Value of Bundled Software

What software is typically included when I purchase a computer system?

The price of most computers includes the operating system, so if you purchase an IBM-compatible computer, you can expect that the latest version of DOS and Windows will be installed on the hard drive by the vendor or manufacturer. Many computer vendors also include applications software such as a word processing package or personal finance manager. Multimedia computer systems usually include several CD-ROMs, such as encyclopedias, fact books, and games.

All other factors being equal, a system with bundled software will cost only slightly more than a system without bundled software. So bundling is often a good value even if not all of the software meets your needs. The slight increase in the price of a computer system with bundled software is generally less than you would pay if you bought the software separately.

Figure 5-7 ◀
Printers

Dot matrix printers create letters and graphics by striking an inked ribbon with a column of small wires called *pins*. By activating some wires in the column, but not activating others, the printer creates patterns for letters and numbers. The more pins in the column, the better the print quality. Therefore, a 24-pin dot-matrix printer is capable of better quality output than a 9-pin printer. Dot matrix printers create color printouts using a ribbon with bands of colored ink. Color printouts from a dot matrix printer tend to look faded and of low quality.

Dot matrix printer operating costs are low. Replacement ribbon cartridges are usually less than $20. The cost of dot-matrix printing is less than $.01 per page.

Pins

Print head

Ribbon

Paper

A 9-pin print head creates an uppercase letter using a 5 X 7 matrix. The two lower pins of the print head are used for letters that go below the line, such as g, y, and q.

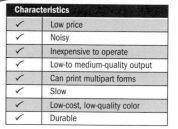

Ribbon

Print head

Dot Matrix printer

9-pin print sample

24-pin print sample

Characteristics	
✓	Low price
✓	Noisy
✓	Inexpensive to operate
✓	Low-to medium-quality output
✓	Can print multipart forms
✓	Slow
✓	Low-cost, low-quality color
✓	Durable

The print quality of a 24-pin dot matrix printer, sometimes referred to as *near letter quality*, is much smoother and easier to read.

Ink-jet printers produce characters and graphics by spraying ink onto paper. The print head is a matrix of fine spray nozzles. Patterns are formed by activating selected nozzles. An ink-jet printer typically forms a character in a 20 X 20 matrix, producing a high-quality printout.

Color ink-jet printers cost a little more, but produce much higher-quality output than color dot-matrix printers. Using special paper, some color ink-jet printers can produce vivid, high-quality, color printouts. The other option for color output, a color laser printer, is far beyond the budget of most home or small business users. Ink-jet printers are inexpensive to operate, requiring only a new ink cartridge or ink refill. Estimated cost per page is about $.01.

Paper output here

Single-sheet papertray

Ink-jet printer

Choosing the Right Printer

What kind of printer should I buy?

Recall that in Chapter 1 you learned about the three categories of printers: dot matrix, ink-jet, and laser.

Occasionally a computer vendor offers a *hardware bundle* that includes a computer, printer, and software. More often, however, printers are sold separately so consumers can choose the quality, features, and price they want. Ink-jet and personal laser printers are most popular with today's consumers because they provide high-quality print on plain paper.

If you want color printouts, color ink-jet printers offer the best price-performance value because of the high price of color laser printers and the poor quality of color dot matrix printers. Figure 5-7 is a guide to the types and features of printers.

Laser printers use the same technology as duplicating machines. A laser charges particles on a drum. Then, a powdery black ink called *toner* onto paper. In the past, the price of laser printers limited their use to businesses and large organizations. Laser printer prices have decreased, however, making them affordable for individuals.

Color laser printers work by reprinting each page for each primary color. For each reprint, the paper must be precisely positioned so each color is printed in exactly the right spot. This dramatically increases the complexity of the print mechanism and the amount of time required to print each page. Like color photocopies, color laser printers are relatively uncommon due to their high price.

Operating costs of laser printers include replacement toner cartridges and print drums. The estimated cost of laser printing is about $.05 per page.

A laser charges a pattern of particles on a drum which picks up a powdery black sustance called toner. The toner is transferred onto paper that rolls

Laser

Drum

Single-sheet paper feed tray

Toner   Paper

Laser printer

Laser print sample

R

Now that you have completed the section on desktop computers, see how well you can interpret the specifications in the MicroPlus ad by answering Question 3 in the Chapter Review.

Characteristics	
✓	Moderate to high price
✓	High-quality output
✓	More expensive to operate
✓	Cannot print multipart forms
✓	Fast
✓	Quiet
✓	Expensive, high-quality color
✓	Durable

Print head nozzles

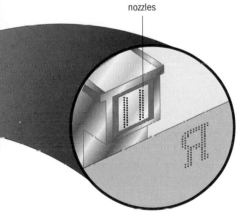

Characteristics	
✓	Moderate price
✓	High-quality output
✓	Inexpensive to operate
✓	Cannot print multipart forms
✓	Slow
✓	Quiet
✓	Low-cost, low-quality color
✓	Durable

R

Ink-jet print sample

Quick Check

1 The three families of microprocessors are _____, _____, and _____.

2 The amount of RAM you need in your computer depends on _____ and _____.

3 The two most popular types of hard drive are _____ and _____.

4 VESA and PCI are types of _____.

5 High resolution and small _____ are two characteristics of a monitor with a clear image.

6 If you want to display photographic-quality images at 640×480 resolution, you need a video adapter with at least _____ of video memory.

7 Modem speeds of 14,400 or 28,800 _____ are typical for today's computer systems.

8 The best value for color printing is a(n) _____ printer.

Consumer's Guide to Notebook Computers

5.2

When shopping for a notebook computer, you'll notice that many of the technical specifications are the same as for desktop computers—processor type and speed, amount of RAM, hard disk capacity, and bundled software. The purpose of this section is to point out additional considerations you need to make when comparing and evaluating notebook computers like the one advertised in Figure 5-8.

Figure 5-8
MicroNote computer ad

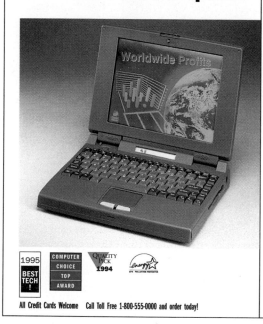

MicroNote Computer

For dependable computing on the go, the MicroNote can't be beat. As powerful as a desktop computer, with built in sound capabilities and active matrix display, this notebook is designed to meet your most exacting computer needs.

- 80486DX4-100 MHz
- 8 MB RAM max 32 MB
- 3¹/²-inch 1.44 MB floppy drive
- 520 MB hard drive
- 9.5 inch active matrix VGA display
- Local bus video with 1 MB video RAM
- External VGA and keyboard port
- PCMCIA type III slot
- One parallel and one serial port
- Touch Pad
- 16-bit stereo Sound-Blaster®-compatible sound
- Advanced power managment
- NiMH battery with hot swap
- 5.7 lbs.

*ON-SITE SERVICE AVAILABLE FOR HARDWARE ONLY AND MAY NOT BE AVAILABLE IN CERTAIN REMOTE AREAS. SHIPPING AND HANDLING EXTRA. ALL RETURNS WILL BE EXCHANGED FOR LIKE PRODUCT ONLY. ALL RETURNS MUST BE IN ORIGINAL BOX WITH ALL MATERIALS. CALL FOR AN RMA NUMBER. DEFECTIVE PRODUCTS WILL BE REPAIRED AT MICROPLUS DISCRETION. THE COST FOR RETURNED MERCHANDISE IS NOT INCLUDED WITH ANY MONEY-BACK GUARANTEE. PRICES AND AVAILABILITY SUBJECT TO CHANGE WITHOUT NOTICE.

1995 BEST TECH!

COMPUTER CHOICE TOP AWARD

QUALITY PICK 1994

All Credit Cards Welcome   Call Toll Free 1-800-555-0000 and order today!

The Advantage of PCMCIA Cards

There doesn't seem to be much room in a notebook computer case—how do I add expansion cards?

A **PCMCIA slot** (Personal Computer Memory Card International Association) is a special type of expansion slot developed for notebook computers, which do not have space in the case for full-size expansion slots and cards. A PCMCIA slot is a small, external slot into which you can insert a PCMCIA card.

PCMCIA cards, also called **PC cards**, are credit-card-sized circuit boards that incorporate an expansion card and a device. So, for example, some PCMCIA cards contain a modem, others contain memory expansion, and others contain a hard disk drive. You can plug in and remove PCMCIA devices without turning the computer off, unlike traditional expansion cards. In this way you can switch from one PCMCIA device to another without disrupting your work, as shown in Figure 5-9.

PCMCIA slots are categorized by size. Type I slots accept only the thinnest PCMCIA cards such as memory expansion cards. Type II slots accept most of the popular PCMCIA cards—those that contain modems, sound cards, and network cards. Type III slots accept the thickest PCMCIA cards, which contain devices such as hard disk drives. Many notebooks provide a multipurpose PCMCIA slot that will accept two Type I cards, two Type II cards, or one Type III card.

PCMCIA cards

▶ **Figure 5-9**
Using PCMCIA
cards

PCMCIA card
inserted into
PCMCIA slot of a
notebook computer.

Phone jack on PCMCIA
modem card.

Comparing Notebook Displays

Is it true that the screen image on a notebook computer is not as good as the image on a desktop computer?

Notebook computers do not use monitors because they are big and heavy, and they require too much electrical power to run on batteries. Instead, notebooks have a flat panel liquid crystal display. A **liquid crystal display (LCD)** uses a technically sophisticated method of passing light through a thin layer of liquid crystal cells to produce an image. The resulting flat panel screen is lightweight and compact.

Notebook LCDs are either passive or active matrix. A **passive matrix screen** relies on timing to make sure the liquid crystal cells are illuminated. As a result, the process of updating the screen image does not always keep up with moving images, and the display can appear blurred. Passive matrix displays are available in monochrome and color versions. A computer with a monochrome passive matrix screen costs several hundred dollars less than a computer with a color passive matrix screen.

An **active matrix screen** updates more rapidly and provides image quality similar to that of a monitor. Active matrix screens are essential for a crisp display of animations and video. However, active matrix screens are difficult to manufacture—approximately 80% are rejected due to defects—and add significantly to the price of a notebook computer.

Most notebook computers have a VGA or SVGA port for an external monitor. The advantage of an external monitor is the high-quality display. The disadvantage is that you need to disconnect the external monitor when you transport the computer.

Multimedia Notebooks: Pros and Cons

Can I use a notebook computer for multimedia computing?

Notebook computer manufacturers have found it difficult to pack a CD-ROM drive and sound card into a small notebook case, but they have been making progress. Notebooks with built-in CD-ROM drives and sound cards are available, even though they are slightly heavier and more expensive than their non-multimedia counterparts.

You can use a docking station as an alternative to built-in multimedia components. A **docking station** is essentially an additional expansion bus into which you plug your notebook computer. The notebook provides the processor and RAM. The docking station provides expansion slots for cards that would not fit into the notebook case. It allows you to purchase inexpensive expansion cards and peripherals designed for desktops, instead of the more expensive devices designed specifically for notebooks. You sacrifice portability—you probably won't carry your docking station and external CD-ROM drive with you—but you gain the use of low-cost, powerful desktop peripherals. Figure 5-10 illustrates how a docking station works.

Figure 5-10
Notebook docking station

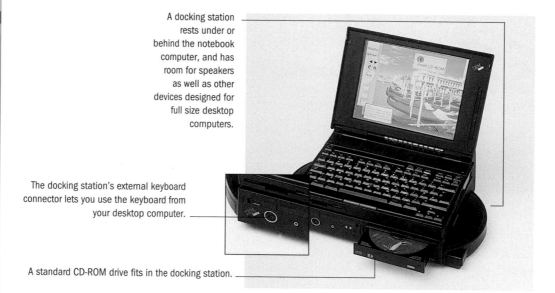

A docking station rests under or behind the notebook computer, and has room for speakers as well as other devices designed for full size desktop computers.

The docking station's external keyboard connector lets you use the keyboard from your desktop computer.

A standard CD-ROM drive fits in the docking station.

If you don't need multimedia capabilities, a port replicator makes it more convenient to connect and disconnect your notebook computer from devices such as an external monitor, mouse, and keyboard. A **port replicator** is an inexpensive device that connects to a notebook computer by a bus connector plug; it contains a duplicate of the notebook computer's ports. Port replicators do not include expansion slots and typically cannot be used to add a sound card or CD-ROM drive to your notebook computer.

Why would you want a port replicator? Suppose that when you use your notebook computer at home you plug in an external monitor, a full-size keyboard, and a printer. Every time you want to travel with your notebook, you must unplug each of these devices, then plug them in again when you return home. It is more convenient to plug the external devices into a port replicator, then plug the port replicator into the bus connector of the notebook. In this way, you only have one plug to connect, instead of many, as Figure 5-11 shows.

VGA monitor port — Mouse port — Keyboard port — Parallel port — Serial port

A typical notebook computer has many ports. Plugging and unplugging devices can be inconvenient if you are frequently traveling with the computer.

A port replicator plugs into a notebook computer using a special connector port and contains ports for external devices. When you want to take the computer traveling, you can leave the external devices plugged into the port replicator and unplug the port replicator from the computer.

▶ **Figure 5-11**
Notebook port replicator

Which Notebook Pointing Device Is for You?

Isn't it clumsy to use a mouse with a notebook computer?

Although a mouse is the standard pointing device used with desktop computers, a mouse can be inconvenient to carry and use while traveling. Most notebook computers include an alternative pointing device. The three most popular options—built-in track ball, track point, and touch pad—are explained in Figure 5-12.

▶ **Figure 5-12**
Notebook pointing devices

A track point is a small eraser-like device embedded among the typing keys. To control the on-screen pointer, you push the track point up, left, right, or down. Buttons for clicking and double-clicking are located in front of the spacebar.

Track point

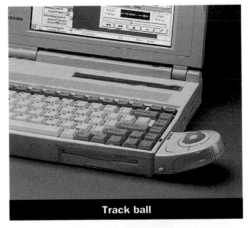

Track ball

A track ball is like an upside-down mouse. By rolling the ball with your fingers, you control the on-screen pointer. Buttons for clicking are often located above or to the side of the track ball.

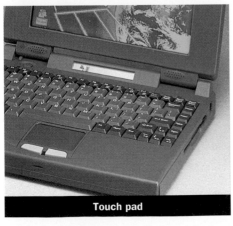

A touch pad is a touch-sensitive device. By dragging your finger over the surface, you control the on-screen pointer. Two buttons equivalent to mouse buttons are located in front of the touch pad.

Touch pad

Considerations for Notebook Power Sources

How long will a notebook computer run on batteries?

Most notebook computers operate on power from either rechargeable batteries or a wall outlet. Because notebooks are designed for portability, the computing time provided by batteries is important. For example, an executive who frequently travels to Asia might want at least eight hours of computing time during the 14-hour flight.

The length of time a notebook computer can operate from battery power depends on many factors. Fast processors, active matrix LCDs, and additional peripheral devices demand significant power from notebook computer batteries. Notebook manufacturers attempt to reduce power consumption by building power-saving features into their computers. These features automatically switch off the hard disk drive, LCD display, or even the processor if you do not interact with the computer after a short period of time. These devices are reactivated when you press a key or move the mouse.

On battery power, notebook computers typically provide two to four hours of operating time before the batteries need to be recharged. Most notebook computers use one of three types of batteries: Nicad (nickel cadmium), NiMH (nickel-metal hydride), or Lithium ion. Nicad batteries typically store less power than NiMH or Lithium ion batteries of equivalent size and weight. Therefore, Nicad batteries provide the shortest operating times. Most ads for notebook computers indicate the battery type and estimated computing times. Consumers need to be aware that many ads indicate maximum operating times. An ad that proclaims "Runs *up* to six hours!" might mean that the battery can supply six hours of operating time with no additional devices attached and with minimal use of the hard disk drive. Under typical working conditions the computer may run for significantly less than six hours on a charge.

The easiest way to extend the operating time of your computer is to purchase extra batteries. When the first battery wears down, you can swap in a new battery and get back to work. Some notebook computers allow you to insert several batteries at the same time; as soon as one is discharged, the notebook switches to the next. Switching batteries while the computer is on is called a **hot swap**.

Most notebook computers require an external AC adapter to plug into a wall outlet or recharge the batteries. This adapter—about the size and weight of a small brick—can add significantly to the traveling weight of the notebook. Some notebook computers have eliminated the external adapter and require only a power cable to plug into a wall outlet. It is a good idea to use AC power whenever possible, such as when you use your notebook at home. Using AC power saves your batteries for when AC power is not available.

Now that you have completed the section on notebook computers, see how well you can interpret the specifications in the MicroNote ad by answering Question 4 in the Chapter Review.

Quick Check

1. In a notebook computer, a(n) _____ slot provides an expansion port for credit-card-sized circuit boards and devices.

2. A(n) _____ matrix LCD display is required for acceptable display of animation and video on notebook computers.

3. A(n) _____ provides an additional expansion bus to which a notebook computer can be connected.

4. A(n) _____ makes it more convenient to connect and disconnect peripheral devices from a notebook computer.

5. The three pointing devices used with notebook computers as alternatives to a mouse are _____, _____, and _____.

6. A battery-powered notebook computer is using a(n) _____ feature if the screen goes blank when you don't type anything for a while.

Product Life Cycles

The computer industry is dynamic. Expensive new models eagerly awaited by consumers and highly touted by industry analysts appear all too soon in discount catalogs. You just master the features of one word processor version when a new version appears. Product advertisements and announcements, like the one in Figure 5-13, frequently appear in national magazines and newspapers, as well as in computer industry publications.

This glitzy roll-out of Microsoft Windows 95 included full-page ads in national newspapers, television ads, and product rallies.

Initially announced for delivery in 1994, Microsoft releases its system on August 24, 1995. Microsoft chairman Bill Gates promotes his company's upcoming product.

Figure 5-13
Product announcement

Can the savvy consumer take advantage of the dynamics of the computer industry? To some extent, the answer is yes. Consumers who understand the computer industry are more likely to make wise purchasing decisions and avoid costly mistakes.

Hardware Product Life Cycle

Does the computer industry introduce new models annually like the automotive industry?

Automobile manufacturers introduce new models every year. The new models incorporate new and improved features and, therefore, give customers an incentive to buy. Computer manufacturers also introduce new models—and for the same reasons as their counterparts in the automotive industry. But the computer industry is not on an annual cycle; the computer marketplace seems rather chaotic with new product announcements and pre-announcements, ship dates, and availability dates all occurring at irregular intervals.

In the computer industry, the life cycle of a new computer model typically includes product development, product announcement, introduction, maintenance, and retirement. Let's look at the aspects of the hardware product life cycle that affect purchasing decisions.

Product Announcement

I saw a great product announcement, but no one has it in stock. Why?

A **product announcement** declares a company's intention of introducing a new product. Products are announced at trade shows and press conferences.

Ideas for new products are everywhere; users express their needs for improved features, engineers produce more efficient designs, scholars publish new theories, and competitors announce new products. Periodically, hardware manufacturers evaluate ideas for new products and decide which new products could most increase profits. As part of the evaluation process, a manufacturer considers how many people might be interested in buying the product, the costs required to produce the product, the time it will take to bring the product to market, and the product's effect on the competition.

Although sometimes a product announcement means that a new product is now on store shelves, this is not always the case. Often a product announcement is a "trial balloon," designed to assess customer interest and to see what countermoves the competition might make. Therefore, a product announcement often means, "We're thinking of making this product; what would happen if we did?" Manufacturers also use product announcements as a way to prevent consumers from buying competitors' products. These announcements mean, "We've got a hot new product coming out soon...wait for it...don't buy from the competition!"

As a consumer, you should be wary of making purchasing decisions based on product announcements. A product announcement can precede the actual product by several years. Sometimes, products are announced but are never made or marketed. These products are referred to as **vaporware**.

Product Introduction, Maintenance, and Retirement

Why are products so expensive when they are first introduced?

When a hardware product is first introduced, the hardware manufacturer usually establishes a suggested list price slightly higher than the previous generation of its products. Initial supplies of the product are generally low while manufacturing capacity increases to meet demand; consumers who want the scarce product must pay a higher price.

Figure 5-14
Pentium prices

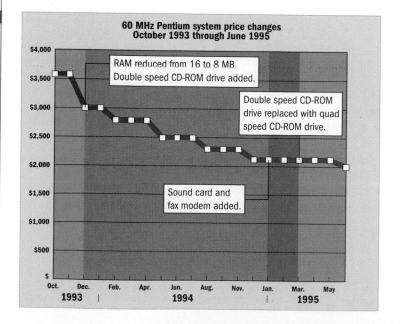

As supply and demand for the product reach an equilibrium, the price of the product decreases slightly. Usually the price decrease is due to discounting by dealers, rather than a change in the manufacturer's list price. Manufacturers tend to maintain a slightly high list price; this practice gives their dealers room to give customer discounts. In Figure 5-14, you can see that the price of computers using the Pentium processor dropped significantly during the first year after their introduction.

► **Figure 5-15**
Microcomputer product line

When a new product becomes available, it is usually added to the manufacturer's current product line, as shown in Figure 5-15. The prices of the older products, such as the 486DX2-66, are reduced to keep them attractive to buyers. Gradually, the oldest products are discontinued as demand for them declines.

New products offer the latest features and usually sell for a premium price. Older products don't include the latest features and must be sold at a discounted price. Very old products are usually available at super-low, close-out prices. For the consumer, this means that the latest generation of products is the most expensive, while products from a previous generation are less expensive and might offer good performance for the price.

Figure 5-16
Price performance curve

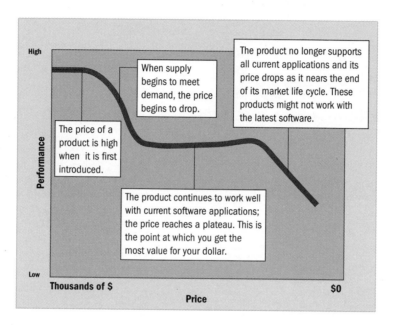

The price and performance of the computers in a typical microcomputer product line can be illustrated by a curve, as shown in Figure 5-16. The products in the middle of a typical microcomputer product line—those that are 8 to 18 months old—tend to offer the best performance for the price.

Software Product Life Cycle

What's the difference between a version and a revision?

Companies that produce computer software are referred to as **software publishers**. Software, like hardware, begins with an idea that is then shaped by a design team and marketing experts. Product announcements are information-gathering tools for software publishers, just as they are for hardware manufacturers, and the software industry also has its share of vaporware. The software life cycle, however, is somewhat different from the hardware life cycle.

A new software product can be an entirely new product, a new **version** (also called a **release**) with significant enhancements, or a **revision** designed to add minor enhancements and eliminate bugs found in the current version. Before you buy software, you should be familiar with the difference between versions and revisions, as illustrated by Figure 5-17.

New software products are usually released with a major advertising campaign. New versions of an existing product also are often released with much fanfare as companies tout the latest features and advantages that the new version has over competitors' products. New versions of

Software publishers typically are not also hardware manufacturers. Most of the software written for IBM-compatible computers is produced by software publishers other than IBM.

software are often offered at discounted prices to owners of the older versions to encourage them to update to the new version and to discourage them from switching to a competing product.

The original software *version* is generally 1.0.

The software publisher releases a *revision* to fix bugs or make small changes in features. The revision number is seperated from the version number by a period.

Version number — Revision number

1.2

A major improvement to a software product would be indicated by a new *version* number—in this case, version 2.0.

Version 1.0   Version 1.1   Version 1.2   Version 2.0

Figure 5-17
Software versions and revisions

Revisions are often made available to current owners of the software at little or no cost. However, revisions are often released with little publicity because software companies can't afford to have every owner of the product request the new revision. This is especially true for revisions that fix bugs that are infrequently encountered by users. Sometimes customers don't know a revision is available until they call the publisher's technical support line with a problem. If the problem has been fixed in the latest revision, the technical support person informs the customer of the existence of the revision and arranges for the customer to receive it.

Alpha and Beta Testing

Why does software have bugs?

Once a software publisher begins serious development of a new software product or a new version of a current product, programming teams code the program according to the design specifications. The program code is tested by programmers and software testers employed by the publisher, a process known as **alpha testing**.

Modern programs are so large, however, that it is virtually impossible to test every logical branch of the program or to find out how the program interacts with the many programs and hardware devices that might be found on the computer systems of typical users. Therefore, the publisher sends the software to selected users for testing under realistic conditions. This phase of testing is referred to as **beta testing**. Software in this phase is called a **beta version**. The users who test the software are referred to as **beta testers**.

Beta testers use the beta version and report any problems to the publisher, who then tries to fix the problems before publishing the final version of the software. Beta testers usually do not get paid for their work, but they might receive a complimentary copy of the finished product.

Sometimes a software product undergoes several rounds of beta testing before it is ready for market. Generally, even after extensive alpha and beta testing, the software still contains some bugs that will be corrected in subsequent revisions and versions.

Introductory Offers

Do those ads really mean that I can upgrade my brand x word processor to the latest version of brand y for only $99?

When a new software product first becomes available, it often appears on the market at a special introductory price to entice customers. Several software products that now carry a list price of $495 were introduced at a special $99 price.

Another type of introductory offer might be called "switch and save." The way this works is that customers can switch to a new software product for a special price—often $129—if they own a competitor's product. Microsoft ran an aggressive switch-and-save campaign in 1992, hoping to convince WordPerfect users to switch to Microsoft Word for Windows. Microsoft ran full-page ads with the headline, "No wonder WordPerfect users prefer Word for Windows. It has 'easy' written all over it." The ads offered Word for Windows at a special $129 price to people with current licenses for competing word processing software, such as WordPerfect, MultiMate, WordStar, and DisplayWrite.

Software Product Line

Although you might purchase computer hardware that is not the latest model, you should purchase only the most current software version. The cost of a new version is usually comparable to that of the previous version, but you get more features.

Should I upgrade whenever the software publisher offers a new version?

Soon after a new version of a product is released, the software publisher usually stops selling earlier versions. For example, WordPerfect Corporation discontinued version 4.2 of its word processing software soon after it released version 5.0. When a new product is released for a different operating system or computer type, however, other versions of the software are still maintained in the product line. For example, WordPerfect was first produced for IBM-compatible computers. A short time later, a new product, WordPerfect for the Macintosh, was produced. Both products remained in the product line.

When a publisher offers a new version of the software you are using, it is usually a good idea to upgrade, but you can wait for several months until the initial rush for technical support on the new product decreases. If you don't upgrade, you might find that the software publisher offers minimal technical support for older versions of the program. Also, if you let several versions go by without upgrading, you might have to purchase the software at full price when you do decide to upgrade.

Quick Check

1. What are the five phases in the life cycle of a computer hardware product?

2. Many companies use a(n) _____ as a "trial balloon" to assess customer interest and see how the competition will respond.

3. Products that are announced, but never shipped are called _____.

4. The _____ is the point in the price-performance curve at which a typical home user might buy computer hardware.

5. A new _____ of a software product features significant enhancements, whereas a _____ of a software product eliminates bugs and adds only a few enhancements.

6. A software publisher sends a(n) _____ version of a product to selected customers so they can test the product under realistic conditions.

The Computer Industry: Tiers, Channels, and the Press

The **computer industry** consists of the corporations and individuals that supply goods and services to people and organizations that use computers. The computer industry is in a continual state of change as new products appear and old products are discontinued; as corporations form, merge, and die; as corporate leadership shifts; as consumers' buying habits evolve; and as prices steadily continue to decrease. You will be a better informed consumer if you understand the tiered structure of computer companies, the five market channels from which you can purchase hardware and software, and the types of publications encompassed by the computer press.

Market Tiers

What accounts for price differences for computers with the same specifications from different vendors?

Since 1981, hundreds of companies have produced IBM PC clones and other personal computers. Industry analysts often refer to three tiers or categories of microcomputer companies, although not all analysts agree on which companies belong in each tier.

The top tier consists of large companies that have been in the computer business for more than ten years and have an identifiable percentage of total computer sales—companies such as IBM, Apple, Compaq, Digital, Toshiba, Epson, AT&T, and Hewlett-Packard. The second tier includes newer companies with high sales volume, but with somewhat less financial resources than companies in the first tier. Most analysts place companies such as Gateway and Dell in the second tier. The third tier consists of smaller startup companies that sell primarily through mail order.

Computer prices vary by tier. Computers from the top-tier vendors generally are more expensive than computers offered by second- or third-tier vendors. For example, a computer with specifications similar to the MicroPlus computer featured in the ad at the beginning of this chapter might cost $2,699 from a first-tier vendor, $2,199 from a second-tier vendor, and $1,999 from a third-tier vendor.

Why do these prices vary by tier? Because first-tier companies often have higher overhead costs, management is often paid higher salaries, and substantial financial resources are devoted to research and development. The first-tier companies are responsible for many of the innovations that have made computers faster, more powerful, and more convenient. Also, many consumers believe that computers sold by first-tier companies are better quality and are a safe purchasing decision. They believe there is less risk that computers from first-tier companies will quickly become obsolete or that the vendor will go out of business.

Computers from second-tier companies are generally less expensive than those from the first tier, although the quality can be just as good. Most IBM-compatible computers are constructed from off-the-shelf circuit boards, cables, cases, and chips. This means that the components in the computers sold by second-tier companies are often the same as those in computers sold by the first tier. The quality of the off-the-shelf parts, however, is not uniform; it is difficult for the consumer to determine the quality of parts.

Second-tier companies often maintain their low prices by keeping the price of their corporate operations low. These companies have a limited research and development budget. Also, they try to maintain a relatively small work force by contracting with another company to provide repair and warranty work.

Computers from third-tier companies often appear to be much less expensive than those in other tiers. Sometimes this reflects the low overhead costs of a small company, but other times it reflects poor-quality components. A consumer who is knowledgeable about the market and has technical expertise can often get a bargain on a good-quality computer from a third-tier company. But some consumers think it's risky to purchase computers from third-tier companies. Third-tier companies are smaller and perhaps more likely to go out of business, leaving their customers without technical support.

Marketing Channels

Is it safe to buy a computer by mail?

Computer hardware and software are sold by marketing outlets or "channels," as shown in Figure 5-18.

Figure 5-18
Marketing channels

Distribution centers stock products from many different manufacture's and then sell the products to retailers.

Manufacturer's produce products and ship them to VARs, distribution centers, computer centers, computer retailers, and mail-order suppliers.

Some manufacture's ship products directly to customers.

Mail-order suppliers specialize in taking phone orders and shipping products to customers using U.S. mail or courier services.

VARs generally modify products or assemble them into complete hardware and software solutions that are targeted at specific businesses.

Computer retailers stock products from several manufacture's and sell these products to customers.

A **computer retail store** purchases computer products from a manufacturer or distribution center and then sells the products to consumers. Computer retail stores are either small local shops or nationwide chains that specialize in the sale of microcomputer software and hardware. The employees at computer retail stores are often knowledgeable about a variety of computer products and can help you select a hardware or software product to fit your needs. Many computer retail stores also offer classes and training sessions, answer questions, provide technical support, and repair hardware products.

Computer retail stores can be a fairly expensive channel for hardware and software. Their prices reflect the cost of purchasing merchandise from a distributor, maintaining a retail storefront, and hiring technically qualified staff. A computer retail store is often the best source of supply for buyers who are likely to need assistance after the sale, such as beginning computer users or those with complex computer systems such as networks.

Mail-order suppliers take orders by mail or telephone and ship the product directly to consumers. Mail-order suppliers generally offer low prices but provide limited service and support. A mail-order supplier is often the best source of products for buyers who are unlikely to need support or who can troubleshoot problems with the help of a technical support person on the telephone. Experienced computer users who can install components, set up their software, and do their own troubleshooting are often happy with mail-order suppliers. Inexperienced computer users might not be satisfied with the support and assistance they receive from mail-order suppliers.

Value-added resellers (VARs) combine commercially available products with special hardware or software to create a computer system designed to meet the needs of a specific industry. Although VARs charge for their expertise, they are often the only source for a system that really meets the needs of a specific industry. For example, if you own a video rental store and want to automate your store, the best type of vendor might be a VAR. The VAR can offer you a complete hardware and software package that is tailored to the video rental business. This means that you do not need to piece together a computer, scanner, printer, and software components for a computer system to keep track of video rentals. VARs are often the most expensive channel for hardware and software, but their expertise can be crucial in making sure that the hardware and software work correctly in a specific environment.

Manufacturer direct refers to hardware manufacturers that sell their products directly to consumers using a sales force or mail order. The sales force usually targets large corporate or educational customers where large volume sales can cover costs and commissions. Manufacturers also use mail order to distribute directly to individual consumers. Manufacturers can sell their products directly to consumers for a lower price than when they sell them through retailers, but they cannot generally offer the same level of support and assistance as a local retailer. In an effort to improve customer support, some manufacturers have established customer support lines and provide repair services at the customer's place of business.

The Computer Press

Where can I get reliable information in order to make computer purchases?

Computer publications provide information on computers, computing, and the computer industry. The type of computer publication you need depends on the kind of information you are trying to obtain.

Computer Magazines contain articles and advertisements for the latest computer products. One of the earliest computer magazines, *Byte*, began publication in August 1975 and still remains one of the most widely read sources of computer information. The success of *Byte* might be attributed to its wide coverage of computers and computing topics. Many magazines that featured only a single type of computer, such as the Apple II, had staying power only as long as the computer maintained good sales. There are exceptions, however, magazines for specific computers, such as *MacWorld*, have a healthy subscription list.

Computer magazines generally target users of both personal and business computers. Articles often focus on product evaluations, product comparisons, and practical tips for installing hardware and using software. These magazines are full of product advertisements, which are useful if you want to keep informed about the latest products available for your computer. You can find computer magazines on virtually any newsstand and at your public library.

Computer Industry Trade Journals have a different focus than computer magazines because they target computer professionals, rather than consumers. Computer trade journals, such as *InfoWorld* and *Computer Reseller News*, focus on company profiles, product announcements, and sales techniques. Often free subscriptions to trade journals are given to corporate decision makers because advertisers want them to be aware of their products. Trade journals are not always available on newsstands, and subscriptions are not always available to the general public.

Computing Journals offer an academic perspective on computers and computing issues. Such journals focus on research in computing, with articles on such topics as the most efficient sorting technique to use in a database management system, the implication of copyright law for educational institutions, or the prevalence of spreadsheet use by executives in Fortune 500 companies. Academic journals rarely advertise hardware and software products because it might appear that advertisers could influence the content of articles.

An article in a computing journal is usually "refereed," which means that it is evaluated by a committee of experts who determine if the article is original and based on sound research

Project 12 at the end of this chapter guides you to some of these sites to discover what kinds of information you can expect to find at Internet World Wide Web sites.

techniques. The best place to find computing journals is in a university library. Some of the most respected journals in the computing field include *Communications of the ACM* (Association for Computing Machinery), *Communications of the IEEE* (Institute of Electrical and Electronics Engineers), *SIAM* (Society of Industrial and Applied Mathematics) *Journal on Computing*, and *Journal of Information Science*.

Internet Sites are an excellent source of information about the computer industry and computer products. Several computer magazines and trade journals maintain Internet sites with articles from back issues. Current issues are also available from some sites for a fee.

Many computer companies have Internet sites where consumers can access up-to-date information about products and services. Here you can usually find product specifications, product announcements, sales literature, technical support forums, and pricing information.

Figure 5-19
Industry analysts

MARKETING

Windows 95 Buzz Will C

By Don Clark
Staff Reporter of THE WALL STREET JOURNAL

Companies don't usually rush to buy ads in another company's infomercial, and the Rolling Stones don't usually sell rights to their songs for television ads.

But then, none of the old rules seem to apply to the selling of Windows 95.

Microsoft Corp. has already caused a marketing frenzy in the computer world during the long delayed introduction of the new computer operating system, which will make its debut next Thursday. Now, it is orchestrating a buzz that is reaching far beyond the tech world, involving a wide range of business partners — including the Stones, whose "Start Me Up" will be a sort of Windows 95 theme song, anchoring TV ads set to start airing Thursday evening.

Microsoft is believed to be spending about $200 million of its own money marketing and advertising Windows 95. But marketing experts say the product is getting 10 times that amount in free publicity from other companies' ads and the effects of a tidal wave of news coverage. Even the Doonesbury comic strip is featuring the new system this week.

"Microsoft has been in the news almost on a daily basis," said Rajiv Lal, a professor of marketing at Stanford University business school. "It's an amazing thing for a company that was perceived as being nerdy."

The latest uproar followed leaks to London newspapers that the Stones had agreed to let Microsoft use "Start Me Up" in Windows 95 TV spots. In one 60-second commercial, the song, from the Stones' 1981 album "Tattoo You," will be heard throughout. A button labeled start is a key new feature for navigating through the software and a consistent theme in Microsoft's print and broadcast advertising.

It is the first time Stones songwriters

they own the copyright, except tising related to the group's ow The Stones have had other co ventures, though, including a Stones Visa and MasterCard i October 1994 by the Chevy Chase Chevy Chase, Md.

British press reports said Mi set a price of $12 million for the song, but one person familiar matter put the true figure at clo million, an amount that would a record in the field. Microsoft comment on the price. "You can get what you want, but if you're you get what you need," said Al music licensing expert and reti president of Time Warner's Warn pell Music unit.

People familiar with one of dows 95 commercials said that with a view of the Windows 95 s and Mr. Jagger's voice singing " Up." Viewers then see a fast MTV-like assemblage of images, which feature people using Micros ucts, among them kids, students workers, and executives.

Microsoft hasn't broken down keting expenditures for Windows has projected that advertising for all of its products will tot $200 million in the year ending 1996, up from $100 million the pric

DOONESBURY copyright 1995 G.B. Trudeau. Re

You can get better acquainted with the views of industry analysts by doing Project 6 at the end of this chapter.

Industry Analysts

Who's got the inside scoop on computer companies and products?

The computer industry has many **industry analysts** who monitor industry trends, evaluate industry events, and make predictions about what the trends seem to indicate. Computer industry analysts range from professional financial analysts, who report on the computer industry for the *Wall Street Journal* and *Forbes* magazine, to the "rumor-central" analysts, who spark up the back pages of trade journals and computer magazines with the latest gossip about new products.

If you want to invest in a computer corporation's stock, the financial analysts might offer some good insights. If you want to invest in a personal computer, the rumor-central columns are the place to get the scoop about product shortages, hardware glitches, software bugs, and impending customer service problems. Figure 5-19 contains an example of a *Wall Street Journal* market analysis for the rollout of Windows 95.

Quick Check

1 Computer vendors are often categorized into three _____ based on market share and financial resources.

2 List the four marketing channels in the computer industry.

3 A(n) _____ is a computer publication designed for computer professionals, rather than the general consumer.

4 A(n) _____ sells complete computer solutions for a specific industry such as video stores or medical offices.

5 Articles in _____ journals are usually accurate because they are refereed by a committee of experts before being published.

User Focus:
Computer Shopping Strategies

If you are like most consumers in pursuit of a good computer value, you will talk to sales people, read computer magazines, look through computer catalogs, and chat with your friends who own computers. Here are some shopping strategies that should help you purchase a computer that meets your needs within a budget you can afford.

Determine Your Needs and Budget

Where do I start?

Start by setting a budget and stick to it! Computer vendors have very carefully priced the computers in their model line so that you will be tempted to spend "just a few hundred dollars more" to get a model with more features. The trouble is that if you decide to spend that few hundred dollars, you will be tempted to spend just a little more to get even more features.

Once you have established a budget, consider how you plan to use the computer. A computer can be a valuable tool for completing your college degree, it can be a useful educational tool for your children, and it can increase your competitive edge in your career. Consider these factors before you begin shopping for a computer:

Notebook or desktop? If you plan to carry your computer with you, a notebook computer is the optimal choice. However, a notebook costs more than a similarly configured desktop, so you will pay for portability or give up features.

Multimedia? If you want to use multimedia applications, you should buy a system with a CD-ROM drive and sound card. Multimedia notebooks can be pricey, but a docking bay might allow you to add multimedia capabilities and still stay within your budget.

Compatibility? Most computers sold today are IBM compatible. However, you should consider a Macintosh computer if most of the computers in your school are Macintoshes, if the computer is for your children who are using Macintosh computers in school, or if Macintosh is the major computer used in your career field.

Printer? Remember that you must include the cost of a printer in your budget. Unless you need to print multipart forms, you should not buy a dot matrix printer. A black-and-white ink jet printer is in the same price range, but it uses single-sheet paper and produces better print quality. Inexpensive laser printers, referred to as "personal laser printers," cost $100 to $300 more than a black-and-white ink-jet printer. Also consider a printer's operational cost. If you are on a very limited budget, it is easier to replace a $15 ink cartridge than a $100 toner cartridge.

Collect the Facts

What information do I need?

Before you make a decision, shop around to collect information on pricing, features, and support. Although you might be tempted to buy the computer with the lowest price and best features, don't forget to consider the warranty and the quality of the support you are likely to get from the vendor. The checklist in Figure 5-20 will help you gather facts about pricing, features, and support.

Figure 5-20
Comparison data sheet

Computer Purchase Data Sheet

Computer brand, model, and manufacturer: _____
Processor type: _____
Processor speed: _____ MHz
RAM capacity: _____ megabytes
Type of bus: ❑ EISA ❑ ISA ❑ MicroChannel ❑ Local Bus ❑ PCI
Number and size of floppy disk drives: _____
Capacity of hard drive: _____ megabytes
Speed of CD ROM drive: _____ ms
Capacity and speed of tape drive: _____
Amount of cache memory: _____ kilobytes
Monitor screen size: _____ inches
Monitor resolution: _____ by _____
Type of video adaptor: ❑ VGA ❑ SVGA
Amount of video memory: _____ megabytes
Number of parallel ports: _____
Number of serial ports: _____
Number of SCSI ports: _____
Number of expansion slots: _____
Operating system: _____
Mouse included: ❑ Yes ❑ No
Sound card and speakers included: ❑ Yes ❑ No
Value of bundled application software: $ _____
Does it have good expansion capabilities? ❑ Yes ❑ No
Does it have an upgrade path for new technologies, such as new processors? ❑ Yes ❑ No
Does the vendor have a support team in place that will meet my needs? ❑ Yes ❑ No
Are technical support hours sufficient? ❑ Yes ❑ No
Is it inexpensive to get support? ❑ Yes ❑ No
Can I contact technical support personnel without being put on extended time? ❑ Yes ❑ No
Are technical support people knowlegeable? ❑ Yes ❑ No
Can I get my computer fixed in an acceptable time period? ❑ Yes ❑ No
Are the costs and procedures for fixing the computer acceptable? ❑ Yes ❑ No
What is the warranty period? _____ years
Does the warranty cover parts and labor? ❑ Yes ❑ No
Are other users satisfied with this computer? ❑ Yes ❑ No
Is the manufacturer a well-financed and stable company? ❑ Yes ❑ No
Are the computer parts and components standard? ❑ Yes ❑ No
Price: _____

Evaluate the Facts

How do I make the decision?

After you have collected the facts, your decision might be obvious. In an ideal situation, a local vendor with a reputation for excellent support is selling a computer with features and price comparable to those sold by many reputable mail-order vendors. In the real world, however, your local vendor's price might be higher, and then your decision is not so clear. You might want to make a decision support matrix like the one shown in Figure 5-21.

Figure 5-21
Decision support
worksheet

1. List at least two possible options. This worksheet is designed to help you choose between Computer #1 and Computer #2.

2. List the factors that are important criteria for making your selection.

3. Assign a "weighting factor" to each criterion using a scale of 1 to 10.

4. After you reasearch the options, assign a raw score for each factor.

5. Add a formula in the spreadsheet to multiply the raw score by the weighting factor to produce a weighted score.

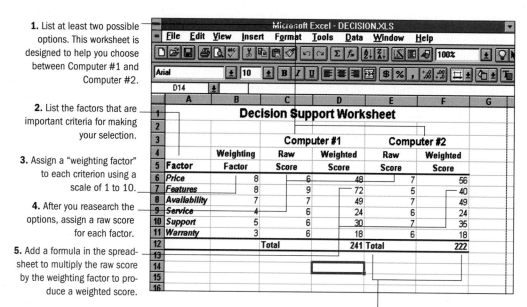

6. Add a formula in the spreadsheet to total the weighted scores for each option. The option that has the hightst total is the best system for you to purchase.

Project 11 at the end of this chapter helps you work with a decision support worksheet like the one in Figure 5-21.

End Note

One strategy for buying a computer is to decide how much you want to spend and then buy whatever computer a major manufacturer offers at that price. You probably won't get a great deal. You might not even get a computer that really meets your needs. But you will have a computer. If you would like to be a more effective consumer in today's computer marketplace, you must understand the terminology in computer ads; and use magazines, journals, and the Internet to keep up-to-date on the latest computer models. In many respects it is part of keeping up with current events. By browsing through an occasional computer magazine and by paying attention to computer-related events in the news, you can keep fairly up-to-date.

Review

1. Make a list of the key points you need to remember about buying a desktop computer.

2. Make a list of the additional factors you must consider when buying a notebook computer.

3. Demonstrate your understanding of the terminology and issues involved in purchasing a computer by answering the following questions about the computer ad in Figure 5-1.

    a. The microprocessor in the MicroPlus computer would be categorized in which microprocessor family?

    b. The software that you could run with the MicroPlus computer would not generally be compatible with which other types of computers?

    c. Is the amount of RAM cache in the MicroPlus computer adequate considering the type of processor in the computer?

    d. Does the MicroPlus computer have enough RAM to run Windows 95?

    e. About how much would it cost to upgrade the MicroPlus computer to 32 MB of memory?

    f. Why does the MicroPlus computer come with only one floppy disk drive?

    g. How fast is the CD-ROM drive?

    h. What is the advantage of the local bus used by the hard drive?

    i. How many types of buses does the MicroPlus computer include?

    j. Can you add a second internal hard disk drive to the MicroPlus computer? Why or why not?

    k. Would you be able to display photographic-quality images at 1024×768 resolution? Why or why not?

    l. Would you be able to run multimedia software on the MicroPlus computer? Why or why not?

    m. What bundled software, if any, is included with the MicroPlus computer?

    n. If you purchase the MicroPlus computer and a week after you receive it, the monitor stops working, what is the MicroPlus company policy on repairs?

4. Demonstrate your understanding of the MicroNote computer ad in Figure 5-8 by answering the following questions:

    a. Who manufactures the processor for the MicroNote computer?

    b. How would you expand the MicroNote computer to include a modem?

    c. Can you disconnect the monitor from your desktop computer and connect it to the MicroNote?

    d. Is the display on the MicroNote suitable for multimedia applications?

    e. Can the MicroNote computer use Macintosh software? Why or why not?

    f. What options would you have if you wanted to connect a CD-ROM drive to the MicroNote?

    g. Can you switch batteries while the MicroNote computer is on?

    h. Can you display photographic quality images at 1024×768? Why or why not?

    i. Which two of the equipment options do you think would be most important for your computing needs if you owned the MicroNote computer?

5. For each of the following computer components, indicate the unit of measurement used to describe the component's capacity:

microprocessor speed	microprocessor word size
hard disk capacity	disk drive access time
floppy disk capacity	CD-ROM drive speed
RAM capacity	video memory
disk cache capacity	bus speed
bus capacity	screen resolution
image clarity	modem speed

6. Draw a diagram to illustrate the life cycle of a computer hardware product.

7. Describe the characteristics of each of the three market tiers in the computer industry.

8. List the advantages and disadvantages of purchasing a computer from each computer industry market channel.

9. Describe the differences among computer magazines, trade journals, and computing journals.

10. Your parents are thinking of buying a computer. Because you are taking a computer course, they turn to you for advice. The first thing you tell them is to decide how much they want to spend. Think about everything you have learned in this chapter—especially the tips in the User Focus section. Based on what you have learned, compose a letter to your parents giving them advice about buying a computer.

Projects

1. The *Computer Shopper* Experience The story about Matt at the beginning of this chapter is fairly realistic. Many people purchase mail-order computers, and the *Computer Shopper* is the most popular source of information for mail-order prices. Suppose you decide to buy a computer, and you decide your budget is $2,000. You don't need to buy a printer because your friend is giving you a useable, but older printer. Look through the ads in a recent issue of the *Computer Shopper* to find the best computer that fits your computing needs and your budget. Write the list of features, the price, and the vendor for the computer, as well as the month and page of the issue. Then explain why you think this computer is the best one for the money.

2. Product Announcements Find a product announcement in a computer magazine. How would you classify this announcement? Is it a trial balloon, an anticipated ship date, or a product release? How can you tell? Was it written by a vendor or by a reporter?

3. Today's Microprocessors Microprocessor technology changes rapidly. New models arrive every couple of years, and the clock speed for a particular model seem to increase every few months. As you learned in this chapter, computers that contain state-of-the-art microprocessors are usually priced at a premium. Because the latest microprocessors are so expensive, the most popular computers—those that are purchased by the most people—tend to contain a previous model microprocessor. When you are in the market for a computer, it is useful to be able to differentiate between the state-of-the art microprocessors and previous models.

Browse through several computer magazines to determine which microprocessor is most popular and which microprocessor is currently state-of-the-art. Write a brief description of your findings. Include the following information:

   a. The clock speed, processor model name or number, and word size for the most popular microprocessor.

   b. The clock speed, processor model name or number, and word size for the state-of-the-art microprocessor.

   c. A brief explanation of what factors helped you determine that these particular microprocessors are the most popular and the most state-of-the-art.

   d. A bibliography of your sources.

4. Comparison Shopping Comparison shopping is a good strategy for finding the best deal in a computer system. Use the hardware checklist in Figure 5-20 to gather comparative information about two computer systems. You can gather the information from a computer magazine, the Internet, or from a local computer retail store. Be sure you exercise courtesy, especially if you visit a small retail store. Let the salesperson know that you are working on a class project, and recognize that the sales person's priority is shoppers who intend to actually buy a computer. Your instructor might suggest that you and one or two other students do this project as a small group.

5. Computer Industry Although the computer industry is less than half a century old, it has more than its share of good luck and hard luck stories. The history of each computer company has contributed in some way to the current state of the computer industry. Select a well-known company in the computer industry such as IBM, Digital, Microsoft, Apple, Compaq, Hewlett-Packard, Cray Research, or Toshiba. Use library and/or Internet resources to research the history of the company and trace the events that led to the company's current status in the computer industry. Write a report that summarizes your research. Follow your instructor's requirements for the length of your report.

6. The Latest "Scoop" Different industry analysts tend to give their readers the scoop on many of the same "hot topics." It's fascinating to see how the rumors spread and how analysts see events from different perspectives. Read at least 10 industry analysts' columns from several computer magazines published in the same month and year. Although 10 columns might sound like a lot, they are not long and many are fairly entertaining. Summarize what you read by indicating the topics that were "hot" that month and how the analysts agreed or disagreed.

7. Your Dollar Buys a Lot More Today You have probably heard that computer technology changes at an amazing speed. Today, your money buys much more computing power than it did in 1990. How much more? Look through the computer ads in back issues of computer magazines for June 1990, June 1993, and June 1995. Create a chart that shows the changes in the specifications for computers for a price of $2,000. Be sure you compare the processor type, processor speed, RAM capacity, hard disk drive capacity, screen resolution, and bus type.

8. Product Comparison Reviews Many computer magazines feature extensive product comparison reviews in which several hardware or software products are evaluated and compared. For example, a magazine might feature a comparison and evaluation of seven word processing software packages or eight notebook computers.

Suppose you are working for an organization and your job is to select hardware and software products.

 a. Describe the organization for which you work, then specify which type of product (notebook computers, word processing software, group scheduler, and so on) you are looking for and why.

 b. Explain the important factors that will influence your decision such as budget or special features that your organization requires from the product.

 c. Find and read an appropriate comparative review in a recent computer magazine.

 d. Based on the comparative review, which product would you recommend? Why?

9. Careers in Computer Sales Computer industry careers related to computer and software sales include retail sales representative, retail store manager, technical support line representative, customer service representative, and phone sales representative. Select one of these careers. Use interviews, if possible, or library resources to determine what educational background is required, the entry level pay scale, the maximum salary, and the job description.

10. Your Compatibility Needs When you purchase a computer, it is likely you will want to maintain compatibility with the type of computers used in your field. For example, if most elementary schools use Apple computers and your field is elementary education, you might have a strong reason for purchasing an Apple computer instead of an IBM compatible. For this project, research the type of computers most typically used in your field or major. Keep a lookout for hard data, such as the number of Apple II computers still in use in schools. Write a one- to two-page report describing your findings; conclude with the computer you would purchase today to prepare for your career of the future. Your instructor might suggest that you do this project in a small group with other students who have similar career goals.

11. Using a Decision Support Spreadsheet for Buying a Computer A decision support spreadsheet like the one in Figure 5-21 helps you prioritize your computing needs and compare the value of several computers based on these priorities. For this Project, do the following:

 a. Create a spreadsheet like the one shown in Figure 5-21.

 b. Modify the factors listed in column A to reflect your computing needs.

 c. Modify the weighting factors in column B to reflect their importance to you.

 d. Gather information about two different computer systems that you might consider purchasing.

 e. Give each computer a raw score for each factor. For example, if Computer #1 has all the features you seek, enter a 10 in cell B7. If Computer #2 only has half the features you want, enter a 5 in cell E7.

 f. Notice which computer has the highest total score. This should be the best computer for your needs.

 g. Somewhere on the spreadsheet include a short description of each computer, including its brand name, price, and model.

 h. Print out your spreadsheet. Be sure to include your name.

12. Computer Companies on the Internet Many hardware and software companies maintain Internet sites. A major purpose of these sites is to distribute information to potential and existing customers. Access the Web page for one of the following companies, then answer questions a through d:

 http://www.microsoft.com
 http://www.ibm.com
 http://www.intel.com
 http://www.apple.com

 a. How would you characterize the information at this site? Is it primarily sales, technical, and/or company background?

 b. Give an example of information at this site that would help you decide whether you wanted to buy a particular product.

 c. Would you be able to use this site to contact a company representative? If so, how would you do this?

 d. Even if you weren't thinking of purchasing a product from this company, describe in detail something at the site you found to be interesting.

Resources

- *Computer Shopper. The* magazine for people who buy computers by mail order. Each issue is packed full of computer ads from vendors in all marketing tiers. Hidden between the ads, you'll actually find articles with helpful hints and product evaluations.

- Freiberger, P. and M. Swaine. *Fire in the Valley: The Making of the Personal Computer.* Berkeley: Osborne/McGraw Hill, 1984. This book provides energetic coverage of the development of the micro-computer from the first microprocessor through the Altair, CP/M, IMSAI, Microsoft, Apple, and the IBM PC. The authors include many photos and anecdotes about the colorful figures who played prominent roles in the early days of the microcomputer industry.

- Rodgers, W. *THINK: Biography of the Watsons and IBM.* New York: Stein and Day, 1969. Rodgers wrote an unauthorized but lively account of IBM and its leaders. Published in 1969, this book ends before the advent of the microcomputer and is, therefore, an account of the "glory days" of mainframe computing.

- Rogers, E. and J. Larson. *Silicon Valley Fever: Growth of High-Technology Culture.* New York: Basic Books, 1982. Rogers, a professor of International Communi-cation at Stanford University, and Larson, a Silicon Valley research scientist, teamed up to create a very readable account of the impact of technology on the businesses and people of Silicon Valley. The legends are all here: the multimillion-dollar companies that started in a garage, the teenagers who became corpo-rate magnates, the most successful public stock offer-ing in history, and the spreadsheet empire that went from rags to riches and back to rags.

- *http://www.awa.com* Downtown anywhere is a World Wide Web site with many of the amenities of a cyber-space city: museums, travel, sports, education, and, of course, shopping! This is an excellent site for checking out current computer pricing.

- *http://www.cexpress.com* Computer Express bills itself as "Your Online Superstore." It is a great place to browse for computer hardware and software. You can even download demos of many software products.

- *http://www.internet.net* This is the Internet site for the Internet Shopping Network. Here you will find several stores selling computer hardware and software, so it is a good place to look if you're interested in current computer pricing and features.

Lab Assignments

 When buying from a mail-order or Internet computer vendor, consumers don't have an opportunity to take various computer models for a "test drive." They make a computer purchase decision based solely on a list of specifica-tions. Thus, it is essential to understand the specifica-tions in computer ads. In this Lab, you will find out how to use a Shopping Glossary to interpret the specifications.

1. Click the Steps button to learn how to use the Shop-ping Glossary. As you proceed through the Steps, answer all of the Quick Check questions that appear. After you complete the Steps, you will see a Quick Check Summary Report. Follow the instructions on the screen to print this report.

2. Click the Explore button and read the ad for the VectorMicro VP5-120 Computer system. Use the Shopping Glossary to define the following terms:

   a. Write-back cache, b. EIDE, c. DRAM

   d. Baud, e. Wavetable , f. EDO memory

3. In Explore, read the ads for the ZeePlus Multimedia Value Pak and the ZeePlus Multimedia Pro computers. The two systems differ substantially in price—$1,129 for the Multimedia Value Pak and $1,599 for the Multimedia Pro computer. If you purchase the more expensive sys-tem, what additional features do you get?

4. In Explore, read the ad for the ZeePlus Multimedia Pro Computer and the and Nevada Tech Systems P5/120 Multimedia Computer. If you get a system configured with 8 MB RAM, 850 MB hard disk, and a Pentium 120 MHz processor, what is the price difference between these two systems? What factors might account for this price difference?

5. In Explore, read the ads to find a notebook computer that's priced within $100 of the VP5/120 desktop com-puter. Make a list of the features the desktop computer has, that the notebook computer does not have. Which one would you buy? Why?

6. Photocopy a computer ad from a recent issue of a computer magazine. On a separate sheet of paper, write each specification (for example, Intel Pentium processor). For each specification, define each term (for example, Intel is a microprocessor manufacturer, Pentium is a type of microprocessor in the x86 family). Write out all acronyms (for example, RAM means random access memory). If you have difficulty with some of the terms and acronyms, click the Explore button and use the Shopping Glossary.

Quick Check
Answers

5.1

1. x86, 68000-series, PowerPC

2. the operating system and application software you intend to use

3. EIDE, SCSI

4. local buses

5. dot pitch

6. 1 MB

7. bps

8. inkjet

5.2

1. PCMCIA

2. active

3. docking station

4. port replicator

5. track point, touch pad, track ball

6. power saving

5.3

1. product development, product announcement, introduction, maintenance, retirement

2. product announcement

3. vaporware

4. plateau

5. version, revision

6. beta

5.4

1. tiers

2. computer retail store, mail-order suppliers, value-added resellers, manufacturer direct

3. trade journal

4. value-added reseller

5. computing journals

Glossary/Index

A

AC adapters, notebook computers, 5-18

academic journals, 5-28–5-29

accelerated video adapter A type of video card that uses graphics coprocessor chips designed to perform video functions at very high speed, 5-10

access time, hard disk drives, 5-7, 5-8

active matrix screen A notebook LCD screen that updates rapidly and provides image quality similar to a monitor, 5-15

alpha testing The software testing phase in which a computer program is tested by programmers and software testers employed by the publisher of a software product, 5-23

AMD, 5-4

Apple Computer, Inc., 5-5, 5-26

application software, bundled with new computers, 5-11

AT&T, computer vendor, 5-26

B

batteries, notebook computers, 5-18

baud rate The number of times the state or frequency of a communications line can change per second, 5-11

bay An opening in a microcomputer case for mounting disk, CD-ROM, and tape drives, 5-9

beta tester A user who performs beta testing on a software product, 5-23, 5-23–5-24

beta testing The software testing phase when selected users test a computer program and report bugs to the publisher, 5-23, 5-23–5-24

beta version Software used in beta testing, 5-23

bits per second (bps) The number of data bits transmitted by a modem in one second, 5-11

bugs, testing software, 5-23–5-24

bundled software, 5-11

buying computers, 5-27–5-28, 5-30–5-31
    desktop computers. *See* buying desktop computers
    notebook computers. *See* buying notebook computers
    strategies, 5-30–5-31

buying desktop computers, 5-4–5-13
    bundled software, 5-11
    bus and slot types, 5-8–5-9
    case selection, 5-9
    CD-ROM drive speed, 5-6–5-7

C

D

Local Area Networks and E-mail

Local Area Networks
and **E-mail**

In the decade between 1976 and 1986 the microcomputer industry boomed. Microcomputer companies made record profits. *Time* magazine named the microcomputer "Man of the Year." Yet, while mainframe users enjoyed the connectivity provided by electronic mail and shared files, microcomputer users were generally isolated on their standalone computers. Communication between microcomputers was jokingly referred to as "the sneaker net"—meaning that to transfer a file from one computer to another, you put the file on a floppy disk, then walked with the disk to another computer. White Reeboks were popular corporate footwear at the time.

The idea that microcomputer users could benefit by connecting their computers into a network became feasible about 10 years ago with the introduction of reliable, reasonably priced software and hardware designed for microcomputer networks. The availability of this hardware and software ushered in a new era of computing, which increasingly provides ways for people to collaborate, communicate, and interact.

The purpose of this chapter is to help you understand the type of local area computer networks you would typically find in a college, university, or business. This chapter emphasizes the user perspective, beginning with a tour of network resources, then presenting practical information on network hardware and software including network applications such as groupware and electronic mail.

CHAPTER**PREVIEW**

In this chapter you will learn how computer networks and electronic mail work. The concepts you learn are useful for effectively using microcomputer networks, such as those in your school labs or in a business where you work. You'll learn how to select a secure password and how to log into a network. You'll also learn how to share files with other users, and you'll pick up some tips for using electronic mail. When you have completed this chapter you should be able to:

■ Describe the resources you would find on a typical local area network

■ Explain how using a computer on a network is different from using a standalone computer

■ List the advantages of using a local area network

■ Explain the difference between sharing files on a network and using groupware

■ Describe how processing differs on networks that use dedicated file servers, peer-to-peer capability, client-server architecture, and host-based time-sharing

■ Describe the types of software you can use on a local area network

■ Explain how software licenses for networks differ from those for standalone computers

■ Explain how a network uses store-and-forward technology for e-mail

E-mail

Local Area Networks

A **computer network** is a collection of computers and other devices that communicate to share data, hardware, and software. A network that is located within a relatively limited area such as a building or campus is referred to as a **local area network** or **LAN**. A network that covers a large geographical area is referred to as a **wide area network** or **WAN**. In this chapter you will learn about local area networks.

Local area networks are found in most medium-sized and large businesses, government offices, and educational institutions. Worldwide an estimated 25 million computers are connected to local area networks.

Not all LANs are the same. Different types of networks provide different services, use different technology, and require users to follow different procedures. The information in this chapter describes how a majority of microcomputer networks work. However, any specific network you use might work differently and require different user procedures. Don't hesitate to ask questions when you use an unfamiliar network.

Network Resources

What's the advantage of a computer network?

A computer that is not connected to a network is referred to as a **standalone computer**. When you physically connect your computer to a local area network, using a cable or other communications channel, your computer becomes a **workstation** on the network and you become a "network user."

Your workstation has all its usual resources, referred to as **local resources**, such as your hard drive, software, data, and printer. You also have access to **network resources**, which typically include application software, storage space for data files, and printers other than those with your local workstation.

On a network, application software and storage space for data files are typically provided by a network server. A **network server** is a computer connected to the network that "serves," or distributes, resources to network users. A **network printer** provides output capabilities to all the network users. Each device on a network, including workstations, servers, and printers, is referred to as a **node**. Locate the workstations, network server, and other network resources in Figure 6-1.

Figure 6-1 ◄
Local and network resources

The microcomputers connected to a network are referred to as **workstations.**

A **network printer** is a network resource because any workstation on the network can send files to it.

Workstation

The **network server** is a network resource. It distributes or "serves" application programs and data files to the workstations. The hard disk drive of the network server is, therefore, shared by the workstations on the network.

Workstation

Data is sent from one device on the network to another over a cable or by wireless signal.

Your computer is a workstation on the network. Your workstation's memory, processor, and disk drives are your **local resources**, as are the program and data files stored on your hard disk.

Your local workstation

The main advantage of a computer network is that all the users can share resources, instead of users each maintaining their own. For example, a LAN permits many users to share a single printer. Most organizations with LANs are able to reduce the total number of printers needed, reduce printer maintenance costs, and use the money saved to buy higher quality printers.

The Login Process

Do I have to do anything special to access network resources?

Even if your computer is physically connected to a network, you cannot use network resources until you log into the network. When you log in, you formally identify yourself to the network as a user.

During the login you are prompted to enter your user ID and password. Your **user ID**, sometimes referred to as your **user name**, is a unique set of letters and numbers. Your **password**, a special set of symbols known only to you and the network administrator, gives you security clearance to use network resources. Your user ID and password are the basis for your user account. A **user account** provides access to network resources and accumulates information about your network use by tracking when you log in and log out.

On most networks, users can select their own passwords. If you have this option, you should select a secure password so other people cannot log in as you and access your files. Your password should be unique, yet something you can remember. How do you select a secure password? Refer to the chart in Figure 6-2 for some password do's and don'ts.

Do	Don't
• Select a password that is at least five characters long.	• Select a password that is a word that can be found in the dictionary.
• Try to use numbers as well as letters in your password.	
• Select a password you can remember.	• Use your name, nickname, Social Security number, birth date, or name of a close relative.
• Consider making a password by combining two or more words.	
• Consider making a password by using the first letters of the words in a poem or phrase.	• Write your password where it is easy to find—under the keyboard is the first place a password thief will look.
• Change your password periodically.	

▶ **Figure 6-2**
Password do's and don'ts

Entering a valid user ID and password is the beginning of the **login process**. As the login process continues, your workstation is connected to network drives, allowing you to use programs and data files stored on a server. The login process also connects your workstation to network resources such as a network printer. The next two sections explain how this works.

A network administrator, also called a network supervisor, is the person responsible for maintaining a network. One of the network administrator's jobs is to create your account and provide you with a user ID and starter password. You can find out more about network-related careers in Projects 4 and 5 at the end of this chapter.

Drive Mapping

How does my computer access data files and application software from a network server?

Your workstation gains access to the file server and its hard drive when the server hard drive is *mapped* to a drive letter. **Mapping** is network terminology for assigning a drive letter to a network server disk drive. For example, on a typical workstation with a floppy drive A: and a hard drive C:, the login process maps the server hard drive as drive F:.

Once a drive letter has been mapped, you can access data files and application software from that drive just as you would from your local hard disk drive. Drive mappings vary from one network to another, depending on the needs of the organization and its users. One organization might map the server drive as F:, while another organization might map the server drive as J:. In other organizations, multiple drives on more than one server might be mapped as F:, I:, J:, and Z:. As a network user, you will find it useful to know the drive mapping so you can more easily find programs and files. Figure 6-3 shows the drive mapping available to a workstation in a network with a single server.

Figure 6-3
A typical workstation drive map

The server hard disk drive becomes drive F:.

Network server

Network printer

Your workstation floppy disk drive is your drive A:.

Your workstation hard drive is your drive C:.

Workstation

On your workstation, the login process assigns drive letters for the server drives. After the drives are mapped, you can view a directory of drive F: and access files on it just as you access files on drives A: or C:.

Using Programs on a Network

When I start a program supplied by a network server, is it the same as starting a program on a standalone computer?

You should remember from Chapter 4 that when you launch a program on a standalone computer, it is copied from your hard disk into RAM. Suppose you want to use a word processing program that is stored on the hard disk of a network server. Will the program be loaded into the memory of the server or into the memory of your workstation?

When you start a program that is stored on a server, the program is copied to the RAM of your workstation. Once the program is in memory, it runs just as if you had started it from your workstation hard disk drive. Figure 6-4 shows how this works.

You might wonder if more than one user on a network can simultaneously use the same program. One advantage of a network is that with proper licensing many users can access a program at the same time. This is called **sharing** a program. For example, while Lotus 1-2-3 is running on your workstation, other users can start the same program. The network server sends a copy of Lotus 1-2-3 to the RAM of each user's workstation.

Sharing programs is effective for several reasons. First, less disk storage space is required because the program is stored only once on the server, instead of being stored on the hard disks of multiple standalone computers. Second, when a new version of the software is released, it is easier to update one copy of the program on the server than to update many copies stored on standalone computers. Third, purchasing a software license for a network can be less expensive than purchasing single-user licenses for each workstation on the network.

Figure 6-4
Starting a program that is stored on the file server

If several users try to start a program at the same time, does it take longer than when only a single user starts the program? To find out, do Project 2 at the end of this chapter.

Using Data Files on a Network

Is there any advantage to storing data files on the server instead of my local hard disk?

Suppose that while connected to a network, you create a document using a word processing program. You can store the document either on your local hard disk or on the server hard disk. If you store the file on your local hard disk, you can access the file only from your workstation. However, if you store the file on the hard disk of the server, you, or any other user, can access the file from any workstation on the network, as shown in Figure 6-5.

Figure 6-5
Network file access

You can store a file, such as **Report.Doc**, on your local hard disk. When you do this, the file can be accessed only from your workstation.

Network server

When you store a file, such as **Market.Doc**, on the server hard disk, other users can also access the file. Therefore, **Market.Doc** is accessible to any workstation on the network.

Make sure you understand that more than one person can typically access a program file from the server, but typically only one person at a time can access a particular data file.

Although a *program file* on the file server can be accessed by more than one user at the same time, most of the *data files* on a network server can be opened by only one user at a time. When one user has a file open, it is **locked** to other users. File locking is a sensible precaution against losing valuable data. If the network allowed two users to open and edit the same data file, both users could make changes to the file; but one user's changes might contradict the other user's changes. Whose changes would be incorporated in the final version of the file?

Suppose two users were allowed to make changes to the same file at the same time. Each user would open a copy of the original file and make changes to it. The first user to finish making changes would save the file on the server. So far so good—the first user has replaced the original version of the file with an edited version. Remember, however, that the second user has been making revisions to the *original* file, but she has no idea of the first user's revisions. When the second user saves her revised version of the file, the changes made by the first user are overwritten by the second user's version, as shown in Figure 6-6.

The original document is not well written and the percentage is wrong. Sam and Gracie both decide to fix it.

▶ **Figure 6-6**
Why networks lock files

If Sam and Gracie were allowed to open the document at the sametime, they could edit the document in two different ways.

Sam stores the edited document on the server, but when Gracie stores her version of the document on the server, it overwrites Sam's version, erasing all of his work.

If you have a local printer in addition to a network printer, you can typically select the printer you want to use.

Using a Network Printer

How does my word processing software know it is supposed to send documents to the network printer instead of to my local printer?

Most application software sends files you want to print to the printer that is connected to your computer's parallel port. But network workstations often do not have local printers. Instead, they need to access a network printer. Figure 6-7 shows how data sent to your workstation's parallel port is **captured** and **redirected** to the network printer.

Figure 6-7
Capturing your workstation printer port

2. The process of logging into a network captures your parallel port and diverts data headed for your printer to the network instead.

Network printer

To network printer →

3. The data travels over the network to the network printer, where it is printed.

Parallel port

Detour

RAM

1. When your workstation is not attached to the network, the file you want to print is sent to the parallel port and out to your printer.

Workstation

What happens if a network printer receives more than one file to print? Most networks would not allow two files to travel simultaneously over the network. However, it is possible that before the printer has completed one printout, other files arrive to be printed. Files sent to a network printer are placed in a **print queue**. A print queue is a special holding area on a network server where files are stored until they are printed. When more than one user sends a file to the print queue, the files are added to the print queue and printed in the order in which they are received.

Figure 6-8 shows what happens when one user sends a document to the printer before another user's printout is completed.

3. Ceo.Doc arrives at the print queue. Before the printer completes this print job, **Gnp.Doc** arrives at the print queue.

Figure 6-8
The network print queue

1. The user at this workstation sends **Ceo.Doc** to be printed. The file is captured on its way to the parallel port and diverted to the network printer.

Ceo.Doc

Print Queue:
1. **Ceo.Doc**
2. **Gnp.Doc**

Workstation

Server

4. The print queue prints out the documents in the order they arrive, so the printer prints **Ceo.Doc** first, then it prints **Gnp.Doc**.

2. The user at this workstation sends **Gnp.Doc** to be printed. The file is captured on its way to the parallel port and diverted to the network printer.

Gnp.Doc

Workstation

Quick Check

1 A network _____ is a computer connected to a network that distributes files to network users.

2 _____ is network terminology for assigning a drive letter to a file server disk drive.

3 A(n) _____ provides access to network resources and accumulates information about your use of the network.

4 Assuming proper licensing, while Jenny uses a spreadsheet program from the file server, Atkin can also use this spreadsheet program at the same time. True or False?

5 While Sandi is editing a word processing document called **Budget.Doc**, Karl can also edit this document at the same time. True or False?

6 When a network printer is assigned to your workstation, any data sent to the workstation's parallel port is _____ and _____ to the network printer.

6.2 | Network Hardware

In the previous section, you looked at local area network resources and learned about the advantages of computer networks. Now let's look at network hardware.

Network Interface Cards and Cables

What establishes the physical connection for the computers in a network?

A network interface card is the key hardware component for connecting a computer to a local area network. A **network interface card** or **NIC** (pronounced "nick") is a small circuit board designed to plug into an expansion slot on a computer main board. Each workstation on a network must have a NIC. The network interface card sends data from your workstation out over the network and collects incoming data for your workstation.

Different types of networks use different types of network interface cards. If you want to add a computer to a network, you need to know the network type so you can purchase the appropriate NIC. Popular network types include **Ethernet**, **Token Ring**, **ARCnet**, **FDDI**, and **ATM**.

Most network interface cards contain a cable connector into which you plug the cable that connects workstations, network servers, and other devices. On the back of your computer, you might see one of the cable connectors like those shown in Figure 6-9.

Figure 6-9
A network interface card and cable connectors

A network interface card is a circuit board that plugs into one of the computer's expansion slots. This NIC is designed for a desktop computer. The NICs for many notebook computers are PCMCIA cards.

An RJ-45 network connector accepts an RJ-45 plug.

A plastic RJ-45 plug connects network hardware devices using twisted-pair wire similar to telephone wiring.

A BNC connector accepts a T-connector.

The T-connector links network hardware using coaxial cable similar to cable television wiring.

Instead of using cables, some **wireless networks** use radio or infrared signals to transmit data from one network device to another. The network interface cards on a wireless network contain the transmitting devices necessary to send data to other devices on the local area network. Wireless networks are handy in environments where wiring is difficult to install.

Network Servers

When I use a network, is my data processed locally or on the network server?

You have already learned the general functions of a network server. However, there are different kinds of network servers. They are explained in this section. When you use a standalone computer, all your data is processed by your computer's microprocessor. The device that processes your data when you are connected to a network depends on the type of servers included on your network.

A **dedicated file server** is devoted only to the task of delivering programs and data files to workstations. As you can see in Figure 6-10, a dedicated file server does not process data or run programs for the workstations. Instead, programs run using the memory and processor of the workstation.

A key feature of a network with a dedicated file server is that the server stores files and data, but the workstations process the data.

▶ **Figure 6-10**
A dedicated file server

The dedicated server sends application software files to the workstations, where they are run using the workstations' microprocessors.

I've got a lot of software and data files. I can send to any workstation, but don't ask me to process any data!

Application software

The dedicated server sends data files to the workstations to be processed.

Data files

Data files and application software are stored on the dedicated server, but the server does not process the data in the files or run the applications.

When I need software, I ask the server to send it.

Dedicated file server

When I need a data file, I can get it from the server.

Workstation 1

Workstation 2

Workstation 3

A typical local area network uses a microcomputer as a file server. However, a minicomputer or a mainframe computer can also be a file server.

In some cases, a network computer performs a dual role as both file server and workstation. This is referred to as a **non-dedicated server** or **peer-to-peer** capability.

"Dedicated file server" does not mean a network has only one server. Many networks have more than one dedicated file server.

When you use a non-dedicated server, your computer functions like a normal workstation, but other workstations can access programs and data files from the hard disk of your computer, as shown in Figure 6-11.

Figure 6-11
A non-dedicated
file server

I'm running Lotus 1-2-3, but I can send Lotus 1-2-3 software or **Budget.Doc** to any workstation.

A non-dedicated server stores data files and application software that is sent to workstations. This non-dedicated server/workstation stores the Lotus 1-2-3 program and the Budget.Doc data file. Even though this workstation acts as a server, you can also use it as a workstation to run an application such as Lotus 1-2-3. If this was a dedicated file server, you could not use it to run programs.

Lotus 1-2-3
Budget.Doc

Non-dedicated file
server/workstation

Do Project 1 at the end of this chapter to find out more about the network at your college or university.

More than one computer on a network can be a non-dedicated server. This non-dedicated server/workstation has provided the Microsoft Office software to one of the other workstations.

I'm running the Microsoft Office software that came from another server/workstation.

Microsoft Office

WordPerfect
Adobe Illustrator

This non-dedicated server/workstation is running the Microsoft Office software it received from one of the other workstations. If requested, it could supply WordPerfect or Adobe Illustrator software to other non-dedicated server/workstations on the network.

Budget.Doc

I can send Microsoft Office software to any workstation.

Budget.Doc

Microsoft Office

Microsoft Office

Non-dedicated file
server/workstation

Non-dedicated file
server/workstation

A key feature of a peer-to-peer network is that workstations also perform the role of server by storing and distributing data and programs.

A **print server** stores files in a print queue and sends each queued file to the network printer. A **print job** is a file that has been sent to the printer. Print jobs are processed locally on workstations that have a local printer, but a print server controls the print jobs on a network server. A print server can be the same computer as the file server, or it can be another micro, mini, or mainframe computer connected to the network.

An **application server** is a computer that runs application software and forwards the results of processing to workstations as requested. An application server makes it possible to use the processing power of both the server and the workstation. Also referred to as **client-server architecture**, use of an application server splits processing between the workstation *client* and the

Client-server architecture is becoming increasingly popular in corporations. Project 3 at the end of this chapter helps you find more information on this topic.

network *server*. Suppose you want to search for a particular record in a 50,000-record database stored on a network server. Study Figure 6-12 to see how client-server architecture makes use of the processing capacity of both the workstation and server.

Figure 6-12
Client-Server
architecture

A key feature of a client-server network is that the data sent by the server can be processed, not just viewed, by the workstations.

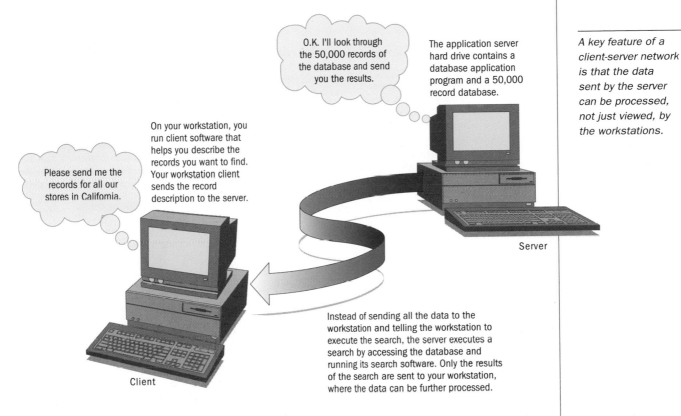

On your workstation, you run client software that helps you describe the records you want to find. Your workstation client sends the record description to the server.

Please send me the records for all our stores in California.

O.K. I'll look through the 50,000 records of the database and send you the results.

The application server hard drive contains a database application program and a 50,000 record database.

Server

Instead of sending all the data to the workstation and telling the workstation to execute the search, the server executes a search by accessing the database and running its search software. Only the results of the search are sent to your workstation, where the data can be further processed.

Client

Some networks include a **host computer**, usually a minicomputer or a mainframe with attached terminals. When you use a host computer from a terminal, all the processing takes place on the host. Your **terminal** has a keyboard and a screen, but it does not have a local storage device, and it does little or no processing on its own.

Connecting terminals to a host computer provided relatively low-cost computer access before powerful microcomputer networks became available. For economic reasons, many organizations have not yet moved important data and programs from mainframe hosts to microcomputers. Can you use a microcomputer to access the data stored on a mainframe host computer?

You can access a host computer from a microcomputer workstation by using terminal emulation software. **Terminal emulation software** makes a microcomputer appear to the host as a terminal. While the terminal emulation software is active, your microcomputer does very little local processing, as you can see in Figure 6-13 on the following page.

Although a system containing a host computer and terminals fits our general definition of a *network*, it is more customary to call it a **time-sharing system**. Because terminals can do little or no processing of their own, every terminal must wait for the host to process its request. The terminals essentially *share* the host's processor by being allocated a fraction of a second of processing time.

A key feature of networks with a mainframe host is that all the processing takes place on the host, not on workstations or terminals.

Now that you have looked at different server models—dedicated server, non-dedicated server, print server, application server, and host—you should be able to see that the device that processes your data depends on the type of server or servers connected to your local area network.

Figure 6-13 ◄
Mainframe host

The host accepts commands from terminals and sends back a display of results. Because the terminals do not have processing power of their own, they cannot further process the results they receive. For example, if your terminal receives a list of 50 people sorted by address, you could not sort the list by last name on your terminal. You would have to ask the host to sort the list and send you the new results.

Quick Check

Make sure you can explain the difference between a dedicated file server, peer-to-peer (non-dedicated server), client-server (application server), and host (time-sharing system).

1 The circuit board that connects a computer to a local area network is called a(n) _____.

2 If a network computer functions both as a file server and as a workstation, it is referred to as a(n) _____.

3 A(n) _____ is devoted to the task of delivering program and data files to workstations.

4 Client-server architecture takes advantage of the processing capabilities of both the workstations and the server. True or false?

5 On some networks, a(n) _____ computer processes data, then outputs the results on the screen of a terminal.

Software for Networks

The software on a local area network typically includes specialized network software as well as many of the same applications you might use on a standalone computer.

Network Operating System

Does a network require any special software?

A network requires **network software** or a **network operating system** to control the flow of data, maintain security, and keep track of user accounts.

Network operating systems such as **Novell NetWare**, **Banyan Vines**, and **Lantastic** are software packages designed exclusively to control network data flow. Network software is sometimes included as a component of popular computer operating systems such as Windows for Workgroups, Windows 95, UNIX, and OS/2.

A network operating system usually has two components: server software and client software. **Network server software** is installed on a file server and controls file access from the server hard drive, manages the print queue, and tracks user data such as IDs and passwords. **Network client software** is installed on the local hard drive of each workstation and is essentially a device driver for the network interface card. When your computer boots up, the network client software is activated and establishes the connection between your workstation and other devices on the network.

Standalone Applications

Do I need to buy a special version of my favorite application software to use it on a network?

Most applications designed for standalone computers can be installed on a network server, which sends them to individual workstations as requested. Most of your favorite word processing, spreadsheet, graphics, and presentation software will work on a network just as they do on a standalone computer.

Some applications that you use on a standalone computer have built-in features for networking that appear only when the software is installed on a network. For example, when your word processing software is installed on a network, it might show you a dialog box that lets you send files to another person on the network.

As you learned in Section 6.1, a network can supply an application to more than one person at a time by copying the program into the memory of the workstations. This capability applies to most standalone software. Therefore, software designed for standalone computers can usually be used on a network by more than one user at a time. However, most applications designed for standalone computers do not allow more than one person at a time to work on the same *data file*.

Groupware

Is there a way for two or more people to work together on the same data file?

When local area networks were first introduced, the concept of sharing files was limited to a sequential process in which one user at a time could work on a document. However, this process did not support many of the organizational activities that require collaboration and communication among employees. For example, in most organizations, people exchange information using memos, phone conversations, and face-to-face meetings. Employees collect, organize, and share information, which must be stored in a centralized repository. Documents and forms flow through

Windows 3.1 does not include network software. Therefore, if your school uses the Windows 3.1 operating system, your school network also requires a network operating system such as Novell NetWare.

In Chapter 2 you learned that a device driver is software that enables a computer to use a specific device. You can go back to Chapter 2, Section 2 to review device drivers.

Groupware encompasses a wide variety of software designed to enhance workgroup activities. For in-depth coverage of groupware, refer to the book Groupware, Workflow, and Workgroup Computing, *cited in the Resources list at the end of this chapter.*

organizations, picking up required signatures and approvals. Employees contribute sections of text that are compiled into a single report.

A **workgroup** is basically two or more people who work on the same project. Recent advances in workgroup technology have provided ways for local area networks to help workgroups become more efficient by coordinating group work and sharing information. Groupware is an important aspect of workgroup technology.

Figure 6-14
Groupware

Groupware software such as Collabra Share and Lotus Notes help work groups collaborate on projects.

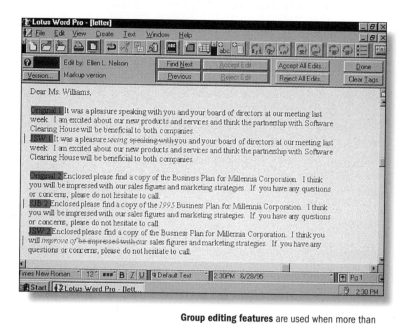

Group editing features are used when more than one person revises a document. Each person's revisions are separately marked to show who made each change. A document can be open by more than one person at a time, however, users will not be able to see each other's edits until their work is saved.

Group scheduling programs generally simplify the process of scheduling meetings. You just select the people that need to attend the meeting, and the group scheduling program finds a date and time when everyone can attend. The meeting appears as a tentative appointment on each person's individual schedule. Each user can then confirm the meeting or send a reply indicating that he or she cannot attend.

recommended meeting time

times when participants have other appointments

Groupware is application software that supports collaborative work, usually on a local area network. As you read the description of the groupware applications in Figure 6-14 consider how you might apply them for school projects or in your career.

Document routing, also referred to as **workflow management**, electronically forwards a document to a series of people for approval. As soon as one person signs off on the document, it is forwarded to the next person in the routing list. Some systems make it easy to check the status of a document to find out who has signed off on the document and who is currently holding it.

Figure 6-14
Groupware
continued

Loan application form

Loan manager evaluated application

Evaluated

Desktop videoconferencing provides a live video image of each participant in a real-time conference. Videoconferencing requires special software on each participating workstation, as well as a small video camera and video input board. Most videoconferencing systems provide optimal image quality using networks or dedicated communication lines, although some systems allow limited videoconferencing using modems and telephone lines.

Bank board members approve

Approved

Branch manager processes loan

Processed

Software Licenses for Networks

Can an organization buy just one copy of a software package and put it on the network for every one to use?

You might want to review the Software Copyright section in Chapter 2 to see why it is illegal for more than one person to use a software package unless the software license specifically allows it.

It would be very inexpensive for an organization to purchase a single copy of a software package, then place it on the network for everyone to use. In an organization with 100 users, for example, word processing capability might cost $295 for a single copy, instead of $29,500 for 100 copies. However, using a single-user license for multiple users violates copyright law.

Most single-user software licenses allow only one person to use the software at a time. However, many software publishers also offer a **network license** that permits use by multiple people on a network. Typically, such a network license will cost more than a single-user license, but less than purchasing single-user licenses for all of the users. For example, a word processing software package that costs $295 for a single-user license might have a $5,000 network license that allows up to 100 people to use the software. Network licenses are available for most software packages by contacting the software publisher.

Quick Check

1. Novell NetWare would be classified as a(n) _____ system.

2. True or false? When run on a network, most application software designed for standalone computers allows only one person at a time to access the same data file.

3. If an organization is planning to use software on a network, it should purchase a(n) _____ so multiple users can legally use the software.

4. If you are a team leader and you want your team members to collaborate on a project using the network, you might try to find a(n) _____ product.

5. If you were the manager of a loan department in a bank, you might request _____ groupware so the network will automatically send loan applications to each member of your department for processing and approval.

User Focus:
Electronic Mail

Electronic mail, or **e-mail**, is correspondence conducted between one or more users on a network. E-mail is a more efficient means of communication than ground or air mail. Rather than waiting for a piece of paper to be physically transported across the country, you can send an electronic version of a message directly to someone's electronic "mail box." E-mail also helps you avoid frustrating "telephone tag."

How E-mail Works

When I send an e-mail message does it go directly to the recipient's workstation? What if the recipient's workstation is not turned on?

An **e-mail message** is essentially a letter or memo sent electronically from one user to another. An **electronic mail system** is the hardware and software that collects and delivers e-mail messages. Typically, a local area network provides electronic mail services to its users. The software on the network server that controls the flow of e-mail is called **mail server software**. The software on a workstation that helps each user read, compose, send, and delete messages is called **mail client software**. Electronic mail systems are often classified as groupware because they facilitate communication among members of a workgroup.

E-mail messages are *stored* on a server. When you want to read this mail, the server *forwards* the messages to your workstation. Hence e-mail is called a **store-and-forward** technology. Because the server stores the messages, your workstation does not need to be on when someone sends you e-mail (Figure 6-15).

The Lotus Notes mail client software handles each user's personal mail box.

Icons and tools help you easily read mail, send mail and replies.

The Lotus Notes window shows you a list of arriving messages; the time they were sent, the sender's name and the subject of each message.

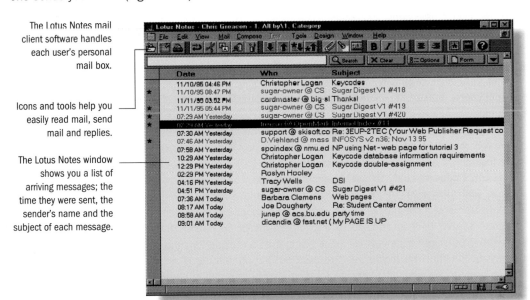

▶ **Figure 6-15**
Using e-mail

Your e-mail is transmitted through an electronic mail system and stored on a host or network server in an area you can think of as your **mailbox**. When you log into the electronic mail system and check your mail, the message is listed as new mail. You can choose to display and read the mail on your computer screen, print it, delete it, reply to it, forward it, or save it on disk.

Some e-mail systems allow you to send an **attachment**, which is a file such as a word processing document, worksheet, or graphic that travels through the e-mail system along with an electronic mail message. For example, suppose you receive e-mail from your department head about the proposed budget for next year. Your department head writes that there is a spreadsheet attachment called Budget containing the budget figures. To see the attachment after you read the e-mail message, your computer starts your spreadsheet program and opens the file Budget.

Some electronic mail systems offer features such as **priority mail**, which immediately alerts the recipient that an important e-mail message has arrived; **return receipt**, which sends a message back to you when a recipient receives your message; **carbon copy**, which sends a copy of the message to another user; and **group addressing**, which allows you to send a copy of an e-mail message to all members of a group at the same time.

What if you want to send e-mail to someone who is not connected to your computer network or host? Many e-mail systems are connected to other e-mail systems through electronic links called **gateways**. When you send an e-mail message to a user on another computer network, the message is transferred through the gateway to a larger e-mail system, which delivers the message to the recipient's network or host computer system.

Managing Your E-mail

I know how to write letters and memos—is there anything special I need to know about writing e-mail messages?

E-mail is not exactly the same as using the post office. With e-mail you can send messages right away—your letters don't sit around waiting for you to take them to the post office. You can send the same message to multiple people as easily as to a single person. It is easy to send replies automatically to messages you receive as well.

The advantages of e-mail can also create potential problems—for example, you might regret the contents of a message sent off in haste. Also, it's easy to accumulate an overwhelming number of messages in your mail box. Here are some tips to help you avoid e-mail problems:

Read your mail regularly. When you use electronic mail, your correspondents expect a quick response. You lose much of the advantage of e-mail if you check your mailbox only once every two weeks!

Delete messages after you read them. Your e-mail is stored, along with everyone else's, on a file server where storage space is valuable. Leaving old messages in your mailbox takes up space that could be used more productively.

You don't have to reply to every e-mail message. The purpose of some e-mail messages is to give you information. Don't reply unless you have a reason to respond, such as to answer a question. Sending a message to say "I got your message" just creates unnecessary mail traffic.

If you receive mail addressed to a group, it might be better to reply only to one person in the group. You might receive mail as a member of a mailing list; the same message will be sent to everyone on the list. If you use the automatic reply feature of your e-mail system, your message is likely to be sent to everyone on the list. Do this only if your reply is important for everyone to see.

Think before you send. It is easy to write a message in haste or in anger and send it off before you have time to think it through. If you're upset, write your message, but wait a day before you send it.

Don't write anything you want to remain confidential. Remember that with electronic mail forwarding messages is easy. Suppose you write something unflattering about Rob in an e-mail message to Julie. Julie can easily forward your message to Rob.

Don't get sloppy. Your e-mail is a reflection of you, your school, and your employer. Use a spellchecker if one is available; if not, proofread your message before you send it. Use standard grammar, punctuation, and capitalization. A message in all uppercase means you're shouting.

E-mail Privacy

Is my e-mail confidential?

You should be aware that your e-mail might be read by someone other than the recipient. Although the U.S. justice system has not yet made a clear ruling, current legal interpretations indicate that e-mail is not legally protected from snooping. You cannot assume that the e-mail you send is private. Therefore, you should not use e-mail to send any message that you want to keep confidential.

Why would an employer want to know the contents of employee e-mail? You might immediately jump to the conclusion that employers who read employee e-mail are snooping. This might be the case with some employers who, for example, want to discover what a union is planning. However, some employers read employee e-mail to discover if any illegal activities are taking place on the computer system. Many employers are genuinely concerned about such activities because they could, in some cases, be held responsible for the actions of their employees.

Also, the network administrator sometimes sees the contents of e-mail messages while performing system maintenance or when trying to recover from a system failure. Even if an employer does not intentionally read e-mail exchanges, technical difficulties might still expose the contents of e-mail messages to people other than the intended recipient.

End Note Local area networks have come a long way since the days of the sneaker net; they now provide connectivity for workgroups using groupware and for individuals exchanging e-mail. Although local area networks provide connectivity within a limited geographical area, electronic mail gateways provide connections between these small networks.

Review

1. Use your own words to answer the questions in italics below each heading in the chapter.

2. List each of the boldface terms used in this chapter, then use your own words to write a short definition.

3. List three reasons why sharing programs is effective for an organization.

4. Suppose Latisha Simms needs to select a password for herself. Rank the following, listing the most secure password first: XX32nsa (a totally random selection of letters and numbers), LASIMMS (for Latisha Alexandra Simms), RRRYBGDTS (the first letters of row, row, row your boat gently down the stream), SMMIS (Latisha's last name spelled backwards), Henry (Latisha's husband's name).

5. Create a sentence outline of Section 6.1 that highlights the main concepts network users need to know.

6. Explain the difference between sharing files on a network and using a groupware product on a network.

7. Fill in the following table to summarize the characteristics of different network servers:

	File Server	Print Server	Non-dedicated Server	Client-Server	Host
Are shared files stored locally?					
Are shared programs stored locally?					
Does some, all, or none of the processing take place on the server?					
Does some, all, or none of the processing take place on the terminals or workstations?					

8. Explain the purpose of network server software and network client software.

9. Describe four types of groupware.

10. Summarize the software licensing issues that pertain to local area networks.

11. Explain how store-and-forward technology applies to electronic mail systems.

Projects

1. Your School Network Research your school network to answer the following questions:

   a. What is the network operating system?

   b. What drives are mapped to a student workstation?

   c. Is the file server a micro, mini, or mainframe computer?

   d. Is the print server a different device than the file server?

2. Network Operating System Efficiency Network operating systems are designed to optimize the process of sending program and data files to workstations. This means that the amount of time it takes multiple users to open the same file should not be much longer than it takes a single user to open the file. How efficient is the file server in your lab? To find out, form a team of three to five class members and do a through d:

   a. Using a stopwatch or the second hand of your watch, record the number of seconds it takes a word processing software application to start on a workstation in your lab. For example, if your lab has WordPerfect for Windows, click the WordPerfect icon to highlight it, then start timing when you press the Enter key to launch the program. Stop timing when the word processor is ready for you to start typing.

   b. Exit the word processing application to get ready for the second part of the test.

   c. Position each member of your team at other workstations on the network. Each team member should click the word processing icon so it is highlighted. One of the team members should give a signal so all the team members press the Enter key at the same time. Each team member should record how long it takes before the word processing application is ready for typing.

   d. Record each team member's results. Prepare a one-page document in which you summarize your experiment and results. Be sure you explain exactly how you carried out the experiment—how many members were on your team, which lab you used, and which software you used. Also, present your conclusions about the efficiency of your network server.

3. Client-Server Architecture in Corporations Client-server architecture is becoming more and more popular in corporations. To find out more about client-server computing, use library and Internet resources to look for case studies and articles about corporations using client-server applications. Write a one-page or two-page description of an effective use of client-server computing. Be sure to include a list of references.

4. Networks in Action Make an appointment to interview the network supervisor in an organization or business related to your career field. To prepare for the interview, make a list of questions you will ask about how the network works and how it is used. Use the topics in this chapter to help organize your questions about network hardware, network software, applications software, and groupware. After the interview, write a two- to three-page summary of your findings. Include the name of the person you interviewed, the business or organization, and the date of the interview. In addition to the report summarizing your findings, submit a list of your questions.

5. Network Careers The companies that produce network operating systems encourage computer professionals to obtain professional certification to demonstrate their knowledge of networking. Such certification is often one of the qualifications listed in ads for network supervisor jobs. Novell offers certification as a CNE (Certified NetWare Engineer) or a CNA (Certified NetWare Administrator). Microsoft also offers a certification program for its Windows NT operating system. Write a one- to two-page paper that describes Microsoft's or Novell's certification process. Include the answers to the following questions: What is the process for certification? What is the cost? How would you prepare for the certification exam? What sort of jobs would you qualify for once you are certified?

Resources

INTERNET OPTIONAL

6. E-mail Smileys E-mail has spawned a language of *emoticons*, or *smileys*, that are composed of keyboard characters. For example, the smiley ;-) looks like a person winking. You could use this smiley in an e-mail message to indicate that you are joking. Lists of smileys have been published on the Internet and in books, computer magazines, and newspapers. Find a list of smileys and select five that you would like to use. Make a list of your five smileys and describe what each means. Submit your list and indicate the source of your selection.

7. Anonymous E-mail? When you send e-mail, your user ID is automatically attached to your message. This return address indicates who sent the message (in case you forgot to include your name), lets your correspondents easily send you replies, and helps the mail system return messages that have incorrect addresses. Recently, some networks have offered a way to send anonymous e-mail. What are the pros and cons of anonymous mail? Under what circumstances would you want to send anonymous mail? Would you expect people to abuse this capability? Discuss this issue in a small group or research the issue individually. Write a one-page summary of your position on whether people should be allowed to send anonymous e-mail.

8. E-mail Ethics Assume that you are the network administrator at a small manufacturing company. While doing some maintenance work on the electronic mail system, you happen to view the contents of a mail message between two employees. The employees seem to be discussing a plan to steal equipment from the company. What would you do? Write a one-page essay explaining what you would do and describing the factors that affected your decision.

9. E-mail Practice Learn how to use the e-mail system available on your school network. Briefly describe how you do each of the following:

  a. Compose and send a message.

  b. Reply to a message you received.

  c. Delete a message you received.

  d. Forward a message you received to someone other than the person who sent the message.

  e. Send a carbon copy of the message.

  f. Send a message to a mailing list.

- **Derfler, F. and L. Freed**. *How Networks Work.* Emeryville, CA: Ziff-Davis Press, 1993. This illustrated guide to networks is the place to begin if you want to learn more about networks.

- **Feibel, W.** *Novell's Complete Encyclopedia of Networking.* San Jose: Novell Press, 1995. This is an excellent reference for definitions of technical terms. Although it is published by Novell, whose networking products are used world wide, the information is relevant to local and wide area networks of all types.

- *http://www.microsoft.com* Microsoft Windows 95 and Windows NT operating systems contain network capabilities. Microsoft encourages computer developers and network administrators to become certified Microsoft network administrators. You can learn more about Microsoft's networks and certification programs at their Internet site.

- *http://www.novell.com* Novell, Inc. publishes Novell NetWare, the most popular microcomputer network operating system. Novell's Internet site contains a copious amount of information about local area networks, network certification, and Novell products.

- **Khoshafian, S. and M. Buckiewicz.** *Introduction to Groupware, Workflow, and Workgroup Computing.* New York: John Wiley & Sons, 1995. A complete, clearly written and well-documented book about groupware and its role in organizations. Especially useful are its conceptual illustrations, such as Figure 1.16, Time and Place Interactions.

- **Sanderson, D.** *Smileys.* Sebastopol, CA: O'Reilly & Associates, 1993. A collection of more than 650 smileys and answers to your deepest questions, such as "Why are smileys sideways?" Tilt your head for some examples: =l:-) Abe Lincoln, :`-(crying, :-? smoking a pipe.

Lab Assignments

Answers

E-mail

 E-mail that originates on a local area network with a mail gateway can travel all over the world. That's why it is so important to learn how to use it. In this Lab you use an e-mail simulator, so even if your school computers don't provide you with e-mail service, you will know the basics of reading, sending, and replying to electronic mail.

1. Click the Steps button to learn how to work with e-mail. As you proceed through the Steps, answer all of the Quick Check questions that appear. After you complete the Steps, you will see a Quick Check Summary Report. Follow the instructions on the screen to print this report.

2. Click the Explore button. Write a message to re@films.org. The subject of the message is "Picks and Pans." In the body of your message, describe a movie you have recently seen. Include the name of the move, briefly summarize the plot, and give it a thumbs up or a thumbs down. Print the message before you send it.

3. In Explore, look in your In Box for a message from jb@music.org. Read the message, then compose a reply indicating that you will attend. Carbon copy mciccone@music.org. Print your reply, including the text of JB's original message before you send it.

4. In Explore, look in your In Box for a message from leo@sports.org. Reply to the message by adding your rating to the text of the original message as follows:

Equipment:	Your Rating:
Rollerblades	2
Skis	3
Bicycle	1
Scuba gear	4
Snow mobile	5

Print your reply before you send it.

5. Go into the lab with a partner. You should each log into the E-mail Lab on different computers. In Explore, look at the Addresses list to find the user ID for your partner. You should each send a short e-mail message to your partner. Then you should check your mail for a message from your partner. Read the message and compose a reply. Print your reply before you send it. (Note: Unlike a full-featured mail system, the e-mail simulator does not save mail in mailboxes after you log off.)

6.1

1. server
2. Mapping
3. account (or user account)
4. True
5. False
6. Captured, redirected

6.2

1. network interface card
2. non-dedicated server
3. file server
4. True
5. Host

6.3

1. network operating
2. True
3. network license
4. groupware
5. Document routing

Glossary/Index

F

FDDI (Fiber Distributed Data Interface) A high speed network standard capable of transmitting data at 100 megabits per second, 6-12

files
  access limitations on networks, 6-8–6-9
  attachments, 6-21–6-22
  locking, 6-8–6-9
  multiple, printing, 6-10–6-11

file servers
  dedicated, 6-13

G

gateway An electronic link that connects e-mail systems, 6-22

group addressing A feature of an e-mail system that allows you to send a copy of an e-mail message to all members of a group at the same time, 6-22

group editing features A feature in groupware that allows more than one person to edit a document at a time, 6-18

group scheduling programs Groupware software that finds a date and time that is convenient for everyone involved to meet, 6-19

groupware Software that is designed to help people collaborate on projects, 6-18

H

hard disks, storing data files, 6-8

hardware
  e-mail, 6-21
  local area networks. *See* network hardware

host computer Usually refers to a mainframe or mini-computer that is the central computer in a system of connected terminals, 6-15

I

infrared signals, local area network data transmission, 6-12

L

Lantastic A network operation system software package designed to control network data flow, 6-17

licenses, software. *See* software licenses

local area network (LAN) A network that is located within a relatively limited area such as a building or campus, 6-4–6-11
  data files, 6-8–6-9
  drive mapping, 6-6
  electronic mail. *See* electronic mail (e-mail)
  hardware. *See* network hardware
  login process, 6-5
  printers, 6-10–6-11
  program files, 6-7, 6-8
  resources, 6-4–6-5
  storing data files, 6-8
  types, 6-12

local resources The resources available to a standalone computer, such as hard drive, software, data, and printer, 6-4

locked A precaution against losing data on a network that allows only one user at a time to open a data file, 6-8

locking files, 6-8–6-9

login process The process you use to access network resources, including entering your user ID and password, 6-5

logging in, local area networks, 6-5

The Internet and the Information Highway

The Internet and the

The data jack slipped smoothly into the socket just behind Kyle's ear. He flipped the switch on his computer. The power light blinked green, and the universe shifted.

Information Highway

He looked out over a computer-generated landscape of surrealistic terrain and fantastic buildings. Messages swirled and pulsed down massive conduits, creating data links between heavily guarded corporate computing centers. The World Health Organization cube spun lazily, tipped on one of its corners. Kyle considered it briefly. It is open to the public. Lots of free data. In the distance—the towers of the Library of Congress. More free data. Interesting, but not what Kyle was after today.

He turned his attention to the golden pyramid. He'd heard rumors on the street that this was the computing headquarters of a major drug cartel. Kyle studied it carefully. It was surrounded by a translucent security globe. Really tough to get at that data, but his job was on the line. The data was critical to the prosecutor's case.

This is a vision of **cyberspace**—a computer generated mental image of a computer world. The term *cyberspace* was coined in 1984 by science fiction writer William Gibson. Today the term cyberspace has been popularized by journalists writing about worldwide information networks. No, you cannot plug your brain into a computer to prowl around in cyberspace. But your computer can provide you access to a digital "information highway" that winds through a landscape of useful and fascinating information, on topics as diverse as hip hop music and military academies. In this chapter you will discover the astonishing potential of the information highway.

CHAPTER**PREVIEW**

In this chapter you will learn how to use a computer to access information from commercial information services and the Internet. First, you will take an on-line tour to get a flavor of the tremendous variety of information available on the information highway. You will learn about the software that helps you navigate through the vast landscape of data along the information highway. You will learn how to subscribe to a commercial information service. And finally, you will learn how to connect your own computer to the Internet. When you have completed this chapter, you should be able to:

■ List examples of the information available on the information highway

■ Compare and contrast the information and services available on the Internet with those available on commercial information services

■ Describe how to subscribe to a commercial information service

■ Describe how Gopher, Usenet, Telnet, FTP, and the World Wide Web help you access information on the Internet

■ Explain the elements of an Internet address

■ Explain how Internet communications software such as SLIP and PPP are used to establish an Internet connection

■ Follow good "netiquette" when using on-line services

■ Discuss the elements of virtual reality that are currently available on-line

LAB

**The Internet:
World Wide Web**

7.1

Touring the **Information Highway**

Before you go on-line for a drive on the information highway, it's a good idea to get a general idea of what you are likely to find. Section 7.1 presents an overview of the information highway and a sample of what's available on it.

The term "on-line service" has two meanings. It can be a synonym for a commercial information service, or it can refer to services offered on-line, such as e-mail.

Information Highway Map

What is the information highway?

The **information highway** is a world-wide network of computers linked by telephone lines and satellites. The "towns" or **sites** on the information highway are computers of all descriptions—micros, minis, and mainframes. The "roads" that connect the computers are communications systems provided by common carriers such as AT&T, MCI, and the French telephone company, Minitel. The "cars" that travel along the information highway carry information of all kinds. This information, sometimes referred to as **on-line information**, includes reports, magazine articles, books, photographs, music, film clips, library card catalogs, advertisements, computer programs, stock market quotes, and U.S. government publications. The information highway also provides services, called **on-line services**, to help you find information and communicate with other people.

A WAN (wide area network) connects computers in widely scattered geographic locations, as opposed to a LAN, which connects computers in a building or small campus.

You can access the information on this highway using a microcomputer and a communications link such as a modem or network. The information highway includes a huge computer network called the Internet and an assortment of commercial information services that provide information for a fee.

The **Internet** is a collection of local, regional, and national computer networks that are linked together to exchange data and distribute processing tasks. These networks can communicate because they use the same networking language. The Internet is similar to a WAN because it covers a wide geographical area. However, each network on the Internet is independently administered, so the Internet lacks the cohesive structure of a single WAN.

Figure 7-1
Commercial information services + the Internet = the information highway

To use the Internet, you must have an account on a network that is connected to the Internet, and your network administrator must approve your account for Internet use. If your school network is connected to the Internet, it is likely that you have access to the Internet from the computers in your lab.

A **commercial information service**, sometimes called an **on-line service**, provides access to computer-based information and services for a fee. To use a commercial information service, you subscribe to it, just like you do to a magazine or newspaper. Commercial information services range from small neighborhood bulletin boards that run on a single microcomputer, to large corporate enterprises using multiple mainframes to provide information to customers in the U.S., Europe, and Asia.

If someone were to draw a simplified diagram or "map" of the information highway it might look like Figure 7-1.

Hundreds of users

Small information service

Millions of home computers

Large comercial information service

Internet host computer

Internet host computer

I-way Rte L

Internet host computer

I-way Rte I

Computer lab network

University host computer

Neighborhood bulletin board service

Hundreds of home computers

KEY

▢ Internet host computer

━ Internet

━ Commerical service

━ Other service

Trip Log

What's out there on the information highway?

To get an idea of what's on the information highway, you can follow this student's account of one day's on-line activities.

—**9 a.m.** I'm in the lab first thing this morning to check my e-mail. Today, I've got two messages. The first is from my Chemistry lab partner. She missed class yesterday. I send her a reply so she knows what the instructor assigned. The other message, signed "Dad," reminds me that Mom's birthday is coming up. Dad subscribed to a commercial information service when he found out that e-mail can travel virtually anywhere on the information highway—even between his commercial service and the network here at school.

—**9:05 a.m.** Got to shop for Mom's birthday present. With a couple of mouse clicks, I'm accessing an on-line shopping mall. The stores include Hammacher Schlemmer, Hilyard and Hilquist, Omaha Steaks, FTD Flowers, Global Plaza, Sharper Image, and Celestial Seasonings. I zap right over to the FTD Flowers store (Figure 7-2). My mom loves flowers, so I order a bouquet for her, using my newly acquired MasterCard. Mom should get them tomorrow.

▶ **Figure 7-2**
FTD flowers on-line store

—**9:10 a.m.** I access headline news to get a quick overview of current events and sports scores. Our rivals on the gridiron got trounced, so it looks like our team will make it to the semi finals.

—**9:30 a.m.** I want to see if anyone in the Bikes discussion group replied to my message about the best tires to use for riding in snow. A **discussion group** is an on-line forum for discussing issues with a group of people. I've participated in on-line discussion groups on basketball, skydiving, Star Trek, and fitness, to name a few.

Now I'm really into mountain bikes, and I get a lot of useful information from the Bikes discussion group. I entered my question about snow tires three days ago, so someone should have replied. Let's see.

My question seems to have opened the floodgates to a lengthy discussion of the dangers of riding in the snow. Well, some of us can't afford a car. O.K. Here's a message about tires. It looks like the tires I have are about the best for winter riding. Good. I don't have to invest in new tires.

—**10:00 a.m.** I log into another discussion group on elementary school education. It's my major and I think its a good idea to keep informed of innovations in my field. Most of the participants are university professors. I don't usually post any messages; I just *lurk*—that's the term for people who watch discussions, but don't participate. I might participate more when I feel more knowledgeable. I glance at the clock. I'm late for my 10:00 class. Time to log out. I'll come back later.

—**1:00 p.m.** My friend Coreen has a computer in her dorm room; but when she runs some multimedia software, Windows freezes up. She thinks something must be wrong with her CD-ROM drive. Most computer hardware manufacturers have technical support information on line, so we go to the lab and log in. We find information about Coreen's CD-ROM drive. It appears that the trouble she has with multimedia software is caused by her video driver software, not the CD-ROM.

We hop over to the on-line site for ATI, the manufacturer for Coreen's video card, and we think we've found a solution.

To fix the problem with Coreen's computer, she needs to install updated driver software for her video card. ATI allows us to legally download a copy of the software. **Download** means electronically transporting a file from a host computer to a local computer. We download the updated driver software from the manufacturer's site and store it on a floppy disk. Coreen can take the disk to her dorm room and install the updated driver on her computer.

While we're on-line, Coreen wants to get the newest dungeon levels for her Doom adventure game. Unfortunately this popular site is busy, so we decide to try another time.

—**1:15 p.m.** Coreen leaves, but I need some information for a paper I'm writing on alternative music. My first stop on-line is at the Library of Congress (Figure 7-3). I look through their card catalog but I can't read the books on-line. I jot down four references. After logging out of the Library of Congress, I connect to our campus library to see if we have these books. We have three of the four books. I can probably get the fourth book through interlibrary loan.

Figure 7-3 ◄
Accessing the
Library of Congress
card catalog

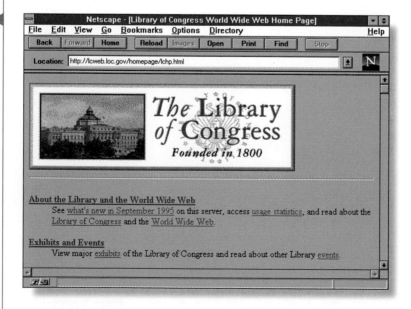

—**1:30 p.m.** I look for more on-line information on alternative music. My favorite index to information is at the "Yahoo" site. I log into Yahoo and quickly find a list of alternative music information, including the Indie List Digest, an on-line magazine called a *zine* (Figure 7-4). I browse through the zine and print out a few particularly interesting pages.

Yahoo!   Write Us   Add URL   Search   Info

Entertainment:Music:Genres:Alternative/Indie

- Alternative Radio List for London and Surrounding Areas
- Alternative Underground
- Artists(80)
- Benno - Swedish alternative music - Info, soundfiles and more stuff devoted to the Swedish indie scene.
- Blank Generation Web - Featuring New York scene of 70s-80s. From Velvet Underground to Sonic Youth, and of cours
- Buddy Project, The - a clearinghouse for musical collaboration and other original works of music.
- Cabco Art in Motion - Promoting independent works for all types of music, spoken arts, and the unusual.
- CassetteNet - Independent cassette labels on the WWW
- Daddy Upright

► **Figure 7-4**
Using Yahoo to locate information on alternative music

I notice a new music video by my favorite hip hop group. I put on earphones so the sound track doesn't disturb other students in the lab. I watch the 30-second video clip. Pretty cool.

—**2:00 p.m.** I see it's 2:00. Science fiction author Ray Bradbury is hosting a chat session on another part of the "net." I tune in. In a **chat session** many people participate in an on-line discussion by typing in their comments. As soon as a participant presses the Enter key, his or her comment is displayed on the chat screen. Other participants can respond, and their responses will also immediately appear on the screen, creating a continuous dialog.

In this chat session, Ray Bradbury answers questions about how science fiction has changed in the last 20 years. Interesting stuff.

—**2:30 p.m.** Time flies when I'm on-line. I've got to log off so I can get those alternative music references from the library before my 3:00 class.

Quick Check

1 The term _____ was originally coined by science fiction writer William Gibson to refer to a computer-generated reality that people could experience by connecting their brain to a computer network.

2 The _____ is a collection of local, regional, and national computer networks that are linked together to exchange data and distribute processing tasks.

3 A(n) _____ charges its subscribers a fee to access information.

4 A(n) _____ is an on-line discussion in which participants post a question or comment, then log in later after other participants have had a chance to respond.

5 When you participate in a(n) _____, all the participants can view your comments as soon as you press the Enter key.

6 The process of transferring files containing text, graphics, music, or video clips from a remote computer to your computer is called _____.

7.2

Commercial Information Services

Figure 7-5
A basic model
of a commercial
information system

The concept of a commercial information service is relatively easy to grasp, so it's a good place to begin before tackling the complexities of the Internet. The first commercial information services provided access to information stored on a mainframe host computer. Using a modem, subscribers could dial into the service's mainframe using terminal emulation software. Once connected, subscribers could view data, run programs, and download files. An important characteristic of commercial information services is that even today they are based on a model in which many computers use terminal emulation software to access a remote host computer (Figure 7-5).

Computers with terminal emmulation software connected by dial-up telephone lines

Mainframe host computer

Commercial Service Providers

What are the major commercial information service providers?

Four of the largest commercial information services are America Online, CompuServe, Microsoft Network, and Prodigy. Each service has about two million subscribers. Study Figure 7-6 to get an idea of the services offered by the "Big Four" service providers.

Figure 7-6
The "Big Four"
service providers

Prodigy

Prodigy. Established in 1990 as a joint venture between IBM and Sears Roebuck & Co., Prodigy is the most family-oriented of the "Big Four" on-line services. It rigorously maintains only G-rated material in all its data. Prodigy claims to have more female subscribers than other services. It pioneered a homework helper for school children and also offers an on-line version of Sesame Street where children can interact with Big Bird to learn their ABCs. For adults Prodigy provides the latest news stories, sports scores, movie reviews, and *Consumer Reports* articles. Prodigy also provides electronic mail, Eaasy Sabre travel reservations, Fodor's on-line travel guide, on-line shopping, current news, encyclopedia, financial information, and discussion groups. Links to many Internet services are also available. Prodigy has an easy-to-use graphical interface. A unique feature of Prodigy—and a feature that you might not like—is that advertisements pop up on your screen from time to time.

▶ **Figure 7-6**
The "Big Four"
service providers
(continued)

CompuServe. Established in 1979, CompuServe is the oldest of the services. It originally catered to business users, but now appeals to a very broad audience. For excellent news coverage, financial information, and computer technical support, CompuServe is one of the best information services. CompuServe electronic mail is easy to use, and its discussion groups cover almost every conceivable topic. For travelers, CompuServe services include Eaasy Sabre travel reservations, the Zagat restaurant Survey, and State Department travel briefings. Of interest to entrepreneurs are Standard and Poor's Company Information, Business Demographics, Entrepreneurs' Small Business Forum, and Citibank's Global Report. For entertainment, you can read Roger Ebert's movie reviews, or select from over 18 single and multiplayer games. Shop on-line at Electronic Mall stores such as JCPenney, Land's End, Hammacher Schlemmer, and Barnes & Noble. Microsoft, IBM, Apple, Novell, and many other computer companies have active forums and technical support on CompuServe. You will find on-line versions of computer publications such as *Dr. Dobbs Journal, PC World, PC Week, and MacWeek.*

The CompuServe user interface reflects the legacy of command line user interfaces. The standard way to navigate CompuServe is to use menus and commands such as GO NEWS or GO WEATHER. The advantage of this user interface is that CompuServe can be accessed by virtually any type of computer with standard communication software. Special software from CompuServe is required only if you want to use Windows or Macintosh-style menus instead of non-graphical menus and GO commands.

America Online. Often abbreviated as AOL, America Online was established in 1985. AOL has a reputation as the flashiest of the commercial information services. It pioneered celebrity chat sessions—the rock band Depeche Mode went on-line to interact with fans. AOL also provides access to MTV Online and has excellent news coverage. On AOL you'll find the top news stories from the *New York Times*, the *Chicago Tribune*, and *Time* Magazine. You'll also find automotive tips in the on-line version of *Car & Driver* magazine, computer product reviews from *PC World* magazine, transcripts of C-Span broadcasts, and articles from *Atlantic Monthly* magazine. AOL's Center Stage features a schedule of dates when you can chat on-line with celebrities including well-known actors, authors, musicians, entrepreneurs, and athletes. For the young crowd, the Academic Assistance center provides elementary school students with a forum where their questions are answered by teachers, educators, and experts. *Comptons Encyclopedia* is on-line as a resource for school reports. For fun, AOL offers a photo tour of Walt Disney World, and kids' clubs for young astronomers, environmentalists, and Star Trek fans. AOL's graphical user interface makes navigation easy.

Figure 7-6
The "Big Four"
service providers
(continued)

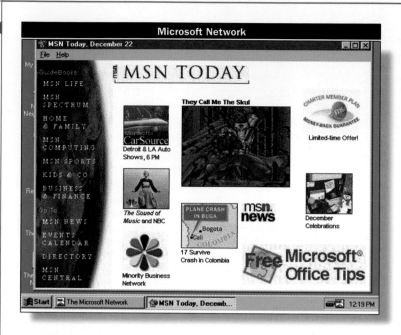

Microsoft Network. Founded in 1995, Microsoft Network (often abbreviated MSN) is the newest giant in the commercial information service industry. Industry watchers attribute its rapidly growing popularity to the fact that software for the Microsoft Network is included with Windows 95. MSN provides e-mail, discussion groups, chat rooms, games, download service, and access to the Internet. The core clientele of MSN is young professionals with a strong interest in computers and technology. Microsoft provides technical support for many of its software products and is expanding its technical offerings in an attempt to match CompuServe's excellent technical support services.

On-line Services

Why would I want to subscribe to a commercial information service?

The type and variety of services offered by a commercial information service depend on the size of the service, but generally include electronic mail, discussion groups, chat sessions, downloads, computer technical support, on-line shopping, reference information, government documents, educational opportunities, interactive games, and connections to other commercial information services, including the Internet.

If you have free access to the Internet provided by your school, you might not want to pay for a subscription to a commercial information service. However, many people do not have free Internet access, but would still like to send and receive e-mail, participate in on-line discussions, shop on-line, and have access to on-line information. For these people, a commercial information service might be the right choice.

Use Project 6 to gather current rate information since the rates charged by commercial information services change frequently.

Fees

Is it expensive to use a commercial information service?

It is easy to accumulate large bills for your on-line activities. Many subscribers lose track of time while they are in the middle of an on-line project and forget that the meter is running. Some commercial information services have fairly complex rate structures; so understanding these rates will help you stay within your budget.

Most commercial information services have a number of **basic services** included in a monthly flat fee. Monthly fees are typically about $10. Basic services usually include access to current news reports, games, discussion groups, on-line shopping, and electronic mail. Even if you do not use the service during a month, you are billed the monthly flat fee. Many services limit the number of hours per month covered by the flat fee. For example, you might be limited to five hours a month. Additional hours cost extra.

You might be charged additional fees, called **surcharges**, for premium services. A **premium service** is information that has been designated as more valuable by the commercial information service. More valuable often means that customers will pay extra for this service. For example, many business-related services such as airline reservations, up-to-the-minute stock reports, and legal searches are often premium services.

Premium service billing depends on what type of information you are accessing. You could be billed per item of information, per report, per search, or per hour. For example, on CompuServe you are billed 1.5 cents for each stock quote, $5 for a money market report, $9 for a database search, and $28 an hour for access to the Airline Guides Travel Service.

Connect time refers to the number of minutes your computer is connected to the service. Connect time charges vary depending on the time of day and the speed of your modem connection. For example, between 8:00 a.m. and 5:00 p.m. the connect time rate might be $10 per hour, while the rate after 5:00 p.m. is only $6. Slower modem speeds have lower connect time charges.

Subscribing to a Commercial Information Service

How do I subscribe?

Even if you currently have free Internet access, when you graduate you might want to subscribe to a commercial information service. Or, your parents might ask you to help them get on-line. Let's walk through the steps you would take to subscribe to a commercial information service.

1. **Obtain a startup kit.** To subscribe to a commercial information service, you should first request the service's startup kit for the operating system you use. The startup kit typically contains disks with the service's communication software, a user manual, and a temporary user ID and password, as shown in Figure 7-7.

▶ **Figure 7-7**
Prodigy startup kit

You can request the startup kit by telephone, fax, or mail. Kits are also available at computer stores and packaged in computer magazines. Most kits are free and include some free access time on-line.

2. **Make sure your computer has a modem.** In addition to the startup kit, you will need a modem. The modem connects your computer to your telephone line, which is the communication link between your computer and the on-line service. A fast modem is an advantage for quickly navigating through on-line menus and downloading files.

3. **Install communications software provided in the startup kit.** When you receive the startup kit, you must install the communications software on your computer. Once installed, you can use the software to begin the subscription process.

4. **Select a local access number.** A **local access number** is a telephone number in your local area code that your modem can dial to connect with the on-line service. A list of these numbers is already programmed into the software provided with the startup kit. By entering your area code and city, you will be able to see a list of numbers to choose from. After you select a number, the software stores it so you can use it whenever you dial in.

5. **Dial in.** Follow the on-screen prompts to have your modem dial the local access number and connect to the on-line service.

6. **Log in.** You will be prompted for a user ID and password. A temporary user ID and password is supplied in the startup kit. You can change the password later to one that is more personalized.

7. **Provide information for your subscription.** The on-line subscription process usually continues with a request for your name and address. Enter the information as requested.

8. **Select a billing option.** If you want your monthly fees billed to your credit card, you must provide your card number. If you want to pay by check, you must supply your checking account number.

9. **Choose your unique user ID and password.** Most services allow you to select your own user ID and password. You should make a note of them and put the note in a secure place. Many people don't use their on-line service regularly and consequently forget their user ID and password. When you have selected a user ID and password, the subscription process is complete and you're on line.

Quick Check

1. Commercial information services are based on a model in which a number of _____ use terminal emulation software to access a(n) _____ computer.

2. What are the four largest commercial information services?

3. On most commercial information services, _____ include services such as electronic mail, current news, games, discussion groups, and on-line shopping.

4. _____ refers to the length of time your computer is attached to a commercial information service.

5. When deciding to subscribe to an information service, it is important to make sure it has a(n) _____ so you don't have to make long distance calls to connect.

The Internet

The history of the Internet begins in 1957 when the Soviet Union launched Sputnik, the first artificial satellite. In response to this display of Soviet technical expertise, the U.S. government resolved to improve its science and technical infrastructure. One of the resulting initiatives was the Advanced Research Projects Agency (ARPA), created by the Department of Defense. ARPA swung into action with a project to design a computer system that could survive nuclear attack. The plan was to construct a network of geographically dispersed computers that would continue to function even if one of the computers on the network was destroyed. In 1969 four computer networks were connected to each other and called ARPANET. Connecting two or more networks creates an **internetwork** or **internet**, so ARPANET was one of the first examples of an internet (with a lowercase i). Gradually, more and more networks were connected to the ARPANET, and it became known as the Internet (with an uppercase I). So, the Internet is essentially a network of networks, as shown in Figure 7-8.

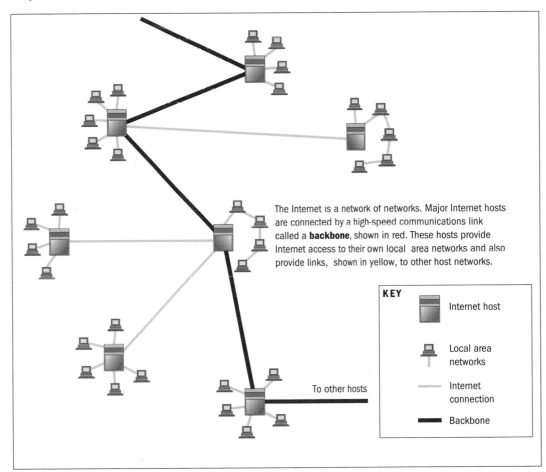

The Internet is a network of networks. Major Internet hosts are connected by a high-speed communications link called a **backbone**, shown in red. These hosts provide Internet access to their own local area networks and also provide links, shown in yellow, to other host networks.

KEY

	Internet host
	Local area networks
	Internet connection
	Backbone

To other hosts

▶ **Figure 7-8**
The Internet is a network of networks

Compare the structure of the Internet to the much simpler structure of a commercial information service illustrated in Figure 7-5.

Today, the Internet is the largest and most widely used network in the world, connecting over 20,000 computer networks, in more than 130 countries, with an estimated 30 million users.

Each of the networks included in the Internet is referred to as a **site**. The graph in Figure 7-9 shows the incredible increase in the number of Internet sites over the past 30 years.

Figure 7-9
Internet growth

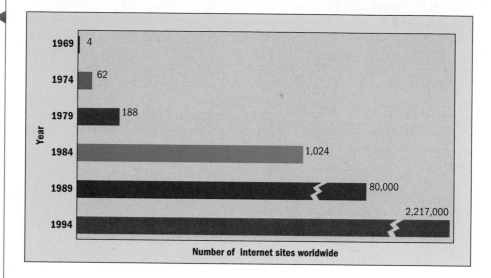

Number of internet sites worldwide

The Internet is unique in many ways—not just because of its incredible size. Although each of the smaller networks connected to the Internet is owned by an individual, a corporation, an educational institution, or a government agency, no one "owns" the Internet. This accounts for the chaotic organization of information on the Internet. On the Internet, no one screens the data, so it is easy to get "junk" along with quality information. Further, no one decides where information is stored on the Internet—you will rarely find all the data pertaining to a topic stored in one location.

With more than 2 milliion sites computers providing information on the Internet and no centralized directory of services, even experienced users have a hard time navigating through the seemingly endless miles of information. Is the information on the Internet worth the trouble it takes to find it? To answer this question let's look at what you can find on the Internet and show you some of the tools you can use to facilitate your search.

Internet Services and Access Software

What kind of information can I find on the Internet?

Imagine a commercial information service such as CompuServe, but a thousand times larger and without a main menu. That's the Internet. Many services provided by CompuServe, America Online, Microsoft Network, and Prodigy are also available on the Internet. Like commercial information services, the Internet offers electronic mail, discussion groups, government documents, computer technical support, on-line shopping, interactive entertainment, and downloadable software, music, graphics, and video clips. The Internet has more information than commercial information services. On the Internet there are *thousands* of discussion groups and *millions* of documents.

Compared to a commercial information service, the Internet requires a wider variety of software to access information. When you are a Prodigy subscriber, for example, you use only one type of software to access Prodigy's on-line services—the communications software supplied in Prodigy's startup kit lets you send mail, participate in discussion groups, read the news, download software, and so on. Using Internet services is not so simple. Many different software packages are available to help you access different types of information and services, such as writing e-mail, participating in discussion groups, looking for information, accessing library card catalogs, and so on.

The trend today is to use a single software package to access most Internet services. However, it is still handy to understand the different types of software available to access information and services. With this understanding you will be able to decide which software you need to access the information *you* want on the Internet.

On-line Activity	Service	Software Tool
Send electronic mail	E-mail	Lotus cc:Mail, Eudora, Pegasus, Microsoft Mail, and other mail client software
Find and view information on a wide variety of topics	World Wide Web	Web browser such as Netscape, Mosaic, Lynx, Winweb
Download files of text, graphics, music, animations, and videos	FTP	FTP software, Netscape, Mosaic, Gopher client software
Run programs on a remote host, play interactive games, use remote library card catalogs	Telnet	Telnet client software
Search for documents, databases, library card catalogs	Gopher	Gopher client software, Netscape, Mosaic
Participate in on-line discussion groups	Usenet	Newsreader software

Figure 7-10
Internet retrieval and communications software

In the rest of Section 7.3 you will learn about Internet information retrieval and communications software. Use Figure 7-10 as a guide.

Internet E-mail

Is Internet e-mail different than e-mail on a LAN?

Internet e-mail is essentially the same as e-mail on a LAN or commercial information service. Learning about Internet e-mail has two advantages. First, you learn how to send mail to virtually anyone who has an e-mail box anywhere in the world. Second, you get a better idea of how the Internet works.

To send mail over the Internet, you must have access to e-mail on a computer that is connected to the Internet. When you want to send mail over the Internet, you simply compose the message on your computer using your e-mail client software, address the message, and tell your e-mail system to send it. Each person with access to Internet e-mail has a unique Internet address. An Internet e-mail address looks something like this:

president@whitehouse.gov

The first part of the address, *president*, is the **user ID**—in this case the user ID of the President of the United States. The **@ sign** separates the user ID from the machine name. A **machine name** is the unique set of numbers and letters that identifies each computer connected to the Internet. In the example, the machine name is *whitehouse*, a computer in Washington D.C. that handles the White House Internet connection. A period separates the machine name from the domain name. The **domain name** groups the computers on the Internet into the following categories: com (commercial), edu (educational), gov (nonmilitary government), mil (military), org (other organizations), or net (network resources). In the address *president@whitehouse.gov*, the domain is *gov*, indicating that the *whitehouse* computer is maintained by a non-military agency of the government.

When you send e-mail, your local mail server software examines the machine name in the address of each message. Those messages addressed to users on the local machine are delivered by the local mail server. Messages addressed to users on other machines are sent out over the Internet.

A mail client is the software you use to compose and send e-mail. The messages you create with one mail client can be read by someone who uses a different mail client.

What happens to e-mail when it leaves your local network? How does the message travel from your local network to the recipient? The answers to these questions reveal how the Internet works.

Recall that the Internet is a collection of networks. With over 20,000 of these networks, it would be impossible for your school to have direct links to every network on the Internet. So, e-mail is rarely sent directly from your network to the recipient's network. Instead, an e-mail message is handed from one network to another until it reaches its destination. Figure 7-11 shows how the Internet routes e-mail from a student at the University of Alaska to a student at the University of the Virgin Islands.

Figure 7-11
Internet e-mail
routes

When you make long-distance telephone calls, your call is routed across the country from one telephone station to another. When you send e-mail on the Internet, your message is routed similarly from one Internet computer to another.

1. The message originates from a computer in a student's apartment one block from the University of Alaska, Fairbanks campus. The message travels over the telephone lines to the University of Alaska.

2. From the University of Alaska, the message travels to one of the main Internet hosts in Washington state.

3. Now the message travels to Boston on the Internet **backbone**—high speed connections between main Internet hosts.

4. Still on the backbone, the message travels to Boston, then to North Carolina.

5. The message leaves the backbone and proceeds to Florida, where it is sent to Puerto Rico, then to the Virgin Islands.

The World Wide Web

What's the easiest way to access information on the Internet?

Currently, some of the best organized and most accessible information on the Internet is available through a service called the **World Wide Web**, abbreviated WWW, but often referred to as "the Web." The information available on the World Wide Web covers almost every conceivable topic, and the information is often presented in multimedia format with graphics, music, or video clips. You can use the World Wide Web to take a tour of the Louvre Museum in Paris, view the Library of Congress African-American collections, read a Stephen King novella (complete with sound effects), check out the latest tunes on the Underground Music Archive, create a sports newsletter that will report on your favorite teams, purchase merchandise from the Worldwide Marketplace, and more.

The official description of the World Wide Web is a "wide-area hypermedia information retrieval initiative aiming to give universal access to a large universe of documents." The World Wide Web consists of pages, called **Web pages,** that contain information on a particular topic. In addition to topic information, a Web page might also include one or more links to other Web pages. **Links** are pointers to other Web pages that make it easy to follow a thread of related information, even if the pages are stored on computers located in different countries. Figure 7-12 shows a conceptual model of how the World Wide Web works.

If you want a quick review of hypertext and hypermedia, reread Section 2.4 in Chapter 2.

Figure 7-12
How the World
Wide Web works

Lab

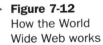

**The Internet:
World Wide Web**

1. Honolulu Community College (HCC), maintains an exhibit containing images, video clips, narration, and text about dinosaurs. Each image, video and document is a separate **page**, stored as a file on the HCC computer. You can jump from one page to another at HCC. For example, you can begin at the introductory screen, called a **home page**.

2. From the home page, you can jump to a page about iguanadons.

3. From this page you can jump to a page that contains a movie.

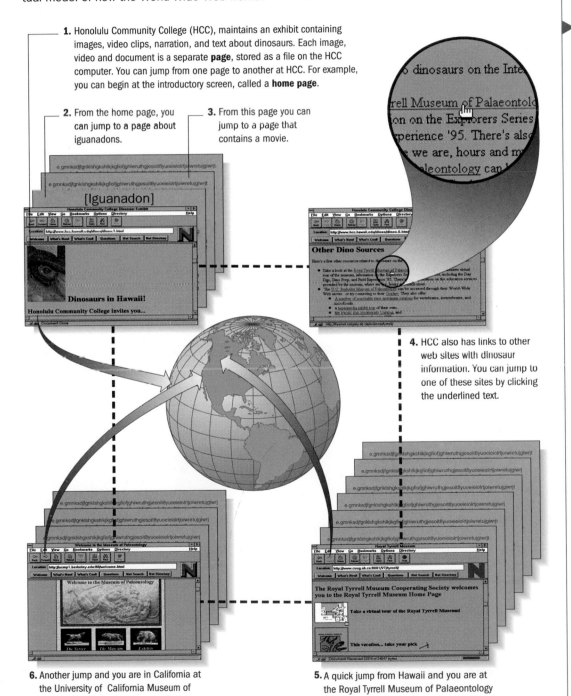

4. HCC also has links to other web sites with dinosaur information. You can jump to one of these sites by clicking the underlined text.

6. Another jump and you are in California at the University of California Museum of Paleontology where even more Web pages on dinosaurs are stored.

5. A quick jump from Hawaii and you are at the Royal Tyrrell Museum of Palaeontology in Alberta, Canada where additional Web pages on dinosaurs are stored.

At many schools students create their own Web pages, using an HTML editor. In Project 10 at the end of this chapter you will create your own Web page.

To offer World Wide Web service, an Internet site must set up Web server software and format its information into pages using a Hypertext Markup Language (HTML) editor. An **HTML editor** creates links between pages, displays links in boldface underlined text, and positions graphics.

Each Web page has a unique address called a **uniform resource locator (URL)**. To access a Web page, you must either follow a link or type a URL. You can find listings of Web page URLs in books, such as *Walking the World Wide Web*, and in Internet magazines, such as *Wired*. You can also access an on-line directory of Web pages using the URL *http://www.yahoo.com*.

A URL is similar to an e-mail address. For example, Honolulu Community College is the Web site for a dinosaur exhibit. The URL for this exhibit is:

http://www.hcc.hawaii.edu/dinos.1.html

And that's just a short URL! Let's look at each part of the URL to see what it means.

http:// Web pages are sent between sites using HyperText Transfer Protocol (HTTP). The *http://* at the beginning of the dinosaur URL indicates that this is a Web page. Whenever you see a long string of characters that begins with http://, you know it is referring to a Web page.

www.hcc.hawaii.edu Some elements of this URL might look familiar—*www.hcc.hawaii.edu* is the Internet address for the World Wide Web server at Honolulu Community College. Many Web server addresses begin with *www*. The *.edu* indicates this is a site maintained by an educational institution.

The Resources section at the end of this chapter contains more sources for WWW URLs.

/dinos.1.html The last part of the URL, */dinos.1.html*, refers specifically to the dinosaur Web page. Honolulu Community College might have other Web pages, such as *dinos.2.html* and *dinos.3.html*. This last part of the URL differentiates among the pages at a particular site.

To access World Wide Web information, you need a computer with Internet access and software called a Web browser. A **Web browser** displays the text, graphics, and links for a Web page. It also helps you follow the links from one Web page to another. Popular Web browser software packages are Netscape, Mosaic, Lynx, and Cello. Figure 7-13 shows you how to use a Web browser to access information on the World Wide Web.

Figure 7-13
Using the Netscape Web browser

When you start the Web browser, it displays the home page of your Internet service provider. From this page you can jump to other Web pages anywhere on the World Wide Web.

You can use the File menu to print out pages or save them on your local hard disk drive.

If you know the URL of the page to which you want to jump, you can type the URL in this box. All World Wide Web URLs begin with **http://**.

You can jump to linked documents by clicking any of the underlined text. On most Web browsers, the pointer changes to a hand when it is positioned over a text or graphical link.

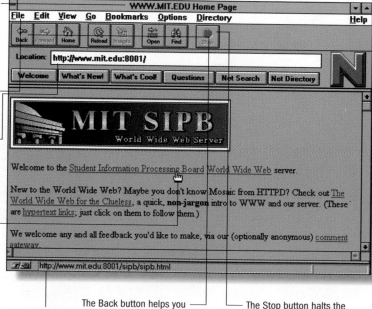

The status bar keeps you updated. Here the status bar shows that the pointer is positioned on a link to Student Information Processing located at **http://www.mit.edu.8001/sipb/sipb.html**. If you select this link, the status bar shows how long it will take for the page to be transmitted.

The Back button helps you navigate to pages you have previously viewed. The Forward button shows you the next page in the sequence.

The Stop button halts the transfer of a page. Sometimes the pages are very large, and you won't want to wait for them.

FTP

Can I download software and graphics files from the Internet?

Named after the yellow pages you use in the telephone book to find products and services, *The Internet Yellow Pages* is one of many published guides to find information on the Internet. Suppose you're interested in some new productivity software. *The Internet Yellow Pages* lists many Internet sites where you can obtain software, such as the Garbo Internet site, described as: "Software, software, software! This anonymous FTP site has gobs of software for DOS, Windows, Macs, and UNIX machines."

FTP (File Transfer Protocol) is a method for transferring files from one computer to another. The files can contain software, text, graphics, sound, animation, or video clips. Usually, the transfer takes place from a host computer to your microcomputer. If you want to download files from the Internet, you will generally use FTP software. **FTP software** connects your computer to a remote host computer called an **FTP server**. Your computer then essentially becomes a part of the FTP server's network.

Once your computer is connected to a remote host, you can look through the directory of files stored on the host. When you find the file you want, you can instruct the FTP software to transmit a copy of the file to your computer's hard disk. If the file you transferred contains software, you can install the software and run it on your computer. If the file you download contains data, you can edit that data using the appropriate type of word processing, graphics, or spreadsheet application software.

On most hosts, you must log in before you can access the files stored on its disks. But what if you don't have an account on the remote host? You can't expect to have an account on every Internet host, so you log in as an *anonymous* user. **Anonymous FTP** means that anyone without an account on a host computer can use FTP software to log in using the user ID "anonymous."

Not every Internet host accepts anonymous logins. You can find lists of those that do in *The Internet Yellow Pages* and similar Internet directories. Alternatively, you can find FTP sites using an on-line Internet service called Archie. **Archie** searches a special FTP database to find all the hosts that contain the file you need and that allow anonymous FTP.

For security reasons, an anonymous user is rarely given access to all the data on a remote host. Anonymous users are given access only to those files available for downloading. Figure 7-14 shows an FTP session in which a user downloads a to-do list manager from the Garbo FTP server.

What is the difference between the World Wide Web and FTP? You access the World Wide Web to read Web pages and follow links to related information. FTP helps you download data and program files onto your hard disk, which you can later view, run, or edit using your application software.

1. The FTP software connects to the host **garbo.uwasa.fi** at the University of Vaasa, Finland. The host is an anonymous FTP server, so you are allowed to log into the computer as an anonymous user.

▶ **Figure 7-14**
A typical
FTP session
(continued on next page)

Figure 7-14
A typical FTP
session
(continued)

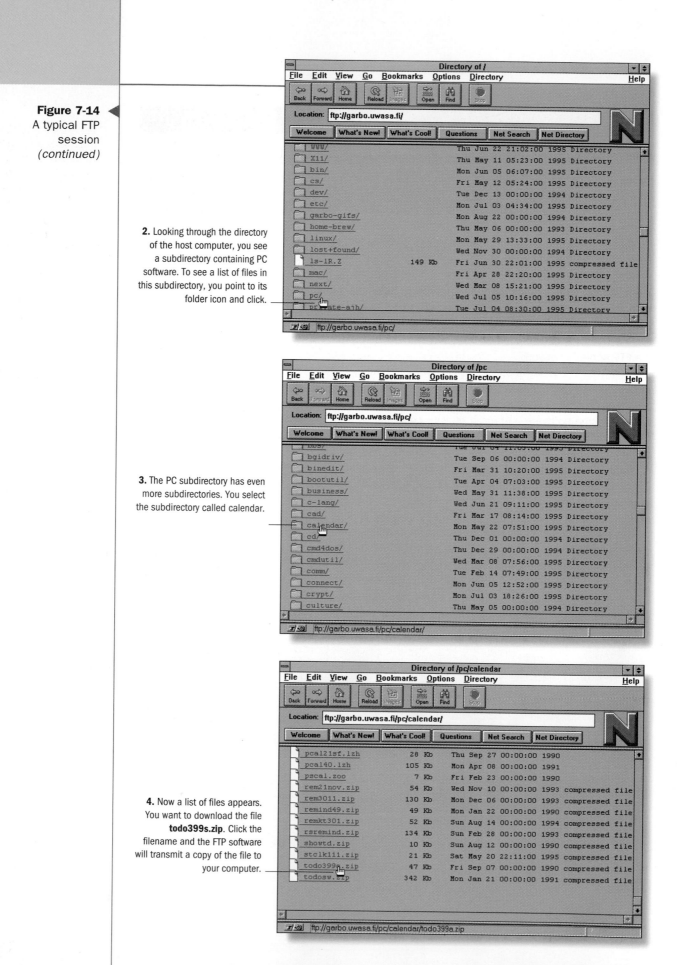

2. Looking through the directory of the host computer, you see a subdirectory containing PC software. To see a list of files in this subdirectory, you point to its folder icon and click.

3. The PC subdirectory has even more subdirectories. You select the subdirectory called calendar.

4. Now a list of files appears. You want to download the file **todo399s.zip**. Click the filename and the FTP software will transmit a copy of the file to your computer.

Telnet

Can I play interactive games with other Internet users?

Some Internet activities require you to run a program on a remote host. For example, you might want to run a program that lets you play backgammon with other players from around the country. Or, suppose you are visiting a friend at another school and you want to read the mail stored in your e-mail box on your own campus.

Telnet is an Internet service that establishes a connection between your computer and a remote host so you can use the processing power of a remote host to run software. You would need to run software on a remote host if the software was not written for the type of computer you have, if the software is too complex for your computer's processor, or if copyright restrictions prevent you from downloading the software.

To use Telnet, your computer must have Telnet software. When you use **Telnet software**, your computer is connected to the remote host and essentially becomes part of the host's network. Once the Telnet connection is established, you can use the resources of the host computer to send mail, run programs, copy files, create files, and so forth.

A popular entertainment on the Internet is MUDing. A **MUD (Multiple User Dimension)** is a computer-generated environment in which you talk to other participants, solve puzzles, and explore computer-generated objects around you. A MUD is text-based—the computer provides you with narrative descriptions of the environment. A **MOO (Multi-user Object-Oriented)** is similar to a MUD, but uses graphics. MUDs and MOOs are often called virtual reality because the computer generates a virtual environment—one that does not exist. Although current MUDs and MOOs, like the one in Figure 7-15, are mostly used for entertainment, they could also be used for activities such as virtual business meetings, virtual classrooms, and virtual town forums.

When you use Telnet, your computer acts as a terminal for the remote host. You might want to review the relationship between terminals and mini/mainframe hosts in Section 1.2 of Chapter 1.

If you want to learn more about virtual reality, MUDs, and MOOs, try Project 7 at the end of this chapter.

Figure 7-15
A MOO

You can select an "avatar" as a graphical representation of your on-line character.

Participants in the MOO type comments on their keyboards. You can interact with the six participants closest to your avatar.

This map shows you different rooms you can explore. Your current location is the main room, indicated by the center box.

Gopher

What does a Gopher have to do with the Internet?

Gopher is a menu-driven Internet service that helps you locate information. The best analogy for Gopher is the directional signs used on roadways (see Figure 7-16).

Figure 7-16
The signs point you in the right direction

How is Gopher different from the World Wide Web? Both Gopher and WWW help you locate information by jumping from one Internet site to another. The World Wide Web places the links within documents. Gopher links are not in the documents, but in the menus that direct you to the documents.

Internet host computers that offer Gopher service are referred to as **Gopher servers**. The original Gopher server was developed in 1991 at the University of Minnesota. Now there is a worldwide network of linked Gopher servers, referred to as **Gopherspace**. Although it is a relatively new service on the Internet, Gopher will probably be replaced by the World Wide Web because the Web has a graphical user interface that is easier to use.

To use Gopher, you need Gopher software on your computer, and you need to connect to a Gopher server. Using Gopher is easy. The Gopher server shows you a menu of options, and you select the one you want. Many of the Gopher menu items are links to other Gopher sites.

As with Windows menus, Gopher menus use certain menu conventions to indicate what type of information a menu option points to. Figure 7-17 shows how these menu conventions appear in a typical Gopher session.

Figure 7-17
Menu conventions in a typical Gopher session

1. The Gopher client software connects you to the Gopher server you request—in this case the Gopher server at the University of Minnesota.

2. The Gopher menu displays a list of resources.

3. The folder icon in front of a menu option indicates that the option leads to another menu.

4. The binocular icon indicates that the menu option will lead to a screen that asks for search specifications, instead of scrolling through the menus. For example, you could search for "Africa."

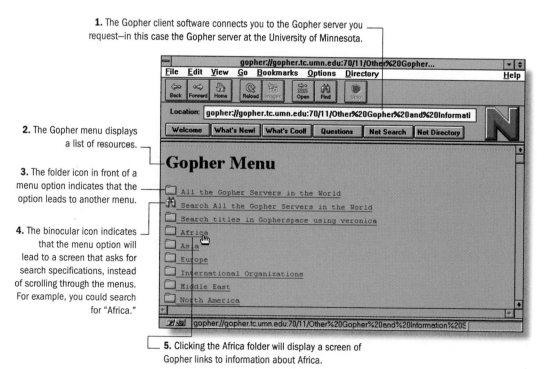

5. Clicking the Africa folder will display a screen of Gopher links to information about Africa.

6. A search for "Africa" results in a menu of Internet resources related to Africa. Each of the folders on this menu represents a different Gopher server. You can select one of the Gopher servers to see what information it contains.

7. Click this reference to see information from the ANC.

8. The African National Congress Gopher server displays its available information.

9. If you click a menu option that has a page icon, you will see the text of the document.

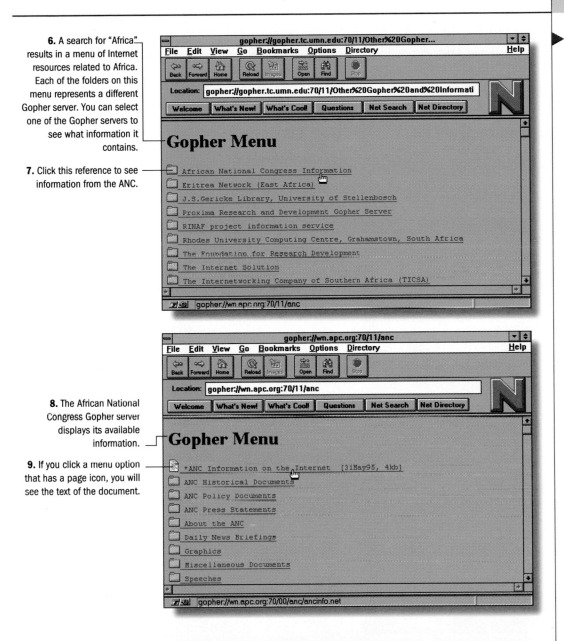

Figure 7-17
Menu conventions in a typical Gopher session *(continued)*

Usenet Newsgroups

Can the Internet help me if I don't have a lot of time to spend looking for information, but I want to keep current on certain topics?

Usenet is an Internet service that maintains thousands of discussion groups involving millions of people from all over the world. Each discussion group focuses on a particular topic such as music, business, computers, education, civil rights, and so on. Many of these groups foster scholarly discussion on topics, with postings contributed by reliable researchers and subject-area experts. Other discussion groups are more informal and the information posted might not be as reliable.

Usenet is often referred to as **the News** or **Netnews** because it was originally used as a sort of bulletin board for posting messages and news items. For the same reason, Usenet discussion groups are called **newsgroups** and user comments in the discussion are called **articles** or **postings**. Today, however, newsgroups carry little of what we think of as headline news. Instead, they carry conversations among the members of a group.

Figure 7-18 ◀
A Usenet thread

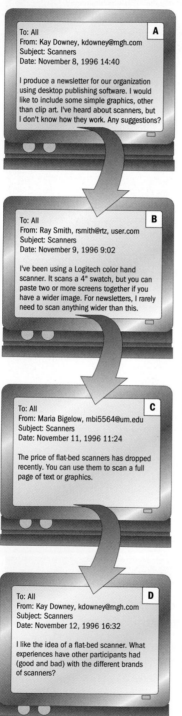

Kay Downey initiates a discussion about scanners on November 8. Her question is added to the newsgroup transcript.

As other users log into the newsgroup, they read Kay's posting. They can post a reply at any time. Here, participants Smith and Bigelow post replies on November 9 and November 11.

On November 12, Kay logs into the newsgroup again and reads the transcripts for November 9, 10, 11. She sees the replies from Smith and Bigelow, then continues the thread by posting another question.

The chat session you read about at the beginning of this chapter is synchronous, because all the participants were on-line at the same time. Discussion groups are asynchronous because the participants do not need to be on-line at the same time.

Usenet conversations are **asynchronous**—they do not take place in real time. For example, suppose Shirley is a member of a marine biology discussion group. Her research on water quality in coral reefs has turned up some rather starting results, and she would like to know if other researchers have found anything similar. She posts her research results on Monday along with a request for comments and additional data. Over the next several days, other members of the group respond. Later in the week when Shirley checks the newsgroup, she reads these responses. The handy thing about Usenet is that you can tune in when you have time, read all the postings since you last logged in, and post your response.

Some discussion groups are moderated, others are not. A **discussion group moderator** screens contributions to the discussion. This might involve eliminating postings that were mistakenly sent to the discussion group, routing personal messages to individual subscribers, and ensuring that the context of postings do not violate the ethical or editorial code of the organization that provides the site for the discussion group.

Sometimes a newsgroup has several conversations going at the same time. The sequence of comments for a particular conversation is called a **thread**. Some threads continue for years. Others are very short. In Figure 7-18 you can read the transcript of a Usenet thread.

To read Usenet articles, you use newsreader software. **Newsreader software** keeps track of the newsgroups you use and provides the commands you use to read articles, follow threads, and post replies.

When you participate in newsgroups, you should be aware of some unwritten rules, referred to as **netiquette**—a term made from combining the words *net* and *etiquette*.

Put your best foot forward. When you post a message to a newsgroup, your message is a reflection of you and your organization. Try to use correct grammar and spelling.

Use conventions to avoid misunderstandings. When you post a message that contains sarcasm or a joke, some readers might misunderstand your point. Identify the jokes and sarcasm in your postings using smileys like :-) for jokes and ;-) for sarcasm. Don't capitalize your entire message—your on-line readers will interpret this as shouting.

Help readers follow the thread. When you respond to a posting, provide the context for your response by including a portion of the original message in your reply.

Be brief. Keep your postings short and to the point.

Avoid flames. A **flame** is a nasty or insulting message posted to an Internet newsgroup or commercial information service discussion. If you reply to a flame with another flame, you could find yourself in the middle of a "flame war." Most on-line pros consider flame wars a waste of time. You can avoid these wars by ignoring flames that come your way. Also, when you post messages, choose your words carefully so you don't inadvertently offend other participants.

Read before you ask. Before you post questions to a newsgroup, take the time to understand the current threads and to read transcripts of previous discussions. Newsgroup participants do not like to answer the same questions repeatedly.

Personal messages belong on e-mail. If you have a personal message for one member of a newsgroup, use e-mail instead of posting it to the entire newsgroup. The other participants will thank you when they don't have to read these personal messages.

Quick Check

1 When you connect two or more networks, you form a(n) _____ .

2 The _____ is the largest and most widely used network in the world.

3 Identify each part of the Internet address **coco@canine.com**.

4 Which Internet service would you use to access the URL *http://physics7.berkeley.edu/home.html?*

5 If you want to find information by making selections from a series of menus, you would use the Internet service known as _____ .

6 If you want to download a file from an Internet host, but you don't have an account on that host, you can use an Internet service called _____ .

7 To run a program on a remote host, you can use the Internet service called _____ .

8 A(n) _____ is a computer-generated virtual reality in which you can explore graphical objects and interact with other participants.

9 The set of unwritten rules of proper behavior on the Internet is called _____ .

User Focus:

7.4

Connecting to the Internet

If your school has Internet access, your Academic Computing department has installed the hardware and software you need to access the Internet from your school lab, and possibly from your dorm room. But what if you want to access the Internet from your computer at home? To access the Internet from your home computer, you must set up the necessary computer equipment, locate an Internet service provider, install the appropriate software on your computer, then dial in.

Set Up Equipment

What special equipment do I need to access the Internet?

The basic equipment for setting up on-line communications is a computer, a modem, and a telephone line. The equipment you use does not change the activities you can do on-line, but it can affect the speed at which you can accomplish these activities.

The speed of your computer is only one factor that affects the speed at which you can send or receive data on-line.

IBM-compatible computers, Macintoshes, and PowerPCs can all connect to on-line services. A fast computer such as a 133 MHz Pentium speeds up some activities such as viewing graphics on-line. However, the overall speed of on-line activities is limited by the speed of the host computer, the speed of your modem, and the speed of your communications link.

A modem converts the data from your computer into signals that can travel over telephone lines. It also translates arriving signals into data that your computer can store, manipulate, and display. A fast modem speeds the process of sending and receiving data, so a 28.8K bps modem provides you with faster on-line response than a 14.4K bps modem. Faster modems are more expensive—you should buy the fastest modem you can afford.

The telephone line that you use for voice communications is suitable for on-line activities as well. Corporations sometimes use faster communications links such as ISDN or T1. Your telephone line, though not the speediest communications link, is certainly the least expensive.

When you are using your telephone line for on-line activities, you can't simultaneously use it for voice calls; while you are on-line, people who call you will get a busy signal. If you pick up the telephone receiver to make an outgoing call while you are on-line, your on-line connection will terminate.

Locate an Internet Access Provider

Who will provide me with an Internet connection, and how much will it cost?

An **Internet access provider** supplies you with a user account on a host computer that has access to the Internet. When you connect your personal computer to the host computer using a modem and the appropriate software, you gain access to the Internet. Your school might provide Internet access for students and faculty who want to use the Internet from off campus. An Internet connection provided by an educational institution is typically free. Many commercial information services such as CompuServe, Prodigy, Microsoft Network, and America Online provide Internet access. Expect to pay additional monthly or connect time fees for this service.

Internet connections are also offered by some telephone companies, cable TV companies, and independent telecommunications firms. These firms charge between $20 and $30 per month for Internet access. Unlike commercial information services, they usually do not maintain their own on-line information, discussion groups, or downloadable software.

Install Communications Software

Where do I get the communications software I need?

Your Internet access provider should supply you with **Internet communications software** that allows your computer to transmit and receive data using Internet communications protocol. A **communications protocol** is a set of rules that ensures the orderly and accurate transmission and reception of data. An analogy in human communication is that during a conversation only one person speaks at a time. Communications protocols help computers recognize when a message starts and stops. They standardize which part of the transmission is an address and which is the message. They also help a computer recognize when a transmission error has occurred, so the data can be retransmitted.

All computers connected to the Internet must use a communications protocol called **TCP/IP (Transmission Control Protocol/Internet Protocol)**. Standard TCP/IP software handles Internet communication between computers that are directly cabled to a network. **SLIP (Serial Line Internet Protocol)** and **PPP (Point to Point Protocol)** are versions of TCP/IP designed to handle Internet communications for a computer that connects to the Internet using a modem. When you want to access the Internet from a computer using a modem, you must use PPP, SLIP, or other similar communications software. This is the communications software you receive from your Internet access provider.

In the past, luck played an important role in establishing successful computer communications. Today, the communications software supplied by most Internet access providers is self-configuring; in other words, the first time you run the software, it examines your computer system and automatically selects the appropriate software settings. You have to deal with technical specifications only if your computer equipment, modem, or telephone line are not standard.

Install Browsers and Other Software

How do I get the other software I need to access information and services on the Internet?

In addition to Internet communications software, you must have software that helps you access Internet information and services such as e-mail, the World Wide Web, and FTP. You will probably want to start with e-mail client software and a Web browser. This software is typically supplied by your Internet access provider. You can add additional software as you need it.

Some text, graphical, sound, and video information on the Internet is stored in special file formats. This information can be viewed only if you use special software, referred to as a **viewer**. You can usually download the viewer you need from the site that provides the specially formatted text, graphical, sound, or video file.

To install an e-mail client, Web browser, or viewer, follow the instructions that accompany the software. If you obtained the software on disk, open a file called "readme" on the disk for instructions. If you downloaded the software, you should find installation instructions at the on-line site.

You can refresh your memory about Internet software by referring back to Figure 7-10.

Dial In

After my hardware is set up and my software is installed, how do I dial in to the Internet?

Most Internet communications software is represented by an icon on your computer's desktop or start screen. You start the software by clicking this icon, and it automatically establishes a connection to the Internet. Figure 7-19 shows what happens when you dial in.

Figure 7-19
Dialing into the Internet

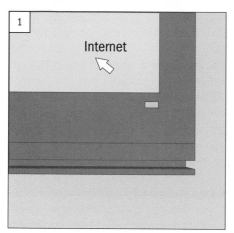

Click the Internet icon supplied by your Internet service provider.

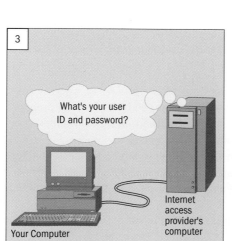

By clicking the Internet icon, you tell the computer to load your Internet communications client software. Your communications client will probably use SLIP or PPP to handle the TCP/IP protocols as your computer transmits and receives data through your modem.

Your communications client dials into Internet service provider. Usually, your communication client has stored the telephone number, so you do not need to enter it each time you want to connect.

If your communications client has stored your user ID and password, it will automatically log you in. Some people prefer to enter their password manually for better security.

End Note

The information highway has received much publicity. Many people agree that such a vast information network has potential to improve the quality of our lives. It provides us with an opportunity to interact with people of diverse backgrounds, engage in life-long education, and enrich our knowledge of the global community.

Fifty years ago a new technology called television promised similar advantages. Today, many people believe that television has failed. They point to inane soap operas, an overabundance of graphic violence, the commercialization of gratuitous sex, and popularity of talk shows featuring bizarre human experiences.

Will the information highway also fail to fulfill its potential? The answer to this question is difficult to predict. The amount of information available on-line is growing. Much of this data is useful, but other information is of questionable value. On-line computer technical support helps thousands of people keep their computers operational, but who is helped by on-line instructions for manufacturing homemade bombs? Satellite photographs from NASA's on-line database contribute to our knowledge of the universe, but what is the contribution of graphical images of sexual exploitation? In many ways, the information highway is a reflection of the interests as well as the problems of our society. Its development is worth watching throughout your lifetime.

Review

1. Below each heading in this chapter, there is a question in italics. Look back through the chapter and answer each of these questions using your own words.

2. Think about the terms *information highway*, *cyberspace*, *Internet*, and *commercial information service*. Using your own words, write a definition of each. Make sure your definitions clearly explain the differences between these terms.

3. Make a list of the services offered by large commercial information services such as CompuServe.

4. List the steps for subscribing to a commercial information service.

5. Define the following terms:

a. basic service

b. premium service

c. connect time

6. Define the following terms:

a. internetwork

b. download

c. URL

d. virtual reality

e. TCP/IP

f. communications protocol

g. MUD

h. MOO

7. Describe in your own words each of the following Internet services:

a. e-mail

b. Telnet

c. FTP

d. Gopher

e. World Wide Web

f. Usenet

8. Suppose you have access to the Internet. For each of the following situations, indicate which Internet service(s) you would use:

a. You are having a problem with the CD-ROM drive on your Macintosh, and you want some help figuring out what might be wrong.

b. You want to download a file of information about the Voyager spacecraft from seds.lpl.arizona.edu.

c. You want to find an Internet site with information on international business.

d. You want to correspond with your friend at Colorado State University.

e. You want to try out a MUD called "Island."

f. You want to join a discussion group on desktop publishing.

g. You want to see what's at the Internet site *http://symbolicnet.mcs.kent.edu.*

h. You are doing DNA research, and you want to use a DNA modeling program that runs on the University of Michigan Medical School computer.

i. You want to take an on-line tour of the Treasures of the Czars exhibit, viewing graphics of the items in the exhibit and reading about their history.

9. Make a list of at least five differences between the Internet and commercial information services.

10. In an Internet address, such as **president@ whitehouse.gov**, the *gov* domain name specifies that the Internet site type is *government*. What are the other Internet domain names and their site types?

Projects

1. The Great Internet Hunt For several years Rick Gates hosted a monthly Internet scavenger hunt. The object of his hunt was to find information on the Internet. The hunt in this project is a little different from Gates' hunt. For this hunt, there are 10 questions. The questions are located at the CTI Web site, *http://www.vmedia.com/cti/concepts2/chap7np.html.* Go to this site and print out the questions. Each question carries a point value between 1 and 5. Answer as many questions as you can using the Internet or other resources. For your answer you must write down the location of the information on the Internet—the URL, FTP site, newsgroup name, and so on. You must also supply at least a one-page printout to verify that you actually visited the site.

2. Internet: Past, Present, Future Use Internet or library resources to write a research paper about the Internet. In your paper be sure to answer, but do not limit yourself to, the following questions:

a. What are the key events in the development of the Internet? Include a time line of these key events.

b. What is the Internet's current status?

c. What changes are likely to take place in the future?

d. What ethical issues do you think are raised by the existence of the Internet?

3. Censored! Prodigy, which bills itself as a family information service, monitors the content of its services to remove X-rated and R-rated text and graphics. However, no such policing occurs at most other Internet services.

The Internet and commercial information services provide a growing forum for discussions on a wide range of topics. Recently, some on-line observers have begun to question the advisability of information exchanged over the Internet. Megabytes of Internet storage space are devoted to X-rated images. Several Usenet groups regularly discuss the details of making bombs and hollow point bullets. Other groups discuss methods of torture. In a well-publicized incident, a discussion group participant described in gory detail how he was going to murder a female college student.

Free speech laws protect the rights of Americans to express themselves, but should the Internet, which is supported with public taxes, provide a forum for such information and discussions? Senator James Exon does not think so and has sponsored Senate Bill 314: the Communications Decency Act, which would make it a federal crime to annoy, abuse, threaten, or harass anyone on-line. Further, it would be a crime to transmit anything "obscene, lewd, filthy, or indecent." Do you think this Act violates free speech?

For this project, research the issue of on-line censorship. Write a position paper arguing for or against censorship. Support your position with facts and examples. Be sure to include a bibliography. After you complete your research, your instructor might suggest that you discuss your ideas in a small group session.

4. Yellow Pages Printed Internet directories such as *The Internet Yellow Pages* help you find information on the Internet. Browse through an Internet directory, such as those listed in the Resources section of this chapter. Find an example of each of the following, and write down the site name, address, or URL:

a. A World Wide Web site that relates to your academic major or career plans.

b. An anonymous FTP site that contains something you would like to download.

c. A Usenet newsgroup that focuses on a topic related to one of your hobbies or leisure time interests.

If you have Internet access, collect a sample of information from each site using download capabilities or the Print menu. When you turn in your project include a cover page that describes why you selected each site and the value of the information you found.

5. No One Knows You're a Dog In a novel called *Ender's War,* two children are catapulted to national prominence because they have innovative ideas about how to solve critical social and economic issues. No one knows they are children, however, because they communicate their ideas on a public information service, which is the central political forum in their society. This brings up an interesting issue, humorously alluded to in the P. Steiner cartoon in Figure 7-20 on the next page.

Figure 7-20 ◀

"On the Internet, nobody knows you're a dog."

Discuss this issue in a small group. In your discussion address questions a through e.

a. Does a communication medium that depends on the written word, rather than on videos, reduce cultural, class, ethnic, and gender bias?

b. According to pollsters, in 1980 many Americans voted for Ronald Reagan because they didn't like his opponent's southern accent. Do you think the election would have been different if campaigning was carried out over the Internet?

c. There is evidence that the younger generation does not like to read and write. Do you think this generation needs a communications medium that is more like television?

d. Do you believe that on-line communications have the potential to reduce biases in our society?

e. Can anyone in your group relate an experience when on-line communication would have been preferable to face-to-face communication?

6. Compare Commercial Information Services The rates for commercial information services such as Compu-Serve, Prodigy, and America Online change frequently. Rather than provide you with outdated information in this chapter, this project will help you compare the rates and services of commercial information services. Select three of the following commercial information services: Compu-Serve, Prodigy, America Online, eWorld (for Macintosh users), Delphi, Microsoft Network, or ImagiNation. Use library resources or materials provided by your instructor to complete the following table for the three services you selected.

Criteria	Service 1	Service 2	Service 3
Need special communications software?			
Setup kit available for DOS?			
Setup kit available for Windows?			
Setup kit available for OS/2?			
Setup kit available for Mac OS?			
Basic monthly fee:			
How many free hours included in basic fee?			
Connect charge for additional hours at 1200 baud:			
Connect charge 2400 baud:			
Connect charge at 9600 baud:			
Connect charge at 14.4K baud:			
Surcharge for discussion groups (Y/N)?			
Database search surcharge (Y/N)?			
Prime time surcharge (Y/N)?			
Number of free e-mail messages included in basic service			
Fee for additional e-mail messages:			
Internet connection available?			
World Wide Web browser available?			

7. Virtual Reality: MUDs, MOOs, Goggles, and Doom Writer William Gibson envisioned a time when people would connect their brains directly to a computer to experience a virtual world in cyberspace. Technology and medical science have not found a way to make a direct connection between our brains and a computer, but today virtual reality takes other forms. On the Internet, MUDs and MOOs provide virtual environments for games, meetings, and socializing. On microcomputers, the multiplayer game Doom provides hours of virtual reality adventure. Using equipment, such as the stereo-optic goggles and sensor gloves shown in Figure 7-21, you can see and manipulate objects that do not exist.

Figure 7-21 ◀

Use your library and Internet resources to learn more about virtual reality. You might also try some virtual reality experiences. If you have Internet access, participate in a MUD or MOO. Play a virtual reality computer game such as Doom or Myst. If available, try out virtual reality goggles.

Now suppose you are asked to produce a three-minute TV news segment on virtual reality. Based on the information you gathered from your library, the Internet, and your personal experiences, write the narrative and describe the images and video clips you would show.

8. Connecting Your Own Computer to the Internet
Suppose you have a computer at home or in your dorm room. You want to connect it to the Internet. To complete this project, answer the following questions:

   a. Does your school offer Internet connections to students who have their own computers? If so, how do you sign up for an account? What is the name of the Internet communications client? If you use your school's Internet connection, are all Internet services available? Which ones are and are not?

   b. If your school does not offer an Internet connection for students' home computers, which commercial service would you select? Explain why.

9. Good Netiquette Design a mini-poster of the rules of good netiquette. You can decide what audience your poster targets: children, high school students, college students, business people—you could even select a specific business. Try to use words and images that will appeal to your target audience.

10. Your Own Web Page Use an HTML editor to design your own Web page. Your instructor will provide you with instructions for locating your HTML editor and for submitting your home page either on disk or on your network.

Resources

- **Benedikt, M.** (ed.) *Cyberspace: First Steps*. Cambridge, MA: The MIT Press, 1993. Michael Benedikt is the editor of this collection of articles about cyberspace—its history, current status, and future potential. Looking at the authors' occupations gives you some idea about the direction of cyberspace research. Contributors include a science fiction writer, architects, computer interface experts, artists, sociologists, anthropologists, and computer engineers.

- **Gibson, W.** *Neuromancer*. New York: Ace books, 1984. Neuromancer is the science fiction novel that started a new genre of cyberspace sci-fi. Gibson paints a world in which Japanese influence has slowly enveloped Western pop culture, and in which the search for information—or even entertainment—means plugging your brain into a computer.

- **Hahn, H. and Stout, R.** *The Internet Yellow Pages*, second edition. Berkeley, CA: Osborne McGraw-Hill, 1995. Find it all here. A fun, but informative listing of thousands of Internet sites.

- **Hoffman, P.** *The Internet*. Foster City, CA IDG Books Worldwide, 1994. This is the companion book to public television's The "Internet Show." It is a great guide for beginners who want an overview of the Internet. Explanations are clear and nicely illustrated.

Internet sites with information about the Internet:

- A multimedia course on the history and status of the Internet at: *http://www.nlm.nih.gov/LECTURES.dir/internet_course.dir/starting_page.html*

- A timeline and growth statistics for the Internet at: *http://tig.com/IBC/Timeline.html*

- Excerpts from talks and tutorials on the Internet at: *http://town.hall.org/university/index.html*

- Lots of Internet info at *http://www.internic.net*

- **Kent, P.** *The Complete Idiot's Guide to the Internet*, second edition. Indianapolis, IN: Alpha Books, 1994. Don't let the title insult you. This book covers some fairly technical material, but the explanations are well done. You'll hardly realize that you're learning anything, but you are—lots of information about connecting to the Internet, sending e-mail, participating in newsgroups, Telnetting, FTP-ing, and Web browsing.

- **Stoll, C.** *Silicon Snake Oil: Second Thoughts on the Information Highway*. New York: Doubleday, 1995. Stoll, a seasoned Internet user, takes a cautionary—some might say reactionary—view of the effect of the information highway on society. He contends that we often mistake information for knowledge and cautions that cyberspace is no substitute for experience in the real world. He also suggests that the ease of firing off your opinion to an on-line discussion fosters flames, rather than reasoned debate.

- **Turlington, S.** *Walking the World Wide Web*. Chapel Hill, NC: Ventana Press, 1995. A clearly-written book about the World Wide Web and the Mosaic Web browser. Also contains a terrific list of web sites. Ventana Press has its own web site: *http://www.vmedia.com*.

- **Wired** This is the magazine of choice among Internet aficionados. It's artsy, glitzy, and off-beat; but it has some high quality articles with non-conventional perspectives. Senior columnist Nicholas Negroponte is well known for his work at the MIT Media Lab. *Wired* has an Internet site at *http://wired.com*.

Lab Assignments

The Internet: World Wide Web

 One of the most popular services on the Internet is the World Wide Web. This Lab is a Web simulator that teaches you how to use Web browser software to find information. You can use this Lab whether or not your school provides you with Internet access.

1. Click the Steps button to learn how to use Web browser software. As you proceed through the Steps, answer all of the Quick Check questions that appear. After you complete the Steps, you will see a Quick Check Summary Report. Follow the instructions on the screen to print this report.

2. Click the Explore button on the Welcome screen. Use the Web browser to locate a weather map of the Carribean Virgin Islands. What is its URL?

3. A SCUBA diver named Wadson Lachouffe has been searching for the fabled treasure of Greybeard the pirate. A link from the Adventure Travel Web *www.atour.com* site leads to a Wadson's Web page called "Hidden Treasure." In Explore, locate the Hidden Treasure page and answer the following questions:

a. What was the name of Greybeard's ship?

b. What was Greybeard's favorite food?

c. What does Wadson think happened to Greybeard's ship?

4. In the Steps, you found a graphic of Jupiter from the photo archives of the Jet Propulsion Laboratory. In the Explore section of the Lab, you can also find a graphic of Saturn. Suppose one of your friends wanted a picture of Saturn for an astronomy report. Make a list of the blue, underlined links your friend must click to find the Saturn graphic. Assume that your friend will begin at the Web Trainer home page.

5. Enter the URL *http://www.atour.com* to jump to the Adventure Travel Web site. Write a one-page description of this site. In your paper include a description of the information at the site, the number of pages the site contains, and a diagram of the links it contains.

6. Chris Thomson is a student at UVI and has his own Web pages. In Explore, look at the information Chris has included on his pages. Suppose you could create your own Web page. What would you include? Use word processing software to design your own Web pages. Make sure you indicate the graphics and links you would use.

7.1

1. cyberspace

2. Internet

3. commercial information service (or on-line service)

4. discussion group

5. chat session

6. downloading

7.2

1. computers, host (mainframe)

2. Prodigy, CompuServe, America Online, Microsoft Network

3. basic services

4. connect time

5. local access number

7.3

1. internet (or internetwork)

2. Internet

3. coco = user ID, @canine = machine name, com = domain name

4. World Wide Web

5. Gopher

6. Anonymous FTP

7. Telnet

8. MOO

9. netiquette

Glossary/Index

Data Security and Control

CHAPTER**PREVIEW**

In this chapter you learn about threats to the data stored on computer systems. With this information, you can begin to assess your risk of losing important data, becoming the target of computer vandalism, or being affected by inaccurate data. You will find out why data backup is one of the most effective security measures for protecting your data. On a practical level, you will learn how to disinfect disks that contain viruses, make backups, and design an effective backup plan for your data. After you have completed this chapter you should be able to:

- List some of the causes for lost or inaccurate data

- Describe how you can protect your computer data from damage caused by power problems and hardware failures

- List at least five symptoms that might indicate your computer is infected by a virus

- Differentiate between the terms virus, Trojan horse, worm, logic bomb, and time bomb

- Describe techniques for avoiding, detecting, and eradicating a computer virus

- Explain why special computer crime laws are necessary

- Describe the process of risk management

- List the advantages and disadvantages of the most popular data security techniques

Data Security
and Control

According to legend, the war between the Trojans and the Greeks continued for more than nine years, until one of the Greek leaders conceived a brilliant plan. He ordered his men to create a huge wooden horse. When it was completed, a few Greek soldiers hid inside and the Greek army pretended to sail away. In the morning, the Trojans found a magnificent horse statue at the city gates. Believing that the horse was a gift, the Trojans pulled it into the city and spent the day celebrating what they thought was a great victory. Late that night, the Greek soldiers hidden inside the horse crept out and opened the city gates for the waiting Greek army.

What does the Trojan War have to do with computers? Like the city of Troy, modern computer users are under siege. They are battling computer criminals, pranksters, viruses, equipment failures, and human errors. There is even a modern software version of the Trojan horse that might erase your data after you unknowingly bring it into your computer system.

Today's computer users battle to avoid lost, stolen, and inaccurate data. **Lost data**, also referred to as **missing data**, is data that is inaccessible, usually because it was accidentally removed. **Stolen data** is not necessarily missing, but it has been accessed or copied without authorization. **Inaccurate data** is data that is not accurate because it was entered incorrectly, was deliberately or accidentally altered, or was not edited to reflect current facts.

This chapter begins by describing mistakes and equipment failures that inadvertently cause lost or inaccurate data. Next, the focus moves to intentional acts of vandalism and computer crime in which data is tampered with or stolen. The section on risk management explains the steps you can take to protect your data. This chapter concludes with an in-depth look at a most important computing activity—data backup.

LAB

Data Backup

What Can Go Wrong

T he data on a computer system is important, but events occur that destroy data or make it inaccurate. For example, people make mistakes. Suppose you store your English Composition term paper on your home computer, but before you turn it in, you inadvertently erase it. Another example is hardware failure. The medical records that a doctor stores on the clinic's computer are important for the correct treatment of patients. What happens if the power goes off or the hard drive fails and no one can access the data? Disasters also occur. The client records that your medical insurance provider stores on its computer system ensure accurate and expedient reimbursement for your medical expenses. What if the insurance provider's computer system is destroyed by fire? The list of examples like these seems endless, but the point remains the same: Important data stored on computers is vulnerable to human error, power problems, hardware failure, and natural disasters.

Operator Error

What's the most likely cause of lost or inaccurate data?

Despite all the sensational press coverage of computer criminals and viruses, the most common cause of lost data is operator error. **Operator error** refers to a mistake made by a computer user. At one time or another, everyone who has used a computer has made a mistake. A few examples will illustrate that it is not an exclusive club.

- Working late at night the President's press secretary finished the final revisions for the next day's speech. Intending to make a copy of the speech as a backup, he mistakenly copied the old version of the speech over the new version.
- The head of the information systems department at a Fortune 500 firm was in a hurry to copy some files onto a floppy disk. Grabbing a disk without a label and thinking it was unformatted, she shoved it in the disk drive and started the formatting process. Unfortunately, the disk contained her only copy of a report that had been mailed from the Houston office.
- A clerk in the medical records office of a metropolitan hospital was embarrassed to learn that he had billed a patient for 555 aspirins instead of 5.

It might seem that nothing can prevent operator error. After all, mistakes do happen. However, the number of operator errors can be reduced if users pay attention to what they're doing and establish habits that help them avoid mistakes.

Many organizations have reduced the incidence of operator errors by using direct source input devices. A **direct source input device**, such as a bar code reader, collects data directly from a document or object, without human intervention. This reduces the possibility of input errors that occur because of such human mistakes as typing the wrong number.

Good user interface design can also reduce operator error. Computer software designers can help prevent mistakes by designing products that anticipate mistakes that users are likely to make and that help users avoid them. For example, Microsoft Windows 95 users can activate a feature that requests confirmation before the computer carries out any activity that might destroy data. Figure 8-1 shows a Windows 95 dialog box that asks for confirmation before a file is deleted.

1. The user selects the file Sales Summary. Pressing the Delete key initiates an operation that will, in effect, destroy the data in the selected file.

2. The Microsoft Windows 95 operating system displays a prompt asking the user to confirm the Delete. The file is deleted only if the user clicks the Yes button.

Figure 8-1
Confirmation dialog box helps reduce operator error

Although a power failure results in lost data from RAM, it is unlikely to cause data loss from disk because magnetic storage does not require power to maintain data.

Power Failures, Spikes, and Surges

If the power goes out, will I lose all my data?

A **power failure** is a complete loss of power to the computer system. Although you can lose power by accidentally bumping the computer on/off switch, a power failure is usually caused by something over which you have no control, such as a downed power line or a malfunction at the local power plant.

Data stored in RAM is lost if power is not continuously supplied to the computer system. Even a brief interruption in the power supply, noticeable only as a flicker of the room lights, can force your computer to reboot and lose all the data in RAM.

An uninterruptible power supply is the best protection against power problems. An **uninterruptible power supply**, or **UPS**, is a device containing a battery and other circuitry that provides a continuous supply of power. A UPS is designed to provide enough power to keep your computer working through momentary power interruptions and to give you time to save your files and exit your programs in the event of a longer power outage. A UPS for a microcomputer costs from $100 to $600,

Figure 8-2
An uninterruptible power supply

A UPS contains a battery that keeps your computer going for several minutes during a power failure. The battery does not supply indefinite power, so in the event of a power failure that lasts more than two or three minutes you should save your work and turn off your computer.

A light on the case lets you know that the UPS is charged and ready.

To connect a UPS, plug it into a wall outlet, then plug your computer and monitor cables into the outlets on the UPS.

depending on the power requirements of the computer and the features of the UPS. Most computer dealers can help you determine your computer's power requirements and recommend the appropriate size and features for a UPS that meets your needs. Figure 8-2 shows a typical UPS.

Two other common power problems are spikes and surges. Both of these can damage sensitive computer components. A **power spike** is an increase in power that lasts only a short time—

Figure 8-3
A surge protector

A surge suppressor is a small device that contains two to six electrical outlets, so you can plug in your computer, monitor, and printer.
It protects your equipment from electrical spikes and surges. It does not have a battery and cannot keep your computer running if the power goes off.

Power spikes and surges are potentially more damaging than a power failure. They can destroy the circuitry that operates your hard disk drive, so you lose access to all the data it contains.

less than a millionth of a second. A **power surge** lasts a little longer—a few millionths of a second. Malfunctions in the local generating plant and the power distribution network can cause surges and spikes. Lightning can also cause a surge that damages computer equipment circuitry. Power surges and spikes are potentially more damaging than power failures. A surge or spike can damage your computer's main board and the circuit boards on your disk drives, putting your computer out of action until the boards are replaced.

Many experts recommend that you unplug your computer equipment, including your modem, during electrical storms. Unfortunately, there is not much you can do to increase the reliability of the local power system. However, the same UPS you use to provide a few minutes of power in the event of a power loss will also filter out power surges and spikes. As a low-cost alternative, you can plug your computer into an inexpensive **surge protector**. Just remember that a surge protector does not protect the data in RAM if the power fails. Figure 8-3 explains how a surge protector works.

Hardware Failure

How reliable are the components of my computer system?

The reliability of computer components is measured as **mean time between failures**, or **MTBF**. This measurement is somewhat misleading to most consumers. For example, you might read that your hard disk drive has an MTBF of 125,000 hours, which is about 14 years. Does this mean your hard drive will work for 125,000 hours before it fails? Unfortunately, the answer is no.

The MTBF is an estimate based on laboratory tests of a few sample components. The tests are conducted in a regulated laboratory environment where power problems, failure of other components, and regular wear and tear do not exist. A 125,000 hour MTBF means that, *on average*, a hard disk drive like yours is likely to function for 125,000 hours without failing. The fact remains, however, that your hard disk drive might work for only 10 hours before it fails. With this in mind, plan for hardware failtures, rather than hope they won't happen.

Much of the equipment that fails does so within the first hours or days of operation, but after that it can be expected to work fairly reliably until it nears the end of its useful life. The failure rate of computer components is illustrated by the graph in Figure 8-4.

Figure 8-4
Failure rate of computer equipment during its useful life

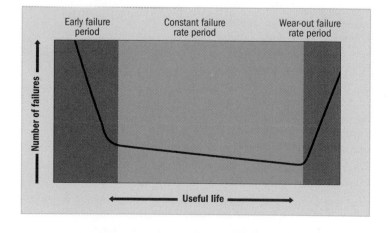

The effect of a hardware failure depends on the component that fails. Most hardware failures are simply an inconvenience. For example, if your monitor fails, you can obtain a replacement monitor, plug it in, and get back to work. On the other hand, a hard disk drive failure can be a disaster because you might lose all the data stored on the hard disk drive. The impact of a hard disk drive failure is considerably reduced if you have complete, up-to-date backups of the programs and data files on your hard disk.

Fires, Floods, and Other Disasters

Should I buy insurance for my computer?

Computers are not immune to unexpected damage from smoke, fire, water, and breakage. However, it is not practical to barricade your computer from every potential disaster. Many insurance policies provide coverage for computers. Under the terms of many standard household and business policies, a computer is treated like any other appliance. You should make sure, however, that your insurance policy covers the full cost of purchasing a new computer at current market prices.

Replacing your damaged computer equipment will not replace your data. Some insurance companies provide extra coverage for the data on your computer. This coverage would provide you a sum of money to cover the time it takes to reload your data on a replacement computer. However, being able to reload your data assumes that you have a backup of your data. Without a backup, much of your data cannot be reconstructed. For a business, the situation is even more critical. Customer accounts, inventory, daily transactions, and financial information are difficult, if not impossible, to reconstruct.

To summarize, a good insurance policy provides funds to replace computer equipment, but the only insurance for your data is an up-to-date backup tape or disk.

Quick Check

1. The most common cause of lost data is _____ .

2. As a result of a power failure your computer will lose all the data stored in RAM and the hard drive. True or false?

3. A(n) _____ contains a battery that provides a continuous supply of power to your computer during a brief power failure.

4. A(n) _____ protects your computer from electrical spikes and surges, but it does not keep your computer operating if the power fails.

5. The circuitry on your computer circuit boards can be damaged by accidentally turning off your computer. True or false?

6. MTBF tells you how often an electronic device needs to be serviced. True or false?

7. The failure of which computer component is potentially the most disastrous?

8. The best insurance for your data is _____

Viruses, Vandalism, and Computer Crime

8.2

Data stored on micro, mini, or mainframe computers can be damaged, destroyed, or altered by vandalism. The vandals are called **hackers**, **crackers**, or **cyberpunks**. The programs these hackers create are colorfully referred to by various sources as *malware*, *pest programs*, *vandalware*, or *punkware*. More typically, these programs are referred to as *viruses*. What would you do if you saw the message in Figure 8-5 on your computer screen?

Figure 8-5
A virus alert: real or fake?

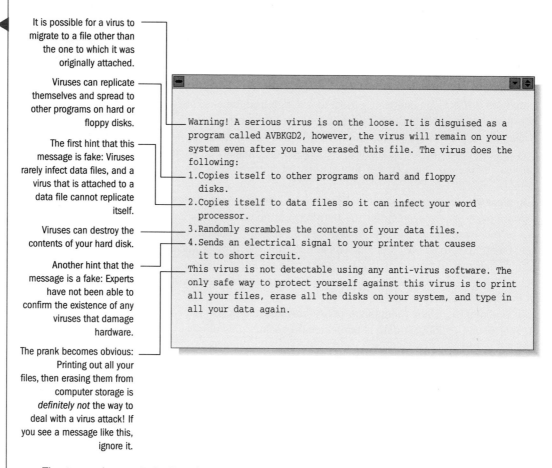

It is possible for a virus to migrate to a file other than the one to which it was originally attached.

Viruses can replicate themselves and spread to other programs on hard or floppy disks.

The first hint that this message is fake: Viruses rarely infect data files, and a virus that is attached to a data file cannot replicate itself.

Viruses can destroy the contents of your hard disk.

Another hint that the message is a fake: Experts have not been able to confirm the existence of any viruses that damage hardware.

The prank becomes obvious: Printing out all your files, then erasing them from computer storage is *definitely not* the way to deal with a virus attack! If you see a message like this, ignore it.

```
Warning! A serious virus is on the loose. It is disguised as a
program called AVBKGD2, however, the virus will remain on your
system even after you have erased this file. The virus does the
following:
1.Copies itself to other programs on hard and floppy
  disks.
2.Copies itself to data files so it can infect your word
  processor.
3.Randomly scrambles the contents of your data files.
4.Sends an electrical signal to your printer that causes
  it to short circuit.
This virus is not detectable using any anti-virus software. The
only safe way to protect yourself against this virus is to print
all your files, erase all the disks on your system, and type in
all your data again.
```

The term *virus* technically refers to only one type of trouble-making program created by hackers. Hackers also cause mischief with programs such as Trojan horses, time bombs, logic bombs, and worms. As you'll learn in this chapter, each of these programs behaves differently when attacking a computer system.

Viruses, Trojan horses, time bombs, logic bombs, and worms lurk on disks and computer bulletin boards waiting to destroy data and cause mischief to your computer system. Understanding how these programs work is the first line of defense against attacks and pranks.

Computer Viruses

Exactly what is a computer virus?

A **computer virus** is a program that attaches itself to a file and reproduces itself to spread from one file to another. A virus can destroy data, display an irritating message, or otherwise disrupt computer operations. The jargon that describes a computer virus sounds similar to medical jargon. Your computer is a "host," and it can become "infected" with a virus. A virus can reproduce itself and spread from one computer to another. You can "inoculate" your computer against many viruses. If your computer has not been inoculated and becomes infected, you can use anti-viral software to "disinfect" it.

A computer virus generally infects the executable files on your computer system, not the data files. When you run an infected program, your computer also runs the attached virus instructions to replicate or deliver its payload. The term **payload** refers to the ultimate mission of a virus. For example, the payload of the "Stoned" virus is the message, "Your PC is now stoned." Figure 8-6 illustrates how a computer virus spreads and delivers its payload.

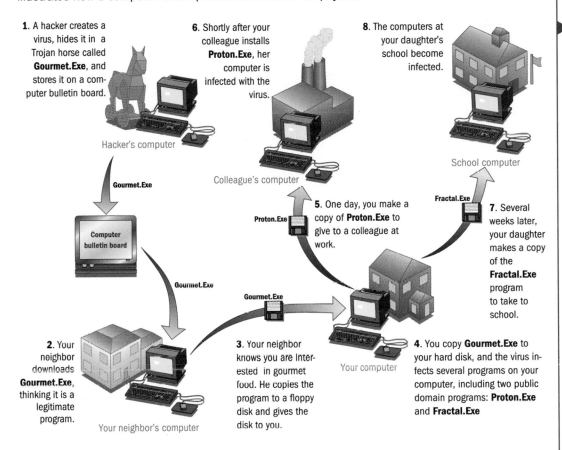

1. A hacker creates a virus, hides it in a Trojan horse called **Gourmet.Exe**, and stores it on a computer bulletin board.

Hacker's computer

Gourmet.Exe

Computer bulletin board

Gourmet.Exe

2. Your neighbor downloads **Gourmet.Exe**, thinking it is a legitimate program.

Your neighbor's computer

3. Your neighbor knows you are interested in gourmet food. He copies the program to a floppy disk and gives the disk to you.

Gourmet.Exe

4. You copy **Gourmet.Exe** to your hard disk, and the virus infects several programs on your computer, including two public domain programs: **Proton.Exe** and **Fractal.Exe**

Your computer

5. One day, you make a copy of **Proton.Exe** to give to a colleague at work.

Proton.Exe

6. Shortly after your colleague installs **Proton.Exe**, her computer is infected with the virus.

Colleague's computer

7. Several weeks later, your daughter makes a copy of the **Fractal.Exe** program to take to school.

Fractal.Exe

8. The computers at your daughter's school become infected.

School computer

Figure 8-6
How a computer virus works

The term "host" has several meanings. It can refer to a computer that has contracted a virus. It can also refer to the main computer in a network.

Most viruses attach themselves to executable files because these are the files that your computer runs. If a virus attaches to an executable file that you rarely use, it might not have an opportunity to spread and do much damage. On the other hand, **boot sector viruses**, which infect the system files your computer uses every time you turn it on, can cause widespread damage and persistent problems. Only a few viruses, such as Cinderella and Frodo, are designed to infect data files. Because a virus needs to be executed to spread, a data file can only be a carrier; it cannot deliver the payload.

Experts say there are over 2,000 viruses. However, 90% of virus damage is caused by fewer than 10 viruses. The extent of damage varies with the virus. Research conducted by Computer Security BBS found that 64% of those surveyed had experienced a computer virus attack in the past 12 months. Forty-nine percent of these cases resulted in damaged or lost data. Figure 8-7 gives you some idea of the financial consequences of virus infections.

Figure 8-7
Impact of virus infections

Impact of virus damage

51%

17%

26%

6%

Disastrous: Loss over $100,000 and/or more than 3 days to fix

Severe: Loss under $100,000 and/or 2–3 days to fix

Moderate: Some loss of data and/or 1–2 days to fix

Minimal: No data/revenue lost and/or less than a day to fix

A key point to understand about viruses is that they contain instructions that the computer must perform for the virus to spread or deliver its payload.

The symptoms of a virus infection depend on the virus. The following symptoms *might* indicate that your computer has contracted a virus. However, some of these symptoms can have other causes.

- Your computer displays annoying messages such as "Gotcha! Arf Arf," "You're stoned!," or "I want a cookie."
- Your computer develops unusual visual or sound effects. For example, characters begin to disappear from your screen or the sound of a flushing toilet comes from your computer's speaker.
- You have difficulty saving files.
- Your computer suddenly seems to work very slowly.
- Files are mysteriously missing.
- Your computer reboots unexpectedly.
- Your executable files unaccountably increase in size.

Viruses are just one type of program in a large category of software designed by hackers to disrupt or damage the data on computers. After looking at other software in this category, you'll find out how to avoid and minimize the damage they cause.

A Modern Trojan Horse

How can I avoid being fooled by a Trojan horse?

At the beginning of this chapter, you learned about the legendary Trojan horse. A modern software version waits to surprise unwary computer users. In the context of computing, a **Trojan horse** is a computer program that appears to perform one function while actually doing something else. A Trojan horse sometimes, but not always, harbors a virus. For example, suppose a hacker writes a program to format hard disk drives and embeds this program in a file called **Sched.Exe.** The hacker then distributes disks containing this Trojan horse and posts it on computer bulletin boards where other users are likely to assume it is a free scheduling program. Users who download and run **Sched.Exe** will discover that the program has erased all the files on their hard disk. This Trojan horse does not harbor a virus because it does not replicate itself. Figure 8-8 shows how this type of Trojan horse program works.

Another popular Trojan horse looks just like the login screen on a network. However, as a user logs in, the Trojan horse collects the user's ID and password. These are stored in a file that a hacker can access later. Armed with a valid user ID and password, the hacker can access the data stored on the network. As with the earlier example, this Trojan horse does not harbor a virus. The hacker's program, designed to defeat network security measures, does not replicate itself.

It is easy to be fooled by Trojan horse programs because they are designed to be difficult to detect. Keep your ears open for information about the latest computer pranks circulating in your local area. Also, be suspicious of anything out of the ordinary on your computer system. For example, if your login screen looks a little different one day, check with your technical support person.

1. The harmless-looking file called **Sched.Exe** is really a Trojan horse that contains a program to format the hard drive.

Sched.Exe

Format C:

4. The command to run the Sched program instead activates the format program, and the contents of the hard disk are destroyed.

No files on drive C:

Run Sched

2. A user innocently puts the disk containing **Sched.Exe** in drive A:.

3. Next, the user tries to run the Sched program, assuming that it is a free scheduling program.

Figure 8-8
How a Trojan horse works

Think of a Trojan horse as a container that hides a secret program. That program might be a virus or a time bomb, or simply a program that, when run, carries out a nasty task such as formatting your hard disk.

Time Bombs and Logic Bombs

Can a virus lurk in my computer system without my knowledge?

Although a virus usually begins to replicate itself immediately when it enters your computer system, it will not necessarily deliver its payload right away. A virus or other unwelcome surprise can lurk in your computer system for days or months without discovery. A **time bomb** is a computer program that stays in your system undetected until it is triggered by a certain event in time, such as when the computer system clock reaches a certain date. A time bomb is usually carried by a virus or Trojan horse. For example, the Michelangelo virus contains a time bomb designed to damage files on your hard disk on March 6, the birthday of artist Michelangelo. March 6 is an odd date for a time bomb attack. Hackers seem to favor dates such as Halloween, Friday the 13th, and April Fool's day for time bomb attacks.

A notorious time bomb appeared in December 1989. Many hospitals and medical clinics received an innocent-looking package containing "AIDS Information" software from a company called PC Cyborg. The process of installing the software also installed a time bomb. After the computer was booted a certain number of times, the time bomb scrambled the data on the hard disk. Next, the bomb displayed an invoice demanding payment before the method for unscrambling the hard disk data was revealed.

A **logic bomb** is a computer program that is triggered by the appearance or disappearance of specific data. A logic bomb can be carried by a virus or Trojan horse. Alternatively, a logic bomb could be a standalone program. For example, suppose a programmer in a large corporation believes that she is on the list of employees to be terminated during the next cost-cutting campaign. Her hostility overcomes her ethical judgment, and she creates a logic bomb program that checks the payroll file every day to make sure her employment status is still active. If the programmer's status changes to "terminated," her logic bomb activates a program that destroys data on the computer.

Worms

Is a worm some type of virus?

"At 2:28 a.m. a besieged Berkeley scientist—like a front-line soldier engulfed by the enemy—sent a bulletin around the nation: *We are currently under attack...* Thus began one of the most harrowing days of the computer age." This lead story in *The Wall Street Journal* reported the now famous Internet worm that spread to more than 6,000 Internet host computers. A software **worm** is a program designed to enter a computer system—usually a network—through security "holes." Like a virus, a worm reproduces itself. Unlike a virus, a worm does not need to be attached to an executable program to reproduce.

The software worm that attacked the Internet entered each computer through security holes in the electronic mail system, then used data stored on the computer to, in effect, mail itself to other computers. The worm spread rapidly, as shown in Figure 8-9.

Figure 8-9 ◀
A worm attacks the internet

2. After arriving at the host, the worm begins to propagate, filling up storage space and slowing processing time. The worm also looks at information stored on the host to locate other connected hosts.

4. Hosts protected by security systems do not allow the worm to enter.

University of Maryland host computer

Security system

Massachusettes Institute of Technology host computer

1. The worm enters a host computer through the electronic mail system.

3. Copies of the worm attempt to use the electronic mail system to travel to other hosts.

Los Alamos host computer

5. Unprotected hosts are invaded. The worm again begins to propagate and look for other connected hosts.

University of California at Berkeley host computer

The Internet worm was not designed to destroy data. Instead, it filled up storage space and dramatically slowed computer performance. The only way to eradicate the Internet worm was to shut down the electronic mail system on the Internet hosts, then comb through hundreds of programs to find and destroy the worm, a process that took up to eight hours for each host.

Avoidance and Detection

Can I protect my computer from viruses and other types of attacks?

Computer viruses and other types of malicious software typically lurk on disks containing public domain software or shareware and on disks containing illegal copies of computer programs downloaded from bulletin boards. Disks and programs from these sources should be regarded as having a high risk of infection.

You learned in Chapter 3 that a WORM drive is a computer storage device that writes data once, but can read that data many times. A software worm has no relationship to a WORM drive.

You can generally avoid a computer virus if you do not use high-risk disks or programs. If you need to use a disk that you suspect might be infected, you can use a virus detection program to check for viruses before you run any programs from the disk.

A **virus detection program**, or **anti-virus program**, examines the files stored on a disk to determine if they are infected with a virus, then disinfects the disk, if necessary. Virus detection programs use several techniques to find viruses. As you know, a virus attaches itself to an existing program. This often increases the length of the original program. The earliest virus detection software simply examined the programs on a computer and recorded their length. A change in the length of a program from one computing session to the next indicated the possible presence of a virus.

In response to early virus detection programs, hackers became more cunning. They created viruses that insert themselves into unused portions of a program file but do not change its length. Of course, the people who designed virus detection programs fought back. They designed programs that examine the bytes in an uninfected application program and calculate a checksum. A **checksum** is a value that is calculated by combining all the bytes in a file. Each time you run the application program, the virus detection program recalculates the checksum and compares it to the original. If any byte in the application program has been changed, the checksum will be different, and the virus detection program assumes that a virus is present. The checksum approach requires that you start with a copy of the program that is not infected with a virus. If you start with an infected copy, the virus is included in the original checksum, and the virus detection program never detects it.

Another technique used by virus detection programs is to search for a signature A **signature** is a unique series of bytes that can be used to identify a known virus, much as a fingerprint is used to identify an individual. The signature is usually a section of the virus program, such as a unique series of instructions. Most of today's virus detection software scans for virus signatures; for this reason, virus detection software is sometimes referred to as a "scanner."

The signature search technique is fairly quick, but it can identify only those viruses with a known signature. To detect new viruses—and new viruses seem to appear every week—you must obtain regular updates for your virus detection program that include new virus signatures.

Some viruses are specifically designed to avoid detection by one or more of these virus detection methods. For this reason, the most sophisticated virus protection schemes combine elements from each of these methods.

A common misconception is that write protecting your disks prevents virus infection. Although a virus cannot jump onto your disk when it is write protected, you have to remove the write protection each time you save a file on the disk. With the write protection removed, your disk is open to virus attack.

What to Do If You Detect a Computer Virus

What should I do if my computer gets a virus?

If you detect a virus on your computer system, you should immediately take steps to stop the virus from spreading. If you are connected to a network, alert the network administrator that you found a virus on your workstation. The network administrator can then take action to prevent the virus from spreading throughout the network.

If you are using your own computer system and you detect a virus, you should remove it to prevent any further damage. There are two methods for removing a virus. First, you can attempt to restore the infected program to its original condition by deleting the virus with the disinfect function of virus detection software. However, depending on how the virus attached itself to the program, it might not be possible to remove the virus without destroying the program. If the virus cannot be removed successfully, you must use the second method: erase the infected program,

Virus scanners are not the same as flat-bed or handheld scanners. When you see the term "scanner" in the context of computer viruses, it refers to virus detection software that searches or "scans" your files to root out viruses.

Recall from Chapter 3 that you can write-protect your floppy disk by opening the small write-protect window. When the write-protect window is open, the computer cannot save files on your disk.

test the system again to make sure the virus has been eliminated, then reinstall the program from the original disks. In cases where the virus has infected most of the programs on the system, it's often best to make a backup of your data files (which are unlikely to have been infected) reformat the hard disk, and install all the programs again from backup copies of the original disks.

With either method, you must also test and, if necessary, remove the virus from every floppy disk and backup used on your computer system. If you don't remove every copy of the virus, your system will become infected again the next time you use an infected disk or restore data from an infected backup. You should also alert your colleagues, and anyone with whom you shared disks, that a virus might have traveled on those disks and infected their computer system.

Computer Crime

Is it a crime to spread a computer virus?

The accounting firm of Ernst & Young estimates that computer crime costs individuals and organizations in the United States between $3 billion and $5 billion a year. "Old-fashioned" crimes that take a high-tech twist because they involve a computer are often prosecuted using traditional laws. For example, a person who attempts to destroy computer data by setting fire to a computer might be prosecuted under traditional arson laws.

Traditional laws do not, however, cover the range of possibilities for computer crimes. Suppose a person unlawfully enters a computer facility. That person might be prosecuted for breaking and entering. But would breaking and entering laws apply to a person who uses an off-site terminal to "enter" a computer system without authorization? And what about the situation in which a person steals a file by copying it without authorization? Is the file really "stolen" if the original remains on the computer?

Most states have computer crime laws that specifically define computer data and software as personal property. These laws also define as a crime the unauthorized access, use, modification, or disabling of a computer system or data.

In early 1995, cybersleuth Tsutomu Shimomura tracked down a hacker who broke into dozens of corporate, university, government, and personal computers. Before his arrest, the hacker stole thousands of data files and more than 20,000 credit card numbers. "He was clearly the most wanted computer hacker in the world," commented assistant U.S. attorney Kent Walker. The hacker's unauthorized access and use of computer data are explicitly defined as criminal acts by computer crime laws.

Under most state laws, intentionally circulating a destructive virus is a crime. Study the excerpt from a typical computer crime law in Figure 8-10 to see what is specifically defined as illegal.

State authorities have jurisdiction over computer crimes committed in one state, but crimes that occur in more than one state or across state boundaries are under federal jurisdiction. The Computer Fraud and Abuse Act of 1986 makes it a federal crime to access a computer across state lines for

Figure 8-10
Excerpt from a state computer crime law

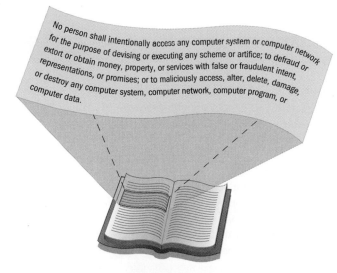

No person shall intentionally access any computer system or computer network for the purpose of devising or executing any scheme or artifice; to defraud or extort or obtain money, property, or services with false or fraudulent intent, representations, or promises; or to maliciously access, alter, delete, damage, or destroy any computer system, computer network, computer program, or computer data.

fraudulent purposes. This act also specifically outlaws the sale of entry pass codes, passwords, and access codes that belong to others.

In a well-publicized espionage case, dramatized in a documentary called *Computers, the KGB, and Me*, hackers used an unclassified military network and the Internet to piece together details on current military research in the United States, which they then sold to the KGB. The hackers, based in Germany, used stolen passwords and telephone access codes to set up communications links from Europe to Virginia, and on to California. The communications crossed state lines, so under the Computer Fraud and Abuse Act the case was placed under federal jurisdiction. With FBI assistance, the case was ultimately cracked by Cliff Stoll, a computer operator of an Internet host computer at the Lawrence Berkeley Laboratory in California.

Laws are made to deter criminals, bring them to trial if they are caught, and punish them if they are convicted. But laws don't actually protect your data. That is something you need to do by making frequent backups and taking steps to prevent unauthorized access to data.

Quick Check

1 A(n) _____ is a program that reproduces itself when the computer executes the file to which it is attached.

2 A(n) _____ is a software container that might contain a virus or time bomb.

3 A(n) _____ is a program that reproduces itself without being attached to an executable file.

4 Suppose that your computer displays a weird message every time you type the word "digital." You might suspect that your computer has contracted a(n) _____ .

5 Three sources of disks that should be considered a high risk of virus infection are _____ , _____ , and _____ .

6 What are three symptoms of a computer virus infection?

7 Many virus detection programs identify viruses by looking for a unique series of bytes called a(n) _____ .

8 Computer crime laws define _____ and _____ as personal property.

Data Security and Risk Management

Data security is the collection of techniques that provide protection for data. Sometimes computer users cite Jeff Richards' Laws of Data security as tongue-in-cheek advice on how to attain foolproof security:

1. Don't buy a computer.

2. If you buy a computer, don't turn it on.

Richards' Laws emphasize the point that it is not practical to totally protect computer data from theft, viruses, and natural disasters. In most situations, providing total security is too time-consuming, too expensive, or too complex. For example, if you are using your computer primarily for word processing, it is too time-consuming to make daily backups, too expensive to keep your data in a fire-proof vault, and too complex to implement password security. On the other hand, if you take no precautions, one day you will be sorry.

In the context of computers, **risk management** is the process of weighing threats to computer data against the amount of data that is expendable and the cost of protecting crucial data. The steps in risk management are as follows:

1. Determine the likely threats to computer data. In the case of individual computer users, the major threats are hardware failure, operator error, and vandalism.

2. Assess the amount of data that is expendable. For this assessment you must ask yourself how much data you would *have* to re-enter if your hard drive was erased and how much of your data would be forever lost because it could not be reconstructed.

3. Determine the cost of protecting all of your data versus protecting some of your data. Costs include time as well as money.

4. Select the protective measures that are affordable, effective against the identified threats, and easy to implement.

If you have your own computer, you can assess your level of risk by doing Project 2 at the end of this chapter.

In the rest of Section 8.3, you'll learn the advantages and disadvantages of the most popular data security techniques that reduce the risk of data loss. These techniques apply to micro, mini, and mainframe computer data. As you read, you'll notice that many of these techniques apply to organizations. This information is also important for you as an individual for three reasons. First, it is likely that you will work with computers within an organization when you graduate, so you will share the responsibility with your coworkers for that organization's data. Second, many organizations maintain data about you such as your credit rating, educational record, and health records. You have a vested interest in the accuracy and the confidentiality of this data. Finally, you currently have data stored on disks that might be time-consuming to reconstruct. You should consider using two of the techniques discussed in this section—backup and virus detection—to secure your own data.

Establish Policies

How can an organization educate its employees on the rules for acceptable computer use?

In a computing environment, **policies** are the rules and regulations that specify how a computer system should be used. Policies are most often determined by management and used by large organizations to stipulate who can access computer data. Policies also help an organization define appropriate uses for its computers and data.

Here are some excerpts from computer policies of private, government, and educational organizations:

- All full-time employees are entitled to an e-mail account, which may be used to exchange messages with other employees on the intercompany network. In the normal course of system maintenance the content of e-mail messages might be read by computer center staff. In addition, management reserves the option to read e-mail messages when there is cause to believe that those messages might be used for illegal or unethical transmission of data.
- Employees are provided with desktop computers to enhance their productivity. These computers may be used for work-related tasks. However, employees are prohibited from using company computers for games, personal financial management, or other activities not related directly to their job description.
- To protect the corporate network from viruses, employees must not install any software that has not been pre-approved by the information systems department. If such software is found on corporate computers, it will be erased immediately and the employee responsible for its installation will be liable for any damages incurred.
- Software piracy is strictly prohibited. Employees who violate this policy will be dismissed.
- The company owns all the data stored on company computers. Unauthorized use or appropriation of data from company computers will be prosecuted to the fullest extent of the law.

The advantages of policies are that they define how a computer system should be used, make users aware of limits and penalties, and provide a framework for legal or job action for individuals who do not follow policies. Policies are an inexpensive building block in the overall structure of data security. Policies do not require any special hardware or software. The cost of policies is the time it takes to compose, update, and publicize them. The disadvantage of policies for data security is that some users disregard policies.

Follow Procedures

What's the difference between policies and procedures?

It might seem that nothing can be done to prevent operator error. After all, mistakes do happen. However, many mistakes can be prevented. Successful computer users develop habits that significantly reduce their chances of making mistakes. These habits, when formalized and adopted by an organization, are referred to as **procedures**. Procedures help reduce human errors that can erase or damage data. Some examples of procedures are these:

- Save your files frequently as you work so you don't lose too much data if the power fails.
- When you format a disk, always view a directory of its contents first to make sure the disk in the drive is the one you want to format.
- Use virus detection software immediately to scan any files that you have downloaded from acomputer bulletin board, commercial information service, or the Internet.
- When entering long columns of data, check off each number as it is entered.
- Before closing out a month, accounting personnel must make a backup.

By now you might have already figured out how policies and procedures differ. Policies are rules and regulations that apply to computer use in a general way. Procedures describe steps or activities that are performed in conjunction with a specific task. Because procedures are more specific, they generally take longer to write than policies, making them somewhat more costly for an organization to create and document.

The major advantage of procedures is reducing operator error. However, procedures have two disadvantages. First, they must be kept up to date as equipment and software change. Second, there is no way to make sure that people follow them.

Use Audit Controls

How can an organization determine if employees are following procedures?

Audit controls monitor the accuracy and efficiency of a computer system. They also track employee activities as well as machine operations to help an organization determine if employees are following procedures. Here are some examples of audit controls:

- A security log audits network usage by recording the time, date, and user ID for each login.
- Audit controls track the time and date each file is opened or modified, as well as the user ID of the person who accesses the file.
- Input data from invoices, receipts, or other paper documents is compared to data stored on the computer system.
- Groupware routes documents for review or approval, tracking the time and date when the document is received in each office.
- Software monitors the number of keystrokes per hour for each data entry operator.

A disadvantage of audit controls is the cost of the software and the time taken by a manager to review the summary reports it produces. Audit controls are sometimes criticized for their "big brother" approach to employee supervision; most employees do not like to have their activities so closely monitored.

Restrict On-line Access to Data

Can people be prevented from accessing data so they can't steal or tamper with it?

The most common way to restrict access to a computer system is with user IDs and passwords. When you work on a multiuser system or network, you generally must have a user ID and password. Data security on a computer system that is guarded by user IDs and passwords depends on password secrecy. If users give out their passwords, choose obvious passwords, or write them down in obvious places, hackers can easily break in. Figure 8-11 shows how the length and composition of passwords affect the chances of unauthorized access.

Figure 8-11
How password length and composition affect the chances of unauthorized access.

	Example	Number of Possibilities	Average Time to Discover
Any short or long name	Ed, Christine	2,000 (a name dictionary)	5 hours
Any short or long word	It, electrocardiogram	60,000 (in a spell checker)	7 days
Two words together	Whiteknight	3,600,000,000	1,140 years
Mix of initials and numbers	JP2C2TP307	3,700,000,000,000,000	1,200,000,000 years
First line of a poem	Onceuponamidnightdreary	10,000,000,000,000,000,000,000,000,000	3,000,000,000,000,000,000,000 years
First two letters of each word in a poem	Onupamidr	100,000,000,000,000	32,000,000 years

Passwords are a first line of defense against unauthorized access. What if a hacker breaks in anyway? One way to limit the amount of damage from a break-in is to assign user rights. **User rights** are rules that limit the directories and files that each user can access. When you receive a user ID and password for a password-protected system, the system administrator gives you rights that allow you to access only particular directories and files on the host computer or file server. For example, in your computer lab, you might have only read rights to the directories that contain software. This would prevent you from deleting or changing the programs on lab computers. Most networks and host computers allow the system administrator to assign user rights, such as those shown in Figure 8-12.

Rights	Description
Erase rights	Allow you to erase files
Create rights	Allow you to create new files
Write rights	Allow you to save information in existing files
Read rights	Allow you to open files and read information
File find rights	Allow you to list files with a directory command

▶ **Figure 8-12**
User rights

Granting users only the rights they need helps prevent both accidental and deliberate damage to data. If users are granted limited rights, a hacker who steals someone's password has only those rights granted to the person from whom the password was stolen.

Hackers occasionally gain unauthorized access to computer systems through something called a trap door. A **trap door** is a special set of instructions that allows a user to bypass the normal security precautions and enter the system. Trap doors are often created during development and testing; they should be removed before the system becomes operational.

In the 1983 film *WarGames*, a trap door was the key to preventing widespread nuclear destruction. A young hacker breaks into a secret military computer that has been programmed to deal with enemy nuclear attacks. The hacker begins to play what he thinks is a detailed computer game. The computer, however, thinks it is an actual attack. Soon the computer passes the stage at which it can be stopped from launching nuclear missiles, except by a trap door designed by the reclusive programmer who created the original program. The trap door provides a way for the programmer to bypass official military channels and access the computer's fail-safe program. A special password is required to enter the trap door, and in the exciting climax of the film, the hacker races against time to get the password and gain access to the computer deep within the military installation in Cheyenne Mountain. In this fictional example, a trap door helped save the world. In general, however, if a trap door is not removed, it becomes a possible means of entry for any hacker who discovers it.

Restricting on-line access with passwords and user rights and closing trap doors might discourage some hackers and slow others, but it is possible that some might still slip through.

Encrypt Data

Is there any way to prevent criminals from using stolen data?

When an unauthorized person reads data, the data is no longer confidential. Although password protection and physical security measures are taken to limit access to computer data, hackers and criminals can still access data.

Encryption is the process of scrambling or hiding information so it cannot be understood until it is decrypted, or deciphered, to change it back to its original form. Encryption provides a last line of defense against the unauthorized use of data. If data is encrypted, unauthorized users obtain only scrambled gibberish instead of meaningful information. Edgar Allan Poe, the American writer famous for his tales of horror, was quite interested in secret codes. He was convinced that it was impossible to design an unbreakable method of encryption. You might be familiar with simple encryption and decryption techniques, such as the one shown in Figure 8-13.

Figure 8-13 ◀
Encryption by
simple substitution

| 17 | 21 | 15 | 20 | 8 | 20 | 8 | 5 | 18 | 1 | 22 | 5 | 14 | 14 | 5 | 22 | 5 | 18 | 13 | 15 | 18 | 5 |

1. This a message encrypted using a simple substitution technique in which the number of each letter's position in the alphabet represents the letter.

2. The key to this encryption looks like this. The 17 in the encrypted message is the "Q," the 21 is the letter "U," and so forth. This is a very simple encryption technique.

A	B	C	D	E	F	G	H	I	J	K	L	M	N	O	P	Q	R	S	T	U	V	W	X	Y	Z
1	2	3	4	5	6	7	8	9	10	11	12	13	14	15	16	17	18	19	20	21	22	23	24	25	26

Quoth the Raven "Nevermore"

3. Once you know the key, you can the decipher the message to see that it is the famous quote from Edgar Allan Poe's poem "The Raven."

Encryption by simple substitution is easy to decipher, but there are many effective encryption techniques that virtually guarantee the security of computer data. This fact worries law enforcement agencies in the U.S. government. Recently, the National Security Agency proposed that something called the Clipper Chip encryption scheme become a standard for all public, private, and government encryption. The **Clipper Chip** is designed to provide secure transmission of voice and data communications while providing a trap door that law enforcement agencies could use to decipher messages. If a law enforcement agency obtained a court order allowing it to tap into encrypted voice or data communications, it could then use its own special key to decipher the messages.

Understandably, a controversy has arisen over the Clipper Chip. Law enforcement agencies say they must have a way to decipher messages; it's not very useful to obtain a search warrant if criminals have encrypted their data with a scheme that could take more than a thousand years to decipher. But opponents of the Clipper Chip maintain that the government has no right to require citizens to use a specific encryption method just so the government can break it. Some people believe that the Clipper Chip is equivalent to the government requiring citizens to use a certain type of lock on their house or business; a lock to which the government holds the master key.

Software is available to encrypt data on micro, mini, and mainframe computers. The cost of this software varies with its sophistication. Regardless of its cost, encryption software is virtually a necessity for some businesses—such as financial institutions that transmit and store funds electronically.

You can discuss the pros and cons of the Clipper Chip in Project 4 at the end of this chapter.

Restrict Physical Access to the Computer System

If it is so easy for hackers to access data from networked computers or terminals, or over phone lines, is there any point to keeping computers locked up?

In 1970, during the Vietnam War, anti-war activists bombed the Army Mathematics Research Center at the University of Wisconsin. A graduate student was killed, the building was damaged, and the computer, along with 20 years of accumulated research data, was destroyed. One of the best ways to prevent people from damaging equipment is to restrict physical access to the computer system. If potential criminals cannot get to a computer or a terminal, stealing or damaging data becomes more difficult. Here are some ways to physically protect computer equipment and data:

- Restrict access to the area surrounding the computer to prevent physical damage to the equipment.
- Keep data backups in a locked vault to prevent theft and to protect against fire or water damage.
- Keep offices containing computers locked to prevent theft and to deter unauthorized users.
- Lock personal computer keyboards in desk drawers at night to prevent access to data on the hard disk drive.
- Lock the computer case to prevent theft of components such as RAM and processors.
- Store floppy disks in a locked cabinet.

Restricting physical access makes it more difficult for unauthorized personnel to destroy equipment and data. You have probably heard about computerized screening techniques that identify people based on voice patterns, finger prints, palm prints, retinal patterns, or handwriting. Researchers are also working on ways to use computers to identify faces as explained in Figure 8-14.

Figure 8-14 ◀ Screening techniques

One way for a computer to identify a face is to compare it to a stored photograph on which key reference points, and the distance between them, has been clearly marked. In real life, however, a person might be wearing glasses, eye makeup, or have an injury that would not match the stored reference points.

Researchers at MIT are working on a computerized system that would "teach" a computer to recognize a face using a set of generalized characteristics such as a "high forehead" and "thin lips" that the computer generates by comparing the face to a training set of many faces. Using this technique a computer can recognize a face with glasses on or off, with different makeup, or with small injuries.

Restricting physical access to computers has disadvantages. Locks and other screening measures can make it more difficult for authorized users to access the computer system. Also, restricting physical access will not prevent a determined criminal from stealing data. Access from a remote location is more difficult, but it might not be impossible. Finally, although restricting access might deter intentional acts of destruction, it will not prevent accidents.

Provide Redundancy

Can anything be done to minimize the damage from accidents?

Accidents can destroy data and equipment. The result is **downtime**, computer jargon for the time a computer system is not functioning. The most dependable way to minimize downtime is to duplicate data and equipment. You will learn about duplicating data in Section 8.4. Duplicating equipment simply means maintaining equipment that duplicates the functions critical to computing activities. This is sometimes referred to as **hardware redundancy**. Figure 8-15 shows some of the equipment that can be used to provide hardware redundancy.

Hardware redundancy reduces an organization's dependency on outside repair technicians. If it maintains a stock of duplicate parts, an organization can swap parts and be up and running before the manufacturer's repair technician arrives. Duplicate parts are expensive, however, and these costs must be weighed against lost revenue or productivity while repairs are underway.

► **Figure 8-15**
Hardware
redundancy

An extra printer in case the main
printer breaks down.

A duplicate file server
to maintain network
communications in
case of a breakdown
in the server disk drive
or main board.

RAID storage to keep copies of data on several
platters in case one platter is damaged.

A UPS or generator to provide electricity
in case of a power failure.

Install and Use Virus Detection Software

How effective is virus detection software?

Virus detection software finds and eradicates many viruses, but it is not 100% reliable. It will fail to detect viruses without a known signature, **polymorphic viruses** that change after they infect your computer, and viruses that use **stealth technology**, to hide from virus detection programs. Virus detection software generally does not detect Trojan horses unless they carry a virus. When virus detection software does not detect a virus in an infected computer, it is called a "false negative report." Sometimes virus detection software tells you that your computer is infected, but a virus is *not* actually present. This is a "false positive report." False negative and false positive reports are infrequent. Virus detection software generally succeeds in detecting and eradicating most widespread viruses, so you should include it in your software collection.

There are many virus detection programs, produced by different software publishers. You can purchase these programs from your local computer dealer or by mail order. Shareware virus detection programs are available from computer bulletin boards and shareware dealers. The cost of a virus detection program for microcomputers is generally less than $100.

Virus detection software can both detect viruses and eradicate them. But this software works only if you use it. You should run your virus detection program periodically to check if any viruses have found their way into your computer system. If viruses are a recurring problem in your computing environment, you might want to configure your virus detection software to continually monitor the behavior of your computer files and alert you if it spots signs of virus-like activity.

In Project 8 you have the opportunity to compare the price and features of popular virus detection software packages.

There is no "magic pill" that will protect your computer from hackers, crackers, and cyberpunks. However, you can reduce the risk of infection if you:

- Install and use virus detection software.
- Keep your virus detection software up to date.
- Make frequent backups *after* you use virus detection software to scan your files for viruses.
- Download software only from virus free sources. Use a virus detection program to scan downloaded software before you use it.
- Exercise care with disks that contain shareware or pirated software. Scan them before you run or copy any files from these disks.

Make Backups

If I implement only one security measure, should it be a backup?

A **backup** is a duplicate copy of a file or the contents of a disk drive. If the original file is lost or damaged, you can use the backup copy to restore the data to its original working condition. Backup is probably the best all-round protection for your data. It provides data protection from hardware failures, vandalism, operator error, and natural disasters, as long as you do the following:

- Make frequent backups. You can't restore data that you haven't backed up; so if you wait a month between backups, you could lose a month's worth of data.
- Scan for viruses before you backup. If your computer is infected with a virus when you back up, your backup will also be infected.
- Store your backup away from your computer. If your backup is next to your computer, a fire or flood could also damage your backup.
- Test your backup. Before you depend on your backups, make sure that you can restore data from your backup to your hard disk. You would not want to discover that your backup files were blank because you didn't correctly carry out the backup procedure. The major disadvantage of backups is user forgetfulness and procrastination. You will learn more about backups in Section 8-4.

Quick Check

1. _____ is the process of weighing threats to computer data against the amount of data that is expendable and the cost of protecting crucial data.

2. A(n) _____ is a rule designed to prohibit employees from installing software that has not been pre-approved by the information systems department.

3. Software that monitors the number of keystrokes per hour for each data entry employee would be classified as a(n) _____.

4. Procedures help reduce human errors that can erase or damage data. True or false?

5. If a network administrator assigns _____, users can access only certain programs and files.

6. Hackers sometimes gain unauthorized entry to computer systems through a(n) _____ that is not removed when development and testing are complete.

7. The Clipper Chip is a method of _____ that scrambles data so it cannot be understood until it is decrypted.

8. _____ is computer jargon that refers to the time a computer system is not functioning.

9. If your virus detection software tells you that your computer is infected when it really is not, the software has given you a false _____ report.

User Focus:
Backup

Losing all your data is one of the most distressing computing experiences. It might be the result of a hardware failure or a virus. Whatever the cause, most users experience only a moment of surprise and disbelief before reaching the depressing realization that they might have to recreate all their data and reinstall all their programs. A backup can pull you through such trying times, making the data loss a minor inconvenience, rather than a major disaster.

Industry experts recommend that all computer users make backups. Sounds simple, right? Unfortunately, this advice tells you what to do, not how to do it. It fails to address some key questions: How often should I make a backup?, What should I back up?, and What should I do with the backups? To keep your data safe, you need a data backup plan, one tailored to your computing needs. To devise your data backup plan, you should consider factors such as the value of your data, the amount of data stored on your computer, the frequency with which your data changes, and the type of backup equipment you have. As these factors change, you need to revise your plan. For example, the backup plan you use while in college is likely to change as you pursue your career. In this section of the chapter you will learn about the advantages and disadvantages of various backup tools and techniques, so you can select those appropriate for your own data backup plan.

Lab

Data Backup

Backup Equipment

Does my computer need a tape drive so I can make backups?

Tape backups are the most popular microcomputer backup solution for small businesses, and they are gaining popularity with individuals as the price of tape drives decreases. When you make a tape backup, data from the hard disk is copied to a magnetic tape. If the data on the hard disk is lost, the backup data is restored by copying it from the tape to a functional hard disk drive. Tape backup requires tapes and a tape drive, costing less than $300. However, you can back up your data without a tape drive.

Many microcomputer users back up their data onto floppy disks. This method is unrealistic for backing up the entire contents of today's high-capacity disk drives—a drive with 500 MB capacity would require at least 350 floppy disks for a complete backup! However, backing up every file is not necessary. Many users back up only those directories that contain data files. In the event of a hard disk failure, these users would need to reinstall all their software from original disks, then copy their data files from the backups.

If you use the computers in a college computer lab, your situation is somewhat unique because you store your data on a floppy disk instead of the hard disk. An effective way to back up if you're in this situation is to make a copy of your disk using the Copy Disk utility, described in the next subsection, "Backup Software."

Usually, backups are stored on magnetic media such as disk or tape. However, you can also use a printout of your data for backup purposes. To restore the data from a printout, you can use a scanner or you can retype it. With either restoration method, you can easily introduce errors, so paper backups should be considered only as a last resort.

Backup Software

Do I need special software to make backups?

A backup is essentially a copy of data. You must use software to tell the computer what to copy. There are three types of software you might use: a copy utility, a disk copy program, or backup software.

A **copy utility** is a program that copies one or more files. You can use a copy utility to copy files between a hard disk and a floppy disk, between two floppy disks of any size, from a CD-ROM to a hard disk, or from a CD-ROM to a floppy disk. A copy utility is usually included with a computer operating system. With Windows 3.1, the File Manager includes a copy utility. With Windows 95, the copy utility is available in the Windows Explorer and from the File menu.

The **Copy Disk** utility is a program that duplicates the contents of an entire floppy disk. You can use a Copy Disk utility only to copy all the files from one floppy disk to another floppy disk of the same size. You cannot use the Copy Disk utility for files on a hard disk drive. The Copy Disk utility is provided with most microcomputer operating systems, including DOS and Windows. You can use Windows 95 the procedure shown in Figure 8-16 to duplicate the floppy disk you use for this course.

Figure 8-16
Using Copy Disk
to back up
a floppy

1. Put your original disk in the floppy disk drive.

Floppy A:

2. Click the 3½ -inch Floppy (A:) icon.

File
Open
Explore
Find
Copy Disk

3. Pull down the File menu and select Copy Disk.

4. Follow the instructions on the screen. When prompted, take your original disk out of the drive and replace it with your backup disk.

Original

Backup

Backup software is designed to manage hard disk backup to tapes or diskettes. When you use backup software you can select the files you want to back up. Most operating systems include backup software. However, if your tape drive requires special proprietary backup software, you should use the backup software included with the tape drive, instead of the software provided with the operating system. Backup software is becoming quite sophisticated. Many packages offer automated features that allow you to schedule automatic backups and back up only those files that have changed since the last backup.

Types of Backups

Should I back up everything on my disk?

A **full backup** is a copy of all the files on a disk. A full backup is very safe because it ensures that you have a copy of every file on the disk—every program and every data file. Because a full backup includes a copy of every file on a disk, it can take a long time to make one for a hard disk. While the backup is in progress, the computer cannot generally be used for other tasks. Some users consider it worth the time because this type of backup is easy to restore. You simply have the computer copy the files from your backup to the hard disk, as shown in Figure 8-17.

When you use the Copy Disk utility to make a backup of a floppy disk, you are making a full backup of the floppy.

Backup   Restore

1. Back up all files from the hard disk drive to a backup tape.

2. Suppose the hard drive fails. You must restore all the files from the backup to the hard disk drive.

▶ **Figure 8-17**
Full backup

A **differential backup** is a copy of all the files that have changed since the last full backup. You must, therefore, maintain two sets of backups—a full backup that you make infrequently, say once a week, and a differential backup that you make more frequently, say once a day. It takes less time to make a differential backup; than to make a full backup; however, restoring data from a differential backup is a little more complex. To restore your data after a differential backup, you first restore data from the last full backup, then restore the data from the latest differential backup, as shown in Figure 8-18.

Figure 8-18
Differential backup

Backup

Restore

Monday   Tuesday Wednesday

Tape 1   Tape 2   Tape 1   Tape 2

1. Make a full backup on Monday evening.

2. On Tuesday evening use a different tape to back up only the files that have been changed since the full backup.

3. On Wednesday evening, back up only the files that have been changed since the full backup. These are the files you changed or created on Tuesday and Wednesday. Put these files on the same tape you used for Tuesday's backup.

4. Now, suppose the hard disk fails. To restore, first load the full backup onto the hard disk drive. This step restores the files as they were on Monday evening.

5. Next, load the data from the differential backup tape. This step restores the files you changed on Tuesday and Wednesday

An **incremental backup** is a copy of the files that have changed since the last backup. When you use incremental backups, you must have a full backup and you must maintain a series of incremental backups. The incremental backup procedure is similar to the differential backup procedure, but there's a subtle difference. With a differential backup, you maintain one full backup and one differential backup. The differential backup contains any files that were changed since the last full backup. With an incremental backup procedure, you maintain a full backup and a series of incremental backups. Each incremental backup contains only those files that changed since the last incremental backup. To restore the data from a series of incremental backups, you restore the last full backup, then sequentially restore each incremental backup.

Incremental backups take the least time to make and provide a little better protection from viruses than other backup methods because your backup contains a series of copies of your files. However, incremental backups are the most complex type of backup to restore, as shown in Figure 8-19.

Backup

Restore

Monday   Tuesday   Wednesday

Tape 1   Tape 2   Tape 3   Tape 1   Tape 2   Tape 3

1. Make a full backup on Monday evening.

2. On Tuesday evening, back up only the files that have been changed or created on Tuesday.

3. On Wednesday evening, back up only the files that have been changed or created on Wednesday.

4. Now, suppose the hard disk fails. To begin the restore process, first load the data from the full backup.

5. Next, load the data from Tuesday's incremental backup. This step restores the work you did on Tuesday.

6. Finally, load the data from Wednesday's incremental backup. This step restores the work you did on Wednesday.

Backup Schedule

How frequently should I make a backup?

Any data backup plan is a compromise between the level of protection and the amount of time devoted to backup. To be absolutely safe, you would need to back up your data every time you change the contents of a file, which would seriously reduce the amount of work you could complete in a day. Realistically, however, you should make backups at regular intervals. The interval between backups will depend on the value of your data—what that data is worth to you or your employer in terms of time and money.

An individual using a personal computer might not be particularly worried about the consequences of data loss. Data backup for such an individual should be quick and easy to complete and should reduce some of the inconvenience of data loss. However, it would not necessarily restore all data or programs. A backup schedule that offers this minimal amount of protection would require a once-a-week backup of those data files that have changed since the last backup, as shown in Figure 8-20.

In the event of a hard disk drive failure, an individual who uses this backup plan would have to reinstall all software from original disks and restore all the

March						
Sun	Mon	Tue	Wed	Thu	Fri	Sat
			1	2	3	4
5	6	7	8	9	10	11
12	13	14	15	16	17	18
19	20	21	22	23	24	25
26	27	28	29	30	31	

data from the backup disks. The data entered or changed since the last backup would be lost. If the last backup was made at the end of the day on Monday and the hard disk failed on Thursday, the data from Tuesday, Wednesday, and Thursday would be lost.

A more rigorous backup plan would be required for more valuable data, particularly if the data was produced by an application, such as an accounting system or payroll program, that operates on a weekly or monthly cycle. Every time you use an accounting system, for example, you do not use all the files that contain your data. Therefore, a file could be damaged by a virus or disk error, but you might not know it for several days or weeks until you try to access the file. In the meantime you might have made backups that contain the damaged file.

A more sophisticated backup procedure, one that you might use with an accounting system, would typically combine daily, weekly, and monthly backups to allow data to be reconstructed at any point before file damage occurred. The daily backups are incremental backups, one performed each day of the week, except for the day during which the weekly backups are performed. The weekly backups are a series of three full backups, one for each week of the month, except the week when you make the monthly backup. The monthly backups are a series of twelve full backups, each performed just before month-end closing. This backup procedure for an accounting application is illustrated in Figure 8-21.

The data backup plan illustrated in Figure 8-21 is not guaranteed to protect against all data loss. Suppose you were using an accounting system and a virus strikes one of the files in July. You don't notice it until the end of the month. Your last weekly backup contains the virus, but the backup for June does not. You can restore the data for January through June from the June backup. You might have to reenter the July data. However, without your backup you would have to reenter all the data!

Figure 8-21 ◀
Backup schedule for an accounting system

| | Daily incremental backup | | Weekly full backup | | Monthly full backup |

As you can see, a backup does not guarantee data security. However, it does provide a solid level of protection for the problems that are most likely to damage data.

End Note The amount of data stored on computer systems, combined with the vulnerability of those systems, creates a potentially risky situation. A surprising amount of personal data about you is stored on computers. All of it might not be accurate. It can be accessed and altered by criminals. It can be destroyed by hardware failure, human sabotage, or natural disaster. The same can be said for national security data or the data that keeps the world financial market running smoothly. One of the main issues of the computer age concerns the security and ethical use of computer data. Risk management has, therefore, become a necessity in most organizations.

In the story of the Trojan War, the Trojans seem so naive. Who would be so foolish as to pull such a suspicious horse into the city? But you have learned that today's computer users are often just as naive about modern technology. They install programs on their computers without checking for viruses, they store massive amounts of data without backups, and they transmit sensitive data without first encrypting it. The Trojans fell for the wooden horse trick the first time, but it is a mistake they would be unlikely to repeat. Will modern computer users repeat their mistakes or learn to take precautions? Now that you've read this chapter, what will you do?

Review

1. Use your own words to answer the italicized questions that appear under each section heading in this chapter.

2. List each of the boldface terms used in this chapter, then use your own words to write a short definition of each term.

3. Complete the following chart to review the factors that cause data loss or misuse. List the factors you learned about in this chapter in the first column. Then place an X in the appropriate column to indicate if the factor causes data loss, inaccurate data, stolen data, or intentionally damaged data. Some factors might have more than one X.

Factor	Unintentional data loss	Inaccurate data	Stolen or misused data	Intentional data loss or damage
Operator error				
[You fill in the rest of the factors]				

4. Complete the following chart to summarize what you have learned about Trojan horses, time bombs, logic bombs, and software worms.

Type	Spreads by	Triggered by
Virus		
Trojan horse		
Worm		
Time bomb		
Logic bomb		

5. Make a check list of steps to take if you suspect that your computer is infected with a virus.

6. List the four steps in the risk management process.

7. Make a list of the data security techniques discussed in Section 8.3, Data Security and Risk Management. Then indicate the advantages and disadvantages of each technique.

8. Use your own words to write descriptions of full, incremental, and differential backup procedures. Make sure your descriptions clearly explain the difference between incremental and differential backups.

9. Thinking back over the entire chapter, what was the most useful concept you learned? What questions do you have about data security that still remain unanswered?

10. On a sheet of paper, list all the reasons you can think of for making a backup of computer data.

Projects

1. Lost Data: What's Your Experience? Describe a situation in which you or someone you know lost data stored on a computer. What caused the data loss? What steps could have been taken to prevent the loss? What steps could you or the other person have taken to recover the lost data?

2. Risk Management: A Personal Perspective Assess the risk to the programs and data files stored on the hard disk of your computer by answering the following questions:

   a. What threats are likely to cause your data to be lost, stolen, or damaged?

   b. How many files of data do you have?

   c. If you add up the size of all your files, how many megabytes of data do you have?

   d. How many of these files are critical and would need to be replaced if you lost all your data?

   e. What would you need to do to reconstruct the critical files if the hard disk drive failed and you did not have any backups?

   f. What measures could you use to protect your data from the threats you identified in the first question? What is the cost of each of these measures?

   g. Balancing the threats to your data, the importance of your data, and the cost of protective measures, what do you think is the best plan for the security of your data?

3. Lost Weekend: Full, Incremental, and Differential Backups Assume that your hard disk drive fails on a Friday afternoon. Explain how you would restore your data over the weekend if you had been using each of the following backup systems:

   a. A full backup every Friday evening

   b. A full backup every Friday evening with a differential backup on Wednesday night

   c. A full backup every Friday evening with an incremental backup Monday through Thursday evenings

4. The Clipper Chip Debate In this chapter you learned that the U.S. government wants to standardize all encryption using the Clipper Chip.

   a. Using library or Internet resources, research the controversy surrounding the Clipper Chip.

   b. In a small group, discuss the concerns raised by the plans for the Clipper Chip encryption method. Be sure to discuss whether you think the Clipper Chip is a good idea. Can you or anyone in your group think of any alternative methods that would protect the privacy of individual citizens while providing a way for law enforcement agencies to perform their job effectively?

   c. After you examine the issues, write a two-page paper that is a dialog between two people— one who supports the government's plan for the Clipper Chip and one who doesn't.

5. The Internet Worm The Internet worm created concern about the security of data on military and research computer systems, and it raised ethical questions about the rights and responsibilities of computer users. Select one of the following statements and write a two-page paper that argues for or against the statement. You might want to use the Internet or library resources to learn more about each viewpoint. Be sure you include the resources you used in a bibliography.

   a. People have the "right" to hone their computing skills by breaking into computers. As a computer scientist once said, "The right to hack is held higher than the right of someone to tell you not to. It's an inalienable right."

   b. If problems exist, it is acceptable to use any means to point them out. The computer science student who created the Internet virus was perfectly justified in claiming that he should not be convicted because he was just trying to point out that security holes exist in large computer networks.

   c. Computer crimes are no different from other crimes, and computer criminals should be held responsible for the damage they cause by paying for the time and cost of replacing or restoring data.

6. Understanding an Acceptable Use Policy Obtain a copy of your school's student code or computer use policy, then answer the following questions. If your school does not have such a policy, create one that addresses these questions.

   a. To whom does the policy apply—students, faculty, staff, community members, others?

   b. What types of activities does the policy specifically prohibit?

   c. If a computer crime is committed, would the crime be dealt with by campus authorities or by state law enforcement agents?

   d. Does the policy state the penalties for computer crimes? If so, what are they?

7. You Be the Jury The company that publishes a popular statistical software package leases its software for a one-year period. The software contains a time bomb, set with the lease expiration date. Each day, the time bomb checks the date. When the current date exceeds the date in the time bomb, the leased software stops working. When customers renew the lease, they receive a series of commands that resets the time bomb for the new expiration date.

In a small group discuss the similarities and differences between the time bomb used by the statistical software publishers and that used by PC Cyborg, which was discussed in the "Time Bombs and Logic Bombs" subsection of Section 8.2.

Suppose both of these software publishers were sued by irritated customers. If you were a juror, what would your verdict be in each case?

8. Virus Detection Software If you suspect your computer has become infected, it is useful to immediately activate virus detection software to scan your files for a virus. With the continued spread of viruses, virus detection software has become an essential utility in today's computing environment. Many virus detection software packages are available in computer stores, on computer bulletin boards, and on the Internet. Find information about three virus detection software packages and fill out the following comparison chart.

	Software 1	Software 2	Software 3
Product name			
Publisher			
Price			
Current version			
Update frequency			
Special features			

Resources

- **Cohen, F.** *A Short Course on Computer Viruses.* New York: Wiley & Sons, 1994. Fred Cohen is a guru in computer virus research. He has written this book for the non-technical reader. One of the interesting aspects of this book is Cohen's discussion of "friendly" viruses.

- *comp.risks (risks@csl.sri.com)* comp.risks is an Internet Usenet discussion group on topics related to computer security and risk management. Transcripts of the discussions are available from *http://catless. nci.ac.uk/Risks.*

- *comp.virus (virus-l@lehigh.edu)* comp.virus is a moderated discussion of computer viruses. The site also provides a list of answers to frequently asked questions about viruses.

- **Denning, J.**, ed. *Computers Under Attack: Intruders, Worms and Viruses.* New York, ACM Press, 1990. This book is a collection of papers, some classics, that provide a well-balanced overview of the technical, legal, and ethical issues surrounding network loopholes, computer viruses, and worms.

- **Hrushka, J.** *Computer Viruses and Anti-Virus Warfare,* 2nd ed. New York, Ellis Horwood, 1992. This book is a very clear introduction to computer viruses, worms, and so on. It has several unique features, including screen shots of virus payloads, a profile of virus writers, and the source code for a simple virus detection program.

- *http://www.symantec.com* This is the Web site for the company that publishes Symantec AntiVirus software. At this site you will also find information about Norton AntiVirus software.

- *http://www.mcafee.com* At this Web site, you can find information about the popular MacAfee VirusScan software.

- *http://www.sands.com* This Web site contains information about Dr. Solomon's Anti-Virus Toolkit.

- *http://www-swiss.ai.mit.edu/6095/articles/froomkin-metaphor/text.html* The HTML version of an excellent paper by A. Michael Froomkin on cryptography, the Clipper Ship, and the U.S. Constitution.

- *http://draco.centerline.com:8080/~franl/clipper/about-clipper.html* A Web page that contains links to many sites with information about the Clipper.

- *http://cpsr.org/dox/home.html* The organization, Computer Professionals for Social Responsibility, maintains this Web site where you can find information about computing ethics.

- **Kahn, D.** *The Codebreakers.* New York: Macmillan, 1976. This is one of the classic books on the history of cryptography. The book is huge—over 1,000 pages—and extensively referenced. Don't let that discourage you from checking this book out from your library. It is written in a captivating style, and you can dip in anywhere and sample tales of intrigue—such as how the Greeks established the first system of military cryptography, how the English broke the "unbreakable" German enigma code during World War II, and how to interpret messages from outer space.

- **Linowes, D.** *Privacy in America.* Chicago: University of Illinois Press, 1989. This well-researched book is sure to motivate you to think about the kind of data that government and private computer systems are accumulating about you. The book concludes with a series of guidelines for protecting your personal privacy.

Lab Assignments

- **Neumann, P.** *Computer Related Risks*. New York: ACM Press, 1995. Peter Neumann is the moderator of the Internet Risks Forum and writes the popular column "Inside Risks" in the professional journal, *Communications of the ACM*. This book is full of documented examples of security breaches. The examples are summarized in table format at the end of each chapter, providing an easy-to-understand overview of the challenge that risk managers face.

- **Slade, R.** *Guide to Computer Viruses*. New York: Springer-Verlag, 1994. Slade's *Guide* is fun to read and packed full of well-researched and accurate accounts of the most widespread PC, Mac, and UNIX viruses. Chapter 5 contains a detailed checklist of the steps that an individual or business should take to protect data from viruses, worms, and other "malware."

- **Stephenson, N.** *Snow Crash*. New York: Bantam Books, 1992. Computer viruses have opened new horizons for science fiction writers, providing good plot twists. In *Snow Crash*, a universal virus spreads to humans as well as computers. Experienced computer hackers are particularly susceptible to one form of this virus, triggered by a particular graphic display on their screens. Although this book is fiction, it shows a good understanding of computers and computer viruses.

- **Stoll, C.** *The Cuckoo's Egg*. New York: Doubleday, 1987. While monitoring user accounts on a large research computer system, the author of this book noticed a $0.75 discrepancy that mushroomed into an international hunt for hackers who were selling U.S. military data to the KGB. This book has all the elements of an espionage thriller, but the story is true and contains a wealth of factual information on computer security. Stoll gave a presentation at Cisco NetWorkers '94 called "Stalking the Wily Hacker." You can access this presentation on the Internet at *http://town.hall.org/university/security/stoll/cliff.html*.

- *Understanding Computers: Computer Security*. Alexandria, VA: Time-Life Books, 1986. A lavishly illustrated, in-depth look at computer security, the methods that hackers use to avoid it, and the improved methods used to foil them. Although written 10 years ago, most of the basic principles of data security presented in this book have not changed, so it is still a good basic reference.

Data Backup

 The Data Backup Lab gives you an opportunity to make tape backups on a simulated computer system. Periodically, the hard disk on the simulated computer will fail, which gives you a chance to assess the convenience and efficiency of different backup procedures.

1. Click the Steps button to learn how to use the simulation. As you work through the Steps, answer all of the Quick Check questions that appear. After you complete the Steps, you will see a Summary Report of your Quick Check answers. Follow the directions on the screen to print this report.

2. Click the Explore button. Create a full backup every Friday using only Tape 1. At some point in the simulation, an event will cause data loss on the simulated computer system. Use the simulation to restore as much data as you can. After you restore the data, print the Backup Audit Report.

3. In Explore, create a full backup every Friday on Tape 1 and a differential backup every Wednesday on Tape 2. At some point in the simulation, an event will cause data loss on the simulated computer system. Use the simulation to restore as much data as you can. Print the Backup Audit Report.

4. In Explore, create a full backup on Tape 1 every Monday. Make incremental backups on Tapes 2, 3, 4, and 5 each day for the rest of the week. Continue this cycle, reusing the same tapes each week. At some point in the simulation an event will cause data loss on the simulated computer system. Use the simulation to restore as much data as you can. Print the Backup Audit Report.

5. Photocopy a calendar for next month. On the calendar indicate your best plan for backing up data. In Explore, implement your plan. Print out the Backup Audit Report. Write a paragraph or two discussing the effectiveness of your plan.

Answers

8.1

1. operator error

2. false

3. uninterruptible power supply (UPS)

4. surge protector

5. false

6. false

7. hard disk drive

8. up-to-date backup

8.2

1. virus

2. trojan horse

3. worm

4. virus

5. public domain software, shareware, and illegal copies of computer programs downloaded from bulletin boards

6. weird messages, unusual sound effects, difficulty saving files (or missing files, unexpected reboots, increased executable file size)

7. signature

8. computer data and software

8.3

1. risk management

2. policy

3. audit control

4. true

5. user rights

6. trap door

7. encryption

8. downtime

9. positive

Glossary/Index

access
   data, restricting, 8-18–819
   physical, restricting, 8-21–8-22

access codes, selling, 8-14–8-15

anti-virus programs. *See* virus detection software

application software. *See* programs

audit controls Measures that monitor the accuracy and efficiency of a computer system, 8-18

backup A duplicate copy of a file or the contents of a disk drive, 8-24

backup software Software designed to manage hard disk backup to tapes or diskettes, 8-27, 8-25–8-27

backups, 8-3, 8-24, 8-25–8-30
   equipment, 8-25
   hard disk, 8-5
   protecting against computer crime, 8-14–8-15
   schedule, 8-29–8-30
   software for, 8-25–8-27
   types, 8-27–8-29
   virus disinfection, 8-13

boot sector virus A virus that infects the systems files every time you turn the computer on, 8-9

bulletin boards
   virus detection software, 8-23
   viruses, 8-11

C

checksum A value calculated by combining all the bytes in a file, 8-13

Cinderella, 8-9

Clipper Chip A chip designed to provide secure transmission of voice and data communications while providing a back door that law enforcement agencies could use to decipher messages, 8-21

Clipper Chip encryption scheme, 8-21

computer crime, 8-14–8-15. *See also* computer viruses; time bombs; Trojan horses; vandalism
   stolen data, 8-3
   stolen passwords, 8-18–8-19

Computer Fraud and Abuse Act of 1986, 8-14

Data Representation

Data
Representation

It was April 18, 1775, the eve of the American Revolution. The Massachusetts Minutemen were huddled around a plank table planning a defense strategy against well-armed and professionally trained British troops. The deployment of the outnumbered revolutionary troops was a critical element in the Minutemen's defense plan. They needed to know the route of the British attack force. If they sent a scout to collect this information how would he communicate the British route of attack? The Minutemen solved this problem by using the plan recounted in Longfellow's poem about Paul Revere's famous ride:

One if by land, and two if by sea;
And I on the opposite shore will be,
Ready to ride and spread the alarm
Through every Middlesex village and farm.

The Minutemen devised a simple plan. The Old North Church tower was visible for miles. As a signal for Paul Revere, either one or two lanterns would be lit in the church tower. One lantern meant the British were coming by land. Two lanterns meant the British were coming by sea. But what if some of the British troops arrived on land and others arrived by sea? Would the Minutemen need another lantern for this third possibility? The answer to this question is clear when you understand data representation and information theory, the topics of this chapter.

In Chapter 5 you were introduced to the use of binary numbers and ASCII and EBCDIC codes to represent data. In this chapter, you will pursue the subject of data representation in more depth and discover how computers store graphical, video, and sound data.

CHAPTER**PREVIEW**

The information in this chapter will help you understand why your files are stored in different formats and the significance of file extensions such as .Pcx, .Tif, .Wmf, .Mid, and .Wav. You will learn how to use compression software to shrink the size of files and save storage space on your disks. When you have completed this chapter, you should be able to:

- Explain how information theory applies to the data representation codes used by computers

- Determine how many bits are needed to represent a given number of messages

- Define the key characteristics of ASCII, ANSI, EBCDIC, and Unicode

- Explain the difference between bitmap and vector graphics

- Calculate the storage space required for a monochrome, grayscale, or color bitmap graphic

- Explain the difference between waveform audio and MIDI music

- List the advantages and disadvantages of data compression

- Use the file extension to identify the format used to compress file data

Data
Representation

Information Theory

The Minutemen could have positioned 20 or 30 lanterns on a hillside to spell out the words "LAND" or "SEA." Instead, if we accept Longfellow's account of the historical evening in 1775, the Minutemen used a simple code in which one light meant "by land" and two lights meant "by sea." It seems that the Minutemen selected a fairly efficient way to convey information. Was there an even more efficient way? You can answer this question using **information theory**, the study of the most efficient way to represent or encode information. Information theory is an important concept for computer and software design. If information is represented efficiently, it can be stored in a small amount of space and it can be transmitted quickly.

Using information theory, computer scientists have designed various ways of encoding and storing information. The way information is encoded and stored in a computer is referred to as a **file format**. A computer stores the data for your word processing documents in a file format different from the file format it uses to store your graphics data or audio data. In this chapter you'll learn about different ways of encoding data and the file formats this encoding produces.

Efficiently Storing and Transmitting Information

Could the Minutemen have sent their message with fewer than two lanterns?

Some methods for storing and transmitting information are more efficient than others. Using information theory, you can evaluate the efficiency of the Minutemen's code. Then you can apply what you learn to understanding the efficiency with which computers store and transmit information.

The Minutemen had two possible messages to convey. We'll refer to these possible messages as "units of information." One of these units of information was "by land." The other unit of information was "by sea," as shown in Figure 9-1.

Figure 9-1
Paul Revere's code

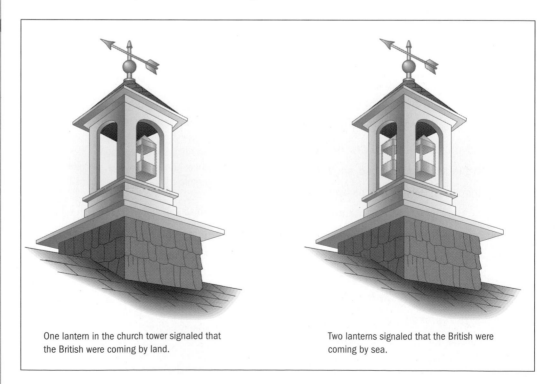

One lantern in the church tower signaled that the British were coming by land.

Two lanterns signaled that the British were coming by sea.

Information theory tells us that the Minutemen could have used a more efficient code, using one lantern instead of two. Figure 9-2 shows that with one lantern, it is possible to convey up to two units of information; the lantern can be on or off, representing "yes" or "no," "land" or "sea," "true" or "false," and so forth.

In the on state, the lantern indicates the British are coming by land.

or

In the off state, the lantern indicates the British are coming by sea.

▶ **Figure 9-2**
One lantern can convey up to two units of information

How does this apply to computers? As you learned in Chapter 4, a computer is an electronic device that stores and manipulates electrical currents that represent bits—0s and 1s. Think of a bit as the equivalent of one lantern. A bit can be a 1 or a 0, just as a lantern can be on or off. The on state of the lantern corresponds to a 1 bit, and the off state of the lantern corresponds to a 0 bit. A computer can use a single bit (one lantern) to store and convey up to two units of information; a 1 bit might correspond to "yes" and a 0 bit might correspond to "no;" a 1 bit might correspond to "land" and a 0 bit might correspond to "sea," and so forth.

Now, if a computer uses two bits (two lanterns) or three bits (three lanterns) how many different units of information can it convey? Figure 9-3 shows that two bits can convey four units of information.

0   0
OFF   OFF

Message 1:
"The British aren't coming."

1   0
ON   OFF

Message 2:
"The British are coming by land."

0   1
OFF   ON

Message 3:
"The British are coming by sea."

1   1
ON   ON

Message 4:
"Some of the British are coming by land, but others are coming by sea."

▶ **Figure 9-3**
Representing information using two bits

Instead of lanterns, you can think of coins. How many permutations of heads (H) and tails (T) can you produce using two coins? Four: HH, HT, TH, TT

Figure 9-4 ◀
Representing
information
using three bits

Figure 9-4 shows that three bits can convey eight units of information.

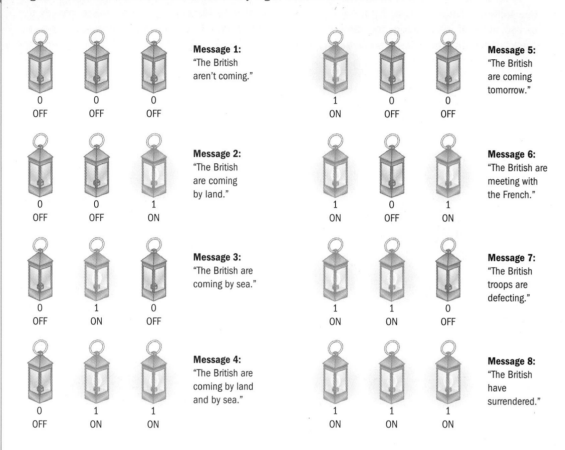

Message 1:
"The British
aren't coming."

0
OFF

0
OFF

0
OFF

Message 5:
"The British
are coming
tomorrow."

1
ON

0
OFF

0
OFF

Message 2:
"The British
are coming
by land."

0
OFF

0
OFF

1
ON

Message 6:
"The British are
meeting with
the French."

1
ON

0
OFF

1
ON

Message 3:
"The British are
coming by sea."

0
OFF

1
ON

0
OFF

Message 7:
"The British
troops are
defecting."

1
ON

1
ON

0
OFF

Message 4:
"The British are
coming by land
and by sea."

0
OFF

1
ON

1
ON

Message 8:
"The British
have
surrendered."

1
ON

1
ON

1
ON

The number of units of information that you can convey is simply the number of different combinations you can make with a given number of bits. There is a pattern to this. With one bit, you can convey two units of information. With two bits, you can convey four units of information. With three bits, you can convey eight units. The pattern is 2, 4, 8; these numbers are all powers of 2, as shown in Figure 9-5.

Figure 9-5 ◀
Powers of 2

$$2^0 = 1$$

$$2^1 = 2$$

$$2^2 = 2 \times 2 = 4$$

$$2^3 = 2 \times 2 \times 2 = 8$$

$$2^4 = 2 \times 2 \times 2 \times 2 = 16$$

$$2^5 = 2 \times 2 \times 2 \times 2 \times 2 = 32$$

$$2^6 = 2 \times 2 \times 2 \times 2 \times 2 \times 2 = 64$$

$$2^7 = 2 \times 2 \times 2 \times 2 \times 2 \times 2 \times 2 = 128$$

$$2^8 = 2 \times 2 \times 2 \times 2 \times 2 \times 2 \times 2 \times 2 = 256$$

We now have a rule about conveying information: The maximum number of different units of information you can convey with n bits is 2^n. For example, if you use four bits (or four lanterns), the exponent n is 4. The maximum number of units you can convey is 2^4 or $2 \times 2 \times 2 \times 2$, which is 16. So, if you use four bits, you can convey a maximum of 16 different units of information. Figure 9-6 summarizes this rule.

| When you use one bit (one lantern)... | | ...you can convey up to two (2^1) messages. | Message one: 0 Message two: 1 |

| When you use two bits (two lanterns)... | | ...you can convey up to four (2^2) messages. | 00 01 10 11 |

| When you use three bits (three lanterns)... | | ...you can convey up to eight (2^3) messages. | 000 100 001 101 010 110 011 111 |

| When you use four bits (four lanterns)... | | ...you can convey up to sixteen (2^4) messages. | 0000 0100 1000 1100 0001 0101 1001 1101 0010 0110 1010 1110 0011 0111 1011 1111 |

▶ **Figure 9-6**
The maximum number of different units of information you can convey with n bits is 2^n

If you have a certain number of bits (or lanterns), you can use the rule in Figure 9-6 to determine how many different messages you can send. Now turn the rule around. If you know how many messages you might want to convey, how can you determine the minimum number of bits you need? For example, suppose that Paul Revere wanted to know how many British troops were in the advance force—he thinks there might be as many as 50. How many bits (lanterns) would the Minutemen need to convey any number between 1 and 50? You can determine this by figuring out what power of 2 provides an adequate number of messages. What power of 2—what exponent—would provide at least 50 different messages?

Suppose the Minutemen use three lanterns. The exponent would be 3, so the Minutemen could send 2^3 messages (8 messages)—not enough to report 50 troops. Four lanterns provide 2^4 messages (16 messages)—not enough. Five lanterns provide 2^5 messages (32 messages)—still not enough. Six lanterns provide 2^6 messages (64 messages)—the Minutemen would need at least six lanterns to send up to 50 different messages.

To make sure you understand the relationship between the number of bits and the units of information those bits can convey, try Chapter Review Question 3.

Representing Numbers

How could the Minutemen arrange six lanterns in the church tower to convey the number 50?

Information theory tells us that the Minutemen could use six lanterns to convey the message that 50 British troops would attack. Which of the lanterns would be off and which would be on to send this message?

Although the Minutemen, like the rest of us, are accustomed to working with the decimal number system (base 10), the binary number system (base 2) would provide a more efficient way for the Minutemen to transmit numbers to Paul Revere. The binary number system uses only two digits, 0 and 1, which correspond to the off and on states of a lantern.

The decimal number 50 is 110010 in binary. To convey the number 50, the Minutemen would arrange six lanterns as follows: on-on-off-off-on-off, as shown in Figure 9-7.

Figure 9-7
Six lanterns represent the number 50

Binary digits	1	1	0	0	1	0
Place value	2^5 thirty-twos	2^4 sixteens	2^3 eights	2^2 fours	2^1 twos	2^0 ones
Binary to decimal conversion	1×32 +	1×16 +	0×8 +	0×4 +	1×2 +	0×1 = 50 (decimal)

Computers can use on and off bits to store decimal numbers in binary format. For example, a pattern of on and off bits corresponding to the lanterns in Figure 9-7 could be used to represent the number 50.

Information theory tells us, however, that the binary number system has limitations. For example, many early microcomputers had only an 8-bit word size. What is the largest decimal number that one of these computers could store in binary format? If your answer is 255, you are correct. If you assign 1s to all eight bits, you have the binary number 11111111, which is equivalent to the decimal number 255. So, using the binary number system, an 8-bit computer could not work with numbers greater than 255 or less than 0. Such a computer would not be very useful, so computer scientists devised alternative ways to use on and off bits to represent large numbers. Because these alternatives use the binary digits 0 and 1, they are referred to as **binary codes**. If computing is your major, you will learn about these other binary codes in your more advanced courses.

You have now seen how the Minutemen could use lanterns to represent numbers and how a computer can use a series of 1s and 0s to represent a number. Next, you'll learn how computers store letters and punctuation symbols.

If you need to review how binary numbers work, revisit the Binary Numbers Lab in Chapter 4. Project 8 shows you how to use a software tool to convert binary numbers into their decimal equivalent.

A binary code is not the same thing as the binary number system. There are many binary codes. These codes use 0s and 1s to represent any type of character or numeric data. For example, a binary code might represent Sunday as 01 and Monday as 10. The binary number system is another example of a binary code. In the binary number system 01, 10, 11, 100 are equivalent to the decimal numbers 1, 2, 3, 4.

Representing Characters

How many lanterns would the Minutemen need to send messages composed of words?

Suppose the Minutemen wanted to send more elaborate messages—messages that required a certain sequence of lighted lanterns for each letter in the alphabet. **Character representation** refers to the way non-numeric data, such as a letter of the alphabet or a punctuation mark, is represented by a series of bits. A **character representation code**, also referred to simply as a *code*, is a series of bits that represents a letter, symbol, or numeral. For example, if you want to represent each of the 26 characters in the alphabet, how many lanterns or bits would you need?

If you use four bits, you can convey 16 (2^4 or $2\times2\times2\times2$) different units of information, but that is not enough for all the letters in the alphabet. If you use five bits you can convey 32 (2^5 or $2\times2\times2\times2\times2$) different units of information. Five bits is enough to represent the 26 characters in the alphabet, plus you could encode six additional items, such as punctuation symbols.

It turns out, however, that five bits are not enough to represent the characters and symbols typically used in written communication. Let's see why.

Written English uses uppercase and lowercase versions of each letter of the alphabet and a variety of symbols for punctuation and abbreviations, such as $ # @ & +. If you count these letters, symbols, and the numerals 0 through 9, 95 different characters must be represented. Therefore, more than five bits are required.

As computers evolved from the primitive number crunchers of the 1940s and 1950s, several character representation codes emerged. The three character representation codes most widely used are ASCII, ANSI, and EBCDIC. A fourth code, Unicode, has been proposed for future worldwide use.

ASCII (American Standard Code for Information Interchange) is the most widely used coding scheme for character data. A file of data encoded using ASCII is referred to as an **ASCII file** or as "a file in ASCII format." The standard ASCII code uses seven bits to represent 2^7 symbols (128 symbols), including uppercase and lowercase letters, special control codes, numerals, and punctuation symbols. A table or matrix is often used to provide a compact reference to the ASCII code. Figure 9-8 shows you how to use a matrix to find the ASCII code for the lowercase letter "a."

To learn more about how computers represent text, do the Text Representation section of the Data Representation Lab.

2. The three binary digits at the top of the column show you the values of the leftmost bits.

1. Locate the lowercase letter "a" in the matrix.

The ASCII code for the lowercase letter "a" is 1100001.

3. The four binary digits at the beginning of the row show you the values of the rightmost bits.

Figure 9-8
An ASCII matrix

You learned the basics of ASCII and EBCDIC in Chapter 4. In this chapter, you focus on how information theory answers questions such as "Why does the ASCII code use seven bits?" or "Why doesn't my word processing software produce Japanese characters?"

The **ANSI** (American National Standards Institute) code uses eight bits to represent each character. Microsoft Windows uses the ANSI code to store the documents you create with Windows applications. The 8-bit ANSI code can convey up to 2^8, that is, 256, units of information, so it can be used to code 256 letters and symbols.

The first 128 of the characters of the ANSI code are the same as those defined by the ASCII code, but with an additional zero as the leftmost bit. For example, the letter "a" is represented by the ASCII code 1100001 and by the ANSI code 01100001. In addition to the 128 characters represented by the ASCII code, the ANSI code represents 128 other characters such as the copyright symbol ©, the pound sterling symbol £, and foreign language characters such as á, ê, and æ.

EBCDIC (Extended Binary Coded Decimal Interchange Code) is an 8-bit character representation code developed by IBM for its mainframe computers. EBCDIC does not use the same code as ASCII or ANSI for the initial 128 characters. For example, in EBCDIC the letter "a" is represented by 10000001.

Communication between computers that use different character representation codes can sometimes be a problem. For example, suppose you create a document on your computer using a Microsoft Windows application and you want to send it to an IBM mainframe. Your document is stored in ANSI format, but the mainframe expects documents in EBCDIC. When you send the letter "k" using the ANSI code 01101011, the mainframe decodes this as a comma using EBCDIC. To avoid this problem, one of the computers must translate the data from ASCII to EBCDIC. This task can be handled by software on either the sending or the receiving computer.

Standard ASCII defines 128 characters, which is sufficient for the numbers, letters, and punctuation marks used in English. ANSI represents all these characters plus many of the characters used in European languages. EBCDIC represents the standard alphabet and an assortment of control codes. However, none of these coding schemes supports alternate character sets such as Hebrew, Cyrillic, or Arabic. These coding schemes also do not support languages such as Japanese or Chinese, which require thousands of different symbols.

To compare ASCII and EBCDIC, refer back to Chapter 4 for a table of ASCII and EBCDIC codes.

Unicode is a 16-bit code that can represent over 65,000 different characters. Theoretically, Unicode can represent every character in every language used today, as well as characters from languages that are no longer used. Such a code would be very helpful in international business and communications, where a document might need to contain sections of text in Japanese, English, and Chinese. Unicode also facilitates the **localization** of software, that is, the modification of software for use in specific countries. With Unicode, a software developer can modify a computer program to display on-screen prompts, menus, and error messages in different languages for use in specific countries or regions. Both Microsoft and Apple have announced plans to add Unicode support to their operating systems.

Quick Check

1 _____ is an area of research that describes how the amount of information you can convey depends on the way you encode the information.

2 If the Minutemen wanted to send up to eight units of information, they would need _____ lanterns.

3 If you code data using the _____ number system, 255 is the largest number that an 8-bit computer can work with.

4 The _____ code uses seven bits to represent 128 symbols, including uppercase letters, lowercase letters, control codes, and punctuation symbols.

5 _____ and _____ are 8-bit codes used by computers to represent characters, symbols, and control codes.

6 _____ is a 16-bit code used to represent every character in every language used today.

7 When a software developer modifies a computer program to display prompts, menus, and error messages in different languages, it is referred to as _____ of software.

8 Using the ASCII table in Figure 9-8, what is the ASCII code for the letter "K"? _____

Representing Graphics and Video

Graphics, such as photographs and drawings, are quite different from documents that contain numbers and text. Obviously, computers cannot store and transmit graphics using character representation codes such as ASCII. However, computers must somehow encode graphics as 1s and 0s to store and transmit them electronically. How does this work?

There are two very different approaches to encoding graphics for computer systems: bitmap and vector. The differences between these two graphical coding schemes affect the image quality, the amount of space required to store the image, the amount of time required to transmit the image, and the ease with which you can modify the image.

Bitmap Graphics

How does a computer store graphical data?

Computers store **bitmap graphics** using a code that indicates the state of each individual dot, or pixel, displayed on the screen. The simplest bitmap graphics are monochrome. A **monochrome graphic** contains only the colors white and black. To understand how a computer codes monochrome bitmap graphics, think of a grid superimposed on a picture. The grid divides the picture into cells, each equivalent to a pixel on the computer screen. With monochrome graphics, each cell, or pixel, can be colored either black or white. If the section of the photo in a cell is black, the computer represents it with a 0 bit. If the section of the photo in a cell is white, the computer represents it with a 1 bit. Each row of the grid is represented by a series of 0s and 1s, as shown in Figure 9-9.

To learn more about bitmap graphics, try the Monochrome Graphics and Color Graphics sections of the Data Representation Lab.

The original picture.

The computer examines each cell in the matrix. If the cell is white, it is coded as a 1. If the cell is black, it is coded as a 0. This pattern of 0s and 1s is stored on disk to represent the graphic.

The computer divides the picture into a matrix equivalent to the resolution of the screen. Here you see only a small part of the entire matrix.

▶ **Figure 9-9**
Storing a monochrome bitmap graphic

With monochrome graphics, the number of bits required to represent a full-screen picture is the same as the number of pixels on the screen. The number of *bytes* required to store the image is the number of bits divided by 8. To see how this works, study the calculation in Figure 9-10.

Figure 9-10
Calculating the size
of a monochrome
bitmap graphic

Recall from Chapter 1 that a pixel is a dot of light on a computer screen. The resolution of a monitor is measured by the number of pixels displayed horizontally and vertically on the screen.

1. Multiply the horizontal by the vertical resolution of the screen:

640 x 480 = 307,200 pixels

This calculates the number of pixels on the screen. Because a monochrome graphic uses only one bit to represent each pixel, this also calculates the number of *bits* needed to store the graphic.

2. It is more conventional to measure storage requirements in bytes rather than bits. Because there are eight bits in a byte, divide the total number of bits by 8 to calculate the number of bytes required for the graphic:

307,200 ÷ 8 = 38,400 bytes

This calculates the number of *bytes* needed to store the graphic.

Monochrome graphics are similar to old-fashioned paper cut-out silhouettes, whereas grayscale graphics are similar to black-and-white photographs.

As you saw in Figure 9-10, a monochrome graphic displayed at 640 by 480 resolution requires 640×480 or 307,200 bits. With eight bits per byte, the graphic requires 38,400 bytes, a relatively small amount of storage space. However, monochrome graphics are seldom used because their two-dimensional appearance is not very realistic.

Grayscale graphics are somewhat more realistic than monochrome graphics. **Grayscale graphics** display an image using shades of gray or "gray scales." The more gray shades used, the more realistic the image appears. To represent grayscale graphics, like the one in Figure 9-11, a computer uses a more complex coding scheme than for monochrome graphics.

Figure 9-11
A 256-grayscale
bitmap graphic

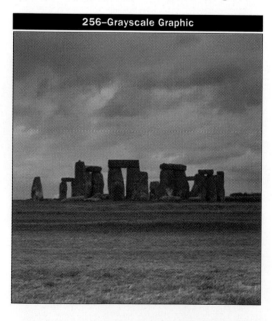

256–Grayscale Graphic

A computer typically represents grayscale graphics using 256 shades of gray. How many bits are required for a 256-grayscale picture? You can answer this question by applying information theory. In a 256-grayscale graphic, each pixel can be white, black, or one of 254 shades of gray—a total of 256 different possibilities. How many bits are needed to convey 256 units of information? The answer is eight: 2^8 is 256. Therefore, a 256-grayscale graphic requires eight bits (one byte) for each pixel. A full-screen 256-grayscale graphic at 640 by 480 resolution requires 307,200 bytes, as shown by the calculation in Figure 9-12.

Multiply the horizontal by the vertical resolution of the screen:

640 x 480 = 307,200

This calculates the number of pixels on the screen. A 256-grayscale graphic uses one byte to represent each pixel, so this is also the number of *bytes* needed to store the graphic.

▶ **Figure 9-12**
Calculating the size of a 256-grayscale graphic

For more realism, computers can display color images. A computer represents color graphics using either 16, 256, or 16.7 million colors. For a 16-color image, each pixel can have one of 16 colors. To represent these 16 different units of information, you need only four bits of storage space for each pixel. A full-screen 16-color image requires 153,600 bytes of storage space.

A 256-color image requires one byte for each pixel. A 256-color image requires 307,200 bytes—twice as much storage space as a 16-color image, but the same amount as a 256-grayscale image.

A photographic-quality image displays up to 16.7 million colors and is called a **24-bit** or **true-color graphic**. To represent 16.7 million colors requires 24 bits (3 bytes) for each pixel. A true-color image requires six times as much storage space as a 16-color image. Is there a difference in the image quality of 16-, 256-, and true-color images? You can judge for yourself by comparing the appearance of the images in Figure 9-13.

▶ **Figure 9-13**
A comparison of color graphic images

True Color Graphic

256–Color Graphic

16–Color Graphic

16–Color Dithered Graphic

Files that contain graphics can be quite large, as you have seen. Such large files also require lengthy transmission or download times. For example, it could take up to three minutes to download a 256-color, 640 by 480 bitmap image from an Internet site to your computer at home. A 16-color graphic would take only half as long to download. Two techniques are used to decrease graphics storage space and transmission time. First, the size of graphics files can be reduced by a technique known as compression, which is discussed in Section 9.4 of this chapter. Second, a technique called **dithering** reduces a 256-color graphic to a 16-color graphic. Dithering is a popular technique for reducing the size of graphics on Internet World Wide Web pages. Dithering uses only 16 colors, but it uses patterns composed of two or more colors to produce the illusion of additional colors and shading, relying on the human eye to blend colors and shapes. For example, an area of solid amber on a 256-color image can be dithered into a pattern of yellow and red dots in a 16-color image, as shown in Figure 9-14.

Bitmap graphics are used for realistic images such as scanned photos. The filename extensions .Bmp, .Pcx, .Tif, .Jpg, and .Gif typically indicate files that contain bitmap images. File extensions are often used as the name of the file format; a file with a .Gif extension is usually called a "GIF file."

Because bitmap graphics are coded as a series of bits that represent pixels, you can modify or edit this type of graphic by changing individual pixels. To modify a bitmap graphic, you use **bitmap graphics software**, sometimes referred to as **photo editing software** or **paint software**. Software packages such as Microsoft Paint, PC Paintbrush, Adobe Photoshop, or Micrografx Photomagic let you zoom in on a section of a picture so you can modify individual pixels more easily. Because making large-scale changes pixel by pixel can be a tedious process, bitmap graphics software provides additional tools to cut, copy, paste, and change the color of sections of a picture.

Bitmap graphics software gives you the capability to modify photographic-quality images. For example, you can retouch or repair old photographs and design eye-catching new pictures using images you cut and paste from several photos.

In Project 4 you get a chance to surf the Internet and compare the types of graphics you see at different sites.

To find out more about bitmap graphics software, do Project 5 at the end of this chapter.

You can see samples of vector graphics in the Vector Graphics section of the Data Representation Lab.

Vector Graphics

What's the difference between vector graphics and bitmap graphics?

Vector graphics consist of a set of instructions that recreates a picture. When you create a vector graphic, you draw lines and shapes in various colors. The computer then translates these lines and shapes into a set of instructions that can recreate your graphic. The computer stores the instructions instead of the actual picture. Figure 9-15 explains more about vector graphics.

Vector graphics do not look as realistic as pictures created with bitmap graphics. Vector graphics, however, have several important advantages. First, a vector graphics image is likely to require much less storage space than a bitmap image. The storage space required for a vector graphics picture depends on its complexity. Each instruction requires storage space, so the more lines, shapes, and fill patterns the picture contains, the more storage space it requires. The vector graphics picture shown in Figure 9-15 requires only 4,894 bytes of storage.

Filled circle tool

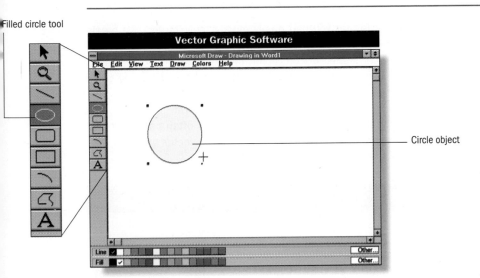

Circle object

Figure 9-15
Vector graphics

When you use vector graphics software to draw a picture, you use drawing tools to create shapes or objects. For example, you can use the filled circle tool to draw a circle that is filled with a solid color. The data for creating the circle is recorded as an instruction such as CIRCLE 40 Y 200 150, which means create a circle with a 40-pixel radius, color it yellow, and place the center of the circle 200 pixels from the left of the screen and 150 pixels from the top of the screen.

Clouds

Filled circle

Filled rectangle

Stonehenge

Using drawing tools, you can create geometric objects such as filled rectangles or circles. You can also create irregular shapes by connecting points to create the outline of a shape. The clouds and Stonehenge objects in this picture were created using this technique. Irregular shapes are recorded as a list of coordinate points to indicate their position on the screen. For example, the upper-left corner of Stonehenge is at location 95 350.

The objects you create with the drawing tools can be assembled into a picture by changing the position, size, and color of the objects. The drawing software adjusts the instructions accordingly. For example, if you enlarge the circle from a radius of 40 to a radius of 60, the instruction that the computer stores for the circle changes to CIRCLE 60 Y 200 150.

A second advantage of vector graphics is that you can easily modify the pictures you create using vector graphics software. You can think of the parts of a vector graphics picture as separate objects that you can individually stretch, shrink, distort, color, move, or delete. For example, your vector graphics picture might contain a sun that you created with a yellow circle. You could easily move the sun to a different location in the picture, enlarge it, or change its color.

Files that contain vector graphics typically have file extensions such as .Wmf, .Dxf, .Mgx, and .Cgm. Vector graphics software is referred to as **drawing software**, and it is often packaged separately from the paint software used to produce bitmap graphics. Popular vector graphics software packages include Micrographx Designer and CorelDRAW.

Digital Video

How do computers store video data?

A video is composed of a series of frames. Each frame is essentially a still picture, which could be represented using the same techniques as bitmap graphics. However, video displays 30 frames per second, which means that digital video recording requires tremendous storage capacity.

As you have seen, a full-screen 256-color image at 640 by 480 resolution requires 307,200 pixels. Multiply this number by 30 to calculate how many bytes are needed for each second of video—that's 9,216,000 bytes, or about 9 megabytes, for one second of video. A two-hour movie would require 66,355,200,000 bytes, more than 66 gigabytes! It would be only marginally possible to play back such a digitally recorded video, even using the most powerful supercomputer. As you will learn later in this chapter, video data requires some special coding techniques to produce a video file of manageable size.

Lab

Data Representation

Quick Check

1 A(n) _____ graphic is represented using a code that indicates the state of each pixel displayed on the screen.

2 A 256-grayscale graphic requires _____ bits for each pixel.

3 A technique called _____ reduces a 256-color graphic to a 16-color graphic and is frequently used to reduce the size of graphics files stored on the Internet.

4 _____ graphics are stored as a series of instructions on how to recreate the objects in the picture.

5 Which of the following file extensions indicate vector graphics formats? .Bmp, .Wmf, .Dxf, .Tif, .Cgm, .Gif, .Pcx, .Mgx

6 A 1-gigabyte hard drive can easily store the digital data for a full-length movie. True or false?

Representing Sound

Computers can record, store, and play back sounds such as voices and music. Sound or audio data can be represented in two very different ways: as a waveform or as MIDI music. The difference between the two is much like the difference between a tape recording and a player-piano roll.

Waveform Audio

How do computers store music?

Waveform audio is a digital representation of sound. To digitally record sound, samples of the sound waveform are collected at periodic intervals and stored as numeric data. Music, voice, and sounds can all be recorded as waveforms. Figure 9-16 shows how a computer digitally samples a waveform.

The distance between peaks is called the frequency. The frequency indicates the tone or note. When the peaks are far apart, the sound is low. When the peaks are close together, the sound is high.

The height of the wave is recorded for each sample. Eight bits are used to record each sample, so the height of a wave is measured on a scale of 0 to 255.

If you assume the height does not change between each sample, you can draw a vertical line between the height of each. The result is a digitized representation of a sound wave, known as a "stepped wave form."

▶ **Figure 9-16**
Sampling a soundwave

The height of a sound wave is called the amplitude. The amplitude indicates the loudness of the sound.

To sample the wave, each second of the wave's duration is divided into thousands of segments. It is too difficult to show all such samples here, so only 30 samples are shown for this wave.

The samples approximate the shape of the wave, but the details of what the sound wave does between samples are lost.

The height of this wave is 155 and is coded as binary 10011011.

The difference between waveform audio and MIDI music is analogous to the difference between bitmap and vector graphics. Just as a bitmap is a digitized representation of an actual picture, waveform audio is a digital representation of a real sound. And as a vector graphic is a set of instructions for recreating a picture, MIDI music is a set of instructions for recreating a sound.

Sampling rate refers to the number of times per second the sound is measured during the recording process. The sampling rate is expressed in Hertz (Hz). One thousand samples per second is expressed as 1,000 Hz or 1 KHz (kilohertz). Higher sampling rates increase the quality of the sound recording but require more storage space than lower sampling rates.

The audio CDs you buy at your favorite music store are recorded at a sampling rate of 44.1 KHz, which means a sample of the sound is taken 44,100 times per second. Each sample requires two bytes of storage space. At a sampling rate of 44.1 KHz, one second of music requires 88,200 bytes. A stereo recording requires twice as much storage space because you are essentially making two recordings to achieve the stereo effect. When you sample music at 44.1 KHz, you can store only eight seconds of stereo music on a 1.44 megabyte floppy disk. Forty-five minutes of music, the length of a typical rock album, requires about 240 megabytes.

To conserve space, applications that do not require such high-quality sound use much lower sampling rates. Voice is often recorded with a sampling rate of 11 KHz or 11,000 samples per second. This results in lower-quality sound, but the file is about one-fourth the size of a file for the same sound recorded at 44.1 KHz.

The waveform files you record and store on your computer generally have .Wav, .Mod, or .Voc file extensions. To record or play back waveform files, you need music software. Such software is usually included with sound cards. Alternatively, you can use the Windows 3.1 Sound Recorder application or the Windows 95 Media Player application. In addition, many Internet FTP sites have downloadable music shareware.

MIDI Music

Can I use MIDI to store voice and music data?

MIDI (Musical Instrument Digital Interface) files contain the instructions that MIDI instruments and MIDI sound cards use to recreate sounds. MIDI files store and recreate musical instrument sounds, but not voice.

MIDI is a music notation system that allows computers to communicate with music synthesizers. The computer encodes the music as a sequence and stores it as a file with a .Mid, .Cmf, or .Rol extension. A **sequence** is analogous to a player-piano roll that contains punched information indicating which musical notes to play. A MIDI sequence contains instructions including the pitch of a note, when a note begins, what instrument plays the note, the volume of the note, and the duration of the note.

MIDI coding is fairly complex, but MIDI software packages such as Cakewalk, Cadenza, and Sequencer Plus have helped hundreds of musicians use computers to compose and record their music. MIDI files are much more compact than waveform files. Three minutes of MIDI music requires only 10 kilobytes of storage space, whereas three minutes of waveform music requires 15 megabytes.

Quick Check

1 _____ audio is analogous to bitmap graphics, whereas _____ music is analogous to vector graphics.

2 The _____ rate refers to the number of times per second a sound is measured during the recording process.

3 Human speech should be recorded at a higher sampling rate than music. True or false?

4 A MIDI sequence is a digital recording of human speech. True or false?

5 Which of the following file extensions indicate data stored as waveform audio? .Wav, .Mid, .Cmf, .Mod, .Voc

Data Compression

Despite the use of information theory to design effective coding schemes for representing characters, graphics, and sounds, the files that contain such data can be quite large. As you learned earlier in this chapter, one second of video requires 9 megabytes, a full-screen bitmap graphic requires 307,200 bytes, and a forty-five minute waveform sound file might be as large as 240 megabytes. These large files can be a problem for the following reasons:

- Large files require large amounts of storage space, quickly filling up a hard disk.
- Large files are likely to become fragmented and reduce the efficiency of your disk drive.
- Opening a large file and locating a particular item of information in the file requires extra time.
- If you want to store a large file on floppy disks for safekeeping or transfer it to another computer, you need many floppy disks.
- Large files require lengthy transmission time.

If you could reduce the size of a file without losing any of the data contained in the file, you would be able to avoid these problems.

Data compression is the general term used for recoding data so it requires fewer bytes of storage space. Data compression is reversible, so the data can be returned to its original form. The process of reversing data compression is sometimes referred to as **uncompressing**, **decompressing**, **extracting**, or **expanding** a file. Figure 9-17 will help you visualize how compression affects the number of bytes required to represent the data in a file.

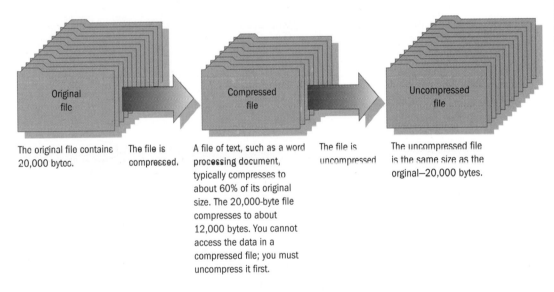

Figure 9-17
Data compression

The original file contains 20,000 bytes.

The file is compressed.

A file of text, such as a word processing document, typically compresses to about 60% of its original size. The 20,000-byte file compresses to about 12,000 bytes. You cannot access the data in a compressed file; you must uncompress it first.

The file is uncompressed

The uncompressed file is the same size as the orginal—20,000 bytes.

There are two types of data compression: disk compression and file compression. **Disk compression** shrinks your files and places them in a special volume on your hard disk. A **disk volume** is a disk or an area of a disk that has a unique name and is treated as a separate disk. Disk compression creates a **compressed volume** containing data that has been recoded to use storage space more efficiently. When you want to use a file from the compressed volume of the disk, the computer automatically expands the file to its regular size. When you store a file on the compressed volume, the computer automatically shrinks it.

The advantage of disk compression is gaining storage space without purchasing additional hardware. You can effectively double your computer's storage capacity by using disk compression. For example, using disk compression you can store 640 MB of data on a 320 MB hard disk. Disk compression has two potential drawbacks. First, if you decide that you no longer want a compressed volume on your drive you must have enough drive space for all the files in their uncompressed size. Many users, taking advantage of the extra storage space provided by disk compression, would not have this space available. The second drawback is that a file error in the compressed volume could mean the loss of all the data in that volume. Regular backups are important for compressed disks.

To compress a disk, you must use a **disk compression utility**. Popular disk compression utilities include DoubleSpace, DriveSpace, Stacker, SuperStor, and AddStor. The Windows 95 operating system includes a disk compression utility.

The second data compression technique, **file compression**, shrinks one or more files into a single smaller file. Unlike disk compression, which creates a disk volume, file compression creates a compressed file. You cannot use this compressed file until it has been uncompressed. PKZIP is a popular shareware file compression utility. In computer jargon, compressing a file is sometimes called **zipping**; uncompressing a file is called **unzipping**.

The advantage of file compression is that you can zip selected files and fit them on a single floppy disk. The disadvantage is that you must manually unzip the files before you use them. Suppose you have five files that require 1.79 MB of storage space and you want to move these files from one computer to another. You can use a file compression utility to zip these files to fit on a single 1.44 MB floppy disk. You can then take the floppy disk to another computer and unzip the files to their original size so that you can use them.

Software publishers frequently use file compression so they can deliver software on fewer floppy disks. With such software, the publisher provides instructions for unzipping and installing the software files.

Using a file compression utility, you can shrink text and .Bmp files by 70%. However, some other types of files hardly shrink at all because they are already stored in a compressed format. In the next sections you will learn why compression utilities shrink text and .Bmp files, but do not have much effect on .Tif and .Pcx files.

Text File Compression

How does a compression utility shrink my document files?

Text files contain many repeating patterns of words and spaces, so compression utilities can shrink text files to less than half of their original size using compression techniques such as adaptive pattern substitution and pointers. **Adaptive pattern substitution** is a compression technique designed specifically to compress text files. This compression technique scans the entire text and looks for patterns of two or more bytes. When it finds such a pattern, it substitutes a byte pattern that is not used elsewhere in the file and makes a "dictionary" entry. Let's look at a simple example.

Using adaptive pattern substitution, how much can you compress the phrase, "the rain in Spain stays mainly on the plain, but the rain in Maine falls again and again"? The uncompressed phrase is 88 bytes long, including spaces and punctuation. Look at Figure 9-18 to see how adaptive pattern substitution compresses this phrase.

1. The original file contains 88 characters, or 88 bytes. Remember that spaces and punctuation "count" when you determine the number of bytes.

2. The # sign is substituted for each occurrence of the word "the." The word "the" is three bytes, but the # sign is only one byte. This substitution saves two bytes for each occurrence of the word.

3. The ^ sign replaces each occurrence of "in." This substitution saves one byte for each occurrence.

```
the rain in Spain
stays mainly on the plain,
but the rain in Maine
falls again and again
```

```
# r@ ^ Sp@
stays m@ly on # pl@,
but # r@ ^ M@e
falls ag@ and ag@
```

4. The @ sign replaces each occurrence of the letters "ain." This substitution saves two bytes for each occurrence.

6. The compressed file is 64 characters, or 64 bytes. The dictionary is 11 bytes. The compressed file, then, is 75 bytes. This is 13 bytes less than the original file size—about a 20% reduction.

```
# the
@ ain
^ in
```

5. The compression software maintains a dictionary entry for each substitution, so the file can be uncompressed to its original state.

▶ **Figure 9-18**
Text compression: Adaptive pattern substitution

In Project 2 you can try compressing a short file using pointers.

Another text compression technique scans a file and looks for repeated words. When a word occurs more than once, the second and all subsequent occurrences of the word are replaced with a number. The number acts as a "pointer" to the original occurrence of the word. Figure 9-19 shows how this works.

2. The second and third time the word "the" occurs, it is replaced by a pointer that means "this word should be the same as the first word in the file." The # sign is a special character that means the number that follows is a pointer, not a part of the actual text.

1. The original file is 88 bytes, including spaces and punctuation.

3. The second occurrence of the word "rain" is replaced by a pointer to the second word in the file.

```
the rain in Spain
stays mainly on the plain,
but the rain in Maine
falls again and again
```

```
the rain in Spain stays
mainly on #1 plain, but
#1 #2 #3 Maine
falls again and #16
```

4. The second occurrence of the word "in" is replaced by a pointer to the third word in the file. This substitution does not reduce the size of the file because the original word was two bytes and the substitution also requires two bytes. For this reason, most compression programs do not substitute a pointer for words that are only two characters.

6. The compressed file is 83 bytes. For this text sample, the compression reduced the file size by only six bytes. Generally, the larger the file, the better the compression because words are likely to be repeated with more frequency.

5. The second occurrence of the word "again" is replaced by a pointer to the sixteenth word. Notice that the pointer requires three bytes: the # symbol, the 1, and the 6.

▶ **Figure 9-19**
Text compression: Using pointers to compress a file

Graphics File Compression

Can I use a compression utility to shrink a graphics file?

Uncompressed bitmap graphics files are very large; however, they often contain repetitive data, such as large blocks of the same color, that can be compressed. **Run length encoding** is a compression technique that looks for patterns of bytes and replaces them with a message that describes the pattern. As a simple example, suppose a section of a picture had 167 consecutive

To find out more about data compression, do the Compressed Graphics section of the Data Representation Lab.

white pixels and each pixel is described by one byte of data. The process of run length encoding compresses this series of 167 bytes into as few as two bytes, as shown in Figure 9-20.

Figure 9-20 ◀
Run length
encoding of
graphics

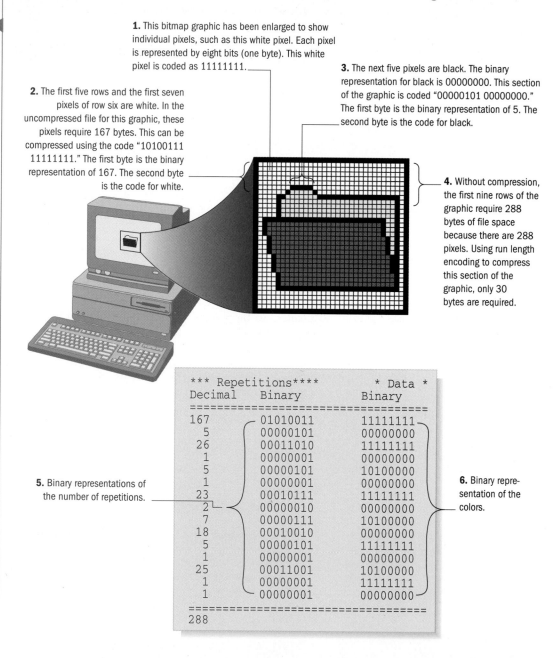

1. This bitmap graphic has been enlarged to show individual pixels, such as this white pixel. Each pixel is represented by eight bits (one byte). This white pixel is coded as 11111111.

2. The first five rows and the first seven pixels of row six are white. In the uncompressed file for this graphic, these pixels require 167 bytes. This can be compressed using the code "10100111 11111111." The first byte is the binary representation of 167. The second byte is the code for white.

3. The next five pixels are black. The binary representation for black is 00000000. This section of the graphic is coded "00000101 00000000." The first byte is the binary representation of 5. The second byte is the code for black.

4. Without compression, the first nine rows of the graphic require 288 bytes of file space because there are 288 pixels. Using run length encoding to compress this section of the graphic, only 30 bytes are required.

5. Binary representations of the number of repetitions.

6. Binary representation of the colors.

| *** Repetitions**** | | * Data * |
Decimal	Binary	Binary
167	01010011	11111111
5	00000101	00000000
26	00011010	11111111
1	00000001	00000000
5	00000101	10100000
1	00000001	00000000
23	00010111	11111111
2	00000010	00000000
7	00000111	10100000
18	00010010	00000000
5	00000101	11111111
1	00000001	00000000
25	00011001	10100000
1	00000001	11111111
1	00000001	00000000
288		

Files with .Bmp extensions usually contain bitmap images that have not been compressed. Files with .Tif, .Pcx, and .Jpg extensions contain bitmap images that have been compressed. A .Tif extension refers to files that have been compressed using **TIFF** or Tag Image File Format. Files stored in .Pcx format use a different compression technique. Files with a .Jpg extension have been compressed into **JPEG** (Joint Photographic Experts Group) format using lossy compression. **Lossy compression** loses some of the original data for the graphics; in theory, the human eye won't miss the lost information. When you save a graphic, most graphics software lets you select whether you want the image stored in BMP, TIFF, PCX, or JPEG file format. Once you have stored a file in compressed format, you generally cannot make it much smaller by using a file compression utility such as PKZIP. Therefore, you can use PKZIP to significantly shrink .Bmp files, but .Pcx, .Tif, or .Jpg files will not shrink significantly.

Video File Compression

Is there a way to compress large video files?

You learned earlier in this chapter that video is composed of a series of frames, each of which is essentially a bitmap image. You also learned that storing the bitmap images for a full-length film requires more than 66 gigabytes of storage space. Clearly, this is beyond the capacity of today's personal computer systems. It is possible, however, to display video on your personal computer by reducing the number of frames displayed per second, reducing the size of the video window, or coding only the changes that take place from one frame to the next.

Video for Windows and **QuickTime** are formats used to encode, compress, store, and play back video segments on computers. A **video segment** is a series of frames or individual images shown in quick succession. The number of frames per second directly affects the perceived smoothness of the segment. High-quality video displays 30 frames per second. Lower-quality video displays only 15 frames per second; that video might appear jerky but is acceptable for some computer applications, such as training videos or animated product catalogs.

Another technique that makes video display possible on a microcomputer is reducing the image size. Displaying an image on one-quarter of your screen requires only a fourth of the data required to display a full-screen image, so most computer video applications use only a small window on your computer screen.

There are many techniques for compressing video data, and the details of these methods are quite complex. A simple example will give you a general idea of how one video compression technique works. Suppose you have a video segment that doesn't change very much from one frame to the next. A "talking head" is a good example; the mouth and eyes change from frame to frame, but the background remains fairly stable. Instead of recording all the data for each frame, a compression program might store only the changes from one frame to the next. Storing only the changes requires far less data, saves storage space, and reduces the time required to display the data.

When you store a graphic, your graphics software will add a file extension to indicate the file format. For example, if you store a file in JPEG compressed format, your software will add a .Jpg extension to indicate how it was compressed.

Most software you use to develop computer video also provides compression options to reduce the size of your video files.

Quick Check

1 _____ is a technique for recoding data so it requires fewer bytes of storage space.

2 Disk compression creates a compressed _____ on your hard disk.

3 The advantage of _____ is that you can compress selected files and fit them on a single floppy disk.

4 A technique called _____ compresses text files by substituting a small byte pattern for reoccurring sequences of characters.

5 JPG files have been compressed with a technique called _____ compression that loses some of the data from the original image.

6 One technique for reducing the size of video files is to reduce the number of frames displayed per second. True or false?

User Focus:
Using a Compression Utility

PKZIP is a popular file compression utility that you can obtain by mail from a shareware distributor, download from the Internet, or purchase from a local computer store. This software is effective for reducing the size of text and .Bmp files. Let's take a specific example to see how you might use this software. Suppose you have a 1.8 megabyte file called **Clients.Doc** on your hard disk (drive C) in a folder called REPORTS. The file contains information about the customers for a mail-order business that you want to give to your coworker. You want to put this file on a single 1.44 megabyte floppy disk that you inserted in drive A. Because **Clients.Doc** requires 1.8 megabytes, it will not fit on a single floppy disk in its uncompressed state.

Compressing a File with PKZIP

How do I use PKZIP to compress a file?

To compress the file for your coworker, you'd first need to be sure you have the PKZIP program on your computer. You could use the Windows File Manager or Explorer to locate it. You would run PKZIP by double-clicking its name. To compress the **Clients.Doc** file, you would type the command pkzip a:clients.zip c:\reports\clients.doc.

As a result of this command, the computer would compress **Clients.Doc** to make a smaller file on drive A called **Clients.Zip**. The .Zip file extension is your clue that the file is compressed.

Unzipping a File

Does my coworker need to uncompress the file before using it?

Because it is not possible to use a compressed file directly, your coworker must uncompress the **Clients.Zip** file. To do this, your coworker must first locate and start the PKUNZIP program. The command pkunzip a:clients.zip c:\reports "unzips" or uncompresses the file and places the uncompressed version on your coworker's C drive. Figure 9-21 summarizes how to use PKZIP and PKUNZIP.

Figure 9-21
Using PKZIP

1. Select the MSDOS prompt.

Microsoft Excel
Microsoft PowerPoint
Microsoft Schedule+
Microsoft Word
MS-DOS Prompt
The Microsoft Network
Windows Explorer

C:>pkzip a:clients.zip c:\reports\clients.doc

2. Type the command **pkzip a:clients.zip c:\reports\clients.doc** then press Enter. This command tells the computer to use the PKZIP program to put a compressed file on drive a: called **clients.zip**. The compressed file is created from the file **clients.doc** in the REPORTS folder of drive C.

Figure 9-21
Using PKZIP
(*continued*)

pkunzip a:clients.zip c:\reports

Compress

Uncompressing

3. The PKZIP program creates a compressed version of the file on drive A. The .Zip extension is your clue that the file is compressed. The original uncompressed file is still on the hard disk in drive C. If you do not want to store the original version of the file, you can delete it. You can now give this disk to your coworker.

4. Your coworker cannot use this file in its compressed form. The file must be uncompressed first. To uncompress the file, go to the MSDOS prompt and enter the command: **pkunzip a:clients.zip c:\reports** then press Enter. This command tells the computer to use the PKUNZIP program to uncompress the file on drive A: called **Clients.Zip**. It also tells the computer to put the uncompressed file in the REPORTS folder of drive C. PKUNZIP decides what to name the file, so you do not include a filename.

End Note   On the evening of April 18, 1775, Paul Revere saw the lantern signal in the tower of the Old North Church, mounted his horse, and sped off on his famous ride. Did the British come by land or by sea? It is interesting that most people remember the code, "one if by land, and two if by sea," but have forgotten (or never knew) if the British actually came by land or by sea. Perhaps this reflects a genuine fascination with codes and the impact of information theory in an age when computers have become an indispensable aspect of everyday life. On the other hand, it may reflect the enduring value of poetry and remind us that technology, though indispensable, is only one aspect of our complex culture.

Review

1. Use your own words to answer the italicized questions under each of the section headings.

2. List each of the boldface terms used in this chapter, then use your own words to write a short definition.

3. Complete the following chart to show how many units of information you can convey with a given number of bits:

Number of Bits	1	2	3	4	5	6	7	8
Number of Units of Information	2	4	8					

4. Perform the calculations necessary to complete the following table:

Screen Width in Pixels	640	640	640	640
Screen Height in Pixels	480	480	480	480
Graphics Type	Mono-chrome	16-color	256-color	True-color
Number of Bytes Required	38,400			

5. List the characteristics of the ASCII, ANSI, EBCDIC, and Unicode character representation codes.

6. A monochrome graphic with two colors per pixel requires one bit to represent each pixel. A color graphic with 16 colors per pixel requires four bits to represent each pixel. How many bits per pixel are required for a color graphic with four colors per pixel?

7. Describe the difference between bitmap graphics and vector graphics.

8. Describe the difference between waveform audio and MIDI music.

9. List five problems associated with large files.

10. Describe the difference between disk compression and file compression.

11. Make a list of the file extensions mentioned in this chapter, then for each extension on your list indicate the type of data it contains (text, graphics, sound) and whether the data in the file is stored in a compressed format.

Projects

1. Your Own Bitmap Graphics Make two photocopies of the grid in Figure 9-22 or make two 8×8 grids on graph paper. Using the first grid, fill in the pixels on the grid to reconstruct an 8-pixel by 8-pixel one-bit monochrome graphic from the following binary codes: 00100000, 01010000, 10001010, 10001111, 11111010, 10001000, 10001000, 10001000. Using the second grid, create your own graphic, then convert it into binary format.

Figure 9-22

2. Try Your Hand at Text Compression One way to compress text is to replace repeated occurrences of words with a pointer to the first occurrence of that word. Using a vertical bar and a number as your pointer, write out the compressed form of the following paragraph:

A computer system is composed of a computer and peripheral devices, such as a printer. The components of a computer system that you can see and touch are referred to as hardware. Software refers to the nonphysical components of a computer system, particularly the programs, or lists of instructions, that are needed to make the computer perform a specific task.

3. Modern, Classical, and Rock Use your library and Internet resources to find more information about MIDI music and write a two- to three-page report. You might want to address questions such as: To what extent do musicians use computer-generated music today? Which modern, classical, and rock composers or performers make extensive use of computer-generated music? How has computer-generated music enhanced the sound quality, creativity, or appeal of modern music?

4. Dithering on the Internet Surf the Internet, looking at the graphics used by various World Wide Web sites. See if you can determine by the appearance of the graphic or by the file size whether a graphic is 16-color, dithered, or 256-color. You might find it useful to do the Bitmap Graphics section of the Data Representation Lab before you tackle this project. Write a one-page report summarizing your findings. Include the sites you visited, your conclusions about the type of graphics used, and printouts of one or two graphics.

5. Graphics Software Software publishers produce a variety of graphics software packages that differ based on the type of graphics supported and the tools they provide to manipulate graphics. Use current computer magazines to research graphics software packages. Write a paper describing three of the software packages you read about. Indicate the key features, the graphics formats supported, and the price of each package. Finally, indicate which package you would purchase and why.

6. Unzip It You learned that PKZIP is a shareware utility for compressing files. The User Focus section of this chapter describes how to use it. For this project, you must access the CTI Web site, *www.vmedia.com/cti/concepts2*, and download the

PKZIP shareware in file **PkZ204G.Exe** to your floppy disk. You should also download the file **Surprize.Zip.** Next you must install PKUNZIP to your floppy disk. From Windows File Manager (Windows 3.1), pull down the File menu and select Run. From the Start menu (Windows 95) select Run. In the box type A:PKZ204G to set up the software. Be sure you pay attention to the shareware agreement. Now use PKUNZIP to unzip the file **Surprize.Zip** on your floppy disk. Follow the instructions in the **Readme.Txt** file to complete the project.

7. Globalization, Localization, and Unicode Current trends in the globalization of communications and business require the use of computers. Much of the data, such as financial transactions, is usable regardless of local language. However, the programs that manipulate that data are generally most effective if they are localized so users do not have to translate screen prompts and error messages. Using your library resources, write a two- to three-page paper on software localization and how it contributes to globalized communications and business.

8. Converting Binary to Decimal to Hexadecimal Although today's computer users rarely need to deal with binary, octal, or hexadecimal numbers, the Windows calculator provides a quick and easy way to convert numbers if you need to do so. For this Project, complete a through e, then fill out the table in f.

   a. On a computer with the Microsoft Windows operating system, look for the Windows Calculator program. In Windows 3.1 it is in the Applications program group. In Windows 95 it is on the Programs menu. If you can't find the Calculator program, ask your technical support person for help.

   b. Start the Windows Calculator.

   c. Click the View menu, then click Scientific.

   d. To convert from decimal to binary, make sure the Decimal button is selected. Then enter a decimal number such as 255. Click the Binary button and the calculator will show the binary equivalent, in this case 11111111.

   e. To convert from binary to decimal, make sure the Binary button is selected, then enter a binary number such as 101. Click the Decimal button to show the decimal equivalent, in this case 5.

f. Fill in the following table:

Decimal	Binary (Base 2)	Octal (Base 8)	Hexa-decimal (Base 16)
10			
	10		
		10	
			10
32			
	111011		
		77	
			B
255			
	1101101		
		33	
			FE

9. Another Picasso? You learned that bitmap graphics require quite a lot of storage space. You can create your own bitmap image and see for yourself. Use Microsoft Paintbrush (Windows 3.1), Microsoft Paint (Windows 95), or any available paint software to create a simple graphic. Store the graphic on a floppy disk in .Bmp format. Print your graphic and don't forget to sign your original work of art! To find the size of your graphic file, you will probably need to use File Manager or Window Explorer. Write the file size on your printout.

Resources

- **Asimov, I.** *One, Ten, Buckle My Shoe, Adding a Dimension.* New York: Doubleday, 1964. If you haven't had your fill of binary numbers, you might want to read Asimov's perspective on the subject.

- **CyberPress Publishing.** Visit this Web site to find a collection of graphical elements designed for use on Web pages. Also, you'll find links to other graphics pages and tutorials on creating Web page backgrounds and 3-D art.

- **Deken, J.** *The Electronic Cottage.* New York: Bantam Books, 1981. For an alternative explanation of how computers use binary numbers, refer to Chapter 3 of *The Electronic Cottage.* In this chapter, the author uses a unique bucket-and-hose analogy to explain how computers communicate.

- *http://www.eeb.ele.tue.nl/midi/index.html* You will want to access this Web site if you are interested in MIDI music. Here you will find information for beginning and experienced MIDI connoisseurs, along with links to many other Web sites with MIDI information and downloadable music files.

- **Internet Arts Museum.** This site contains a variety of original art that you can download for free. *http://www.rahul.net/iamfree.*

- **Longfellow, H. W.** *Tales of a Wayside Inn [1863-1874], pt. 1, The Landlord's Tale: Paul Revere's Ride.* If you can't remember if the British came by land or by sea, you can find Longfellow's poem in most anthologies of American verse. You might have memorized sections of the poem in elementary school. Historians do not agree about whether it presents an accurate account of the events of April 18, 1775.

- *Multilingual Computing* (208-263-8179, info@multi-lingual.com) This magazine is devoted to technical and sociological issues of localized software design. Here you will find articles on Unicode, machine translation, localization, internationalization, and globalization of software. In addition, you will find advertisements and reviews of books and software development tools for localizing software.

- **Shannon, C. E. and W. Weaver.** *The Mathematical Theory of Communication.* Urbana, IL: University of Illinois Press, 1949. This is a classic publication on information theory. Although the approach is rather technical, this book is required reading for serious students of computer information systems and computer science.

- **The Web Museum.** The Web version of the Louvre Art Museum is so popular that special Internet sites called "mirror sites" have been set up all over the world to accomodate the more than 200,000 weekly cyber visitors. Check out this site for art of all types: *http://www.sunsite.unc.edu/wm.*

Lab Assignments

Data Representation

A computer stores many types of data—text, graphics, sound, animation, and video. Digital computers, such as the microcomputers you use, store all these different types of data as the electronic equivalent of 1s and 0s. How is it possible to reduce a long document or complex graphic to a series of 1s and 0s? In this Lab you'll find out how this is done.

1. Click the Steps button to learn how text, monochrome graphics, color graphics, and vector graphics are stored. As you proceed through the Steps, answer all of the Quick Check questions that appear. After you complete the Steps, you will see a Quick Check Summary Report. Follow the instructions on the screen to print this report.

2. Click the Explore button. Suppose you are a computer and you need to sort a list containing words, numbers, and symbols. Look up the ANSI representation for the first character of each item on the list. Then, sort the list according to this ANSI code. The item with the lowest ANSI code should be first in the list. The list is as follows:

```
age
5
Tree
]
Apple
05
10
```

3. Using Explore's Quick Convert, find the ANSI code for your first and last name. Write this on paper. Then write the decimal equivalent to the ANSI code for your first and last name.

4. Suppose you are a computer, and you receive the following 1s and 0s from your modem. Using Explore's ANSI Table, convert these 1s and 0s into the letters, numerals, and symbols you would display on the screen.

```
01010100   01101000   01100101
00100000   00110100   00100000
01101111   01100110   00100000
01001000   01100101   01100001
01110010   01110100   01110011
```

5. Suppose you are a computer, and you receive a monochrome graphics file containing a string of 1s and 0s. Using Explore's Monochrome Grid, create this graphic, then print it.

```
00000000
01000100
11101110
```

```
11111110
01111100
00111000
00010000
```

6. Using Explore's Monochrome Grid, convert the following decimal numbers into a monochrome graphic, then print it.

8, 12, 254,255, 254, 12, 8, 0

7. Suppose you are a computer, and you must send a monochrome graphic to another computer over a local area network. Using Explore's Monochrome Grid, convert the following graphic into 1s and 0s, then print it.

▶ **Figure 9-23**

8. Suppose you are a computer, and you receive a 16-color graphics file containing a string of 1s and 0s. Using Explore's 16-Color Grid, recreate this graphic, then print it.

```
11111111   11001111   11001111   11001111
11111111   11000100   01000100   11001111
11111111   11001100   01001100   11001111
11111111   11111100   11001100   11111111
11111111   11111111   00101111   10101111
11111111   11111111   00101010   10101111
11111111   11111111   00101010   11111111
11111111   11111111   00101111   11111111
```

9. Using Explore's Vector Draw, recreate a vector graphic from the following set of instructions. Print your completed graphic.

Shape	Color	Top	Left	Width	Height
Circle	red	73	212	50	50
Circle	blue	137	212	50	50
Circle	green	202	212	50	50
Rounded rectangle	black	39	200	73	241

Quick Check

Answers

9.1
1. Information theory
2. 3
3. binary
4. ASCII
5. ANSI, EBCDIC
6. Unicode
7. localization
8. 1001011

9.2
1. bitmap
2. 8
3. dithering
4. Vector
5. .Wmf, .Dxf, .Mgx, .Cgm
6. false

9.3
1. Waveform, MIDI
2. sampling
3. false
4. false
5. .Wav, .Mod, .Voc

9.4
1. Compression
2. volume
3. file compression
4. adaptive pattern substitution
5. lossy
6. true

Glossary/Index

Communication Systems Infrastructure

Communications Systems Infrastructure

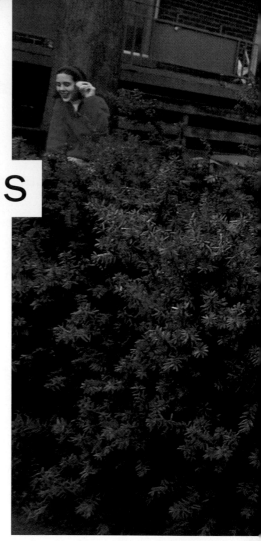

Communications means getting information from point A to point B. Communications technology can be simple or sophisticated. Link two cans together with string and you have a simple "telephone." Link two computers using modems, telephone lines, satellites, and fiber-optic cables and you have a sophisticated communications system.

In today's communications environment, even machines hold conversations, such as the following:

Beeeeeep [Translation: Is anybody there?]

Peeeep [Translation: Hello, I'm here.]

Chuuussssh [Translation: Good, we need to talk.]

Burrrrrr [Translation: I didn't get that.]

Whaaaan [Translation: Well, do you understand this?]

Zzzhuussst [Translation: Wait, you're going too fast for me.]

Burrrzzzzz [Translation: Let's try it slower, OK?]

Chirp [Translation: Yes, we're all set!]

This beeping, chushing, and chirping conversation might seem bizarre, but it takes place millions of times a day as one modem calls another and establishes communications. Fax machines hold similar conversations. Radio signals carrying thousands of talk and news shows pulse through the air. Cables and satellites carry hundreds of television programs. LANs, WANs, and the Internet transport millions of documents and images. We are, in fact, surrounded by data, transmitted over a **communications infrastructure** made up of telephone lines, cable television lines, satellites, computer networks, and microwave, radio, and television transmitters.

Although most of the systems in this communications infrastructure were originally designed for other purposes (such as carrying voice communications), they are being pressed into service to transport computer data. Today, individuals and organizations are taking advantage of this vast communications infrastructure to gather, transmit, and locate computer-based information.

The purpose of this chapter is to show how the communications infrastructure provides many pathways for transporting computer-generated information. This chapter begins with an overview of today's communication systems. Next, Section 10.2 presents basic terms and concepts important to understanding how computers and other devices transmit data. The focus then shifts to how communications concepts apply to local area networks. This chapter ends with how to configure a modem—an important skill for computer users who want to connect to the communications infrastructure.

CHAPTER**PREVIEW**

In this chapter you will learn how to access computer-based data from telephones, cellular phones, fax machines, and other computers. You will learn the basic terminology of data communications and some technical details about how modems and LANs transport data. You will also find out how to set up a modem, so you can use your home computer to access data on the Internet, LANs, information services, and bulletin boards. When you have completed this chapter, you should be able to:

■ Explain Shannon's communications system model

■ Discuss the advantages and disadvantages of data communications over telephone, cellular phone, cable television, Internet, and private communications systems

■ Describe how packet switching works for data transmission

■ Define bandwidth and discuss how it affects data communications

■ Explain the differences in simplex, half duplex, full duplex, and echoplex protocols

■ Explain how a computer uses odd or even parity

■ Differentiate between synchronous and asynchronous communications protocols

■ Describe how devices communicate on local area networks

■ List today's popular LAN standards and LAN communications protocols

■ Explain the differences between communications and collision handling on Ethernet and token-passing networks

■ Understand how to connect and configure a modem for dial-up communications

LAB

Building a Network

10.1 Communications Systems

A **communications system** is the combination of hardware, software, and connecting links that transport data. In 1949, Claude Shannon, an engineer at the prestigious Bell Labs, published an article that described a communications system model. In this model, data from a source is encoded and sent over a communications channel where it is decoded by a receiver. According to Shannon, the effectiveness of communication depends on the efficiency of the coding process and the channel's resistance to interference called "noise." Study Figure 10-1 to get an overview of Shannon's communications system model.

Figure 10-1 ◄
Shannon's communications system model

What's the difference between communication and communications? We tend to use the term communication to describe a message or an exchange of messages between two people. If we want to talk about technology-aided exchange of information, we usually add an "s" and use the term communications.

4. The encoded message travels by means of a **channel** or **communications link**. A communications link might include telephone wiring, fiber-optic cable, microwaves, or satellites.

Source → Encode → Channel → Decode → Receiver

Noise

1. The **source** originates or initiates the communication. The source might be a person or a computer.

2. The **message**, represented here by a folder, is the information that the source wants to communicate to the receiver. The message might be a document, picture, sound, or numeric data.

3. The message is **encoded** by changing its format into one that can be transmitted. In a modern communications system, a message typically is encoded into an electronic signal that can be sent over telephone lines, broadcast by radio waves, or transmitted as microwaves.

5. Noise, such as electrical interference, sometimes disrupts a transmission. The message can become garbled unless the communications system has the capability to check for errors and correct them.

6. The message is decoded at the end of the transmission. **Decoding** usually means reversing the coding process that occurred before the message was sent.

7. The **receiver** is the destination for the message. The receiver can be a person, a computer, or another communications device.

Figure 10-2 ◄
Five-tiered telephone system

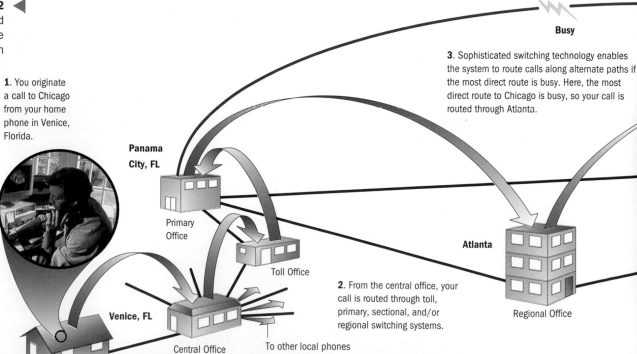

1. You originate a call to Chicago from your home phone in Venice, Florida.

3. Sophisticated switching technology enables the system to route calls along alternate paths if the most direct route is busy. Here, the most direct route to Chicago is busy, so your call is routed through Atlanta.

Busy

Panama City, FL

Primary Office

Toll Office

Venice, FL

Central Office

To other local phones

2. From the central office, your call is routed through toll, primary, sectional, and/or regional switching systems.

Atlanta

Regional Office

Today's communications systems evolved from early courier services such as the Pony Express and Wells Fargo. Technology began to shrink the globe, so to speak, in 1844 when Samuel Morse sent the first telegraph message. By the turn of the century, more than one million miles of telegraph lines linked cities and continents. The telegraph was soon upstaged by a new communications system based on the telephone. Riding on the coattails of the telephone system came the cellular phone system. At the same time, cable television services began stringing thousands of miles of cable to deliver "pay TV." In addition to these commercial communications systems, many businesses established private communications systems such as private branch exchanges (PBXs) and local area networks (LANs). The rest of this section explains how individuals and organizations use these communications systems to send and receive computer data.

The Telephone System

What are the advantages and disadvantages of using the telephone system to communicate computer data?

In 1876 Alexander Graham Bell transmitted the first telephone message, and over the next century his company, now known as AT&T, built a communications empire. Telephone companies use a five-tier switched network to transmit calls. At each level of the network, a switching station, referred to simply as a **switch**, routes calls toward their destination. The first tier of this network physically connects each telephone in a city to a local switch in what's called a **central office (CO)**. The second tier links several local offices to toll switches. Connections then fan out to primary switches, sectional offices, and regional offices. Each tier of the telephone network serves a wider geographical region, as shown in Figure 10-2.

If you're a history buff, you might like to delve more deeply into the history of our communications infrastructure by doing the Communications Archeologist Project at the end of this chapter.

4. In Chicago, a central office forwards the call along the last segment of its journey to the receiver's phone.

Figure 10-2
Five-tiered telephone system *(continued)*

Chicago

Central Office

Regional Office

In Figure 10-2 notice that your telephone is directly connected only to the central office. Long distance calls are routed through toll, primary, sectional, and regional switches that you share with other telephone subscribers.

When the computer age dawned in the middle of this century, the telephone system connected virtually every home and business in Australia, Europe, and the United States, and a substantial number in Asia, Africa, and South America. Looking back, a marriage between telephones and computers seemed inevitable. Computers provide lightning fast data processing and tremendous capacity for storing data. The telephone system provides the pipeline for sending that data throughout the world.

Computer and telephone technologies, however, were not originally designed to be compatible. Telephones communicate using analog audio signals, but computers are digital devices that operate by turning voltages on and off. To send computer data over phone lines, it is necessary to convert digital pulses into analog audio waves. A device called a **modem** prepares computer data for transmission by converting digital pulses into audio tones, one tone representing a one bit, the other tone representing a zero bit. A modem also receives data by converting audio tones into digital pulses.

The term "modem" is derived from the words "modulate" and "demodulate." In communications terminology, **modulation** means changing the characteristics of a signal, as when a modem changes a digital pulse into an analog signal. **Demodulation** means changing a signal to its original state, as when a modem changes an audio signal back to a digital pulse.

Modulating a digital signal allows computers, fax machines, and other digital devices to use the telephone system for data transport. With a modem, computer users can connect their computers to the Internet. Banks use telephone lines to electronically transfer funds worldwide in a matter of seconds. Automated fax-back services provide customers with faxed information on topics they request. Universities provide registration and course scheduling using touch-tone phones. Franchise managers can access centralized warehouses to check product availability. Meetings between participants in different cities can take place using **desktop videoconference** technologies that transmit full-motion video captured by a camera attached to a computer. The number of applications for home and business continues to grow.

Inexpensive access is the primary advantage of the telephone system for computer communications. Most people have telephone service, so an inexpensive modem is all that's required to set up communications. Computer communications are virtually indistinguishable from voice communications, and so service charges are the same as for voice calls.

Plain old telephone service (called **POTS** by communications industry insiders) provides business and residential customers with dial-up lines. A **dial-up line** is a non-dedicated communications channel that creates a connection when you dial, then destroys the connection when the call is completed. POTS has limited carrying capacity. Using the latest modem technology, these lines have a maximum data transport capacity of about 30 kilobits per second. Some applications, such as videoconferencing, require more capacity than provided by these lines. Telephone companies are scrambling to offer higher capacity service such as ISDN, T1, and T3.

ISDN (Integrated Services Digital Network) service transports data digitally over dial-up or dedicated lines. A **dedicated line**, also called a **leased line**, is a permanent connection between two locations. Phone companies offer two grades of ISDN service: a basic service with 64 kilobits per second capacity and an enhanced service with 2 megabits per second capacity. **T1 service** provides 1.5 megabits per second capacity over a dedicated line. **T3 service** uses fiber-optic cables to provide dedicated service with a capacity of 45 megabits per second.

Many businesses pay higher rates to access high-capacity lines, but these services are not available in all areas. For many data communications applications, the telecommunications infrastructure is only as good as its weakest link. For example, suppose a law firm wants to have a videoconference between its home office in Washington, D.C., and a Nashville hotel, where one of the firm's lawyers is staying. If the Washington office has ISDN service but the hotel has only POTS lines, the POTS line would limit the speed of data transmission. At both sites the video images would appear as a series of still images instead of full-motion video.

A dial-up line makes a temporary connection when you dial. A dedicated line maintains a permanent connection between two designated locations.

Pulse and rotary dialing do not correspond to analog or digital telephone service. Most telephones equipped with touch-tone dialing still communicate using analog audio signals.

The Cellular Phone System

Can I use a computer with a cellular phone?

The **cellular phone system** was designed for mobile communications—for example, police cars that need to communicate with headquarters while on patrol and for business people who need to keep in touch with clients while traveling.

Instead of sending analog signals over a telephone cable to a central office, a cellular phone uses FM radio waves to communicate with a base station tower. Towers are spaced in the middle of a limited geographical area called a **cell**. Each cell provides 50 to 70 radio channels, one for each simultaneous call within the cell. From the tower, calls are routed to lines provided by the telephone system; calls to other cellular phones are routed to the tower currently serving that phone. When a call is in progress and you move from one cell to another, your call is switched from one tower to another.

Adjacent cells cannot use the same radio channels, but non-adjacent cells can. To see how this works, study Figure 10-3, which depicts each cell as a hexagon and represents groups of channels by a color.

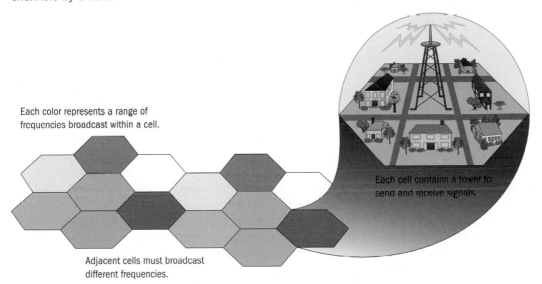

Each color represents a range of frequencies broadcast within a cell.

Each cell contains a tower to send and receive signals.

Adjacent cells must broadcast different frequencies.

Figure 10-3
Cell radio frequencies

Although the cellular phone system requires no cables, you can still transmit and receive computer data. Most cellular phone companies offer digital service; however, most cellular phone users send their data using cellular analog service. This unusual state of affairs exists because digital computer pulses must still be converted into a radio signal for cellular transmission. Conventional modem technology already provides inexpensive digital-to-analog conversion. With the help of another inexpensive converter box, called a **data module**, the signals from a conventional modem are easily transmitted over cellular analog service. You can use the same modem on a cellular system as on the regular telephone system. Figure 10-4 shows you how to connect a computer to a cellular phone.

Figure 10-4
Cellular computer
communications

The advantage of computer communication on the cellular phone system is mobility. Police can access local and national law enforcement computer databases while on patrol. Sales representatives can check their computerized scheduler and read e-mail while traveling. Repair technicians can access troubleshooting databases while on site. In the aftermath of natural disasters, essential data can still flow between government and service agencies.

The disadvantages of cellular communications include cost, reliability problems, and lack of security. Communications charges are considerably higher than the regular telephone system. You pay for **air time**, the number of minutes you are connected to towers when you place calls *and* when you receive calls. Per-minute charges vary from 30 cents to more than a dollar. Add to this any long distance charges you incur from a long distance service provider and surcharges for **roaming** calls placed outside of your local calling area.

Cellular transmissions are susceptible to more interference than communications that travel over regular telephone lines. Overloaded cellular channels are noisy with transmissions that sometimes spill over from other cells and with static caused by electrical equipment, high-tension wires, and other transmitting devices. Channel noise will cause your modem to drop the connection, forcing you to restart communications.

Communications over the cellular system are literally floating in the air and easy to intercept with the right equipment. When transmitting sensitive or confidential data over a cellular phone system, it is advisable to encrypt it.

The Cable Television System

Does the cable television system offer any facilities for computer communications?

In the past 20 years, cable television systems have connected an estimated 90% of the homes in the United States to cable stations. **Cable TV (CATV)** stations receive broadcasts via satellite, then rebroadcast them to homes via cables. Users pay a fee for this service, depending on the number and type of channels to which they subscribe. Figure 10-5 illustrates CATV technology.

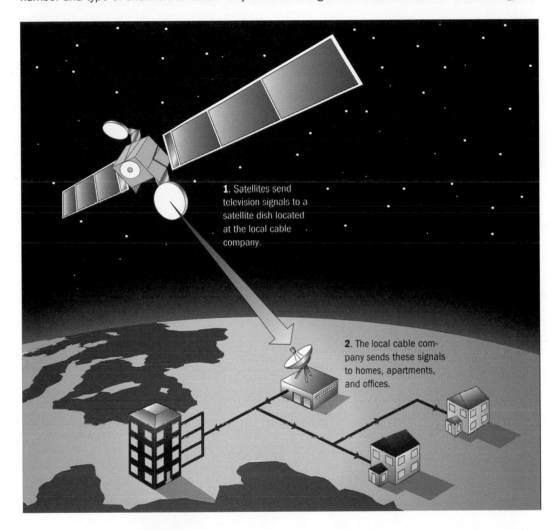

Figure 10-5
Cable television system technology

1. Satellites send television signals to a satellite dish located at the local cable company.

2. The local cable company sends these signals to homes, apartments, and offices.

The potential advantage of cable television systems for data communications is their cables. These cables, connected to every subscriber's home, have a carrying capacity of 4 to 10 megabits, far in excess of the capacity provided by POTS lines. Using a similar technology as the cables used in many local area networks, CATV cables are capable of carrying computer-based video, audio, and teleconferencing in addition to regular programming.

So why is your modem connected to the telephone system instead of the cable television system? The disadvantages of today's cable television system stem from its history as a one-way delivery channel. CATV signals are sent to homes, but there is no provision for signals to flow from homes back to the station, though two-way communication would be possible with the installation of additional sending and receiving devices. Another problem is the isolation of each cable company. Because local cable companies receive programming from satellites, there is no need to interconnect the various cable companies. Unless such connections were available, computer communications would be limited to the area served by the local cable company.

Cable company operators have spotted an opportunity to widen their market and are currently studying the technical and financial requirements. Stay tuned to see if a consortium of independent cable operators can challenge the telephone company's dominion in computer communications.

The Internet

Can the Internet take care of all my data communications needs?

The Internet began as an experiment to "nuke-proof" military communications. The original system, called ARPAnet, connected four sites: Stanford University, the University of California at Los Angeles and at Santa Barbara, and the University of Utah. To maintain communications in case a nuclear attack destroyed the connection between any of these two sites, the network employed packet-switching technology. **Packet switching** is a message delivery technique that divides a message into smaller units called packets. Each packet is addressed to its destination, but it might travel a different route than other packets. At the receiving end of the transmission, all the packets are gathered and reassembled. Packets can be routed to avoid congested or inoperable communications links, as shown in Figure 10-6.

Figure 10-6
Packet switching

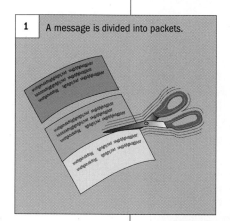

1 A message is divided into packets.

2 Each packet is addressed to its destination.

3 A packet might travel the shortest path to its destination.

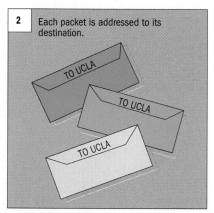

4 If a route is congested with heavy traffic or inoperable, packets can be rerouted via other links.

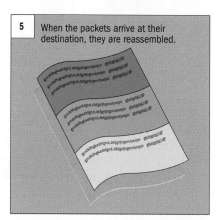

5 When the packets arrive at their destination, they are reassembled.

The original ARPAnet computers were connected by a dedicated digital line, but it was soon possible to dial in to these computers using a modem and analog telephone line. Today, these two types of connections still exist. Most Internet host computers are connected by dedicated lines. Users who want to access these hosts from home use a modem and a POTS line.

The Internet transports data in many formats, including text, graphics, sound, and video. With high-speed connections it is possible to establish full-motion videoconferencing over the Internet. Researchers are also studying the feasibility of Internet-based commercial video and radio services.

Both organizations and individuals have discovered the advantages of the Internet for transporting data across the globe. Businesses are increasingly using the Internet to transport data between their local area networks. In addition, businesses and universities often press the Internet's World Wide Web into service, using Web pages to post announcements, schedules, and other internal information.

Data transfer over the Internet backbone and between Internet servers is fast and dependable. However, most individuals who access the Internet do so using slow analog dial-up lines. Most experts agree that the Internet in its current form will not meet the data transport needs of a growing population of users, especially for graphics, audio, video, or teleconferencing applications. Plans to improve Internet technology are on the drawing board, but one of the main stumbling blocks is a feasible alternative to the slow communications links currently available for the "last mile" connection from Internet host computers to millions of homes.

Private Communication Systems

Is there any advantage to setting up a private communications network?

The telephone companies and other service providers generally furnish reliable communications channels backed by technical expertise and professional service. However, businesses sometimes have limited negotiating power when it comes to fees and services. To gain more financial and technological control, many organizations prefer to construct a private communications system. A **private communications system** is operated in-house to service intra-business communications needs. For communications outside the business, a private communications system usually connects to a commercial carrier such as the telephone system. Private branch exchanges and local area networks are typical private communications systems.

A **private branch exchange (PBX)** is essentially a mini-telephone system that includes the cables, telephones, and switching systems for communications within a building or campus. PBX equipment can be purchased or leased, but no monthly or per-call charges are assessed by an external service company. PBXs primarily carry voice communications, although technically they have the capability to carry computer data also.

A **local area network (LAN)** connects computers within a limited geographic area. Used mainly to exchange computer data, a LAN can be purchased, installed, and operated by an individual or business without fees or surcharges from external service companies. LANs can be connected to other communications systems to exchange computer data with other computers and networks. In Section 10.3 you'll take a more detailed look at LAN communications technology.

Quick Check

1. In a communications system, a source encodes data and sends it along a(n) _____.

2. The telephone system was designed to carry _____ audio signals.

3. POTS lines provide a temporary connection, but _____ lines provide a high-capacity permanent connection between two locations.

4. It is impossible to use a regular modem on a cellular phone system. True or false?

5. CATV cables offer a higher carrying capacity than POTS lines. True or false?

6. _____ switching is a message delivery technique that divides a message into smaller units, each addressed to its destination.

7. Most people who access the Internet do so using _____ lines.

8. Two popular private communications systems are _____ and _____.

10.2 | Data Communications

Data communications is the process of transmitting and receiving data in an orderly way so the data that arrives at its destination is an accurate duplication of the data that was sent. When data travels a short distance, such as when you send data from your computer to your printer, it is referred to as **local communications**. When data travels a long distance, the communication is referred to as **telecommunications**; the prefix "tele" is derived from a Greek word that means "far" or "far off."

The difference between a short distance and a long distance is somewhat arbitrary. For example, if your computer sends data to a printer in the next room, that transmission of data is regarded as local communications. However, if you phone the person in the next room, you are transmitting data over a telecommunications device. Because the same basic communications concepts apply to both local communications and telecommunications, in this chapter we will not further distinguish between the two.

Basic data communications concepts are the building blocks for understanding how data travels on a communications system. These concepts come in handy when you install, configure, or upgrade a local area network. In addition, these concepts help you set up modems, fax machines, and cellular data transfers.

In Section 10.1, you got an overview of today's communications systems. Here in Section 10.2, you will take a closer look at general communications concepts that apply to all communications systems.

Communications Signals

Exactly what is transmitted when I send a message?

When you use a modem to send a document from your computer to another computer or fax machine, symbols such as "A" and "!" don't somehow squirt through the phone cables. Instead, most of today's communications systems transmit messages and data in the form of electromagnetic signals. You can think of these signals as waves that ripple through cables (telephone, telegraph, CATV, Internet) or through the air (cellular phone, radio, broadcast TV, satellite and microwave transmissions.)

Like ocean waves, electromagnetic waves are characterized by their spacing and their height. The spacing between waves is referred to as the **frequency**. Waves that are spaced close together have a higher frequency than waves spaced far apart. The height of an electromagnetic wave is referred to as its **amplitude** (Figure 10-7). Waves with higher amplitudes are more powerful, louder in the case of sound waves, than waves with low amplitudes.

Figure 10-7
Wave frequency and amplitude

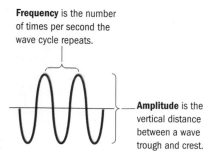

Frequency is the number of times per second the wave cycle repeats.

Amplitude is the vertical distance between a wave trough and crest.

Signal frequency is measured in Hertz (Hz). The sound signals that travel over phone lines have frequencies between 300 Hz and 3,000 Hz. Computer communications carried out using telephone company equipment use the same frequencies allocated to voice transmissions. For example, when sending a string of 1s and 0s for an ASCII code, a 0 is transmitted as a 1,070 Hz wave and a 1 is transmitted at 1,279 Hz.

Although we usually think of a wave as a smooth curve, waves can have different shapes. These shapes are referred to as **wave forms** or **wave patterns**. Analog signals may represent an unlimited range of values and, therefore, have a smooth, curved wave form. Digital signals, on the other hand, represent discrete values within a limited range and, therefore, have a square wave pattern. Compare the analog and digital wave patterns shown in Figure 10-8.

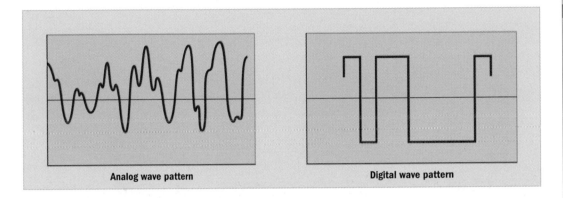

Analog wave pattern   **Digital wave pattern**

▶ **Figure 10-8**
Analog and digital wave patterns

Communications devices convert the frequency and wave form of signals that represent messages so that these signals can travel over a communications system. Let's look at an example. Your computer internally stores and moves the characters in a document as digital signals. To transmit this data over a phone line, a modem converts the digital signals into analog signals that travel over the wires in a phone cable. If you are sending this data across the country, it is likely to be further converted into a different frequency so it can be transmitted between the phone company's microwave towers. Alternatively, the signal might be converted into light waves and sent through a fiber-optic cable. If your data is traveling to a cellular phone, it will be further converted to a radio wave so it can be broadcast from the cellular tower.

You can compare an analog wave to the sweep of the second hand on an analog watch—it moves through a smooth curve. A digital wave, like the numbers on a digital watch switch abruptly from one value to another.

Channels and Communications Media

What technology options are available for carrying communications signals?

A **communications channel** is a physical or logical path for a signal transmission. For example, telephone cables provide a physical path for analog audio signals. However, a one-to-one correspondence between a channel and a communications link, such as a cable, does not exist. A single cable might be able to provide multiple channels. For instance, a CATV cable can carry the signals for many television programs, each on its own channel.

A **communications medium** carries one or more communications channels and provides a link between transmitting and receiving devices. The media most frequently used in today's communications systems include twisted-pair cable, coaxial cable, fiber-optic cable, microwave, radio waves, and infrared transmission.

A **twisted-pair cable** consists of pairs of copper wire twisted together. Each wire is covered with a thin layer of insulating plastic. The wires are bundled together to form a cable, as shown in Figure 10-9.

Figure 10-9
Twisted-pair cable

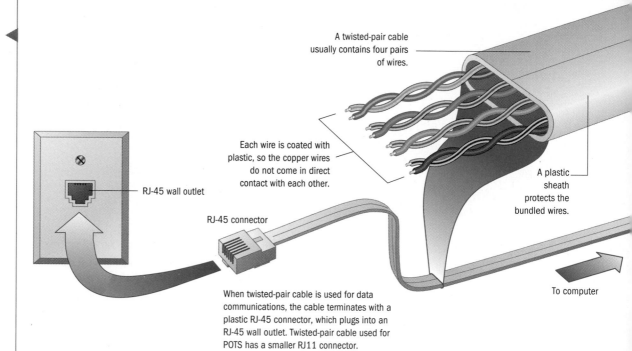

A twisted-pair cable usually contains four pairs of wires.

Each wire is coated with plastic, so the copper wires do not come in direct contact with each other.

A plastic sheath protects the bundled wires.

RJ-45 wall outlet

RJ-45 connector

To computer

When twisted-pair cable is used for data communications, the cable terminates with a plastic RJ-45 connector, which plugs into an RJ-45 wall outlet. Twisted-pair cable used for POTS has a smaller RJ11 connector.

Figure 10-10
Coaxial cable

Coaxial cable, often called **coax cable**, (pronounced "co-ax") is a high-capacity communications cable consisting of a copper wire conductor, a non-conducting insulator, woven metal outer shielding, and a plastic outer coating, as shown in Figure 10-10.

An insulator separates the center wire from the metallic sheath.

A T-shaped connector at the back of the computer attaches to a network interface card.

A metal BNC connector links the cable to a T-shaped connector on the back of the computer for data communications. Your cable TV connector is somewhat smaller.

Coaxial cable has a copper wire core.

The entire cable is protected with a braided copper shielding and a plastic coating.

Coaxial cable is used for cable television where its high capacity allows it to carry signals for more than 100 television channels simultaneously. It also provides good capacity for data communications and is used in situations where twisted-pair cable is not adequate to carry the required amount of data.

Coaxial cable used to be one of the most widely used cables for connecting computers in local area networks, however, today it is being replaced by twisted-pair cable, which is less expensive and easier to install. But for situations where high bandwidth is required, both coaxial cable and twisted-pair cable are being replaced by fiber-optic cable.

Fiber-optic cable is a bundle of extremely thin tubes of glass. Each tube, called an **optical fiber**, is much thinner than a human hair. A fiber-optic cable usually consists of a strong inner support wire; multiple strands of optical fiber each covered by a plastic insulator; and a tough outer covering, as shown in Figure 10-11.

A plastic coating protects the bundle of fibers.

A metal wire strengthens the cable so it cannot be bent at an angle that would break the glass fibers.

The cable contains many glass fibers.

The fiber and cladding are encased in a plastic coating.

The fiber is wrapped in a "cladding" that helps reflect the light that travels through the fiber.

The core of each fiber is a perfectly formed glass tube with a diameter less than that of human hair.

Figure 10-11
Fiber-optic cable

Fiber-optic cables do not conduct or transmit electrical signals. Instead, miniature lasers or LEDs (light emitting diodes) send pulses of light through the fibers. Electronics at the receiving end of the fiber convert the light pulses back into electrical signals. Each fiber is a one-way communications channel, which means that at least two fibers are required to provide a two-way communications link. Fiber-optic cable has a very high capacity so it is capable of transmitting large amounts of data.

Radio waves provide wireless transmission for mobile communications, such as cellular telephones, and in situations where it is difficult or impossible to install cabling, such as in remote, geographically rugged regions. Wireless communications channels are generally slower than cables, and they are more susceptible to static and radio interference.

Microwave transmission sends a high-frequency radio signal from a ground or satellite microwave transmitting station to a microwave receiving station. Microwave transmission is line-of-sight transmission, which means that no obstacles, such as mountains or buildings, can be located between the transmitting and receiving stations. Microwave transmissions can also be affected by heavy rain and snow, which block the microwaves. Microwave stations cannot be more than 25 or 30 miles apart because at farther distances, the curve of the earth blocks transmission. To avoid this problem, many communications systems use communications satellites. Communications satellites are generally placed in geosynchronous orbits about 22,300 miles above the earth. A satellite in a **geosynchronous orbit** stays above the same part of the earth by orbiting around the earth at the same speed as the earth rotates.

Infrared transmissions use a frequency range just below the visible light spectrum to transport data. Infrared is a popular communications medium for local area networks in buildings where cabling is difficult. An inexpensive device attached to each computer sends and receives infrared signals.

Bandwidth

Why do some communications systems have a higher capacity than others?

The capacity of a communications system depends on the bandwidth of the channels it uses. **Bandwidth** is the range of frequencies that a channel can carry. The bandwidth of an analog signal is expressed in Hertz (Hz) and is calculated by subtracting the lowest channel frequency from the highest one, as shown in Figure 10-12.

Figure 10-12
Calculating bandwidth

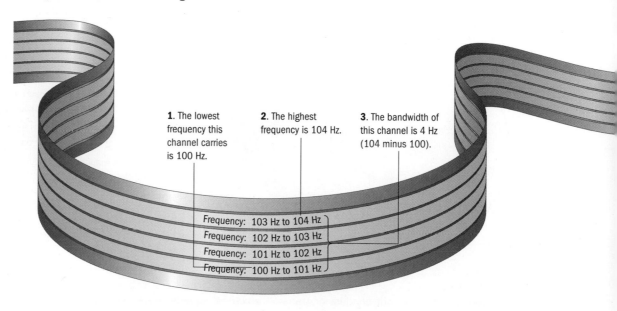

1. The lowest frequency this channel carries is 100 Hz.

2. The highest frequency is 104 Hz.

3. The bandwidth of this channel is 4 Hz (104 minus 100).

Frequency: 103 Hz to 104 Hz
Frequency: 102 Hz to 103 Hz
Frequency: 101 Hz to 102 Hz
Frequency: 100 Hz to 101 Hz

Bandwidth is simply a measure of the amount of data a channel can carry. Just as a large pipe can carry more water than a small pipe, a channel with a large bandwidth can carry more data than a channel with a small bandwidth.

Of the communications media discussed so far in this chapter, twisted-pair and coaxial cables have the least bandwidth. Radio waves used for microwave, cellular phone, and satellite transmissions have much higher bandwidths. Fiber-optic cable has the highest potential bandwidth.

Transmission Speed

How fast can computer data travel over a communications channel?

The speed of digital communications is measured in bits per second (bps). Although bandwidth is a measure of the capacity of a communications channel, it does not necessarily coincide with the speed at which you can transmit your data. Many communications channels work something like an airport conveyor belt. The conveyor belt moves at a constant speed. If you have three pieces of luggage and you are the only person on the plane, your bags will arrive one right after another. However, if you have just arrived on a full 747, your bags will be intermixed with those of hundreds of passengers and it will take longer for you to get them. The packets of data you send over a communications channel are like pieces of luggage. When a communications channel is busy, it takes longer to send and receive data.

Digital communications speeds are measured in bits (not bytes) per second.

Signal Direction

Do all channels send and receive data?

You use a CB radio differently from the way you use the telephone—with a CB radio, you must press a button when you are ready to send and release the button when you want to receive; with a telephone you don't have to take any action to switch between talking and listening. The way you use a communications device—whether you need to press a button to talk, for example—depends on the communications mode.

Simplex communication allows communication in only one direction. A radio transmitter uses simplex communication—it can transmit, but it cannot receive signals.

Half-duplex communication allows you to send or receive, but not to do both at the same time. A CB radio is an example of half-duplex transmission. The CB radio is in receive mode until you press the "talk" button.

Duplex or **full-duplex communication** allows you to send and receive at the same time. A telephone line is an example of full-duplex communication; most computer communications take place in this mode.

Some communications are sent and then echoed back to the sender as a means of checking accuracy. This type of communication is referred to as **echoplex**, or simply as an **echo**. Echoplex is useful in situations when it is important to be absolutely certain that data was transmitted accurately.

Transmission Mode

Is there any way to stuff more data down a channel?

Communications engineers have developed many ways to speed up communications. This has been a key area of research for computer communications, which are not limited (as are human communications) by the pace of human speech.

Most communications take place serially: One piece of information follows another. For a computer, **serial transmission** means that a byte is broken down into individual bits that are transmitted one after another over the communications medium. Faster data transfer can be achieved by **parallel transmission**, in which all the bits for an entire byte are sent at the same time. Parallel transmission requires a communications media that can carry simultaneous units of data. In computer systems, this is usually achieved using a parallel cable that contains one wire for each bit.

Serial transmission is typically used for modem and network communications. Parallel transmission is typically used for sending data to a printer.

Communications Protocols

How does a communications channel deal with interference?

In Shannon's communications system model, noise sometimes interferes with transmissions. For example, suppose that you were sending a message to a business colleague, "Let's meet at the exhibition hall at 5:00 p.m. for dinner." As the sequence of bits for the word "hall" travels across the communications channel, some interference changes a single bit. The "a" in the word "hall," which was transmitted as 01100001, arrives at its destination as 01101001, which is the ASCII code for the letter "i." When "hall" is changed to "hill," the meaning of your message has been altered. This is a fairly innocent example, but transmission errors that change letters or numbers—such as a digit on your paycheck—could have disastrous effects.

To ensure that the data you transmit is not altered by noise or interference, both the sending and the receiving computers must follow a set of communications protocols. **Communications protocols** are rules that ensure the orderly and accurate transmission and reception of data. A simple manual communications protocol is to include the zip code when you address packages you send by U.S. mail. If you omit the zip code, the package might not arrive at its destination.

Without protocols, data communication is impossible. When two devices communicate they must agree on protocols for starting and ending a transmission, recognizing transmission errors, sending data at the right speed, and formatting or packaging the data.

Parity

Can a computer detect if it has received data altered by line noise?

Computers use error-checking protocols to ensure accurate delivery of data. One error-checking protocol uses a **parity bit** to describe the number of 0s or 1s in a sequence of data. The transmitting computer attaches a parity bit to the transmitted data. The parity bit is either a 0 or a 1, depending on the protocol. With **even parity**, the number of 1 bits in a data block is an even number. With **odd parity**, the number of 1 bits in the data block is an odd number. Let's look at an example.

Suppose that a computer is sending the ASCII code 0011001 under an even parity protocol. The ASCII code contains three 1's—an odd number. Because even parity requires an even number of 1s, the computer must attach a 1 and send out the code 10011001. The computer that receives the 10011001 checks to make sure it contains an even number of 1s. If it does not, a bit probably got changed during transmission and the data will need to be retransmitted. Study Figure 10-13 to find out more about how the computer assigns parity bits.

The 8-bit ANSI code for the letter "A" has an even number of 1 bits.

For even parity, the computer adds a 0 parity bit. By doing so, the data block, which is now 9 bits, still has an even number of 1 bits.

The 8-bit ANSI code for the letter "Q" has an odd number of 1 bits.

For even parity, the computer adds a 1 parity bit. By doing so, the data block now has an even number of 1 bits.

3. When the data block arrives, the receiver checks the total number of 1 bits. There is an odd number of 1 bits, which is not correct under even parity. The receiver transmits a message back to the sender requesting that the data block be transmitted again.

2. Noise in the channel changes the second bit from 1 to 0.

1. The computer transmits the data block that contains the ANSI code for the letter "A" including the 0 parity bit.

Figure 10-13
Parity

When a computer adds a parity bit to ANSI or EBCDIC-encoded data, each character requires nine, instead of eight, bits. However, the parity bit is removed when the data reaches its destination, so storage requirements do not increase.

Synchronous and Asynchronous Protocols

How does the receiving computer know when the transmission begins and ends?

A major challenge with serial communications is coordinating the transmission and the reception. The transmitting computer sends a series of bits, but if the receiving computer misses the first three bits of a serial transmission, the message would be hopelessly garbled, as shown in Figure 10-14.

1. The word "Hello" is encoded as ANSI, then transmitted. Each set of 8 bits represents one character. In a successful transmission, "Hello" arrives at its destination.

2. If the receiving device misses the first 3 bits of data, the message becomes garbled.

3. These 3 bits were missed by the receiving device.

4. When the first 3 bits are missed, the receiving device regards the next 8 bits as an ANSI code. The last 5 bits from the letter "H" and the first 3 bits from the letter "e" are 01000011, or the letter "C".

Figure 10-14
A garbled data transmission

There are two ways to coordinate serial communication, referred to as synchronous and asynchronous protocols. Using **synchronous protocol**, the sender and the receiver are synchronized by a signal called a clock. The transmitting computer sends data at a fixed rate, and the receiving computer expects the incoming data at the same fixed rate. Much of the communication that takes place on the main circuit board of a computer is synchronous; however, communication between two microcomputers rarely uses the synchronous protocol.

Computers typically use asynchronous protocol when they communicate using modems. Using **asynchronous protocol**, the sending computer transmits a start bit to indicate the beginning of the data. Next, the sending computer transmits the data as a series of bits, called a block. The end of each block is indicated by transmitting one or more stop bits, as shown in Figure 10-15.

Figure 10-15
Asynchronous
protocol

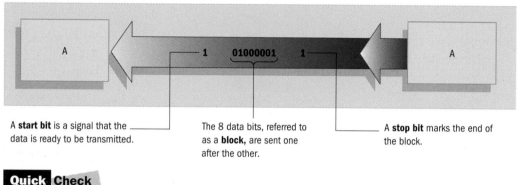

A **start bit** is a signal that the data is ready to be transmitted.

The 8 data bits, referred to as a **block,** are sent one after the other.

A **stop bit** marks the end of the block.

Quick Check

1 _____ is the range of frequencies that a channel can carry.

2 The speed of digital communications is measured in _____ per second.

3 A telephone line is an example of a(n) _____ channel, whereas a radio is an example of a simplex channel.

4 Communication _____ are rules that ensure the orderly and accurate transmission and reception of data.

5 A computer using _____ parity would need to add a 1 bit to 11011100 before sending it.

6 Most data communications are asynchronous. True or false?

Local Area Network Communications

Lab

Building a Network

ocal area networks are an integral part of today's computing environment. Therefore, it is likely that you might participate in constructing, configuring, or upgrading a network. To understand network communications, you can apply what you have learned so far about communications systems and data communications.

Think of a network as a railroad system that transports cargo (data) between destinations (workstations). Like railroad tracks, network cables provide physical connections between workstations. Network software does the work of shipping companies, "packing" each shipment (message) into acceptable containers, making sure each container is addressed to the correct destination, and verifying that each container arrives at its final destination. Network hardware directs the flow of data over network cables, in much the same way that railroad dispatchers direct the movement of trains on the railroad tracks to prevent collisions and to make sure that each train arrives at its assigned destination.

Network Connections

How are the devices on a LAN connected to each other?

A computer network might transfer data or messages between hundreds of devices, much like a railroad system delivers freight to hundreds of towns. In a railroad system, each town is connected to the rest of the system by a track. In a computer network, each network device is connected to the rest of the network by cable, radio waves, or infrared beam. Today's networks rely mostly on cable connections.

Network cable is typically arranged in one of two ways. Cables can branch out to each workstation from a central device called a **concentrator**, **hub**, or **MAU (multistation access unit)**. Alternatively, the cable can run directly from one workstation to another, connecting them in a series, as shown in Figure 10-16.

► **Figure 10-16**
Network cabling

Cables branch out from a central hub, concentrator, or MAU.   Cables run from one workstation to another.

Each device on a network requires a network interface card to establish a data pathway between a computer and the network communications channel. A network interface card plugs into an expansion slot in the computer main board or into a PCMCIA slot. A cable plugged into the interface card connects the computer to the rest of the network, as diagrammed in Figure 10-17.

Figure 10-17
Network interface
card connections

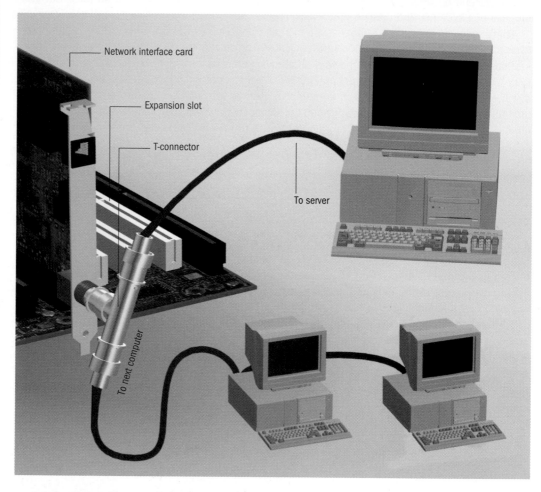

A network interface card supports a particular network standard. A **network standard** is a set of communications protocols for orderly transmission of data. Every device on a network must use the same network standard or else it cannot communicate and share the network resources. Popular network standards include Ethernet, Token Ring, and ARCnet.

Ethernet, the most popular network standard, typically transmits data at 10 megabits per second. Ethernet network interface cards are available from many manufacturers at very competitive prices. **Token Ring**, the second most popular network standard, transmits data at either 4 megabits or 16 megabits per second. Token Ring network interface cards are usually more expensive than Ethernet cards. **ARCnet**, a third network standard, transmits data at either 2 megabits or 20 megabits per second.

Other network standards support much higher transmission rates. **FDDI**, **ATM**, and **Fast-Ethernet** transmit data at 100 megabits per second. These high transmission rates are ideal for high-traffic applications, such as network access to multimedia and video.

All the devices on a network must use the same network standard. Therefore, new devices added to a network must use the same type of network interface card as the other devices on the network. For example, all the devices on an Ethernet network must use Ethernet cards.

Network Data Packets

When I send a document to the network server, does the entire file travel as a single transmission?

A railroad dispatcher makes sure that a train arrives at its destination. However, the dispatcher doesn't pack the cargo on the train, address individual boxes, or unpack the cargo at the destination. These tasks are handled by a shipping company. Network software works like a shipping company to package and address messages, then unpack them at the destination workstation.

To see how the network software works, let's suppose that you are working with a data file stored on the file server. When you open or save this file, it is sent between your workstation and the file server. The network does not send the entire data file as a unit because transmitting a long file ties up the entire network until the transmission is complete. Instead, the network transmits the file as a series of messages, called **packets**. Each packet contains the address of the destination workstation, the "return address" of the sending workstation, and a small segment of the data file. The network software on the receiving workstation reassembles the complete file from the segments that arrive in each packet.

Network software uses a **network communications protocol**, which specifies the structure of the packets. To send and receive packets successfully, the sending and receiving workstations must use software with the same network communications protocol.

The most widely used network communication protocols are TCP/IP, IPX, LAT, and AFP. **TCP/IP (transmission control protocol/Internet protocol)** is used on microcomputer, minicomputer, and mainframe networks. TCP/IP is frequently used on UNIX systems and is the basis for communication on the Internet, the world's largest computer network. **IPX (Internetwork packet exchange)** is the protocol used by Novell NetWare, the most popular microcomputer network software. **LAT (local area transport**, also known as **DECnet)** is a network protocol developed by Digital Equipment Corporation (DEC) for use with its minicomputers. **AFP** was developed by Apple Computer, Inc. for AppleTalk networks and Apple Macintosh computers.

Transmitting Data Over a Network

How does a network interface card transmit a packet to a specific workstation?

A railroad system needs dispatchers to direct trains to their appropriate destinations and make sure that trains do not collide. Network interface cards and network switching devices perform functions similar to those of a railroad dispatcher—directing data to the appropriate workstation and trying to prevent collisions.

The way a network distributes packets to workstations depends on the network standard. An Ethernet network distributes packets quite differently from a Token Ring network. On an Ethernet network, before a network interface card sends a packet, it checks to see if the network is busy. If another network interface card is sending a packet, it waits and tries again later. If the network is not busy, the network interface card broadcasts the packet to every device on the network. Every device receives the packet, but it is accepted only by the device to which it is addressed.

Sometimes, two devices on an Ethernet network simultaneously check the network and see that it's not busy. These two devices then send packets at the same instant. When two packets are sent at the same time, it's called a **collision**. Ethernet networks use a method called **carrier sense multiple access with collision detection (CSMA/CD)** to deal with collisions. When messages collide, both devices stop sending and wait for a random period of time before attempting to send again. You can probably see why it is essential that both devices wait a random period of time. If the devices were designed to wait for a specific period of time, both would wait and try again at the same time, resulting in another collision. They would continue to wait and collide,

Packets were discussed earlier in this chapter in conjunction with packet-switching networks. Refer back to the first frames of Figure 10-6 for an illustration of how data is divided into packets.

It is easy to confuse network standards and network protocols. Network standards such as Ethernet, Token Ring, and ARCnet apply to network hardware. Network protocols such as TCP/IP and IPX apply to network communications software.

Ethernet and Token Ring are two of the most popular types of networks. This section explains some of the major differences in how these two networks operate.

wait and collide, and never send the message. Figure 10-18 shows how packets are transmitted on an Ethernet network.

Figure 10-18
How Ethernet works

1. One of the workstations checks the network to make sure it is not busy, then broadcasts a packet. The packet is addressed to workstation #21, but all the workstations receive it. Every workstation examines the address of the packet, but only the workstation to which it is addressed reads it.

2. If the workstations simultaneously check the network, find it is not busy, and send packets at the same time, a collision occurs.

3. When a collision occurs, a special signal travels over the network to indicate that it is "jammed." This signal lasts a fraction of a second, then the network is again ready for traffic. The two workstations that had sent simultaneous packets each wait for a random length of time before trying to send their packets again.

On a token-passing network, such as Token Ring or ARCnet, a special message called a **token** continuously travels around the network. The token carries a signal to indicate whether the token is busy or available to carry a packet. If a device wants to send a packet, it waits for the token. If the token is busy, the device must wait. If the token is available, the device attaches the packet to the token, sets a signal to indicate the token is busy, and sends the token on its way. As the token passes each device, the network interface card checks the address and accepts the packet if it is addressed to that device. The token and message continue traveling around the network until they return to the sending device. The sending device then removes the packet, sets the signal to indicate the token is available, and sends the token on down the cable. The token prevents collisions. Figure 10-19 shows how packets are transmitted on token-passing networks.

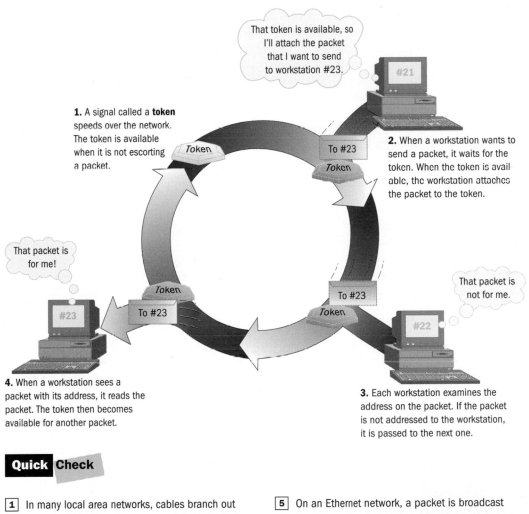

Figure 10-19
How token passing works

Quick Check

1. In many local area networks, cables branch out to each workstation from a central device called a(n) _____ .

2. Ethernet, Token Ring, and ARCnet are popular network _____ .

3. Network _____ packages and addresses data before it is sent over the network.

4. TCP/IP, IPX, and LAT are examples of network _____ .

5. On an Ethernet network, a packet is broadcast to all the network devices, not just the device to which it is addressed. True or false?

6. When packets collide on an Ethernet network, the packet with the highest address goes first. True or false?

7. On some networks a special message called a(n) _____ continuously travels around the network carrying packets.

User Focus:

10.4

Setting Up a Modem

The data communications concepts you learned in this chapter are not abstract concepts. Communicating with another computer using a modem is common today; to do so you must be able to configure your modem and communications program correctly.

Suppose you just purchased a new modem and want to try it out by calling a local computer bulletin board, where you can leave messages for other computer users, play games, and search for information. How do you connect your modem to your computer and then set it up to communicate with the bulletin board?

The steps you take to set up your modem depend on the brand of modem you purchased, the type of computer you have, and the operating system your computer uses. This User Focus section provides some general guidelines for setting up modem communications. You'll learn about connecting a modem to your computer and telephone, configuring your communications software, setting communications protocols, and dialing automatically. You'll also discover where people typically run into problems while trying to get their modem to work correctly.

Connecting a Modem to Your Computer

How do I connect a modem to a computer?

When you purchase a modem, you can select one of two types: external or internal. An **external modem** is housed in its own box and is connected by cable to a serial port on a computer. An **internal modem** is a circuit board that plugs into an expansion slot inside a computer. Both internal and external modems function identically. Some people prefer external modems because they can be easily moved from one computer to another and because they have a display panel that can be used to diagnose communication problems. Other people prefer internal modems because they take up less desk space, don't require a cable, and are generally less expensive.

To connect your modem to the telephone system you must unplug the cable from the back of your telephone and plug it into the modem. If you want to use the phone as well as the modem, you must connect another piece of cable from your modem to your telephone, as shown in Figure 10-20.

Figure 10-20
Connecting a modem to your computer and phone

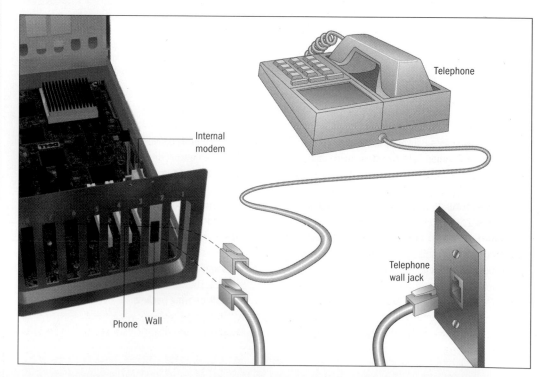

Configuring Communications Software

How does the computer know how to use a modem?

Your communications software orchestrates the interconnected functions of the modem, computer, and telephone system. Your next step is to configure your communications software by supplying information about the modem, computer, and phone system.

Windows 95 uses its plug-and-play feature to detect newly installed equipment automatically and search its equipment database for the information needed to operate a new device. If you don't have a plug-and-play operating system, you must use communications software to configure your modem manually. Your communications software might show you a screen like the one in Figure 10-21.

You will also need to enter information about your telephone service, such as whether you have tone or pulse dialing capability.

If your communications software was supplied with your modem, all the modem-specific settings should have been entered by the manufacturer.

You will need to enter computer-specific information such as the COM port on your computer to which your modem is attached.

Figure 10-21 Using communications software to manually configure your modem

Usually, your communications software comes with typical settings already entered. You need only change those settings that are different for your computer system. Two settings that typically differ from one computer to another are the COM port used for the modem and whether your phone supports pulse or tone dialing.

IBM-compatible computers have up to four serial communications ports: COM1, COM2, COM3, and COM4. If your computer has a mouse, it usually uses serial port COM1. Because your modem cannot use the same port as another device, it should use COM2. If you try to use a modem and you don't hear a dialing sound when the communications program should be dialing, the modem might be connected to one serial port while the communications software is sending its commands to another. In this case, you must configure your communications software to use a different COM port.

When you want to communicate with another computer, the modem must "dial" the telephone number for the other computer. The modem can dial the number for you, but it must be set up for pulse or touch-tone dialing, depending on the type of telephone service you have. Your communications software can help you specify the type of telephone service so the modem can use the correct dialing signals.

Setting Protocols

How do I set communications protocols for the various computers with which I want to communicate?

Communications protocols vary, depending on the computer at the other end of your connection. For example, the protocols you use to connect to the Internet are different from those you would use to connect to a bulletin board or a commercial information service such as CompuServe. Your communications software helps you select the protocols for a communication session.

The protocols you set for a typical dial-up connection include transmission speed, word size, stop bits, and parity. Suppose that you want to contact a local bulletin board at 555-9509. You talked to the bulletin board operator who told you to set up your communications protocols for eight data bits, no parity, and one stop bit.

The bulletin board requires an eight-bit word. This means the bulletin board sends data in packets of eight bits. Document files, as well as graphics and sounds files, must be divided into eight-bit packets as they are sent.

Communications with the bulletin board require one stop bit. You learned in this chapter that a stop bit is an extra bit sent after each block to indicate that the complete block has been sent. Start bits and stop bits are used with asynchronous communication to coordinate the sending and receiving devices.

The bulletin board requires no parity. You know that a parity bit is used to check for transmission errors caused by noise in the channel. With even parity, the number of 1 bits in a data block must be an even number. With odd parity, the number of 1 bits in the data block is odd. If a communications system uses no parity, it does not use a parity bit to detect errors.

Your communications software provides you with a mini-database where you can enter the number of the bulletin board along with the correct communications protocols. Once you have entered this information and saved it, you can use it any time you want to communicate with this bulletin board, as shown in Figure 10-22.

Figure 10-22
Selecting a number using communications software

Clicking the Data List button displays a database of phone numbers.

Here is one person's list of frequently called bulletin boards and commercial information services.

The computer dials this number to establish a connection.

The database includes the communications settings needed for each connection. For example, 19200-8-N-1 means connect at 19200 bps, use 8 data bits, no parity, and 1 stop bit.

Dialing

Both my telephone and computer are connected to the wall jack. Do I just dial the phone to begin computer communications?

When you want to initiate computer communications, your computer needs to dial the number. To do this, you select the bulletin board from the mini-database in your communications software. The communications software tells the modem to send the dialing signals out to the phone cable. Most modems have a speaker, so you can hear the tones as the number is dialed. You should be able to hear the phone ring at the bulletin board. The bulletin board's modem will answer with a high-pitched tone. Then begins a conversation of tones, squawks, and hisses like the one described in the beginning of this chapter as the two modems agree on protocols. Soon, you should see the bulletin board's welcome message, and you're ready to communicate!

End Note
Computers are no longer isolated devices, thanks to a communications infrastructure that integrates telephone lines, satellites, and radio transmitters. This evolving communications infrastructure is also having a profound effect on the way people work and socialize. Here's one person's account:

"I guess you could call me a telecommuter because I work at home, but I like to think of myself as a virtual employee. To my coworkers it seems like I'm right next door. Actually, I live and work in a different city. I have two phone lines at home—one for voice communications and one for my computer and my fax machine. I also have a voice mail system at "corporate" that takes calls from my customers. Many of them don't know I'm virtual.

"My desktop videoconference system lets me attend meetings without leaving home. I can instantly fax documents to my customers and coworkers. FedEx drives up to my door to collect documents that cannot be transmitted electronically because they require signatures. I don't need to trek to the library to do market research. Instead, I fire up my computer and surf the Internet. I avoid telephone tag by sending e-mail. If the person I need to contact doesn't have an e-mail account, I use AT&T's message delivery system—they place the call and deliver the message.

"Entertainment? Of course I have cable TV, but I spend more time answering e-mail from my friends. It's a great way to keep in touch and it's nice to know that I can just fire off a message to my friends in Germany or India and it will be in their mailbox within minutes. OK, I admit that I spend time playing virtual reality games on the Internet. I also hang out with other people in my profession through Internet Usenet groups and chat rooms on commercial information services. That's where I heard about this graduate course at Colorado State University. I registered and took the course. Never went to campus. I watched televised lectures and submitted all my coursework using the Internet. It was actually fun."

This is today. Imagine the future!

Review

1. Arrange the boldface terms in this chapter into one of the following categories: communications services, communications protocols, communications devices, communications channels, miscellaneous.

2. Without looking back in this chapter, try to sketch out Shannon's communications system model and add appropriate labels. When your sketch is complete, compare it to Figure 10-1 and make any necessary corrections.

3. List and describe some of the different services offered by telephone companies for data communications.

4. Describe how you could use the cellular phone system for data communications.

5. List the advantages and disadvantages of CATV systems for data communications.

6. Design a poster illustrating how packet switching works.

7. This chapter provided an example of simplex (radio), half-duplex (CB radio), and full-duplex (telephone) communications. Can you think of at least one more example of each?

8. Suppose you are a computer packaging data for transmission and you must assign a parity bit. Given each of the following bytes and the required parity, fill in the table to indicate if you would add a 1 or a 0 as the parity bit:

Byte	Parity	Parity bit (1 or 0)
10000011	even	
11100100	even	
00000000	even	
10011001	odd	
10000111	odd	
11111110	odd	

9. Suppose you are a fifth grade teacher and your students are asking you questions about your school's local area network. You decide to explain how a network works by using a railroad analogy. Either write a short lesson or design a series of posters explaining how LAN communications work.

10. Review Section 10.4 and distill the information into a series of numbered steps that someone could follow to set up a 14.4 bps modem to dial in to a bulletin board that uses a seven-bit word size, one stop bit, and even parity.

Projects

INTERNET
OPTIONAL

1. Communications Archeologist Using information from this chapter, from your library, and the Internet, make a list of important artifacts (objects) in the evolution of communications systems. Make sure you can associate a date with each of these artifacts. Now suppose it is the year 2500 and you are an archeologist newly arrived from another planet. You see these artifacts in a museum. How would you use them to explain the evolution of communications systems on planet Earth? Write a report detailing your theories about the evolution of Earth communications systems, using diagrams, time lines, and other visual elements.

INTERNET
OPTIONAL

2. Modem Shopping In today's computing environment, a modem is an essential piece of equipment for accessing the Internet, commercial information services, and bulletin boards. Suppose you have a computer and want to purchase a modem. Look in current computer magazines or in an online shopping mall for a modem ad. When you find one, answer the following questions:

a. Where did you find the ad? (List the magazine, issue, and page number, or list the Internet source and its URL.)

b. Who manufactures the modem?

c. What is the speed of the modem?

d. Is it an internal or an external modem?

e. Does this modem come with communications software?

f. Does the modem have additional features such as fax capability? If so, what are these additional features?

3. 2001 Today In 1945 a young British engineer and aspiring writer (who later wrote the science fiction classic, *2001: A Space Odyssey*) conceived the idea of artificial satellites that would orbit the earth in geosynchronous orbit. It was not until 1960 that the United States launched an inflatable satellite called Echo I, which transmitted and received voice, music, and data from Earth. Satellite technology opened up new horizons in communications, now incorporated in telephone and CATV systems. Use your library and Internet resources to learn more about satellite technology. Then create a brief information brochure describing satellite technology. You can select your target audience (elementary school children, college students, seniors, science club members, etc.). Your instructor might specify that you should use word processing or desktop publishing software to produce your brochure.

4. The Scoop on Data Communications Suppose you are a news reporter for your student newspaper. What do you think other students would like to know about using their computers for data communications? Write a two-page article targeted at student use of the communications infrastructure available at your school.

5. Communications in the Workplace Your career field probably makes extensive use of communications technologies. To prepare for your career you should understand which communications technologies are used and how to use them. Research and write a paper describing how communications technologies are used in your career field. At the end of the paper, include a list of these technologies. Check off those that you currently know how to use.

6. Communications Tour Arrange to tour an office at your school or a local business. As part of the tour, interview your tour guide about technologies used for internal and external communications. Don't forget low-tech options such as U.S. mail. Create a diagram to illustrate what you learned about the flow of communications into and out of the office you toured.

7. Claude Shannon Many of today's communications technologies are based on Claude Shannon's theories of communication, now referred to as information theory. One of Shannon's biographers describes the impact of information theory as "ranging from the efficient transmission systems for communication for the Voyager and Galileo spacecraft, the efficient coding of television and speech, the analysis of radar systems, and the error-correcting encoding endemic in computers and compact discs, and on to new insights in cryptography and to many rather general appli-

cations in a host of fields." Write your own mini-biography of Shannon, describing how his work is reflected in today's communications technologies. Your instructor will give you guidelines for the length of the paper and the format for page layout and footnotes.

8. The Road Ahead The Internet is increasingly used as a general communications service. What began as a conduit for transmitting text-based documents has evolved into a channel for documents, graphics, sound, and video. The press has dubbed the Internet the "Information Superhighway." Most experts agree, however, that the Information Superhighway is not yet a reality. As Microsoft chairman Bill Gates points out in his book *The Road Ahead*, "Today's Internet is not the information highway I imagine, although you can think of it as the beginning of the highway." What is the Information Superhighway? To find out, research in your local library (including Gates' book) and on the Internet. From the information you collect, create a table that shows in one column what's available on the Information Superhighway today and in another column what's anticipated for the Information Superhighway of the future.

9. Is It Shrinking? We've all heard people exclaim that communications are shrinking the globe. It's an understandable image for a world in which you can pick up a telephone and call someone in Singapore or watch television images of events taking place right now in virtually any country in the world. But how does this technology affect people? What are the advantages and the disadvantages of instant access and worldwide communications? Make a list of at least 10 advantages and disadvantages. Then do a little research to find out what the experts think. Write an essay that presents your opinion about how society can best deal with the impact of new and planned communications technologies. Your instructor will give you guidelines for the essay's length and format.

10. Distance Learning and the Virtual Classroom In this chapter's End Note you heard from someone who had taken a university course without going to campus. Referred to as "distance education," such courses are being taken by an increasing number of students who complete them at home with the use of computer and communications technology. Suppose you were enrolled in a distance education program this semester. How would you receive and submit your assignments, do research, and communicate with your instructors and with other students? Imagine that you had access to any computer and communications technologies that exist today, and suppose that money is no object—what would be your ideal distance education environment? Write a paper describing a typical "school day" with your ideal distance education environment and explain the technologies you would use for the courses you are taking this semester.

Resources

- *Communications.* Alexandria, VA: Time-Life Books, 1986. This book is an excellent reference on the history of the telecommunications industry, and it presents fundamental concepts of communications in a clear and interesting format. The editors of this series have done a good job of selecting timeless, underlying concepts that do not change over time. Consequently, the relatively old publication date does not significantly influence the book's value as a reference.

- **Feibel, W.** *Novell's Complete Encyclopedia of Networking.* San Jose: Novell Press, 1995. The introduction to this book contains a warning, "This book is not up to date, and never has been. If you read this paragraph again tomorrow, the book will be even less up to date than it is today." Nonetheless, this book contains a very complete description of the terms and concepts important to networking and data communications. The printed edition of the book also includes a CD version so you can search and cross reference online.

- **Gates, W.** *The Road Ahead.* New York: Penguin Books, 1995. As chairman of the most successful software company in history, Bill Gates could be expected to have some valuable insights on the direction of computing and communications. Gates produced this book as his contribution to discussions about how to develop the Information Superhighway. He provides a collection of the many social and technical issues that need to be addressed as we move forward in this age of information.

- *http://dist_ed.alaska.edu* The University of Alaska Distance Learning Center site contains many references and resources related to distance education. Here you will also find plentiful links to other distance education sites.

- *http://globeandmail.ca/Editorial/Archives* A Canadian publication, *The Globe and Mail* contains supplements and columns that focus on communications, computers, and technology. One of the supplements, Highway00.html, contains a collection of articles on the Information Superhighway.

- *http://www.hotwired.com/wired/scenarios* A featured topic from the December 1995 issue of *Wired* magazine, this site contains the text of a series of articles written by futurists such as Paul Saffo, Stewart Brand,

John Perry Barlow, and Bruce Sterling. Where is technology taking us? Browse through these Web pages to find out.

- *http://www.math.washington.edu/~hillman/entropy. html* This site contains the text of *A Primer on Information Theory* by Thomas D. Schneider, written for people who are "made a little nervous by the word logarithm." You'll need a PostScript viewer for your browser software to read the text.

- *http://www.open.ac.uk* The Open University is one of the largest and most respected distance education institutions in the world, with more than 200,000 graduate and undergraduate students. At this site you can learn a lot about distance education.

- *http://www.openu.edu* The Open University in Florida offers undergraduate and graduate courses in business, entrepreneurship, and professional development. Its Web site contains interesting material about traditional versus non-traditional systems of education.

- *http://www.racal.com/networking.html* This is an excellent Web site for information on data communications—modems, LANs, ISDN, and so on. The Ethernet section even includes a drawing of the first Ethernet system by its inventor, Robert Metcalfe.

- *http://www.well.com/user/hlr/texts/tft6.html* At this site you will find the full text of Chapter Six from the book *Tools for Thought: The People and Ideas of the Next Computer Revolution.* This chapter focuses on Claude Shannon and his work on entropy and information theory.

- **Seyer, M. D.** *RS-232 Made Easy: Connecting Computers, Printers, Terminals, and Modems.* Englewood Cliffs, NJ: Prentice Hall, 1991. If you haven't had enough of the train analogy and want to learn more about data communications, this is the book for you. Want to know how a digital wave form is similar to a box car followed by a flat car? How is a dial-up line similar to a draw bridge? The answers to these questions will help you understand all about communications.

- *The Internet Unleashed.* Indianapolis: Sams Publishing, 1994. This is a *huge* book—more than 1,300 pages— and most of it focuses on the Internet. However, it has an excellent section about using the telephone system for data communications.

- **Toffler, Alvin.** *Creating a New Civilization: The Politics of the Third Wave.* Atlanta: Turner Publishing, 1995. Toffler, a well-respected futurist, addresses many issues facing modern society, including the impact of technology.

Lab Assignments

Building a Network

 How many times have you waited in line to use the computers in your school labs? Here's your chance to become a computer lab manager and see if you can please all the students who use your labs. In the Building a Network Lab, you control a simulated computer network that provides services to student computer labs and to students dialing in from home. By monitoring usage and installing new equipment, see if you can make all your students happy!

1. Click the Steps button to learn how to use the simulation to monitor and configure the network. As you work through the Steps, answer all of the Quick Check questions that appear. After you complete the Steps, you will see a Quick Check Summary Report of your answers. Follow the directions on the screen to print this report.

2. In Explore, use File/Open to set up the network configuration stored as **msu.net**. Record the statistics for one day in Figure 10-23 provided, then answer questions a through e.

- a. How many hours during the day are more than 25% of the lab users without computer access?
- b. Are remote users satisfied with the level of dial in service?
- c. Would you characterize the printer load as high or low?
- d. Is the current demand exceeding the capacity of the file server?
- e. What should you do to improve the network to meet demand?

Figure 10-23

Time	Lab users without work-stations	Remote users without access	File server load	Printer load
8:00				
9:00				
10:00				
11:00				
Noon				
1:00				
2:00				
3:00				
4:00				
5:00				
6:00				
7:00				
8:00				
9:00				
10:00				
11:00				

3. In Explore, install a network hub and a file server in the Tech Room. Install a print server with an attached printer in Lab 1. Install another print server and attach a printer in Lab 2. Install three workstations in Lab 1 and five workstations in Lab 2. Record the statistics for one day in Figure 10-24, then answer questions a through e.

a. How many hours during the day are more than 25% of the lab users without computer access?

b. Are remote users satisfied with the level of dial in service?

c. Would you characterize the printer load as high or low?

d. Is the current demand exceeding the capacity of the file server?

e. What should you do to improve the network to meet demand?

Figure 10-24 ◀

Time	Lab users without work-stations	Remote users with-out access	File server load	Printer load
8:00				
9:00				
10:00				
11:00				
Noon				
1:00				
2:00				
3:00				
4:00				
5:00				
6:00				
7:00				
8:00				
9:00				
10:00				
11:00				

4. In Explore, use File/Open to set up the network configuration stored as **wfcc.net**. Use no more than 30 devices to construct what you think is an optimal network for the students in the simulation. (Hint: Don't forget to save your network frequently on your floppy disk as you are working on it.) Make sure you test your network for at least five days. The percent of students unable to access workstations and modems should rarely go above 25%. Server and printer loads should never reach 100%. After you are satisfied with your network, print out your network configuration report.

Quick Check

Answers

10.1

1. channel

2. analog

3. dedicated (leased)

4. false

5. true

6. Packet

7. dial up (POTS)

8. LANS, PBXs

10.2

1. bandwidth

2. bits

3. duplex

4. protocols

5. even

6. true

10.3

1. hub (concentrator)

2. standards

3. software

4. protocols

5. true

6. false

7. token

Glossary/Index

G

half-duplex communication Communication that can send or receive, but cannot do both at the same time, 10-17

Hertz (Hz), 10-12

hubs, LANs, 10-21

infrared transmission Transmissions that use a frequency range just below the visible light spectrum to transport data, 10-16

internal modem A modem on a circuit board that plugs into an expansion slot inside a computer, 10-26

Internet, 10-10–10-11
    TCP/IP protocol, 10-23

IPX (Internetwork packet exchange) A popular microcomputer network protocol developed by Novell for use with the NetWare local area network software, 10-23

ISDN (Integrated Services Digital Network) Telephone service that transports data digitally over dial-up or dedicated lines, 10-6

LAT (local area transport) A network protocol developed by Digital Equipment Corporation (DEC) for use with DEC minicomputers; also called DECnet, 10-23

leased lines, 10-6

LEDs (light emitting diodes), 10-15

local area network (LAN) A network that connects computers within a limited geographic area, used mainly to exchange computer data, 10-1110-5, 10-11, 10-21–10-25
    connections, 10-21–10-22
    data packets, 10-22–10-23
    data transmission, 10-23–10-25

local communications Transmitting and receiving data over a short distance, such as when sending data from a computer to a printer, 10-12

Macintosh computers, 10-23

MAUs (multistation access units), LANs, 10-21

media, communications, 10-13–10-16

message Information that the source wants to communicate to the receiver, 10-4

microwave transmission Signals sent over a short to medium distance from a microwave transmitting station to a microwave receiving station, 10-16

modem A peripheral device that converts the digital signals used inside your computer to an analog or voice signal that can be transmitted over the phone lines, 10-6, 10-26–10-29
    cellular phone system, 10-7–10-8
    connecting, 10-26
    dialing, 10-29
    protocols, setting, 10-28
    software configuration, 10-27

modulation The process of changing the characteristics of a signal, as when a modem changes a digital pulse to an analog signal, 10-6

Morse, Samuel, 10-5

network communications protocol The rules that specify the structure of packets transmitted over the network, 10-23

network interface cards, 10-21

network standard A set of communications protocols that provides for the orderly transmission of data on a network, 10-22

networks
    Internet, 10-10–10-11
    ISDN, 10-6
    local. *See* LANs (local area networks)
    telephone, 10-4–10-6

noise Any interference that disrupts the communication process, 10-4

odd parity Error-checking protocol in which the number of one bits in the data block is an odd number, 10-18

optical fiber A single glass tube, thinner than a human hair, in a fiber-optic cable, 10-15, 10-15–10-16

packet A small section of a large file that is transmitted on a network. A packet consists of the address of the destination workstation, the address of the sending workstation, and a small segment of a data file, 10-23, 10-22–10-23

Information Systems in Organizations

The musicians played "Rule Britannia," and the dignitaries assembled. The Queen arrived. Michael Abercrombie stepped forward confidently. His gray eyes absorbed every detail, and a slight smile played on his lips as the short ceremony began. Several of the dignitaries whispered to each other. "Amazing archeological discovery..." "Excellent head for business..." "...Grandfather would be proud..."

An explorer, with a degree in archeology from Oxford, Michael Abercrombie played a principal role in unearthing artifacts that radically altered theories about the migration of ancient people across continents. Michael is also the chief executive officer of the venerable establishment, Abercrombie & Livingston Outfitters, Ltd, purveyors of expedition equipment and supplies. Founded in 1892 by Michael's grandfather, A&L Outfitters has provisioned hundreds of expeditions that push the envelope of human skill and knowledge. In addition to supplies, A&L provides highly respected expertise on appropriate gear for any terrain or climate. A&L's main offices are located in London. Branch outlets are spread across the globe in Telluride, Katmandu, Geneva, Lima, Guatemala City, and Dar es Salaam.

A&L relies on a computerized information system to conduct business efficiently and effectively. An **information system** collects, maintains, and provides information to people. Today, many information systems are computerized. These computerized information systems can be defined as the computers, peripheral devices, programs, data, people, and procedures that work together to record, store, process, and distribute information. In this chapter, the terms "information system" and "computer information system" are used interchangeably to refer to information systems that are computerized.

Information Systems in **Organizations**

A&L's information system is designed to maintain a high level of customer satisfaction and provide expertise on expedition conditions and equipment. Customer satisfaction and the success of expeditions depend on A&L's ability to deliver equipment to the right place at the specified time. A&L's reputation as a dependable source of expertise on local conditions depends on access to information from diverse sources.

This chapter describes how computer systems like the one at A&L Outfitters—a fictitious company—help businesses and organizations function effectively.

CHAPTER**PREVIEW**

As you read this chapter, you should think about the relationship between people, organizations, and information. Consider the ways you interact with organizations: You make purchases from sales organizations, you are a student in an educational organization, you will probably have a career as an employee of an organization—you might even create your own organization. The information you learn in this chapter will help you interact with organizations as a client, customer, employee, or founder. After you have completed this chapter you should be able to:

- Provide examples of mission statements from for-profit and non-profit organizations

- Classify the activities that take place in a typical business

- Discuss some trends that affect the way organizations operate

- Describe the information needs of executives, managers, and workers

- Provide examples of office automation that make significant improvements in the way an organization operates

- Describe the transaction processing systems typically used in businesses

- Differentiate between an MIS and a DSS

- Explain how an expert system works

11.1 Organizational Structure

An **organization** is a group of people working together to accomplish a goal. You are probably a member of an organization, such as a student club, a fraternity or sorority, a sports team, or a political party. You also deal with many organizations every day: your school, stores, banks, and government agencies. Many organizations use computers to operate more effectively, gather information, and accomplish tasks. In this section, you'll review some basic concepts about organizations and businesses. These concepts give you a foundation for understanding how computers and related technologies enhance organizational activities.

Types of Organizations

What's the difference between an organization and a business?

You have learned that an organization is a group of people working together toward a goal. Any organization that seeks profit by providing needed goods and services is called a **business**. A&L Outfitters is an example of a business that was formed to make a profit selling expedition equipment. Some organizations are formed to accomplish political or charitable goals that do not include amassing personal profit. These organizations are known as non-profit organizations.

Every organization has a **mission**—a goal or plan. All the activities that take place in an organization, including those activities that involve computers, should contribute to this mission. The written expression of an organization's mission is called a **mission statement**. A mission statement describes not only an organization's goals, but also how those goals will be accomplished. For example, the mission of A&L Outfitters is to make a profit by providing high-quality equipment and services for professional expeditions in mountain, jungle, and polar environments.

In Project 1, you can work with mission statements for a variety of organizations.

Organizational Activities

Are there activities that all organizations have in common?

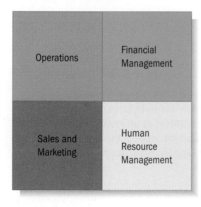

Figure 11-1
Four functional groups common to most organizations

Computer and communications technologies help organizations carry out many activities. It is useful to look at some of the broad categories of organizational activities where information systems are applied. Most organizational activities fall into four functional groups, shown in Figure 11-1: operations, financial management, sales and marketing, and human resource management.

An organization must carry out its primary activity. A university educates students. An automobile manufacturer makes cars. A hospital provides health care. A&L Outfitters sells expedition equipment and provides expedition support services. The primary activities of an organization are called **production** or **operations**.

Would you classify accounting activities at H&R Block tax offices as operations or as financial management? The primary activity (operations) at H&R Block is accounting—the tax return preparation it does for clients. The financial management functional group also does accounting—H&R Block must keep an eye on its own income and expenses as a business.

Every organization must manage its money. A university tracks tuition payments, payroll, and maintenance expenses. An automobile maker tracks manufacturing costs, payroll expenses, and income from sales. A hospital tracks patient bills, insurance payments, staff wages, and suppy expenses. A&L Outfitters tracks the cost of the equipment it sells, customer payments, and expenses for salaries, rents, and business taxes. Tracking the flow of money through an organization is referred to as **accounting** or **financial management**.

Most organizations need to promote their activities. A university needs to let prospective students know what educational services it provides. An automobile manufacturer must advertise its products. A hospital needs to convince patients that it can best serve their health care needs. A&L Outfitters advertises its products and services in specialized mountaineering and expedition magazines. Advertising and promoting an organization is called **sales and marketing**, or **public relations**.

Organizations are made up of people. University faculty, staff, and administrators; automotive workers and managers; and health care workers in a hospital must be hired, evaluated, and supervised. A&L Outfitters hires sales associates, experienced expedition consultants, purchasing agents, shippers, maintenance workers, and managers. It must keep track of these employees' salaries and benefits, evaluate how well they perform their jobs, and plan how to best use each employee's skills and talents. Keeping track of employees in an organization is referred to as **human resource management**.

Computers are increasingly being deployed to assist the tasks in all four of these functional groups. You'll read about some specific examples later in this chapter.

Trends and Challenges

Today's organizations can't function without computers, right?

Computers are certainly an important aspect of organizational activity. Organizations exist in a rapidly changing and competitive environment in which opportunities and threats abound. A well-known business analyst, Michael Porter, created the Five Forces model, shown in Figure 11-2, to illustrate the potential effects of these opportunities or threats.

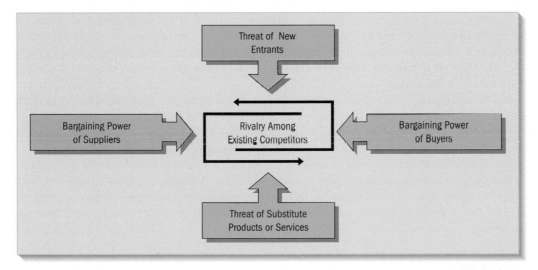

Figure 11-2
Five Forces model

Although the word "threat" sounds negative and "opportunity" sounds positive, both threats and opportunities can ultimately be beneficial if an organization makes an appropriate response, such as installing useful technology.

To be successful in its mission, an organization must respond effectively to opportunities and threats. But what is an effective response? An organization has a choice of three fundamental strategies. First, it can become better at what it does, for example, by lowering costs and prices, by improving its products or services, or by offering better customer service. A second response is to change the structure of an industry. For example, the film industry previously generated income only from movie theater ticket sales. Video rental stores significantly redefined this industry by providing an alternative way to view films. As a third response, an organization can create a new product or service. The music industry responded to pirated music tapes by promoting difficult-to-copy audio CD technology.

Business analysts continuously devise variations of these three fundamental strategies. Currently popular strategies include use of technology, downsizing, total quality management, re-engineering, "just in time" inventory, and employee empowerment. Let's look at how A&L has responded to some of the challenges it faced throughout the years.

A&L was founded in 1892. At first it had only one office, located in the heart of London. Business was conducted in person and by mail until the new century dawned and A&L installed a revolutionary technology, the telephone. The telephone enhanced communications between A&L, its customers, and its suppliers. However, the telephone did nothing to change the basic way employees processed and shipped customer orders—everything was done manually.

Business boomed in the roaring '20s, and A&L expanded by opening branch offices in Nepal and Turkey. Orders from these branches were phoned or telegraphed into the London office for processing. During World War II, patriotic managers and employees focused their efforts on supply logistics for British troops. After the war, A&L's business focus again turned to expeditions, and two more outlets were established. "Automation" was fashionable, and so A&L installed a system of pneumatic tubes to transport order forms quickly from the salesroom to the warehouse. **Automation** is the use of electrical or mechanical devices to improve manufacturing or other processes.

Further expansion in the 1960s and 1970s forced the company to consider **computerization** for tracking inventory. A&L purchased a minicomputer and hired information system staff to write programs to process orders and track inventory. The computer system was a success—A&L managers always knew what was in stock and could place timely orders to restock the warehouse.

Despite the computerized inventory system, customers were defecting to competitors who promised faster delivery. A&L employed a technique called TQM to increase customer satisfaction by decreasing shipping times. **TQM (total quality management)** is a strategy in which an organization makes a commitment to analyzing and implementing ways to improve the quality of its products or services. A&L used computers to track the entire shipping process, and managers analyzed this data to devise a plan to streamline shipping operations.

Shipping operations were streamlined by distributing some of the warehousing operations to the outlets. Each outlet now kept its own stock of frequently ordered products, ready for immediate delivery. Employees in the outlets were empowered to make more decisions, such as what to stock for their local markets. **Employee empowerment** means giving employees the authority to make business decisions.

A&L's centralized minicomputer system was not designed for this distributed inventory structure, so A&L managers decided to move to a completely new computerized inventory system. They decided to "rightsize" by moving inventory from the minicomputer to networked microcomputers. **Rightsize** means to find the most effective configuration for computer resources.

A&L's ability to effectively react to challenges has kept its business profitable for generations. Technology and computers have played a major part in A&L's effective response. However, technology is not an answer to all problems faced by organizations. Employee and product development are also likely to play an important part of an overall strategy for continued business success.

Strategies labeled by buzz words like "total quality management" are usually refinements of the three fundamental strategies: improve what you do, change the industry structure, or create a new product.

In many companies, rightsizing means moving operations from a mainframe or minicomputer system to networked microcomputers. This is sometimes also called downsizing.

Quick Check

1. What's the difference between an organization and a business?

2. All the activities that take place in an organization should contribute to the organizational _____.

3. List the four functional groups of organizational activities.

4. Organizations must successfully respond to _____ and _____, or they will cease to exist.

5. Three fundamental strategies for responding to changes in the business or organizational environment are _____, _____, and _____.

6. _____ is a strategy in which an organization makes a commitment to analyzing and implementing ways to improve the quality of its products and services.

7. Many companies _____ by moving operations from a mainframe computer to a microcomputer network.

People, Decisions, and Information

Every organization requires people. Some organizations, such as IBM and AT&T, employ tens of thousands worldwide. How does an organization coordinate the activities of its employees? Most organizations have an organizational structure that arranges employees in ascending order of authority and pay. An organizational chart such as the one in Figure 11-3 depicts the hierarchy of employees in an organization such as A&L Outfitters.

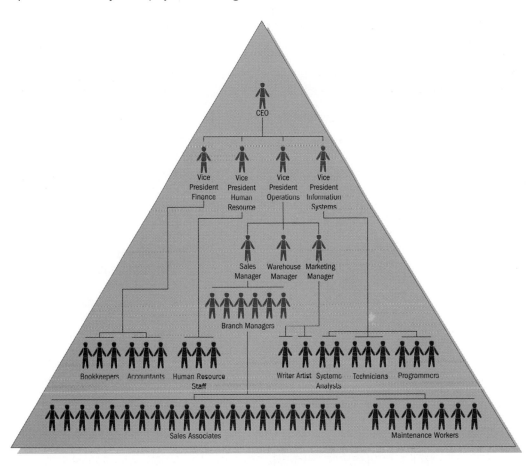

▶ **Figure 11-3**
Organizational chart

At the top of most organizations is a single individual. As you progress down the organizational chart, each level fans out to encompass more employees. With this in mind, you can see how a triangle or pyramid like the one in Figure 11-4 can be used to represent the composition of employees in an organization.

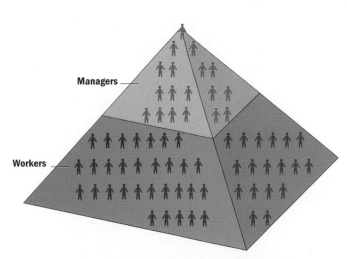

People in the organization pyramid can be classified as either workers or managers. **Workers** are the people who carry out the organization's mission. For example, they assemble cars, write newspaper articles, sell merchandise, answer telephones, lay bricks, cut trees, or fix engines. Workers are usually supervised by managers.

Managers make decisions about how an organization will carry

▶ **Figure 11-4**
Organization pyramid

out its activities. They decide organizational goals and plan what steps to take to achieve those goals. Managers approve new products and authorize new construction. They also monitor, coordinate, evaluate, and supervise the activities of workers.

Workers and managers all perform activities that contribute to the success of an organization. Their activities frequently require decisions. Those decisions are based on information that is often supplied by an information system. To appreciate the significance of an information system, it's useful to understand the information needs and the types of decisions made by people in the organization pyramid.

Workers

Do workers use information systems?

In today's workplace, a high percentage of workers use information systems and other computer or communications technologies. The technology available to a worker depends on what the organization provides and what is needed to do the job. Every worker's situation is unique, but it is possible to make some generalizations about the technology that workers use by looking at worker classifications. Some business experts classify workers as information workers, service workers, or goods workers. These workers are the foundation of the organization pyramid, as shown in Figure 11-5.

Figure 11-5
Worker classifications in the organization pyramid

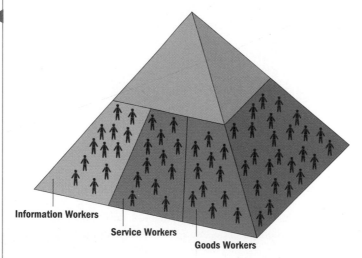

Information Workers

Service Workers

Goods Workers

Information workers produce and manipulate information. Examples of information workers include architects, writers, computer programmers, secretaries, and accountants. These workers often make extensive use of information systems. A computer is one of the information worker's most important tools.

Service workers are employees whose primary activity is delivering services to customers. Examples of service workers include waiters, sales associates, taxi drivers, nurses, and receptionists. Service workers often use information systems, but their main focus is person-to-person interaction.

Goods workers create and manipulate physical objects. Examples of goods workers include farmers, construction workers, assembly line workers, miners, mechanics, and plumbers. Goods workers sometimes use computerized equipment and robots to manipulate physical objects.

A&L employees include information workers and service workers. Like many of today's businesses, A&L does not have goods workers because it does not manufacture any products. According to the Department of Labor, less than 20% of the labor force in the United States is employed as goods workers. England, Canada, France, and Germany have workforces with similar compositions.

Figure 11-6 describes the jobs of A&L service and information workers.

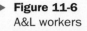
Figure 11-6
A&L workers

Accountants and bookkeepers are information workers. They keep track of cash flowing in and out of the business. Some bookkeepers are responsible for sending customer bills and recording customer payments. Others make sure that A&L promptly pays its expenses for inventory, phone, electricity, and so on.

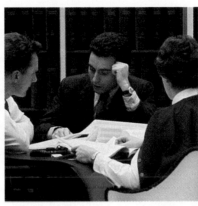

Sales associates are service workers. They help customers by taking orders and recommending products.

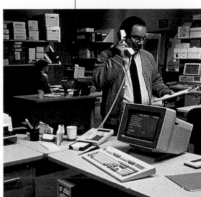

Systems analysts and programmers are information workers. They use computers to plan and implement changes to A&L's information system.

The Human Resource staff consists of secretarial and clerical information workers. They continually monitor employee contracts, insurance policies, and other benefit programs.

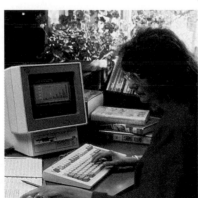

A&L's in-house writer and artist are information workers. The writer produces advertising copy and product descriptions, assisted by the artist, who supplies graphics. Both use computers to produce their work, and they make extensive use of on-line information services for ideas.

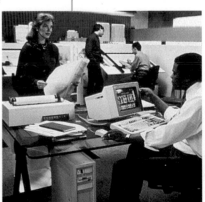

A&L's technicians are service workers who install, move, and repair in-house computers.

Cashiers, classified as service workers, keep the stores running smoothly.

Managers

What managerial tasks are enhanced by information systems?

Just as there are different types of workers, there are also different types of managers, with different responsibilities in an organization. Managers are classified as executive managers, middle managers, or supervisors, as shown in the revised organization pyramid in Figure 11-7.

Figure 11-7
Managerial levels of the organization pyramid

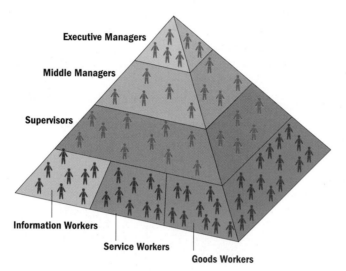

Executive Managers

Middle Managers

Supervisors

Information Workers

Service Workers

Goods Workers

Executive managers, sometimes referred to as **senior managers**, make long-range plans and goals for the organization. Executives are the entrepreneurs who create new businesses under the expectation that they will be a long-range success. They select the mission statement for an organization. They also cultivate business relationships with bankers, politicians, and other industry leaders in case their influence is needed in the future. This emphasis on long-range and future goals is referred to as **strategic planning**.

A&L's founder stated the company's mission as "providing the highest quality expedition equipment and exceptional customer service." Today, Michael Abercrombie, A&L's chief executive officer, is trying to anticipate market changes in the next five to ten years. He is using A&L's information system to assist with this planning effort.

Middle managers are responsible for designing ways to achieve the plans laid out by executive managers. In general, middle managers decide how to deploy human, financial, and natural resources to achieve organizational goals. This type of action planning is referred to as **tactical planning**.

Think of strategic planning as deciding "what" an organization will do. Tactical planning emphasizes "how" a goal will be reached.

At A&L, middle managers are responsible for figuring out how to achieve the founder's goals of providing the highest quality equipment and exceptional customer service. Several years ago, a group of managers made plans to create a quality assurance lab to test new products. The managers used data from A&L's information system to identify financial resources for the new test lab. Using these financial resources, they found a suitable location and hired employees to staff the lab. The managers now use the information system to monitor the ongoing expenses of the lab.

Supervisors are managers who deal primarily with day-to-day operations. They schedule and monitor workers and processes. Scheduling and monitoring are sometimes referred to as **operational planning**. At A&L, the quality assurance lab supervisor receives a list of new products. Using computerized scheduling capabilities provided by A&L's information system, the supervisor assigns each product to a tester and schedules the test date. After testing a product, test results are stored in the information system so they can be accessed by sales associates who are consulting with customers.

Problems and Decisions

For what purpose do workers and managers use information systems?

One of the major functions of an information system is to help people make decisions in response to problems. Problems occur at all levels of an organization and require strategic, tactical, or operational solutions and decisions. All problems are not alike, but they can be classified into three types: structured, semi-structured, and unstructured.

Everyday, run-of-the-mill, and routine problems are called **structured problems**. When people make decisions in response to structured problems, the procedure for obtaining the best solution is known, the objective is clearly defined, and the information necessary to make the decision is easy to identify. An example of a structured problem is figuring out which customers should receive overdue notices. The information for this decision is usually stored in a file cabinet or in a computer system. The method for reaching a solution is to look for customers with an outstanding balance, then check whether the due date for their payment falls before today's date.

Semi-structured problems are less routine than structured problems. When solving a semi-structured problem, the procedure for arriving at a solution is usually known; however, it might involve some degree of subjective judgment. Also, some of the information regarding the problem might not be available, might lack precision, or might be uncertain. An example of a semi-structured problem at A&L is whether to decrease inventory levels of cold-weather equipment in response to global warming trends. Inventory and sales information on cold-weather equipment exists for past years. However, information on global warming, though it exists, is not definitive. To determine future inventory levels of cold-weather equipment, someone at A&L will have to make an educated guess based on historical inventory data and inconclusive information on climatic changes.

Unstructured problems require human intuition as the basis for decision making. Information relevant to the problem might be missing, and few, if any, parts of the decision can be tackled using concrete models. An example of an unstructured problem at A&L would be the selection of a new company logo. The decision is likely to be based on someone's artistic tastes, rather than on hard data.

Computer information systems help people solve structured, semi-structured, and even unstructured problems. However, the degree of assistance an information system provides will vary with the problem. Traditionally, computers have contributed most to solving structured, routine, and repetitive problems. Although some computer tools can be applied to unstructured problems, these problems are still often resolved based on someone's "gut feeling."

Information and Information Analysis Tools

Where do computers get the information that they supply to the workers and managers who make decisions?

Information systems are designed to collect information that workers and managers need to make decisions. This information comes from both internal and external sources. Organizations generate **internal information** about inventory levels, cash flow, personnel, customers, orders, sales, and so on. Today, this internal information is increasingly generated with the help of computerized input devices such as terminals, bar-code readers, and personal computers. Once it is generated, the information is stored in an information system.

Organizations collect **external information** from outside sources. Using Internet resources and other communications capabilities, it is becoming increasingly easy to collect external information about competitors' products, pricing, finances, and plans. Such information is often available from a company's Web site or from sites housing business publications or analysis.

Decision support software like DecideRight contains a tool you can use to analyze information. A decision support system, on the other hand, often includes a collection of such tools, and it contains the data necessary for making a decision.

Organizations can also collect external information, such as mailing lists and credit reports, about potential customers. Other readily available external information includes patent information, demographics, labor statistics, maps, and government documents. External information, unlike internal information, is typically not stored permanently in an organization's information system. Instead, it is collected when needed for a specific purpose, then erased later when it is no longer needed.

Information systems supply workers and managers with reports and information analysis software tools to manipulate information. Most information systems periodically produce a fixed set of reports, such as daily cash register receipts or monthly sales summaries. In addition, some information systems allow users to customize their own reports to provide the right information in the right format for making a decision.

Information analysis tools help people model problems, then find a logical path to a solution or decision. Information analysis tools include spreadsheets, flow charts, and special-purpose analysis software. Software such as DecideRight, shown in Figure 11-8, is designed to help weigh the factors that must be considered in a decision.

Figure 11-8
DecideRight software

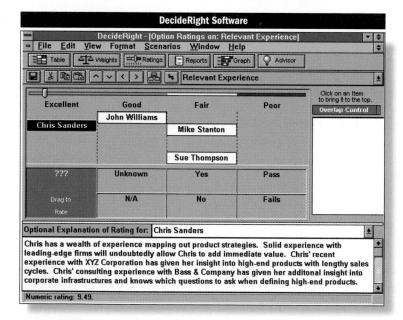

A manager trying to decide who to hire, might use a software tool, such as DecideRight. Each candidate for the job is rated according to a series of factors. So far, Chris Sanders seems to be the best person for the job. Her rating is excellent and her numeric rating is 9.49, as shown at the bottom of the screen.

Quick Check

1. Draw an organization pyramid showing the three types of managers and three types of workers.

2. Less than 20% of the U.S. labor force is _____ workers.

3. The managerial activity that emphasizes long-range and future goals is called _____.

4. Middle managers are typically responsible for _____ planning.

5. _____ problems require human intuition as the basis for decision making.

6. _____ information is generated by the organization itself, whereas _____ information is collected from sources outside the organization.

Information Systems

T he purpose of an information system is to improve the effectiveness of an organization by providing useful, accurate, and timely information. For example, a computerized information system helps A&L Outfitters improve the effectiveness of its operations by providing data communications among outlets, tracking orders from customers, scheduling shipments to expedition base camps, and tracking inventory at each branch outlet.

An information system might have one or more of the following components or subsystems: an office automation system, a transaction processing system, a management information system, a decision support system, and an expert system. Let's take a closer look at each of these systems.

An important point to remember is that a successful information system supports activities that are defined by the organization's mission.

▶ **Figure 11-9**
Office automation

Office Automation

Does an information system automate routine office tasks?

As its name suggests, an **office automation system** "automates," or computerizes, routine office tasks such as producing documents, tracking schedules, making calculations, and facilitating interoffice voice and written communication. Word processing, spreadsheet, scheduling, and electronic mail software are integral parts of most office automation systems. Study Figure 11-9 to learn how computers automate routine tasks in a typical office.

The office automation system at A&L uses electronic mail to overcome the problem of communicating between outlets in seven time zones. Word processing software helps with routine correspondence, such as responses to inquiries from potential customers, congratulatory messages to successful expeditions, and letters to suppliers. Desktop publishing software provides a cost-effective way to prepare A&L's quarterly newsletter. In the London office, scheduling software maintains appointment calendars for A&L sales agents and executives.

Old Way

New Way
Memos and other routine communications are created using word processing software, then sent using electronic mail.

Old Way

New Way
Scheduling software maintains appointment calendars for individual employees, arranges committee and group meetings, and schedules conference rooms.

Old Way

New Way
Voice mail digitally records incoming messages and reduces the amount of "telephone tag" required to contact someone.

Old Way

New Way
Word processing and database software produce customized form letters and mailing labels.

Old Way

New Way
Database software maintains the type of information stored on a Rolodex or in a card file.

Old Way

New Way
Spreadsheet software helps employees perform routine calculations.

Old Way

New Way
Word processing software or specialized forms software creates paper-based or electronic forms, such as job application forms and registration forms.

Old Way

New Way
Desktop publishing software and laser printers help produce advertising brochures, posters, newsletters, and catalogs.

Old Way

New Way
Presentation graphics software produces professional visuals, which can be displayed in meetings using a computer projection device.

A new trend in office automation is groupware. **Groupware** is software that helps people collaborate on projects. In organizations many projects or procedures are not completed by only one person. Reports, for example, are often the product of more than one person's efforts—many people might participate by contributing sections of a report, reviewing a draft document and suggesting changes, or approving a final version of the report. A groupware word processor would facilitate this process: It allows more than one person to access the report file, it records the changes and comments made by each person, and it contains a routing mechanism for approvals. In addition to word processing, groupware is available for scheduling, project planning, and decision making.

Transaction Processing

How does an organization collect information on production or operations?

In an information system context, a **transaction** is an event that requires a manual or computer-based activity. When you order a product by mail or when you buy merchandise in a store, you are involved in a transaction. When you make a phone call or when you pay your phone bill, you are also involved in a transaction. Most transactions require a sequence of steps. For example, to pay your phone bill, you must receive the bill, write a check for the amount, and place the check in the mail. Then, the post office must deliver your payment to the phone company, and the phone company must record the payment. For the transaction to be successful, all the steps of the transaction must be completed. If even one step fails, the entire transaction has failed.

Production or operations activities usually involve one or more transactions. A **transaction processing system** keeps track of all the transactions for an organization by providing a way to collect, display, modify, or cancel transactions. The transaction data is stored in one or more files. Usually, a transaction processing system does not produce elaborate reports. Instead, it produces basic reports, such as those that list the transactions contained in a file. Figure 11-10 diagrams the processes that take place in a typical transaction processing system.

Figure 11-10 ◄
Characteristics of a transaction processing system

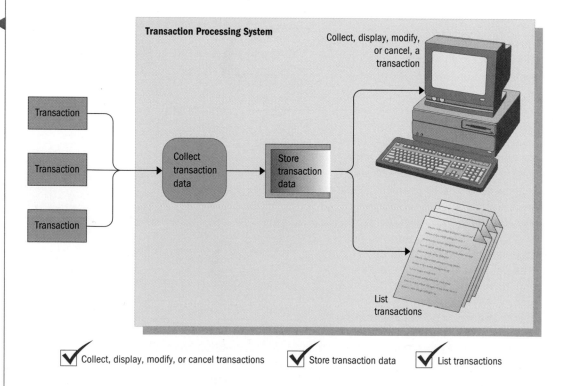

Transaction Processing System

Collect, display, modify, or cancel, a transaction

Transaction

Transaction

Transaction

Collect transaction data

Store transaction data

List transactions

✓ Collect, display, modify, or cancel transactions   ✓ Store transaction data   ✓ List transactions

Some examples of transaction processing systems that are found in businesses today include these:

- An **order-entry/invoice system** provides a way to input, view, modify, and delete customer orders. It helps track the status of each order, and it creates invoices.
- A **point-of-sale (POS) system** records items purchased at each cash register and calculates the total amount due for each sale. Some POS systems automatically verify credit cards, calculate change, and identify customers who have previously written bad checks.
- An **inventory control system** tracks information about inventory such as the cost, price, and quantity in stock. When an item is sold, it is removed from inventory. When a new item arrives, it is added to the inventory.
- A **general accounting system** records the financial status of a business by keeping track of income, expenses, and assets.

Transaction processing systems at A&L Outfitters computerize order entry, invoicing, inventory control, and general accounting. Study Figure 11-11 to learn how A&L's order entry system processes transactions for customer orders.

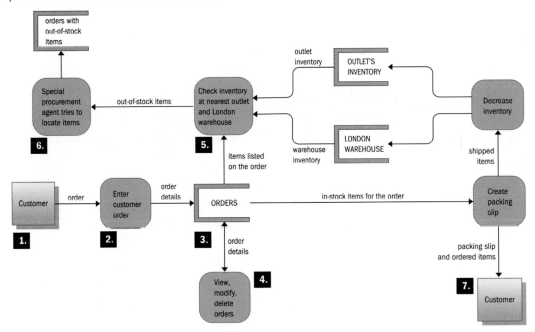

Figure 11-11
A&L Outfitter's transaction processing system

1. A customer wants to order equipment and supplies.

2. A sales representative takes an order from a customer by entering the customer's selections on a microcomputer connected to A&L's network. Occasionally, A&L agents are dispatched to remote locations, where they take orders on a notebook computer, then send the completed order to the London office using a modem.

3. The order is stored on the network file server.

4. Sales associates can modify an order if a customer wants to add or change items. If an expedition is canceled, the order can be deleted.

5. Each item on the order is checked against the existing inventory. If it is not in stock at the local outlet, a telecommunications link to London checks to see if the item is available from the central warehouse.

6. Ordered items that are not in stock locally or in the central warehouse are tracked down by a special procurement agent.

7. A list of available items becomes the packing slip that accompanies the shipment to the customer.

A transaction processing system is designed mainly for use by clerical personnel to record transactions. Most transaction processing systems generate a limited number of reports that provide a basic record of completed transactions. However, managers need more sophisticated reports to help them understand and analyze data. These reports are usually created by a management information system.

Management Information Systems

How can the data collected by a transaction processing system be presented in a format more conducive to decision making?

A **management information system**, or **MIS**, generally uses the data collected by a transaction processing system but manipulates that data to create reports that workers and managers can use to make routine business decisions in response to structured problems. As Figure 11-12 shows, an MIS is characterized by the production of routine reports that managers use for structured and routine tasks.

Although they are called management information systems, *these systems also provide valuable information to workers—especially information workers.*

Figure 11-12
Characteristics of a management information system

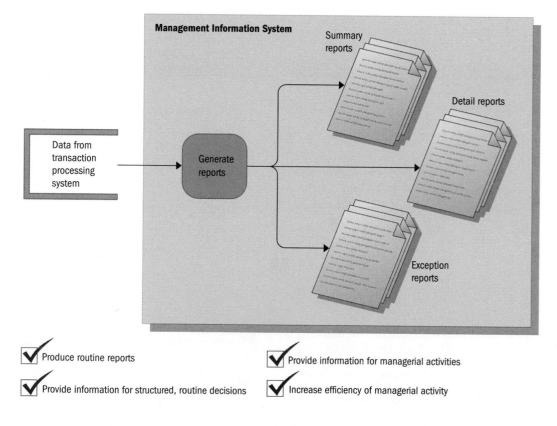

☑ Produce routine reports

☑ Provide information for structured, routine decisions

☑ Provide information for managerial activities

☑ Increase efficiency of managerial activity

One of the major goals of an MIS is to increase the efficiency of managerial activity. As you learned earlier in this chapter, different levels of management have different information needs. In response to these different needs, a management information system produces several types of reports. A **detail report** is an organized list, for example, a report of inventory items alphabetized by product name. Such reports are suitable for some supervisory activities, but they are rarely used for tactical or strategic planning. A **summary report** combines or groups data and often shows totals. For example, a summary report might show the total annual sales for the past five years. Summary reports are useful in tactical and strategic planning. An **exception**

report contains information that is outside of normal or acceptable ranges, such as a reorder report showing low-stock items in inventory. Workers use exception reports to take action, such as restocking inventory. Managers also use exception reports to analyze potential problems, such as continued inventory shortages or large numbers of customers making late payments.

The A&L management information system supplies managers of branch outlets with many reports, produced on a daily, weekly, or monthly basis. Once a day, the managers at each branch outlet receive a summary report showing the number of orders filled, the total amount due for the orders, the number of payments received, and the total amount of all the payments. On a weekly basis, the inventory manager of each branch outlet receives a report that lists inventory items that need to be reordered. Every month each branch outlet manager receives a summary report of total income and expenses for the branch. Also on a monthly basis, the Vice President of Sales in the London office receives a summary report showing income and expenses for all the branches, along with the total profit for the entire company.

To create these reports, the MIS sorts, extracts, and totals the data from the transaction processing system. The specifications for most of these reports were created by A&L's information systems department when the MIS system was designed. Managers at A&L can request additional customized reports if the current reports do not meet their needs. However, as is the case in many businesses, the information system personnel at A&L have many projects that are behind schedule, and they would not be able to find the time to add a new report to the processing routine for several months.

Because managers cannot quickly obtain customized reports, A&L's MIS system is not very flexible. For example, it does not provide a way for a manager to easily obtain a customized report that compares sales at the Katmandu outlet with those at the Geneva outlet. However, A&L managers can create customized reports on demand using the corporate decision support system.

Decision Support Systems

Can managers and workers get information relevant to problems that weren't anticipated when the information system was designed?

A **decision support system**, or **DSS**, allows users to manipulate data directly and produce on-demand reports. A DSS is designed to help managers and workers make non-routine decisions, such as solving semi-structured problems in which the decision might be based on imprecise data or might require "guesstimates." Decision makers use a DSS to design decision models and make queries. A **decision model** is a numerical representation of a realistic situation, such as a cash flow model of a business that shows how income adds to cash accounts and expenses deplete those accounts. A **decision query** is a question or set of instructions that describes the data that needs to be gathered to make a decision.

A decision support system derives its name from the fact that it "supports" the decision maker, that is, it provides the tools the decision maker needs to examine the data. However, a DSS does not make decisions—that remains the role of the human decision maker.

A DSS typically includes modeling tools, such as spreadsheets, so managers can create a numerical representation of a situation and explore "what-if" alternatives. A DSS also typically includes statistical tools so managers can study trends before making a decision. A DSS usually includes data from the organization's transaction processing system, but it might also include or access external data such as stock market reports, as shown in Figure 11-13.

Figure 11-13
Characteristics of a decision support system

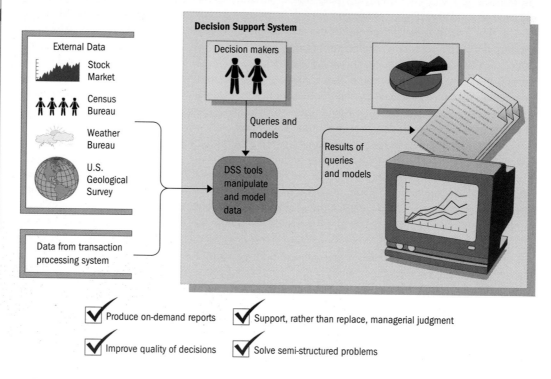

✓ Produce on-demand reports   ✓ Support, rather than replace, managerial judgment

✓ Improve quality of decisions   ✓ Solve semi-structured problems

The managers at A&L Outfitters use their DSS to tackle diverse problems because it contains a good selection of decision support tools. For example, one A&L branch outlet manager is using the DSS to project next year's sales of cold-weather camping equipment. To make this projection, he first retrieves from the A&L transaction processing system the data on the past two years' sales of each item of cold-weather camping equipment. He then transfers the data into a spreadsheet so he can manipulate it and examine several "what-if" scenarios. He uses the DSS link to a commercial information service to filter through articles about camping, recreation, and weather. For example, the manager discovers that weather systems last year were especially intense. Because of the bad weather, expeditions to cold climates were not advisable and sales of cold-weather equipment declined.

Next, the manager uses the DSS to search through an A&L database that contains information on all the expeditions of the past five years. The DSS helps him create a graph showing that expeditions to cold regions declined last year after a steady increase for the previous three years. Should he gamble and assume that last year was an unusual deviation in a steadily increasing cold-weather equipment market? By manipulating the data in the spreadsheet, the manager looks at best- and worse-case scenarios and decides that it is not too risky to order 5% more cold-weather camping equipment.

Expert Systems

Do information systems ever make decisions?

You've just seen how a DSS helps a manager manipulate the data necessary to make a decision. However, the DSS does not make a decision. The manager must analyze the data and reach a decision. The DSS does not substitute for the judgment of the manager, which is appropriate in situations where trained professionals are making decisions. However, in many organizations, it would be useful if every decision did not need to be made by a highly paid expert.

For example, A&L customer service would improve if sales associates were allowed to decide whether a customer is allowed to buy on credit. If sales associates could make this decision they would not need to consult with a manager before they could give the customer credit approval. Customers would probably be pleased if sales associates could make this decision. However, uninformed credit decisions could result in a high number of uncollectable accounts. What if the computer could examine a customer's credit history, determine the credit risk using the same criteria as an experienced credit analyst, and then decide whether to extend credit? This process would be like having a credit analyst working with every sales associate. Customer service would improve with minimal risk.

An **expert system**, or **knowledge-based system**, is a computer system designed to analyze data and produce a recommendation or decision. As the name implies, an expert system is a computerized expert. To create an expert system, the knowledge of an expert about a particular type of decision is captured in a set of facts and rules called a **knowledge base**. A knowledge base is stored in a computer file and then manipulated by software called an **inference engine**. When it is time to make a decision, the inference engine begins analyzing the available data by following the rules in the knowledge base. If the expert system needs additional data, it checks external databases, looks for the data in a transaction processing system, or asks the user to answer questions, as shown in Figure 11-14.

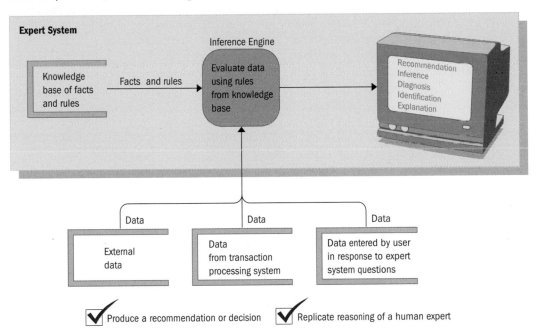

▶ **Figure 11-14**
Characteristics of an expert system

An expert system is not a general-purpose problem solver or decision maker. Each expert system is designed to make decisions in a particular area or "domain." For example, an expert system created for use at the Campbell Soup Company captured the knowledge of an expert cooking-vat operator to help less experienced employees troubleshoot problems that might arise as the soup cooks. Other expert systems have been developed to locate mineral deposits, diagnose blood diseases, evaluate corporate financial statements, underwrite complex insurance policies, and recommend stock purchases.

Expert systems are sometimes created using a computer programming language, but more often they are created using an expert system shell. An **expert system shell** is a software tool used for developing expert system applications. An expert system shell is an expert system without any rules. The shell contains the inference engine and a method for entering the rules for the

An expert system shell is analogous to a pasta machine. It provides a hopper that you use to enter ingredients and a device (inference engine) to mix and extrude the dough. However, you must provide the recipe and ingredients (rules) for the type of pasta you want to create.

knowledge base. To create the expert system, you use the shell to enter the rules, then use the inference engine to test the rules and make certain the decisions they produce are correct.

A&L Outfitters does not currently have an expert system, but the special procurement agent is trying to convince management to explore the possibility of using an expert system to fill orders more efficiently. You'll learn more about expert systems in the next section of this chapter.

Quick Check

1 Word processing software is likely to be part of a(n) _____ system.

2 An information system that collects information when customers purchase merchandise is a point-of-sale system that would be classified as a(n) _____ processing system.

3 A(n) _____ system is characterized by the production of regularly scheduled reports that managers use for structured and routine tasks.

4 A(n) _____ report contains information that is outside of normal, or acceptable, ranges, such as a reorder report showing inventory items that need to be restocked.

5 A(n) _____ system provides users with the ability to manipulate data directly and produce customized reports on demand.

6 A(n) _____ system is designed to capture the knowledge of a specialist in the form of rules. These rules are the basis for the computer to make a decision in response to a problem.

7 A(n) _____ contains an inference engine and a method for analyzing data, but it does not contain any rules.

Creating Expert System Facts and Rules

What's really fascinating about an expert system is its ability to make inferences based on the rules and data in a knowledge base. This ability essentially means that an expert system can "think for itself" to draw conclusions from a set of facts. For example, read through the facts in Figure 11-15 about the British royal family and see if you can determine how William and Henry are related.

Charles is a male, his mother is Elizabeth, his father is Philip, and he is married to Diana.

Andrew is a male, his mother is Elizabeth, his father is Philip, and he is married to Fergie.

William is a male, his mother is Diana, his father is Charles, and he is single.

Henry is a male, his mother is Diana, his father is Charles, and he is single.

You were probably able to infer from these facts that William and Henry are siblings—brothers, actually. What could a computer do with these facts? Computers, as you have probably heard, know only the facts they have been given. If you want a computer to know that William and Henry are brothers, you have to explicitly enter this fact. This was true until expert systems and logic programming were developed. Now, however, we can give an expert system the set of facts in Figure 11-15 and a general rule about siblings, such as "If two people have the same mother or father, they are siblings." The expert system can then use this rule to infer that William and Henry are siblings.

Because the sibling rule is generic—because it doesn't mention any specific people—the expert system can also use it to make inferences about other people in the knowledge base who are siblings. Suppose for a moment that you are the expert system's inference engine. Using the sibling rule, can you find any other siblings in the knowledge base shown in Figure 11-15?

Knowing that the purpose of an expert system is to use rules to make inferences based on a series of facts, you can see that the core activity for creating an expert system is writing facts and rules for the knowledge base. Let's take a closer look at the characteristics of facts and rules.

▶ **Figure 11-15**
Royal family knowledge base

Notice that the general rule about siblings mentions nothing specific about William and Henry, yet the expert system is able to apply the rule to conclude that they are siblings.

If you look at the facts in the knowledge base you will see that Charles and Andrew are siblings because they have the same mother and father.

Facts

How do I write the facts for a knowledge base?

A fact is a basic building block of a knowledge base. You can think of a fact as a statement or simple sentence. For example, here is a knowledge base with three simple facts:

Elizabeth is a female.
Charles is a male.
Elizabeth is Charles' mother.

Once the facts are in a knowledge base, you can ask questions and the expert system will search through the facts to produce an answer. For example, You might ask, "Is Charles a male?" and the expert system would respond with the answer "Yes." Or, you might ask, "Who is Charles' mother?" and the expert system would answer, "Elizabeth." These answers seem obvious to you because you have seen the relevant rules in the knowledge base. However, in a realistic situation, the knowledge base might contain hundreds of facts about British royalty dating back to the ninth century. You could ask "Who was Athelstan's son?" The expert system could tell you that King Athelstan, who ruled from 925 to 940, had a son named Edmund.

The way you write the facts for a knowledge base depends on the development tool you use. When you use an expert system shell, you might be able to type the facts as simple sentences,

In many ways, the facts in a knowledge base are similar to those in a database. You can make queries of either a database or a knowledge base to search through the facts for answers.

such as "Elizabeth is a female." If you use a programming language, such as PROLOG, to construct your expert system, you might use a shorthand notation called **predicate logic**. Suppose you want to enter a fact about William's parents. Instead of entering a rule like "William's mother is Diana and his father is Charles," you can use the predicate logic shorthand, parents('William', 'Diana', 'Charles'). Using predicate logic, you put facts into the framework described in Figure 11-16.

Figure 11-16 ◀
Expressing facts
using predicate
logic

Related elements enclosed in parentheses.

Use a period at the end of the fact.

parents('William', 'Diana', 'Charles').

The predicate describes the relationship of the elements in parentheses.

Commas separate elements.

Use single quotes around proper names.

Figure 11-17 ◀
British royalty facts
in predicate logic
format

At the beginning of this User Focus section, you looked at a series of facts that described the British royal family. Figure 11-17 shows these facts written in predicate logic.

person('Charles', male, 'Elizabeth', 'Philip', 'Diana').

person('Andrew', male, 'Elizabeth', 'Philip', 'Fergie').

person('William', male, 'Diana', 'Charles', single).

person('Henry', male, 'Diana', 'Charles', single).

Rules

Can I use predicate logic for rules, too?

As with facts, the way you enter the rules for an expert system depends on the development tool you use. You'll be disappointed to learn that most development tools do not allow you to enter rules in free-form English. Even though you might think of the siblings rule as "Any two people who have the same mother or father are siblings," you will not be able to use this wording when you enter the rule. The reason most expert system development tools do not accept free-form English rules is that such rules are often too ambiguous for the computer to use in making inferences. Therefore, a more structured format for writing rules is required. In general a development tool requires you to use IF...THEN format or predicate logic to write rules.

IF...THEN format requires rules to begin with an IF clause. The IF clause is followed by a THEN clause. For example, suppose you want to write a rule that if two people have the same father they are related. Using the IF...THEN format, your rule would be:

```
IF father-of-person1 = father-of-person2
THEN person1 and person2 = related
```

The IF...THEN format also allows you to connect clauses with the words AND, OR, and NOT. You could write the following rule to identify brothers:

```
IF father-of-person1 = father-of-person2
AND mother-of-person1 = mother-of-person2
AND person1=male
AND person2=male
THEN person1 and person2 = brothers
```

The format for predicate logic rules is a little more abstract, but it's fun to figure out how this shorthand works. First, think of the rule as the *outcome* followed by a series of facts that would make the outcome true. For example, you would think about the siblings rule as "Person A and Person B are siblings *if* Person A has a mother and father *and* Person B has the same mother and the same father."

Now take each clause, beginning with "Person A and Person B are siblings." How would you express this in predicate logic? You would write siblings (PersonA, PersonB). You make PersonA one word to show that it is one thing. If you wrote it "Person A" (with a space) the computer might think it was two things: one Person and some other thing called A. It is important to capitalize PersonA. That way the computer knows that you're not referring to someone named "PersonA," such as a man named "Mr. PersonA." Instead, PersonA means any person, and the computer needs to figure out that person's name.

Next, how would you express "Person A has a mother and father" in predicate logic format? You would write person(PersonA, Mother, Father). Again, you capitalize Mother and Father to tell the computer that it needs to substitute some real mother and father names here. Can you guess how to express the clause, "Person B has a mother and father?"

When you write the clause person(PersonB, Mother, Father) how does this imply that Person B has *the same* mother and father as Person A? In the rule for Person B you used "Mother" and "Father," the same as you did in the rule for Person A. If you had written person(PersonB, Ma, Pa), you would be implying that Person A has different parents from Person B.

Now you need to join these clauses together. You use the symbols :– for *if*. You use a comma to represent the word "and." Your completed rule is shown in Figure 11-18.

When you use predicate logic, capitalized words that you do not surround with apostrophes are treated as variables.

siblings(PersonA, PersonB):-   Person A and Person B are siblings if

person(PersonA, Mother, Father),   Person A has a Mother or Father and

person(PersonB, Mother, Father).   Person B has [the same]Mother and [the same] Father

▶ **Figure 11-18**
The sibling rule expressed in predicate logic

As you can see, creating the facts and rules for an expert system exercises your mind. In everyday activities, you probably don't think about how you think. How did you look at the facts about British royalty and infer which were siblings? You "just did it," right? But when you write facts and rules for an expert system, you have to become aware of your own mental processes—how you analyze information and make decisions. The people who create expert systems have a job that is sometimes complex and often introspective. Their goal, however, is to create an expert system in which all the details of a decision are hidden from the user. Therefore, using an expert system is much easier than creating one.

End Note   At the end of the ceremony, the Queen proclaimed Michael Abercrombie a knight of the realm. His friends, gathered for the event, good-naturedly greeted him as *Sir Michael*. Michael smiled as he reflected on his business and archeological adventures. There were moments on a few expeditions when he didn't know if he would survive. And there were times when business competition threatened the survival of A&L. But, somehow, clear thinking, a willingness to adapt, and sheer persistence managed to save the day.

The modern business environment is rapidly changing and exceedingly competitive. The very survival of a business can depend on its ability to respond to threats and understand the opportunities provided by technological advances, such as computer information systems.

On a personal level, your future in a profession, organization, or business may be closely linked to your ability to adapt to rapid technological change. If you can learn to deal effectively with technological changes, you will greatly increase your chances for a successful and satisfying career.

Review

1. Divide a sheet of paper into four quadrants labeled Operations, Sales and Marketing, Human Resource, and Financial Management. In each quadrant list at least five examples of a specific organization's activities. For example, in the Operations quadrant you might list "A computer manufacturer assembles microcomputers."

2. Complete the following table, indicating if each activity is part of operations, financial management, sales and marketing, or human resource management.

Activity	Activity Type
A worker assembles cars at an automobile plant	
A restaurant owner plans newspaper ads for the restaurant	
A store manager trains new employees in a clothing store	
A manager calculates total monthly sales	
A member of a recycling group speaks to a service organization to explain how the group encourages home owners to recycle bottles and cans	

3. Complete the following table, indicating the type of computer system represented by each example. The first one is filled in for you.

Example	Type of Computer System
System used to write reports and schedule meetings in a law office	Office automation
System used to sell airline tickets at a travel agency	
System used to analyze automobile problems and determine the most likely cause and solution to the problem	
System used by an executive who wants to find out how many toasters the Wichita store sold in October	

4. Refer to Michael Porter's Five Forces model in Figure 11-2. For each of the following events, indicate if it would be classified as bargaining power of suppliers, threat of new entrants, bargaining power of buyers, threat of substitute products or services, or rivalry among existing competitors.

a. The value of the dollar falls in world markets, making Japanese car imports very expensive.

b. Luxury-car makers move into the utility vehicle market, offering upscale competition to the once popular Jeep Cherokee.

c. 3½-inch disk drives become popular with computer users.

d. The Mideast war results in serious oil shortages.

e. Cable TV companies offer two-way communications links for sending computer data.

5. Without looking back in this chapter, draw an organization pyramid showing the three levels of management and the three categories of workers.

6. Classify the following as information workers, goods workers, or service workers:

secretaries	construction workers	miners
electricians	dock workers	cashiers
beauticians	actors	writers
scientists	welders	chefs

7. Kooler Inc. manufactures plastic coolers suitable for camping and recreational use. The senior management of the firm includes the President, the Vice President for Operations, the Vice President for Finance, and the Vice President for Sales and Marketing. Each vice president is in charge of one or more departments, as described below.

The Vice President for Operations is responsible for three departments: Shipping, Maintenance, and Human Resource. The Vice President for Finance is in charge of the Finance department. The Sales and Marketing departments are the responsibility of the Vice President for Sales and Marketing.
Draw an organizational chart showing how Kooler Inc. is structured.

8. List the three fundamental strategies that an organization can use to respond to threats or take advantage of opportunities.

9. Create a summary table or grid to illustrate the differences between structured, semi-structured, and unstructured problems.

10. List three examples of transaction processing systems. For each system, explain the type of data that is entered into the system and describe one or two reports that the system might produce.

11. Explain the difference between a detail report, a summary report, and an exception report.

12. Create a chart or table that summarizes the characteristics of transaction processing systems, management information systems, decision support systems, and expert systems.

13. Look at the following knowledge base expressed in predicate logic format. Does the rule at the end identify brothers, sisters, friends, or cousins? If an expert system uses this knowledge base, what will it infer?

```
male(charlie).
male(linus).
male(sam).
male(george).
female(lucy).
female(pattie).
female(amanda).
female(anne).
parents(linus, amanda, sam).
parents(lucy, amanda, sam).
parents(pattie, anne, george).
related(X,Y):-
        female(X),
        parents(X, Mother, Father),
        female (Y),
        parents(Y, Mother, Father).
```

Projects

INTERNET OPTIONAL

1. Mission, Threats, and Opportunities
Suppose you are a management consultant for one of the following well-known companies. The company needs to produce a mission statement, and it is your job to help. The company also wants to know what factors might influence its business in the future. Pick one of the companies. Do some library or Internet research to get some background information on the company. Write a mission statement for your company, then use Michael Porter's Five Forces model as the basis for listing five forces that you think are likely to affect your company's business in the next year or two.

    Ben and Jerry's Ice Cream
    NIKE
    Black & Decker
    Harley-Davidson
    Mattel
    Intel
    Royal Caribbean Cruise Line

2. Charting an Organization Interview someone from an organization or business. Draw an organizational chart showing the structure of the organization.

3. Organizational Activities Think of any real or hypothetical business or non-profit organization. Assume that the organization is divided into four departments—operations, financial management, sales and marketing, and human resource management. Write a one-paragraph summary of the types of activities that would be handled by each of the four departments.

4. Responding to a Threat Assume that you are the manager of a movie theater. Local video rental businesses have boomed, and attendance at movies has declined. Write a short paper explaining how you would deal with this threat and keep the movie theater profitable.

5. Taking Advantage of Opportunities Assume you are the manager of a medium-sized snowmobile company. Jet skis are just becoming popular. Write a short paper explaining why you think your company should or should not get into the jet ski business

6. Evaluating Strategies Assume that you are the president of a national fast-food chain. The board of directors has proposed that you empower the employees at the local outlets by allowing them to make decisions about menu items, restaurant decor, and general operations. List three possible advantages to this approach. List three possible disadvantages to this approach.

7. Researching Decision Support Systems Assume you are the Information Systems Director for a manufacturer of office furniture. The president of the company has asked you to learn more about decision support systems. Use the library or the World Wide Web to search for more information about current decision support systems. Make a list of 10 DSS resources and write a one-sentence description of each.

8. The Russian Royal Family Your organization is preparing a Web site containing genealogical information on royal families from around the world. You have been asked to collect the information on the Russian czars. Use your library or the Internet to find the full name, mother's name, father's name, spouse's name, and siblings for each of the last three Russian czars. Record this information as if you were going to use it in a knowledge base. Use the predicate logic syntax you learned in Section 11.4.

Resources

- **Berk, J. and S. Berk.** *Total Quality Management: Implementing Continuous Improvement.* New York: Sterling Publishing Co. Inc., 1993. Find out more about TQM.

- **Clocksin, W. and C. Mellish.** *Programming in PROLOG,* 3rd ed. New York: Springer-Verlag, 1987. This is the classic textbook on programming with the PROLOG computer language. If you are interested in learning more about declarative language and expert systems, this book is excellent.

- **Davis, G. and M. Olson.** *Management Information Systems: Conceptual Foundations, Structure, and Development,* 2nd ed. New York: McGraw-Hill, 1985. This book is the most widely cited concepts text on MIS.

- *Expert Systems* magazine Web site *http://info.learned.co.uk/li/publicat/esbasic.htm* Here is where you will find the Web site for *Expert Systems*, an international journal of knowledge engineering and neural networks. The site contains a list of articles in recent issues, but not the text of the articles themselves. There is, however, a link to reviews of expert systems books.

- **Mizuno, S. and Y. Akao,** eds. *QFD: The Customer-Driven Approach to Quality Planning and Development.* Tokyo, Japan: Asian Productivity Organization, 1994. A well-regarded reference to Quality Function Deployment, the Japanese approach to quality control.

- **NASA Web site on TQM** *http://mijuno.larc.nasa.gov/dfc/tqm.html* This is a NASA Web site devoted to total quality management that includes short articles, a bibliography, list of TQM societies, and links to other TQM Web sites.

- **Porter, M.** *Competitive Advantage: Creating and Sustaining Superior Performance.* New York: Free Press, 1985. Porter explains his Five Forces model in the context of business competition and industrial management.

- **Royal geneology Web site,** *ftp.cac.psu.edu/~saw/royal/* This site contains information on royal families from around the world.

- **Turban, E.** *Decision Support and Expert Systems.* New York: Macmillan, 1988. This is an excellent text on computer applications for management support. The explanations are clear, and many examples illustrate the concepts.

- **Yourdon, E.** *Modern Structured Analysis.* Englewood Cliffs, New Jersey: Yourdon Press, 1989. Everything you wanted to know about systems analysis and design.

Quick Check

Answers

11.1

1. An organization is a group of people working together toward a goal. A business is similar, but the goal is to produce a profit.

2. mission

3. operations, financial management, sales and marketing, human resource management

4. opportunities, threats

5. a. become better at what it does

   b. change the industry structure

   c. create a new product or service

6. total quality management (TQM)

7. downsize (rightsize)

11.2

1.

2. goods

3. strategic planning

4. tactical

5. unstructured

6. internal, external

11.3

1. office automation

2. transaction

3. management information system (MIS)

4. exception

5. decision support

6. expert system

7. expert system shell

Glossary/Index

 A

accountants, 11-9

accounting systems, 11-15

accounting The process of tracking the flow of money through an organization; also called financial management, 11-4

advertising, 11-4–11-5

artists, 11-9

AT&T, 11-8

automation The use of electrical or mechanical devices to improve manufacturing or other processes, 11-6

 B

bookkeepers, 11-9

business Any organization that seeks profit by providing needed goods or services, 11-4

 C

computerization The use of computers to automate business processes, 11-6

 D

decision model A numerical representation of a realistic situation, decision query A question or set of instructions that describes the data that is required to make a decision, 11-17

decision query A question or set of instructions that describes the data that is required to make a decision, 11-17

decision support system (DSS) A system that provides data and modeling tools that managers use to make structured and semi-structured decisions, 11-17, 11-17–11-18

detail report A complete list of transactions, usually in chronological order, such as a list of inventory items alphabetized by product name, 11-16

 E

employee empowerment Giving employees the authority to make business decisions, 11-6

empowerment, 11-6

exception report A list of records that match a condition outside of the usual range or limits, 11-16

exception reports, 11-16

Developing Effective Information Systems

Developing Effective

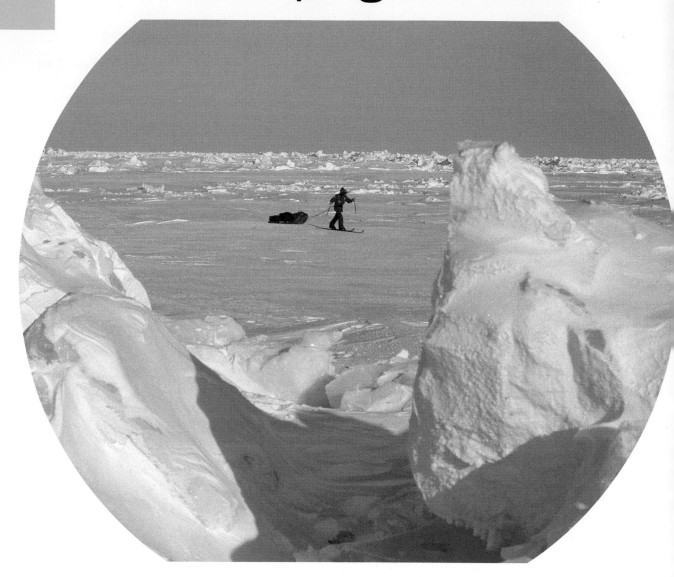

Three men sat around a kitchen table in Oslo, Norway. "So we'll try it!" one said, and the rest agreed. It was the beginning of a daring attempt to cross 413 nautical miles of shifting ice, snow drifts, and frigid water between Canada and the North Pole without assistance from sled dogs, snowmobiles, or resupply flights. Each man would pull a specially designed Kevlar and fiberglass sled containing food, water, and fuel. Each sled would weigh 265 pounds fully loaded.

The expedition members knew that their success depended on having the right gear and provisions, so they immediately contacted Abercrombie & Livingston Outfitters, Ltd. of London. The expedition's order was routed to the A&L branch in Telluride, Colorado—the closest A&L location to the expedition's staging area in Resolute, Canada.

Information Systems

Unfortunately, several items needed by the expedition were not in stock in the Telluride branch. The team couldn't wait for the back-ordered items to arrive with the next scheduled inventory shipment, so a helpful store manager called other A&L outlets, found the items at the Geneva outlet, and had the items shipped to the Telluride branch. The team received the necessary equipment in time, but the process required significant effort on the part of a motivated store manager.

To provide better service to its customers, A&L management decided to upgrade its information system. One of the objectives of the upgrade was to help managers check other outlets to find out-of-stock items. If a local branch does not have a particular item in stock, the upgraded system should check to see which other branches have the item in stock, then identify the branch that can ship the item most quickly and at the lowest cost.

The computer industry abounds with tales of information systems, developed at great expense, that didn't meet expectations because they didn't work correctly, were too complex to use, or weren't flexible enough to meet changing business needs. As Frederick Brooks observes in his book *The Mythical Man-Month*, "One can expect the human race to continue attempting systems just within or just beyond our reach, and software systems are perhaps the most intricate and complex of all man's handiwork."

Whether you are part of a team to develop a complex corporate information system, or whether you are developing a small information system for your own use, you will be more likely to succeed if you analyze the purpose of the information system, carefully design the system, test it thoroughly, and document its features.

This chapter describes the process A&L used to plan and implement the upgrade to its information system. It begins with an overview of the entire development process. It then takes a more detailed look at how to analyze needs, design a new system, construct the system, implement it, and maintain it.

CHAPTER**PREVIEW**

In this chapter you'll find out how to create or upgrade an information system—how to determine what needs to be done, how to design and construct the system, how to test the system to make sure it works correctly, and how to maintain the system. The User Focus section introduces you to an important development tool, data flow diagrams. When you have completed this chapter, you should be able to:

- Explain the system development life cycle

- Understand the difference between a systems analyst and a programmer

- Understand the difference between a problem statement and a solution

- Use the PIECES framework to identify problems in an information system

- Explain how data flow diagrams, data dictionaries, and structured English document the way an information system works

- Understand the difference between system requirements and application specifications

- Differentiate between a request for proposal and a request for quotation

- Discuss the difference between software engineering and knowledge engineering

- Explain the difference between unit testing, integration testing, system testing, and acceptance testing

- Explain the advantages and disadvantages of direct conversion, parallel conversion, phased conversion, and pilot conversion when switching to a new system

LAB

System Testing

12.1 | Analyze Needs

Creating an information system can be compared to building a house. You don't just grab a hammer and start nailing pieces of wood together. It is important to have a plan. An information system is similar to a house in this respect. If you want to end up with a successful product, you must plan before you begin construction. A **system development life cycle** (SDLC), is an outline of a process that helps develop successful information systems. Several variations of the SDLC exist, but most of them are similar to, or variations of, the one shown in Figure 12-1.

Figure 12-1 ◀
System development life cycle

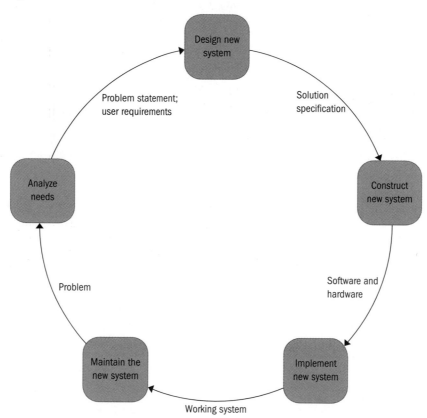

The major activities of the analysis phase of the SDLC are listed in Figure 12-2.

Figure 12-2 ◀
Analysis activities

- ✓ Select the project team
- ✓ Define the problem
- ✓ Study current system
- ✓ Determine requirements

Select the Project Team

Who participates in the process of building an information system?

Computer professionals called **systems analysts** are often responsible for analyzing information requirements, designing a new information system, and supervising the new system implementation. Systems analysts also create specifications for application software for the new system, then give those specifications to computer programmers, who create computer programs to meet those specifications.

Increasingly, managerial and clerical employees initiate and participate in the development of information systems, as is the case at A&L Outfitters. That's why no one was surprised when the special procurement agent at A&L suggested that it was time to automate part of her job. The special procurement agent and a systems analyst from A&L's information systems department formed a project team to work on the new system.

A **system development project team**, or **project team** for short, is a group of people who are assigned to analyze and develop an information system. The composition of the project team depends on the scope of the project. Larger and more complex projects have large project teams, and a majority of the people on the team are systems analysts or other computer professionals. Smaller projects have fewer members on the project team and a higher percentage of the team members are likely to be users, rather than computer professionals. Figure 12-3 contains some excerpts from the first meeting of the special procurement project team as the special procurement agent explains what she calls the "cross-shipping problem."

Systems Analyst (SA): I'm not very familiar with your job. Would you fill me in?

Special Procurement Agent (SPA): As you probably know, when a customer places an order, it is usually filled with items from the local outlet's inventory. However, if that outlet is out of stock on an ordered item, the computer checks to see if it is available in the London warehouse.

SA: Yes, I know how that works. And if the item is in stock in London, we ship it from London to the outlet.

SPA: Right. But if the item is not in the outlet or the London warehouse, the order comes to me. I try to locate the item by using the DSS system. If I find the item at another outlet, I usually ask them to "cross-ship" the item to the outlet where it was ordered.

SA: By cross-ship, do you mean that one outlet ships the item to another outlet?

SPA: Exactly.

SA: That sounds like you're making effective use of the system. So what's the problem?

SPA: The problem is that it takes time for me to check the inventories and decide which outlet can supply the item fastest and least expensively. I usually don't receive notification for 24 hours; then, with my workload, it might be another day or two before I can tackle it.

SA: I see.

SPA: It's costing the company a lot of money to deliver some of these items, considering the time I spend and the possible delay to the customer.

SA: So I assume you would like to automate the cross-shipping decision, if possible?

SPA: Yes, I think it would be cost-effective.

▶ **Figure 12-3**
Excerpts from the special procurement project team meeting

If you think of an information system as a movie in which computers, software, users, and programmers play the starring roles, the systems analyst is the screenwriter who creates the script that coordinates the actions of all the actors.

When you analyze an information system, ask yourself if any of the PIECES problems apply. For example, ask yourself if there is a Performance problem, if there is an Information problem, and so on.

Define the Problem

How do I begin to analyze an information system?

The first activities in the analysis phase are to define the problem and create one or more problem statements. A **problem statement** is a sentence that identifies what needs to be improved or fixed. Here are some examples of well-defined problem statements for information systems:

- In a garden supply store: The price tags frequently fall off items—especially the plants—so customers have to wait at the registers while an employee checks the price.
- In a casino: Croupiers are not allowed to extend additional credit to a gambler, so everyone at the table must wait while a manager goes to the cashier's cage to check the customer's credit.
- In a police car: Officers do not have access to out-of-state arrest warrants, so they might stop a motorist for a minor violation but fail to make an arrest on a more serious charge.

A common pitfall in the analysis phase is to state a solution, rather than a problem. Solutions are not appropriate at this stage of the SDLC because you should not consider solutions until you understand more about the problem with the current system. Although the following statements might sound reasonable, they are solutions, not problems:

- The garden supply store needs a bar-code reader so cashiers can determine the price of an item even if it doesn't have a price tag.
- The casino should provide floor managers with cellular phones so they can call the cashier's cage for a credit check.
- The police car should be equipped with a computer that can access a national database of outstanding arrest warrants.

James Wetherbe developed the PIECES framework to help identify problems that exist in an information system. Each letter of PIECES stands for a potential problem, as shown in Figure 12-4.

Figure 12-4 ◄ PIECES helps identify problems

Performance
The system has a performance problem if it does not respond fast enough to users or it takes too long to complete processing tasks.

Information
There is an information problem if users don't receive the right information at the right time, in a usable format.

Economics
There is an economics problem if the system costs too much to use.

Control
There is a control problem if information is available to unauthorized users or if authorized users are not given the authority to make decisions based on the information they have.

Efficiency
There is an efficiency problem if too many resources are used to collect, process, store, and distribute information.

Service
There is a service problem if the system is too difficult or inconvenient to use.

At A&L Outfitters the special procurement agent classified the procurement problem as an efficiency problem. Too many resources, that is, too many hours of her time, are devoted to choosing the best location from which to cross-ship items. The special procurement agent and systems analyst at A&L Outfitters created the following problem statement:

> **If a customer orders an item that is out of stock, the current procedures are not efficient for determining whether other outlets have the item in stock, and from which outlet the item could be cross-shipped cost-effectively.**

Study the Current System

Is it important to understand the current system before planning a new system?

Typically, a new information system is designed to replace a system or process that is already in place. It is essential to study the current system carefully and understand its strengths and weaknesses before planning the new system.

Systems analysts use *data flow diagrams*, *data dictionaries*, and *structured English* to document the way a system, or a part of a system, works. Study Figure 12-5 to see how such documentation gives you a better idea of how A&L's current system works.

In Section 12.6, you'll learn how to create data flow diagrams.

Figure 12-5
System documentation

Data Dictionary

A **data dictionary** contains detailed descriptions of the data that flows through the information system.

Data flow diagram

The open rectangle indicates stored data and is referred to as a **data store**. This data store contains data on each item in inventory: such as inventory item number, description, cost, price, location, and quantity on hand.

On a **data flow diagram,** the data that moves through the system is indicated by arrows called **flow lines**. The ordered item data on this flow line includes the item number, description, quantity ordered, price, and order number.

A rounded rectangle indicates a **process** that the system performs on the data.

A square indicates an **external entity**: a person or organization that is not part of the information system.

```
Check Inventory

If the QuantityOnHand at the nearest Outlet>=Qty
   then print item information on packing slip
   otherwise, if QuantityOnHand at the London warehouse>=Qty
       then print item information on packing slip
       otherwise, print the order for the special
       procurement agent.
```

A **process specification** explains what happens to data within a process. Often, process specifications are written in structured English to concisely and unambiguously explain the logic of the process.

Process Specification

Data flow diagrams, data dictionaries, and structured English are valuable tools for analyzing information systems. These tools help analysts produce documentation that is also useful in the design and maintenance phases. However, it can be difficult to keep the diagrams, dictionaries, and structured English specifications for an information system up to date. For example, if the information systems department at A&L decided to rename Qty to QtyOrdered, several revisions would need to be made in the data dictionary and the process specification. It might be easy to miss one of the changes, which could lead to errors and bugs in the information system.

To make it easier to maintain data flow diagrams, data dictionaries, and process specifications, systems analysts use CASE tools. CASE stands for computer aided software engineering. A **CASE tool** is software that is designed for drawing diagrams of information systems, writing process specifications, and maintaining data dictionaries. A CASE tool keeps track of the labels on data flow diagrams, data dictionaries, and process specifications. If you change a label in one place, the CASE tool makes the appropriate revisions everywhere else. Figure 12-6 shows a screen from a CASE tool called Excelerator.

Figure 12-6
A screen from the Excelerator CASE tool

Menus help the analyst modify the diagram and edit the data dictionary.

The analyst uses the rounded rectangle tool to draw the process symbols on the DFD.

This is the process currently being added to the DFD.

The analyst adds the name of the process using the Modify Entity Data Process window.

Additional information about the process can be added, including a process specification.

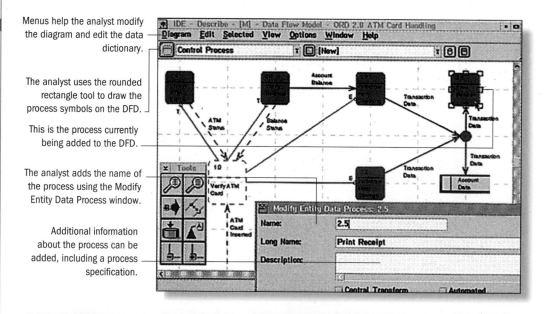

A CASE tool is to a systems analyst what a word processor is to a secretary. CASE tools help analysts create and modify the design documents with which they work.

Determine System Requirements

How do you determine what the new system should do?

System requirements are the criteria for successfully solving the problem or problems you have identified. These requirements will guide you as you design and plan a new information system. Requirements also serve as an evaluation checklist at the end of the development project, so they are sometimes called **success factors**. The information system you create should meet the requirements you defined.

An analyst determines requirements by interviewing users and studying successful information systems that solve problems similar to those found in the earlier stages of analysis.

The special procurement agent at A&L Outfitters created the following list of requirements:

- When the current information system fills an order, it should check stock in all the outlets, then correctly determine the best outlet from which to ship each item.
- The system should be able to determine the best outlet from which to ship without any human intervention.

- **The system should be easy to maintain. When shipping rates or shipping times between outlets change, it should be easy to change that information in the system.**

Another way to determine requirements is to construct a prototype. A **prototype** is an experimental or trial version of an information system. Often the prototype is not a fully functioning system because it is designed only to demonstrate selected features that might be incorporated into a new information system. An analyst demonstrates the prototype to users who evaluate which features of the prototype are important for the new information system.

Quick Check

1 The _____ is an outline of a process that helps develop effective information systems.

2 _____ are often responsible for analyzing information requirements, designing a new information system, and supervising the new system implementation.

3 A(n) _____ is a sentence that identifies what needs to be improved or fixed in an information system.

4 A(n) _____ tool is software that is designed for drawing diagrams of information systems, writing process specifications, and maintaining data dictionaries.

5 _____ , sometimes called _____ , are the criteria for successfully solving a problem or problems.

6 A(n) _____ is an experimental or trial version of an information system that is under development.

12.2 Design the New System

In the design phase, alternate solutions are identified and evaluated, hardware and software are selected, and the specifications for constructing the system are developed, as noted in Figure 12-7.

Figure 12-7
Design activities

- Identify potential solutions
- Evaluate solutions and select the best
- Purchase hardware and software
- Develop application specifications

Identify Potential Solutions

What if there seem to be multiple ways to solve the problem?

There might be more than one way to solve the problem you have identified and meet the requirements you specified in the analysis phase of the SDLC. Some potential solutions might be better than others: more effective, less costly, or less complex. Therefore, it is not a good idea to proceed with the first solution that comes to mind. You should, instead, identify several potential solutions, then compare the advantages and disadvantages of each. Finally, select the solution that provides the most benefits for the least cost.

Remember that information systems include people, procedures, data, hardware, and software. When you identify potential solutions, consider whether there are alternatives in any of these areas. For example, you might consider if there are software alternatives such as purchasing a commercial program, writing custom software, or using an application development tool. Let's see how A&L might look at alternative software solutions for its upgraded information system.

When designing an information system, remember to consider alternative solutions for software, hardware, procedures, and personnel.

An **application development tool**, sometimes called a **4GL** for fourth-generation language, is essentially a type of software construction kit that contains building blocks you can assemble into a software product. Application development tools usually produce applications faster than traditional programming languages. As an analogy, consider baking a cake. You can sift the flour with the salt, mix the sugar, eggs, shortening, and milk, then combine the dry and wet ingredients, and so forth to create a cake "from scratch." This is analogous to creating a software application using a programming language. Another way to bake a cake is with a cake mix. You just add water and eggs, mix, and bake. An application development tool is the programmer's "cake mix" and provides a quicker, easier way to construct an application.

Creating an information system using a programming language takes many months or years and is very costly. Using an application development tool reduces the time and cost somewhat, but application development is still a major effort. Another possibility is to purchase a commercial software application and customize it where possible to fit with the way the organization works. In summary, there are often three alternative software solutions: (1) create the application using a programming language; (2) build the application using an application development tool; or (3) buy a commercial software application.

Evaluate Solutions and Select the Best

How do you choose the best solution?

A spreadsheet or other decision support tool can help you select the best alternative by determining the criteria and ranking alternatives.

After you list alternative solutions, you can evaluate each solution based on its advantages and disadvantages. The project team at A&L Outfitters is considering three software options. They could use a programming language or other software development tool to write a custom module to determine when and where to cross-ship. The advantage of this solution is that a custom program can be designed to meet the procurement agent's requirements exactly. The disadvantage of this solution is that it requires the services of one or more programmers. Considering the backlog of upgrade requests in the information systems department, the module would probably not be available for 18 months.

Another potential solution for A&L is to purchase a commercial software application that already includes the ability to determine when and where to cross-ship. The advantage of this solution is that commercial applications have already been well tested and could be installed very quickly. But it might be difficult to locate a commercial application that would work with the current transaction processing system. Many commercial applications are designed to interact only with other modules purchased from the same vendor. Aside from the cross-shipping problem, A&L is happy with the current transaction processing system and doesn't intend to switch to an entirely new system just to add cross-shipping capability.

Another possible solution is to use an application development tool such as an expert system shell to design an expert system module that determines the feasibility of cross-shipping. An advantage of this solution is that the special procurement agent can play an active role in the development process. Disadvantages of this solution include the time the special procurement agent will have to spend developing the system and the possible trouble she and the systems analyst might have integrating the expert system with the rest of the transaction processing system.

To evaluate the three potential solutions, the special procurement agent creates a list of evaluation criteria:

- **The solution must run on A&L's current hardware.**
- **The software application for the solution must integrate with the current transaction processing system.**
- **The solution must be in place within six months.**
- **The solution must meet the requirements delineated in the analysis phase.**
- **Support for the solution must be available from a vendor, software publisher, manufacturer, or the A&L information systems department.**

After evaluating the alternatives, the project team decides that the best solution is to use an expert system shell to create an expert system that would work with the current transaction processing system. Custom programming would take too long, and the team was unable to locate an appropriate commercial application that would work with A&L's current system.

The project team takes its proposal to management. In most organizations, management approval is necessary for modifications or additions to the current information system. Management approval is also necessary for equipment purchases, software purchases, and time commitments for personnel resources, such as the time it takes to design, create, test, and maintain an information system.

A systems analyst works with users and reports to management, so interpersonal skills are an important qualification for careers in information systems development.

Purchase Hardware and Software

Once you've decided what you want to do and have selected a solution, how do you get started?

Once you select a solution and management has cleared the project to proceed, the next activity is to purchase the hardware and software needed to implement the solution. Typically, more than one vendor sells the hardware and software necessary for the new system, so an organization often has a choice of vendors.

The method for selecting the hardware, software, and vendor depends on the project team's understanding of what is required for the solution. If the team members do not know exactly what hardware and software are needed, they can describe the problem and ask vendors how they would resolve it. If the project team members know exactly what they want, they just need to find a reputable vendor who sells the equipment at a reasonable price.

A **request for proposal**, or RFP, is a document you send to vendors that describes the problem you are trying to solve and the requirements for the solution. The RFP essentially asks the vendors to recommend a solution and describe their qualifications to implement the solution. You

In Project 3 you will look on the Internet for some RFPs produced by real companies seeking assistance with system development.

usually use an RFP when you have not yet selected the equipment or software that meets your needs.

A **request for quotation**, or RFQ, is a request for a formal price quotation on a list of hardware and software. You submit an RFQ when you know the make and model of the equipment and the titles of the software packages you need, but you want to compare prices. Figure 12-8 shows the difference between an RFP and an RFQ.

Figure 12-8
An RFP and RFQ

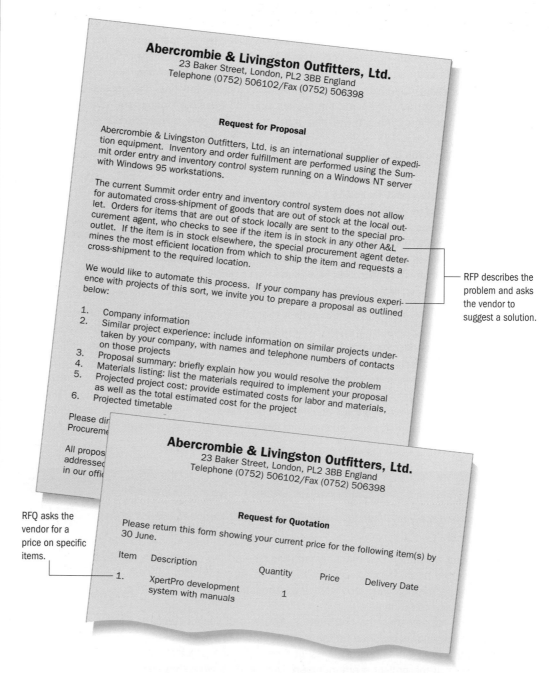

RFP describes the problem and asks the vendor to suggest a solution.

RFQ asks the vendor for a price on specific items.

The special procurement agent and systems analyst at A&L Outfitters explore a variety of expert system development tools. Eventually they select a product called XpertPro. It is an expert system shell that has been used successfully in many companies in Europe and North America. They selected XpertPro because it runs on their current hardware, it is compatible with Windows operating systems, it will integrate with their current transaction processing system, and it appears to provide the capabilities they need. Because the special procurement agent knows exactly what she wants, she asks the A&L purchasing department to send RFQs to vendors who sell XpertPro. When the vendors return the RFQs, the purchasing agent at A&L looks for the vendor that offers the most competitive price and then orders XpertPro from that vendor.

Develop Application Specifications

How do you make sure that the information system that is finally created will meet your needs?

Application specifications describe the way an application should interface with the user, store data, process data, and format reports. The specifications are similar to an architectural blueprint that shows the detailed plan for constructing a building. For large information systems, a systems analyst develops the specifications after interviewing users to determine their information needs. The specifications are then given to a programmer or application developer, who creates the application. In a small information systems project, you as the user might develop your own specifications. Then you might give the specifications to a programmer, or if you have the expertise, you might create the application yourself.

Whether a large or small system is under development, it requires detailed specifications so that the final system solves the problem defined during the analysis phase. At A&L, the specifications for the expert system define the rules for the knowledge base. The project team develops the following rules for the cross-ship expert system:

- If the ordered item is in stock at the outlet nearest the destination of the order, then deliver the item from that outlet.
- If the ordered item is not in stock in any outlet, then send the order to the special procurement agent.
- If the ordered item is in stock at only one outlet, then cross-ship the item from that outlet.
- If the ordered item is in stock in more than one outlet, then cross-ship it from the outlet with the lowest shipping cost and fastest delivery time.

Quick Check

1. In the _____ phase, you should identify several potential solutions, evaluate these solutions, and then select the one that offers the most benefits at the lowest cost.

2. A(n) _____ can help you compare the costs and benefits of several potential solutions.

3. A(n) _____ is a document sent to vendors that describes the problem and the requirements for the solution.

4. You would send out a(n) _____ if you know exactly what hardware and software you want to purchase.

5. _____ describe the way an application should interface with the user, store data, process data, and format reports.

Construct the System

Figure 12-9
Construction
activities

In the construction phase, new hardware and software are installed, applications are created to meet the specifications developed during the design phase, and the new system is tested, as noted in Figure 12-9.

Install Hardware and Software

What's the first step in the construction phase?

Installing hardware and software is the first step in the construction phase. The expert system for A&L Outfitters does not require any new hardware. However, in many development projects, new hardware is required and is installed during the construction phase. New hardware can either replace old equipment or be connected to existing equipment. In either case, new hardware must be tested to make sure it operates correctly. Problems with the hardware or connections to other equipment must be corrected during the construction phase so they do not disrupt the implementation phase.

Many new information systems require new software such as a commercial application, a programming language, an application development tool, or an expert system shell. Before it is used, software must be installed and tested to make sure it works correctly. Software testing can reveal problems that result from incompatibilities with the existing hardware or an incorrect installation of the software. These problems must be corrected before continuing with system construction activities. Other problems might result from bugs, or errors, in the software and must be corrected by the organization that originally wrote the software.

The A&L project team installs and tests the expert system development shell, XpertPro. At this stage, the project team is only testing the *development tool* to make sure it runs on the computer without generating error messages—the rules for the expert system have not yet been entered, so the team is not testing the cross-shipping rules yet. When the team members are sure that the expert system shell operates correctly, they continue with the construction of the cross-shipping system.

Software—even commercial software—isn't perfect. There are always bugs. If you discover bugs during the construction phase, it is important to contact the software publisher to find out when and if the company can fix the bug.

Create Applications

So, you've got the new hardware, new software tools, and complete application specifications. Are you ready to begin?

So far, you have seen that information systems can be constructed using tools such as a programming language, an application development tool, commercial software, or an expert system shell. As Figure 12-10 shows, the construction technique depends on the construction tool.

Figure 12-10
Construction
techniques depend
on the tool

Construction Tool	Construction Techniques
Programming language	Install programming language. Write application modules using programming language. Test application modules separately and as a whole to make sure there are no errors.
Application development tool	Install the application development tool. Use the tool's building blocks to construct application. Test application modules separately and as a whole to make sure there are no errors.
Commercial software	Install the commercial software. Customize software to meet specifications, if possible. Test the software to make sure the customization reflects the specifications.
Expert system shell	Install the expert system shell. Enter facts and rules in the knowledge base. Test the expert system to make sure the rules are correct.

When the applications or programs for an information system are created using a programming language or application development tool, the process is referred to as **software engineering**.

When an information system is constructed using a commercial application, the application has been written and tested by the software publisher. However, the application sometimes needs to be customized. **Software customization** is the process of modifying a commercial application to reflect the needs of the users. Customization might include changing the appearance of the user interface, enabling or disabling the mouse, selecting the menus that appear, and designing forms or reports. The extent to which a commercial application can be customized depends on the options available in the application. For example, some commercial applications provide options for customizing report formats while other commercial applications do not.

When an information system requires the construction of an expert system, the facts and rules for the knowledge base must be entered and tested. The process of designing, entering, and testing the rules in an expert system is referred to as **knowledge engineering**. Because the members of the A&L project team have decided to use an expert system shell to construct the cross-ship application, their major construction activities are to enter and test the facts and rules for the expert system. As with any application, the A&L expert system must meet the design specifications and go through a rigorous testing process to ensure that the facts and rules produce the expected results.

Test Applications

How can you make sure that a new information system works?

A rigorous testing process is the only way to make sure a new information system works. Different types of testing during the construction phase help identify and fix problems before the information system is incorporated into day-to-day business activities.

Application testing is the process of trying out various sequences of input values and checking the results to make sure the application works correctly. Application testing is performed in three ways: unit testing, integration testing, and system testing.

As each application unit is completed, it undergoes **unit testing** to make sure that it operates reliably and correctly. When all units are complete and tested, **integration testing** is performed to ensure that the units operate correctly together. Unit testing and integration testing are usually performed in a test area. A **test area** is a place where software testing can occur without disrupting the organization's regular information system. A test area might be an isolated section of storage on the computer system that runs the organization's regular information system, or it might be on an entirely separate computer system. When problems are discovered during unit testing or integration testing, the cause of the problem is determined and the problem is corrected. Unit testing and integration testing are then repeated to make sure that the problem is corrected and to make sure that no new problems were introduced when the original problem was fixed.

After the unit and integration testing are completed, **system testing** ensures that all the hardware and software components work together. If an existing information system is modified, system testing is performed when the new or modified units are combined with the rest of the existing system. In a completely new information system, system testing is performed to simulate daily work loads and make sure that processing speed and accuracy meet the specifications. System testing is ideally performed in a test area; however, an organization might not have the hardware resources to duplicate its existing information system for testing purposes. In this case, system testing must be performed on the "live," or production, system; this can cause some disruption in the normal functions of the organization.

The A&L project team has one application unit to test: the expert system. To perform the test, the project team places a series of sample orders. The results of the test are examined to see

Application testing is usually the responsibility of the programmers or the project team. A specific test plan is developed and carried out during the construction phase of system development.

Lab

System Testing

if the expert system completes the orders as expected. In most cases, the expert system works, but the team discovers that two orders do not go through correctly. On examining these two orders, the A&L team notices that in both cases, the item was in stock in two locations that had the same shipping cost and the same shipping time. No rule had been entered that told the system which location to select when an item is available in more than one location that has the same shipping time and the same shipping cost. The A&L team added the following rule and retested the system.

- **If more than one outlet has the item in stock and the shipping cost and the shipping time are the same, then ship from the outlet that has more of the items in stock.**

After adding this rule, the team tests the expert system again. This time all the test orders are processed correctly.

The A&L project has only one module, so integration testing is not necessary. For system testing, the project team loads the expert system and a copy of the order system into a test area. The purpose of this testing session is to make sure the order data is correctly communicated between the existing order entry system and the new expert system. The system test goes smoothly, and so it is time for the project team to schedule implementation of the new system.

Quick Check

1 _____ is the process used to create a program using a programming language or application development tool.

2 The process of designing, entering, and testing the rules in an expert system is referred to as _____ .

3 _____ testing verifies correct operation of a particular component.

4 _____ testing verifies correct operation of multiple components working together.

5 A(n) _____ is a place where software testing can occur without disrupting the existing information system.

6 _____ testing ensures that all hardware and software components work correctly together.

Implement the New System

In the implementation phase, the information system is placed into operation. This phase requires careful planning and preparation. The activities that occur in the implementation phase are shown in Figure 12-11.

▶ **Figure 12-11**
Implementation activities

Train Users

How do people find out how to use the new information system?

The expert system for A&L Outfitters works behind the scenes, so it doesn't require any user interaction or training. However, for many new information systems, the users need extensive training on system operation, data entry, and additional procedures. If user training is required, the organization schedules training sessions. Training sessions are sometimes conducted by systems analysts, but might also be conducted by professional trainers or by users from the project team. During the training sessions, users learn how to interact with the interface, how to perform their tasks using the new system, and how to find additional information in user manuals or procedure handbooks. **Procedure handbooks** contain step-by-step instructions for performing a specific job task. A procedure manual takes the place of a complete user manual because in large organizations, employees in a particular department usually perform specific tasks and do not need to know how all the features of the system work.

Procedure manuals contain instructions for carrying out a specific task, whereas a user manual contains general instructions for using all the features of a system.

Convert Data

What happens to the data from the old system?

The data used by the A&L expert system is taken directly from the transaction processing system, so it is not necessary to convert any data before implementing the new system. However, implementation of many new information systems requires data to be converted from a manual or previous computer system to the new system. For example, suppose a local Department of Motor Vehicles office has a manual system for issuing and renewing driver's licenses. It has more than 8,000 records for currently licensed drivers. If this office computerizes, it will need to convert these 8,000 records into electronic format that can be accessed by the new computerized system.

When converting data from a manual system to a computer system, the data can either be typed or scanned electronically into the appropriate storage media. Some organizations have a lot of data that must be converted, and the conversion process can take a long time, require extra personnel, and be quite costly. When converting data from a previous computer system to a new system, a programmer writes conversion software to read the old data and convert it into a format that is usable by the new system.

Convert to New System

How does a business go about switching from the old system to the new system?

System conversion refers to the process of deactivating the old system and activating the new one. System conversion is also referred to as "cutover" or "go live." There are several strategies for converting to a new system.

A **direct conversion** means that the old system is completely deactivated and the new system is immediately activated. Direct conversion usually takes place during non-peak hours to minimize disruption to normal business routines. Direct conversion is risky, however, because if the

Don't confuse system conversion and data conversion—data conversion changes data from one format to another, whereas system conversion changes from one information system to another.

new system does not work correctly, it might need to be deactivated and tested further. In the meantime, the old system must be reactivated and the transactions that were entered into the new system need to be reentered into the old system so business can continue.

A **parallel conversion** avoids some of the risk of direct conversion because the old system remains in service as some or all of the new system is activated. Both the old and the new systems operate in parallel until it can be determined whether the new system is performing correctly. Parallel conversion often requires that all entries are made in both the new and old systems, which is costly in terms of time, computer resources, and personnel. Parallel conversion is fairly safe, but often not practical because of the cost and duplication of effort.

Phased conversion works well with larger information systems that are modularized. In a **phased conversion**, one module of the new information system is activated at a time. After it has been determined that the module is working correctly, the next module is activated, until the entire new system is operating. In a phased conversion, each module of the new system has to work with both the old system and the new system, greatly increasing the complexity and cost of the conversion.

A **pilot conversion** works well in organizations with several branches that have independent information processing systems. The new information system is activated at one branch. After it has been determined that the system works correctly at one branch, it is activated at the next branch. During a pilot conversion, some method must be developed to integrate information from branches using the new system with information from branches still using the old system.

A&L Outfitters has decided on a direct conversion for the following reasons:

- The added expense of a parallel conversion is probably unnecessary because the expert system has been extensively tested and is likely to work correctly.
- A pilot conversion is not possible because all the branch outlets access the same information system.
- Phased conversion would not be feasible because there is only one module.

Acceptance Testing

What about the people who are buying or will be using the system? Do they get a chance to make sure it is working correctly?

After the conversion, an information system undergoes a final test called acceptance testing. **Acceptance testing** is designed to assure the purchaser or user of the new system that the system does what it is supposed to do. The procedures for acceptance testing are usually designed by the users and system analysts, and they often include the use of real data to make sure that the system operates correctly under normal and peak data loads.

At A&L Outfitters, the special procurement agent has allotted a week's time to observe the expert system in operation to make sure it is working acceptably. If the week passes and no major problems appear with the system, the project team will consider the implementation phase complete.

You should recognize that application testing takes place in the construction phase, but acceptance testing takes place in the implementation phase.

Quick Check

1 A(n) _____ contains step-by-step instructions for performing a specific task.

2 _____ is often used to convert data from an old information system into a format that is usable by the new system.

3 Data conversion refers to the process of converting data, while _____ refers to the process of switching from the old system to the new system.

4 _____ conversion means the old system is completely deactivated and the new system is immediately activated.

5 In a(n) _____ conversion, both the new system and the old system remain operational—entries are made in both systems until it is determined that the new system is performing correctly.

6 In a(n) _____ conversion, one module of the new system is activated at a time.

7 In a(n) _____ conversion, the new system is activated in a single branch or location, where it is thoroughly tested before being activated in the rest of the organization.

8 _____ testing is designed to assure the purchaser or user of the new system that the system does what it is supposed to do.

12.5 Maintain the System

Figure 12-12
Maintenance
activities

After a system is implemented, it remains in operation for a period of time. During this time, maintenance activities ensure that the system functions as well as possible. Figure 12-12 shows the major maintenance activities for a typical information system.

The A&L expert system will be maintained along with the rest of the transaction processing system. Information systems personnel will make sure that it is backed up regularly. They will also monitor system performance to make sure the expert system does not create a bottleneck and slow down the rest of the system. The special procurement agent has a copy of the expert system that she can use to make modifications in response to changing conditions, for example, if Federal Express changes its shipping rates.

Some organizations spend as much as 80% or more of their information systems budget on software maintenance. Maintenance tasks come from many sources and follow a U-shaped curve, as shown in Figure 12-13.

Figure 12-13
Factors that
require system
maintenance

The maintenance phase continues until the information system is no longer cost-effective or changes in the organization make the information system obsolete. It is not unusual for an information system to remain in operation for 20 years, but eventually its useful or cost-effective life nears a close. Then it is time to begin the systems development life cycle again.

Quick Check

1 _____ activities include backing up the system, monitoring the system for correct performance, and modifying the system in response to changing conditions.

2 Some organizations spend as much as ____% of their information systems budget on software maintenance.

3 In the early stages of a new information system, much of the maintenance effort is expended dealing with _____.

4 An information system is typically used until it is no longer _____ or until it is made obsolete by changes in the organization.

5 When an information system becomes obsolete, it is time to begin the _____ once again.

User Focus:
Using Data Flow Diagrams

A **data flow diagram**, sometimes called a DFD, graphically illustrates how data moves through a system. You can think of a DFD as a map that traces the possible paths for data traveling from entities such as customers through processes such as printing, or to storage areas. It is much easier to get an overview of an information system by studying a DFD than by reading a lengthy description. Before you learn about DFD details, look at the DFD in Figure 12-14 and see if you can figure out whether it represents A&L's transaction processing system, MIS, DSS, or expert system.

Figure 12-14
DFD of an A&L system

OUTLET INVENTORY

OUTLET INVENTORY

OUTLET INVENTORY

SHIPPING INFO

quantity instock

shipping cost and delivery time

customer order

item on customer order

TPS

EXSYS.QUE

Determine best source

ORDERS.QUE

order with item locations

Print picking ticket

picking ticket

Shipping clerk

DFD Symbols

What's the significance of the different symbols on a DFD?

Standardized symbols shown in Figure 12-15 make it easy for programmers and systems analysts to understand a DFD. Knowing what each symbol signifies will help you draw your own DFDs and will help you identify the A&L system that is depicted in Figure 12-14.

An **external entity** is typically a square box that represents an outside source or destination for data. An external entity might be a customer who places an order, a supplier from which you receive inventory items, or another computer system that provides data. You should label external entities with a singular noun such as "Customer" or "Supplier." The A&L system in Figure 12-14 shows two external entities: TPS (transaction processing system) and Shipping clerk. This system receives data from the A&L transaction processing system and sends data to a shipping clerk.

A **data flow** is a line that represents data as it flows through an information system. Arrows at the end of a data flow indicate

Figure 12-15
Data flow diagram symbols

External entity

Data flow

Process

Data store

*You might have heard of "flow charts." Data flow diagrams are not the same. Flow charts show a sequence of steps for **how** to process data. A data flow diagram shows **what** happens to data in an information system.*

the direction in which data moves. A double-ended arrow indicates that data moves in both directions. You should label data flow lines with the name of a record, such as "order form," or with a field name, such as "Lastname." The DFD for the A&L system in Figure 12-14 shows that the data in this system is a customer order. A customer order contains the customer name and address, as well as the items the customer ordered.

A **process box** is typically a rounded rectangle that contains the name of a process or procedure. A process box might represent an activity such as "Print picking ticket," "Remove duplicates," or "Sort by last name." When you draw a DFD, you label each process box. The label usually begins with a verb such as "Print" or "Sort" to show that a process does something to the data. The DFD for the A&L system in Figure 12-14 contains two processes. You can see from the labels on these processes that this system determines which outlet is the best source for an item that a customer ordered. It also prints a "picking ticket," which is a list of inventory items and their locations that shipping clerks use to find the items they must pack in an order.

A **data store** is depicted as an open-ended rectangle. A data store shows data at rest, such as when data is stored in a file on a hard disk. You can label data stores with the name of the file that contains the data. The A&L system in Figure 12-14 contains four data stores. EXSYS.QUE holds customer orders while they are waiting to be processed. A series of data stores labeled OUTLET INVENTORY each contain a file of inventory items, their prices, and the quantity of each currently in stock. Each OUTLET INVENTORY represents the data stored at one of A&L's branch outlets. The SHIPPING INFO data store contains the rates and shipping times for shipping companies such as FedEx, UPS, and U.S. mail. ORDERS.QUE is a file that contains customer orders and, importantly, the nearest location that has the item in stock.

As you have probably recognized, the DFD in Figure 12-14 depicts A&L's new expert system. The purpose of this system is to figure out the best source for the items ordered by a customer. Obviously, if the item is in stock at the local warehouse, that is the best source. However, if the item is not in stock locally, the expert system will search the inventory of warehouses at other A&L locations. When it finds the item at one or more other warehouses, the expert system will analyze shipping prices and times to select the best source. The system then prints a picking ticket at the appropriate warehouse, so a shipping clerk can pack the item and send it.

Interpreting a DFD

How do I read a DFD so I can understand the information system it represents?

To understand a DFD, you should first look at the external entities to find out where the data originates and where it is ultimately headed. Next, you begin to trace the path of the data by following the arrows. To find out how the data gets processed, you read the labels on the process boxes.

It is important to recognize that the data you are tracing is not the only data in the system. To process the data you are tracing, the information system often requires other data. For example, to determine which outlet is the best source for items on a customer order, the information system needs to look at data stored in the OUTLET INVENTORY and SHIPPING INFO. The annotated DFD in Figure 12-16 highlights some of the important points you can discover from the DFD of A&L's expert system.

Figure 12-16
Annotated A&L DFD

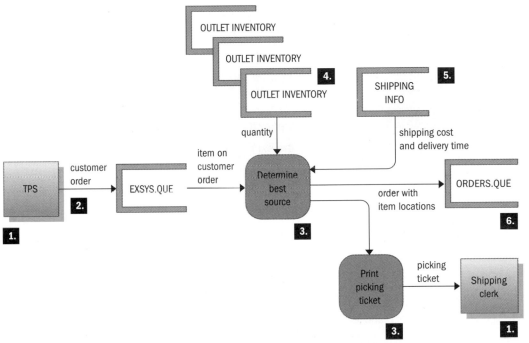

Figure 12-16
Annotated A&L DFD

1. Data originates from the A&L transaction processing system and ends up in the hands of a shipping clerk and in the ORDERS.QUE data store.

2. The data originates as a record called "customer order."

3. The system carries out two processes: It determines the best source for an ordered item, and it prints a picking ticket.

4. To determine the best source for an inventory item, the system checks inventory using data from a series of data stores called OUTLET INVENTORY. Each data store contains the inventory for one A&L warehouse.

5. The system needs to use data from the SHIPPING INFO data store if the item is not in stock at the local warehouse.

6. After the system determines the best source, it now has a customer order that contains a list of ordered items and the warehouse from which each item can be shipped. This data is stored in ORDERS.QUE, where it can be accessed by A&L's other information systems. The order data is further processed by being printed as a picking ticket.

Accuracy and Completeness

How can I tell if a DFD is accurate?

If someone shows you a DFD, it is likely that your feedback is needed on the completeness and accuracy of the data flows and processes. After you have interpreted the DFD and have an overview of the system it depicts, think carefully about each process. Examine the data that enters the process and the data that it produces. Is the data that enters the process sufficient to produce the data that leaves the process? For example, suppose the OUTLET INVENTORY data store was missing from A&L's expert system DFD. Without this data, how could the "Determine best source" process take an order item and produce the name of the outlet that has the item in stock? If OUTLET INVENTORY was omitted, the DFD would not be accurate.

You can also check the DFD for black holes and miracles. A **black hole** is a process that has no output. A process that just "does something" to data, but doesn't put that data anywhere is useless. A **miracle** is a process that has no input. This is an aptly named mistake—like a wizard

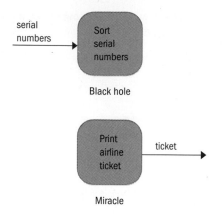

Figure 12-17
Black holes and
miracles

Black hole

Miracle

trying to conjure a bouquet of flowers from thin air, it is impossible for an information system process to process data it doesn't have. The black holes and miracles you see in Figure 12-17 would be errors if you found them on a DFD.

End Note

The Norwegian expedition members carefully checked their gear in Resolute, Canada before their departure. Everything had arrived, including the ski poles that the A&L expert system ordered cross-shipped from the Geneva outlet. "You're the best prepared expedition I've ever seen!" exclaimed the pilot, who flew the Norwegians to their departure point on Ellesmere Island.

The trek was not uneventful. Just six days out, one expedition member injured his back when his sled slipped into a crevasse. They radioed for help and a rescue plane ferried him back to Resolute. Weeks later, a hungry polar bear attack proved almost fatal, but the two remaining expedition members trudged northward and, finally, reached the North Pole on May 4. On May 5 a U.S. Navy research plane established contact with the expedition. "Who are you?" the pilot radioed. "Is there an emergency?"

"No," was the reply. "We are just two Norwegians who skied here from Canada."

Review

1. Arrange each of the boldface terms in this chapter into one of the following categories: analyzing needs, designing the system, constructing the system, implementing the system, maintaining the system, miscellaneous.

2. Write a short explanation of the types of activities that occur in each of the five phases of the system development life cycle.

3. Some of the following statements describe a problem, and others describe a solution. Indicate if each statement is a problem or a solution.

 a. The desk clerks aren't quickly informed of cancellations and sometimes tell people the hotel is full, even when rooms are available due to cancellations.

 b. Notebook computers should be purchased for the sales people so they can prepare quotations without returning to the main office.

 c. When a customer calls and orders an item that is not in stock, the order clerks cannot find out when the item is expected to be back in stock.

 d. The clerk in accounting needs a faster laser printer.

 e. It takes too long to print the current daily reports.

 f. When the public relations department sends ads to a typesetter, it is very expensive and takes at least two days to make a change in the ad copy.

4. Create a table that shows the differences between unit testing, integration testing, system testing, and acceptance testing. Your table should show the purpose of the test, what is tested, and the phase of the SDLC in which it is tested.

5. For each of the problem descriptions, use the PIECES framework to indicate if each should be classified as a Performance, Information, Economics, Control, Efficiency, or Service problem.

 a. Employees are using company computers to print banners for special occasions, using up tractor-feed paper and ribbons.

 b. Customers at the Department of Motor Vehicles must wait while sales clerks walk to computer terminals located in the back of the office, check records, then return.

 c. When order entry clerks complete an order, they must wait 10 seconds while the computer stores the order. During this time, they cannot enter other orders.

 d. When patients are admitted to a hospital, the admitting clerk writes information on a paper form. This information is then sent to data entry, where it is entered into the hospital computer system. The data entry clerks are backlogged, so patient data is not available in the computer system for at least 12 hours.

6. Suppose you want to diagram the data flowing into a mail room. The data comes from the post office and ends up in employee mailboxes. There is one process in which each item is sorted according to its address. Draw a DFD of the mail-sorting system. Make sure you label each symbol on the diagram.

7. Suppose you are a teacher and you want to compute student grades. The data comes from student tests and goes into your grade book. You will take a numeric score such as 76 and convert it into a letter grade A, B, C, D, or F. It is the letter grade that you want in your grade book. Draw a DFD of the grading system. Make sure you label each symbol on the diagram.

Projects

1. Evaluating Possible Solutions Rodney Watson is a systems analyst for U-Fix-It hardware stores. U-Fix-It installed bar-code readers at each register to speed checkouts and improve inventory control. Unfortunately, the clerks are complaining that the bar-code labels are falling off many of the items. When this happens, the clerk must call for someone to go back and check the price of the item. Rodney has identified four possible solutions.

 a. Switch to a bar-code label that has better adhesive on the back so the labels are less likely to fall off.

 b. Modify the system so clerks can check the current price of an item on a computer price list from their terminals.

 c. Print weekly price lists and place them at each register so the clerks can check the price at any item.

 d. Hire additional workers to check prices so customers don't have to wait so long for a price check.

Explain which of these solutions you would select and why you would select that solution. If you need additional information before making a decision, describe the information that you need.

2. Problems and Solutions Jennifer Aho works in the circulation department of *Cycle*, a magazine dedicated to bicycle and triathlon enthusiasts. The MIS department prints a monthly report showing the current number of *Cycle* subscribers in each zip code. Jennifer calculates the total number of subscribers for the current month and enters this total in a worksheet. She then creates a line chart showing the increase or decrease in total subscribers for the current year. It takes Jennifer four hours each month to calculate the total number of subscribers, enter the total on her worksheet, and print the latest copy of the chart.

a. Define the problem.

b. Think of two possible solutions to this problem. Describe each solution.

c. Which solution would you select? Why?

3. Request for Proposal Use your Web browser to search the Web for an actual request for proposal. You can use the search function at *http://www.lycos.com* or any of the other Internet search engines. Try the phrase *request for proposal* as the search string.

Select a request for proposal from the list and write a brief summary of the proposal that includes the following:

a. The URL of the proposal

b. The organization or business that submitted the proposal

c. A brief summary of the problem the organization is trying solve

4. Cool CeeDees, Inc. Assume you are the manager of a music store called Cool CeeDees. You have defined the following problem: "The current cash register and checkout system does not keep track of the titles of the CDs we sell. It takes too much time to manually count the number of copies of each CD remaining in stock in order to determine which CDs must be reordered." Write a one-page request for proposal, asking vendors to recommend a solution to this problem.

5. Purchase Process Most businesses purchase equipment, supplies, or inventory from various vendors. For example, the publisher of Barnett newspapers purchases supplies and equipment for its staff of reporters, editors, advertising agents, and production crew. Suppose a reporter needed a new notebook computer to take on field assignments. Use the data flow diagram in Figure 12-18 to discover how Barnett would track this reporter's purchase order. Write a one-page description of this process.

6. CASE Tools CASE tools are one of the most important items in a systems analyst's tool kit. Suppose you have been recently hired as a systems analyst and your supervisor asks you to find and evaluate three CASE tools. Browse the Web and look in computer trade journals to find three CASE tools. Write a memo to your supervisor to report your progress. In the memo include the name of each CASE tool, the company that produces it, its price, and a short description of its purpose and features.

Figure 12-18 ◄

Resources

- **Brooks, F.** *The Mythical Man-Month: Essays on Software Engineering.* Reading, MA: Addison-Wesley, 1982. This classic book contains a series of essays that examine the problems encountered during the construction of complex information systems. One of the central problems identified by Brooks is the need to develop a conceptual vision of the product.

- *http://dxsting.cern.ch/sting/glossary.html* This long document is a glossary of terms related to software engineering with links to definitions for each term.

- *http://www.aisintl.com/* This site is a good starting point for more information about CASE. It includes discussions, product reviews, user's groups, and additional Web links.

- *http://www.alaska.net:80/~pacrim/cpolar* Here's your chance to be an Arctic explorer. Learn more about a 10-day jet tour of the Arctic with stops in Alaska, Russia, Finland, Norway, Iceland, Greenland, and Canada. No sleds, no skis, and no frostbite!

- *http://www.computer.org/pubs/expert/expert.htm IEEE Expert* provides a comprehensive view of the way intelligent systems are being used in fields ranging from manufacturing to health care to finance. This site contains abstracts of articles from issues dating back to 1985.

- *http://www.cs.cmu.edu/Web/Groups/AI/html/faqs/ ai/expert/part1/faq.html* This is an excellent place to start looking for additional information on expert systems. It includes references and additional information on free, inexpensive, and commercial expert system shells.

- *http://www.ide.com/*
  http://www.intersolv.com/
  http://www.objectware.com/
  http://www.xcase.co.il/ These sites are operated by companies that offer tools for systems analysis and software engineering. They are a good way to find out what is currently available.

- **Martin, J., and C. McClure.** *Diagramming Techniques for Analysts and Programmers.* Englewood Cliffs, NJ: Prentice-Hall, 1985. This books provides an excellent introduction to a variety of charts and diagrams that can be used to document information systems.

- **Turban, E.** *Decision Support and Expert Systems.* New York: Macmillan, 1988. This is an excellent text on computer applications for management support. The explanations are clear, and there are many examples that illustrate the concepts.

- **Wetherbe, J.** *Systems Analysis and Design,* 3rd ed., St. Paul, MN: West Publishing, 1988. James Wetherbe developed the PIECES framework to help systems analysts identify problems in information systems. A section of this text describes the PIECES framework in detail.

- **Yourdon, E.** *Managing the System Life Cycle,* 2nd ed., Englewood Cliffs, NJ: Yourdon Press, 1988. Yourdon, a well-respected authority on information systems, describes a structured approach to creating successful computer information systems.

Lab Assignments

System Testing

 In the System Testing Lab, you are responsible for testing the expert system designed for A&L Outfitters. You will discover if the expert system correctly determines how to cross-ship orders from one A&L outlet to another. If you do all the Lab Assignments in order, you will thoroughly test the system. Your instructor might select these assignments, however; in that case you'll get just a flavor of the system testing process.

1. Click the Steps button to learn how to place test data in A&L's inventory, and how to place test orders. As you proceed through the Steps, answer the Quick Check questions. After you complete the Steps, you will see a Quick Check Summary Report summarizing your answers. Follow the instructions on the screen to print this report.

2. When an item is not in stock at the destination outlet, but is in stock at *one* other outlet, the system should find the outlet that has the item in stock. In Explore, test A&L's system to see if it processes such orders correctly. To do this:

- a. Use the **View/Edit Inventory** dialog box to make sure that only the Geneva outlet has item 3002 in stock.

- b. Place an order on the queue for item 3002 with Katmandu as the destination outlet.

- c. Process the order. The item is not in stock at the destination outlet, Katmandu, so the expert system should search the inventory of other outlets and find the item in Geneva. The picking ticket should show Ship From: Genv and Ship to: Katm.

d. Design a test plan that tests at least one order from each outlet and that tests at least one order for each of the five inventory items. Carry out your test plan and record the results. Does the system correctly process orders for an item that is not in stock at the destination outlet, but is in stock at one of the other A&L outlets? If not, explain what the system does wrong, and how it should work.

3. When an item is not in stock at the destination outlet, but is in stock at *two or more* other outlets, the system should find the outlet with the lowest shipping cost. In Explore, conduct the following tests to see if such orders are processed correctly:

a. Use the **View/Edit Inventory** dialog box to make sure that only the Geneva and Telluride outlets have item 3002 in stock.

b. Place an order for item 3002 with Katmandu as the destination outlet.

c. Process the order. The item is not in stock at the destination outlet, Katmandu, but it is available in Geneva and Telluride. The expert system should select the outlet with the lowest shipping cost.

d. Click the **View Shipping Info** button to check the shipping information. Click **Katmandu**, the destination outlet, to view the cost per pound and the time in days to ship an item to that outlet from each of the other outlets. Of the two outlets where this item is available (Geneva and Telluride), Geneva's shipping cost is lowest. The picking ticket should show Ship From: Genv.

e. Design a test plan of five tests to further test how the system handles orders that are in stock at two or more outlets other than the destination outlet. Carry out your test plan and record the results. Did the system correctly process the orders in your test plan? If not, explain what the system did wrong, and how it should work.

4. When an item is in stock at two outlets with the same shipping cost, the system should find the outlet with the fastest shipping time. In Explore, conduct the following tests to see if such situations are processed correctly.

a. Click the **View Shipping Info** button, then click **Guatemala City** as the destination outlet. Notice that items shipped to Guatemala City from Lima and Geneva have the same shipping cost—$26 per pound. Also notice that items shipped from Lima will arrive faster—shipping takes 2 days from Lima, but 3 days from Geneva. Therefore, if an item is needed in Guatemala City, but it is in stock in Geneva and Lima, the expert system should select Lima. Let's test this.

b. Make sure item 3004 is in stock *only* in Lima and Geneva, then order item 3004 with Guatemala City as the destination.

c. Process the order. Because the shipping cost is the same from Lima and Geneva, the expert system should select the outlet with the fastest shipping time. The picking ticket should show Ship From: Lima.

d. Shipping rates are also the same from Telluride and Guatemala City to Geneva. Set up a test in which item 3005 needs to be shipped to Geneva, but is in stock only in Telluride and Guatemala City.

e. Does the system correctly process an order for an item that is in stock at two outlets with the same shipping cost? If not, explain what the system does wrong, and how it should work.

5. In Explore, test the following scenario: if an item is not in stock in the destination outlet, but is in stock at two other outlets with the same shipping cost and the same shipping time, the system should find the outlet that has the highest quantity of the item in stock.

a. There is one situation in which an item can be in stock in two outlets with the same shipping cost and the same shipping time. This situation arises if an item is in stock in Telluride and Guatemala City and is to be shipped to Katmandu. Make sure Telluride has 2 of item 3005 in stock, and Guatemala City has 5 of item 3005 in stock. Also make sure item 3005 is not in stock in any other outlets.

b. Place an order on the queue for item 3005 with Katmandu as the destination outlet.

c. Process the order. Because there are more of item 3005 in stock in Guatemala City, the picking ticket should show Ship From: Guatemala City.

d. Does the system correctly process an order for an item that is in stock in two outlets with the same shipping cost and the same shipping time? If not, explain what the system does wrong, and how it should work.

Quick Check

Answers

12.1

1. systems development life cycle

2. Systems analysts

3. problem statement

4. CASE

5. System requirements, success factors

6. prototype

12.2

1. design

2. spreadsheet

3. RFP

4. RFQ

5. Application specifications

12.3

1. Software engineering

2. knowledge engineering

3. Unit

4. Integration

5. test area

6. System

12.4

1. procedure handbook

2. Conversion software

3. system conversion

4. Direct

5. parallel

6. phased

7. pilot

8. Acceptance

12.5

1. Maintenance

2. 80

3. bugs or errors

4. cost-effective

5. systems development life cycle

Glossary/Index

A

acceptance testing The final test of an information system in which the purchaser or user of the new system verifies the new system is operating correctly, 12-18

accuracy, data flow diagrams, 12-22–12-23

application development tool A programming environment containing building blocks that can be assembled into an application, 12-10

application specification A document that describes the way an application should interface with the user and how it should store data, process data, and format reports. Also called a 4GL for fourth-generation language, 12-13

application testing The process of trying out various sequences of input values and checking the results to make sure an application works correctly, 12-15

applications
    creating, 12-14–12-16
    testing, 12-15–12-16

B

black hole A process in a data flow diagram that has no output, 12-23

Brooks, Frederick, 12-3

C

CASE tool Software that is designed for drawing diagrams of information systems, writing process specifications, and maintaining data dictionaries, 12-7, 12-7–12-8

completeness, data flow diagrams, 12-22–12-23

customization, software, 12-15

D

data conversion, 12-17

data dictionary A detailed, alphabetical listing of the data elements, data flows, data stores, and processes in an information system, 12-7

data flow A line in a data flow diagram that represents data as it flows through an information system, 12-21, 12-21–12-22

data flow diagram (DFD) A graphical representation of the way data moves through an information system, 12-7, 12-21–12-23
    accuracy and completeness, 12-22–12-23
    interpreting, 12-22

Managing the Data in Files and Databases

Managing the Data
in Files and Databases

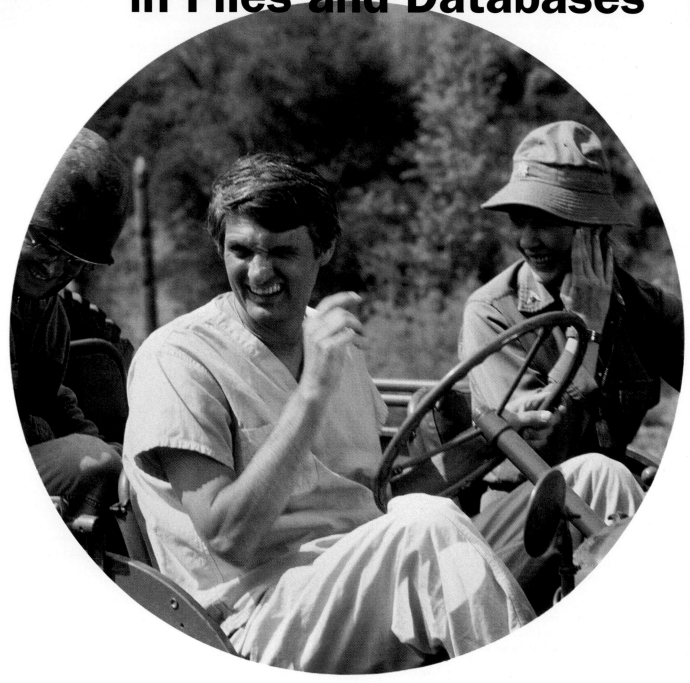

M*A*S*H, a "two thumbs up" film made in 1970, depicted the hijinks of doctors and nurses in a Mobile Army Surgical Hospital (M.A.S.H.) during the Korean War. The film quickly was recast for television and became a hit series. Millions of viewers tuned in to catch the exploits of two irreverent doctors, John McIntyre and Hawkeye Pierce; a clever procurement officer named Radar O'Reilly; and an officious head nurse, Margaret "Hot Lips" Houlihan.

It was during the Korean War that the first commercial electronic computer predicted the outcome of the 1952 presidential election and some experts predicted that five or six of these machines would be sufficient to satisfy the world's data processing needs. Using computers to maintain data in a M.A.S.H. unit was unthinkable back then. Today, however, computers are deployed with U.S. troops all over the world. Computers are also standard equipment in virtually every hospital and medical clinic.

Our society is becoming increasingly information dependent. Information is stored in databases such as course registration schedules, library card catalogs, and Internet World Wide Web pages. Understanding how to plumb these databases for information is a valuable skill in today's information age. This chapter provides an overview of file and database management concepts that will help you do this.

CHAPTER**PREVIEW**

In this chapter you will learn the terminology associated with files and databases. You will discover the advantages and disadvantages of different types of data management software. You will learn about typical data management tasks such as creating files, entering data, searching, sorting, updating, and reporting. And you will learn how to use a query language to search for information. When you have finished this chapter you should be able to:

- Explain the difference between a database and a file

- Define the term "data independence" and explain how it applies to file management systems and database management systems

- Differentiate between a record type and a record occurrence

- Describe the distinguishing characteristics of the four major database models

- Recommend whether to use custom software, file management software, database management software, or object-oriented tools to best solve a data management problem

- Demonstrate how to reduce data redundancy in a file

- List six major database management activities

- Describe the difference between sorting and indexing

- Select an appropriate output format for your data

- Use Boolean logic to construct SQL and Internet search engine queries

LAB

SQL Queries

File and Database Concepts

The term *data file* has several different meanings within the context of computing. You might think of a data file as any file that contains data—word processing documents, graphics, sounds, and so on. You might think of a data file as one that is not an executable or program file. These are valid definitions, but the term *data file* might also refer to a file that contains information organized in a uniform format. An example of this type of file is a telephone directory. All the information is in a uniform format: last name, first name, address, and phone number. Other examples include an inventory list, a library card catalog, and a schedule of university courses.

A file that is organized in a uniform format is formally referred to as a **structured data file** or a **database file**; more commonly, it is referred to as a "data file" or just a "file." Unfortunately, the terms "data file" and "file" do not distinguish files that are organized in a uniform format from those that are in a more free-form format, such as word processor, spreadsheet, graphics, and sound files. Therefore, when you see the term "data file" or "file" in a computer magazine or documentation, you might have to use clues from the context of the article to decide whether "file" means a structured data file or a free-form file. In this chapter, "data file" refers to a file organized in a uniform format, and the concepts you learn in this chapter apply specifically to this type of data file.

The tasks associated with maintaining and accessing the data stored in a data file are often referred to as **data management**. In this chapter, you will learn about data management concepts using data about the employees who work at Midtown General Hospital. The people who work in the Midtown human resource department use some of this data to maintain basic information about each employee, track absenteeism, examine gender equity, and make staffing projections. The payroll department also uses some of the data to generate employee paychecks. The Midtown data is stored in a series of data files. Each of these data files has a **file structure** that describes the way the data is stored in the file. Figure 13-1 shows some of the data in Midtown's Employee file and provides a conceptual overview of data file terminology.

Figure 13-1 ◄
Data file
terminology

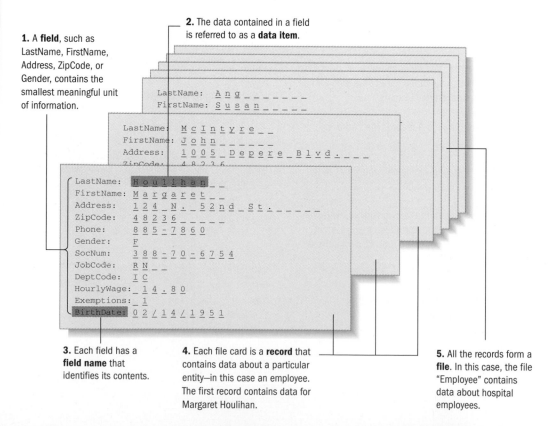

2. The data contained in a field is referred to as a **data item**.

1. A **field**, such as LastName, FirstName, Address, ZipCode, or Gender, contains the smallest meaningful unit of information.

```
LastName:    A n g _ _ _ _ _ _ _
FirstName:   S u s a n _ _ _ _ _
LastName:    M c I n t y r e _ _
FirstName:   J o h n _ _ _ _ _ _
Address:     1 0 0 5 _ D e p e r e _ B l v d . _ _ _ _
ZipCode:     4 8 2 3 6
LastName:    H o u l i h a n _ _
FirstName:   M a r g a r e t _ _
Address:     1 2 4 _ N . _ 5 2 n d _ S t . _ _ _ _ _ _
ZipCode:     4 8 2 3 6 _ _ _ _
Phone:       8 8 5 - 7 8 6 0
Gender:      F
SocNum:      3 8 8 - 7 0 - 6 7 5 4
JobCode:     R N _ _
DeptCode:    I C
HourlyWage: _ 1 4 . 8 0
Exemptions: _ 1
BirthDate:   0 2 / 1 4 / 1 9 5 1
```

3. Each field has a **field name** that identifies its contents.

4. Each file card is a **record** that contains data about a particular entity—in this case an employee. The first record contains data for Margaret Houlihan.

5. All the records form a **file**. In this case, the file "Employee" contains data about hospital employees.

Fields

What's the basic building block for a data file?

As you can see in Figure 13-1, a **field** contains the smallest unit of meaningful data, so you might call it the basic building block for a data file. Each field has a **field name** that describes the contents of the field. For example, the field name BirthDate might describe a field containing an employee birth date.

A field can be either variable-length or fixed-length. A **variable-length field** is like an accordion—it expands to fit the data you enter. A **fixed-length field** has a maximum limit on the number of characters (bytes) it can contain. The data that you enter in a fixed-length field cannot exceed the allocated field length. Moreover, if the data you enter in a field is shorter than the allocated length, blank spaces are automatically added to fill the field. All the fields in Figure 13-1 are fixed length. The underscores indicate the maximum number of characters that each field can contain.

Data Types

Are there any special rules about what data I can enter in a field?

The data you can enter into a field depends on the field's data type. Every field in a file is assigned a data type. From a technical perspective the **data type** specifies the way the data is represented on the disk and in RAM. From a user perspective, the data type determines the way you can manipulate the data.

The two most common data types are character and numeric. A **numeric data type** is assigned to fields containing numbers that you might want to manipulate mathematically by adding, averaging, multiplying, and so forth. As an example, the HourlyWage field in Figure 13-1 is a numeric field, so the data in this field can be multiplied by the number of hours worked to calculate pay. There are two main numeric data types: real and integer. The data in the HourlyWage field is a **real number** because it contains a decimal point. The data in the Exemptions field is a whole number or **integer**.

The **character data type**, also referred to as the **string data type**, is assigned to fields containing data that does not need to be mathematically manipulated. Examples of character data include names, descriptions, cities, and state abbreviations.

Some of the data we call "numbers" does not require a numeric data type. A Social Security "number" is an example of data that looks numeric but would not be mathematically manipulated. Social Security numbers, therefore, are usually stored as character data. Other examples of "numbers" that are generally stored as character data include phone numbers and zip codes.

Some file and database management systems provide additional data types such as date, logical, and memo. The **date data type** would be used when you want to manipulate dates, such as when you want to store 10/15/95, but manipulate it to display "October 15, 1995." The **logical data type** is used to store true/false or yes/no data using minimal storage space. For example, you might want to store data in a field to indicate if an employee has a CPR certificate. You could use a logical field called CPRCert in which you would enter either Y or N. A **memo data type** is also called a **memo field** and usually provides a variable-length text field into which you can enter comments. For example, a manager might use a memo field to make notes about an employee's outstanding job performance.

The concept of data types is a theme that pops up in many computer applications. It is especially important to understand the difference between character and numeric data when you use databases, spreadsheets, and programming languages.

Records

What's the relationship between an entity and a record?

An **entity** is a person, place, thing, or event about which you want to store data. A **record** contains fields of data about one entity. For example, one of the records in Figure 13-1 contains fields of data about the entity Houlihan, Margaret. In a medical office, a patient record contains data such as name, address, and insurance carrier for one patient. In a retail business an inventory record contains data such as part number, cost, and quantity in stock for one inventory item.

A data file with fixed-length fields will have fixed-length records; therefore, the storage space required for each record is the same. For example, every record in the Midtown Employee file contains the same number of characters. You might wonder how this is possible if the data in the fields is different for each record. What if an employee has a very long last name—shouldn't that record be longer than one for an employee with a short last name? The answer is no. Recall that blanks are added to fields that contain data with less than the maximum allocated bytes, so including the blanks, each of the records contains the same number of bytes.

Calculating the record length is important because it helps determine storage needs. Suppose you want to store a data file on a high-density 3½-inch floppy disk. You have approximately 1,440,000 bytes of storage space available. Could you fit 10,000 of the Midtown employee records on this disk? To answer this question, you need to calculate the size of one employee record by summing the field sizes. Figure 13-2 shows you how to calculate the size of one employee record and then, from that calculation, determine the number of records that will fit on a disk.

Don't get confused about the term "fixed-length field." It means that a field such as BirthDate is limited to a maximum of 10 characters. It does not mean that all the fields have a length of 10. In Figure 13-1 you can see that the BirthDate field has a different length from the Address field.

Figure 13-2
Calculating record size and storage requirements

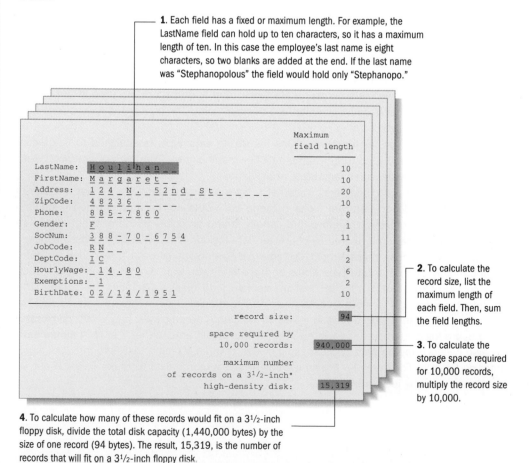

1. Each field has a fixed or maximum length. For example, the LastName field can hold up to ten characters, so it has a maximum length of ten. In this case the employee's last name is eight characters, so two blanks are added at the end. If the last name was "Stephanopolous" the field would hold only "Stephanopo."

		Maximum field length
LastName:	H o u l i h a n _ _	10
FirstName:	M a r g a r e t _ _	10
Address:	1 2 4 _ N . _ 5 2 n d _ S t . _ _ _ _ _ _	20
ZipCode:	4 8 2 3 6 _ _ _ _ _	10
Phone:	8 8 5 - 7 8 6 0	8
Gender:	F	1
SocNum:	3 8 8 - 7 0 - 6 7 5 4	11
JobCode:	R N _ _	4
DeptCode:	I C	2
HourlyWage:	_ 1 4 . 8 0	6
Exemptions:	_ 1	2
BirthDate:	0 2 / 1 4 / 1 9 5 1	10

record size:	94
space required by 10,000 records:	940,000
maximum number of records on a 3½-inch" high-density disk:	15,319

2. To calculate the record size, list the maximum length of each field. Then, sum the field lengths.

3. To calculate the storage space required for 10,000 records, multiply the record size by 10,000.

4. To calculate how many of these records would fit on a 3½-inch floppy disk, divide the total disk capacity (1,440,000 bytes) by the size of one record (94 bytes). The result, 15,319, is the number of records that will fit on a 3½-inch floppy disk.

A record contains the data collected for a particular person, place, thing, or event. Midtown has a record for an employee named Margaret Houlihan and another record for John McIntyre. A record for a specific entity is sometimes referred to as a **record occurrence** to distinguish it from the general record format, which is called a **record type**. This is an important distinction to grasp, so examine Figure 13-3 to be certain you understand the difference.

Figure 13-3
Record types and record occurrences

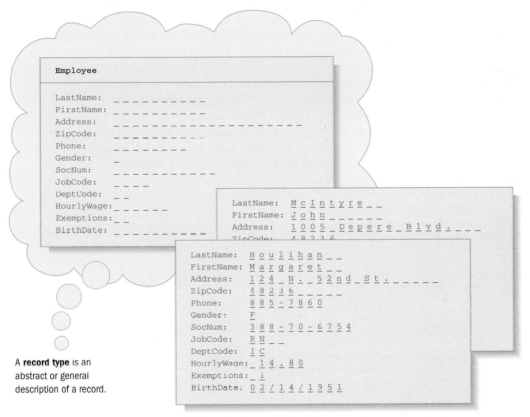

A **record type** is an abstract or general description of a record.

A **record occurrence** is an actual record that can be filled in with data. Here is a record occurrence for Houlihan, and another record occurrence for McIntyre.

"Blocks" is a general category of things analogous to a record type. The actual blocks you use for construction, such as bricks, cement blocks, or Legos, are analogous to record occurrences.

Flat Files

Do all the records in a data file contain the same fields?

The term **flat file** is sometimes used to refer to a data file in which all the records have the same **record format**, that is, the same field names, field lengths, and data types. You could also say that a flat file is a single *record type*. People use the term flat file primarily when they want to distinguish between a single file and a database. The Employee data file shown in Figure 13-1 is a flat file because all the records have the same record format—the same fields, field lengths, and data types.

Flat files are not particularly efficient for complex data management tasks, and they are increasingly being replaced by databases. To find out why, you need to understand what a database is and how it stores data.

Using a flat file is like buying a Lego set that contains only square, white Legos. Your construction options are limited. Using a database is like purchasing the deluxe Lego set with red triangles, small black squares, and wheels—you gain the flexibility to construct much more interesting projects.

Databases

Does a database offer more flexibility by consolidating files that have different record formats?

"Database" is one of those terms that has no single definition. It is sometimes loosely used to describe any data file made up of records and fields. This usage, however, does not distinguish between a flat file and a database, so it is not completely accurate from a technical perspective. It is more accurate to define a **database** as a variety of different record types that are treated as a single unit. This definition implies that several flat files or record types can be consolidated or related in such a way that they can be used as essentially one unit—a database.

In addition to the Employee record type, Midtown stores the following data:

- Job classifications are stored using a record type called Job.
- Department descriptions are stored using a record type called Department.
- Payroll history is stored using a record type called Timecard.

Look at Figure 13-4 to get a general idea of the data Midtown stores.

Figure 13-4
Midtown record types

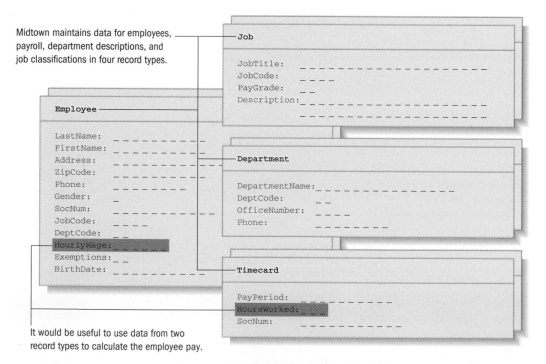

Midtown maintains data for employees, payroll, department descriptions, and job classifications in four record types.

It would be useful to use data from two record types to calculate the employee pay.

To use Midtown's four record types as essentially one unit, they must be consolidated into a database. After you create this database, you can combine the data from more than one record type. For example, you could use the HoursWorked data from the Timecard and the HourlyWage data from the Employee record type to calculate an employee's pay.

To use data from more than one record type, a database maintains relationships. A **relationship** is an association between entities. For example, in the Midtown data there is a relationship between the employee entity and a time card. You could describe this relationship by saying "an employee has a time card." A database lets you define relationships between record types. These relationships provide you with more flexibility for manipulating data than in a single flat file or a group of unrelated flat files. For example, if the Employee records are a flat file and the

Timecard records are another flat file, the procedure to calculate Houlihan's pay is somewhat complex, as shown in Figure 13-5.

► **Figure 13-5**
Using two flat files
to calculate pay

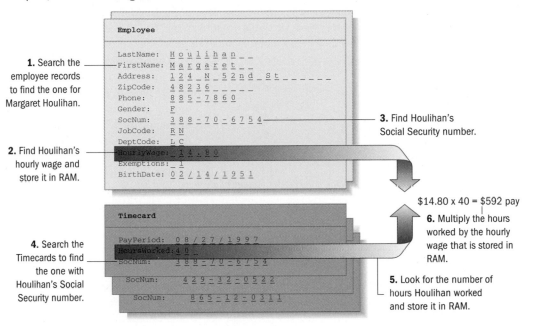

1. Search the employee records to find the one for Margaret Houlihan.

2. Find Houlihan's hourly wage and store it in RAM.

3. Find Houlihan's Social Security number.

4. Search the Timecards to find the one with Houlihan's Social Security number.

$14.80 x 40 = $592 pay

6. Multiply the hours worked by the hourly wage that is stored in RAM.

5. Look for the number of hours Houlihan worked and store it in RAM.

This calculation is easier if you have defined a relationship between the Employee record type and the Timecard record type, as shown in Figure 13-6.

► **Figure 13-6**
Using related
record types to
calculate pay

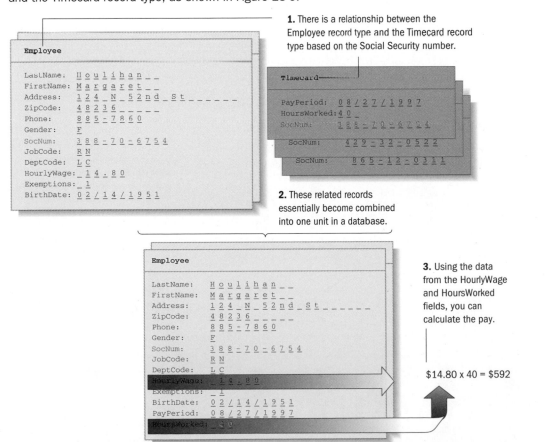

1. There is a relationship between the Employee record type and the Timecard record type based on the Social Security number.

2. These related records essentially become combined into one unit in a database.

3. Using the data from the HourlyWage and HoursWorked fields, you can calculate the pay.

$14.80 x 40 = $592

A **data structure diagram**, shows the relationships between record types. It is a general outline or plan for the way the actual records are related. A data structure diagram helps you visualize the data relationships and design better databases. On a data structure diagram, each record type is shown as a box. There are three possible relationships: one-to-one, one-to-many, and many-to-many. Figure 13-7 shows how these relationships are drawn on a data structure diagram.

Figure 13-7
Diagramming
relationships

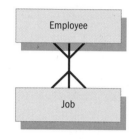

A **one-to-one** relationship is shown by using a single line to connect the boxes that represent record types.

A **one-to-many** relationship is shown by adding a "crow's foot" to the end of the line next to the record type with many occurrences.

A **many-to-many** relationship is shown by adding a "crow's foot" to both ends of the line that connects the record type boxes.

A **one-to-one relationship** means that one record in a particular record type is related to only one record of another record type. For example, each employee has one Social Security card. Also, a particular Social Security card is assigned to only one person. A **one-to-many relationship** means that one record in a particular record type may be related to more than one record of another record type; for example, one employee has many time cards, one job title can be held by many employees, or one department can have many employees.

You can practice drawing data structure diagrams in Review Question 8 and Project 2 at the end of this chapter.

A **many-to-many relationship** means that one record in a particular record type can be related to many records in another record type and vice versa. For example, a department might require personnel with many job descriptions such as nurses, technicians, and physicians. At the same time, a particular job might be required in more than one department; for example, nurses might be required in the intensive care department and in obstetrics.

How can we show the relationships in the Midtown database? By using a data structure diagram like the one in Figure 13-8. Figure 13-9 shows a single occurrence of these relationships so you can study a specific example.

Figure 13-8
Data structure
diagram for
Midtown General
Hospital

▶ **Figure 13-9**
An occurrence of each record type in the Midtown database

There are four major **database models**, and each has a different way of representing relationships between entities. Each database model is described using slightly different terminology, but the concepts of record types, fields, and relationships are useful for understanding all of the models.

In a **hierarchical database**, a "parent" record type can be linked to one or more "child" record types, but a child record type can have only one parent. The relationships between records are established by creating physical links between the stored records. A **physical link** means that the records are stored on the disk medium in such a way that the computer can trace the links from one record to another.

A hierarchical database is effective for data that has fairly simple relationships and when data access is routine and predictable. Hierarchical databases are less effective for data with complex relationships and in situations that require flexible or "on the fly" data access because the relationships are physical links defined at the time the database is created. If you want to add a record type or define a new relationship, you need to redefine the database and then store it in its new form. Study Figure 13-10 for an overview of the hierarchical database model.

Figure 13-10
Hierarchical
database model

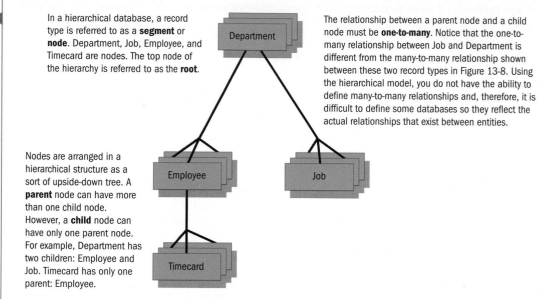

In a hierarchical database, a record type is referred to as a **segment** or **node**. Department, Job, Employee, and Timecard are nodes. The top node of the hierarchy is referred to as the **root**.

The relationship between a parent node and a child node must be **one-to-many**. Notice that the one-to-many relationship between Job and Department is different from the many-to-many relationship shown between these two record types in Figure 13-8. Using the hierarchical model, you do not have the ability to define many-to-many relationships and, therefore, it is difficult to define some databases so they reflect the actual relationships that exist between entities.

Nodes are arranged in a hierarchical structure as a sort of upside-down tree. A **parent** node can have more than one child node. However, a **child** node can have only one parent node. For example, Department has two children: Employee and Job. Timecard has only one parent: Employee.

The model for a **network database** resembles the hierarchical model in many respects. For example, as with the hierarchical model, the network model is a collection of physically linked records in a one-to-many relationship. The physical link is created when the data is stored on tape or disk. There are differences between the two models, however. In a network database, related record types are referred to as a **set**. A set contains an **owner**, which is similar to a parent record in a hierarchical database. A set also includes one or more **members**, roughly equivalent to child records in a hierarchical database.

A network database provides more flexibility than a hierarchical database because it allows member records to have more than one owner. However, as shown in Figure 13-11, many-to-many relationships are not allowed in a set; therefore, the network model does not allow you to define some real-world data relationships.

Figure 13-11
Network database
model

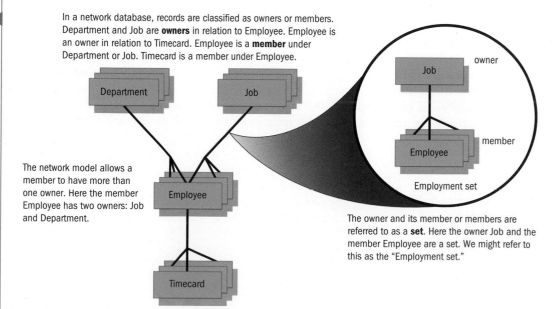

In a network database, records are classified as owners or members. Department and Job are **owners** in relation to Employee. Employee is an owner in relation to Timecard. Employee is a **member** under Department or Job. Timecard is a member under Employee.

The network model allows a member to have more than one owner. Here the member Employee has two owners: Job and Department.

The owner and its member or members are referred to as a **set**. Here the owner Job and the member Employee are a set. We might refer to this as the "Employment set."

A **relational database** is perceived by its users to be a collection of **tables** roughly equivalent to a collection of record types. Today's microcomputer databases most frequently use the relational database model because it offers great flexibility for defining relationships.

The strategy for defining relationships in the relational model is fundamentally different from that of the hierarchical or network models. In the relational model, records are related by the data stored jointly in fields of the records in two files. For example, Margaret Houlihan's Employee record is related to her Timecards because the data in the SocNum fields is the same. The significance of the relational database model is that the tables seem to be essentially independent, but they can be related in many flexible ways. Further, because the tables are a perceptual aid, the user does not need to deal with a physical storage plan for the data on disk. Figure 13-12 provides an overview of relational database structure and terminology.

Figure 13-12
Relational database model

The data for each record type is stored in a **table**, also called a **relation**. A relational database for the Midtown General Hospital would have four tables: Employee, Timecard, Job, and Department.

Data from the two tables can be combined by matching the data in two fields. For example, the data in the Employee and the Timecard tables can be joined by matching the data in the SocNum field.

Table: Employee

LastName	FirstName	Address	SocNum
Ang	Susan	99 Lake Shore Dr.	453-78-2311
Houlihan	Margaret	124 N. 52nd St.	388-70-6754
McIntyre	John	1005 Depere Blvd.	475-66-6245

A row of the table is called a **tuple** and is equivalent to a record. The columns in the table are called **attributes** and are equivalent to fields.

Table: Timecard

PayPeriod	HoursWorked	SocNum
05/26/1997	45	453-78-2311
05/26/1997	40	388-70-6754
05/26/1997	49	475-66-6245
06/02/1997	40	453-78-2311
06/02/1997	40	388-70-6754
06/02/1997	43	475-66-6245

Table: Job

JobTitle	JobCode	PayGrade	Description
Registered Nurse	RN	5	A registered...
Staff Physician	SMD	9	A Staff...

Table: Department

DepartmentName	DeptCode	OfficeNumber	Phone
Intensive Care	IC	S0502	885-7070
Emergency Room	ER	B100	885-1222
Obstetrics	OB	S0301	885-1344
Accounting	AC	AD230	885-4536
Human Resources	HR	AD260	885-1908

An **object-oriented database** organizes data into a hierarchical class of objects defined by **attributes**. An **object** can be manipulated using **methods**. An analogy will explain the meaning of class, object, attribute, and method.

Suppose you have a class of things called "fasteners" that includes objects such as screws and nails. Each object has attributes. A nail has a point, and it has a flat head. A screw has a point, it has a grooved head, and it has spiral ridges on its shaft. What method do you apply to a nail? You pound it with a hammer. What method do you use with a screw? You twist it with a screwdriver. See Figure 13-13.

Figure 13-13 ◄
Classes, objects, attributes, methods

How does this apply to the data at Midtown? A Midtown employee can be described as an *object* with *attributes* such as a last name, first name, and Social Security number. Employee objects are grouped by *class*: registered nurse, clerk, staff physician, and so on. The *method* for paying an employee depends on the class to which an employee object belongs. Registered nurses and clerks are paid by the hour. Staff physicians are paid a salary. Figure 13-14 shows an object-oriented approach to Midtown data.

Figure 13-14 ◄
Object-oriented database model

Class

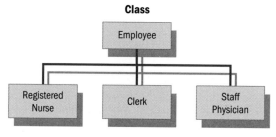

Objects that share common characteristics are grouped into a **class**. The class Employee includes the objects Employee, Registered Nurse, Clerk, and Staff Physician. The Timecard object is a separate class.

Objects

All the objects in a class share certain **attributes**, so all have fields for LastName, FirstName, Address, and so on. Unique attributes can also be assigned to some objects. In this case, staff physicians have a Salary field, whereas RNs and Clerks have an HourlyWage field.

Methods to calculate weekly pay

Find hours worked on Timecard and multiply by HourlyWage

Divide annual salary by 52

The method CalculateWeeklyPay calculates the weekly pay for registered nurses, clerks, and staff physicians. To find the hours worked by each clerk or nurse, the method looks in the HoursWorked field of the Timecard object. Staff physicians are paid based on salary. Therefore, the method CalculateWeeklyPay is different for staff physicians than for registered nurses or clerks.

Using an object-oriented database for Midtown data provides a structure capable of defining complex data relationships. It also provides the flexibility to create variations of a single record type. For example, in the hierarchical, network, and relational models, all the employee records have the same structure, which includes a field for hourly wage. To use these models for salaried employees you would need to design a new record type such as SalaryEmployee. With the object-oriented database, the record type for salaried employees would be only a variation of Employee and would not require a separate series of commands.

The decision of which database model to use is usually made by the **database administrator**, who is responsible for designing and supervising the database. In the past, mainframe databases often followed the hierarchical or network model. During the 1980s the databases that companies and individuals maintained on microcomputers typically followed the relational model, primarily because most database management software for microcomputers supported the relational database model. The new trend is toward the object-oriented model, although the commercial tools for developing and maintaining object-oriented databases have emerged only recently.

Quick Check

1. A(n) _____ field expands as you enter data.

2. What data type should you use for a field that contains Social Security numbers?

3. The abstract or general description of the Midtown employee file is called a record _____, whereas a record that contains the data for John McIntyre is called a record _____.

4. All the records have the same format in a(n) _____ file.

5. A(n) _____ is a diagram that shows the relationships between record types in a database.

6. If you want your database to include methods, you should use a(n) _____ database.

7. A(n) _____ database does not use pointers or physical links, but instead finds related records by examining the contents of fields.

File and Database Software

13.2

oftware helps you design an efficient hierarchical, networked, relational, or object-oriented model for your data. It helps you enter data, manipulate data, and format data into reports. The software you select for these tasks depends on your data model, the flexibility you require for manipulating your data, and the resources you can devote to maintaining your data. In this section you will learn the advantages and disadvantages of custom software, file management software, database management systems, and object-oriented tools.

Custom Software

Because every database is unique, do I need to write my own custom file management software?

Historically, file management tasks were often accomplished using custom software, designed to hold data, such as time cards, and to manipulate that data. To manipulate other data, such as employee records, additional custom software was required. An organization with many different data files would require many custom programs to manipulate the data in those files, as shown in Figure 13-15.

Figure 13-15
Custom file managment software

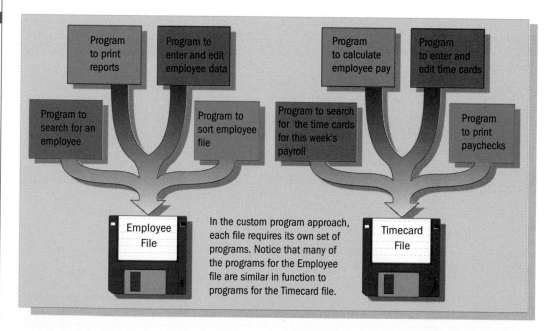

In the custom program approach, each file requires its own set of programs. Notice that many of the programs for the Employee file are similar in function to programs for the Timecard file.

It is possible to create custom software to accommodate hierarchical, network, database, and object-oriented models. However, the complexity of relational and object-oriented models means that most custom software supported hierarchical and networked files. An additional problem with custom file management software is that expensive programmer resources are spent "reinventing the wheel" by writing essentially the same file management programs for each data file. Today, it is rare that an individual or company would use a programming language to write file management software "from scratch." For this reason, businesses and individuals now use commercial file management and database management system software.

File Management Software

Can commercial file management software adapt to my data management needs?

File management software adapts to your data management needs by allowing you to specify field names, select data types, and designate field lengths for each file you create. You then use standard features provided by the software for basic data management tasks such as entering, changing, organizing, displaying, locating, and printing data. Figure 13-16 illustrates how file management software handles the data management tasks common to a number of data files.

▶ **Figure 13-16**
File management software

File management software adapts to different files as a result of a concept called data independence. **Data independence** refers to the separation of data and the programs that manipulate that data. This means that if you change the file structure, for example, by adding a field, the programs that manipulate the data still function. File management software promotes data independence because the file management software is not tied to a particular data file.

File management software is not part of a data file; therefore, you might say that it is **external** to the data. In fact, if you found that you didn't like the file management software you used to create your data files, you could change to different file management software and use it with your existing data files.

In some situations, the basic file management features provided by commercial file management software are not sufficient for the needs of an organization—perhaps the software does not allow enough flexibility in designing reports, or perhaps it does not provide a way to graph the data. If the file management software's basic features are not sufficient, you might require a customized program, but you would typically use it in addition to the commercial file management software.

File management software, generally considered the easiest and least expensive data manipulation tool, does have limitations. Although file management software manages the data in different files, it works with only one file at a time and, therefore, does not recognize any relationships that exist between entities. File management software creates and manipulates only flat files. The file management software in Figure 13-16, for example, cannot find the names of the

What's the difference between data independence and data dependence? Here's an analogy. Data dependence is like an inexpensive hand-held electronic game—it plays only one game because the game is hard-wired into the electronics. Data independence is like Nintendo—you can use the same machine to play different games because the device is separate from the game.

employees who worked more than 40 hours in the pay period beginning 5/16/1997 because the employee names are in one file and the time card data is in another file.

Database Management System

Can I buy commercial software that will let me work with data in more than one file at a time?

A **database management system (DBMS)** is application software that helps you manage the data in more than one file at a time. A DBMS performs the same functions as a file management system, but in addition a DBMS allows you to work with more than one file by defining relationships among record types, as shown in Figure 13-17.

Figure 13-17
Database management system software

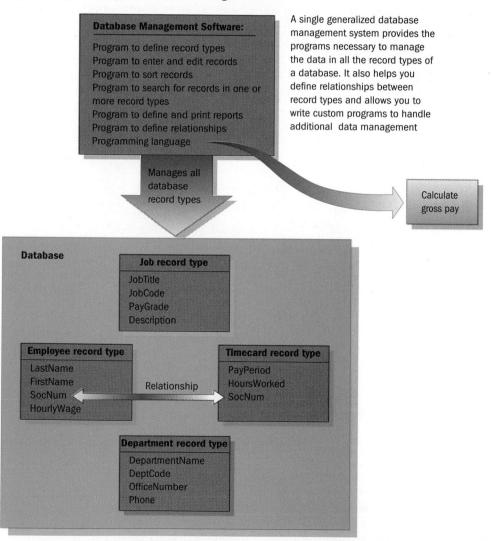

A DBMS typically provides a way to create customized programs for tasks you frequently perform. For example, every two weeks you might want to find all the time cards for the current pay period, then find the hourly wage from each employee's Employee record, and finally calculate total pay. You could use the built-in functions of the database software to do each of these operations, one by one. However, by creating a custom program to do this, you could tell the DBMS to "do payroll" and it would automatically perform all the necessary operations.

Many of today's database management systems provide an option for **client-server** operation. Using a client-server DBMS on a network, **DBMS server software** runs on the network server. This server software processes requests for data searches, sorts, and reports that originate from the **DBMS client software** running on individual workstations. For example, you might want to search an aircraft database for a list of the aircraft used by commercial airlines worldwide. Your DBMS client refers this request to the DBMS server. The server searches for the information and sends it over the network to your workstation. Once at your workstation, you can sort the list and create your own customized report. Client-server operations distribute data processing tasks. If your DBMS did not have client-server capability, the entire database would be copied to your workstation and your software would search for the requested data—a process that would typically take much longer than if the data was processed with the help of the server.

It would be possible to create a database management system using a programming language. However, because a DBMS is quite complex most users elect to purchase a commercial DBMS package. The cost of a database management system can be a worthwhile investment, especially for an organization with many record types and databases to maintain.

Object-Oriented Tools

Can I use a DBMS to create an object-oriented database?

File management systems and database management systems operate on a **passive data set** in which the data simply waits for a program to process it. However, an object-oriented database often includes methods that perform actions on the data. To construct an object-oriented database you should use an **object-oriented database management system (OODBMS)** or a programming language, such as **Smalltalk**, that is designed to manipulate objects and define methods.

With the object-oriented approach the only programs that operate external to the database are those you use to define the objects, methods, and classes for the database. These programs are usually included in the object-oriented database software, although they do not become part of the database itself. Figure 13-18 illustrates the object-oriented approach.

You should review Figure 13-15 through Figure 13-18 so you can remember the differences between the four types of data management software. You can summarize these differences in Review Question 3 at the end of this chapter.

An OODBMS provides a way to define objects, methods, and classes. Most other data management activities, such as sorting, searching, and calculating, are performed by methods incorporated in the database.

▶ **Figure 13-18**
Object-oriented DBMS

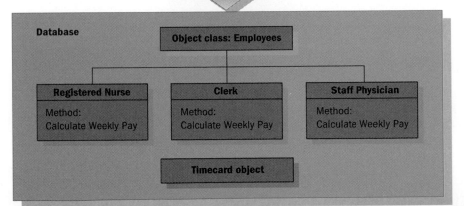

Object-Oriented Database Management System

Define objects
Define methods
Specify classes

Database

Object class: Employees

Registered Nurse

Method:
Calculate Weekly Pay

Clerk

Method:
Calculate Weekly Pay

Staff Physician

Method:
Calculate Weekly Pay

Timecard object

Quick Check

1 Historically, file management tasks were often accomplished by _____ software designed to hold data and to manipulate that data.

2 File management software adapts to different files as a result of a concept called _____ .

3 File management software is external to a data file, but the methods that manipulate data are internal in a(n) _____ database.

4 File management software works with only one file at a time, but if you want to define relationships between data in two or more files you must use _____ software.

5 A(n) _____ DBMS distributes data processing tasks between the workstation and a network server.

6 File management software and database management systems operate on a _____ data set and are therefore not suitable for object-oriented databases.

File and Database Management Tasks

13.3

A **data management environment** refers to the software or program you use to design and manage data, whether you use custom software, file management software, database management systems, or object-oriented tools. Regardless of the data management environment you use, many data management tasks remain the same. In this section you will learn more about specific data management tasks.

Designing the File Structure

Where do I begin?

The key to an effective file or database is the initial design of its structure. With a good structure, the data can be flexibly manipulated to provide meaningful, accurate, and timely information for decision making. Suppose that you are a database administrator faced with the task of designing an effective way to store and manage your organization's data. How do you proceed?

The first step is to determine what data needs to be collected and stored. In other words, you must decide what fields to include. To do this, you might begin by listing the information that is available, as well as any additional information that is necessary to produce the screen output or printed reports that your organization requires. Each piece of information on your list is a candidate for a data field. If you are designing a file or database for the human resource department, for example, you would probably recognize the need for information such as employee name, address, phone number, job code, and birth date. Each of these might become a data field.

The next step in the design process is to decide how to organize the information into fields so it can be used flexibly. For example, would it be better to store an employee name as one field or would it be better to have separate fields for the first name and the last name? If you would like to print mailing labels with the name in the format "Margaret Houlihan" and also print an employee list with the names in the format "Houlihan, Margaret" you would need to have separate fields for the first and the last names. If you did not use separate fields for the first and last names, "Margaret Houlihan" would be entered into a single field. It would then be very difficult to devise a way to separate the first name from the last name and reverse them if you wanted to output the name as "Houlihan, Margaret."

Next, you must decide on the data type for each field. As you learned earlier in this chapter, most data management environments let you select from character, numeric, date, logical, and memo data types. Remember that data you want to use for calculations should be defined as numeric.

After you select data types, you should decide on the format and valid range for each field. The **field format** provides a template for the way data is displayed on the screen and printed. For example, if you specify a field format of XX/XX/XXXX, when you enter 10151997 it appears as 10/15/1997. On the other hand, if you specify the format XX-XX-XXXX, the entry 10151997 appears as 10-15-1997. In addition to dates, other commonly use field formats are shown in Figure 13-19.

In Project 1 you can play the part of a database administrator and design the structure of a gourmet supply store's inventory database.

Currency	$9,999.99
Social Security number	XXX-XX-XXXX
Telephone number	(XXX)XXX-XXXX
Zip code	XXXXX-XXXX

▶ **Figure 13-19**
Field format examples

Notice in Figure 13-19 that to specify the field format, a series of 9s is used when the field type is numeric, but a series of Xs is used when the field type is character.

Many data management environments allow you to use a **range check** to specify what constitutes the range of valid entries in each field and, thereby, decrease errors. For example, you might specify that the HourlyWage field can contain values from $0.00 to $20.00. Then if a user enters $150 instead of $15, the database will not accept the entry.

Your ability to define field formats and range checks depends on the particular data management environment you use. The programming languages used to create custom software generally provide you with the commands necessary to create a section of your program that will display and print fields as you specify. With the object-oriented approach, you would define formats and range checks as methods. Not all file and database management systems provide a way to define field formats and range checks. You would need to refer to the documentation to find out if a particular environment supports these two features.

The next consideration in database design is how to group the fields. Each group you create becomes a record type; or if you are using an object-oriented model, each group becomes an object and the objects may further be grouped into classes. You should structure the groups to reduce storage space requirements and provide the level of access-flexibility required by the people who use the data.

In an object-oriented environment you can also define methods that process the data in each object. A careful consideration of which objects inherit each method will help you produce an efficient object-oriented database.

When you group fields into record types, you essentially make the choice between using a flat file and a database. If you arrange all the fields in a single record type, you are using a flat file structure. If you arrange the fields into more than one record type, you are using a database structure. Let's look at an example.

Suppose the information systems manager of Midtown wants to keep track of computer equipment in case it needs to be replaced or repaired. Should he maintain a flat file or a database? Figure 13-20 shows a flat file, which would keep track of computer equipment and provide the information necessary to send it to a repair center.

To better understand grouping, suppose you were working on a Department of Motor Vehicles database. You'd need fields such as last name, height, eye color, make, model, and year. You'd group some of these fields as "drivers" and some as "cars."

Figure 13-20 ◄
Equipment flat file

Item	Serial Number	Date Purchased	Repair Center	Repair Center Phone	Repair Center Address
Computer	458876	02/12/1995	Epson	415-786-9988	93 Torrance Blvd.
Computer	433877	03/03/1996	IBM	913-559-5877	2 Bradhook Ave.
Printer	6855200	03/03/1996	Epson	415-786-9988	93 Torrance Blvd.
Computer	884411	01/21/1995	Epson	415-786-9988	93 Torrance Blvd.
Modem	B7654D	01/21/1995	High Tech	509-776-7865	4109 Highway 56
Computer	5544998	01/21/1995	IBM	913-559-5877	2 Bradhook Ave.

Using a flat file for this data is not very efficient. The problem with this flat file structure becomes evident when you look at the repair center data. The Epson repair center name, address, and phone number are repeated on many records. If the repair center moves to a different location, a data entry clerk will have to change the address in many records.

Repetition of data is referred to as **data redundancy** and is very undesirable because it makes inefficient use of storage space and makes updating cumbersome. In a well-structured database, the data is stored non-redundantly.

The process of analyzing data to create the most efficient database structure is referred to as **normalization**. There are five normalization procedures, the first of which is to eliminate data redundancy. The remaining normalization procedures are somewhat technical and are best left to more advanced students of database management. To eliminate data redundancy, you remove the repeating fields and group them as a new record type, as shown in Figure 13-21.

► **Figure 13-21**
Eliminating data redundancy

1. To reduce data redundancy, move the repair center data to a new record type called RepairCenter.

2. If you are using a relational model, leave the Repair Center column in the Equipment record type, but duplicate it in the RepairCenter record type. This field establishes the relationship between the tables.

3. The RepairCenter record type needs only one record for each repair center. Compare this new structure with the flat file structure in Figure 13-20, which has more data redundancy because the Epson phone and address information repeats three times.

Record type: Equipment

Item	Serial Number	Date Purchased	Repair Center
Computer	158876	02/12/1995	Epson
Computer	433877	03/03/1996	IBM
Printer	6855200	03/30/1996	Epson
Computer	884411	01/21/1995	Epson
Modem	B7654D	01/21/1995	High Tech
Computer	5544998	01/21/1995	IBM

Record type: RepairCenter

Repair Center	Repair Center Phone	Repair Center Address
Epson	415-786-9988	93 Torrance Blvd.
IBM	913-559-5877	2 Bradhook Ave.
High Tech	509-776-7865	4109 Highway 56

You can try your hand at reducing data redundancy in Project 5 at the end of this chapter.

Entering Records

When can I enter my data?

When you specify the database structure, you essentially design a blank form that will hold data. After the form is complete, you can begin to enter data. As you enter each record, it is assigned a **record number**. The first record you enter becomes record #1. The second record you enter becomes record #2, and so forth. In an object-oriented database, each object receives a unique **object ID number**, which is similar to a record number in some respects. The computer uses record numbers and object IDs to keep track of the data you enter.

Consistency is important for data entry because it affects the efficiency of your searches. Suppose you're entering employee data for registered nurses and you enter "RN" as the job code for some employees, but you enter "NURS" for other employees who hold the same position. If you later want the database software to print a list of all nurses and you ask for all the RNs, the employees you identified as NURS will not be included on the list.

Another issue related to entering consistent data is case sensitivity. **Case sensitivity** means that uppercase letters are not equivalent to their lowercase counterparts. In a case-sensitive database, the state abbreviation MI is not the same as the abbreviation Mi. Not all data management environments are case sensitive. You must read the documentation to determine whether a particular data management environment is case sensitive.

Searching

How do I find a particular record once it is entered?

A realistic file or database contains hundreds or thousands of records. If you want to find a particular record or a particular group of records, scrolling through every record is too cumbersome. Instead, you enter search specifications called a **query**, and the computer will quickly locate the records you seek. For example, if you want a list of everyone who has "Jones" as a last name, you would use a query to tell the computer to look for all the records with "Jones" in the LastName field.

You'll learn more about queries in the User Focus section of this chapter.

Most database management systems have a special query language that you use to state search criteria. A **query language** provides a set of commands you can use to locate and manipulate data. A popular query language for both mainframes and microcomputers is **Structured Query Language**, more commonly called **SQL**.

As an alternative to a query language, many data management environments allow you to query by example. **Query by example** provides you with a blank record into which you enter examples or specifications of the records you want to find. Figure 13-22 shows how you might use query by example on a form for the Midtown employee records.

Figure 13-22
Query by example

When you begin a query by example, the software displays the field names on a blank form.

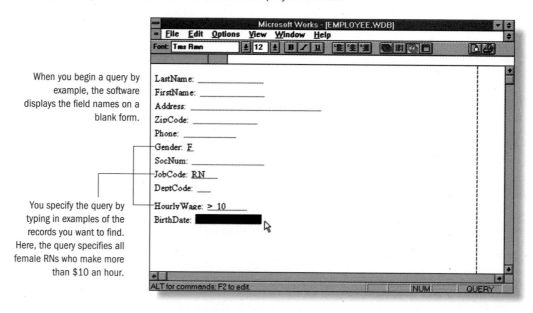

You specify the query by typing in examples of the records you want to find. Here, the query specifies all female RNs who make more than $10 an hour.

Updating Information

What if I want to change some of the data?

Often the reason you search for a particular record is to **update** it, that is, to change it or delete it. The typical process is to enter a query so the computer finds and displays the record you wanted to update. Next, you make the changes and, if necessary, indicate that you want to save the record in its changed format.

Different data management environments have different ways of saving updated records. With many environments, changes are automatically saved as soon as you move to the next record. With other environments, you must issue a command to save the changes you make. To learn the specific procedures for the data management environment you use, you should refer to the software documentation or online Help.

In addition to individual changes, computers make it easy to perform **global updates** to change the data in more than one record at a time. Consider the Employee file in the Midtown General Hospital database. A number of employees are working at $4.35 per hour, the minimum wage set by the government. Suppose that the minimum wage increases to $5.65 per hour. Instead of searching for each employee with an hourly wage of $4.35 and manually changing the numbers to $5.65, you could enter a command such as:

UPDATE EMPWAGE SET HourlyWage = 5.65 WHERE HourlyWage <5.65.

Let's see how this command performs a global update. The UPDATE command means you want to change the data in some or all of the records. EMPWAGE is the name of the file that contains the data you want to change. SET HourlyWage = 5.65 tells the DBMS to change the data in the HourlyWage field to 5.65. WHERE HourlyWage <5.65 tells the DBMS to change only those records in which the current hourly wage is less than $5.65.

Organizing Records

Can I organize my data in different ways?

It is easier to use information if it is presented in a sequence related to how the information is going to be used. For example, if you want to view a list of employees and you are looking for a specific employee by name, it is handy to have the employee records alphabetized by last name. If, on the other hand, you want to view a list of employees to compare hourly wages, it is useful to have the records in numeric order according to the number in the HourlyWage field.

A **sort key** is the field used to arrange records in order. Suppose Midtown managers want employee records arranged alphabetically by last name. The sort key would be LastName. Alternatively, if they want the records arranged by hourly wage, the sort key would be HourlyWage.

There are two ways to organize records in a file; you can sort them or you can index them. If you change the order of the file itself, by essentially rearranging the sequence of the records on the disk, you are **sorting**. Because the records are rearranged, each record receives a new record number to indicate its new position in the file. For example, in a file sorted by last name, the record with the last name that appears first in the alphabet would become record #1.

Sorting is an acceptable procedure for smaller files in which the time to sort the records is minimal. Sorting is also acceptable for files that you don't want sorted multiple ways. However, if you sometimes need to view a file in alphabetical order by last name, but at other times you need to view the file in order by salary, sorting is not very efficient.

An alternative way to organize records is indexing. **Indexing** leaves the records in their original order and retains the original record numbers but creates additional files, called index files. An **index file** allows you to display information in order. Think of an index file as being similar to the index of a book. The index of a book contains topics in alphabetical order, which allows you to find a topic in the index list easily. Next to the topic is a page number that points to the location of the actual information about the topic. Figure 13-23 on the next page shows how an index file lists the contents of the LastName field in alphabetical order, then uses the record number as a pointer to the corresponding record number in the original file.

What makes indexing so flexible is that you can have multiple index files for each of your data files. For example, Midtown could have three index files for the employee data file—one index file to arrange employees by last name, one to arrange employees by hourly wage, and one to arrange employees by job category.

In some database management systems, the distinction between sorting and indexing will help you more effectively utilize the DBMS to organize your data. However, you should be aware that not all data management environments differentiate between the terms "sort" and "index." For example, Microsoft Access uses the term "sort" for procedures that organize data *without* rearranging records.

Figure 13-23
Indexing

1. Records are typically numbered in the order in which they are entered, so the employee record with the earliest start date is record 1.

2. To index the records by last name, the computer creates an index file containing the data in the LastName field.

3. The only other field in the index file contains the original record numbers. Notice that in the orginal table, Susan Ang is record 3. In the index file, Susan's record is listed first because her name is first in the alphabet. Her record number is 3, as it was in the original file.

4. Because the index file contains only some of the information for each employee, the computer uses the index file to look up information from the original database table. To display the first and last names in alphabetical order, the computer looks at the first item in the index file and displays the contents of the LastName field, Ang. To find Ang's first name, the computer looks at record 3 in the table. It finds Susan in the FirstName field and displays it.

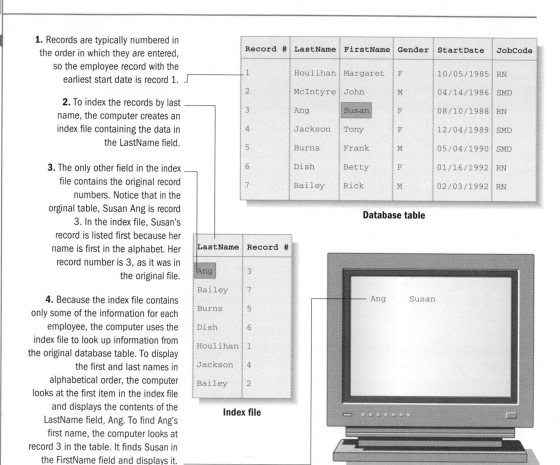

Record #	LastName	FirstName	Gender	StartDate	JobCode
1	Houlihan	Margaret	F	10/05/1985	RN
2	McIntyre	John	M	04/14/1986	SMD
3	Ang	Susan	F	08/10/1988	RN
4	Jackson	Tony	F	12/04/1989	SMD
5	Burns	Frank	M	05/04/1990	SMD
6	Dish	Betty	F	01/16/1992	RN
7	Bailey	Rick	M	02/03/1992	RN

Database table

LastName	Record #
Ang	3
Bailey	7
Burns	5
Dish	6
Houlihan	1
Jackson	4
Bailey	2

Index file

Ang   Susan

Quick Check

1 When designing the structure for a file or database, you might use XXX-XX-XXXX to specify the _____ for Social Security numbers.

2 A(n) _____ helps you prevent data entry mistakes such as entering $1500 instead of $150.

3 The first step of normalization is to eliminate _____ .

4 In a(n)_____ database, Margaret is not the same as margaret.

5 After you _____ a record, many data management environments require you to issue a command to save the changes you made.

6 If you want to group the records in the Midtown Employee database, you could use JobCode as the _____ .

7 If you want to organize a file in multiple ways, it is better to _____ the data rather than to sort it.

8 When you _____ , you enter search specifications in a blank record.

Designing Effective Output

The output from a data file presents information in a format that facilitates making a decision, preparing an analysis, or taking some action. Traditionally, output is presented as words and numbers in reports, but output can assume other formats such as graphs, graphics, and sound. How can you determine the best way to present information? It is useful to know what type of output options are available and the advantages of each type.

Reports

How can I produce a professional-looking report based on the data in a file or database?

In response to a query, your data management environment might display a list of records that match your search criteria. This simple list displays the information you need, but it might not provide it in the optimal format. The list might include some unnecessary fields, it might not include a title or page numbers, it might not display subtotals or totals, and the column headings might not be as descriptive as you would like. If a list is not adequate, you can design a screen-based or printed report that conveys information more effectively. A **database report** is the formatted output of some or all of the data from a database.

The part of a data management environment that provides you with the ability to design reports is called a **report generator**. Usually a report generator helps you create a report template. A **report template** does not contain any data. Instead it contains the outline or general specifications for a report including such things as what to title the report, which fields to include, which fields you want to subtotal or total, and how the report should be formatted. For example, you might create a report template called Midtown Employees, which specifies the following:

- The title of the report is Midtown General Hospital Employees.
- The report contains six columns with data from the LastName, FirstName, SocNum, Gender, StartDate, and JobCode fields.
- The headings for the columns are: Last Name, First Name, Social Security #, Gender, Start Date, and Job Code.
- The report is arranged alphabetically by last name.

This template would produce a report similar to the one shown in Figure 13-24.

You can think of a report template as a form that the computer fills in anytime you tell it to generate a report. You must create the template, but once you have done so, you do not need to specify the format for the report each time you print it.

► **Figure 13-24**
Columnar report

Report title   Report date   Page number

Page 1
08/01/1997

Midtown General Hospital Employees

	Last Name	First Name	Social Security #	Gender	Start Date	Job Code
	Ang	Susan	453-78-2311	F	08/10/1988	RN
	Bailey	Rick	876-77-5465	M	02/03/1992	RN
	Burns	Frank	987-57-4532	M	05/04/1990	SMD
	Dish	Betty	765-43-4325	F	01/16/1992	RN
	Houlihan	Margaret	388-70-6754	F	10/05/1985	RN
	Jackson	Tony	432-67-4362	F	12/04/1989	SMD
	McIntyre	John	475-66-6245	M	04/14/1986	SMD

Column headings

First column contains data from LastName field

Second column contains data from FirstName field

After you use a report generator to design a template for a report, you can produce the report at any time. When you produce the actual report, it is based on the data currently contained in the file. For example, the report in Figure 13-24 was produced on August 1, 1997. This report includes employees who are listed in the database as of August 1. Now suppose that on September 1 your organization hires several new employees who are added to the database. You then use the Midtown Employee report template to print a report on September 2. This report will follow the same format as the previous report, but the new employees will be included.

Types of Reports

Can I use a report generator to produce different kinds of reports?

Most report generators produce reports in columnar, or table, format. Within this format you can produce different kinds of reports to meet a variety of information needs. You want to choose the right type of report to present the right amount of information to make good decisions.

A **detail report** lists transactions, usually in sorted or chronological order. A detail report of daily cash register transactions, for example, contains each of the items sold at each cash register. This report is likely to be a fairly long and not particularly useful, unless a checkout clerk needs to trace back through the day's transactions to reconcile an error. You should create a detail report only when such detailed information is required for a decision.

A **summary report** is a condensed version of a detail report. In a business, summary reports are usually produced for managers. A summary report might show total sales by department, providing a manager with information about which departments are meeting their sales goals. Why not use a detail report for this purpose? A detail report, showing each of the items sold in every department, would not be as useful for this manager for two reasons. First, a detail report requires manual effort to total the sales for each department. Second, the detail report information on specific items sold is not relevant to analyzing whether a department met sales goals.

A **control-break report** is a specific type of summary report in which subtotals are created by category. To produce a control-break report, the report designer must make sure the records are sorted or indexed to reflect the groups on the report. For example, at Midtown, a report that is grouped by department would be sorted or indexed using DeptCode as the key field. Figure 13-25 illustrates the characteristics of a control-break report.

An **exception report** provides a list of records that match a condition outside of the usual ranges or limits. For example, a report that lists customers who have overdue balances would be an exception report—the data in the Date Paid field for these records would be outside the time limit set for payment. The purpose of an exception report is to point out quickly where action needs to be taken, in this case sending out overdue notices.

Graphs

Is there a way to graph the data in a file or database?

A graph represents data visually in a way that can be quickly assimilated and understood. Graphs are appropriate for presenting a summary of data when detailed data is not relevant to the decision process. You can create graphs based on the data in files and databases using graphing software. You can also transfer data from your file or database into a spreadsheet and create a graph using the spreadsheet's graphing capabilities.

A well-designed graph should convey your point within a few seconds. Every graph should have a title, and the important elements of your data should be identified with labels.

A graph with too much data might not be a great improvement over a detailed report. To check whether a graph you create is meaningful, try to write one sentence explaining what the graph

Midtown Department Payroll

Last Name	First Name	Social Security #	Hourly Wage	Hours Worked	Gross Pay
DEPARTMENT CODE: ER					
Bailey	Rick	876-77-5465	$14.80	42.00	$621.60
Brown	Karen	372-17-2227	$10.50	40.00	$420.00
McIntyre	John	475-66-6245	$90.00	55.00	$4,950.00
Nardi	Susan	371-28-1882	$8.50	36.00	$306.00
Peterson	Angela	578-02-0092	$9.50	38.00	$361.00
Smith	Tracy	421-88-1384	$8.45	40.00	$338.00
St. Aubin	Harold	461-28-1228	$9.25	40.00	$370.00
			SUBTOTAL:	291.00	$7,366.60
DEPARTMENT CODE: IC					
Burns	Frank	987-57-4532	$90.00	63.00	$5,670.00
Choi	Lisa	398-13-1883	$8.85	45.00	$398.25
Houlihan	Margaret	388-70-6754	$14.80	45.00	$666.00
Kaefer	Kathryn	387-18-1882	$110.00	44.00	$4,840.00
Matsuzaki	Akiko	443-28-1998	$9.75	44.00	$429.00
Smith	Ralph	538-18-1888	$10.75	42.00	$451.50
			SUBTOTAL:	283.00	$12,454.75
DEPARTMENT CODE: OB					
Ang	Susan	453 78 2311	$14.80	52.00	$769.60
Dish	Betty	765-43-4325	$14.80	42.00	$621.60
Jackson	Tony	432-67-4362	$90.00	58.00	$5,220.00
Nunez	Maria	377-13-1773	$10.60	40.00	$424.00
			SUBTOTAL:	238.00	$7,702.20
				TOTAL:	**$27,523.55**

1. In a control-break report, records are grouped. Here, the records are grouped by DeptCode; all the employees in the ER (emergency room) are listed in one group, all the IC (intensive care) staff are in one group, and so forth.

2. At the end of each group, the report displays subtotals for hours worked and gross pay.

Figure 13-25
A control-break report

shows, for example, "U.S. sales have increased, but foreign sales have decreased" or "Most people support tax reform." If you have trouble writing a descriptive sentence, your graph may not be effective. Another way to test your graph is to show it to friends or colleagues for five seconds. If, in five seconds, they can't identify the main point of the graph, you should probably make some revisions.

Although there are many types of graphs, four types are most often used for business and the social sciences: bar graphs, line graphs, pie charts, and scatter plots. These graphs use different visual elements, bars, lines, pie slices, and dots, to depict data. They differ also in the number of data sets you can depict. A **data set** is a collection of related numbers. For example, a data set might consist of two numbers: the number of male undergraduates who own computers and the number of female undergraduates who own computers.

A **line graph** connects each number in a data set with a line. More lines can be added to the graph to depict additional data sets. Line graphs work well for showing trends over time. For this reason, the horizontal axis of a line graph often shows a series of months or years. Figure 13-26 shows a graph of two data sets: U.S. sales and foreign sales during the period 1991 through 1995.

Figure 13-26
A line graph

A line graph shows trends over time. Typically, the horizontal axis shows days, months, or years.

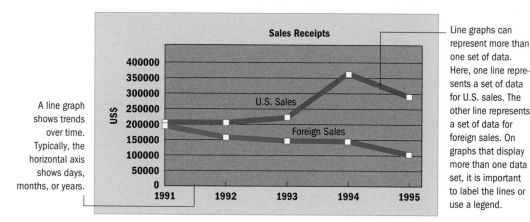

Line graphs can represent more than one set of data. Here, one line represents a set of data for U.S. sales. The other line represents a set of data for foreign sales. On graphs that display more than one data set, it is important to label the lines or use a legend.

A **bar graph** uses blocks or "bars" to represent a set of data. The height of each bar corresponds to the magnitude of the data. A bar graph can depict more than one data set, using another set of bars. Color coding or cross-hatching provides a visual distinction between data sets. Bar graphs work well for showing comparisons because the human eye automatically compares the height of the different bars on a graph. If you find that you have created a bar graph with dates on the horizontal axis, consider using a line graph instead. Figure 13-27 shows a bar graph comparing two data sets: male graduates and undergraduates who own computers and female graduates and undergraduates who own computers.

Figure 13-27
A bar graph

Bar graphs show comparisons. The human eye automatically compares the height of the bars on the graph.

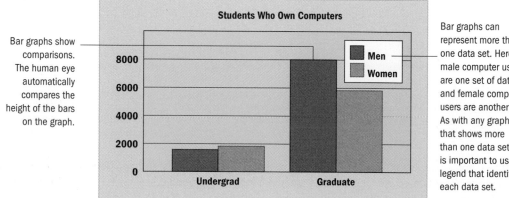

Bar graphs can represent more than one data set. Here male computer users are one set of data, and female computer users are another set. As with any graph that shows more than one data set, it is important to use a legend that identifies each data set.

A **pie chart** depicts data as slices of a circular "pie." The size of the slice corresponds to the magnitude of the data. Unlike line and bar graphs, a pie chart shows only one data set.

Pie charts are most effective when you want to show percentages. The pie chart in Figure 13-28 shows the percentages of voters who support tax reform, who do not support tax reform, and who are undecided.

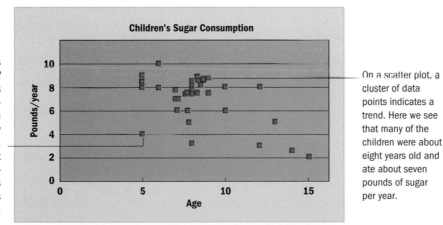

A pie chart is best used to show parts of a whole or percentages. The data for a pie chart comes from only one data set.

Voters Supporting Tax Reform

Undecided 18%

Yes 46%

No 36%

It is useful to show the actual percentages on each slice of the pie, along with the data labels.

Number of voters surveyed = 8,967

Figure 13-28
A pie chart

A **scatter plot**, also called an **x-y chart**, uses a dot to show the location of data pairs. For example, suppose you collect data on 30 children to find out how much sugar each consumes in a year. You are interested to see if children in certain age groups consume more sugar than children in other age groups. For each child you know how much sugar was consumed and the child's age. This is a data pair. For example, a five-year-old might have consumed four pounds of sugar during the year. The data pair would be (5,4). On a scatter plot, a dot placed at the coordinate (5,4) would represent this data pair, as shown in Figure 13-29.

Figure 13-29
A scatter plot

A scatter plot shows the location of data pairs. On this plot, data pairs represent one person of age x who eats y amount of sugar. This data point represents a five–year-old who eats four pounds of sugar a year.

Children's Sugar Consumption

Pounds/year

Age

On a scatter plot, a cluster of data points indicates a trend. Here we see that many of the children were about eight years old and ate about seven pounds of sugar per year.

Characteristics of Effective Output

How can I make my output most effective?

Whether you use reports or graphs you can effectively present information by observing the following guidelines:

- Present only the amount of information necessary to make a decision and to take appropriate action. Too much information makes it difficult to identify and interpret the essential information.
- Present information in a usable format. If subtotals and totals are necessary for making a decision, present them. Your readers should not need to make additional manual calculations.

- Information should be timely. Reports must arrive in time to be used for effective decision making. Some decisions require information periodically, for example, monthly sales reports. Other decisions require ongoing information that will be best satisfied by a continuous display, for example, changing stock prices.
- Information should be presented in a clear and unambiguous format. Make sure you include necessary titles, page numbers, dates, labels, and column headings to help decision makers identify the information.
- Present the information in the format most appropriate for the decision and the decision maker. In many cases a traditional report, organized in rows and columns, is most appropriate. In other cases, graphs might be more effective.

Quick Check

1 A(n) _____ contains the outline or general specifications of a report but does not contain any data.

2 A(n) _____ report summarizes your data by category.

3 A(n) _____ report provides a list of records that match a condition outside of the usual range or limits.

4 A pie chart can depict only one _____, whereas a line or bar graph can depict more than one.

5 To show comparisons, you should use a(n) _____ graph.

6 A(n) _____ graph usually has dates on its horizontal axis.

7 An effective report or graph presents information in the format most appropriate for the decision and the _____.

Using Boolean Logic in Queries

The mathematician George Boole is responsible for defining a system of logic now called Boolean logic or Boolean algebra. Boolean algebra uses three main operations: NOT, AND, and OR. Elements of Boole's system of logic have been universally adopted by database query languages such as SQL and are used to enter queries into search engines that help you find information on the Internet.

According to experts such as Alan Cooper, who claims, "Users don't understand Boolean," some people have difficulty using Boolean logic for search specifications. It is easy to confuse the meaning of Boolean AND and OR because in casual speech we often use these words exactly opposite from the way that Boole defined them. However, the use of Boolean in query languages for databases and Internet searches is so pervasive that it is important for computer users to understand Boole's meanings for AND and OR.

Set Theory

So what's the difference between AND and OR?

To understand the difference between AND and OR, it is useful to think about set theory. **Set theory** is a simple way of depicting what happens when you combine, select, or exclude elements from a group. Imagine a group of things. In set theory, all the things in your group are called "the universe." Graphically, you represent this universe with a rectangle. Now suppose that some of the things in your group are electronic gizmos. You represent these gizmos with a circle, as shown in Figure 13-30.

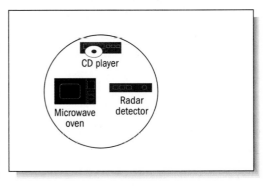

▶ **Figure 13-30**
A circle represents the electronic gizmos in your universe

Your universe might also contain car parts, such as tires, hood ornaments, steering wheels, CD players, and radar detectors. As you expect, you would draw another circle in the universe to represent car parts. The catch is that some car parts are also electronic gizmos (CD players and radar detectors, for example). You show this by overlapping the circles in your universe. Study Figure 13-31 and make sure you understand the four different categories of things in your universe.

Now, here's the part that many people find tricky. Which things in your universe are **electronic gizmos AND car parts**? According to Boole, they are CD players and radar detectors. AND means a thing must fit *both* criteria: It must be both an electronic gizmo and also a car part.

Electronic gizmos that are not car parts.

Car parts that are also electronic gizmos.

Things that are not car parts, nor electronic gizmos.

Car parts that are not electronic gizmos.

▶ **Figure 13-31**
Adding car parts to your universe

Figure 13-32 ◄
Electronic gizmos
AND car parts

*You can practice
drawing diagrams
of Boolean sets in
Review Question 9
at the end of this
chapter.*

Figure 13-33 ◄
Electronic gizmos
OR car parts

Figure 13-34 ◄
NOT (car parts OR
electronic gizmos)

Figure 13-35 ◄
Relational
operators

Lab

SQL Queries

Operator	Description
=	equal to
>	greater than
<	less than
>=	greater than or equal to
<=	less than or equal to
<>	not equal to

To show this on your diagram, color in only the overlapping part of the circles, as shown in Figure 13-32.

Now, what about the things that are **electronic gizmos OR car parts**? OR means a thing fits *either* criterion. So tires, radar detectors, CD players, hood ornaments, steering wheels, and microwave ovens fit the bill. To show this in your universe, color in both circles, as shown in Figure 13-33.

NOT means to select the opposite. For example, what things in your universe are **NOT car parts**? Everything not in the car parts circle. What things are **NOT(car parts or electronic gizmos)**? To figure this out, first do the OR in parentheses. What in your universe is car parts OR electronic gizmos? All the things in the circles. The NOT is what's left—everything outside the circles, as shown in Figure 13-34.

To summarize: AND means a thing must meet both criteria. It is restrictive—it only includes the overlapping area of the two circles. OR means a thing must fit either criterion. It is more inclusive—it includes anything in either circle. NOT means "the other things."

Boolean Queries

How does set theory apply to database queries?

You usually use a query to locate data in a database. Your query essentially tells the DBMS what you want it to find. Most popular query languages use command words, expressions, relational operators, and Boolean operators to formulate a query.

Simple queries are usually accomplished using a command word such as FIND and an expression such as LastName = "Houlihan". A simple **expression** usually has a field name on the left and the specific thing you want to find on the right. The query you use to locate the record for an employee with the last name Houlihan is **FIND LastName = 'Houlihan'**. You can create expressions using any of the **relational operators**: =, >, <, >=, <=, and <>. You can review the meanings of these operators in Figure 13-35.

A complex query, such as one to find only those employees who are registered nurses and have Houlihan for their last name and are female, requires the use of Boolean operators. Let's use the sample set of employees, shown in Figure 13-36, to visualize the results from queries of the Midtown General Hospital Employee database.

When used in a query, the logical operator AND connects two expressions, both of which must be true to match the search criteria. For example, the search criteria *JobCode = 'RN' AND Gender = 'F'* requests only those records for female registered nurses. If Margaret Houlihan is a female and a registered nurse, her record would match the search criteria. Figure 13-37 shows the results of such a search.

The logical operator OR connects two expressions, but only one of them must be true to match the search criteria. The search criteria *JobCode = 'RN' OR Gender = 'F'* would produce all the records for females, regardless of their job code. The search would also produce all the records for registered nurses of either gender.

The logical operator NOT precedes a simple or complex expression and, in a search specification, produces the records that do not match the expression. For example, the expression *NOT JobCode = 'RN'* would produce records for any employee who is not a registered nurse. What about the search criteria *NOT(JobCode = 'RN' AND Gender = 'F')*? Think of it this way: The computer will locate the records for all employees who are registered nurses and female (like Margaret Houlihan, who is a female registered nurse), but it will not produce these records. Instead it will produce all the other records. So, will the search *NOT(JobCode = 'RN' AND Gender = 'F')* produce Rick Bailey? Yes, it will and Figure 13-38 shows why.

What about using NOT and OR, as in the search criteria *NOT(JobCode = 'RN' OR Gender = 'F')*? This time, the computer essentially eliminates any records for registered

Figure 13-36
Midtown employees

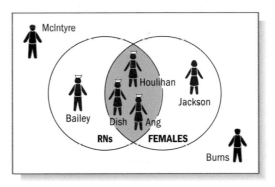

Figure 13-37
JobCode = 'RN'
AND Gender = 'F'

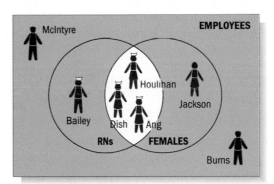

Figure 13-38
NOT (JobCode = 'RN'
AND Gender = 'F')

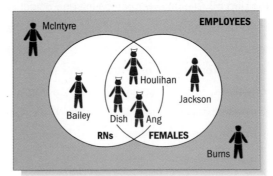

Figure 13-39
NOT (JobCode = 'RN'
OR Gender = 'F')

Compare Figure 13-39 to Figure 13-38 to make sure you understand the difference between the queries **NOT(JobCode = 'RN' AND Gender = 'F')** *and* **NOT(JobCode = 'RN' OR Gender = 'F')**.

nurses. It also eliminates any records for female employees. Figure 13-39 shows a conceptual diagram for this query.

Search criteria can become quite complex. Look at the employee table in Figure 13-40; let's use it to learn how to use a complex query to locate data in the table.

Figure 13-40
Midtown employee
table

LastName	FirstName	Gender	StartDate	JobCode
Ang	Susan	F	08/10/1988	RN
Bailey	Rick	M	02/03/1992	RN
Burns	Frank	M	05/04/1990	SMD
Dish	Betty	F	01/16/1992	RN
Houlihan	Margaret	F	10/05/1985	RN
Jackson	Tony	F	12/04/1989	SMD
McIntyre	Jon	M	04/14/1986	SMD

You might, for example, want to find the salaries of only those female employees who started working after August 1, 1988, but before August 1, 1990, as registered nurses or staff physicians (SMD). The search criteria would be **Gender = 'F' AND (StartDate > 08/01/1988 AND StartDate < 08/01/1990) AND (JobCode = 'RN' OR JobCode = 'SMD')**. The parentheses in this search criteria indicate the order in which the expressions should be evaluated by the DBMS. The expressions in parentheses should be evaluated first.

When you need to do a complex search, you might want to experiment with parts of the search first, to be certain the parts produce what you expect. For example, in the complex search above, you might first test the expression **(StartDate > 08/01/1988 AND StartDate < 08/01/1990)** to be certain it retrieves records with start dates during the correct time period. Once you have tested parts of your query, you can combine them to create your complete query.

You can practice queries in Project 3 at the end of this chapter.

End Note
The final episode of *M*A*S*H* aired on September 19, 1983. On that date, a typical hospital was likely to be using separate minicomputer systems to automate billing, maintain patient records, and track lab results. Microcomputers were just then appearing on the business scene after the launch of the IBM PC in 1982. Microcomputer networking was virtually unheard of. Client-server computing and object-oriented databases were just ideas batted around academia. The Internet consisted of fewer than 1,000 computers; the World Wide Web did not exist.

The infrastructure of a Korean War M.A.S.H. unit seems primitive by today's standards—no computers, irregular communications, a surgical tent instead of an operating room. Ultimately, however, medicine deals with people—the efforts of doctors, nurses, patients, friends, and family to fight disease and heal injuries. That was the appeal of *M*A*S*H*.

Review

1. Look back through this chapter and make sure you can answer the italicized questions under each heading.

2. Complete the following chart to summarize the terminology used as synonyms for the terms "record type," "record," and "field" in hierarchical, network, relational, and object-oriented databases:

	Relational	Hierarchical	Network	Object-oriented
Record Type				
Record				
Field				

3. Complete the following chart to summarize the characteristics of the four types of file and database management software:

	Custom Software	File Management	Database Management	Object-Oriented
Files manipulated with:	a custom program	file management software		
Promotes data independence:	No			
File support:	one at a time			
Manipulates relationships:		no		

4. List the steps you should follow to design a file or database.

5. Create a topic outline for the material presented in the section "File and Database Concepts."

6. Describe the difference between a record occurrence and a record type.

7. Draw a hierarchy diagram showing the relationship among the following terms: file, program file, data file, free-form data file, structured data file, flat file, database, relational database, hierarchical database, network database, object-oriented database.

8. For each of these pairs of record types, draw a data structure diagram showing whether the relationship is one-to-one, one-to-many, or many-to-many.

Author	Book
Musician	CD
Person	Social Security number
House	Mailbox
Doctor	Patient
Car	Tire

9. Suppose you have a universe that contains overlapping circles for golfers and CEOs (chief executive officers). Draw diagrams showing each of the following:

- a. Golfers OR CEOs
- b. Golfers AND CEOs
- c. NOT(Golfers AND CEOs)
- d. NOT(Golfers)
- e. (NOT Golfers) AND (NOT CEOs)
- f. NOT(Golfers OR CEOs)

10. Make a list of the six relational operators you can use in SQL queries.

Projects

1. Gourmet Gallery Suppose you are the database administrator for a large gourmet supply store. You are working with the inventory manager to define an effective record format for a file containing data about the merchandise. The inventory manager gives you a sample of the index cards now being used to keep track of the inventory (Figure 13-41). Use this card to design an effective record format for the inventory data file. To do this:

a. List each field the inventory record should contain. Your field names should be descriptive, contain no more than 10 characters, and be only one word. For example, use "PARTNUMBER", not "PN." Remember to think about how the data might be used for output—the fields you define might not be exactly the same as the fields on the index card.

b. Assign a data type to each field. You may use the following data types: character, numeric, date, and logical.

c. Define the length of each field. You might have to make some intelligent guesses about the field length because you do not know what all the data looks like. For example, you can see from the example that some part numbers are at least 10 characters long, but you might guess that some part numbers will be longer—use your judgment. Be careful about the length of fields that contain dollar values. You should not leave a space for the $ sign, but you should leave a space for the decimal point.

d. Where appropriate, indicate the input or output format for a field, for example, you would use 9999.99 for currency fields.

Figure 13-41 ◄

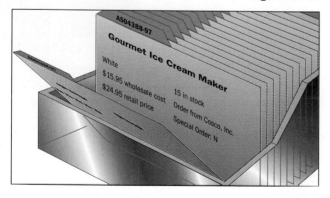

2. Central State University Suppose that you work on the staff at Central State University and you have the following data:

The Management Department (phone: 455-9800) has three graduate faculty: Professors Sharon Smith (office: BA 502, phone: 455-9897), Associate Professor Rico Gomez (office: BA 510, phone: 455-9888), and Associate

Professor Ariel Headly (office: BA 402, phone: 455-9776). S. Smith teaches Quantitative Analysis (course ID:MM525) on Tuesday and Thursday, 7-9 p.m., in room BA 10. She also teaches the Graduate Seminar (course ID: MM698) on Monday, 7-10 p.m., in room BA 21. R. Gomez teaches Personnel Management (course ID: MM560) on Monday and Wednesday, 7-9 p.m., in room BA 20. A. Headly teaches Leadership in Organizations (course ID: MM610) on Thursday, 6-9 p.m., in room BA 20.

a. Draw a data structure diagram showing how you would arrange this data in a hierarchical database, then draw the specific occurrence of the data that was described above.

b. R. Gomez decides to help A. Headly teach the Leadership in Organizations course. Now this course has two instructors. Redraw your data structure diagram using a network model to show this relationship. Also redraw your diagram showing an occurrence of the data.

c. Diagram the tables you would use if you were to structure this data as a relational database.

3. Toy Store Use the printout of a small toy store inventory in Figure 13-42 to determine the result of the queries in a through k below, then write out the queries you would use to find the data indicated in l through t on page 13-40.

How many records would match each of the following queries?

a. Quantity < 50

b. Wholesale > 2.50 AND Wholesale < 4.00

c. Ordered < '7/1/89'

d. Brand = "Nature's Kids" OR Brand = "Plastic Pets"

e. Brand = "Galaxy Toys" AND Brand = "Flying Fun"

f. (Brand = "Flying Fun" OR Brand = "Nature's Kids") AND Retail < 5.00

g. Brand = "Flying Fun" OR (Brand = "Nature's Kids" AND Retail < 5.00)

h. (Color = "Brown" OR Color = "Purple") AND Retail = 4.99

i. Color = "Brown" OR (Color = "Purple" AND Retail = 4.99)

j. Stock > 10 OR Stock < 50 AND Ordered By = "J. Mathers" OR Retail > 10.00

k. NOT(Supplier = "Toy Barn" OR Supplier = "GraphInc")

► **Figure 13-42**
Toy store inventory

Toy	Brand	Supplier	Color	Ordered	Ordered By	Quantity	Wholesale	Retail	Stock
Fortran Learner	Computer Fun	Fun Factory	Yellow	7/1/89	A. Hayes	50	$3.99	$5.39	32
Rocket Racer	Flying Fun	Fun Factory	Red/Blue	7/14/89	A. Hayes	50	$2.50	$3.38	32
Day-Glo Frisbees	Flying Fun	Fun Factory	Lime/Pink	7/1/89	A. Hayes	50	$2.50	$3.38	45
Model Cessna	Flying Fun	Fun Factory	Black	7/1/89	A. Hayes	50	$8.99	$12.14	0
Model Satellite	Flying Fun	Fun Factory	Red/White	6/25/89	A. Hayes	50	$5.50	$7.43	12
Satellite Launcher	Flying Fun	Toy Barn	Silver/Taupe	6/24/89	A. Hayes	50	$12.50	$16.88	10
Kaleidoscope	Galaxy Toys	Toy Barn	Purple	7/14/89	T. Livingston	50	$3.99	$5.39	10
Warp 10 U.F.O.	Galaxy Toys	Toy Barn	Silver/Blue	7/1/89	T. Livingston	50	$2.50	$3.38	40
Space Station	Galaxy Toys	Toy Barn	N/A	7/1/89	T. Livingston	25	$12.50	$16.88	50
Orbitron	Galaxy Toys	Toy Barn	Magenta	6/23/89	T. Livingston	25	$13.99	$18.89	3
Brontosaurus Bruce	Nature's Kids	Graphinc	Olive	7/14/89	T. Livingston	25	$4.99	$6.74	6
Ferdie Frog	Nature's Kids	Toy Barn	Green	7/1/89	T. Livingston	25	$2.50	$3.38	70
Stegosaurus Sam	Nature's Kids	Toy Barn	Brown/Olive	7/1/89	T. Livingston	25	$2.50	$3.38	84
Agatha Alligator	Nature's Kids	Toy Barn	Green	7/1/89	T. Livingston	25	$4.99	$6.74	54
Eight-color Paintset	Non-Toxic Toys	Toy Barn	N/A	7/14/89	J. Mathers	25	$2.99	$4.04	75
Wooden Tugboat	Non-Toxic Toys	Toy Barn	Brown	6/25/89	J. Mathers	50	$6.50	$8.78	23
Wooden Train Set	Non-Toxic Toys	Toy Barn	Brown	6/25/89	J. Mathers	25	$8.50	$11.48	1
Inflatable Crab	Plastic Pets	Toy Barn	Red	7/5/89	J. Mathers	50	$4.99	$6.74	1
Inflatable Lobster	Plastic Pets	Toy Barn	Pink	7/5/89	J. Mathers	50	$4.99	$6.74	18
Inflatable Snails	Plastic Pets	Toy Barn	Green/Olive	7/5/89	J. Mathers	50	$4.99	$6.74	20
Plastic Penguin	Plastic Pets	Toy Barn	Black/White	7/5/89	J. Mathers	50	$4.99	$6.74	20
Micro Mice	Plastic Pets	Toy Barn	White	7/5/89	J. Mathers	50	$4.99	$6.74	21
Vampire Fangs	Plastic Pets	Toy Barn	Pink	7/5/89	J. Mathers	50	$4.99	$6.74	22
Thinking Trees	Plastic Pets	Toy Barn	Brown	7/5/89	J. Mathers	50	$4.99	$6.74	13
Model Mercedes	Rich Folks	Graphinc	Blue/Tan	7/5/89	J. Mathers	50	$4.99	$6.74	4
Model Ferrari	Rich Folks	Graphinc	Red/Blue	7/5/89	J. Mathers	50	$4.99	$6.74	25
Plastic Sushi	Rich Folks	Graphinc	Yellow/Green	7/5/89	J. Mathers	50	$4.99	$6.74	33
Expanding Espresso	Rich Folks	Graphinc	Brown	7/5/89	J. Mathers	50	$4.99	$6.74	27
Rock'n'Roll Ron	Zap Toys	Toy Barn	Magenta/Red	7/5/89	J. Mathers	50	$4.99	$6.74	28
Singing Slugs	Zap Toys	Toy Barn	Green/Olive	7/5/89	J. Mathers	50	$4.99	$6.74	2
Piano Pete	Zap Toys	Toy Barn	Brown	7/5/89	J. Mathers	50	$4.99	$6.74	30
Dan the Drummer	Zap Toys	Toy Barn	Brown	7/5/89	J. Mathers	50	$4.99	$6.74	1
Bronco Buster	Zen Toys	Graphinc	N/A	7/5/89	J. Mathers	50	$4.99	$6.74	23
The Entertainer	Zen Toys	Graphinc	N/A	7/5/89	J. Mathers	50	$4.99	$6.74	33
Flower Child	Zen Toys	Graphinc	N/A	7/5/89	J. Mathers	50	$4.99	$6.74	14

*This data file is included in the Microsoft Works for Windows 3.0 online tutorial.

Write out the query you would use to find:

l. All the toys ordered between July 1 and July 7

m. Any toys with a wholesale cost more than $4.99 that were not ordered by J. Mathers

n. All the Brown toys that retail for more than $10.00

o. Any toys made by Zen Toys or Rich Folks for which there are fewer than 10 in stock

p. Any toys that were ordered by T. Livingston or A. Hayes before 7/1/89

q. The names of any toys from the Toy Barn that retail for between $4.00 and $8.00

r. Any purple toys that retail for less than $5.00 or any green toys that the store has fewer than 10 in stock

s. Any toys that the store ordered in quantities of 50 that do not have a wholesale cost of $4.99

t. Any toys that are pink or red or magenta, and have a retail price less than $10.00

4. Indexing Suppose you have a small file with the following records about computer books:

Record Number	Author	Title	Publication Date
1	Norton, Peter	Programmer's Guide to the IBM PC	1985
2	Craig, John Clark	Visual Basic Workshop	1991
3	Minsky, Marvin	Society of Mind	1986
4	Nelson, Theodore	Literary Machines	1987
5	Wodasky, Ron	Multimedia Madness	1992
6	Waite, Mitchell	Unix Primer Plus	1983

Figure 13-43 ◄

a. Complete the following table to create an index that will organize the records in alphabetical order according to author last name:

Author Name	Record Number
Craig, John Clark	2
Minsky, Marvin	3

b. Create an index table to organize the records by publication date.

5. Normalization Take the first step in the normalization process by eliminating the data redundancy in Figure 13-43. If necessary, create new record types. Assume you are working with a relational database model.

Invoice file

Invoice Number	Customer Name	Address	Date	Item Number	Item	Price	Number Purchased
0010	Jack Wei	503 S. HWY 7	09/01/1994	56887	B&D Hammer	17.69	1
0010	Jack Wei	503 S. HWY 7	09/01/1994	67433	Sand Paper–Fine	4.98	2
0010	Jack Wei	503 S. HWY 7	09/01/1994	2230B	CTR Sink	2.49	1
0011	Sally Zachman	834 N. Front St.	09/01/1994	56887	B&D Hammer	17.69	1
0012	Brad Koski	2910 52nd St.	09/02/1994	56887	B&D Hammer	17.69	2
0012	Brad Koski	2910 52nd St.	09/02/1994	4311A	9-inch Brush	7.89	1

6. Web Search The Internet World Wide Web encompasses a tremendous amount of information stored on computers all over the world. How can you find specific information quickly and efficiently? By using a search engine. Several Web sites provide search engines you can use to find information on computers all over the Web. One of the best search engines is Lycos, located at *http://www.lycos.com.* Lycos lets you tailor your searches using Boolean operators—AND, OR, and NOT. To complete this project use your Web browser to connect to Lycos. Next to the Search box, click Search Options.

Under Search Options, you can enter search words and specify AND or OR. Use Lycos to find the answers to the following questions:

   a. What did Albert Einstein think about socialism?

   b. Where can you find information about the dogs that the Soviets launched into space?

   c. Where can you find a quote from Confucius about learning?

   d. How many sites does Lycos find that contain information about the Magna Carta or about netserfs?

   e. Where would you find information about what netserfs think of the Magna Carta?

Resources

- **Codd, E. F.** "A Relational Model of Data for Large Shared Data Banks." *Communications of the ACM* 13(6), June 1970. Codd developed the relational database model in 1970 and described it in this article. Although the relational database model was thought to be impractical during the 1970s, modern computer architecture now provides the power necessary for its implementation.

- **Date, C. J.** *An Introduction to Database Systems*, 5th edition. Reading, MA: Addison-Wesley, 1990. Date's book is a classic on database management. Date has worked extensively on many database-related theories, including a set of standards for the SQL query language.

- *http://www.lycos.com* Need to search the Internet for information? The Lycos search engine lets you enter sophisticated queries using Boolean operators. Probably the best public search engine on the Internet, Lycos has an extensive link to substantive information.

- *M*A*S*H.* Robert Altman, dir. 20th Century Fox, 1970. This critically acclaimed film was the precursor to a

popular television show that ran for 11 seasons and continues to delight audiences with reruns.

- **Rob, P. and Coronel, C.** *Database Systems: Design, Implementation, and Management.* Belmont, CA: Wadsworth, 1993. This textbook provides a basic introduction to files and databases, with good coverage of object-oriented methodology appropriate for students who are planning to become computer information systems professionals.

Lab Assignments

SQL Queries Lab

To query many relational databases, you use SQL (usually pronounced by saying the letters of the acronym, "S Q L"). IBM developed SQL in the mid 1970s for use in mainframe relational database products such as DB2. In 1986 the American National Standards Institute (ANSI) adopted SQL as the standard relational database language and it is now used extensively on microcomputer databases as well. Understanding how to use SQL is an important skill for many data management jobs. In this Lab, you will get a taste of this powerful and flexible database language. To gain further expertise, you should refer to the course offerings at your school.

1. Click the Steps button to learn how to formulate SQL queries. As you proceed through the steps, answer the Quick Check questions. After you complete the Steps, you will see a Quick Check Summary Report. Follow the instructions on the screen to print this report.

2. In Explore, use the scroll bar to browse through the database to find the answers to the following questions:

   a. What are the names of the staff physicians? (Hint: The JobCode for staff physicians is SMD.)

   b. How many LPNs are in the database?

   c. Who makes more than $20 an hour?

   d. What is Ralph Smith's job?

   e. When was Tony Jackson hired?

3. In Explore, try the following queries and indicate if each accomplishes the result listed:

   a. QUERY: SELECT * FROM Employee order by Hourlywage

      RESULT: Displays employees beginning with the person who is the lowest paid

b. QUERY: SELECT * FROM Employee where Gender = 'F' AND Jobcode = 'SMD'

RESULT: Displays all the female staff physicians

c. QUERY: SELECT * FROM Employee where LastName between 'C' and 'M'

RESULT: Displays all the employees with last names that begin with a C, D, E, F, G, or H

d. QUERY: SELECT * FROM Employee where Gender = 'M' or Hourlywage > 20.00

RESULT: Displays only the men who make more than $20 an hour

e. QUERY: SELECT * FROM Employee where DeptCode <> 'OB' order by BirthDate

RESULT: Displays all the obstetricians' birthdays

4. In Explore, suppose that the database contains thousands of records and it is not practical to browse through all of the records using the scroll bar. Write down the queries you use to do the following:

a. Find the record for Angela Peterson.

b. Find the records for all the Rns.

c. Find all the employees who work in Intensive Care (IC).

d. Find all the employees who make less than $15 an hour.

e. Find all the employees who do not work in obstetrics (OB).

5. In Explore, suppose that the database contains thousands of records and it is not practical to browse through all of the records using the scroll bar. Write down the queries you use to do the following:

a. Find the name of the oldest employee.

b. Find the departments that have female employees.

c. Find out how many employees work in Intensive Care.

d. Find the last names of the female employees who make between $10 and $15 per hour.

e. Get an alphabetized list of male employees who work as Rns or LPNs.

6. Circle the errors in the following SQL queries:

a. SELECT * FROM Employee where DeptCode <> OB order by BirthDate

b. SELECT * FROM Employee where Wages between 10 and 50

c. SELECT * FROM Employee where order = LastName

d. SELECT * FROM Employee where DeptCode <> 'OB' and Hourly Wage > '$10.00' order by LastName

e. SELECT * FROM Employee where FirstName like T*

Quick Check Answers

13.1

1. variable-length

2. character (string)

3. type, occurrence

4. flat

5. data structure diagram (entity relationship diagram)

6. object-oriented

7. relational

13.2

1. custom

2. data independence

3. object-oriented

4. database management system or DBMS

5. client-server

6. passive

13.3

1. field format

2. range check

3. data redundancy

4. case sensitive

5. update

6. sort key

7. index

8. query by example

13.4

1. report template

2. control-break

3. exception

4. data set

5. bar

6. line

7. decision maker

Glossary/Index

update To change or delete a record in a database, 13-25

updating data, 13-25–13-26

variable-length field A field that expands to fit the data entered into it, 13-5

x-y charts, 13-33

Computer Programming

Computer **Programming**

It's Tuesday night. You and a group of friends are studying late when the munchies strike. Pizza sounds really good, but when you and your friends pool all your money, you have a grand total of $24.63—not much to feed eight hungry students. You all agree to call several pizza places to compare prices. One of your friends, looking up from her financial management text, says, "Maximize pizza, minimize cost!"

You call VanGo's Pizzeria first and find out that they have an 8" round pizza with two toppings for $8.99. Next, you call a pizza place named The Venice and discover that they have a 10" square pizza for $11.99. Which one is the better deal? You search for a calculator but can't find one. Your friend with the pocket protector offers to let you use his notebook computer so you can write a program to compare pizza prices. Now what?

This chapter is an introduction to basic concepts of computer programming: problem statements, algorithms, coding, control structures, testing, and documentation. Additional chapter topics include characteristics of computer programming languages and brief descriptions of today's most popular programming languages. This chapter is a stepping-stone for programming activities such as the Visual Programming Lab.

CHAPTER**PREVIEW**

In this chapter, you'll learn about computer programming and find out how to write a program that compares pizza prices. You can apply what you learn about the pizza program to many different problems that a computer can help you solve. You will also learn about the methodology programmers use to specify, code, and test computer programs. Understanding this methodology will be useful if you become involved in software development as a programmer or as a computer user. When you have completed this chapter, you should be able to:

- Describe the difference between a systems analyst and software engineer

- Identify the assumptions and known information in a problem statement

- Describe the relationship between an algorithm, pseudocode, and program code

- List at least four ways to express an algorithm

- Identify control structures in a simple BASIC program

- Describe the difference between syntax and logic errors

- Explain the purpose of program documentation, remarks, and user reference

- List the major characteristics that differentiate programming languages

- List today's most popular computer programming languages

- Describe the difference between a "small" program and a "large" program using the Department of Defense standards

Software Engineering

Software engineering is the systematic approach to the development, operation, maintenance, and retirement of software. Software engineers are responsible for designing software that is used in an information system. The jobs of the systems analyst and the software engineer overlap, but they are not the same. A systems analyst plans an entire information system, including hardware, software, procedures, personnel, and data. A software engineer focuses on the software component of an information system: on software design, coding, and testing. Let's look at the process of software engineering, beginning with problem statements and algorithms, which form the foundation for software design.

Computer Programs

Is it difficult to write a computer program?

In Chapter 2, you learned that a **computer program** is a set of detailed, step-by-step instructions that tell a computer how to solve a problem or carry out a task. You also briefly studied a short program, written in the Pascal programming language, designed to convert feet and inches into centimeters. Where do these instructions come from? Although we speak of "writing a computer program," it is not exactly the same process as writing a letter. When you write a letter, you usually compose it "on the fly;" you are not particularly concerned about the structure, nor are you particularly concerned with efficiency, as long as you communicate your message.

People can tolerate some degree of ambiguity when they communicate. Suppose you write your friend a letter that includes the following statement: "Remember to water my plants and lock the doors. Oh, and don't forget to feed the fish."

You assume your friend knows which plants to water and how much water to use, you hope your friend remembers what to feed the fish, and you assume your friend will feed the fish before leaving the house and locking the door.

Computers don't deal with ambiguity as well as people. So, when you give the computer a set of instructions, you need to be more explicit than you would be with a person. Consequently, you must think of computer programming as a process that is more structured than writing a casual letter to a friend. You must be more precise and less ambiguous.

Writing a computer program is quite a bit more complex than writing a letter. However, the software engineering process offers guidelines that help you achieve a successful outcome to this complex task. Computer programming begins with a problem statement, which is the basis for an algorithm. An algorithm, in turn, is the basis for program instructions. Let's take a closer look at what we mean by problem statement, algorithm, and program instructions.

The Problem Statement

What's a good problem statement for the pizza program?

Problems that you might try to solve using a computer often begin as questions. For example: "Which pizza place has the best deal?" But this question is not stated in a way that helps you devise a way for the computer to arrive at an answer. The question is vague. It doesn't tell you what information is available for determining the best deal. Do you know the price of several pizzas at different pizza places? Do you know the size of the pizzas? Do you know how many toppings are included in the price? The question "Which pizza place has the best deal?" does not explain what "best deal" means: Is it merely the cheapest pizza? Is it the pizza that gives you the most toppings for the dollar? Is it the biggest pizza you can get for the $24.63 that you and your

Like many other disciplines, software engineering is a skill that you learn and develop with practice. For some insights on the discipline from experts, you might want to browse through the book Programmers at Work. *You'll find the citation in the Resources section of this chapter.*

friends managed to scrape together? Study Figure 14-1 and see if you can pose a problem statement that is better than the initial vague question, "Which pizza place has the best deal?"

A **problem statement** defines certain elements that must be manipulated to achieve a result or goal. A well-posed problem statement has three characteristics:

■ It specifies any assumptions that define the scope of the problem.
■ It clearly specifies the known information.
■ It specifies when the problem has been solved.

In a problem statement, an **assumption** is something that you accept as true in order to proceed with the program design. For example, in the pizza problem, you can make the assumption that you want to compare two pizzas. Further, you can assume that some pizzas are round and others are square. To simplify the problem, you might make the additional assumption that none of the pizzas are rectangular, that is, none will have one side longer than the other. This simplifies the problem because you need to deal only with the "size" of a pizza, rather than the "length" and "width" of a pizza. A fourth assumption for the pizza problem is that the pizzas you compare have the same toppings. Finally, you assume that the pizza with the lowest cost per square inch is the best buy.

The **known information** in a problem statement is the information you supply the computer to help solve a problem. For the pizza problem, the known information includes the prices, the shapes, and the sizes of pizzas from two pizza places. The known information is often included in the problem statement as "givens." For example, a problem statement might include the phrase, "given the prices, the shapes, and the sizes of two pizzas... ."

After you specify the known information in a problem statement, you specify how you will determine when the problem has been solved. Usually this means specifying the output you expect. Of course, you cannot specify the answer in the problem statement—you won't know, for example, whether VanGo's Pizzeria or The Venice has the better deal before you run the program. But you can specify that the computer should output which pizza is the better deal.

Suppose you and your friends decide that the best deal means getting the biggest pizza at the lowest price; in other words, the best deal is the pizza that has the cheapest price per square inch. In this case, pizza that costs 5¢ per square inch is a better deal than pizza that costs 7¢ per square inch. The problem is solved, therefore, when the computer has calculated the price per square inch for both pizzas, compared the prices, and printed a message indicating which one has the lower price per square inch. You could write this part of the problem statement as "The computer will calculate the price per square inch of each pizza, then print a message indicating whether Pizza 1 or Pizza 2 has the lower price per square inch."

The values for known information do not have to be known at the time you write the program. For example, if you write a program to manage a video store, you do not need to know the names of the customers when you write the program. The known information in this case is that video stores have customers, who have a name, address, phone number, and so forth.

After thinking carefully about the problem, you have a list of assumptions, a list of known information, and a description of what you expect as output. The complete problem statement for the pizza program is:

Assuming that there are two pizzas to compare, that both pizzas contain the same toppings, and that the pizzas could be round or square, and given the prices, the shapes, and the sizes of the two pizzas, the computer will calculate the price per square inch of each pizza, then print a message indicating which pizza has the lower price per square inch.

This problem statement is rather lengthy. The following format for the problem statement is easier to understand:

ASSUMPTIONS:
There are two pizzas to compare, Pizza 1 and Pizza 2
The pizzas have the same toppings
A pizza is either round or square
Neither of the pizzas is rectangular
The pizza with the lower cost per square inch is the "best buy"
GIVEN:
The prices of two pizzas in dollars
The shape of each pizza (round or square)
The size of each pizza in inches
COMPUTE:
The price per square inch of each pizza
DISPLAY:
"Pizza 1 is the best deal" if Pizza 1 has the lower price per square inch
"Pizza 2 is the best deal" if Pizza 2 has the lower price per square inch
"Neither is the best deal" if both pizzas have the same price per square inch

Now that you have learned how to write a problem statement, we can move to the next step in the programming process—creating an algorithm.

You can practice identifying assumptions and known information in Projects 1 and 2 at the end of this chapter.

Algorithms

How do I formulate an algorithm for the pizza problem?

An **algorithm** is a set of steps for carrying out a task. An algorithm is an abstract idea, but it can be written down and it can be implemented. For example, the algorithm for cooking a batch of macaroni and cheese is a set of steps that includes boiling water, cooking the macaroni in the water, and adding cheese. The algorithm is written down, or expressed, as instructions in a recipe. You can implement the algorithm by following the instructions.

An important characteristic of a correctly formulated algorithm is that by carefully following the steps, you are guaranteed to accomplish the task for which the algorithm was designed. So, if you carefully follow the recipe on the macaroni package, you should be guaranteed of a successful batch of macaroni and cheese.

An algorithm for a computer program is the set of steps that explains how to begin with the known information specified in a problem statement and manipulate that information to arrive at a solution. An algorithm for a computer program is typically first written in a format that is not specific to a particular computer or programming language. This way, the software engineer focuses on formulating a correct algorithm, rather than on expressing the algorithm using the commands of a computer programming language. In a later phase of the software development process, the programmer translates the algorithm into instructions written in a computer programming language so the algorithm can be implemented by a computer.

When you are just beginning to work with computer programming, determining the amount of detail required to express an algorithm might seem difficult. For example, you might wonder if your algorithm needs to specify the steps necessary to do addition—do you need to explain how to "carry"? The detail necessary for the algorithm depends on the computer language you intend to use to write the program. As you become familiar with the commands that a language contains and what each command does, you will gain an understanding of the level of detail required. For the pizza problem, let's suppose that you will use the BASIC computer language. Study Figure 14-2 to understand the level of instructions that are appropriate for algorithms that are the basis for BASIC programs.

Algorithm Task	Example
Assign a value to a variable	Size = 10
Evaluate an expression or "solve an equation"	SquareInchPrice = Price / SquareInches
Ask for information (input) from the user	Enter the Price of a pizza
Display or print the results of calculations	Display the SquareInchPrice
Make decisions	If the pizza is square, calculate SquareInches by multiplying the Size * Size
Repeat some instructions	Repeat the price calculations for as many pizzas as the user wants

Figure 14-2
A sample of the kinds of tasks an algorithm for a BASIC program can specify

To design an algorithm, you might begin by solving the problem yourself and recording the steps you take. If you take this route, remember that to solve the pizza problem you have to obtain initial information on the cost, the size, and the shape of the pizzas. The computer also needs this initial information, so part of your algorithm must specify how the computer gets it. When the pizza program runs, it should request the user to enter the initial information needed to solve the problem. Your algorithm might begin like this:

Ask the user for the shape of the first pizza and hold it in RAM as Shape1.
Ask the user for the price of the first pizza and hold it in RAM as Price1.
Ask the user for the size of the first pizza and hold it in RAM as Size1.

Next, your algorithm should specify how to manipulate this information. You want to calculate the price per square inch, but an instruction like "Calculate the price per square inch" neither specifies how to do the calculation nor deals with the fact that you must perform different calculations for square and round pizzas. A more appropriate set of instructions is shown in Figure 14-3:

Figure 14-3
Algorithm for
calculating
the price per
square inch

1. To calculate the area of a square pizza, multiply the length of one side by the length of the other side. The sides are the same size in a square, so you can use the formula Size1 * Size1.

2. To calculate the area of a round pizza, use the formula for the area of a circle: πr^2. π is approximately 3.142. r^2 is the square of the radius of the circle. The size of a pizza is its diameter, so you need to divide the diameter by 2 to get the radius, using Size1 / 2. Then you need to square the radius. ^2 is the notation you use on a computer to indicate the exponent 2.

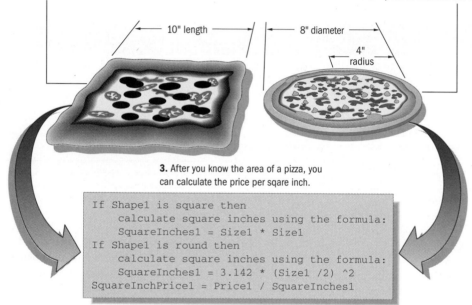

3. After you know the area of a pizza, you can calculate the price per sqare inch.

```
If Shape1 is square then
    calculate square inches using the formula:
    SquareInches1 = Size1 * Size1
If Shape1 is round then
    calculate square inches using the formula:
    SquareInches1 = 3.142 * (Size1 /2) ^2
SquareInchPrice1 = Price1 / SquareInches1
```

The algorithm you have designed so far calculates the price per square inch of one pizza. The algorithm should specify a similar process for calculating the price per square inch of the second pizza:

Ask the user for the shape of the second pizza and hold it in RAM as Shape2.
Ask the user for the price of the second pizza and hold it in RAM as Price2.
Ask the user for the size of the second pizza and hold it in RAM as Size2.
If Shape2 is square then calculate the square inches using the formula:
  *SquareInches2 = Size2 * Size2*
If Shape2 is round then calculate the square inches using the formula:
  *SquareInches2 = 3.142 * (Size2 / 2) ^2*
SquareInchPrice2 = Price2 / SquareInches2

Finally, the algorithm should specify how the computer decides what to display as the solution. You want the computer to display a message telling you which pizza has the lowest square-inch cost, so your algorithm should include something like this:

If SquareInchPrice1< SquareInchPrice2 then display the message "Pizza 1 is the best deal."
If SquareInchPrice2 < SquareInchPrice1 then display the message "Pizza 2 is the best deal."

But don't forget to indicate what you want the program to do if the price per square inch of both pizzas is the same:

If SquareInchPrice1 = SquareInchPrice2 then display the message "Both pizzas are the same deal."

The complete algorithm for the pizza problem is shown in Figure 14-4.

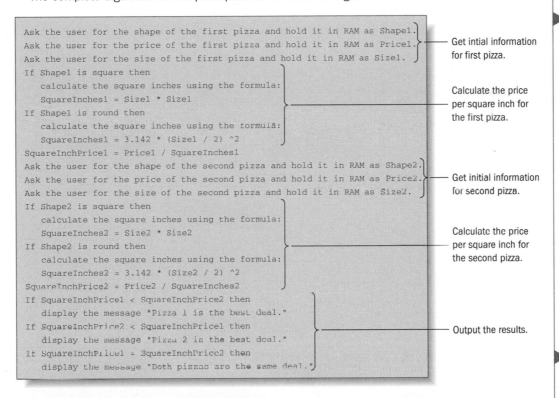

► **Figure 14-4**
Algorithm for pizza problem

— Get intial information for first pizza.

— Calculate the price per square inch for the first pizza.

— Get initial information for second pizza.

— Calculate the price per square inch for the second pizza.

— Output the results.

► **Figure 14-5**
Pseudocode for pizza program

Expressing an Algorithm

What's the best way to express an algorithm?

You can express an algorithm in several different ways. In Figure 14-4, the algorithm for the pizza problem is expressed in **structured English**. Another way to express an algorithm is with pseudocode. **Pseudocode** is a notational system for algorithms that has been described as "a mixture of English and your favorite programming language." Compare the pseudocode for the pizza problem in Figure 14-5 with the structured English in Figure 14-4 to understand some of the differences between these two ways of expressing an algorithm.

```
display prompts for entering shape, price, and size
input Shape1, Price1, Size1
if Shape1 = square then
    SquareInches1 ← Size1 * Size1
if Shape1 = round then
    SquareInches1 ← 3.142 * (Size1 / 2) ^2
SquareInchPrice1 ← Price1 / SquareInches1

display prompts for entering shape, price, and size
input Shape2, Price2, Size2
if Shape2 = square then
    SquareInches2 ← Size2 * Size2
if Shape2 = round then
    SquareInches2 ← 3.142 * (Size2 / 2) ^2
SquareInchPrice2 ← Price2 / SquareInches2

if SquareInchPrice1 < SquareInchPrice2 then
    output "Pizza 1 is the best deal."
if SquareInchPrice2 < SquareInchPrice1 then
    output "Pizza 2 is the best deal."
if SquareInchPrice1 = SquareInchPrice2 then
    output "Both pizzas are the same deal."
```

A third way to express an algorithm is to use a flow chart. A **flow chart** is a graphical representation of the way a computer should progress from one instruction to the next when it performs a task. The flow chart for the pizza problem is shown in Figure 14-6.

Figure 14-6
Flowchart for
pizza program

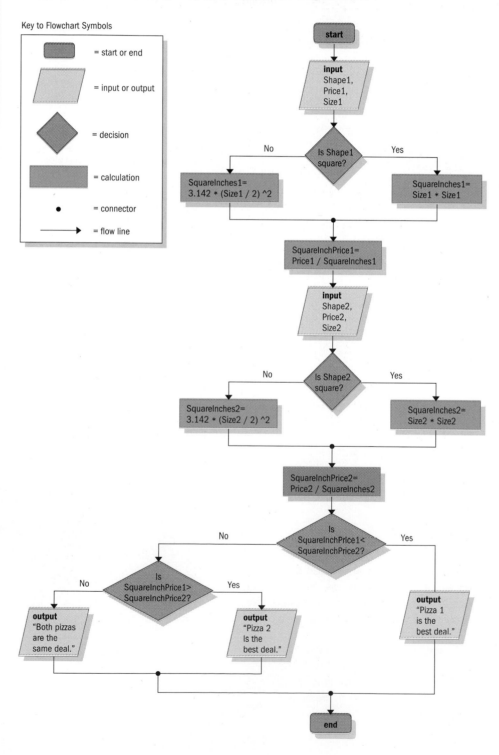

Another way to express an algorithm is to **define the objects** that the computer must manipulate, then specify the method for manipulating each object. This way of expressing an algorithm is useful for designing object-oriented programs, which you will learn more about later in this chapter. Figure 14-7 shows a description of one of the objects for the pizza program.

Object: Calculate Best Deal
Type: Button
Appearance:
Calculate Best Deal
Method:
```
If Shape1 = "square" THEN SquareInches1 = Size1 * Size1
If Shape1 = "round" THEN SquareInches1 = 3.142 * (Size1 / 2) ^2
SquareInchPrice1 = Price1 / SquareInches1
If Shape2 = "square" THEN SquareInches2 = Size2 * Size2
If Shape2 = "round" THEN SquareInches2 = 3.142 * (Size2 / 2) ^2
SquareInchPrice2 = Price2 / SquareInches2
If SquareInchPrice1 < SquareInchPrice2 THEN BestDeal = "Pizza 1 is the
best deal."
If SquareInchPrice2 < SquareInchPrice1 THEN BestDeal = "Pizza 2 is the
best deal."
If SquareInchPrice1 = SquareInchPrice2 THEN BestDeal = "Both pizzas are
the same deal."
```

Figure 14-7
Object descriptions for the pizza program

Quick Check

1. If you have a job as a(n) _____ you would focus on the software component of an information system.

2. Before you write a computer program, you should write a(n) _____ to define the elements that must be manipulated to achieve a result or goal.

3. A(n) _____ is a set of steps for carrying out a task or solving a problem.

4. "A mixture or English and your favorite programming language" is the description of _____.

5. A(n) _____ is a graphical representation of the way a computer should progress from one instruction to the next when it performs a task.

14.2

Coding Computer Programs

Lab

Visual Programming

A problem statement and an algorithm are often combined into a document called the **program specification**, which is essentially a blueprint for a computer program. When the program specification is complete, it is time to begin coding the program. **Coding** is the process of using a computer language to express an algorithm. A person who codes or writes computer programs is called a **computer programmer**.

With many computer programming languages, the coding process means entering commands. With other computer programming languages, you enter or select the characteristics of objects or you enter descriptive statements about the objects.

To code the pizza algorithm using the BASIC computer language, you type a list of commands. Look at the completed program in Figure 14-8 and study the callouts to get a general understanding of the elements of a computer program.

Figure 14-8
BASIC code for the
pizza program

Command words
are shown in boldface.

The program is written as a list of
steps. The computer executes the
steps starting at the top of the list.

Remarks that
begin with REM
explain each
section of
the program.

```
REM   The Pizza Program
REM   This program tells you which of two pizzas is the best deal
REM   by calculating the price per square inch of each pizza.

REM   Collect initial information for first pizza.
INPUT   "Enter the shape of pizza one:", Shape1$
INPUT   "Enter the price of pizza one:", Price1
INPUT   "Enter the size of pizza one:", Size1

REM   Calculate price per square inch for first pizza.

REM   If the first pizza is square, calculate the square inches by multiplying
one side by the other.
If Shape1$ = "square" THEN SquareInches1 = Size1 * Size1

REM   If the first pizza is round, calculate the number of square inches where
REM   pi = 3.142, size / 2 = radius, and (size / 2) ^2 = radius squared:
If Shape1$ = "round" THEN SquareInches1 = 3.142 * (Size1 / 2) ^2
SquareInchPrice1 = Price1 / SquareInches1

REM   Collect initial information for second pizza.
INPUT   "Enter the shape of pizza two:", Shape2$
INPUT   "Enter the price of pizza two:", Price2
INPUT   "Enter the size of pizza two:", Size2

REM   Calculate price per square inch for second pizza.
If Shape2$ = "square" THEN SquareInches2 = Size2 * Size2
If Shape2$ = "round" THEN SquareInches2 = 3.142 * (Size2 / 2) ^2
SquareInchPrice2 = Price2 / SquareInches2

REM   Decide which pizza is the best deal and display results.
If SquareInchPrice1 < SquareInchPrice2 THEN Message$ = "Pizza 1 is the best deal."
If SquareInchPrice2 < SquareInchPrice1 THEN Message$ = "Pizza 2 is the best deal."
If SquareInchPrice1 = SquareInchPrice2 THEN Message$ = "Both pizzas are the
same deal."
Print Message$
END
```

Data is stored
in variables, or
memory locations, in
RAM. The variable
Shape1$ stores text,
such as the word
"round." The $
indicates a text
variable. Other
variables, such
as Price1, store
numbers, and
the variable name
does not include a $.

You can use your library and Internet resources to find out more about computer programming careers when you do Project 11 at the end of this chapter.

Program Sequence

How do I tell the computer the sequence in which it should perform instructions?

The normal pattern of program execution is for a computer to perform each instruction in the sequence established by the programmer. The first instruction in the program is executed first, then the second instruction, and so on through the rest of the instructions in the program. Here is a simple program written in the QBASIC computer language that outputs "This is the first line," then outputs "This is the second line."

```
PRINT "This is the first line."
PRINT "This is the second line."
```

Although most modern programming languages do not use line numbers, older programming languages, such as the original version of BASIC, required programmers to number each instruction like this:

```
100 PRINT "This is the first line."
200 PRINT "This is the second line."
```

If the lines in a program are numbered, a computer begins executing the instruction with the lowest number, then proceeds to the instruction with the next highest number, and so on.

Some algorithms specify that a program execute instructions in an order different from the sequence in which they are listed, skip some instructions under certain circumstances, or repeat instructions. **Control structures** are instructions that specify the sequence in which a program is executed. There are three types of control structures: sequence controls, selection controls, and repetition controls.

Sequence Controls

Is there any way to have the computer follow a different sequence?

A **sequence control structure** changes the sequence, or order, in which instructions are executed by directing the computer to execute an instruction elsewhere in the program. In the following simple QBASIC program, the GOTO command tells the computer to jump directly to the instruction labeled "Finish." The program will never execute the command PRINT "This is the second line."

```
PRINT "This is the first line."
GOTO Finish
PRINT "This is the second line."
Finish: PRINT "All Done!"
END
```

► **Figure 14-9**
Too many GOTOs

```
100     Year = 1997
200     PRINT "The year is"
300     GOTO 1000
400     PRINT "Your lucky number is "
500     GOTO 1200
600     PRINT "Your unlucky number is "
700     Product = 1*9*9*7
800     PRINT Product
900     GOTO 1500
1000    PRINT Year
1100    GOTO 400
1200    Total = 1+9+9+7
1300    PRINT Total
1400    GOTO 600
1500    END
```

Although it is the simplest control structure, the GOTO command is rarely used by skilled programmers because it can lead to programs that are difficult to understand and maintain. In 1968, the journal *Communications of the ACM* published a now famous letter from Edsger Dijkstra, called "Goto Statement Considered Harmful." In his letter, Dijkstra explained that injudicious use of the GOTO statement in programs makes it difficult for other programmers to understand the underlying algorithm, which in turn means that such programs are difficult to correct, improve, or revise. You might think that a few GOTOs in a program are hardly harmful, but just take a look at Figure 14-9 and try to determine what the computer will output.

Experienced programmers prefer to use sequence controls other than GOTO to transfer program execution to a subroutine, procedure, module, or function. **Subroutines**, **procedures**, **modules**, and **functions** are sections of code that are part of a program, but are not included in the main sequential execution path. Figure 14-10 shows the execution path of a program that uses the GOSUB command to transfer execution to a subroutine.

Figure 14-10 ◄
Sequence controls

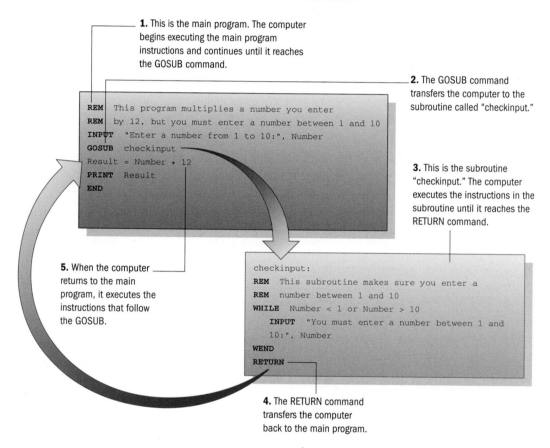

1. This is the main program. The computer begins executing the main program instructions and continues until it reaches the GOSUB command.

2. The GOSUB command transfers the computer to the subroutine called "checkinput."

3. This is the subroutine "checkinput." The computer executes the instructions in the subroutine until it reaches the RETURN command.

```
REM   This program multiplies a number you enter
REM   by 12, but you must enter a number between 1 and 10
INPUT "Enter a number from 1 to 10:", Number
GOSUB checkinput
Result = Number * 12
PRINT Result
END
```

```
checkinput:
REM   This subroutine makes sure you enter a
REM   number between 1 and 10
WHILE Number < 1 or Number > 10
    INPUT "You must enter a number between 1 and
    10:", Number
WEND
RETURN
```

5. When the computer returns to the main program, it executes the instructions that follow the GOSUB.

4. The RETURN command transfers the computer back to the main program.

Selection Controls

Can the computer make decisions as it executes a program?

A **selection control structure**, also referred to as a **decision structure** or **branch**, tells a computer what to do based on whether a condition is true or false. A simple example of a selection control structure is the IF..THEN command. The following program uses the IF..THEN command to decide whether a number entered is greater than 10. If the number is greater than 10, the computer prints "That number is greater than 10!" If the number is not greater than 10, the program does not print this message.

```
INPUT "Enter a number from 1 to 10:", Number
IF Number > 10 THEN PRINT "That number is greater than 10!"
END
```

Screen

N

Repetition Controls

Can a computer perform a series of instructions more than once?

A **repetition control structure,** also referred to as a **loop** or **iteration**, repeats one or more instructions until a certain condition is met. In QBASIC, the most frequently used loop commands are FOR..NEXT and WHILE..WEND. The following simple QBASIC program uses the FOR..NEXT command to print a message three times.

```
FOR N = 1 TO 3
    PRINT "There's no place like home."
NEXT N
END
```

The FOR..NEXT command is used to repeat a series of instructions a specified number of times. To see how this works, pretend that you are the computer executing this FOR..NEXT loop. The variable N is a RAM location in the computer. You can use the box labeled N in the margin.

As the computer, you would also have a screen on which to display output. Use the screen box in the margin. Now, let's walk through the loop.

1. As the computer, the first time you see the instruction FOR N = 1 TO 3, you set N equal to 1. To do this, write the number 1 in the N box in the margin.

2. You would then execute the next instruction, PRINT "There's no place like home." To do this, write the phrase "There's no place like home" in the screen box in the margin.

3. The instruction NEXT sends you back to the command FOR N = 1 TO 3. Because this is the second time you have executed this statement, put a 2 in the N box in the margin (you can erase the 1 that was there previously).

4. You need to check if the value in box N is greater than 3. Why do this? Because the command FOR N = 1 TO 3 means you can continue to loop only if N is 3 or less. Well, N is only 2, so you can proceed.

5. Go to the next instruction, which is PRINT "There's no place like home." So, write this again in the screen box.

6. Moving on, you reach the NEXT statement again, and this sends you back to the FOR statement.

7. Continue by changing the value in the N box to 3. Check the N box to make sure it does not contain a value greater than 3. It doesn't, so continue.

8. The next line instructs you to PRINT "There's no place like home," so write this again in the screen box. The NEXT statement sends you back to the FOR statement. Increase the value in the N box to 4. This time when you check if the value in N is greater than 3, it is. That means the loop is complete and you should jump to the statement past the end of the loop.

9. The next statement is END, so you've completed the program.

Quick Check

1. _____ is the process of using a computer language to express an algorithm.

2. In a BASIC program, the computer executes line 200 before it executes line 100. True or false?

3. A(n) _____ changes the sequence, or order, in which instructions are executed by transferring program execution to instructions elsewhere in the program.

4. Edsger Dijkstra suggested that the _____ statement makes programs difficult to understand, debug, and modify.

5. A(n) _____ structure tells a computer what to do, depending on whether a condition is true or false.

6. A(n) _____ structure repeats one or more instructions until a certain condition is met.

Debugging and Documenting

As you are coding a program, you must test each section of your code to make sure it works correctly. This process is referred to as **debugging** because the process "gets the bugs out" so they don't cause errors when you use the program. As you are coding you should also write **documentation** as a permanent record that explains how your program works.

Testing a Program

How do I know if my program will function correctly?

A computer program must be tested to ensure that it works correctly. Testing often consists of entering test data to see if the program produces correct results. If the program does not produce correct results, the programmer must examine the program for errors, correct the errors, and test the program again.

For example, to test the pizza program, you could run the program and enter data for which you have already calculated the results. Suppose you use a calculator to determine that the price per square inch of an $18.50, 15" square pizza is about $.08. One way to test the program is to run it and enter $18.50 for the price, 15 for the size, and square for the shape. The program should produce the result $.08 for the price per square inch of this pizza. If it doesn't, you know that you made an error when you wrote the program and that you must correct the error.

But testing a single set of values is not enough. At minimum, you should test every statement at least once, and you should test every decision branch. The pizza program has two possible decision branches for calculating the price per square inch. One branch is for square pizzas; the other branch is for round pizzas. Even if you enter a set of test data for a square pizza and the program provides the correct result, you cannot assume the program is working correctly until you also test it with data for a round pizza.

When you find an error, or bug, in a program, it might be a syntax error or it might be a run-time error. A **syntax error** is caused when an instruction does not follow the syntax rules, or grammar, of the programming language. For example, when you want to print a message, you need to use the PRINT command. The command `IF AGE = 16 THEN "You can drive"` will produce a syntax error because the command word PRINT is missing. The correct version of the command is `IF AGE = 16 THEN PRINT "You can drive."`

Syntax errors are very common, but they are easy to detect and correct. Syntax errors can be caused by omitting a command word, misspelling a command word, or using incorrect punctuation, such as a colon (:) where a semicolon (;) is required. Many of today's programming languages detect and point out syntax errors when you are in the process of coding each instruction. Because these languages show you syntax errors when you type each line of code, you typically will have few syntax errors when you test programs written with these languages.

The other type of program bug is a run-time error. A **run-time error** is an error that shows up when you run a program. Run-time errors can be caused by a typing error that results in the correct syntax but does not produce the intended result. For example, suppose you erroneously use the < symbol in the following command for the pizza problem:

```
IF SquareInchPrice1< SquareInchPrice2 THEN PRINT "Pizza 2 is a
better deal than Pizza 1."
```

The command produces the wrong output as a result of the error you introduced when you used the < sign instead of the > sign.

Other run-time errors are classified as logic errors. A **logic error** is an error in the logic or design of the program. Logic errors can be caused by an inadequate definition of the problem or by an incorrect or incomplete solution specified by the flowchart or pseudocode. Logic errors are usually more difficult and time-consuming to identify than syntax errors.

Program errors are classified as syntax errors or logic errors. Syntax and logic errors that appear when a program runs are run-time errors.

Program Documentation

Why do I need to document my programs?

A computer program inevitably must be modified because needs change. Modifying a program is much easier if the program has been well documented. For example, suppose VanGo's Pizzeria and The Venice have both added a new rectangular pizza to their menu. In that case, you and your friends would want to modify the pizza program so you can enter the dimensions of a rectangular pizza. First, you need to understand how the current program works. Although this might seem like a fairly easy task for the short pizza program, imagine trying to understand a 5,000-line program that calculates income tax, especially if you weren't the person who wrote the original program. You might want some additional information to explain the logic behind the program and the formulas that the programmer devised to perform calculations.

Program documentation explains how a program works and how to use it. The documentation you create should be useful to other programmers who need to modify your code and to people who use your program. Typically, program documentation takes two forms: remarks inserted into the program code and "written" documentation.

Remarks are explanatory comments inserted into the lines of code of a computer program. To revise a computer program, a programmer reads through the original program to find out how it works, then makes revisions to the appropriate sections of code. It is easier to understand the original program if the person who writes it places remarks in the program. Remarks are ignored by the computer when it executes the program, but for programmers who must modify the program, these remarks are very handy.

A well-documented program contains initial remarks that explain the purpose of the program. These remarks contain essentially the same information as the problem statement. For example, the pizza program contains the following initial remarks:

```
REM  The Pizza Program
REM  This program tells you which of two pizzas is the better deal
REM  by calculating the price per square inch of each pizza.
```

Remarks are also called comments. Depending on the language, a remark might begin with REM or with a symbol such as (*.

Remarks should also be added to the sections of a program in which the purpose of the code is not immediately clear. For example, in the pizza program, the purpose of the expression 3.142*(size/2)^2 might not be immediately obvious to a programmer reading the code. Therefore, it would be helpful to have a remark preceding the expression, like this:

```
REM  The program calculates the number of square inches in a round
  pizza where
REM  pi = 3.142, size/2 = radius, and (size/2)^2 = radius squared:
SquareInches = 3.142*(size/2)^2
```

There is no hard and fast rule about when you should include a remark in a program. However, if you were to work with a group of other programmers on a project, your group might develop guidelines to ensure that remarks are used consistently throughout the code for the project. As you gain experience writing programs, you will develop a sense for using remarks appropriately.

Written documentation is external to a program and contains information about the program that is useful to programmers and the people who use the program. Written documentation can be paper-based or in electronic format. Because documentation serves two audiences—the programmers and the users—there are two broad categories of written documentation for computer programs: program manuals and user references.

A **program manual** contains any information about the program that might be useful to programmers, including the problem statement and algorithm. Because a program manual is a software development and maintenance tool, it is used by programmers, not users. The **user reference**, or **reference manual**, contains information that helps users learn to use a computer program. Figure 14-11 lists the types of information that might be included in a program manual and a user reference.

▶ **Figure 14-11**
Program documentation

Program Manual

- Problem statement
- Algorithm expressed in:
  Structured English
  Pseudocode
  Flow chart
- Printout of program code

User Reference

- Description of what the program does
- Instructions on how to install the program
- Instructions on how to start the program
- Description of the options or features of the program
- Instructions on what to input
- Pictures of the screens and menus
- Troubleshooting tips

In Chapter 1 you learned that reference manuals are usually organized by feature.

Quick Check

1 Entering known data to see if a program produces the correct results is part of the _____ process.

2 If you ignore the rules or grammar of a programming language, you are likely to get a(n) _____ error.

3 Suppose you run the pizza program and the output indicates Pizza 2 is the best deal. However, your test data shows that Pizza 1 is the best deal. Because this error appeared when you ran the program, it would be classified as a(n) _____ error.

4 _____ errors are the usually the most difficult and time-consuming errors to identify.

5 _____ explains how a program works and how to use it.

6 Programmers insert _____ into programs to explain how the program works and to make it easier for other programmers to modify the program.

7 A(n) _____ is documentation used by programmers, whereas a(n) _____ is documentation designed for the people who use the program.

Programming Language Characteristics

Hundreds of programming languages have been developed over the last 30 years. Some languages were developed to make the programming process more efficient and less error-prone. Some languages were developed to provide an effective command set for specific types of programs, such as business programs or scientific programs. Other languages were created specifically as teaching tools.

Programming languages have characteristics that describe how they work and provide information about the types of computing tasks for which they are appropriate. For example, Pascal can be described as a high-level, procedural, compiled language. When you need to select a language to use for a program, it is useful to understand some of the general characteristics of programming languages and the advantages or disadvantages of these characteristics.

Procedural

Was the pizza program written using a procedural language?

Although a procedural language follows a linear progression, it still may have control structures to branch to subroutines or to repeat instructions.

Languages with procedural characteristics create programs composed of a series of statements that tell the computer how to perform the processes for a specific task. Languages with procedural characteristics are called **procedural languages**. BASIC, the language that you used for the pizza program, has procedural characteristics. The instructions tell the computer exactly what to do: display a message on the screen asking the user to enter the shape of the pizza; display a message asking for the size of the pizza; display a message asking for the price of the pizza; if the shape is square, calculate the square-inch price with the formula SquareInchPrice = Price/Square Inches, and so forth.

As you might guess, procedural languages are well suited for programs that follow a step-by-step algorithm. Programs created with procedural languages have a starting point and an ending point. The flow of execution from the start to the end is essentially linear; that is, the computer begins at the beginning and executes the prescribed series of instructions until it reaches the end, as shown in Figure 14-12.

Figure 14-12
Execution
of procedural
languages

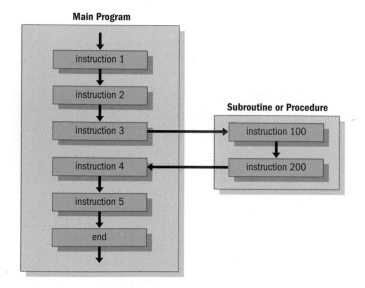

Declarative

Do all languages require the programmer to specify the exact procedure for the solution?

A **declarative language** lets a programmer write a program by specifying a set of statements and rules that define the conditions for resolving a problem. The language has a built-in method for considering the rules and determining a solution.

Unlike programs that are created using a procedural language, programs created with a declarative language do not tell the computer how to solve a problem. Instead, a program created with a declarative language describes what the problem is. For example, Figure 14-13 contains a short program written in the PROLOG language that describes several people and determines which of these people have a sister in the list.

Charlie, Linus, Sam and George are declared to be males.

Lucy, Pattie, Amanda, and Anne are declared to be females.

The relationship between parents and children are described.

The program describes the three criteria for determining if person X is a sister of person Y:

1) Person X must be a female.
2) X has a mother M and a father F.
3) Y has the same mother and father as X.

Figure 14-13
A PROLOG program

Describing a problem and the rules that lead to a solution places an emphasis on words rather than on mathematical formulas. For this reason, declarative languages are useful for programs that manipulate ideas and concepts, rather than numbers.

Low-Level

Our pizza program used commands like PRINT and END. Don't computers understand only ones and zeros?

A **low-level language** requires a programmer to write instructions for the lowest level of the computer system, that is, for specific hardware elements such as the processor, registers, and RAM locations. A low-level language is useful when a programmer needs to directly manipulate what happens at the hardware level. Programmers typically use low-level languages to write system software such as compilers, operating systems, and device drivers.

Each instruction in a low-level language usually corresponds to a single instruction for the processor. Recall that in Chapter 4 you saw how an instruction, such as `MMR M1 REG1`, tells a computer to move a number from a RAM location into a register. Using a low-level language, several instructions are necessary to tell the computer how to do even simple operations, such as add two numbers together. Figure 14-14 shows a section of a program, written in a low-level language, that adds two numbers together.

Figure 14-14
Low-level
instructions

Assembly Language Instructions	Explanation of Instructions	Computer Action
LDA 5	Load 5 in the accumulator	Accumulator: 5
STA Num1	Store the 5 in a memory location called Num1	Accumulator: Num1
LDA 4	Load 4 in the accumulator	Accumulator: 4
ADD Num1	Add the contents of memory location Num1 to the number in the accumulator	Accumulator: 9
STA Total	Store the sum in a memory location called Total	Accumulator: 9 Total: 9
END	Stop program execution	

A **machine language** is a low-level language in binary code that the computer can execute directly. Machine languages are very difficult for humans to understand and manipulate. They were primarily used in the earliest days of computer development when other programming languages were not available.

High-Level

What's the alternative to using a low-level language?

A **high-level language** allows a programmer to use instructions that are more like human language, such as the BASIC command, PRINT "Please wait…" When high-level languages were originally conceived in the 1950s, computer scientists thought they would eliminate programming errors. This was not to be the case—syntax and logical errors are possible even with high-level languages. However, high-level languages significantly reduce programming errors and make it possible to write programs in less time than when using low-level languages. Programs written in high-level languages must be translated into instructions the computer can execute. Therefore, a high-level language must be compiled or interpreted.

Compiled

How does a high-level language produce machine-executable instructions?

A **compiler** translates a program written in a high-level language into low-level instructions before the program is executed. The commands you write in a high-level language are referred to as

source code. The low-level instructions that result from compiling the source code are referred to as **object code**. Figure 14-15 explains more about the compiling process.

2. When the compiler finds a command word, variable name, number, operator, or punctuation mark, it generates a token. A token created by a compiler is a shorthand way of encoding command words. For example, the compiler generates a one-byte token for the variable name NUM1.

1. The source code is examined by part of the computer programming language called a compiler. The compiler scans the source code for command words, numbers, operators, and punctuation marks that it understands. It discards programmer remarks and comments used by the programmer to document the program.

Source code

Scan routine

Tokens

const
    NUM1=5;
    NUM2=4;
var
    TOTAL:integer;
begin

Parser

5 is a value

NUM1 is a memory location

3. The compiler attempts to parse the tokens, that is, to rearrange the tokens into a format that is the same as the machine language.

Object code

Code generator

LDA 5
STA NUM1
LDA 4
ADD NUM1
STA TOTAL
OUT TOTAL
END

4. The compiler uses the information from the parser to generate machine language instructions.

Figure 14-15
A programming language compiler

A compiler is like a person who translates a book from one language to another; the entire book must be translated before it is published.

When you use a **compiled language**, you must compile your program to produce executable program code. Therefore, if you write, compile, and run a program, but then discover that it contains a bug, you must fix your program, then recompile it before you test it again. Once you have compiled your bug-free final version, however, you can run the program without recompiling it.

Interpreted

How is an interpreter different from a compiler?

An **interpreted language** uses an interpreter instead of a compiler to create code that the computer can execute. When you run a program that is written in an interpreted language, the language's **interpreter** reads one instruction and converts it into a machine language instruction, which the computer executes. After the instruction is executed, the interpreter reads the next instruction, converts it into machine language, and so forth. Programs written in interpreted languages take longer to execute because the computer must translate every instruction as it is executed. A program with many loops is especially inefficient in an interpreted language because the instructions contained in the loop are translated multiple times, once for each time the loop is executed.

What is the advantage of an interpreted language over a compiled language? With an interpreted language, you do not need to wait for your program to compile, so the testing process seems to take less time. Figure 14-16 illustrates the concept of a language interpreter.

Figure 14-16
A programming language interpreter

Programming language interpreters work in much the same way as the interpreters at the United Nations who must translate speeches one line at a time while the speech is being presented.

1. The interpreter is a computer program that is part of the programming language environment. The interpreter examines the first word in the first command of the program.

```
Program AddNumbers
const
      NUM1=5;
      NUM2=4;
var
      TOTAL: integer;
begin
      TOTAL: = NUM1=NUM2;
      writein('The total is: ',TOTAL);
end.
```

COMMAND WORDS
begin
end
if
program
readin
writein
while
var

2. The interpreter looks for the command word in a list of valid commands for the language.

4. If the syntax is correct, the interpreter translates the entire command into machine language and sends it to the processor.

```
0010110111000001110101
0100010110000111001
110011000011000100
00010011000110100010
011000110010111
```

0100....

PROGRAM COMMAND SYNTAX

program programname
The word "program" followed by a space then a string of characters

3. If the command is on the list, the interpreter reads the rest of the command and makes sure it conforms to the syntax required for that command.

Object-Oriented

How do objects figure into computer programming?

Object-oriented languages are based on a new approach to programming that uses objects. An **object** is an entity or "thing" that a program manipulates. For example, a button—a rectangular icon on the screen—is an object. You are familiar with the way you can click a button using the mouse. A programmer can use an object-oriented language to define a button object in a program and display the button when the program runs.

An object belongs to a **class**, or group, that has specific characteristics. A common example is the object class called *window*. All window objects, including application windows, belong to the class called *window* and share certain characteristics, such as a title bar and a control-menu box. When a programmer creates a new window object, it acquires, or **inherits**, the characteristics and capabilities of the *window* class. Each specific instance of a window object may also have its own unique characteristics, such as its title, size, or location on the screen. Figure 14-17 shows several objects from an object class.

1. Two objects on the screen are in the class "window": the Document - WordPad window and the Save As window. All windows are rectangular and have a title bar. You can open and close windows, and you can move them around on the screen.

2. The Document - WordPad window is a subclass of "window" object generally referred to as an application window. Windows in this class have a maximize button, a minimize button, and a menu bar.

3. The Save As window is a subclass of "window" called a "dialog box window." It has a title bar, but it does not have a menu bar, a minimize button, or a maximize button.

> Program objects are essentially the same things as the objects in an object-oriented database, but their use is not limited to defining data.

▶ **Figure 14-17**
Objects in the "window" class

The same object can be used in many different programs, thus significantly enhancing programmer productivity. For example, many software applications provide users with a way to save a file, save a file under a new name, open a file, and print a file. If you were programming such applications, it would be handy to have an object to perform these tasks. Anytime you wrote a program that needed to do these tasks, you could simply use this object and avoid "recreating the wheel."

In fact, this object is such an obviously good idea that it already exists. Version 3.1 of Microsoft Windows includes a file called Comdlg.Dll (for COMMon DiaLoG) that contains the menu and dialog box objects for opening, saving, and printing files. Programmers writing programs for Windows don't have to create these menus and dialog boxes from scratch; they can simply include commands in their programs that tell Comdlg.Dll to activate a menu or dialog box.

The Comdlg.Dll object is the reason the File menu in most Windows programs looks the same. These programs all use the Comdlg.Dll object.

Components

Who creates the objects I use in my programs?

In practice, object-oriented programs contain objects that were created by the program designer. However, programmers can also purchase objects called components or libraries. **Components** are prewritten objects that programmers can customize and add to their own programs. Components are available commercially for a few of today's most popular programming languages. Using components is referred to as **component programming**.

For example, suppose you have been hired by a city government to write software to track recyclables. The engineers want to generate graphs periodically to compare amounts of glass, paper, aluminum, and other recyclable materials. A graphing component will help you provide this function in your software. You simply attach the graphing component to the rest of your program code. The engineers also need to fill in government forms. You can purchase a forms component, customize it for the government forms, and attach it to your recycling software.

Programmers can select from a wide array of components that add functions such as spreadsheet-like rows and columns, database management, expert systems, report generation, on-line help, data acquisition, text editing, scientific imaging, and 3-D graphics. Components are advertised in programming language magazines such as *Visual Basic Programmer's Journal*.

Event-Driven

Do all programs follow a set sequence of activities?

A **program event** is an action or occurrence, such as a key press or mouse click, to which a program might respond. An **event-driven language** helps programmers easily create programs that constantly check for and respond to a set of events. Most programs that use graphical user interfaces are event-driven—they display controls, such as menus, on the screen and take action when the user activates one of the controls. To create an event-driven program, code segments are attached to graphical objects, such as command buttons and icons. Users manipulate an object to generate an event, for example, clicking a button labeled "Continue." The event causes the instructions attached to that object to be executed. Figure 14-18 shows a screen from an event-driven program and the program code attached to one of the events.

Event-driven languages are useful for creating programs that feature graphical user interfaces, such as those that run on the Macintosh computer or under the Windows operating system. Although other languages can be used to develop such programs, an event-driven language simplifies the development process.

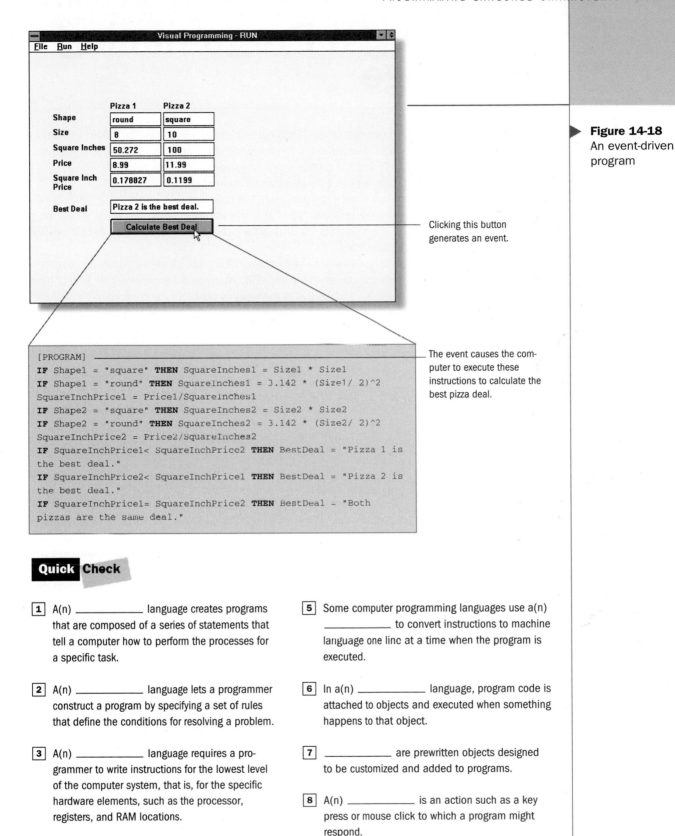

Figure 14-18
An event-driven
program

Clicking this button
generates an event.

The event causes the com-
puter to execute these
instructions to calculate the
best pizza deal.

```
[PROGRAM]
IF Shape1 = "square" THEN SquareInches1 = Size1 * Size1
IF Shape1 = "round" THEN SquareInches1 = 3.142 * (Size1/ 2)^2
SquareInchPrice1 = Price1/SquareInches1
IF Shape2 = "square" THEN SquareInches2 = Size2 * Size2
IF Shape2 = "round" THEN SquareInches2 = 3.142 * (Size2/ 2)^2
SquareInchPrice2 = Price2/SquareInches2
IF SquareInchPrice1< SquareInchPrice2 THEN BestDeal = "Pizza 1 is
the best deal."
IF SquareInchPrice2< SquareInchPrice1 THEN BestDeal = "Pizza 2 is
the best deal."
IF SquareInchPrice1= SquareInchPrice2 THEN BestDeal = "Both
pizzas are the same deal."
```

Quick Check

1 A(n) _____ language creates programs that are composed of a series of statements that tell a computer how to perform the processes for a specific task.

2 A(n) _____ language lets a programmer construct a program by specifying a set of rules that define the conditions for resolving a problem.

3 A(n) _____ language requires a programmer to write instructions for the lowest level of the computer system, that is, for the specific hardware elements, such as the processor, registers, and RAM locations.

4 In a compiled language, _____ is compiled, or translated, into object code, which the computer can execute.

5 Some computer programming languages use a(n) _____ to convert instructions to machine language one line at a time when the program is executed.

6 In a(n) _____ language, program code is attached to objects and executed when something happens to that object.

7 _____ are prewritten objects designed to be customized and added to programs.

8 A(n) _____ is an action such as a key press or mouse click to which a program might respond.

Selecting a Programming Language

Usually, more than one programming language is suitable for a task. So, when you select a language for a project, keep in mind the following questions:

- Do the characteristics of the programming language fit the task at hand?
- Is the language currently used for other applications in the organization?
- Does the organization have expertise using the language?

If the answers to all these questions are "yes," the language you are considering should be a good choice for the project. The descriptions of popular programming languages in this section will help you answer the first question.

BASIC (Beginner's All-purpose Symbolic Instruction Code) was designed as a language for beginning programmers. Since its introduction in 1964, many popular versions of BASIC have been created, including GW-BASIC, shipped with the original IBM PCs, and Microsoft's QBASIC. BASIC has become one of the most popular and widely used programming languages because it is easy to use and available for almost every type of computer system. BASIC is a high-level, procedural language. Most versions of BASIC are interpreted languages, although some versions provide compiling capabilities.

Early versions of BASIC were too limited for the development of sophisticated commercial programs, but newer versions, such as Microsoft's **Visual Basic**, are comprehensive and powerful programming languages suitable for use in professional programming projects. Visual Basic is especially useful for creating event-driven programs that have a graphical user interface.

COBOL (COmmon Business-Oriented Language) is the language most typically used for transaction processing on mainframe computer systems. Developed in 1960, COBOL is a high-level, procedural, compiled language used by thousands of professional programmers to develop and maintain complex programs in large organizations and businesses. COBOL programs tend to be rather long, but they are easy to understand, debug, and maintain. This functionality is particularly important in large organizations where critical programs must be maintained and modified by many different programmers over a period of years.

FORTRAN (FORmula TRANslator), developed in 1954, is the oldest high-level computer language still in use, although it has undergone many changes since its creation. FORTRAN was designed by scientists and is often used to create scientific, mathematical, and engineering programs on mainframes and minicomputers.

Pascal was designed in 1971 to help students learn how to program computers. Pascal is a high-level, procedural, compiled language. The design of the language encourages a structured approach to programming. Despite its structured design, Pascal has gained only moderate popularity as a programming language for professional and commercial applications.

C is the most popular language for developing professional and commercial programs for microcomputer systems. Most major application programs and operating systems are written in C. C is a compiled procedural language that provides both high-level commands and low-level access to hardware. This duality gives the programmer significant flexibility in writing programs. Because of this flexibility, experienced C programmers can make their programs very fast and efficient. However, this flexibility can make C programs difficult to understand, debug, and maintain.

C++ is an object-oriented version of C. Many people believe that the object-oriented nature of C++ will make programmers more productive. However, object-oriented programming requires a significantly different mental perspective from that of procedural programming. Therefore, many programmers experience difficulty using the object-oriented features of C++.

LISP (LISt Processor) and **PROLOG** are declarative languages, often used to develop expert systems. These languages, developed in 1960 and 1971, respectively, have not gained as much popularity as procedural languages, probably because early computer applications were designed to handle tasks that required simple and repetitive calculations—tasks that procedural languages could handle effectively. Tasks that require a computer to perform complex logical operations on character data are better handled by declarative languages.

SQL (Structured Query Language) was developed to provide a standard language for defining and manipulating a database. SQL is a high-level declarative language that allows programmers and users to describe the relationship between the data elements in a database and the type of information they want to derive from the database. Although a database can also be manipulated by a procedural language such as COBOL, SQL is generally regarded as more effective because SQL commands are tailored to database activities.

8086 assembly language is a low-level language consisting of short mnemonic commands that the computer can easily translate into machine language. The 8086 assembly language instruction set is specific to the Intel 8086 microprocessor, and, therefore, programs written in this language can execute only on computers with microprocessors from the x86 family. Today, 8086 assembly language is used primarily for programs, or segments of programs, that must be made as short as possible or that must run as quickly as possible. Professional programmers use 8086 assembly language for the sections of application programs that need to execute quickly and for system software that controls computer hardware.

End Note

The pizza program is a relatively "tiny" program. The commercial programs you use—word processing or spreadsheet programs, for example—are much larger. By the Department of Defense standards, a "small" program is one with fewer than 100,000 lines of code.

A "medium-size" program is one with 100,000 to one million lines of code. A "large" program is one with more than one million lines of code.

Research has shown that on average, one programmer creates 20 lines of code per day, including coding, testing, and documenting. It is not surprising, then, that most commercial programs are written by a team of programmers and take many months, or years, to complete.

What is the point of learning about computer programming if you do not plan to become a programmer? There are several reasons. First, you are likely to use many computer programs during your career, and when you realize that your word processing program contains 750,000 lines of code, you will understand how a few bugs might exist. You will also understand that you, individually, would not want to undertake the task of writing a word processing program; that is a project best left to professional programming teams. Finally, although you would not typically write the productivity software you use, it is possible that you might have the opportunity to develop or participate in the development of software applications that are specific to your needs. Your understanding of computer programming and software engineering will help you plan constructively and participate productively in the development process.

Review

1. Answer the questions listed in the Chapter Preview section at the beginning of this chapter.

2. List each of the boldface terms used in this chapter, then use your own words to write a short definition of each term.

3. Describe how the job of a systems analyst differs from the job of a software engineer.

4. Is there a difference between an algorithm and a computer program? Why or why not?

5. Give an example of a sequence control structure, a selection control structure, and a repetition control structure.

6. Which lines in the program in Figure 14-19 contain branch or loop control structures?

Figure 14-19 ◀

```
INPUT "Employee Name:"; EmpName$
WHILE EmpName$ <> "EOF"
    INPUT "Hours Worked "; HoursWk
    INPUT "Pay RATE    "; PayRate
    GrossPay = HoursWk * PayRate
    IF GrossPay > 50 THEN
        Tax = GrossPay *.12
    ELSE
        Tax = 0
    END IF
    NetPay = GrossPay - Tax
    PRINT "Gross Pay "; GrossPay
    INPUT "Employee Name"; EmpName$
WEND
PRINT "Payroll complete."
END
```

7. Explain the difference between a syntax error and a logic error.

8. Explain the difference between program remarks and written documentation.

9. Fill in the following matrix to summarize the characteristics of today's popular programming languages. Most languages will have more than one characteristic.

	Procedural	Declarative	Low-level	High-level	Compiled	Interpreted	Object-oriented	Component	Event-driven
BASIC									
Visual Basic									
COBOL									
FORTRAN									
Pascal									
C									
C++									
LISP/PROLOG									
SQL									
8086 assembly language									

Projects

1. What Information Do You Need? In this chapter you learned that problem solving requires information. List the known information required to solve the following problems:

   a. Calculate the square footage of a rectangular room

   b. Calculate the amount of gasoline required to drive your car from New York City to San Francisco

   c. Calculate how much it costs to ship a box of books from Dallas, Texas to Portland, Oregon

   d. Calculate how much it would cost to purchase new carpeting for your living room

   c. Calculate your tuition for next semester

2. Assumptions and Known Information To grasp a problem, you must understand the assumptions on which the problem is based and the known information you can use to solve the problem. To practice identifying assumptions and known information, study the following problem. Think about the information you would need to solve the problem yourself. Identify the assumptions and known information.

Problem: Two tourists are planning a walking tour of a city; they plan to visit a bookstore, a science museum, a Thai restaurant, and a craft market. A city map shows the location of each place. According to the legend on the map, one-half inch on the map is a one-mile walk. The tourists want to know how far they will walk from their hotel to each of the places they want to visit.

3. Writing an Algorithm The algorithm is the key to writing an effective computer program. If you as the programmer understand the steps that efficiently carry out a task or solve a problem, you should be able to translate this algorithm into a workable computer program. To try your hand at writing an algorithm, use the problem statement in Project 2. Write an algorithm for determining the total distance the tourists will walk. Hint: Think about the steps you would take to solve this problem using the map, a calculator, and a ruler.

4. Imagine You're a Computer To understand a computer program or debug program code, computer programmers have a trick. They imagine that they are the computer executing the code. By following exactly what the computer should do at each step in a program, a programmer can discover how a program works or which instructions cause problems. Try a simple example. Imagine you are a computer instructed to execute the following BASIC program. Indicate the value of X and Y after you execute each instruction. At the beginning of the program, X and Y are each assigned a value of 0.

```
REM Sample program
X = 10
Y = X * 2
X = X * Y
END
```

5. Find the Errors A friend has written a BASIC program to calculate the number of tanks of gas her car will require to go a specified number of miles. Unfortunately, the program doesn't work correctly. She shows you a printout of the program and asks for your help.

```
REM This program calculates the number
    of tanks of gas
REM required to drive my car a specified
    number of miles.
MilesPerGallon = 22.5
GallonsPerTank = 12
INPUT "Enter the number of miles to
    drive:", MilesToDrive
GallonsRequired = Miles ToDrive /
    MilesPerGallon
TanksRequired = GallonsRequired /
    GallonsPerTank
PRINT "This trip will require:"
PRINT MilesPerGallon
PRINT "tanks of gas."
END
```

A syntax error and a logic error prevent the program from working correctly. Examine the program code carefully to locate the two errors; then write the corrected lines.

Corrected Lines

_____

_____

6. Documentation—Good or Bad? Writing documentation is not an easy task. Many programs have hundreds of features. Organizing these features into a useful reference format and describing the features so that even a beginner can understand them requires good logical and writing skills. How good is the documentation for programs you use? Describe the documentation for a computer program that you have used. Discuss what you like or do not like about the documentation, and indicate how you think the documentation can be improved.

7. Pick a Language—Any Language
Select a computer language. Use your library or Internet resources such as *http://www.yahoo.com/Computers/* to research the language, then answer the following questions:

a. Is this a procedural or a declarative language?

b. Is this a high-level or a low-level language?

c. Is this a compiled language or an interpreted language?

d. Is this an object-oriented language?

e. Is this an event-driven language?

f. When was the language developed?

g. For what purpose was the language developed?

h. Who developed the language?

i. Is the language typically used on micro, mini, or mainframe computers?

8. Batting Averages A baseball player's batting average is calculated by dividing the number of times the player hit the ball by the number of times the player was at bat, minus the number of times the player "walked," as in the formula, Hits / (TimesAtBat – Walks). Write the specifications for a program that calculates a baseball player's batting average. Be sure to include the assumptions, known information, formula for calculation, and output description. Also, create a flowchart to express the algorithm.

9. Grading Computer Literacy Exams Assume your school has a computer literacy exam that students must pass before they can graduate. Scores on the exams can be between 0 and 100. A student must score at least 70 to pass the test. Marsha Murray in the testing office has a list of students and scores for the exam given in December. Write the specification for a program that would allow Marsha to input student names and scores, analyze each score to see if the student passed, and print out a list of student names, scores, and "Passed" or "Failed." Also write pseudocode to express the algorithm.

10. The Card Shark Assume you are talking to a friend on the phone. You know your friend has three cards and they are all in the same suit. For example, your friend might have the two of clubs, the five of clubs, and the eight of clubs. Further, assume that the cards are shuffled so they are in no particular order. You need to tell your friend how to sort the cards so the lowest numbered card is first and the highest numbered card is last. However, you cannot see the cards and your friend cannot communicate with you except to say OK. You need to give your friend general instructions, such as "Take

the first two cards and compare the numbers on them." Write out the instructions, or algorithm, for sorting the three cards.

11. Computing Careers What are the job prospects for computer programmers? Looking at employment ads is one way to find out. To research the employment opportunities in a large city of your choice, look in the classified ad section of a large city newspaper or check out Internet sites such as:

http://www.careermosaic.com
http://www.sjmercury.com/classifieds

Write a summary of your research by answering the following questions:

a. Where did you look for information?

b. How many computer programmer jobs were available?

c. What was the average salary offered?

d. What were the educational requirements for entry-level positions?

e. What programming languages seem to be in greatest demand?

Resources

■ **Cooper, A.** *About Face: The Essentials of User Interface Design.* Foster City, CA: IDG Books Worldwide, 1995. Alan Cooper is well-known as the "Father of Visual Basic." His book, destined to be a classic, tackles important issues of graphical user interface design. You'll find it entertaining and informative.

■ **Dijkstra, E.** "Goto Statement Considered Harmful," *Communications of the ACM* 11; 3. Dijkstra's original letter about GOTO statements was published in the *Communications of the ACM*, a prestigious journal of the Association of Computing Machinery.

■ **Lammers, S.** *Programmers at Work.* Redmond, WA: Microsoft Press, 1986. In this book you will find fascinating interviews with the star programmers of the early microcomputer era, including Bill Gates, Gary Kildall, and Dan Bricklin. The programmers give their views on issues such as "Is programming an art or a science?", "How did you develop your programming skills?", and "What is your programming style?" You will also find some original examples of programs, flowcharts, and program specifications.

■ **McConnell, S.** *Code Complete: A Practical Handbook of Software Construction.* Redmond, WA: Microsoft Press, 1993. A realistic guide to computer programming, written by experienced programmers. This book is well researched and contains abundant references and hard data, yet is easy to read. We think *Code Complete* is destined to become a classic.

■ **Pattis, R.E.** *Karel the Robot: A Gentle Introduction to the Art of Programming.* New York: Wiley, 1981. In this book, the author uses a robot named Karel to teach students intuitively about programming, particularly Pascal. Pattis wrote this book when he was a graduate student at Stanford University. It is entertaining and very easy to understand.

■ **Sigwart, C., G. Van Meer, and J. Hansen.** *Software Engineering: A Project-Oriented Approach.* Irvine, CA: Franklin, Beedle, & Associates, 1990. This book presents a good basic foundation in software engineering. It is well referenced, and the glossary contains relevant definitions selected from the *IEEE Standard Glossary of Software Engineering Terminology.*

■ **Zak, D.** *Introductory Microsoft Visual Basic 2.0/3.0 for Windows.* Cambridge: Course Technology, 1994. If you enjoyed the Visual Programming Lab in this chapter, you might want to learn how to program using the popular Visual Basic language. Zak's book is a quick introduction in tutorial format that will help you quickly learn the basics.

Lab Assignments

Visual Programming Lab

 In the Visual Programming Lab, you use an event-driven, object-oriented programming environment to create simple programs. This Lab provides a "taste" of what it would be like to program in a visual language such as Visual Basic.

1. Click the Steps button to learn how to create a graphical user interface containing buttons, labels, and text boxes. As you work through the Steps, answer all of the Quick Check questions. After you complete the Steps, you will see a Quick Check Summary Report of your answers. Follow the directions on the screen to print this report.

2. In Explore, create a program to calculate the total cost of carpeting a room. Test your program, then print it showing the cost of $12.99/sq. yd. carpeting for a 10 × 14 foot room.

Assume that the room is rectangular. The known information is the length and width of the room, and the price of a square yard of carpet. You must calculate:
■ the square feet of carpet needed (length * width of room)
■ the square yards of carpet needed (square feet/9)
■ total price of carpet (Price per square yard * the square yards needed)

Your user interface should look like the following screen:

3. Suppose you like to shop from catalogs. Your favorite catalog is having a sale—selected merchandise is discounted 10%, 20%, 30%, or 40%. You want to know how much you'll save if you buy some of the merchandise you want. In Explore, create a program to calculate savings. Test your program, then print it showing the savings for a $863 item at 30% discount.

Assume that the items you purchase will be discounted and that there is no additional charge for shipping. The known information is the original price of the item and its discount—10%, 20%, 30% or 40%. Calculate how much you will save. (For example, for a 10% discount, multiply the original cost by .1.) Your user interface should look like the following screen:

4. In your recording studio, studio musicians are paid by the hour, but your sound technicians are salaried. You started to make a program to calculate weekly paychecks, but it doesn't seem to work.

Your assumption is that some employees are salaried and some are hourly. You know the salaries for salaried employees. You know the hourly wage and the hours worked each pay period by the hourly employees. You want to calculate the weekly pay for salaried employees (Wages / 52) and the weekly pay for hourly employees (Wages * Hours).

In Explore, open the program PAY.VPG and test it. Enter 32240 in the Wages box, then click the Salaried button. The output should be 620. Next enter 8 in the Wages box and 40 in the Hours box. Click the Hourly button. The output should be 320. Find what's wrong with this program and correct it. Print your solution.

Answers

14.1

1. software engineer (programmer)

2. problem statement

3. algorithm

4. pseudocode

5. flow chart

14.2

1. Coding (programming)

2. false

3. sequence control structure

4. GOTO

5. selection control (decision or branch)

6. repetition control (loop, iteration)

14.3

1. testing (debugging)

2. syntax

3. run-time

4. Logic

5. Documentation

6. remarks (comments)

7. program manual, reference manual (user reference)

14.4

1. procedural

2. declarative

3. machine (assembly, low level)

4. source code

5. interpreter

6. event-driven

7. Components (libraries)

8. event

Glossary/Index

D

debugging The process of testing each section of code to make sure it runs correctly, 14-17

decision structures, 14-14

declarative language A characteristic of computer languages that lets you write a program by specifying a set of statements and rules that define the conditions for resolving a problem, 14-21

definition of objects One way to express an algorithm that requires that the computer define the objects it must manipulate and specify the method for manipulating each object, 14-11

documentation A permanent record that explains how a program works, 14-17, 14-18–14-19

E

8086 assembly language A low-level computer language written for the Intel 8086 microprocessor family, 14-29

errors, computer programs, 14-17

event-driven language A characteristic of computer languages that helps programmers create programs that constantly check for and respond to a set of event, 14-26–14-27

expressing algorithms, 14-9–14-11

F

flow chart A graphical representation of the way a computer should progress from one instruction to the next when it performs a task, 14-10

FOR..NEXT command
    QBASIC, 14-15

FORTRAN (FORmula TRANslator) The oldest high-level computer language still in use, designed for solving scientific type problems, 14-28

function A section of code that is part of a program but not executed in the sequential execution path, 14-14

G

GOSUB command, 14-14

GOTO command
    QBASIC, 14-13

GW-BASIC, 14-28

H

high-level language A characteristic of computer languages that allow you to use instructions that are more like human language, 14-22

I

IF..THEN command, 14-14

inheritance The ability of an object to acquire the capabilities and characteristics of its class, 14-25
    object class characteristics, 14-25

instructions
    level for algorithms, 14-7
    sequence, 14-13
    structure, 14-4

interpreted language A characteristic of computer languages that use a translator instead of a compiler to create code that the computer can understand, 14-24

interpreter The part of an interpreted language that reads and executes one instruction at a time, 14-24

iterations, 14-15

K

known information The information you supply the computer so it can solve a problem, 14-5

known information, problem statements, 14-5

written documentation Paper-based or electronic external documentation that contains information about a program, 14-18

Answers

Chapter One

1.1

1. accepts input, processes data, stores data, produces output
2. data
3. process
4. memory
5. storage

1.2

1. keyboard, monitor
2. microcomputer
3. terminal
4. minicomputers, mainframes
5. mainframe
6. compatible
7. network

1.3

1. prompt
2. wizards
3. Enter
4. syntax error
5. submenu, dialog box
6. graphical user interfaces
7. cursor, insertion point
8. Ctrl, Alt
9. Windows
10. character-based

Chapter Two

2.1

1. false
2. data
3. program
4. software
5. shareware
6. license
7. system software

2.2

1. multitasking
2. UNIX
3. micro
4. Utility
5. device driver
6. programming language

2.3

1. word processing, spreadsheet, database management
2. integrated software
3. horizontal market software
4. education software
5. desktop publishing

2.4

1. text, graphics, sound, animation, photo images, video
2. false
3. hypertext, hypermedia
4. MPC
5. speakers, sound card, CD-ROM drive, high-resolution color monitor, fast processor (high memory capacity is also acceptable)
6. multimedia kit

Chapter Three

3.1

1. data, information
2. drive letter, subdirectory, subdirectory, filename, filename extension
3. exe, com
4. Most Windows software automatically adds a specific extension to each file created with it.
5. logical
6. root
7. source

3.2

1. kilobytes(megabytes or gigabytes also acceptable), milliseconds
2. magnetic, optical
3. tracks, sectors

4. random, sequential

5. floppy disk, CD-ROM

6. hard disk drive

7. FAT (File Allocation Table)

8. false

Chapter Four

4.1

1. integrated circuit

2. bit

3. byte

4. ASCII, EBCDIC

5. binary

6. bus (or data bus)

4.2

1. Random access memory (RAM)

2. volatile

3. megabytes

4. capacitors

5. SIMM

6. virtual

7. ROM

8. CMOS

4.3

1. microprocessor

2. ALU

3. Control unit

4. opcode, operand

5. fetch, interpret, execute, increment instruction pointer

6. clock rate, word size, cache, instruction set

4.4

1. expansion bus

2. expansion card

3. slot, port

4. parallel, SCSI, serial, MIDI

Chapter Five

5.1

1. Product development, product announcement, introduction, maintenance, retirement

2. the operating system and application software you intend to use

3. EIDE, SCSI

4. local buses

5. dot pitch

6. 1 MB

7. bps

8. inkjet

5.2

1. PCMCIA

2. active

3. docking station

4. port replicator

5. track point, touch pad, trackball

6. power saving

5.3

1. product announcement, introduction, maintenance, retirement

2. product announcement

3. vaporware

4. plateau

5. version, revision

6. beta

5.4

1. tiers

2. computer retail store, mail-order suppliers, value-added resellers, manufacturer direct

3. trade journal

4. value-added reseller

5. academic journals

Chapter Six

6.1

1. server
2. mapping
3. account (or user account)
4. true
5. false
6. captured, redirected

6.2

1. network interface card
2. non-dedicated server
3. file server
4. true
5. host

6.3

1. network operating
2. true
3. network license
4. groupware
5. document routing

Chapter Seven

7.1

1. cyberspace
2. Internet
3. commercial information service (or on-line service)
4. discussion group
5. chat session
6. downloading

7.2

1. computers, host (mainframe)
2. Prodigy, CompuServe, America Online, Microsoft Network
3. basic services
4. connect time
5. local access number

7.3

1. internet (or internetwork)
2. Internet
3. coco = user ID, @canine = machine name, com = domain name
4. World Wide Web
5. Gopher
6. Anonymous FTP
7. Telnet
8. MOO
9. netiquette

Chapter Eight

8.1

1. operator error
2. false
3. uninterruptible power supply (UPS)
4. surge protector
5. false
6. false
7. hard disk drive
8. up-to-date backup

8.2

1. virus
2. trojan horse
3. worm
4. virus
5. public domain software, shareware, and illegal copies of computer programs downloaded from bulletin boards
6. weird messages, unusual sound effects, difficulty saving files (or missing files, unexpected reboots, increased executable file size)
7. signature
8. computer data and software

8.3

1. risk management
2. policy
3. audit control
4. true
5. user rights
6. trap door
7. encryption
8. downtime
9. positive

Chapter Nine

9.1

1. Information theory
2. 3
3. binary
4. ASCII
5. ANSI, EBCDIC
6. Unicode
7. locatization
8. 1001011

9.2

1. bitmap
2. 8
3. dithering
4. Vector
5. .Wmf, .Dxf, .Mgx, .Cgm
6. false

9.3

1. Waveform, MIDI
2. sampling
3. false
4. false
5. .Wav, .Mod, .Voc

9.4

1. Compression
2. volume
3. file compression
4. adaptive pattern substitution
5. lossy
6. true

Chapter 10

10.1

1. channel
2. analog
3. dedicated (leased)
4. false
5. true
6. Packet
7. dial up (POTS)
8. LANS, PBXs

10.2

1. bandwidth
2. bits
3. duplex
4. protocols
5. even
6. true

10.3

1. hub (concentrator)
2. standards
3. software
4. protocols
5. true
6. false
7. token

Chapter 11

11.1

1. An organization is a group of people working together toward a goal. A business is similar, but the goal is to produce a profit.

2. mission

3. operations, financial management, sales and marketing, human resource management

4. opportunities, threats

5. a. become better at what it does

   b. change the industry structure

   c. create a new product or service

6. total quality management (TQM)

7. downsize (rightsize)

11.2

1.

2. goods

3. strategic planning

5. unstructured

6. internal, external

11.3

1. office automation

2. transaction

3. management information system (MIS)

4. exception

5. decision support

6. expert system

7. expert system shell

Chapter 12

12.1

1. systems development life cycle

2. Systems analysts

3. problem statement

4. CASE

5. System requirements, success factors

6. prototype

12.2

1. design

2. spreadsheet

3. RFP

4. RFQ

5. Application specifications

12.3

1. Software engineering

2. knowledge engineering

3. Unit

4. Integration

5. test area

6. System

12.4

1. procedure handbook

2. Conversion software

3. system conversion

4. Direct

5. parallel

6. phased

7. pilot

8. Acceptance

12.5

1. Maintenance

2. 80

3. bugs or errors

4. cost-effective

5. systems development life cycle

4. tactical

Chapter 13

13.1

1. variable-length

2. character (string)

3. type, occurrence

4. flat

5. data structure diagram or entity relationship diagram

6. object-oriented

7. relational

13.2

1. custom

2. data independence

3. object-oriented

4. database management system or DBMS

5. client-server

6. passive

13.3

1. field format

2. range check

3. data redundancy

4. case sensitive

5. update

6. sort key

7. index

8. query by example

13.4

1. report template

2. control-break

3. exception

4. data set

5. bar

6. line

7. decision maker

Chapter 14

14.1

1. software engineer (programmer)

2. problem statement

3. algorithm

4. pseudocode

5. flow chart

14.2

1. Coding (programming)

2. false

3. sequence control structure

4. GOTO

5. selection control (decision structure or, branch)

6. repetition control (loop, iteration)

14.3

1. testing (debugging)

2. syntax

3. run-time

4. Logic

5. Documentation

6. remarks

7. program manual, reference manual (user interface)

14.4

1. procedural

2. declarative

3. machine (assembly, low level)

4. source code

5. interpreter

6. event-driven

7. Components (libraries)

8. event

Glossary/Index

O

object An abstract representation of a real-world entity that has a unique identity, properties, and the ability to interact with other objects, 13-14
> classes, 14-25
> defining, 14-11
> object-oriented databases, 13-14–13-15
> object-oriented languages, 14-25–14-26
> prewritten, 14-25–14-26

object code The low-level instructions that result from compiling your source code, 14-23

object ID A unique number assigned to a specific object; similar to a record number, 13-24, 13-14–13-15
> creating, 13-20

object-oriented database A type of database that deals with data as objects, 13-14

object-oriented database management system (OODBMS) Application software that provides a way to define objects, methods, and classes, 13-20

object-oriented language Computer languages that are based on a new approach to programming that uses objects, 14-25, 14-25–14-26

odd parity Error-checking protocol in which the number of one bits in the data block is an odd number, 10-18

off bits, 4-11

Office (Microsoft program), 2-25

office automation system A system that automates or computerizes routine office tasks such as producing documents, tracking schedules, making calculations, and facilitating voice and written communication, 11-13, 11-13–11-14

offices, integrated software, 2-25

on bits, 4-11

on-line censorship, 7-36

on-line Help, 1-30

on-line information The information, including text, music, film clips, and computer programs, available on the information highway, 7-4

on-line services The services available on the information highway to help you find information and communicate with other people. *See also* commercial information services, 7-4

on-line shopping mall, information highway, 7-5

on-line spell checker, 2-22

on-line Thesaurus, 2-22

one-to-many relationship A relationship in which one record in a particular record type may be related to more than one record of another record type, 13-10, 13-12

one-to-one relationship A relationship in which one record in a particular record type is related to only one record of another data type, 13-10

op code The part of an assembly language instruction that contains a command word for an arithmetic or logical operation. Also called operation code, 4-17

opening a file The process of retrieving data from a storage medium into the computer's memory. Also called reading data or loading data, 3-16

operands The part of an instruction that specifies the data or the address of the data for the operation, 4-17

operating system A set of programs that manages the resources of a computer, including controlling input and output, allocating system resources, managing storage space, maintaining security, and detecting equipment failure. *See also* DOS; Macintosh, 2-8, 2-12
> bundled with new computers, 5-11
> copy utilities, 8-26
> documentcentricity, 3-7
> executable files, 3-5
> FATs, 3-29–3-31
> functions, 2-12–2-14
> identifying, 2-14
> interaction with application software, 2-12, 2-14
> interaction with hardware, 2-12, 2-14
> loading, 4-31–4-32
> local area networks. *See* network operating systems
> microcomputers, 2-14–2-17
> multiuser, 2-13
> MVS, 2-12
> networks. *See* network operating systems
> prompts, 4-33
> revisions, 2-37–2-38
> software requirements, 2-37–2-38
> updating CMOS settings, 4-14
> VMS, 2-12

operational planning Scheduling and monitoring of workers and processes, 11-10

operations The primary activities of an organization; also called production, 11-4

operator error A cause of lost data in which a computer user makes a mistake, 8-4

optical fiber A single glass tube, thinner than a human hair, in a fiber-optic cable, 10-15, 10-15–10-16

optical storage The technology with which data is burned into the storage medium using beams of light to form permanent patterns of small pits in the disk surface, 3-17, 3-17–3-18

OR logical operator, 13-37

order entry/invoice system A transaction processing system that provides a way to input, view, modify, and delete

P